T0183805

Lecture Notes in Computer Science 12217

More information about this series at http://www.springer.com/series/7409

Helmut Degen · Lauren Reinerman-Jones (Eds.)

Artificial Intelligence in HCI

First International Conference, AI-HCI 2020
Held as Part of the 22nd HCI International Conference, HCII 2020
Copenhagen, Denmark, July 19–24, 2020
Proceedings

 Springer

Editors
Helmut Degen
Siemens
Princeton, USA

Lauren Reinerman-Jones
University of Central Florida
Orlando, FL, USA

ISSN 0302-9743   ISSN 1611-3349 (electronic)
Lecture Notes in Computer Science
ISBN 978-3-030-50333-8   ISBN 978-3-030-50334-5 (eBook)
https://doi.org/10.1007/978-3-030-50334-5

LNCS Sublibrary: SL3 – Information Systems and Applications, incl. Internet/Web, and HCI

This Springer imprint is published by the registered company Springer Nature Switzerland AG
The registered company address is: Gewerbestrasse 11, 6330 Cham, Switzerland

Foreword

The 22nd International Conference on Human-Computer Interaction, HCI International 2020 (HCII 2020), was planned to be held at the AC Bella Sky Hotel and Bella Center, Copenhagen, Denmark, during July 19–24, 2020. Due to the COVID-19 coronavirus pandemic and the resolution of the Danish government not to allow events larger than 500 people to be hosted until September 1, 2020, HCII 2020 had to be held virtually. It incorporated the 21 thematic areas and affiliated conferences listed on the following page.

A total of 6,326 individuals from academia, research institutes, industry, and governmental agencies from 97 countries submitted contributions, and 1,439 papers and 238 posters were included in the conference proceedings. These contributions address the latest research and development efforts and highlight the human aspects of design and use of computing systems. The contributions thoroughly cover the entire field of human-computer interaction, addressing major advances in knowledge and effective use of computers in a variety of application areas. The volumes constituting the full set of the conference proceedings are listed in the following pages.

The HCI International (HCII) conference also offers the option of "late-breaking work" which applies both for papers and posters and the corresponding volume(s) of the proceedings will be published just after the conference. Full papers will be included in the "HCII 2020 - Late Breaking Papers" volume of the proceedings to be published in the Springer LNCS series, while poster extended abstracts will be included as short papers in the "HCII 2020 - Late Breaking Posters" volume to be published in the Springer CCIS series.

I would like to thank the program board chairs and the members of the program boards of all thematic areas and affiliated conferences for their contribution to the highest scientific quality and the overall success of the HCI International 2020 conference.

This conference would not have been possible without the continuous and unwavering support and advice of the founder, Conference General Chair Emeritus and Conference Scientific Advisor Prof. Gavriel Salvendy. For his outstanding efforts, I would like to express my appreciation to the communications chair and editor of HCI International News, Dr. Abbas Moallem.

July 2020   Constantine Stephanidis

HCI International 2020 Thematic Areas and Affiliated Conferences

Thematic areas:

- HCI 2020: Human-Computer Interaction
- HIMI 2020: Human Interface and the Management of Information

Affiliated conferences:

- EPCE: 17th International Conference on Engineering Psychology and Cognitive Ergonomics
- UAHCI: 14th International Conference on Universal Access in Human-Computer Interaction
- VAMR: 12th International Conference on Virtual, Augmented and Mixed Reality
- CCD: 12th International Conference on Cross-Cultural Design
- SCSM: 12th International Conference on Social Computing and Social Media
- AC: 14th International Conference on Augmented Cognition
- DHM: 11th International Conference on Digital Human Modeling and Applications in Health, Safety, Ergonomics and Risk Management
- DUXU: 9th International Conference on Design, User Experience and Usability
- DAPI: 8th International Conference on Distributed, Ambient and Pervasive Interactions
- HCIBGO: 7th International Conference on HCI in Business, Government and Organizations
- LCT: 7th International Conference on Learning and Collaboration Technologies
- ITAP: 6th International Conference on Human Aspects of IT for the Aged Population
- HCI-CPT: Second International Conference on HCI for Cybersecurity, Privacy and Trust
- HCI-Games: Second International Conference on HCI in Games
- MobiTAS: Second International Conference on HCI in Mobility, Transport and Automotive Systems
- AIS: Second International Conference on Adaptive Instructional Systems
- C&C: 8th International Conference on Culture and Computing
- MOBILE: First International Conference on Design, Operation and Evaluation of Mobile Communications
- AI-HCI: First International Conference on Artificial Intelligence in HCI

Conference Proceedings Volumes Full List

http://2020.hci.international/proceedings

First International Conference on Artificial Intelligence in HCI (AI-HCI 2020)

Program Board Chairs: Helmut Degen, Siemens Corporation, USA, and Lauren Reinerman-Jones, University of Central Florida, USA

- Esma Aimeur, Canada
- Iman Avazpour, Australia
- Gennaro Costagliola, Italy
- Ahmad Esmaeili, USA
- Mauricio Gomez, USA
- Jennifer Heier, Germany
- Rania Hodhod, USA
- Sandeep Kuttal, USA
- Sushil Louis, USA
- Rob Macredie, UK
- Adina Panchea, Canada
- Giovanni Pilato, Italy
- Robert Reynolds, USA
- Gustavo Rossi, Argentina
- Carmen Santoro, Italy
- Anil Shankar, USA
- Marjorie Skubic, USA
- Davide Spano, Italy
- Roberto Vezzani, Italy
- Giuliana Vitiello, Italy

The full list with the Program Board Chairs and the members of the Program Boards of all thematic areas and affiliated conferences is available online at:

http://www.hci.international/board-members-2020.php

HCI International 2021

The 23rd International Conference on Human-Computer Interaction, HCI International 2021 (HCII 2021), will be held jointly with the affiliated conferences in Washington DC, USA, at the Washington Hilton Hotel, July 24–29, 2021. It will cover a broad spectrum of themes related to Human-Computer Interaction (HCI), including theoretical issues, methods, tools, processes, and case studies in HCI design, as well as novel interaction techniques, interfaces, and applications. The proceedings will be published by Springer. More information will be available on the conference website: http://2021.hci.international/.

General Chair
Prof. Constantine Stephanidis
University of Crete and ICS-FORTH
Heraklion, Crete, Greece
Email: general_chair@hcii2021.org

http://2021.hci.international/

Contents

AI Applications in HCI

Human-Centered AI

Towards Increased Transparency
with Value Sensitive Design

Jacob Dexe[1,2]⬤, Ulrik Franke[1,2(✉)]⬤, Anneli Avatare Nöu[1]⬤,
and Alexander Rad[1]⬤

[1] RISE Research Institutes of Sweden, 164 29 Kista, Sweden
{jacob.dexe,ulrik.franke,anneli.nou,alexander.rad}@ri.se
[2] KTH Royal Institute of Technology, 100 44 Stockholm, Sweden

Abstract. In the past few years, the ethics and transparency of AI and other digital systems have received much attention. There is a vivid discussion on explainable AI, both among practitioners and in academia, with contributions from diverse fields such as computer science, human-computer interaction, law, and philosophy. Using the Value Sensitive Design (VSD) method as a point of departure, this paper explores how VSD can be used in the context of transparency. More precisely, it is investigated (i) if the VSD Envisioning Cards facilitate transparency as a pro-ethical condition, (ii) if they can be improved to realize ethical principles through transparency, and (iii) if they can be adapted to facilitate reflection on ethical principles in large groups. The research questions are addressed through a two-fold case study, combining one case where a larger audience participated in a reduced version of VSD with another case where a smaller audience participated in a more traditional VSD workshop. It is concluded that while the Envisioning Cards are effective in promoting ethical reflection in general, the realization of ethical values through transparency is not always similarly promoted. Therefore, it is proposed that a transparency card be added to the Envisioning Card deck. It is also concluded that a lightweight version of VSD seems useful in engaging larger audiences. The paper is concluded with some suggestions for future work.

Keywords: Value Sensitive Design · Transparency · Explainability · Financial markets · Internet of Things

1 Introduction

With recent advances in Artificial Intelligence (AI), issues pertaining to the ethics and transparency of AI and other digital systems have received much attention. Contributions come from many academic fields, including computer science, human-computer interaction, law, philosophy, and others. Among the

This research was partially supported by Länsförsäkringsgruppens Forsknings- & Utvecklingsfond, agreement no. P4/18.

ⓒ Springer Nature Switzerland AG 2020
H. Degen and L. Reinerman-Jones (Eds.): HCII 2020, LNCS 12217, pp. 3–15, 2020.
https://doi.org/10.1007/978-3-030-50334-5_1

questions explored are how to understand the notions of transparency and explainability in different contexts, how to make existing systems more transparent, what effects transparency can entail, and how to construct systems for increased transparency from the very first design phases.

It is the latter problem of *designing for transparency* that we address in this paper. More precisely, we present some first steps towards applying Value Sensitive Design (VSD), and specifically the Envisioning Cards,[1] to this end. VSD was introduced by Batya Friedman in 1996 [9] as a method to systematically and proactively take account of human values throughout a design process. In the decades since, it has been influential in the design of information systems in general [10] as well as AI in particular [6,15].

While VSD is useful for getting participants to adopt more varied ethical viewpoints, it is also important to make sure that those viewpoints are put into practice. Turilli & Floridi [13] argue that information transparency serves as a *pro-ethical condition*. This means that in order for certain ethical principles to be realized, we need to consider information transparency. For example, sometimes ethical principles might require data transparency, whereas sometimes, ethics might require data to be hidden, but the rules regulating this practice to be transparent. We are therefore interested in seeing whether Envisioning Cards let participants discuss how transparency can act as such a pro-ethical condition, increasing chances that ethical principles are realized.

Thus, in this paper we explore how VSD can be used in new contexts to engage broader audiences and, perhaps more importantly, how and if Envisioning Cards could be amended to not only *highlight* but also *realize* ethical principles in design processes. More precisely, the research questions addressed are the following:

RQ1: Do the VSD Envisioning Cards facilitate transparency as a pro-ethical condition?

RQ2: How can the Envisioning Card tool be improved in order to realize ethical principles through transparency?

RQ3: Can the Envisioning Card tool be adapted to facilitate reflection on ethical principles in large groups?

The remainder of this paper is structured as follows: The next section gives an overview of related work. Section 3 introduces the research method used, followed by a presentation of results in Sect. 4. These are discussed in Sect. 5, before Sect. 6 concludes the paper.

2   Related Work

Transparency in digital systems is a topic well covered in academic literature, and is naturally much more complex than the simplifications made in this article.

First, transparency is not necessarily beneficial in and of itself. As related in the introduction above, Turilli & Floridi [13] call transparency a *pro-ethical*

---

[1] www.envisioningcards.com.

condition, meaning that transparency is a condition for several ethical principles. The condition has two relations—dependence and regulation. For dependence, their argument is that several ethical principles are dependent on transparency in order to be realized—accountability and informed consent among them. Here, information has to be disclosed in some form in order for accountability to "exist in any meaningful way" (quoting from Mallin [11]). For instance informed consent cannot exist without having information to consent to. As for regulation, ethical principles—here the examples are privacy, anonymity and freedom of expression—work by restricting the flow of information, but transparency also enables ethical principles by providing information about "regulatory constraints to the public".

de Laat adopts a somewhat similar instrumental view of transparency, arguing that *full* transparency most often is not desirable, listing several objections [3]: loss of privacy, perverse effects of disclosure, loss of competitive edge, and the limited gains that can be expected from transparency if algorithms are inherently opaque. Instead, he opts for full transparency for oversight bodies only, rather than the general public.

Royakkers et al. [12] bring up social and ethical issues that proceed as a result of digitalization by looking at various technologies, such as Internet of Things, biometrics, robotics, and digital platforms. It turns out that six public (ethical) values recur throughout their investigation [12]: Privacy, autonomy, security, human dignity, justice and balance of power. Increased digitalization in society puts these values under various forms of pressure. Furthermore, it is emphasized that transparency is an issue involved in for example privacy and balance of power. To uphold the ethical values, it is important to elucidate issues involved, such as transparency.

It is also important to relate to the emerging field of AI ethics, as AI systems have an increasing impact on society. It is commonly held that ethical and social values must be reflected in AI design. Dignum [5] discusses transparency as an important ethical construction to understand AI systems. Furthermore, Dignum argues that accountability, responsibility and transparency (ART) are essential principles that should form the basis of AI systems.

Zerilli et al. argue that while transparency and explainability are certainly important, it may be that algorithms are held to an unrealistically high standard [17]. They review evidence of well-known flaws (including transparency problems) in human decision-making, and propose that relevant justification of algorithmic decisions should be similar to human justification. More precisely, they recommend explanations for algorithmic decisions similar to Daniel Dennett's theory of the "intentional stance" [4], rather than explanations based on the technical architectures of tools.

The aim of our paper is not to make a contribution to the theoretical literature on transparency. Our ultimate aim is more empirical, as related in the RQs, even though this paper only represents some first steps. However, we note with satisfaction that questions related to transparency in information systems attract considerable attention, emphasizing the (eventual) importance of empirical research such as ours.

3   Method

The study reported is two-fold, combining a first case where a larger audience participated in a reduced version of VSD, with an emphasis on transparency, with a second case where a smaller audience participated in a more traditional VSD workshop. Both cases took place in December, 2019. Following an introduction of the VSD method, the conditions of the two cases studied are described.

3.1   Value Sensitive Design

Value Sensitive Design (VSD) is a theoretically grounded strategy for the design of technology that attempts to present human values in a fundamental and comprehensive way throughout the design process. It uses an iterative tripartite methodology, consisting of (i) conceptual, (ii) empirical, and (iii) technological investigations around human values [8]. Though the early literature on VSD did not define values explicitly but rather used examples [2], Friedman et al. in later work define a human value as "what is important to people in their lives, with a focus on ethics and morality" [8]. Examples important in technical design include human welfare, privacy, freedom from bias, trust, autonomy, informed consent and identity [8].

Conceptual investigations include philosophically informed analysis with the goal to identify the stakeholders who are influenced by the technical design and also the central values at stake in the design context [8]. The *empirical* investigations are based on the conceptual by identifying values that are important to the stakeholders (both direct and indirect stakeholders) when they use the technology. The significance of the empirical investigation is to obtain information about how stakeholders perceive the technical artifact with respect to the values that are important to them in relation to their social context in which the technology is located [8,10]. The *technical* investigations focus on the technical design and performance. An important aspect of VSD is the focus on both direct and indirect stakeholders, as well as how the technology will promote the human and moral values identified. Each decision will have an impact on usability, stakeholder values and stakeholder access.

In [8] a number of VSD methods are presented which provide guidance on how to conduct a certain type of research or design enquiry. The methods are based on the theoretical constructs of VSD. For example, an important theoretical commitment (conceptual) is to identify the direct and indirect stakeholders in a design project. One practical method is the Envisioning cards, which is like a versatile toolkit that take into account human values during the design process. The method is based on four *envisioning criteria* [7]: (i) stakeholders, (ii) time, (iii) values, and (iv) pervasiveness. The cards can be used by for example designers, technologists and end-users as they are self-explanatory and the

Fig. 1. Data collection in case 1, along with refreshments.

cards support them in the ethical reflection. The cards are "designed to provide opportunities for values-oriented reflection, iteration, and course correction throughout the design, implementation, and evaluation of information tools" according to Davis & Nathan [2]. Davis & Nathan also claim that as of 2015, Envisioning Cards had only been applied in classroom settings in academia.

3.2 Case 1

The first case took place at an event titled *Financial Markets Transparency*, co-hosted by the authors at the Stockholm School on Economics. Following a keynote on financial markets and AI by Paolo Sironi from IBM Watson Financial Services, the VSD Envisioning Cards were used to engage the audience, consisting of 25 people, mostly professionals from the IT and finance sectors. More precisely, four pairs of cards and adapted questions, one for each of the four envisioning criteria, were shown to the audience, as illustrated in Fig. 1. Their answers to the questions were collected using menti.com, and the results were presented to all as they were entered. Participants were free to submit as many responses as they pleased during the time the poll was active, i.e., more than one answer per participant was allowed. Following this data collection, which coincided with some refreshments, three additional experts from academia, industry, and government joined the keynote speaker in a panel. In the panel discussion, the moderator (one of the authors) used the questions and the answers collected as input.

3.3 Case 2

The second case took place within the context of an R&D project conducted jointly between one research institute, one university college, and five commercial

Fig. 2. An illustration of the model: finding ways for the workers to use IoT technology.

companies working with industrial production. The project aim is to find ways for workers in manufacturing to quickly put internet-of-things (IoT) technology to use, without need for additional training or external experts. (To meet this goal, the project has a particular focus on the technology being accessible and understandable, thus lowering the threshold for its use by the factory workers). Two of the authors conducted a 2-h workshop with 5 people (researchers from the research institute) participating in the project. In this case, the VSD methodology was followed more thoroughly, and the Envisioning Cards were again used to introduce new perspectives to the workshop participants and provoke their thoughts.

The workshop started by explaining the purpose and method. Then, participants drew a model of their project on a large paper (see Fig. 2), both to give themselves a shared view of what they were working on, and to give the workshop leaders an insight into what the project was about. Then, in segments of 20 min per category, Envisioning Cards were introduced. For *stakeholders* the cards *Direct Stakeholders* and *Non-targeted Use* were used, for *time Work of the Future* and *Obsolesence*, for *values Choose Desired Values* and *Elicit Stakeholder Views and Values*, and for *pervasiveness Accounting for Culture* and *Widespread Use*. The workshop leaders were active in the discussion, suggesting perspectives and challenging views and arguments of the participants. The results were documented by saving the physical artifacts created in the session, i.e., hand-drawn model illustrations, post-its added to the illustration, and lists pertaining to different Envisioning Cards. After the workshop, the participants were invited to share their impressions and thoughts about the method in order for the workshop leaders to evaluate what effect the participants thought the method had.

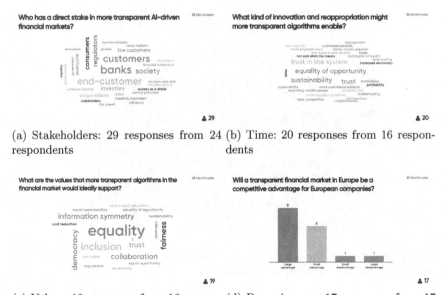

(a) Stakeholders: 29 responses from 24 respondents

(b) Time: 20 responses from 16 respondents

(c) Values: 19 responses from 16 respondents

(d) Pervasiveness: 17 responses from 17 respondents

Fig. 3. Case 1 audience responses to the questions, arranged by envisioning criteria. Each response can contain up to five separate text field inputs.

4 Results

4.1 Case 1

The answers given to the *stakeholders* question (Fig. 3(a)) show a heavy emphasis on consumer perspectives ("consumers", "customers", "end-customer", "hopefully customers", "the customers") and the corporate entities that would adopt more transparent algorithms ("banks", "corporations", "financial institutions", "microbanks"). The *time* question (Fig. 3(b)) offers a less coherent image, but is centered on trust, sustainability and equality. The answers to the *values* question (Fig. 3(c)) highlight equality and inclusion, as well as democracy, trust, collaboration, fairness and information symmetry. The *pervasiveness* question (Fig. 3(d)), finally, is heavily skewed towards transparency being positive for European actors. While we did not test for the prior knowledge and views of participants, the answers give a broader view than the authors had expected—either indicating that the participants were more well versed in the topic than expected, or that the questions actually help re-frame the topic and offer broader perspectives, as VSD aims to.

Fig. 4. The results from the brainstorming with the Envisioning Cards; (i) Stakeholders, (ii) Time, (iii) Values and (iv) Pervasiveness.

4.2   Case 2

The participants initially described their project as focusing on giving production line workers an easy way to implement IoT monitoring and then being able to respond to the input from the IoT system—hopefully giving better overview, quicker response time for service and letting employees take initiatives in developing the production line. The results from the brainstorming with the four categories of envisioning cards are illustrated in Fig. 4 and described in greater detail in the following.

The *stakeholders* cards let the participants first identify actors in the process and their motivations, and then possibilities that the system might be used for things which the participants did not intend. The participants zeroed in on the people who are involved in the work they want to affect, a somewhat narrow definition of stakeholder. The workshop leaders helped the participants expand the definition, which appeared to be useful in later discussions. The *Non-targeted Use* card led the participants to think of the unintended consequences a very adaptable system might have, and the problem with enabling more monitoring in the workplace.

The *time* cards started with a brainstorming session which created a lot of output, but did not foster discussion in the same way the previous cards had. The *Obsolescence* card seemed to not match the project as well as the workshop leaders had anticipated—the participants seemed fairly confident in that technological or methodological obsolescence was not a large concern going forward.

The *values* cards were to be fairly close to what the participants saw as the stand out feature of their project. Despite this, the group mentioned that this was one of the more valuable parts of the workshop, as they had not tried to formulate values—and especially tensions between different stakeholders and values. The latter question opened up lines of thought that the participants claim they had not dealt with before, and was one of the reasons why they stated that they would want to adapt the method themselves when continuing their work in the project.

The *pervasiveness* cards were further from the group's normal line of work. Regarding cultures, they quickly broke the question down to not only deal with culture as in different origins, but also culture in the workplace, and between different roles in a project, e.g., themselves as researchers, and their project partners as line workers or managers at private companies. The final card proved harder to get results from.

The participants in Case 2 were already well versed in workshops and methods for expanding thinking on responsibility and human centered design. However, they stated after the workshop that they had not reflected on a number of the perspectives among the Envisioning Cards, specifically when it came to assigning specific values and reflecting on value tensions, as well as cultural impacts. As an aside, the group also stated that they intend to adopt the VSD method in their project.

However, while the group did reflect on ethical principles and the consequences of using technologies in different ways, they did not explicitly discuss those things in terms of transparency. Inferences could be made from how certain aspects of the process were described (e.g. being able to discuss what problems to solve and how among coworkers requires transparency to some degree) but were not mentioned outright, and aside from wanting to use the method in their project, the participants did not discuss how to realize ethical principles and values that they had identified.

5 Discussion

5.1 Reliability and Validity

Having used two different approaches to the Envisioning Cards, one in line with normal procedures and one where aspects of the Envisioning Cards were used in a very different setting, the reliability of the study is somewhat mixed. For case 2, the participants believe that they reflected on values and ethics in a way that they have not done before, which seems to be in line with the aim and use of the method. However, repeated attempts with the same group have not been performed, which weakens the reliability somewhat as only one instance for applying the method has been realized. In case 1, the Envisioning Cards were applied in an unorthodox way in a single instance. While the results are interesting and noteworthy, reliability is admittedly not as high as it would be with repeated trials on new audiences and new formulations.

In both cases, the validity seems to be good. Case 1 investigates whether adaptation of the Envisioning Cards is possible on larger audiences, and the menti.com system was used by the audience for interaction and engagement in the discussion. Case 2 was, as previously remarked, a fairly standard workshop using Envisioning Cards. The reflections from the participants give an indication of how the method influenced the participants' reasoning.

5.2   Effects of Using Envisioning Cards

Despite Envisioning Cards being a tool that is most often applied to smaller teams, case 1 showed that even in a setting with larger audiences the types of questions posed in the Envisioning Cards do allow participants to reflect on ethical principles to a larger extent than the authors initially assumed. A live word cloud was used to support the participants and gave the ability for them to add multiple answers. The participants could see the word cloud forming and updating (see Fig. 3) both on the auditorium screen and in their respective phones or computers. This allows the audience to react, e.g., 'agreeing' by submitting an identical answer, or 'conversing' by submitting an answer inspired by a previous one. However, this requires instructions to make sure that the audience makes use of this latent interactivity. Such instructions could also alleviate some disadvantages of word clouds, such as similar concepts not identically worded being separately treated (e.g., "customers" and "end-customers" in Fig. 3(a)). As shown in Fig. 3, all of the word clouds had more answers submitted than individuals who submitted responses (and each submitted response could include five separate answers). It can thus be concluded that VSD-inspired questions can indeed be used in larger settings to provide new perspectives.

The Envisioning Cards, unsurprisingly, work best when there is a common design project for all the participants (case 2). The common design project gives a common frame of reference that is a clear benefit compared to what is possible in more loosely assembled audience as in case 1. Symptoms of this in the larger audience include lack of common understanding of the questions discussed (cf., e.g., the "nor (sic!) sure what this means" comment (barely visible) in Fig. 3(b)).

In case 2, the participants managed to make many more values and principles more explicit than in case 1. This is, of course, partly due to the more standard use case for the Envisioning Cards, and perhaps partly due to the participants in case 2 being more versed and in tune with the perspectives that the cards aim at getting participants to discuss. Having a drawing of the entire process (Fig. 2) made the team focus not only on the finished product but also on what it takes to get it there, and where different ethical principles and values come into play. The group used the drawn image of the project as a reference when discussing the various cards, and made amendments along the way when they thought of processes that they had initially forgotten to make explicit.

The participants in case 2 said that the method made them reflect on the possible adverse effects of their project. Previously, while they had worked on human-centred perspectives, they had mainly reflected on positive uses and positive effects, with little or no reflection of possible negative (unintended) implications. The group claimed that the VSD approach helped them see the project and their method in a broader perspective.

5.3   Transparency

In case 1, transparency was introduced as an explicit part of the questions posed, in order to make them more in line with the theme of the seminar. In case 2, we did not explicitly introduce any questions regarding transparency. Therefore case 2 can be used to see if the Envisioning Cards also help participants to connect the dots between what ethical principles are introduced in the workshop, and how to actually realize those principles (as per Turilli's & Floridi's hypothesis about transparency as a *pro-ethical condition* [13]).

However, in the discussions in case 2 transparency was *not* brought up as an explicit condition for realizing ethical principles. The participants did, however, seem to come to a realization that it was necessary to be more explicit and present with the employees in stage 1–3 (see Fig. 2) in order for the actual implementation to be of high quality. The participants concluded that while the *product* itself might not be clear with information output, the *process* ought to be. This realization, by the workshop participants, could be construed as (a particular kind of) transparency being important to realize the ethical value "democratize technology" [16] which was highlighted by the participants as a core value of the product.

6   Conclusion

The results are related to the three questions presented in the introduction.

RQ 1: *Do the VSD Envisioning Cards facilitate transparency as a pro-ethical condition?* It is concluded that while the Envisioning Cards are an effective tool to promote reflection on values and ethical principles, it is not necessarily promoting ways to realize those values and principles through transparency.

RQ 2: *How can the Envisioning Card tool be improved in order to realize ethical principles through transparency?* Going forward—while our research is narrow in scope, we propose that (at least) one additional card be introduced to the Envisioning Card deck, a card in the pervasiveness category to deal with the problem of realizing ethical principles. In short—a transparency card. As stated in the literature, with AI technologies becoming more prevalent, transparency is most likely growing more important for organisations aiming to fulfill ethical principles.

We also suggest further empirical evaluation of end results from design processes, such as actual products or services designed and built, in terms of desirable features that were aimed for in the Envisioning Card session, such as transparency. Though such evaluation may require more time (even considerably more, depending on the context), we believe that this is a very worthwhile empirical endeavor which would shed considerable additional light on what can and cannot reasonably be accomplished using VSD and its Envisioning Cards.

RQ 3: *Can the Envisioning Card tool be adapted to facilitate reflection on ethical principles in large groups?* We conclude that a lightweight version of the method seems useful in engaging larger audiences with the relevant questions and tools that help audiences interact. However, it is also clear that more research is needed to further corroborate this finding.

As for methodology, in case 1 at least two things need to be adjusted for, or developed further. First, there is a need for further investigation into the importance of common understanding of the problem beforehand, e.g., as gained from an introductory lecture to a larger audience, in order to further mimic the workshop setting that the Envisioning Cards are usually applied in. Second, there is a need for further investigation of the impact of particular wordings when paraphrasing the Envisioning Cards for specific contexts, which will undoubtedly prime and anchor [14] participants into particular ways of thinking. But these require serious consideration when extrapolating the VSD method to new settings. We would also suggest further development of VSD for larger audiences, such as case 1, inspired by insights from the literature, e.g., [1]. In an academic setting, the adapted method could also be used in a class setting during a full course, to facilitate the repetition and shared perspectives the method encourages.

Finally, some reflections and further investigations regarding the use of the Envisioning Cards in design projects that fit into case 2. We would like to continue following the process and use the cards over time. Further investigation of the effectiveness of cards on different participants, taking prior knowledge and other demographic factors into account would be welcome. We would also like to further develop what sort of artifacts participants ought to make during the workshop in order to both improve the discussion and, more importantly, give the participants something to come back to when continuing the design process.

Using the VSD in one-off settings leaves several discussions unresolved, such as finding out what participants think about the discussions in between iterations and how the ideas that are developed in the workshops are implemented over time. While this first study did not adopt the iterative process that is suggested in the instructions for the Envisioning Cards, we are confident that it would increase the value of the method and allow the results to be absorbed by the participants to a larger degree.

References

1. Bateman, S., Gutwin, C., Nacenta, M.: Seeing things in the clouds: the effect of visual features on tag cloud selections. In: Proceedings of the Nineteenth ACM Conference on Hypertext and Hypermedia, pp. 193–202. ACM (2008). https://doi.org/10.1145/1379092.1379130
2. Davis, J., Nathan, L.P.: Value sensitive design: applications, adaptations, and critiques. In: van den Hoven, J., Vermaas, P.E., van de Poel, I. (eds.) Handbook of Ethics, Values, and Technological Design, pp. 11–40. Springer, Dordrecht (2015). https://doi.org/10.1007/978-94-007-6970-0_3
3. de Laat, P.B.: Algorithmic decision-making based on machine learning from big data: can transparency restore accountability? Philos. Technol. **31**(4), 525–541 (2017). https://doi.org/10.1007/s13347-017-0293-z
4. Dennett, D.C.: The Intentional Stance. MIT Press, Cambridge (1989)

5. Dignum, V.: Responsible autonomy. In: Proceedings 26th International Joint Conference on Artificial Intelligence, pp. 4698–4704. IJCAI (2017)
6. Dignum, V.: Responsible artificial intelligence: designing AI for human values. ITU J. ICT Discov. (1) (2017)
7. Friedman, B., Hendry, D.G.: The envisioning cards: a toolkit for catalyzing humanistic and technical imaginations. In: Proceedings of the 2012 Annual Conference on Human Factors in Computing Systems, pp. 1145–1148. ACM (2012). https://doi.org/10.1145/2207676.2208562
8. Friedman, B., Hendry, D.G.: Value Sensitive Design: Shaping Technology with Moral Imagination. The MIT Press, Cambridge (2019)
9. Friedman, B.: Value-sensitive design. Interactions **3**(6), 16–23 (1996). https://doi.org/10.1145/242485.242493
10. Friedman, B., Kahn, P.H., Borning, A., Huldtgren, A.: Value sensitive design and information systems. In: Doorn, N., Schuurbiers, D., van de Poel, I., Gorman, M.E. (eds.) Early Engagement and New Technologies: Opening Up the Laboratory. PET, vol. 16, pp. 55–95. Springer, Dordrecht (2013). https://doi.org/10.1007/978-94-007-7844-3_4
11. Mallin, C.: The relationship between corporate governance, transparency and financial disclosure. Corp. Gov. Int. Rev. **10**, 253–255 (2002). https://doi.org/10.1111/1467-8683.00289
12. Royakkers, L., Timmer, J., Kool, L., van Est, R.: Societal and ethical issues of digitization. Ethics Inf. Technol. **20**, 127–142 (2018). https://doi.org/10.1007/s10676-018-9452-x
13. Turilli, M., Floridi, L.: The ethics of information transparency. Ethics Inf. Technol. **11**(2), 105–112 (2009). https://doi.org/10.1007/s10676-009-9187-9
14. Tversky, A., Kahneman, D.: Judgment under uncertainty: heuristics and biases. Science **185**(4157), 1124–1131 (1974). https://doi.org/10.1126/science.185.4157.1124
15. Umbrello, S.: Beneficial artificial intelligence coordination by means of a value sensitive design approach. Big Data Cogn. Comput. **3**(1), 5 (2019). https://doi.org/10.3390/bdcc3010005
16. Yamamoto, Y., Sandström, K., Munoz, A.A.: Karakuri IoT - the concept and the result of pre-study advances in manufacturing technology. In: Advances in Manufacturing Technology XXXII, pp. 311–316. IOS Press (2018). https://doi.org/10.3233/978-1-61499-902-7-311
17. Zerilli, J., Knott, A., Maclaurin, J., Gavaghan, C.: Transparency in algorithmic and human decision-making: is there a double standard? Philos. Technol. **32**(4), 661–683 (2018). https://doi.org/10.1007/s13347-018-0330-6

A Method for Quickly Establishing Personas

Wen-jun Hou[1,2], Xiang-yuan Yan[1,2(✉)] (iD), and Jia-xin Liu[1,2] (iD)

[1] School of Digital Media and Design Arts, Beijing University of Posts and Telecommunications, Beijing 100876, China
1642738174@qq.com
[2] Beijing Key Laboratory of Network Systems and Network Culture, Beijing University of Posts and Telecommunications, Beijing 100876, China

Abstract. The use of personas can help teams better understand the characteristics of users, which leads to more accurately discovery the problems and real pain points that users face. At present, there are two main ways to establish personas. One is to generate personas qualitatively or quantitatively through interviews, questionnaires, etc. These processes are related to the experiences of analysts and the statistical methods used, usually resulting in different conclusions and spending much time. The other is that the technical teams directly obtain the users' operation data on the products and use algorithm models to automatically generate personas. But this method is only suitable for mature products or existing functions, while the questionnaire method has nothing to do with mature products and functions. In this paper, we present persona segmentation through K-Means and PAM clustering algorithms in machine learning for questionnaire data, including mixed data, as an objective, quick, low-cost method for establishing personas. The method consists of four steps: first, design questionnaire. Second, transform the multi variables caused by multiple choice questions into a single variable. K-Means clustering algorithm is used for the continuous data of multi variables. The rule-based clustering method is used for the classified data. Then, cluster the processed data by PAM. The fourth step is to create personas, which are labeled in this paper. In the end, we demonstrate that the method is appropriate to create useful personas by machine evaluation and expert evaluation.

Keywords: Personas · Questionnaire · Clustering algorithm · Machine learning · Label

1 Introduction

Alan Cooper first proposed the concept of persona-technique [1]. It is a fictional character, made up of a demographic profile, 'psychographics' such as goals, attitudes, behaviors and a series of needs [2]. Persona is an abstract representation of a unique group of people who share common goals, attitudes, and behaviors.

© Springer Nature Switzerland AG 2020
H. Degen and L. Reinerman-Jones (Eds.): HCII 2020, LNCS 12217, pp. 16–32, 2020.
https://doi.org/10.1007/978-3-030-50334-5_2

Personas are currently used in many fields, so it is necessary to establish personas quickly and economically. In terms of marketing and user research, personas are widely used to summarize core users of websites and mobile applications or to select participates in tests [3,4,7]. Personas are also used to analyze target groups of marketing campaigns [5,6]. In addition to product recovery and upgrade, personas are also very important. Not only many workers, but most academicians and practitioners also analyze users and create personas [8]. Therefore, if personas can be established quickly and economically, the enterprise work and scientific research can be promoted efficiently.

At present, there are two methods to build personas. The first method is to collect data manually and then build personas qualitatively or quantitatively. Through qualitative data such as interviews, experts cluster users to generate personas. However, this approach has been criticized because of its lack of rigor: developing personas based on a set of interviews with a limited number of users can hardly represent the breadth of real users [9]. Besides, some researchers generate personas quantitatively through questionnaires and statistical methods. Different analysts use different statistical methods, leading to different results [8]. The second is that technical teams directly obtain the users' operation data on the products, such as click, purchase and other behavior data, and automatically generate the personas based on the algorithm model [10–12], but this method is only applicable to the existing products with a large number of users and the teams with high level of technology.

These methods seldom consider how to establish personas objectively, effectively, quickly and economically when there is no product or technical ability.

Generally speaking, the questionnaire is a commonly used quantitative method for personas establishment, which can solve the problem of small sample size and no representativeness, and has nothing to do with whether there are mature products. But for the analysis of questionnaire data, different experts adopt different statistical methods, usually resulting in different conclusions and spending much time. Moreover, it is difficult to design the questionnaire within the limitations of the data type of statistical methods. To solve the above problems, we propose the combination of the questionnaire method and machine learning clustering algorithm to build personas. Thanks to the development of machine learning technology in recent years, the algorithm for clustering classified data, continuous data and mixed data has been very mature. A persona is a group representative of similar users, while clustering algorithms just divide similar users together. So clustering algorithms are very direct methods to build personas.

In this paper, we will focus on the questionnaire; the clustering algorithm of machine learning, and explain how to process the questionnaire data into the data needed by the clustering algorithm. Writing the character narratives will not be considered. Next, we will demonstrate the method's use in a case study creating persona segmentations for the design of Postal Bank Hall in Beijing, China. Finally, the validity of this method is proved by clustering algorithm evaluation and consistency evaluation.

2   Related Work

2.1   Qualitative Personas

The personas were initially established by the qualitative methods [13]. Generally speaking, these methods need to obtain text information through one-to-one interviews and observation. Through analysis and comparison, the most important behavioral variables that can classify users, are determined. Then segmentation process is mostly done with the use of manual techniques, such as affinity diagrams, card sorting exercises and expert panels [5,14]. Besides, semi-automatic Latent semantic analysis [15] and action research with tacit knowledge [16] can also be used in the segmentation process. Finally, based on the collected data, the personas are described. However, the number of users interviewed one-on-one is limited so that the personas cannot represent the breadth of real users [9]. When the number of data increases, human experts are easily affected by their own experience in analysis, resulting in cognitive biases of users, subjective decision and lack of accuracy. So the method proposed in this paper uses the questionnaire to collect data and the machine learning to analyze data to avoid subjective decisions.

2.2   Quantitative Personas

To improve the accuracy of personas, it is more and more common to establish personas in quantitative ways. Originally, the questionnaire is distributed to collect data, and then the personas are produced by statistical techniques. Different experts adopt different methods. McGinn use Factor Analysis to create personas [17], Greaney use Principal Component Analysis [18], and Laporte use Correspondence Analysis [2]. However, these three analysis methods are time-consuming and only work on a single data type. That is to say, the premise of using these methods is that the data must be all continuous data or all classified data, which limits the questionnaire design. Moreover, these methods are still inseparable from the subjective judgment of the analysts, resulting in different conclusions.

Cluster Analysis is an exploratory analysis method without prior knowledge. Some researchers use Cluster Analysis to build personas [8,19], which has the advantages of fast and low cost. However, the clustering algorithms they use are all clustering models in SPSS (an analysis software), which are also only applicable to a single type of data, limiting the design of the questionnaire, and the clustering effect is not very good due to the inability to adjust the parameters.

There are some controversies on personas establishment with Cluster Analysis. It is often criticized because it will identify clusters based on any input data, even if there is no underlying structure in the data [20]. This is the disadvantage of no prior knowledge. However, by high-dimensional data visualization technology, the clustering effect can be expressed and evaluated. Besides, the clustering algorithm is described as a black box [2]. The traditional clustering algorithm is based on mathematics, not a black box, such as K-Means and PAM algorithm.

Therefore, the clustering algorithm in machine learning is expected to be a fast and effective way to build personas without restricting the questionnaire design.

2.3 Automatically Generated Personas

With the abundance of Internet products, some teams began to study how to use big data to build personas. The technical team can obtain the users' click, shopping, browsing and other behaviors data on the product through the deployment of files. Then they generate personas automatically and in real-time [10–12]. The automatic persona generation (APG) can facilitate enterprise personnel to view and analyze data in real-time. APG is also a good solution for changing user data [21]. However, the deployment of APG is massive and the generation algorithm is complex. Most importantly, the premise of establishing APG is the existence of mature products. Therefore, if it is impossible to use APG, but necessary to understand attitudes, views and other information, the method of combining the questionnaire and clustering algorithm in machine learning proposed can be used to build personas quickly, objectively and explicitly.

The main contribution of this paper is:

- We propose a method, combining questionnaire and K-means and PAM clustering algorithms in machine learning to build personas, which can make up for the problem that the statistical analysis takes a long time and that the results of different experts are different.
- Describe the method step by step and specific details. This method can process the mixed data and solve the problem that the existing methods can only deal with a single type of data, which limits the design of the questionnaire.
- Based on the case of Postal Bank Hall, this method was used. The validity of this method was proved by clustering algorithm evaluation and consistency evaluation.

3 Methods

3.1 Overview of Methods

The whole method is divided into four steps.

First, design the questionnaire. In general, personas of a product can be constructed from several aspects, such as user goals, behavior, economic level, demography, and other needs. The designed questionnaire often includes single choice questions, multiple choice questions, matrix questions and so on. The collected data include classified data or continuous data in single variable, continuous data in multi variables and dichotomy data in multi variables caused by multiple choice questions.

Secondly, transform the multi variables caused by multiple choice questions into a single variable. K-Mean is used to analyze the continuous data in multi variables, observe and obtain the clustered results as the transformation results. The rules defined in advance are used to cluster the classified data in multi variables, and the clustered results are taken as the transformation results.

Thirdly, cluster users according to all the processed variables. In the second step, all multivariate data are transformed into single variable data, and then machine learning PAM algorithm is used for clustering. PAM algorithm can cluster continuous data and classified data at the same time. After clustering all cases, clustered results will be produced, which is a group of similar users. This is the first and most critical step in building personas.

Fourth, create personas. We created personas with label in the last, but writing the character narratives will not be considered.

3.2   K-Means Algorithm

Introduction of K-Means. The K-Means algorithm is an unsupervised clustering algorithm that is simple to implement and has a good clustering effect. The idea of K-means algorithm is simple, that is, for a given sample set, the sample set is divided into K clusters according to the distance between the samples, so that the points in the cluster are connected as closely as possible, and the distance of different clusters is as large as possible [22].

The process is to first randomly select the initial point as the centroid, and calculate the similarity between each sample and the centroid. In this algorithm, the similarity is represented by the value of Euclidean distance. The sample points are classified into the most similar classes, and then the centroids of each class are recalculated. This process is repeated until the centroids no longer change. The categories to which each sample belongs and the centroid of each category.

The algorithm flow is as follows:

Suppose the input sample set $D = x_1, x_2, \ldots, x_m$, the number of clusters is K, the maximum number of iterations is N, and the output cluster is divided into $C = C_1, C_2, C_3, \ldots, C_k$. Our goal is to minimize the squared error E (Eq. 1).

$$E = \sum_{i=1}^{k} \sum_{x \in C_i} \|x - \mu_i\|^2 \tag{1}$$

where μ_i (Eq. 2) is the mean vector of the cluster C_i, which can also be called the centroid.

$$\mu_i = \frac{1}{|C_i|} \sum_{x \in C_i} x \tag{2}$$

Step 1: Randomly select K samples from the data set D as the initial centroid vector $\mu = \{\mu_1, \mu_2, \mu_3, \mu_k\}$.

Step 2: Iterate $n = 1, 2, \ldots, N$.

- Divide the initialization cluster. $C_t = \phi, t = 1, 2, \ldots, k$.
- For $i = 1, 2, \ldots, m$, calculate the distance d_{ij} (Eq. 3) between the sample x_i and each centroid vector $\mu_j (j = 1, 2, \ldots, k)$. Mark x_i as the category λ_i corresponding to the smallest d_{ij}, and update $C_{\lambda_i} \cup x_i$ at this time.

$$d_{ij} = \|x_i - \mu_i\|^2 \tag{3}$$

- For $j = 1, 2, \ldots, k$, recalculate the new centroids for all sample points in C_j.
- If none of the K centroid vectors change any more, end the iteration.

Step 3: Enter K divided clusters C, $C = \{C_1, C_2, C_3, C_k\}$.

Clustering Effect Evaluation. The effect of clustering can be judged by the Calinski-Harabasz Index [23]. The formula for calculating its score s is as follows in Eq. 4.

$$s(k) = \frac{tr(B_k)}{tr(W_k)} \frac{m - k}{k - 1} \tag{4}$$

where m is the number of training set samples and k is the number of categories. B_k is the covariance matrix between categories, and W_k is the covariance matrix of the data within the categories. tr is the trace of the matrix.

This indicator represents that the smaller the covariance of the data within a category, the better, and the larger the covariance between categories, the better, such that the Calinski-Harabasz score will be high.

3.3 PAM Algorithm

Introduction of PAM. K-means can only cluster continuous variables, so when final clustering is performed on all data, we choose the PAM clustering method. PAM can use arbitrary distances for calculation, it is not sensitive to "noise" and outlier data, and can accommodate mixed data types, not limited to continuous variables.

The purpose of the PAM algorithm is to give k partitions to n data objects. The basic idea is: first, randomly select a center point for each cluster, and the remaining objects are assigned to the nearest cluster according to their distance or dissimilarity from the center point, and then repeatedly replace the center point with a non-center point to improve the quality of clustering [24]. Whether a non-representative object O_h (or center point) is a good substitute for the current representative object O_i (or center point). For each non-center point object O_j, the quality of the cluster is evaluated by a cost function C_{jih}.

There are four cases for the calculation of the cost function C_{jih}.

- O_j currently belongs to O_i. If O_i is replaced by O_h, and O_j is closest to another O_m, $i! = M$, then O_j is assigned to O_m, then the replacement cost is $C_{jih} = d(j, m) - d(j, i)$.
- O_j currently belongs to O_i. If O_i is replaced by O_h and O_j is closest to another O_h, then O_j is assigned to O_h, and the replacement cost is $C_{jih} = d(j, h) - d(j, i)$.
- O_j currently belongs to O_m, $m! = I$. If O_i is replaced by O_h, and O_j is still closest to O_m, then O_j is assigned to O_m, then the replacement cost is $C_{jih} = 0$.
- O_j currently belongs to O_m, $m! = I$, if O_i is replaced by O_h, and O_j is closest to O_h, then O_j is assigned to O_h, then the replacement cost is $C_{jih} = d(j, h) - d(j, m)$.

Clustering Effect Evaluation. For the K value selection of this clustering algorithm, we use the Silhouette Coefficient. The Silhouette Coefficient combines the Cohesion and Separation of the cluster to evaluate the effect of clustering [25]. The value is between -1 and 1. The larger the S value (Eq. 5), the better the clustering effect.

$$S = \frac{b - a}{max(a, b)}, S \in [-1, 1] \tag{5}$$

a is the average distance between X_i and other samples in the same cluster, called Cohesion. b is the average distance between X_i and all samples in the nearest cluster, called Separation. The nearest cluster is Eq. 6.

$$C_j = argmin_{C_k} \frac{1}{n} \sum_{p \in C_k} |p - X_i|^2 \tag{6}$$

Where p is a sample in a certain cluster C_k, that is, after using the average distance of all samples from X_i to a certain cluster as a measure of the distance from the point to the fail cluster, the cluster nearest to X_i is selected as the nearest cluster [26]. After the Silhouette Coefficient of all the samples are obtained, the average Silhouette Coefficient is obtained by averaging, and the closer the distance between the samples in the cluster, the farther the distance between the cluster samples, the larger the average Silhouette Coefficient, the better the clustering effect.

4   CASE STUDY: Creating Personas for Postal Bank Hall in Beijing

4.1   Questionnaire Design and Data Collection

To establish personas for Postal Bank Hall in Beijing, we designed a questionnaire, which is outlined in Table 1. Collecting user information from five aspects: Faith in Postal Bank, Behavior Attribute, Business Attribute, Economic Level and Demographics, each of which has 1 to 3 different questions. There are 11 questions in total. For example, in terms of Faith in Postal Bank, there are two questions: "how long have you been a postal customer?", "What services are important to you for Postal Bank Hall". Considering the logic of the questionnaire, questions in the same aspect are not distributed in order. Among the 11 questions, Q1, Q5, Q9, Q10 and Q11 are single choice questions, Q2 and Q8 are matrix questions, Q3 are blank filling questions, and Q4, Q6 and Q7 are multiple-choice questions.

We distributed questionnaires to all Postal Bank Hall in Beijing and collected 200 valid and real user data (105 men and 95 women).

Table 1. Questionnaire design outline and types of data collected.

Dimension	Q number	Q	Q type	Data type
Faith in Postal Bank	1	How long have you been a customer of Postal Bank?	Single choice question	Categorical
	6	What services are important to you for Postal Bank Hall	Multiple Choice	Categorical
Behavior Attribute	2	How and how often do you handle postal business	Matrix question	Categorical
	5	Why did you initially choose Postal Bank?	Single choice question	Categorical
	4	The type of business you do in the Postal Bank hall are	Multiple Choice	Categorical
Business Attribute	3	In the Postal Bank Hall, the amount of business you do is	Fill in the blanks	Continuous
Economic Level	7	The most popular sneaker brand you buy are	Multiple Choice	Categorical
	8	In the following seven aspects, your monthly consumption proportions are	Matrix question	Continuous
Demographics	9	Your gender is	Single choice question	Categorical
	10	Your age is	Single choice question	Categorical
	11	Your job is	Single choice question	Categorical

4.2 Data Processing

Multiple-choice questions often result in multiple variables in the same dimension and the value of each variable is 0 or 1. Similarly, matrix questions result in multiple variables in the same dimension, but each variable value is one of 1, 2, 3, etc. Matrix blank filling questions such as proportion collection may cause multiple variables in the same dimension and the value of each variable is continuous data. Combining these multi variables with single variables for clustering will affect the clustering effect and the interpretability of clustering results. Therefore, it is necessary to transform the multi variables caused by multiple questions into a single variable for clustering.

We Propose K-Means to Transform Continuous Data in Multi Variables into Classified Data in Single Variable. In this study, Q8 (In the following seven aspects, your monthly consumption proportions are) is a matrix question, as shown in the Table 2. The collected data is continuous. Every case is a seven-dimensional vector, which is clustered by k-means. We used the Calinski-Harabasz score to evaluate the clustering effect and found that when the number of categories is set to 3, the clustering effect is the best, clustering out three types of consumption concepts, which are shown on the two-dimensional graph of storage and diet (see Fig. 1). By analyzing the center point of classes, we can get the following conclusion.

A: The red spots are affiliate to class A, which is average in all expenses.

B: The green spots are class B, which is spending far greater in the diet, clothing than that in storage management.

C: The blue spots are class C. It is the person who spends more than half of his monthly income on storage management.

The above method can transform multi-variable continuous data into single-variable classified data.

Table 2. Q8 and collected data.

In the following seven aspects, your monthly consumption proportion are	Data
Rice, fruit, tobacco and alcohol	eg. 22 %
Clothes and daily necessities and services	eg. 10 %
Live	eg. 28 %
Traffic and communication	eg. 20 %
Education, culture and entertainment	eg. 7 %
medical insurance	eg. 3 %
Storage management	eg. 10 %

The Classified Data in Multi Variables are Clustered Based on Rules.
In this study, Q4, Q6, and Q7 are multiple-choice questions and the collected data are multivariate binary data. Take Q7 (The most popular sneaker brand you buy are) as an example. The data collected in Q7 are shown in the Table 3.

According to the pre-defined rules, as shown in Table 4, People who only buy Adidas and Reebok belong to category 1. They have strong purchasing power and pursuit of fashion. People who buy both Adidas and WARRIOR belong to category 2. They have purchasing power. People who buy Lining and WARRIOR belong to category 3. They have limited purchasing power and care about cost performance. People who only buy WARRIOR and XDLONG belong to category 4. They have weak purchasing power. Based on this, the classified data in multi variables are transformed into classified data in single variable, as shown in Table 5.

At this point, multi variables are transformed into single variables.

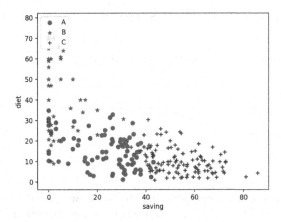

Fig. 1. Data of Q8 was clustered three types of consumption concepts, described in the two-dimensional map of storage and diet. (Color figure online)

Table 3. Nine options and user data for Q7 (The most popular sneaker brand you buy are).

Num	Lining, etc.	New balance, etc.	Adidas, etc.	ANTA, etc.	Reebok, etc.	XDLONG, etc.	WARRIOR, etc.	Other	Never
1	0	1	1	0	1	0	0	0	0
2	1	0	0	1	0	0	0	0	0
3	0	0	1	0	0	0	0	0	0
...	...	...	...	...	...	...	...	...	...
200	0	0	1	0	1	0	0	0	0

Table 4. Pre-defined rules for Q7.

Num	Meaning	Label1	Label2	Label3	Label4	Label5
1	Only buy Adidas and Reebok	Strong purchasing power	Brand believer	Pursuit of fashion	Adidas	Nike
2	Buy both Adidas and WARRIOR	Purchasing power	Fashion	Quality	Adidas	WARRIOR
3	Buy Lining and WARRIOR	Limited purchasing power	Cost performance	Economic	Lining	WARRIOR
4	Only buy WARRIOR and XDLONG	Weak purchasing power	Cheap	Economic	WARRIOR	XDLONG

Descriptive Analysis. Before clustering, it is necessary to understand the overall distribution of data. To explore and analyze the processed data, draw the relationship between any two variables, as shown in Fig. 2. The horizontal and vertical axes are single variables. Except that the businessAmount variable in

Table 5. Multi-variable classified data is transformed into single variable classified data for Q7.

Num	Lining, etc.	New balance, etc.	Adidas, etc.	ANTA, etc.	Reebok, etc.	XDLONG, etc.	WARRIOR, etc.	Other	Never	New value
1	0	1	1	0	1	0	0	0	0	1
2	1	0	0	1	0	0	0	0	0	3
3	0	0	1	0	0	0	0	0	0	1
...	...	...	...	...	...	...	...	...	...	...
200	0	0	1	0	1	0	0	0	0	4

column 6 (row 6) is continuous data, all other data are classified data. In Fig. 2, coordinates (1, 1) (2, 2) (3, 3) (12, 12) are the data distribution of the variable. For example, (1,1) is the data distribution of men and women in gender, and (6,6) is the probability density plot of businessAmount. Other graphs draw the relationship between two variables. For example, (1,3) is the data distribution of job and gender. A half of the figure is the data distribution of men in eight kinds of jobs, and the other is the data distribution of women in eight kinds of jobs. It can be concluded that there is no significant correlation between job and gender because there is no significant difference between the two figures. (1, 6) shows the data distribution of businessAmount and gender. It can be seen that the business amount of men is slightly larger than that of women.

On the whole, there is no obvious correlation between the variables. Although there is a certain relationship between some variables, this relationship is not very obvious, which will not have much impact on the results of clustering.

4.3 PAM Clustering

After all the multi-variables are transformed into single variables and there is no obvious correlation between the variables, users are clustered through PAM, so different types of users are obtained. PAM is suiting for classified data and continuous data. We used Python to complete this work and get the clustering results.

Users are divided into three categories with good effect, and the contour coefficient is 0.45, as shown in Fig. 3. The clustering results are visualized by changing the high-dimensional data into two-dimensional data, as shown in Fig. 3. Three user groups can be seen with large distances between clusters and small distances within clusters. The first group has 48 red dots, the second has 70 green dots, and the third has 82 blue dots.

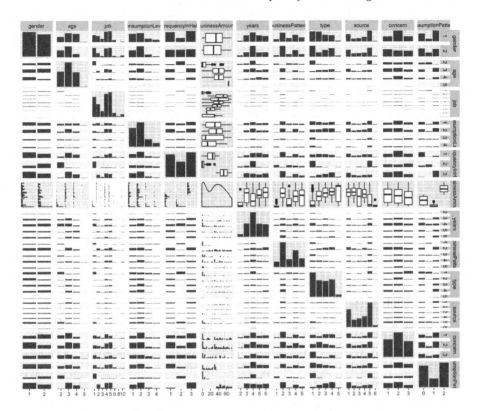

Fig. 2. Overall distribution of data

4.4   Personas with Labels

Analyze the specific characteristics of these three types of user groups. According to the clustering results, the data distributions of all user groups in each variable are obtained. For example, the first type of user group, as shown in Fig. 4, has 19 men (gender. 1), 29 women (gender. 2), 44 people aged 18–25 (age. 2), and the consumption level is evenly distributed among consumption level 1, consumption Level 2, and consumption Level 3. The total business amount handled is 10000 on average Yuan and so on.

Drawing personas with labels are good to help designers better use personas. This work consists of two parts. On the one hand, tag each level of variables. On the other hand, the size of the label is related to the percentage of the level in the variable in each category. For example, 18–25 years old people are the most in Category 1, and "18–25" in Fig. 5 below is the most. It hard to see the

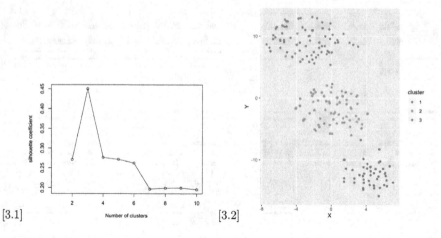

[3.1]

[3.2]

Fig. 3. Contour coefficient and visualization of clustering results (Color figure online)

other age labels because of too few people of other ages. The work was done by Python's package, which can reduce the manual repetitive work. Similarly, the user groups of category 2 and 3 are shown in Fig. 5.

At this point, we have completed the core work of establishing personas: clustering and visualization. Adding other descriptions to personas is not the focus of the study, so it will not be elaborated.

4.5 Assessment

In this study, we mainly evaluate the clustering results from two aspects:

- Clustering effect of the algorithm. In unsupervised learning, the contour coefficient is used to evaluate the clustering effect. The contour coefficient is 0.45 in the case, which shows good performance.
- The consistency with expert clustering. Calculate the consistency of the same data after clustering by experts and machines. 21 pieces of data were randomly selected for clustering by experts. There are 15/21 in the same clustering category, and kappa of 0.571 indicates good consistency.

So it is considered that the results of this machine clustering are acceptable.

```
[[1]]
 gender age          job      consumptionLevel frequencyInHall businessAmount    years
 1:19  2:44   1    :39   1:17          1: 2        Min.   : 0.000   2: 5
 2:29  3: 3   4    : 3   2:13          2:46        1st Qu.: 0.000   3: 9
       4: 1   5    : 3   3:11          3: 0        Median : 1.000   4:31
       5: 0   3    : 1   4: 7                      Mean   : 3.854   5: 2
              6    : 1                             3rd Qu.: 5.000   6: 1
              10   : 1                             Max.   :20.000
              (Other): 0
 businessPattern type   source concern consumptionPatterns
 1:16          1:42   1: 0   1:15   0:18
 2: 2          2: 5   2: 0   2:13   1:30
 3:13          3: 0   3: 3   3:20   2: 0
 4:10          4: 0   4: 1
 5: 7          5: 1   5:40
               6: 4
```

Fig. 4. The data distributions of all user groups in each variable

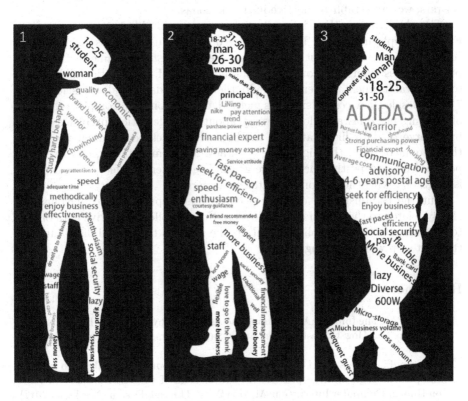

Fig. 5. Personas with labels

5 Conclusion and Future Work

This paper described the use of k-means and PAM clustering algorithms in machine learning to create personas, including four steps:

- Design the questionnaire.
- Process data. By using K-Means and rule-based clustering method, the multi variables caused by multiple choice questions are transformed into a single variable.
- Cluster the users. The groups of similar users can be obtained by PAM that can cluster continuous data and classified data at the same time.
- Create personas with labels according to the clustered results.

With our case study, according to contour coefficient and kappa, we demonstrated that it is a powerful method for continuous data and classified data, although there is a large number of data. Without specifying the number of clusters, we can establish effective initial personas.

The clustering method in machine learning is suitable to create personas. First, principle matching. The definition of similar user groups in persona is consistent with the concept of clustering. Second, fast. The time of the whole process is less than one month from the beginning of the questionnaire design to the establishment of personas, and the time of data analysis is less than 7 days. Besides, low cost. Using this method, one persona can complete the work of creating personas and do not worry about the calculation problems caused by a large of data like statistical methods. For machine learning, the larger the amount of data, the higher the accuracy. Most importantly, effective. The personas created by this method are good. The clustering effect is good and it is consistent with the personas created by experts.

But the establishment of more accurate and representative personas are closely related to the way of data collection. How to collect objective data or how to demonstrate that the collected data is the same as the overall distribution is the next step worth striving for.

References

1. Cooper, A.: The Inmates Are Running the Asylum: Why High Tech Products Drive Us Crazy and How to Restore the Sanity. Sams - Pearson Education, Indianapolis (2004)
2. Laporte, L., Slegers, K., De Grooff, D.: Using correspondence analysis to monitor the persona segmentation process. In: Proceedings of the 7th Nordic Conference on Human-Computer Interaction: Making Sense Through Design (NordiCHI 2012), pp. 265–274. Association for Computing Machinery, New York (2012). https://doi.org/10.1145/2399016.2399058
3. Dong, J., Kelkar, K., Braun, K.: Getting the most out of personas for product usability enhancements. In: Aykin, N. (ed.) UI-HCII 2007. LNCS, vol. 4559, pp. 291–296. Springer, Heidelberg (2007). https://doi.org/10.1007/978-3-540-73287-7_36

4. Reeder, B., Turner, A.M.: Scenario- based design: a method for connecting information system design with public health operations and emergency management. J. Biomed. Inform. **44**(6), 978–988 (2011)

5. Scott, D.M.: The New Rules of Marketing. Wiley, Hoboken (2007)

6. van Laer, T., Lurie, I.: The Seven Stages of the Digital Marketing Cycle. Social Science Research Network, Rochester, NY (2017)

7. Nielsen, L., Storgaard Hansen, K.: Personas is applicable: a study on the use of personas in Denmark. In: Proceedings of the SIGCHI Conference on Human Factors in Computing Systems, pp. 1665–1674. ACM (2014)

8. Brickey, J., Walczak, S., Burgess, T.: A comparative analysis of persona clustering methods. In: Sustainable It Collaboration Around the Globe Americas Conference on Information Systems DBLP (2010)

9. Mulder, S., Yaar, Z.: The User is Always Right. New Riders, Berkeley (2007)

10. Jansen, B.J., Sobel, K., Cook, G.: Classifying ecommerce information sharing behaviour by youths on social networking sites. J. Inf. Sci. **37**(2), 120–136 (2011)

11. Chen, X., Pang, J., Xue, R.: Constructing and comparing user mobility profiles. ACM Trans. Web (TWEB) **8**(4), 1–25 (2014). Article 21

12. Zhang, X., Brown, H.-F., Shankar, A.: Data-driven personas: constructing archetypal users with clickstreams and user telemetry. In: 2016 CHI Conference on Human Factors in Computing Systems, Santa Clara, CA (2016)

13. Cooper, A., Reimann, R.: About Face 2.0: The Essentials of Interaction Design. Wiley Publishing, Indianapolis (2003)

14. Lindgren, A.C., Amdahl, P., Chaikiat, P.: Using personas and scenarios as an interface design tool for advanced driver assistance systems. In: HCII (2007)

15. Miaskiewicz, T., Sumner, T., Kozar, K.A.: A latent semantic analysis methodology for the identification and creation of personas. In: Proceedings of the Twenty-sixth annual SIGCHI conference on Human factors in computing systems, 5–10 April, Florence, Italy, pp. 1501–1510. ACM Press (2008)

16. Mahamuni, R., Khambete, P., Punekar, R.M., Lobo, S., Sharma, S., Hirom, U.: Concise personas based on tacit knowledge - how representative are they? In: Proceedings of the 9th Indian Conference on Human Computer Interaction (IndiaHCI 2018), pp. 53–62. ACM, New York (2018). https://doi.org/10.1145/3297121.3297126

17. McGinn, J., Kotamraju, N.: Data-driven persona development. In: CHI 2008. ACM (2008)

18. Greaney, J., Riordan, M.: The use of statistically derived personas in modeling mobile user populations. In: MobileHCI (2003)

19. Tu, N., Dong, X., Rau, P., Zhang, T.: Using cluster analysis in persona development. In: International Conference on Supply Chain Management and Information Systems (2010)

20. Siegel, D.: The mystique of numbers: belief in quantitative approaches to segmentation and persona development. In: CHI 2010. ACM (2010)

21. Salminen, J., Soon-Gyo, J., An, J., Kwak, H., Jansen, B.J.: Findings of a user study of automatically generated personas. In: Extended Abstracts of the 2018 CHI Conference on Human Factors in Computing Systems (CHI EA 2018), p. 6. ACM, New York (2018). Paper LBW097. https://doi.org/10.1145/3170427.3188470

22. Xu, J., Liu, H.: Web user clustering analysis based on KMeans algorithm. In: 2010 International Conference on Information on Networking and Automation (ICINA). IEEE (2010)

23. Lukasik, S., Kowalski, P.A., Charytanowicz, M., et al.: Clustering using flower pollination algorithm and Calinski-Harabasz index. In: 2016 IEEE Congress on Evolutionary Computation, Vancouver, 24–29 July 2016, pp. 2724–2728. IEEE (2016)
24. Bo, F., Wenning, H., Gang, C., et al.: An improved PAM algorithm for optimizing initial cluster center. In: IEEE International Conference on Software Engineering. Service Science. IEEE (2012)
25. Zhu, L., Ma, B., Zhao, X.: Clustering validity analysis based on contour coefficients. J. Comput. Appl. (12), 139–141 (2010)
26. Zhou, H.B., Gao, J.T.: Automatic method for determining cluster number based on silhouette coefficient. Adv. Mater. Res. **951**, 227–230 (2014)

The Role of Behavioral Anthropomorphism in Human-Automation Trust Calibration

Theodore Jensen[1]([⊠]), Mohammad Maifi Hasan Khan[1], and Yusuf Albayram[2]

[1] University of Connecticut, Storrs, Mansfield, CT 06269, USA
{theodore.jensen,mohammad.khan}@uconn.edu
[2] Central Connecticut State University, New Britain, CT 06053, USA
yusuf.albayram@ccsu.edu

Abstract. Trust has been identified as a critical factor in the success and safety of interaction with automated systems. Researchers have referred to "trust calibration" as an apt design goal– user trust should be at an appropriate level given a system's reliability. One factor in user trust is the degree to which a system is perceived as humanlike, or anthropomorphic. However, relevant prior work does not explicitly characterize trust appropriateness, and generally considers visual rather than behavioral anthropomorphism. To investigate the role of humanlike system behavior in trust calibration, we conducted a 2 (communication style: *machinelike, humanlike*) × 2 (reliability: *low, high*) between-subject study online where participants collaborated alongside an Automated Target Detection (ATD) system to classify a set of images in 5 rounds of gameplay. Participants chose how many images to allocate to the automation before each round, where appropriate trust was defined by a number of images that optimized performance. We found that communication style and reliability influenced perceptions of anthropomorphism and trustworthiness. Low and high reliability participants demonstrated overtrust and undertrust, respectively. The implications of our findings for the design and research of automated and autonomous systems are discussed in the paper.

Keywords: Human-computer trust · Human-automation trust · Anthropomorphism · Computers as Social Actors

1 Introduction

A user's trust has been identified as a critical factor in both the safety and efficacy of interactions with automation and computers [5,10]. Parasuraman and Riley [25] note that human-automation systems can suffer from both *disuse* of reliable and effective automation and *misuse* of unreliable automation, which may result from *undertrust* and *overtrust*, respectively. Thus, it is not necessarily desirable to increase trust, but to promote good 'trust calibration.' A user's trust should be appropriate with respect to that system's capabilities [10].

© Springer Nature Switzerland AG 2020
H. Degen and L. Reinerman-Jones (Eds.): HCII 2020, LNCS 12217, pp. 33–53, 2020.
https://doi.org/10.1007/978-3-030-50334-5_3

Anthropomorphism, or the degree to which an entity is perceived as human-like, is one among numerous approaches to trust-building design in HCI. In general, the notion that greater anthropomorphism makes users more comfortable has motivated the development of humanlike agents (e.g, Apple's Siri, Amazon's Alexa, Google Assistant) as the interface to computing systems. Automated systems researchers have recognized the role of anthropomorphic agents in user perceptions and trust in collaborative tasks (e.g., [36], [35]). As artificial intelligence (AI) continues to drive the development of complex autonomous technologies in various applications, the significance of anthropomorphism or humanness in the interface will only grow. We argue that the process by which a user interacts with an automated system is less straightforward than "more humanlike = good." Rather, anthropomorphic features or social cues in the interface color a user's expectations of the system's future behavior. While greater anthropomorphism may increase trust, this does not necessarily equate to better outcomes. The question of how *appropriateness* of user trust, with respect to system reliability, is influenced by humanlike features remains unanswered.

To investigate this, we designed a 2 (communication style) × 2 (reliability) between-subject study where participants collaborated with a *low* or *high* reliability Automated Target Detection (ATD) system in 5 rounds of gameplay. The task involved classifying a set of 20 images as "Dangerous" or "Not Dangerous." A score incentivized the speed and accuracy with which all of the images were collectively classified. Participants chose how many images to allocate to the automation before each round. *Trust appropriateness* was the difference between a user's allocation in a round and an ideal level of allocation in each reliability condition that maximized the score (i.e., 5 images in low reliability, 15 in high). We attempted to elicit low and high anthropomorphism perceptions via *machinelike* and *humanlike* communication styles, respectively. Machinelike messages were minimal and informational, while humanlike messages were friendly, apologetic, and framed from the perspective of the automation.

We found that both communication style and reliability influenced measures of perceived anthropomorphism, confirming that behavioral cues can affect humanness perceptions without a visually humanlike representation. Humanlike communication was associated with greater perceptions of the automation's benevolence. We also demonstrate the utility of a trust appropriateness measure. Despite the lack of a communication style effect, we found that high and low reliability participants were prone to undertrust and overtrust, respectively. Characterizing trust with respect to good performance in experimental setups can help to inform human-centered design that assists with appropriate trust calibration.

2   Related Work

Much of the prior work on anthropomorphism and social cues in HCI, as well as human-machine trust, is inspired by the Computers as Social Actors (CASA) paradigm [27]. CASA has been applied not only to justify studying the human construct of trust in HCI contexts generally, but to rationalize that a more socially-oriented system will lead to better interactions. We challenge the assertion that more humanlike systems will bring about the best outcomes by investigating the role of perceived humanness in the process of trust calibration. We discuss relevant prior work below.

2.1   Trust in Automation and HCI

A substantial body of work has investigated the notion of "trust" in automation (see [10] and [5] for reviews). Trust has been defined in the organizational psychology literature as *"the willingness of a party to be vulnerable to the actions of another party based on the expectation that the other will perform a particular action important to the trustor, irrespective of the ability to monitor or control that party"* [12]. This definition readily applies to interactions with computers and automated systems. We rely on systems to assist us with a task despite an inability to observe the exact process by which they execute the task. We make ourselves vulnerable to the possibility that the trusted computer fails to assist us.

Trust in automation researchers have suggested "trust calibration" to be a critical consideration when designing systems. That is, rather than necessarily aiming to increase trust, it is most desirable that a user is able to maintain an appropriate level of trust relative to the system's reliability [10]. Trust that is too high can be counterproductive or dangerous. We consider *trust appropriateness* as ultimately more important than trust. The best outcomes will be achieved when a user has an accurate understanding of a technology's strengths and shortcomings.

Despite the breadth of research on the importance of human-computer and human-automation trust, researchers generally investigate whether system features increase trust. Even in the work that acknowledges trust calibration in human-automation interaction, trust is often viewed as an end, without reference to what is an "ideal" level of trust. Actual measures of trust appropriateness or performance are relatively rare (for one measure, see [34]).

McDermott and ten Brink [13] defined "Calibration Points" as moments when automation reliability changes and a user must adjust their level of trust. In practice, changing environmental conditions or inputs that change reliability can affect automation performance and, therefore, necessitate a change in user trust. Appropriate trust occurs when a user adjusts their perceptions and behavior to accommodate changes in reliability at a Calibration Point. Our study involves a static level of reliability where the best automation performance occurred at a predetermined "ideal" level of reliance on the automation. In this way, we quantified trust appropriateness with respect to the ideal level and observed how system features influenced users' calibration to this level throughout extended interaction with the automation.

De Visser, Pak, and Shaw [37] effectively outline how systems may be designed to support appropriate trust calibration via dynamic trust repair mechanisms. Noting the shift from automated to autonomous systems as having a significant impact on the nature of "human-machine relationships," they refer not only to the importance of *trust repair acts* in response to detrimental behaviors by a system, but that of *trust dampening acts* in response to beneficial behaviors [37]. Trust that is too high can be equally as problematic as trust that is too low, and systems can be designed to prevent both.

More recently, de Visser et al. [38] referred to "relationship equity" as a key variable in trust calibration on human-robot teams. Over the course of an interaction, the machine's behaviors and its responses to those behaviors (i.e., dampening and repair acts) influence the accumulated relationship equity between the human and the technological team member. In turn, relationship equity affects trust in the technology in the future. Perceptions of an automated or autonomous teammate's humanness may play a significant role in the interpretation of trust repair and dampening messages and, thus, how relationship equity among teammates develops. We sought to investigate how humanlike features influence users' perceptions of and behavior toward an automated teammate over the course of a collaborative task.

2.2 Computers as Social Actors and Anthropomorphism

As mentioned, a body of research using the Computers as Social Actors paradigm has informed much of the research on trustworthy design. CASA studies have found that social rules learned for human-human interaction often still apply to computers. This has also been referred to as "the media equation" (i.e., "media = real life") [27]. For instance, one study utilizing CASA found that participants are more likely to disclose information to a computer that first discloses to them, as is the case when interacting with another person [15]. Another study found that participants were polite toward computers, in that they were more positive when giving direct feedback to a computer, rather than feedback on a separate machine [20]. This phenomenon has been replicated in various social contexts (see [27]), suggesting that humans have a general tendency to treat computers like people.

Given that participants in early CASA studies were often from technical backgrounds and denied that they would treat computers like people, Nass and Moon [18] suggested that social responses occur due to mindlessness–when computers possess a sufficient amount of social cues, we cannot help but to automatically engage the scripts we use for interacting with other humans. Nass, Steuer, Henriksen, and Dryer [19] opt for the Greek term "Ethopoeia" to describe this automatic process, rather than "anthropomorphism," which they define as a conscious and sincere belief that a non-human is human. Because conscious anthropomorphism is inconsistent with CASA, researchers have more recently argued that anthropomorphism may indeed be a mindless process [8]. While the media equation posits that computers elicit the same social responses as people, there is ample evidence that the degree of humanness influences the strength of the social response. Morkes, Kernal, and Nass [16] suggest that "soft" social responses to communication technologies (SRCT) may be a more appropriate model than the "hard" SRCT implied by the media equation. Soft SRCT implies a continuum of socialness on which entities are perceived, rather than a binary judgment of human or not human.

We use *anthropomorphism* to refer to the assignment of humanlike qualities to an entity by an observer, and the process by which mindless social responses to computers occur. *Anthropomorphic* is used to describe a target that is perceived as humanlike, and more or less anthropomorphic represents the degree to which a target is perceived as humanlike. Degrees of anthropomorphism are synonymous with degrees of socialness, as anthropomorphizing has been referred to as the act of evaluating another entity's "social potential" and informing expectations of that entity's future behavior [21]. A sensitivity to humanness is understandable from an evolutionary perspective, since human intelligence could pose a unique threat to survival [21]. As we face an increasing variety of intelligent and evolutionarily unfamiliar technologies, we may be anthropomorphizing even if we are not actively and consciously considering our technological interaction partner as a human. An understanding of the dynamics of anthropomorphism can critically inform interface design and ensure that the appropriate amount of humanness is employed in a system.

Research on *visual anthropomorphism*, or the extent to which an entity has a humanlike appearance, tends to show that agents with a greater degree of anthropomorphism elicit more positive perceptions than those that appear less humanlike [4,22]. The role of a humanlike appearance in fostering positive perceptions has motivated research and design of systems represented by anthropomorphic software agents as well as humanlike robots.

Currently there is less understanding of *behavioral anthropomorphism*, or the extent to which an entity acts in a humanlike manner. These perceptions may arise more subtly given that an explicit representation of a human is not given. Nass and Moon [18] pointed to various features of computers that may elicit a social response, such as words for output or the filling of roles usually held by people. These may be thought of as behaviorally anthropomorphic features. Parasuraman and Miller [24] investigated the role of "etiquette" in human-automation interaction, manipulating communication style to compare an interruptive system to a patient one. They found that the latter "good etiquette" system improved performance significantly, even compensating for low automation reliability. While etiquette may contribute to perceived humanness, the study did not measure this. The current study explicitly measures how perceptions of anthropomorphism are elicited by the communication style of messages displayed by an automated system.

One group of researchers has observed the effects of anthropomorphism of an automated agent that suggested answers in a number pattern guessing game, using a visual representation and background stories to demonstrate the humanness of the agent [34–36]. In the first study, the appropriateness of participants' compliance with the agent's suggestions is reported, and it appeared that performance with a human agent was better than a computer agent [34]. All three studies demonstrated that, in response to reliability that steadily degraded, there were less drastic trust decrements when the automation was represented by a more anthropomorphic agent [34–36]. Pak, Fink, Price, Bass and Sturre [23] similarly found that a visually anthropomorphic agent led to better performance and greater compliance with advice (i.e., behavioral trust) than a less anthropomorphic agent. Kulms and Kopp [9] found that subjective trust was higher for an agent represented by a human compared to a computer, although there was no agent effect on behavioral trust.

While it is often assumed that anthropomorphism positively influences trust, researchers in various domains have suggested that anthropomorphism may not always have a positive effect on perceptions and interactions. Duffy [3] referred to the careful interplay between humanness perceptions and expectations for robot behavior. Culley and Madhaven [2] specifically called researchers and designers to consider the consequences of inappropriate trust calibration that may result from overly anthropomorphic agents. Moreover, the metaphor of the "uncanny valley" [31] has been used to study the discomfort and unpleasantness that arise when an agent or robot is "too humanlike" [32].

Our study builds on these to investigate how anthropomorphism perceptions elicited by communication style influence an explicit measure of trust appropriateness.

3   Methodology

We conducted a 2 (communication style: *machinelike, humanlike*) × 2 (reliability: *low, high*) between-subject study to observe how users calibrated trust in an error-prone automated system. Reliability determined the percentage of images that the system correctly identified and overall performance when it was relied upon. The communication style of the system's messages was intended to elicit different anthropomorphism perceptions.

Given that prior work has shown positive effects of anthropomorphism on trust, such as less drastic trust declines in the face of degrading performance [34–36] and more positive subjective trust [9], we predicted that participants would have more appropriate trust when the system's communication style "matched" its reliability. In other words, positive associations with greater humanness would lead participants to expect better reliability. Thus, we expected that trust would be less appropriate in the cases where 1) the system acted machinelike but reliability was high, and 2) the system acted humanlike but reliability was low. We formed the following hypotheses:

H1: Participants in the *low reliability-machinelike* group will have more appropriate trust than participants in the *low reliability-humanlike* group.

H2: Participants in the *high reliability-humanlike* group will have more appropriate trust than participants in the *high reliability-machinelike* group.

To test these hypotheses, we designed an online game where participants collaborated with and were able to adjust their level of reliance on an automated system. Participants reported on their perceptions of the system in a post-gameplay survey. The details of our methods are presented below.

3.1   The Target Identification Task

In each of 5 rounds of gameplay, participants classified a subset of 20 images on a map. To manually classify an image, participants clicked on a marker on the map, after which an image of a vehicle was shown in the Vehicle Identification Panel to the right of the map. "Non-dangerous" vehicles had only text on top of them, while "dangerous" vehicles had numbers in addition to text. Participants used "Zoom In," "Zoom Out," and "Rotate" buttons to determine whether the vehicle was dangerous. The manual task was intentionally made simple to reduce variability in individual performance.

While participants manually identified their portion of the images, the ATD system "worked" in parallel on the rest of the images. In reality, the system took a fixed amount of time per image and had accuracy determined by the reliability condition. The low reliability automation correctly identified 60% of its allocated images and the high reliability automation correctly identified 90%, both rounded down to the nearest integer so that the automation always misidentified at least one image. This level of accuracy was chosen based on prior work finding that a decision aid with less than 70% accuracy is considered worse than no aid [41], although our task involved reliance on automation's simultaneous performance rather than decisions to comply with an aid's suggestions.

The round ended when all 20 images had been classified. The gameplay interface is shown in Fig. 1.

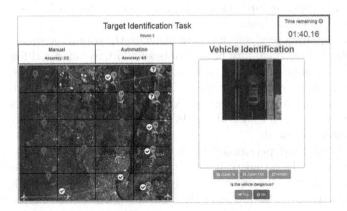

Fig. 1. *Target Identification Task interface.* The map with markers for each image is shown on the left. A check mark indicates a correctly classified image, an "X" incorrectly identified manual images, and a "?" for images unable to be identified by automation. Manual and automation accuracy are updated above the map. On the right, participants use various buttons to inspect and classify the current image. The timer at the upper right counts down from 2 minutes.

3.2   Scoring

Participants received a score representing their performance in each round, which was motivated as follows. Manual classification involved clicking multiple times and was more time consuming than automated classification. However, the automation was not perfect and could lead to low accuracy based on the reliability condition. We told participants that their "Round Score" credited speed (overall time spent to classify the 20 images) and accuracy (overall percentage of correctly identified images). Participants had to decide how willing they were to rely on the automation to quickly assist in classifying images despite the risk to overall accuracy.

In reality, the Round Score was determined solely by the number of images allocated to the automation in a given round. The best Round Score occurred for an "ideal" number of images in each reliability group: 5 images for low reliability, 15 for high. Round Scores decreased linearly with the distance away from this value. Moreover, while we told participants that their Round Score was up to 100 points, we limited the maximum score to 90 points so that it was not obvious when ideal calibration had been achieved. We added a small, randomly generated "noise" amount to each Round Score so that it appeared that scoring varied based on performance.

Trust appropriateness was characterized with respect to the ideal value. For instance, allocating 18 images to the high reliability automation is indicative of overtrust, 10 of undertrust, and 15 of appropriate calibration. This allowed us to observe how the communication style and reliability manipulations influenced the degree of miscalibration.

This fixed scoring mechanism was in line with the ostensible speed and accuracy incentives. Low reliability participants should have allocated fewer images to the automation because of its reduced accuracy, although they still needed to rely on it to achieve reasonable speed. High reliability participants should have allocated more images to the automation because it did not greatly compromise accuracy, although they still should have helped to identify some images to achieve reasonable speed.

To motivate good performance, we told participants that they would be rewarded a bonus based on their cumulative Round Scores in addition to the compensation they would receive for completion of the study. In reality, all participants first received $2 immediately following participation and a $2 bonus after we were no longer recruiting participants. The timing of the bonus ensured that workers were not able to reveal to other workers that an additional $2 was rewarded regardless of performance.

3.3   Feedback Page and Message Design

Following each round of the game, a feedback page (Fig. 2) was shown containing three elements: 1) the Round Score for the previous round, 2) a message noting the number of errors made by the automation, and 3) the allocation decision for the next round.

The Round Score was shown with a colored gauge indicating where the score fell out of 100 possible points, as well as the compensation amount ostensibly associated with that score (100 points = \$0.40).

Fig. 2. *Feedback page.* The Round Score is shown in the upper left along with its ostensibly associated compensation amount. The feedback message is displayed in the upper right panel. In the lower panel, participants choose how many images to allocate to the automation for the next round. Text in both the feedback message and the allocation panel is determined by a participant's communication style condition.

The design of the feedback messages was based on research investigating the effects of trust repair messages following system errors. For instance, Tzeng [33] found that apologies by computers led to more positive impressions. Jensen et al. [7] found that a self-blaming automated system ("I was unable...") was perceived as more trustworthy than one blaming its developers for errors ("The developers were not able...") using the same collaborative game used in the current study. Moreover, Sebo, Krishnamurthi, and Scassellati [30] and Quinn, Pak, and de Visser [26] have noted how apologies and denials by robots and automation influence future trust.

In line with this prior work, the humanlike text was designed using first-person (the automation referred to itself as "I"), an apology when reporting errors and, in general, social niceties intended to elicit the perception of humanness. On the other hand, the machinelike text was designed to be minimal, informational, and impersonal. The manipulation is similar to that in Parasuraman and Miller's [24] etiquette study, although they used interruptive or patient timing of messages and did not measure perceived humanness of the automated system. After gameplay, we tested whether the humanlike communication style led to greater perceived anthropomorphism with two different scales. The text we displayed on the feedback page in each condition is shown in the second column of Table 1.

Table 1. *Introduction and feedback messages for each communication style condition.* Introduction messages were shown after the instruction page and prior to Round 1 of gameplay. Feedback messages were shown after each round of gameplay. The portion of each message regarding the allocation decision was shown in a separate panel from the rest of the message. "X" represents the number of images that the ATD system could not identify in the previous round and "Y" represents the subsequent round number.

	Introduction	Feedback
Machinelike	Target Identification Task	X images unable to be identified
	Number of images allocated to automation for Round 1	Number of images allocated to automation for Round Y
Humanlike	Hello! Welcome to the Target Identification Task. I will use these messages to communicate with you about my performance	I am sorry that X images were unable to be identified
	Please let me know how many images I should classify in Round 1	Please let me know how many images I should classify in Round Y

3.4 Study Procedure

Participants were recruited on Amazon Mechanical Turk (MTurk) and restricted to workers 18 years or older, living in the United States, and having completed at least 1000 Human Intelligence Tasks (HIT's) with an approval rate of at least 95%. Upon accepting the HIT, participants were shown an information sheet describing the general study procedure and were asked whether they consented to participate. Those who gave consent were forwarded to our online game.

First, an instruction page was displayed describing the Target Identification Task. After reading about the task and game controls, participants were required to correctly answer a series of multiple choice questions about the game. This included a question confirming their understanding of the importance of speed and accuracy for performance. These motivational details were critical so that there was risk and reward in relying on the ATD system, both components of a trusting relationship. One multiple choice question also confirmed that participants were using audio so that they would hear the sound effects accompanying correct and incorrect image identifications.

After completing the instruction page, an introduction message was displayed, followed by the allocation decision for Round 1. The introduction text was the first manifestation of the communication style, and is shown in the first column of Table 1 for each group. Participants played the first round of the game after confirming their allocation decision.

After the feedback page that followed the fifth round of the Target Identification Task, participants were forwarded to a post-gameplay survey. Only those who completed all 5 rounds of gameplay and the survey were compensated.

3.5   Survey Measures

The post-gameplay survey was hosted on our university's Qualtrics server. Participants first responded to a series of demographic questions regarding gender, age, race, education level, and video gaming frequency before reporting on their experience in the game.

Game-Related Questions. Two items were used to assess the perceived reliability of both automated and manual identification. For instance, the automation item asked, "How reliable was the automation? Specifically if the automation analyzed 100 images, how many would it correctly identify?" Two additional items assessed the perceived speed of automated and manual identification. The automation item in this case asked, "How fast was the automation? Specifically, if the automation analyzed images for one minute, how many would it identify?"

Then, in one multiple answer item, participants were asked to select which factors contributed to their score, with the following options in order: "None of the below," "All of the below," "The automation's accuracy," "Your accuracy," "The automation's speed," and "Your speed." This was used to confirm that participants were not aware of the fixed scoring mechanism.

Perceived Behavioral Anthropomorphism. To check the effect of the communication style manipulation, we included 4 of the items from the anthropomorphism index of the Godspeed questionnaire [1] rated on 5-point semantic differential scales with reference to the ATD system (Fake/Natural, Machine-like/Humanlike, Unconscious/Conscious, Artificial/Lifelike). The Godspeed scale was developed for robotic systems, and so the "Moving rigidly/Moving elegantly" item was not relevant given our automated system's lack of physical embodiment.

Three additional perceived behavioral anthropomorphism (PBA) items were developed for the current study referring specifically to the humanness of the system's behavior and messages. Participants rated agreement with the statements, "The system communicated with me like a human would," "My interaction with the system felt like one with another person," and "The system acted in a humanlike manner" on a 7-point Likert scale.

Individual Differences in Anthropomorphism. The Individual Differences in Anthropomorphism Questionnaire (IDAQ) was developed by Waytz, Epley, and Cacioppo [39] and has been found to predict trust in technology [40]. Items were rated on an 11-point scale from "Not at all" to "Very much." Sample items include, "To what extent do cows have intentions?" and "To what extent does the average computer have a mind of its own?"

Perceived Trustworthiness Characteristics. We measured subjective trust in the ATD system by adapting perceived ability, integrity, and benevolence items from McKnight, Choudhury, and Kacmar [14], originally from Mayer and Davis [11]. Prior work on automated systems has found that these trusting perceptions are influenced by information about system performance and process [6] as well as system accuracy and attribution of blame for errors in a similar image classification task [7]. These "trusting beliefs" can help to paint a thorough picture of how humanness relates to automation perception and behavior beyond unidimensional subjective trust measures.

We included 3 attention check questions throughout the survey asking for a specific multiple choice answer (e.g., "Please select 'Disagree' for this statement").

The study was approved by the University of Connecticut Institutional Review Board (IRB).

4   Evaluation

A total of 158 participants completed the study. We first removed the data of 27 participants who incorrectly answered at least one of the attention check questions. Next, in the multiple answer item, only one of the remaining participants answered "None of the below" when asked which factors contributed to their score, suggesting that this participant did not think their score was actually based on performance. All subsequent analyses were conducted on the remaining 130 participants, with the group distribution shown in Table 2.

Table 2. *Group distribution.* Number of participants in each experimental condition.

Group	n
Low reliability, machinelike	30
Low reliability, humanlike	33
High reliability, machinelike	34
High reliability, humanlike	33

The sample consisted of 71 (54.6%) males and 59 (45.4%) females, and there were 106 (81.5%) white, 11 (8.5%) African American, 5 (3.8%) Hispanic, 5 (3.8%) Asian, and 3 (2.3%) Native American participants. The average age was 37.2 years ($SD = 11.7$). Regarding education level, 57 (43.8%) participants reported having at least a 4-year college degree. When asked how often they play games on a computer or mobile device, 54 (41.5%) said they play daily, 41 (31.5%) a few times a week, and 35 (26.9%) a few times a month or less.

A Chi-square test revealed that the experimental groups did not significantly differ in terms of gender ($\chi^2(3) = 0.29$, $p = 0.96$). A Fisher's Exact Test likewise found that groups were similar in terms of race ($p = 0.49$). Lastly, Kruskall-Wallis Tests found that there were no significant differences in age ($\chi^2(3) = 3.20$, $p = 0.36$), education level ($\chi^2(3) = 0.97$, $p = 0.81$), or gaming frequency ($\chi^2(3) = 3.11$, $p = 0.38$). Thus, group differences can be attributed to our manipulations.

We expected that participants would rate manual identification as more accurate than automated identification, and automated identification as faster than manual identification. Given the non-normal distributions of these responses, two Wilcoxon Signed-Ranks Tests (the non-parametric equivalent of a paired t-test) confirmed this prediction. Participants reported that, out of 100 images, they would correctly identify significantly more ($M = 86.9$, $SD = 17.0$) than the automation ($M = 72.6$, $SD = 17.8$)($p < 0.001$) and that, in one minute, the automation would identify significantly more images ($M = 57.1$, $SD = 31.5$) than they would ($M = 34.5$, $SD = 28.0$)($p < 0.001$). Consistent with Mayer, Davis, and Schoorman's definition of trust [12], participants had to decide how willing they were to be vulnerable to the ATD system's lower accuracy, with the expectation that it would help improve their speed.

4.1 Manipulation Checks

Participants accurately reported the number of images they would expect the automation to correctly identify out of 100 in both the low ($M = 60.5$, $SD = 15.0$) and high ($M = 84.0$, $SD = 11.5$) reliability groups. A Mann-Whitney U-test confirmed that this difference in perceived reliability between groups was significant ($U = 328.50$, $p < 0.001$).

Next, we tested the effect of the automation's communication style on perceived anthropomorphism measured using the 4 established Godspeed items ($\alpha = 0.94$) and the 3 PBA items developed for this study ($\alpha = 0.91$). The IDAQ scale ($\alpha = 0.91$) was entered as a covariate for each test to control for individual anthropomorphic tendencies and because it reduced the error term in both cases[1].

A 2 (reliability) $\times$ 2 (communication style), Analysis of Covariance (ANCOVA) on the Godspeed measure yielded a significant main effect of reliability ($F(1, 125) = 9.00$, $p = 0.003$, $\eta_p^2 = 0.067$) when controlling for the IDAQ ($F(1, 125) = 25.51$, $p < 0.001$, $\eta_p^2 = 0.160$). High reliability participants ($M_{adj} = 2.96$, $SE = 0.13$) reported greater Godspeed perceived anthropomorphism than low reliability participants ($M_{adj} = 2.41$, $SE = 0.13$). However, the main effect of communication style was not significant ($F(1, 125) = 2.07$, $p = 0.153$, $\eta_p^2 = 0.016$).

---

[1] Estimated marginal means are reported at the mean IDAQ score of 4.17.

A separate ANCOVA on the PBA measure yielded significant main effects of both reliability ($F(1, 125) = 4.29$, $p = 0.040$, $\eta_p^2 = 0.033$) and communication style ($F(1, 125) = 10.56$, $p = 0.001$, $\eta_p^2 = 0.078$) when controlling for the IDAQ ($F(1, 125) = 18.39$, $p < 0.001$, $\eta_p^2 = 0.128$). High reliability participants ($M_{adj} = 4.14$, $SE = 0.17$) reported greater perceived anthropomorphism than low reliability participants ($M_{adj} = 3.63$, $SE = 0.18$). Also, participants in the humanlike condition ($M_{adj} = 4.28$, $SE = 0.17$) reported greater perceived anthropomorphism than those in the machinelike condition ($M_{adj} = 3.49$, $SE = 0.17$).

There are three important conclusions from these results. First, individual tendencies appear to play a significant role in perceptions of anthropomorphism of automation. Second, the PBA items may measure something slightly conceptually distinct from the Godspeed items, given that the latter were not significantly influenced by communication style. The Likert-style PBA items were more explicit in their reference to system behaviors being humanlike. Third, the high reliability system was consistently perceived as more humanlike than the low reliability system. When the system was more accurate and could handle more of the task load, it was considered more humanlike. It is worth noting that participants responded to the perceived anthropomorphism items after the entire interaction. Perceptions of humanness may have been influenced to a greater extent by communication style initially, especially when they only saw the introduction message and had not watched the system in action. Over time, observation of the automation's performance grew to inform humanness perceptions to a greater extent.

4.2   Allocation to the Automation and Trust Appropriateness

To test hypotheses $H1$ and $H2$, we operationalized a participant's *trust appropriateness* for each round of gameplay as the difference between their allocation to the ATD system for that round and the ideal allocation amount for their reliability condition (5 images for low reliability, 15 for high). Negative values represent undertrust of the automation and positive values represent overtrust. Mean trust appropriateness for each group across the 5 rounds of gameplay is shown in Fig. 3.

Trust appropriateness was submitted to a repeated measures analysis of variance (rm-ANOVA) with round of the game as the within-subject factor and reliability and communication style as between-subject factors. There was a significant main effect of reliability on trust appropriateness ($F(1, 126) = 192.64$, $p < 0.001$, $\eta_p^2 = 0.605$)[2]. Regardless of round, high reliability participants tended to undertrust the automation ($M_{adj} = -2.63$, $SE = 0.32$) whereas low reliability participants tended to overtrust ($M_{adj} = 3.64$, $SE = 0.33$).

Moreover, there was a significant interaction between round and reliability ($F(4, 504) = 13.32$, $p < 0.001$, $\eta_p^2 = 0.096$). Post-hoc comparisons were conducted with a Bonferroni adjustment to $\alpha = 0.05/10 = 0.005$. Low reliability participants' trust appropriateness in Round 1 ($M = 5.19$, $SD = 3.40$) was

---

[2] Levene's test was violated only for first round trust appropriateness.

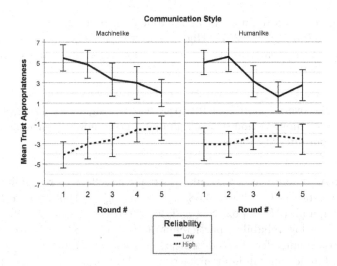

Fig. 3. *Group mean trust appropriateness.* Means for each group's trust appropriateness over the 5 rounds of gameplay are shown. Error bars display 95% confidence interval.

significantly different than in Round 3 ($M = 3.21$, $SD = 4.32$)($p = 0.001$), Round 4 ($M = 2.25$, $SD = 4.20$)($p < 0.001$), and Round 5 ($M = 2.37$, $SD = 3.96$)($p < 0.001$). Round 2 trust appropriateness ($M = 5.19$, $SD = 3.94$) was also significantly different from Round 3 ($p = 0.002$), Round 4 ($p < 0.001$), and Round 5 ($p < 0.001$). High reliability participant's trust appropriateness in Round 1 ($M = -3.62$, $SD = 4.14$) was significantly different than in Round 4 ($M = -1.96$, $SD = 3.25$)($p = 0.004$). Lack of differences between the later rounds suggest that participants' found a relatively stable level of trust after observing the automation perform throughout the game. However, appropriate trust was never achieved by either reliability group. One sample t-tests using a Bonferroni-adjusted significance level confirmed that group mean trust appropriateness in each round was significantly different from 0.

The interaction between communication style and reliability was not significant, and thus $H1$ and $H2$ were not supported.

4.3   Perceived Trustworthiness

To observe whether our manipulations influenced subjective trust, we conducted a multivariate analysis of variance (MANOVA) on the perceived ability, integrity, and benevolence of the ATD system. We found significant main effects of both reliability ($F(3, 124) = 23.64$, $p < 0.001$, Wilks' $\lambda = 0.636$, $\eta_p^2 = 0.364$) and communication style ($F(3, 124) = 3.07$, $p = 0.030$, Wilks' $\lambda = 0.931$, $\eta_p^2 = 0.069$) and conducted a series of follow-up univariate ANOVA's. The significance level for follow-ups was Bonferroni-adjusted to $\alpha = 0.05/3 = 0.0167$.

Ability. There was a main effect of reliability on perceived ability ($F(1, 126)$ = 68.04, $p < 0.001$, $\eta_p^2 = 0.357$). High reliability participants ($M = 5.81$, SD = 0.87) rated the system's ability higher than low reliability participants ($M =$ 4.23, $SD = 1.29$).

Integrity. The overall model for integrity was not significant, suggesting that reliability and communication style manipulations did not influence participants' rating of system integrity items.

Benevolence. There was a marginally significant effect of reliability on perceived benevolence ($F(1, 126) = 4.68$, $p = 0.032$, $\eta_p^2 = 0.036$) where high reliability participants ($M = 4.62$, $SD = 1.36$) rated the system as slightly more benevolent than low reliability participants ($M = 4.15$, $SD = 1.26$). Additionally there was a main effect of communication style ($F(1, 126) = 6.34$, $p = 0.013$, $\eta_p^2 = 0.048$). Participants in humanlike groups ($M = 4.67$, $SD = 1.15$) rated the system as more benevolent than those in machinelike groups ($M = 4.11$, $SD =$ 1.46).

5   Discussion

We believe our method and findings offer valuable insights into the synthesis of research on CASA, anthropomorphism, and trust in automation as follows.

5.1   System Behaviors and Anthropomorphism

First, we wanted to observe whether perceptions of anthropomorphism could be elicited by subtle system behaviors and features, and not just visual cues to humanness that are often studied. Nass and Moon [18] suggested that one cue that may lead to social responses to computers is the filling of roles normally held by people. In our study, the automation may have been perceived as humanlike because it was performing the same task as each participant. Likewise, the mere presence of words for communication may have been enough of a cue to perception of the system as a social entity.

On top of these features common across groups, we sought to demonstrate that the communication style of system messages would elicit differences in perceptions of humanness. We found that the system's communication style influenced our PBA measure, but not the Godpseed measure. This may point to differences in what our explicitly-worded Likert items measured compared to the more general phrasing of the Godspeed items. Among the 3 PBA items, one referred specifically to the system's communication, while the 5 Godspeed items noted general characteristics of the automation.

Additionally, reliability affected both the PBA and Godspeed measures. Participants perceived the more accurate system as more humanlike. Prior findings on the relationship between accuracy and humanness are mixed. One study similarly found that a more smoothly operating robot was perceived as more humanlike [29]. Another found that greater inconsistency between a robot's spoken instructions and gestures actually led to greater perceived anthropomorphism [28].

In light of communication style's lack of effect on the Godspeed measure, it seems that reliability carried a greater weight in perceptions of the automation on our experiment. Had perceived anthropomorphism been measured early in the interaction, perhaps before participants observed the automation's performance, communication style may have shown a stronger effect. Nonetheless, this suggests that anthropomorphism may be a relatively dynamic perception with respect to an entity. Further research is needed to understand the extent to which systems represented by a humanlike agent are consistently perceived as humanlike, or whether perceptions of humanness change based on familiarity or the observation of certain behaviors.

In general, this finding lends to the idea that perceptions of a system's anthropomorphism are drawn from how it acts, and not just what it looks like. We encourage further work identifying specific features or system actions that lend to perceptions of *behavioral anthropomorphism*. For instance, the messages in the current study were consistent across rounds. Messages that change over time may act as a cue to more dynamic and humanlike behavior, and therefore have a more substantial influence on trust in a system.

The more accurate system may also have been perceived as more humanlike due to a greater sense of similarity, given that participants felt that they were more accurate than the automation. Prior work has found that computers with personalities that are similar to the user elicit more positive impressions [17].

We found that humanlike communication style participants perceived the system as more benevolent than machinelike communication style participants. In fact, the effect of communication style on perceived benevolence ($\eta_p^2 = 0.048$) was slightly larger than that of system reliability ($\eta_p^2 = 0.036$). The humanlike messages appeared to express that the system had the capacity to care for the user. This supports previously found positive perceptual benefits of apologies by computers [33]. Prior work has also found that self-blame by an automated system following errors leads to perceptions of greater benevolence compared to blame of system developers [7]. As of yet, however, the relationship between benevolence perceptions and behavioral outcomes such as reliance has not been demonstrated in the human-automation context. Future work in this area may help to better understand the relationship between anthropomorphism, trustworthiness perceptions, and performance.

5.2 Trust Calibration and Appropriateness

A second goal of the current study was to demonstrate a relationship between humanlike system design features and trust appropriateness. As mentioned, the communication style manipulation did not strongly influence behavioral trust. Within our experimental setup, the influence of the scoring mechanism may have been too dominant to observe such an effect. Speed and accuracy incentives as well as the clear representation of performance given by the Round Score may have reduced the salience of the communication style. A task that was more social in nature than the Target Identification task or a stronger manipulation of anthropomorphism could have amplified the effect we hoped to observe.

Nonetheless, we believe the quantifiable measure of trust appropriateness employed in this study sheds light on the importance of trust calibration as a design goal. Our participants gradually calibrated their trust to a more appropriate level over the course of the game. Participants in the low reliability group demonstrated overtrust. The degree of overtrust was significantly greater in the first two rounds compared to the later three. On the other hand, participants in the high reliability group generally demonstrated undertrust. A lack of significant differences between rounds (except for between Rounds 1 and 4) suggests that these participants may have been better calibrated initially. Without considering what represents an "appropriate" level of trust, prior work tends to miss the fact that increasing trust is not always desirable.

This measure was not without its limitations. For one, the predetermined ideal levels of trust for both groups generally led to longer times for each round. The shortest round durations would be more likely to occur at more equal levels of allocation, especially when the speed of manual classification increased with experience. For instance, 10 manual and 10 automated images would likely lead to less overall time than the ideal 5 manual and 15 automated in the high reliability condition. Although we motivated participants to perform both quickly and accurately, while also fixing the score to motivate certain levels of allocation, MTurk users' desire to complete HIT's quickly may have incentivized speed to a greater extent. This was likely especially true for low reliability participants, since the ideal level of allocation for their score was associated with a great deal of effort in manually identifying 15 images.

Our study also defined trust appropriateness in a specific way. Reliability was represented as a fixed percentage of images that the automation would classify correctly. Thus, calibration of trust involved building an understanding of this percentage and finding what level of allocation would optimize performance. In practice, other types of trust calibration may be more prevalent, as noted in McDermott and ten Brink's [13] idea for Calibration Points. Understanding the situations in which system reliability changes and adjusting behavior accordingly is a critical aspect of the calibration process. Further research is needed to clarify how anthropomorphism and agents that represent systems help or hinder the goal of appropriate trust in contexts where reliability is dynamic.

6   Conclusion

In this study, we sought to observe whether perceptions of behavioral anthropomorphism influenced the extent to which individuals were able to calibrate their trust in an automated system to an appropriate level. We found that, while both communication style and reliability influenced measures of perceived anthropomorphism, only reliability significantly influenced the appropriateness of participants' trust in the automation throughout the game. In particular, low reliability participants tended to overtrust the automation while high reliability participants tended to undertrust. The humanlike system was perceived as more benevolent than the machinelike system. Further research is needed to identify other system features and behaviors that elicit behavioral anthropomorphism perceptions. Additionally, we hope that the measure of trust appropriateness that we employed inspires other researchers to focus on trust calibration, rather than simply increasing levels of trust.

Acknowledgments. The authors would like to thank Md Abdullah Al Fahim and Kristine Nowak for their insights while preparing this experiment and manuscript.

References

1. Bartneck, C., Kulić, D., Croft, E., Zoghbi, S.: Measurement instruments for the anthropomorphism, animacy, likeability, perceived intelligence, and perceived safety of robots. Int. J. Soc. Robot. **1**(1), 71–81 (2009). https://doi.org/10.1007/s12369-008-0001-3
2. Culley, K.E., Madhavan, P.: A note of caution regarding anthropomorphism in HCI agents. Comput. Hum. Behav. **29**(3), 577–579 (2013)
3. Duffy, B.R.: Anthropomorphism and the social robot. Robot. Auton. Syst. **42**(3–4), 177–190 (2003)
4. Gong, L.: How social is social responses to computers? The function of the degree of anthropomorphism in computer representations. Comput. Hum. Behav. **24**(4), 1494–1509 (2008)
5. Hoff, K.A., Bashir, M.: Trust in automation: integrating empirical evidence on factors that influence trust. Hum. Factors **57**(3), 407–434 (2015)
6. Jensen, T., Albayram, Y., Khan, M.M.H., Buck, R., Coman, E., Fahim, M.A.A.: Initial trustworthiness perceptions of a drone system based on performance and process information. In: Proceedings of the 6th International Conference on Human-Agent Interaction, pp. 229–237. ACM (2018)
7. Jensen, T., Albayram, Y., Khan, M.M.H., Fahim, M.A.A., Buck, R., Coman, E.: The apple does fall far from the tree: user separation of a system from its developers in human-automation trust repair. In: Proceedings of the 2019 on Designing Interactive Systems Conference, pp. 1071–1082. ACM (2019)
8. Kim, Y., Sundar, S.S.: Anthropomorphism of computers: is it mindful or mindless? Comput. Hum. Behav. **28**(1), 241–250 (2012)
9. Kulms, P., Kopp, S.: More human-likeness, more trust? The effect of anthropomorphism on self-reported and behavioral trust in continued and interdependent human-agent cooperation. Proc. Mensch und Comput. **2019**, 31–42 (2019)
10. Lee, J.D., See, K.A.: Trust in automation: designing for appropriate reliance. Hum. Factors **46**(1), 50–80 (2004)
11. Mayer, R.C., Davis, J.H.: The effect of the performance appraisal system on trust for management: a field quasi-experiment. J. Appl. Psychol. **84**(1), 123 (1999)
12. Mayer, R.C., Davis, J.H., Schoorman, F.D.: An integrative model of organizational trust. Acad. Manag. Rev. **20**(3), 709–734 (1995)
13. McDermott, P.L., Brink, R.N.T.: Practical guidance for evaluating calibrated trust. In: Proceedings of the Human Factors and Ergonomics Society Annual Meeting, vol. 63, pp. 362–366. SAGE Publications, Los Angeles (2019)

14. McKnight, D.H., Choudhury, V., Kacmar, C.: Developing and validating trust measures for e-commerce: an integrative typology. Inf. Syst. Res. **13**(3), 334–359 (2002)
15. Moon, Y.: Intimate exchanges: using computers to elicit self-disclosure from consumers. J. Consum. Res. **26**(4), 323–339 (2000)
16. Morkes, J., Kernal, H.K., Nass, C.: Effects of humor in task-oriented human-computer interaction and computer-mediated communication: a direct test of SRCT theory. Hum.-Comput. Interact. **14**(4), 395–435 (1999)
17. Nass, C., Lee, K.M.: Does computer-generated speech manifest personality? An experimental test of similarity-attraction. In: Proceedings of the SIGCHI conference on Human Factors in Computing Systems, pp. 329–336. ACM (2000)
18. Nass, C., Moon, Y.: Machines and mindlessness: social responses to computers. J. Soc. Issues **56**(1), 81–103 (2000)
19. Nass, C., Steuer, J., Henriksen, L., Dryer, D.C.: Machines, social attributions, and ethopoeia: performance assessments of computers subsequent to" self-" or" other-" evaluations. Int. J. Hum.-Comput. Stud. **40**(3), 543–559 (1994)
20. Nass, C., Steuer, J., Tauber, E.R.: Computers are social actors. In: Proceedings of the SIGCHI conference on Human factors in computing systems, pp. 72–78. ACM (1994)
21. Nowak, K.L.: Examining perception and identification in avatar-mediated interaction. In: Sundar, S.S. (ed.) Handbooks in Communication and Media. The Handbook of the Psychology of Communication Technology, pp. 89–114. Wiley-Blackwell (2015)
22. Nowak, K.L., Biocca, F.: The effect of the agency and anthropomorphism on users' sense of telepresence, copresence, and social presence in virtual environments. Presence Teleoperators Virtual Environ. **12**(5), 481–494 (2003)
23. Pak, R., Fink, N., Price, M., Bass, B., Sturre, L.: Decision support aids with anthropomorphic characteristics influence trust and performance in younger and older adults. Ergonomics **55**(9), 1059–1072 (2012)
24. Parasuraman, R., Miller, C.A.: Trust and etiquette in high-criticality automated systems. Commun. ACM **47**(4), 51–55 (2004)
25. Parasuraman, R., Riley, V.: Humans and automation: use, misuse, disuse, abuse. Hum. Factors **39**(2), 230–253 (1997)
26. Quinn, D.B., Pak, R., de Visser, E.J.: Testing the efficacy of human-human trust repair strategies with machines. In: Proceedings of the Human Factors and Ergonomics Society Annual Meeting, vol. 61, pp. 1794–1798. SAGE Publications, Los Angeles (2017)
27. Reeves, B., Nass, C.I.: The Media Equation: How People Treat Computers, Television, and New Media Like Real People and Places. Cambridge University Press, New York (1996)
28. Salem, M., Eyssel, F., Rohlfing, K., Kopp, S., Joublin, F.: To err is human (-like): effects of robot gesture on perceived anthropomorphism and likability. Int. J. Soc. Robot. **5**(3), 313–323 (2013)
29. Salem, M., Lakatos, G., Amirabdollahian, F., Dautenhahn, K.: Would you trust a (faulty) robot? Effects of error, task type and personality on human-robot cooperation and trust. In: 2015 10th ACM/IEEE International Conference on Human-Robot Interaction (HRI), pp. 1–8. IEEE (2015)
30. Sebo, S.S., Krishnamurthi, P., Scassellati, B.: "I don't believe you": investigating the effects of robot trust violation and repair. In: 2019 14th ACM/IEEE International Conference on Human-Robot Interaction (HRI), pp. 57–65. IEEE (2019)

31. Seyama, J., Nagayama, R.S.: The uncanny valley: effect of realism on the impression of artificial human faces. Presence Teleoperators Virtual Environ. **16**(4), 337–351 (2007)
32. Strait, M., Vujovic, L., Floerke, V., Scheutz, M., Urry, H.: Too much humanness for human-robot interaction: exposure to highly humanlike robots elicits aversive responding in observers. In: Proceedings of the 33rd annual ACM conference on human factors in computing systems, pp. 3593–3602. ACM (2015)
33. Tzeng, J.Y.: Toward a more civilized design: studying the effects of computers that apologize. Int. J. Hum.-Comput. Stud. **61**(3), 319–345 (2004)
34. de Visser, E.J., et al.: The world is not enough: trust in cognitive agents. In: Proceedings of the Human Factors and Ergonomics Society Annual Meeting, vol. 56, pp. 263–267. SAGE Publications, Los Angeles (2012)
35. de Visser, E.J., et al.: A little anthropomorphism goes a long way: effects of oxytocin on trust, compliance, and team performance with automated agents. Hum. factors **59**(1), 116–133 (2017)
36. de Visser, E., et al.: Almost human: anthropomorphism increases trust resilience in cognitive agents. J. Exp. Psychol. Appl. **22**(3), 331 (2016)
37. de Visser, E.J., Pak, R., Shaw, T.H.: From 'automation' to 'autonomy': the importance of trust repair in human-machine interaction. Ergonomics **61**(10), 1409–1427 (2018)
38. de Visser, E.J., et al.: Towards a theory of longitudinal trust calibration in human-robot teams. Int. J. Soc. Robot. **12**, 459–478 (2019). https://doi.org/10.1007/s12369-019-00596-x
39. Waytz, A., Cacioppo, J., Epley, N.: Who sees human? The stability and importance of individual differences in anthropomorphism. Perspect. Psychol. Sci. **5**(3), 219–232 (2010)
40. Waytz, A., Heafner, J., Epley, N.: The mind in the machine: anthropomorphism increases trust in an autonomous vehicle. J. Exp. Soc. Psychol. **52**, 113–117 (2014)
41. Wickens, C.D., Dixon, S.R.: The benefits of imperfect diagnostic automation: a synthesis of the literature. Theor. Issues Ergon. Sci. **8**(3), 201–212 (2007)

Transparency and Trust in Human-AI-Interaction: The Role of Model-Agnostic Explanations in Computer Vision-Based Decision Support

Christian Meske[(✉)] and Enrico Bunde

Freie Universität Berlin, Garystraße 21, 14195 Berlin, Germany
c.meske@fu-berlin.de

Abstract. Computer Vision, and hence Artificial Intelligence-based extraction of information from images, has increasingly received attention over the last years, for instance in medical diagnostics. While the algorithms' complexity is a reason for their increased performance, it also leads to the 'black box' problem, consequently decreasing trust towards AI. In this regard, "Explainable Artificial Intelligence" (XAI) allows to open that black box and to improve the degree of AI transparency. In this paper, we first discuss the theoretical impact of explainability on trust towards AI, followed by showcasing how the usage of XAI in a health-related setting can look like. More specifically, we show how XAI can be applied to understand *why* Computer Vision, based on deep learning, did or did not detect a disease (malaria) on image data (thin blood smear slide images). Furthermore, we investigate, how XAI can be used to compare the detection strategy of two different deep learning models often used for Computer Vision: Convolutional Neural Network and Multi-Layer Perceptron. Our empirical results show that i) the AI sometimes used questionable or irrelevant data features of an image to detect malaria (even if correctly predicted), and ii) that there may be significant discrepancies in how different deep learning models explain the same prediction. Our theoretical discussion highlights that XAI can support trust in Computer Vision systems, and AI systems in general, especially through an increased understandability and predictability.

Keywords: Explainability · Artificial Intelligence · Deep learning · Computer Vision · Trust · Healthcare

1 Introduction

The progress in the field of Artificial Intelligence (AI) has led to its wide-spread application in different areas, like the finance or health sector [1, 2]. In this context, especially Computer Vision, which refers to machine learning models to extract information from images (e.g., to detect objects), is one of the many research areas in which AI-based systems have achieved high performance or even outperform humans. Already in 2012, a neural network was able to surpass the accuracy of humans when classifying traffic signs [3]. The basis of many breakthroughs in this field was built on

© Springer Nature Switzerland AG 2020
H. Degen and L. Reinerman-Jones (Eds.): HCII 2020, LNCS 12217, pp. 54–69, 2020.
https://doi.org/10.1007/978-3-030-50334-5_4

the development of deep learning methods. This is a popular branch of machine learning, which simulates structures of the human cerebral cortex and uses large datasets for training and application of multi-layer neural networks [4].

Deep learning is increasingly being examined in the healthcare domain. For example, it can be applied for medical imaging in areas such as radiology (chest radiography), pathology (whole-slide imaging), ophthalmology (diabetic-retinopathy) and dermatology (e.g. skin condition) [5] or parasite detection (malaria) [6, 7]. Despite the breakthroughs and progress in this context, one challenge regarding deep learning approaches is its 'black box' characteristic [8]. Due to the high degree of complexity of deep learning-based approaches such as neural networks, there is no inherently comprehensive understanding of the internal processes [9]. AI systems that suffer from this problem are often referred to as opaque [10]. In consequence, there is the trade-off between performance and explainability: while the performance of models increases, the explainability of these approaches decreases [11]. In order to create more transparency, to open the black box and to generate explanations regarding the decisions of AI systems, methods of Explainable Artificial Intelligence (XAI) have been developed. XAI aims to "produce explainable models, while maintaining a high level of learning performance (prediction accuracy); and enable human users to understand, appropriately, trust, and effectively manage the emerging generation of artificially intelligent partners" [12].

In this paper we will focus on XAI and its potential influence on trust. The multi-disciplinary research on trust is conducted, for instance, in philosophy, psychology, sociology, marketing, information systems (IS) or human-computer interaction (HCI) [13, 14]. Due to the fact that AI becomes more powerful and is increasingly used in critical situations with potentially severe consequences for humans (e.g., autonomous driving, medical diagnostics), trust towards such systems is an important factor. In the different streams of trust research, there are varying concepts and definitions [13]. We use a concept established by Söllner et al. [14] and thus handle trust as a formative second-order construct.

Our goal is to implement two different neural networks as the basis of a Computer Vision system to detect a disease (malaria) in images (thin blood smear slide images): A Convolutional Neural Network (CNN) and a Multi-Layer Perceptron (MLP). The dataset was obtained from Kaggle and originally stems from the official National Institute of Health. It contains 27,558 images for two classes with 13,779 images for each of the classes 'parasitized' and 'uninfected'. We then aim to generate explanations with the XAI method Local Interpretable Model-Agnostic Explanations (LIME) and use those for the comparison of both neural networks. Overall, we propose the following two research questions. RQ1: How can XAI increase trust in AI-based Computer Vision systems? RQ2: How can XAI methods be used to validate and compare the decision strategy of different AI-based Computer Vision systems?

The paper is structured as follows: First, relevant literature on AI, deep learning and trust is presented. Afterwards, we describe our research design, including the implemented MLP and CNN as well as LIME. This is followed by the results for our implemented neural networks and the generated explanations, and a discussion on the relevance of XAI with respect to trust as well as implications for research and practice. The Paper ends with a conclusion.

2 Relevant Literature

2.1 Artificial Intelligence and Decision Support Systems in Health-Care

AI techniques, especially deep learning models, are increasingly applied in the health sector and fulfil different purposes such as analyzing, interpreting, categorizing, or annotating clinical images [15, 16]. Because of the advancements of such AI systems, innovations such as AI-based decision support systems (DSS) for all organizations in general, and especially for health care providers or even as apps for private individuals, are increasingly developed [17, 18]. Therefore, it can be stated, that the role of technological decision support in health-care increased [19]. Especially the role of AI is gaining importance, as it is able to integrate various datatypes, which will be used to produce predictive models. Yet, the data collection is a complex process [20, 21]. Another reason for the growing interest in AI is based on its performance for different applications. AI was examined in the context of healthcare and DSS with different focuses. For example, machine learning approaches were investigated for predicting the outcome of individual cancer patients, and can help to improve personalized medicine [22]. Another case, where AI has been investigated, is the detection of autism spectrum disorder, which is usually based on behavioral observations, yet there are different approaches to use AI algorithms for detection in data [23]. Moreover, AI-based approaches are investigated for the detection of diabetes and prediction of blood glucose [24]. AI is also being applied for the detection and supervision of illnesses like Parkinson's disease [25] or the diagnosis of asthma [26]. Additionally, such advanced analytics can be implemented to assess whether patients have taken the medications as prescribed or to improve the adherence [27]. Possible benefits from AI for DSS in the healthcare context could include disburden professionals from repetitive tasks, enable timely reaction to critical situations, and to reduce costs, time as well as medical error [27, 28]. Decision support systems in general can hence be described as "[…] one of the greatest potential benefits of a digital health care ecosystem" ([21], p. 1).

2.2 Computer Vision and Artificial Neural Networks

Computer Vision is a discipline, where deep learning models have helped to significantly increase accuracy [29]. For instance, in the health-care sector, AI-based image interpretation is a well-researched task within medical imaging. There are further areas of application such as image denoising, auto segmentation or image reconstruction [30]. Within the health context there are different image types that are being investigated, whereby diagnostic images are by far the most used health data type [31]. Further concrete application examples of deep learning and computer vision in the health context are the examination of abnormal findings in retinal fundus images [32], recognition of skin conditions such as skin cancer [33] or in the context of neuroscience, the detection of Alzheimer's disease through medical image classification [34]. In our work, we focus on two specific types of neural networks in a Computer Vision system: MLP and CNN. Both neural networks can be categorized as deep learning approaches, whereby deep learning itself is a sub-category of machine learning [34]. Artificial neural networks are inspired by the biological neural network of mammalians.

The functional unit of this network is the perceptron, which partitions the input data in separate categories [34, 35]. The perceptron is an important element for modern neural networks, which today are composed hierarchically into a network [34].

MLP can also be described as the quintessential example for a deep learning model [36]. Today MLPs are often still applied, e.g., for a comparison between neural networks [37]. CNNs present an approach of state-of-the-art neural networks and are frequently applied for image-level diagnostics, which can be justified with the fact that for many tasks they achieve human-level performance [29]. CNNs are generally composed of different layers, i.e. convolutional, pooling and fully connected layers, whereby the convolutional layer is relevant for the identification of patterns, lines or edges [38]. Pooling layers reduce the number of features, which is done through the aggregation of similar or even redundant features [34]. In general, the CNN gathers different representations across the layers, where they learn individual features of the image [39].

2.3 Explainable Artificial Intelligence

The high accuracy of AI has not only been achieved due to an increased performance of hardware but also because of increasingly complex algorithms as used in deep learning approaches. There is hence a trade-off between performance and explainability [11]. Consequently, one of the major issues with AI for DSSs lies in the problem, that they are perceived as black boxes, even by developers. This problematic circumstance hinders the adoption of AI by different stakeholders, for instance due to concerns regarding ethical and responsible clinical implementation of DSSs [21]. For instance, decision trees achieve a rather low performance, yet a high degree of explainability, in contrast to more sophisticated approaches such as neural networks, which can reach a high performance, yet they show a rather low degree of explainability [12]. To solve these problems and to allow for more transparency, methods of "Explainable Artificial Intelligence" (XAI) are developed. The aim of XAI research can be described as to make AI systems more intelligible and human-understandable, which hence become more transparent without decreasing their performance [40, 41]. The reasons and motivations for the implementation of XAI methods can be manifold. They can help to increase trust of the user, to better understand and validate the AI systems, to comply with regulations such as the General Data Protection Regulation, and also have an impact on the compliance behavior of employees [42, 43]. XAI as a research area has hence a lot of potential to increase trust in AI-based decisions and the underlying algorithms, yet brings new challenges with it, such as what a trustworthy explanation should look like [40]. In literature (e.g., [40]) there are different overarching objectives for XAI: explain to justify (or as we would call it, explain to 'comply'), explain to control, explain to improve and explain to discover (which we would call explain to 'learn' *about* and *from* the system). In addition, so we argue, the goal to comply and to control AI are interconnected, as are the goals to learn and to improve. Eventually, so we argue, the four goals allow individuals and organizations to achieve the overriding objective of *managing* AI. A summary of XAI objectives is depicted in the following Fig. 1.

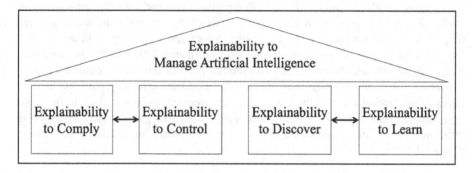

Fig. 1. Objectives of Explainable Artificial Intelligence (XAI).

There are numerous overview papers, which establish different categories for the various XAI methods (e.g. [40, 44, 45]). For our study, we decided to apply the XAI method Local Interpretable Model-Agnostic Explanations (LIME) as described in more detail in Sect. 4.2 of the research design.

3   Theoretical Background: Trust and Human-Computer Interaction

Currently, we can observe a digital transformation of workplaces [46]. In this context, trust is an important component and influences if or how, for instance, AI-based systems will be adopted [44, 45, 47]. Especially with regard to critical applications of AI such as for autonomous driving or medical diagnostics, trust plays a major role [48, 49]. There are additioan reasons why it is necessary to investigate trust [50]. For example, the risk or the uncertainty associated with a technological interaction can be reduced [14] or the experience with a technology can be created more positive and meaningful [51]. Trust is defined as "[…] the willingness of a party [trustor] to be vulnerable to the actions of another party [trustee] based on the expectation that the other will perform a particular action important to the trustor, irrespective of the ability to monitor or control that other party." ([52], p. 712, cited in [14]). We adapt two possible roles of IT artifacts [14] and apply them to the relationship between a human user and an explanation interface (IT artifact): the explanation interface has the role of the trustee, whereas the human is the trustor. Another role for the explanation interface is the mediator role between human users, who are again the trustors, and the AI system as the trustee (visualized in Fig. 2).

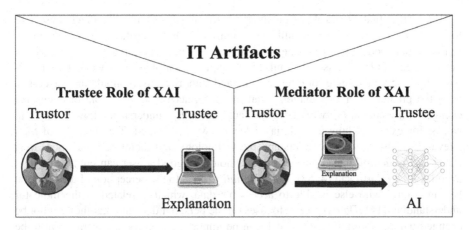

Fig. 2. Two roles of XAI and explanation interfaces in trust research (modified from [14]).

We are particularly interested how trust towards an explanation or explanation interface can be increased. For the assessment of trust from human users towards an explanation interface, we have adapted the model for trust in IT artifacts, hereinafter referred to as the trust framework [14]. We find this framework suitable for our study, since it is designed for the conceptualization of trust in IT artifacts, which can also represent AI-based Computer Vision systems or explanation interfaces. According to this framework, trust is constituted by the performance, process and purpose of the IT artifact. We are especially interested in the subdimensions of the Process of the IT artifact, on which XAI and explanation interfaces can have an influence: *user authenticity, understandability, predictability, confidentiality, authorized data usage* and *data integrity* (see Fig. 3).

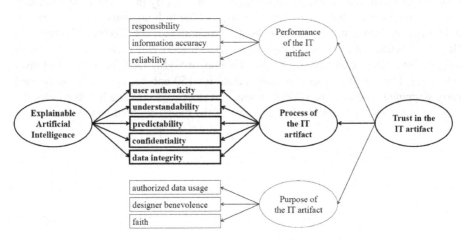

Fig. 3. Trust framework for IT artifacts (modified from [14], p. 7).

We argue, that the explanation interface of an AI system will affect these five formative indicators and hence, influence the trust in the IT artifact. *User authenticity* can be understood as the user's perception that no other user can act unauthorized, in his own name [14]. This is important, for example, when physicians work with an AI-based DSS only themselves or other specific and authorized users should have access to view the prediction or explanation in an interface, access sensible data or even take changes. *Understandability* refers to the fact, that a user understands how the system works, for example, how a (malaria) detection was generated. This point is of high relevance as users want to understand the technology and therefore build more trust [12, 14]. *Predictability* can answer the question how good a user can predict the next actions of the IT artifact [14, 53]. *Confidentiality* refers to the perception of the user that he can control who else is able to access his data, which is related to the indicator understanding [14]. *Data integrity* focuses on the personal data and that they cannot be changed without being noticed, which can be important as users in general want to be in control of their data [14].

4   Research Design

4.1   Implementing the Multi-Layer Perceptron and Convolutional Neural Networks

Our goal is to train two AI-based Computer Vision models, an MLP and a CNN, to detect malaria in cell images. We then want to use XAI to understand and compare the detection (or 'decision') strategy of each model to increase trust. We have implemented both models with keras and computed the metrics (i.e. accuracy, recall, f1-score) through the scikit-learn classification report. Table 1 provides an overview of the architectures of both deep learning models. As it can be seen, the MLP is a simple multi-layered neural network, while the CNN is inspired by the VGG-16 architecture, whereby we have created a slimmer version here, due to limitations of the computing infrastructure. Furthermore, we have used a batch size of 32, Rectified Linear Unit (ReLu) as activation function, Dropout for regularization, Stochastic gradient descent as optimizer, binary cross entropy as loss function, and a Sigmoid function as last layer activation. The training process would operate for 150 epochs, though we have used early stopping to monitor the validation loss, if it stopped decreasing for 10 epochs, the training was cancelled, and the best weights of the model restored and saved.

Table 1. Overview of the architectures for the MLP and CNN.

MLP	CNN
Dense layer (128, Relu)	Convolutional layer (32, 3 × 3, 1, Relu)
Dense layer (128, Relu)	Global average pooling (2 × 2)
Dense layer (128, Relu)	Convolutional layer (64, 3 × 3, 1, Relu)
Dropout (0.5)	Global average pooling (2 × 2)
Dense layer (1, Sigmoid)	Convolutional layer (128, 3 × 3, 1, Relu)
	Global average pooling (2 × 2)
	Convolutional layer (256, 3 × 3, 1, ReLu)
	Global average pooling (2 × 2)
	Convolutional layer (512, 3 × 3, 1, ReLu)
	Global average pooling (2)
	Dense layer (1024, Relu)
	Dense layer (1024, Relu)
	Dropout (0.5)
	Dense layer (1, Sigmoid)

4.2 Local Interpretable Model-Agnostic Explanations and the Investigated Data Set

The decision to use Local Interpretable Model-Agnostic Explanations (LIME) was made because an XAI method was required, which can be implemented for both models (CNN and MLP). LIME was introduced in 2016 [54] and is also offered as a python library, which simplifies integration into the development environment. In addition, LIME has already been investigated and examined in various tasks such as the classification and explanation of lymph node metastases [55] or recognition of facial expressions [56]. After a few tests, we decided to visualize the two most relevant regions on an explanation for malaria detection. When we had more regions visualized, the problem arose that in part the meaningfulness of the explanation was lost, due to an overload of highlighted regions in the image. Regions that represent the predicted class are highlighted in green (for instance the class: malaria) and regions that stand against the predicted class are highlighted in red (for the class: no malaria).

The dataset was obtained from Kaggle [57] and originally stems from the official National Institute of Health (NIH), which hosts a repository for this dataset [58]. The dataset contains 27,558 images: 13,779 of the class 'parasitized' cell images and 13,779 of the class 'uninfected' cell images. Figure 4 visualizes five randomly selected, exemplary images for both classes. The images of the dataset where of different sizes, so they had to be resized (128×128 pixels). The data was investigated by Rajaraman et al. [6, 7] with a focus on the performance of different neural networks. This gives us some comparative metrics, regarding the performance of our own neural networks. Although the focus was not on presenting new benchmarks, it can be argued that performance can also influence the quality of the explanation.

Parasitized Examples

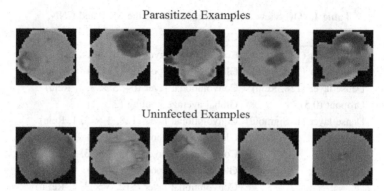

Uninfected Examples

Fig. 4. Exemplary images for both classes parasitized (first row) and uninfected (second row). (Color figure online)

5   Results

5.1   Performance of the Computer Vision-Based Malaria-Detection

In the following section we present the performance-related metrics of the artificial neural networks. We will compare the results of the two approaches using the conventional metrics accuracy, recall and f1-score. Rajaraman et al. [6, 7] presented benchmark results for different state-of-the-art architectures, such as VGG-16 (accuracy: 95.59%) or VGG-19 (accuracy: 99.09%). Our overall goal was not to exceed these values, yet they can serve as a benchmark. With our own CNN model, we were able to achieve comparable results. Moreover, the CNN has been shown to be a much more powerful and efficient model compared to the MLP. Table 2 gives an overview of the results of the two neural networks, as well as the results achieved for accuracy, recall and the f1-score. Furthermore, the values achieved are shown per class and as a weighted average. The results verify the assumption, that the CNN would outperform the MLP for all metrics.

Table 2. Results of the malaria detection based on the CNN and MLP.

Neural network	Class	Accuracy	Recall	F1-Score
CNN	Parasitized	**94.5%**	97.9%	96.2%
	Uninfected	**98.1%**	94.4%	96.2%
	Weighted average	**96.3%**	96.1%	96.2%
MLP	Parasitized	71.0%	62.0%	67.0%
	Uninfected	67.5%	77.5%	72.2%
	Weighted average	70.2%	69.8%	69.6%

5.2   Results of the Application of Explainable Artificial Intelligence

In the exemplary LIMEs, the two most relevant regions are highlighted. If only one region can be seen in an image, it means that the two most relevant regions were next to

Original Input Image   CNN LIME   MLP LIME
(Class Parasitized)   (Class Parasitized)   (Class Parasitized)

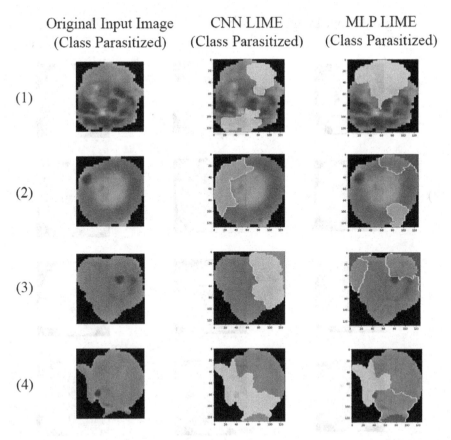

Fig. 5. Comparison of LIMEs for the *Correct* AI-based classification of *Parasitized* cells. (Color figure online)

each other. These can be regions which *support* the decision for its predicted class (green) or which *oppose* the predicted class (red). In Fig. 5, four different examples for the parasitized class are depicted. In the first row we see, for example, that the original image contains relevant regions in the lower half of the image. The CNN's explanations are relatively intuitive. For example (1) a region is highlighted which clearly marks a conspicuous region and a second region, which highlights a mix of conspicuous and inconspicuous areas at the same time. This contrasts with the LIME of the MLP, in which two adjacent regions with two regions lying side by side are marked, which for the most part only include completely irrelevant regions (e.g. (2) and (3)).

Figure 6 shows some LIMEs for the 'uninfected' class. It can be seen again that the CNN correctly highlights regions that stand for the uninfected class, whereby the MLP again highlights regions that may speak for and against the uninfected class. It is interesting that small irregularities in the image are often included in the explanations. For example, this could indicate that the CNN can distinguish the relevant regions from parasitized and uninfected examples, using this ability for classification. Another

Original Input Image   CNN LIME   MLP LIME
(Class Uninfected)   (Class Uninfected)   (Class Uninfected)

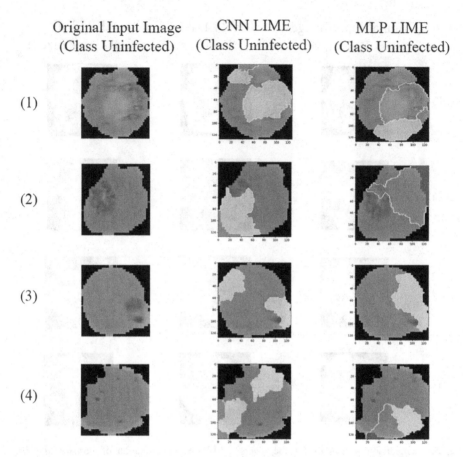

Fig. 6. Comparison of LIMEs for the *Correct* AI-based classification of *Uninfected* cells. (Color figure online)

observation is that in many LIMEs it can be seen that the black borders of the images are often included in the explanation and highlighted as a relevant area, even though this data feature should not play a role for the classification.

6 Discussion

The evaluation based on the metrics showed that the CNN exceeded the MLP. The CNN was able to achieve more than 96% for all metrics (accuracy, recall, f1-score). These results illustrate how powerful deep learning-based computer vision approaches have become. The results also show that AI-based decision support can be a great support for humans. The better performance of the CNN is also reflected in the LIMEs. For the most part, the CNN has applied comprehensible decision strategies, detecting relevant features in the cell images, while the MLP often marked irrelevant areas of the cell image, even if correctly classified. An interesting observation was that not all conspicuous regions were highlighted in the LIMEs. In fact, it was more often a mix of relevant and irrelevant regions, which contradicts human expectations and can influence the human-computer trust relationship. Another behavior that can be classified as undesirable behavior is the following. Very often, the black borders of the images were marked as relevant regions in the LIMEs of both models. Yet, they should be unimportant for the classification task.

Based on these findings, in the following we will conceptually discuss and reflect on the adapted trust framework, especially regarding aspects of the *Process of the IT artifact*. To make this discussion more comprehensible, we refer to the following fictitious scenario: a physician implemented a DSS and receives an explanation for a certain prediction, which are presented in an explanation interface.

User authenticity plays an important role for the assessment and development of trust. A user (e.g. physician) should be able to be sure that no other user can carry out actions on their behalf, e.g., prescribing medication. This indicator can be transferred to the explanation interface, as it can help to prevent unauthorized persons from accessing it through a personalized login or lock screen. In addition, metadata can be sent for actions that are triggered based on the results in the explanation interface, for example the person who edited data, the time and the device from which an action was initiated, so that user authenticity could be implemented and evaluated in the explanation interface.

Understandability is an indicator, which focus directly on the explanation as the goal of XAI: making the results of an AI system more understandable to humans [40]. However, the application scenario, target group and the implemented AI models such as CNN or MLP play a major role here. For complex approaches such as neural networks, there are a variety of XAI methods to open the black box and generate explanations (e.g. LIME) [44, 45]. The explanations of certain predictions, also called local explanations in contrast to global explanations regarding the whole AI model, highlight the relevant data features and hence make the decision strategy comprehensible.

Predictability is also a relevant indicator, which in our case, is intended to indicate how well a user can use the current explanations to evaluate how the system will handle, for example, new and unknown data. Therefore, the questions 'Why did you do that' or 'Why not something else? should not come up for the user; rather the user should be able to answer these questions himself through the explanation or explanation interface [12].

Confidentiality is also linked to the indicator *understandability* [14]: the user wishes to understand how the system works and wants to be in control. In this context, confidentiality refers to questions regarding who else has access to the data or the system. For example, a personalized interface could be created, which is only intended for a specific user and therefore lead to a high degree of confidentiality.

Data integrity is similar to the indicator *user authenticity* since this aspect also addresses the explanation interface rather than the sole explanation. It is about the extent to which personal data is processed and that changes to this data should be traceable. Here, for example, the relevant data could also be displayed in the explanation interface, which was used for the prediction so that the user can see and examine it or even experiment with different data.

7 Conclusion

In this study, we investigated how explanations can help to increase trust in AI. Moreover, we were able to demonstrate how to implement XAI to better understand AI in a critical area such as disease detection based on deep learning-based approaches. In doing so, we were able to achieve a certain degree of explainability, which, in addition to the conventional metrics, enabled us to use a further instrument for the comparison of two neural networks. It was also possible for us to increase the explainability without sacrificing performance. We can use the explanations in the form of LIMEs to control the AI's prediction. Based on the visual explanations, we can quickly identify the relevant areas of a predicted class and compare them with our own interpretation of the data and critically reflect on the prediction or decision recommendation. It was also possible to identify a certain level of undesirable behavior, as sometimes areas from the black, irrelevant borders of an image was used to classify malaria. Moreover, a relevant realization was that the mere presentation of an explanation is not be enough for an end-user to evaluate the trustworthiness of an AI. Here, it would be necessary to set up an explanation interface and to augment it with further relevant elements (e.g. the predicted class or confidence).

There are various ways how future research can build on our work. One possibility would be to examine how the quality and performance of the deep learning models can be increased with the help of AI explanations. This could be achieved, for example, by data augmentation (i.e. additional data being generated from the existing data). Moreover, it is still unsolved, how to generate knowledge from AI explanations, or in other words, to learn from what the machine has learned. In addition, it could be examined how the explanations of a CNN differ from those of a Recurrent Neural Network for Computer Vision. Future research should also deal with the evaluation of the adapted trust framework. Another option would be to establish design principles for personalized explanation interface of DSSs, and evaluate those in empirical settings of human-AI interactions.

References

1. Grace, K., Salvatier, J., Dafoe, A., Zhang, B., Evans, O.: Viewpoint: when will AI exceed human performance? Evidence from AI experts. J. Artif. Intell. Res. **62**, 729–754 (2018)
2. Maedche, A., et al.: AI-based digital assistants. Bus. Inf. Syst. Eng. **61**(4), 535–544 (2019)
3. Ciresan, D., Meier, U., Masci, J., Schmidhuber, J.: Multi-column deep neural network for traffic sign classification. Neural Netw. **32**, 333–338 (2012)
4. Lu, Y.: Artificial intelligence: a survey on evolution, models, applications and future trends. J. Manag. Anal. **6**(1), 1–29 (2019)
5. Kulkarni, S., Seneviratne, N., Baig, M.S., Khan, A.H.H.: Artificial intelligence in medicine: where are we now? Acad. Radiol. **27**(1), 62–70 (2020)
6. Rajaraman, S., et al.: Pre-trained convolutional neural networks as feature extractors toward improved malaria parasite detection in thin blood smear images. PeerJ **6**, 1–17 (2018)
7. Rajaraman, S., Jaeger, S., Antani, S.K.: Performance evaluation of deep neural ensembles toward malaria parasite detection in thin-blood smear images. PeerJ **7**, 1–16 (2019)

8. Teso, S., Kersting, K.: Explanatory interactive machine learning. In: Conitzer, V., Hadfield, G., Vallor, S. (eds.) AIES'19: AAAI/ACM Conference on AI, Ethics, and Society, pp. 239–245. Association for Computing Machinery, New York (2019)
9. Schwartz-Ziv, R., Tishby, N.: Opening the blackbox of Deep Neural Networks via Information (2017). https://arxiv.org/abs/1703.00810. Accessed 09 Feb 2020
10. Zednik, C.: Solving the black box problem: a normative framework for explainable artificial intelligence. Philos. Technol. 1–24 (2019)
11. Gunning, D., Aha, D.W.: DARPA's Explainable Artificial Intelligence (XAI) program. AI Mag. **40**(2), 44–58 (2019)
12. DARPA: Explainable Artificial Intelligence (XAI), DARPA program Update 2017, pp. 1–36 (2017). https://www.darpa.mil/attachments/XAIProgramUpdate.pdf. Accessed 27 Jan 2020
13. Corritore, C.L., Kracher, B., Wiedenbeck, S.: Online trust: concepts, evolving themes, a model. Int. J. Hum. Comput. Stud. **58**(6), 737–758 (2003)
14. Söllner, M., Hoffmann, A., Hoffmann, H., Wacker, A., Leimeister, J.M.: Understanding the formation of trust in it artifacts. In: George, J.F. (eds.) Proceedings of the 33rd International Conference on Information Systems, ICIS 2012, pp. 1–18 (2012)
15. Jayaraman, P.P., et al.: Healthcare 4.0: a review of frontiers in digital health. Wiley Interdisc. Rev. Data Min. Knowl. Discov. **10**(2), e1350 (2019)
16. Gilbert, F.J., Smye, S.W., Schönlieb, C.-B.: Artificial intelligence in clinical imaging: a health system approach. Clin. Radiol. **75**(1), 3–6 (2020)
17. Meske, C., Amojo, I.: Social bots as initiators for human interaction in enterprise social networks. In: Proceedings of the 29th Australasian Conference on Information Systems (ACIS), paper 35, pp. 1–22 (2018)
18. Kemppainen, L., Pikkarainen, M., Hurmelinna-Laukkanen, P., Reponen, J.: Connected health innovation: data access challenges in the interface of AI companies and hospitals. Technol. Innov. Manag. Rev. **9**(12), 43–55 (2019)
19. Poncette, A.-S., Meske, C., Mosch, L., Balzer, F.: How to overcome barriers for the implementation of new information technologies in intensive care medicine. In: Yamamoto, S., Mori, H. (eds.) HCII 2019. LNCS, vol. 11570, pp. 534–546. Springer, Cham (2019). https://doi.org/10.1007/978-3-030-22649-7_43
20. Stieglitz, S., Meske, C., Ross, B., Mirbabaie, M.: Going back in time to predict the future - the complex role of the data collection period in social media analytics. Inf. Syst. Front. **22**(2), 395–409 (2018). https://doi.org/10.1007/s10796-018-9867-2
21. Walsh, S., et al.: Decision support systems in oncology. JCO Clin. Cancer Inf. **3**, 1–9 (2019)
22. Ferroni, P., et al.: Breast cancer prognosis using a machine learning approach. Cancers **11**(3), 328 (2019)
23. Song, D.-Y., Kim, S.Y., Bong, G., Kim, J.M., Yoo, H.J.: The use of artificial intelligence in screening and diagnosis of autism spectrum disorder: a literature review. J. Korean Acad. Child Adolesc. Psychiatry **30**(4), 145–152 (2019)
24. Woldaregay, A.Z., et al.: Data-driven modeling and prediction of blood glucose dynamics: machine learning applications in type 1 diabetes. Artif. Intell. Med. **98**, 109–134 (2019)
25. Gi-Martin, M., Montero, J.M., San-Segundo, R.: Parkinson's disease detection from drawing movements using convolutional neural networks. Electronics **8**(8), 907 (2019)
26. Spathis, D., Vlamos, P.: Diagnosing asthma and chronic obstructive pulmonary disease with machine learning. Health Inf. J. **25**(3), 811–827 (2019)
27. Eggerth, A., Hayn, D., Schreier, G.: Medication management needs information and communications technology-based approaches, including telehealth and artificial intelligence. Brit. J. Clin. Pharmacol. 1–8 (2019)

28. Khanna, S.: Artificial intelligence: contemporary applications and future compass. Int. Dent. J. **60**(4), 269–272 (2010)
29. Esteva, A., et al.: A guide to deep learning in healthcare. Nat. Med. **25**(1), 24–29 (2019)
30. Lewis, S.J., Gandomkar, Z., Brennan, P.C.: Artificial intelligence in medical imaging practice: looking to the future. J. Med. Radiat. Sci. **66**, 292–295 (2019)
31. Jiang, F., et al.: Artificial intelligence in healthcare: past, present and future. Stroke Vascul. Neurol. **2**(4), 230–243 (2017)
32. Son, J., Shin, J.Y., Kim, H.D., Jung, K.-H., Park, K.H., Park, S.J.: Development and validation of deep learning models for screening multiple abnormal findings in retinal fundus images. Ophthalmology **127**(1), 85–94 (2019)
33. Chen, M., Zhou, P., Wu, D., Hu, L., Hassan, M.M., Alamri, A.: AI-Skin: skin disease recognition based on self-learning and wide data collection through a closed-loop framework. Inf. Fusion **54**, 1–9 (2020)
34. Valliani, A.A., Ranti, D., Oermann, E.K.: Deep learning in neurology: a systematic review. Neurol. Ther. **8**(2), 351–365 (2019)
35. Rosenblatt, F.: The perceptron: a probabilistic model for information storage and organization in the brain. Psychol. Rev. **65**(6), 386–408 (1958)
36. Goodfellow, I., Bengio, Y., Courville, A.: Deep Learning. MIT Press, Cambridge (2016)
37. Jang, D.-H., et al.: Developing neural network models for early detection of cardiac arrest in emergency department. Am. J. Emerg. Med. **38**(1), 43–49 (2020)
38. Kim, M., et al.: Deep learning medical imaging. Neurospine **16**(4), 657–668 (2019)
39. Saba, L., et al.: The present and future of deep learning in radiology. Eur. J. Radiol. **114**, 14–24 (2019)
40. Adadi, A., Berrada, M.: Peeking inside the black-box: a survey on Explainable Artificial Intelligence (XAI). IEEE Access **6**, 52138–52160 (2018)
41. Gunning, D., Stefik, M., Choi, J., Miller, T., Stumpf, S., Yang, G.-Z.: XAI – explainable artificial intelligence. Sci. Robot. **4**(37), eaay7120 (2019)
42. Dosilovic, F.K., Brcic, M., Hlupic, N.: Explainable artificial intelligence: a survey. In: Proceedings of 41st International Convention on Information and Communication Technology, Electronics and Microelectronics, Opatija Croatia, pp. 210–215 (2018)
43. Kühl, N., Lobana, J., Meske, C.: Do you comply with AI? Personalized explanations of learning algorithms and their impact on employees compliance behavior. In: 40th International Conference on Information Systems, pp. 1–6 (2019, forthcoming)
44. Guidotti, R., Monreale, A., Ruggieri, S., Turini, F., Giannotti, F., Pedreschi, D.: A survey of methods for explaining black box models. ACM Comput. Surv. (CSUR) **51**(5), 93 (2018)
45. Ras, G., van Gerven, M., Haselager, P.: Explanation methods in deep learning: users, values, concerns and challenges 1–15 (2018). arXiv:1803.07517. Accessed 27 Jan 2020
46. Meske, C.: Digital workplace transformation – on the role of self-determination in the context of transforming work environments. In: Proceedings of the 27th European Conference on Information Systems (ECIS), pp. 1–18 (2019)
47. Yan, Z., Kantola, R., Zhang, P.: A research model for human-computer trust interaction. In: Proceedings of the 2011 IEEE 10th International Conference on Trust, Security and Privacy in Computing and Communications, pp. 274–281 (2011)
48. Mühl, K., Strauch, C., Grabmaier, C., Reithinger, S., Huckauf, A., Baumann, M.: Get ready for being chauffeured: passenger's preferences and trust while being driven by human automation. Hum. Factors, pp. 1–17 (2019)
49. Qasim, A.F., Meziane, F., Aspin, R.: Digital watermarking: applicability for developing trust in medical imaging workflows state of the art review. Comput. Sci. Rev. **27**, 45–60 (2018)
50. Gulati, S., Sousa, S., Lamas, D.: Design, development and evaluation of a human-computer trust scale. Behav. Technol. **38**(10), 1004–1015 (2019)

51. McKnight, D.H., Carter, M., Thatcher, J.B., Clay, P.F.: Trust in specific technology: an investigation of its components and measures. ACM Trans. Manag. Inf. Syst. (TMIS) 2(2), 12–32 (2011)
52. Mayer, R.C., Davis, J.H., Schoorman, F.D.: An integrative model of organizational trust. Acad. Manag. Rev. 20(3), 709–734 (1995)
53. Muir, B.M., Moray, N.: Trust in automation. Part II. Experimental studies of trust and human intervention in a process control simulation. Ergonomics 39(3), 429–460 (1996)
54. Ribeiro, M.T., Singh, S., Guestrin, C.: "Why should I trust you?" Explaining the predictions of any classifier. In: Proceedings of the 22nd ACM SIGKDD International Conference on Knowledge Discovery and Data Mining, pp. 1135–1144 (2016)
55. de Sousa, I.P., et al.: Local interpretable model-agnostic explanations for classification of lymph node metastases. Sensors 19(13), 2969 (2019)
56. Weitz, K., Hassan, T., Schmid, U., Garbas, J.-U.: Deep-learned faces of pain and emotions: elucidating the differences of facial expressions with the help of explainable AI methods. TM-Tech. Mess. 86(7–8), 404–412 (2019)
57. Kaggle Malaria Cell Images Dataset. https://www.kaggle.com/iarunava/cell-images-for-detecting-malaria. Accessed 27 Jan 2020
58. National Library of Medicine – Malaria Datasets. https://lhncbc.nlm.nih.gov/publication/pub9932. Accessed 27 Jan 2020

Defining a Human-Machine Teaming Model for AI-Powered Human-Centered Machine Translation Agent by Learning from Human-Human Group Discussion: Dialog Categories and Dialog Moves

Ming Qian[1][✉] and Davis Qian[2]

[1] Pathfinders Translation and Interpretation Research,
513 Elan Hall Road, Cary, USA
qianmi@pathfinders-transinterp.com
[2] School of Information Science, University of North Carolina,
Chapel Hill, USA
davisq@live.unc.edu

Abstract. The vision of human-machine symbiosis is that a human will work closely and harmoniously with the machine. We study interactions among human translators to help define potential Human-Machine Interface (HCI) and Human-Machine Teaming (HMT) models for human-centered machine translation systems. The role of the machine, in this context, is to be an AI-based agent serving as a real-time partner. The questions we ask are that if we have such an agent, what are the main functions of the agent, how does the agent interact with a human translator in a way where they can work symbiotically as partners, what human deficiencies can be augmented by an AI-based agent and how, and what kind of human behaviors should the AI-based agent mimic. We used a data set collected from an online translation study group composed of certified and highly experienced translators (both English-to-Chinese and Chinese-to-English), and altogether we analyzed several hundred dialogs between these translators related to the translation results. Each dialog always started with an initial comment and would focus on one of many possible categories. The first question we asked was which categories were discussed more frequently than the others, and why. At both the word level and above the word level, three dominating categories were found: source misunderstanding, target expression problem, and confirmation on good translation. In addition, we found that the more than half of the dialogs focused only at the word-level. The second question we asked was whether a discussion (represented by a dialog) was effective or not. What we found was that the most common pattern was the one associated with "simple but effective" dialog, while constructive dialogs were conversely very infrequent. Based on these findings, we derive the HCI/HMT design implications for an AI-based translation agent: provide better capability beyond the word/phrase level to complement human deficiencies; focus on building algorithms to support better source understanding and target expression delivery; provide quick information search and retrieval to support real-time interaction; provide confirmation to a human partner's good translation with reasons and explanations; provide help regarding source understanding and

H. Degen and L. Reinerman-Jones (Eds.): HCII 2020, LNCS 12217, pp. 70–81, 2020.
https://doi.org/10.1007/978-3-030-50334-5_5

target language delivery based on the native language of the human partner; act in the role of a "lead translator" who has better domain and linguistic knowledge, superior cognitive capability, and unique analytic perspectives to complement human deficiency; and perform in-depth constructive dialogs with human partners by stimulating thought.

Keywords: Human-Machine Teaming · Human-machine interaction · Artificial intelligence · Machine translation · Human-human teaming · Dialog · Teaming · Human-centered · Explanation · Argument

1 Introduction

1.1 Machine-First Human-Optimized Model Versus Human Augmentation Model

Translating a large amount of content relying solely on human power is impossible. At the same time, machine translation (MT) results are not perfect (Machine translations must sacrifice quality for speed, convenience, or cost). Rather than using countless man-hours and effort for entire translations or living with unsatisfactory machine-generated results, a machine-first human optimized model has been the status quo. Post-editing is the process whereby humans amend machine-generated translation to achieve an acceptable result [1]. Human linguists have a better understanding of context and utilize better creativity to complement machine power to generate a large amount of contents with reasonable quality in a short period of time.

The main problem of this approach is that human editors can only do minor editing —they can make the final text understandable, but style, terminology, grammar, and syntax might not be perfect. Studies found that most professional translators surveyed rated the post-editing experience negatively. The reasons are "lack of creativity, tediousness of the task, and limited opportunity to create quality." [2] The reason is that standard post-editing interfaces violate basic precepts of human-computer interaction (HCI) design. It is impossible for human translators to clean up all the problematic translations generated by the MT system [3].

Interactive and adaptive MT systems like the one developed by Lilt (https://labs.lilt. com/) have emerged on the market by taking on the idea of an augmented translator made more productive by machine assistance (machine continuously learns in real-time from human feedback). This type of system tries to put the human back in the center of the translation process.

1.2 Human-Machine Symbiosis and Human-Human Collaboration

Human-machine symbiosis [4] has been identified as one of the primary challenges of HCI research. The ideal vision of human-machine symbiosis is one where humans are coupled to machines in a harmonious way. To achieve this, related technology needs to exhibit characteristics typically associated with human behavior and intelligence [4].

In this study, we study collaborations among human translators to help define potential Human-Machine Interface (HCI) and Human-Machine Teaming (HMT) models for future human-centered machine translation systems in which an AI-based agent serves as a real-time partner. We are interested in finding answers on the following questions: If we have an AI-based agent as a machine translation assistant, what are the main functions of the agent? How does the agent interact with a human translator so they can work holistically as partners? What human deficiencies can be augmented by an AI-based agent and how? What kind of human behaviors should the AI-based agent mimic? What level of expertise should a human translator expect from an AI-based agent?

2   Methodologies

2.1   Translators' Study Group

Human translators practice in order to gain competency in understanding the source language and generating appropriate target language based on that understanding. One way for translators to improve their skills is to have a group dialog in which they: (1) explain/discuss their understanding of the source text and context; (2) explain/discuss their target language choices; (3) have a dialog/argument about differing opinions, with the goal of building a consensus. The treasure trove of information encoded in these explanations, discussions, and dialogs can be of great use for defining potential Human-machine interfaces and interactions.

We used a data set collected from an online translation study group. The group was composed of 32 members, of which 11 were American Translator Association (ATA) certificated translators (specializing in English to Chinese, or Chinese to English language pairs), and 9 members who either held graduate degrees in translation, had multiple years of experience working for well-respected translation companies, or had experience translating published books. The goal of this study group was to improve translation skills and help the participants prepare for ATA certification exams. The format of the group study was as follows: every member translated an assigned piece, then all versions produced were put into a shared document where everybody could comment on the other members' results and a back and forth dialog could ensue from multiple comments on the same piece. In this paper, we studied 10 translation pieces (five of them were English → Chinese translation pieces and the other five were Chinese → English translation pieces) and analyzed 292 dialogs when group members discussed the translation results on these pieces.

2.2   Research Questions

A dialog always started with an initial comment. The initial comments would focus on various categories such as:

(1) a word, phrase, or terminology
(2) grammar
(3) sentence structure
(4) punctuation
(5) logic relation
(6) misunderstanding on the source language content
(7) faithfulness of target language delivery based on source language understanding

(8) quality of target language delivery
(9) ...

Therefore, the first question we asked is which categories from the above list were discussed more frequently than the others, and why. For example, a human translator can easily identify a misused word, but have a harder time identifying problematic sentence structures due to cognitive constraints and knowledge limits. Consequently, easily identifiable categories would be discussed more and hard to identify categories would be discussed less. From the perspective of human-machine symbiosis, machines can augment human capabilities on these hard tasks by automatically identifying the hard to identify categories for the human.

The next question we asked is whether a discussion (represented by a dialog) is effective to generate better source understanding or better target language delivery. For example, the initial comment raised a question on the usage of a phrase, but there was no follow-up discussion. This indicated a discussion associated with no actual dialog move, or an ineffective dialog move. Then, we summarized all the dialogs and found out what percentage of them were ineffective, effective, or very effective. From the perspective of human-machine symbiosis, we wanted to identify the defects of human-human dialog and see whether machines could augment humans in these problematic areas.

2.3 Dialog Categories

Table 1 lists all the dialog categories defined at the sentence level and above. Table 2 lists all the dialog categories we defined at the word level.

Table 1. Dialog categories.

Category description	Examples
Confirmation on good translation (sentence-level and above)	- *This translation is very concise but accurate. I learned a lot from the way you handled this* - *Very smooth and natural, good job!* - *I like the approach to handle the Chinese expression "但是同时......" by using the English conjunction word "while"*
Wrong or missing logical relation	- *Missing a "but" here. As a result, the logical relation broke away from the previous sentence*
Target language expression can be improved	- *Missing subject in this sentence* - *The expression "in the aspect of" is not natural in English; replace it with "in terms of" or "with regard to"*
Misunderstanding on source language content	- *The original text did not emphasize "why", instead it only said that it does not work* - *There is ambiguity here. A reader can interpret "we" as Tencent Lab, Tencent, China, or the AI industry all around the world*
Word/phrase level sub-categories	*See sub-category definitions and examples in Table 2*
Incorrect punctuation	- *English and Chinese have different parentheses formatting*

Table 2. Dialog categories (at the word-level).

Category description	Examples
Confirmation on good translation on word/phrase	- *This word 'expire' is very accurate in this context* - *Excellent choice of words here*
Better word choice suggested based on context understanding	- *Bargaining should be translated as* "谈判" *instead of* "协商" *based on the historical context*
Bad translation due to misunderstanding on source language content	- *It is not about taking advantage of the complexity.* *It is about simplifying the complexity*
Poor target language expression	- *"positive surprise" is not a natural English expression, "pleasant surprise" is better*
Translation is too literal	- 太长太绕口了 *(too lengthy, too wordy)*
Inconsistent usage of one source word at different places	- *The word "Progressive" was translated as* "开明"*in the first section, but here it was translated as* "进步"

2.4   Types of Collaborative Dialog Moves

We identify four types of collaborative dialog moves [5] towards an initial comment: (1) no dialog moves; (2) ineffective dialog moves; (3) simple but effective dialog moves; (4) constructive dialog moves such as argumentative moves (indirect check, challenge, and counterarguments), and constructive moves (adding information, explaining information, evaluating information, transforming information, summarizing information, etc.).

Explanation, in this context, serves as a mechanism through which the translators' opinions can be connected and brought to the subject matter (e.g., "I used this word because I wanted to make the English translation as close to the style of an English paper's editor") and serve the broad function of guiding reasoning (e.g. "MO is usually used in reference to criminal acts, but it can be used within other contexts sometimes. What do you think?") A well-explained dialogue move is an effective move while an ineffective dialogue move is usually associated with bad explanation (e.g. "I felt at that moment that I should use that word").

3   Analysis Results and Discussions

3.1   Text Sources for Translation Materials

Table 3 lists the titles and source links for the original text for the English-to-Chinese translation exercises. Table 4 lists the titles and source links for the original text for the Chinese-to-English translation exercises.

Table 3. Titles and links for the English-to-Chinese translation pieces (originals).

Title	Source link
Scientific Management and Reduced Working Hours	https://greprepclub.com/forum/og-vpr-20-21-22-23-during-the-1920s-most-advocates-of-sci-2842.html
After Neoliberalism	https://www.ips-journal.eu/regions/global/article/show/after-neoliberalism-3522/
Emma Watson: the Perfect Student	https://twitter.com/fredimagazine/status/879406554700808194
Banana and Diplomacy	https://archive.org/stream/jstor-25120060/25120060_djvu.txt
How Business School Deans Would Change MBA Rankings	https://poetsandquants.com/2018/02/07/how-business-school-deans-would-change-mba-rankings/?pq-category=admissions

Table 4. Titles and links for Chinese-to-English translation pieces (originals).

Title	Source link
中国与古巴的合作发展与展望	http://www.ccg.org.cn/Event/View.aspx?Id=10600
日本农业经济学科本科教育的发展及启示	http://www.xml-data.org/ZGNYJY/html/23d09194-72ef-4f37-9126-c28fcb4ef81a.htm
施一公: "中国式科研"误国误民	http://www.sohu.com/a/301445553_425345
第五次技术和产业革命	https://www.chainnews.com/articles/058916200669.htm
AI医疗落地面临的挑战	https://www.leiphone.com/news/201811/yp5huhUeS4H3zhJw.html

3.2 Dialog Categories

Table 5 shows the dialog topic statistics for the five English-to-Chinese translation pieces, and since more than half of the dialogs focus on words/phrases, Table 6 shows the specific statistics for the word-level dialog topics regarding the same five English-to-Chinese translation pieces.

Table 5. Statistics on the dialog categories for five English-to-Chinese translation pieces (sentence level and above).

Paper no.	Confirm good translation	Logic relation problem	Target language expression problem	Misunderstanding the source	Word-level dialogs	Wrong punctuation
1	3	1	5	1	10	0
2	8	0	3	4	21	2
3	2	2	1	1	11	4
4	0	0	1	1	7	3
5	0	0	0	0	17	0
Total	13	3	10	7	66	9
%	12	2.8	9.3	6.5	61	8.3

Table 6. Statistics on the dialog categories for five English-to-Chinese translation pieces (word/phrase level).

Paper no.	Incorrect within context	Source misunderstanding	Too literal	Confirm good translation	Inconsistent usage	Poor target delivery
1	2	4	2	6	0	0
2	1	2	3	10	1	5
3	0	4	0	1	0	6
4	0	4	1	2	0	0
5	0	3	2	10	0	2
Total	3	17	8	29	1	13
%	4.2	24	11.3	40.8	1.4	18.3

Table 7 shows the dialog topic statistics for the five Chinese-to-English translation pieces, and again, since more than half of the dialogs focus on words/phrases, Table 8 shows the specific statistics for the word-level dialog topics regarding the same five English-to-Chinese translation pieces. Figures 1 and 2 show percentage comparison at the sentence level and above, and at the word level.

Table 7. Statistics on the dialog categories for five Chinese-to-English translation pieces (sentence level and above).

Paper no.	Confirm good translation	Logic relation problem	Target language expression problem	Misunderstanding the source	Word-level dialogs	Wrong punctuation
1	0	0	9	3	6	0
2	0	0	6	1	7	1
3	5	0	7	8	22	1
4	0	0	1	0	22	0
5	9	0	11	6	52	1
Total	16	0	34	18	109	3
%	8.9	0	18.9	10	60.6	1.6

Table 8. Statistics on the dialog categories for five Chinese-to-English translation pieces (word/phrase level).

Paper no.	Incorrect within context	Source misunderstanding	Too literal	Confirm good translation	Inconsistent usage	Poor target delivery
1	0	2	4	0	0	0
2	0	2	4	1	0	0
3	0	9	8	5	0	0
4	1	2	0	4	0	15
5	1	14	2	13	0	22
Total	2	29	18	23	0	37
%	1.8	26.6	16.5	21.1	0	34

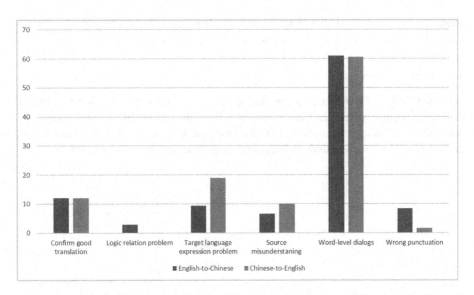

Fig. 1. Percentage comparison of various dialog categories between Chinese-to-English and English-to-Chinese translation pieces at sentence level and above.

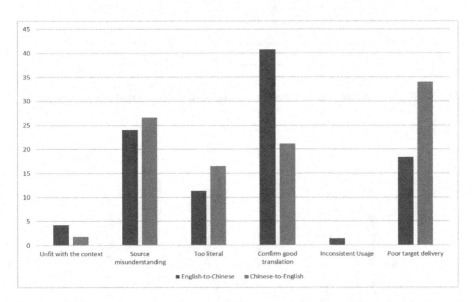

Fig. 2. Percentage comparison of various dialog categories between Chinese-to-English and English-to-Chinese translation pieces at word level.

We can observe that word-level comments are dominating (>50%), and the next three large categories are *confirmation of good translation, source misunderstanding, poor target expression delivery* at both the sentence level and above, and at the word level. At the word level, literal translation is also a significant category, but literal translation can also be classified as poor target expression delivery.

3.3 Dialog Types

Figures 3 and 4 show statistics on dialog move types for the English-to-Chinese translation sample pieces and the Chinese-to-English translation sample pieces. For different dialog categories, simple but effective dialog seems to the dominant dialog move types. Constructive dialogs happened sometimes but not very frequently.

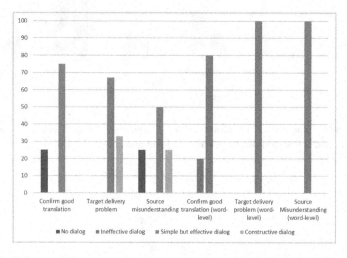

Fig. 3. Statistics on dialog move types for the English-to-Chinese translation sample piece.

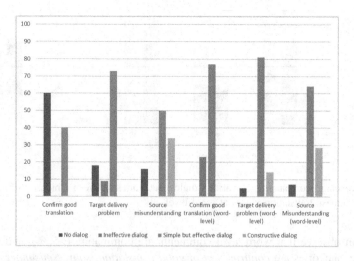

Fig. 4. Statistics on dialog move types for the Chinese-to-English translation sample piece.

3.4 Interpreting the Results and Implications for HCI/HMT

Based on the results listed in Sect. 3.3, we summarize the observations and the design implications for HCI/HMT in Table 9.

Table 9. Observations made based on collected statistics and their HCI design implications.

Observations made based on collected statistics on the sample data	Design implications for Human-centered machine translation HCI/HMT
More than half of the dialogs focused on discussions related to words/phrases. To capture problems beyond the word level, better knowledge, skill, and cognition level are required.	An AI-based solution designed to identify issues beyond the word/phrase level can be very helpful. It can supplement a human's natural deficiency for this task.
Two dominant dialog categories discussed were misunderstanding of the source content and target language delivery problems.	AI-based solutions should focus on building algorithms to perform source understanding and target expression delivery.
Human-to-human interactions have many confirmations on good translation (e.g. "Good!"; "I am impressed"; "will save this example in my notebook"; "Why didn't I think of this expression?"); but about half of these confirmation comments do not contain further explanation.	An AI-based agent should provide confirmation and feedback to human users' translation because it resembles the human behavior. In addition, the AI-based agent should be designed to provide reasoning and explanations behind the confirmations.
For target language expression delivery, a human translator has fewer problems if the target language is their native language, while they have more problems if the target language is not their native language. For example, a native Chinese speaker has more problems with English expressions compared to Chinese expressions. The statistics reflect this observation because most of the study group are native Chinese speakers.	An AI-based agent should change its level of monitoring on target language expression delivery based on the native language of its human partner. A native speaker needs less assistance from the agent while a non-native speaker needs more.
Even though most of the study group members are native Chinese speakers, in terms of source understanding, more misunderstandings were found in the original Chinese text than were found in the English translation. The reason could be that native Chinese speakers are more familiar with Chinese, so it is easier for them to identify a misunderstanding in Chinese than in English.	An AI-based agent should provide help on understanding based on the native language of its human partner.
One dominant type of dialog move was the "simple but effective" dialog move, which is usually performed by a lead translator figure who has more knowledge and authority than the other group members.	An AI-based agent could act in the role of a "lead translator" who has better knowledge or authority than its human partner. For example, the AI-based agent can be programed to have more domain knowledge

(*continued*)

Table 9. (*continued*)

Observations made based on collected statistics on the sample data	Design implications for Human-centered machine translation HCI/HMT
	or linguistical knowledge, better cognitive sensitivities related to certain features (e.g. numbers, emotion, formality), and analytic perspectives.
A significant number of dialogs initiated with a comment seeking discussion, but no dialog happened, mainly due to either lack of knowledge, or the large amount of time and effort required to do research before an effective feedback could be provided.	An AI-based agent should be designed to provide feedback and useful knowledge snippets in a timely fashion.
Constructive dialogs did not happen that often, but when they did, it led to better understanding and improved target delivery.	An AI-based agent should be designed to perform in-depth constructive dialogs with its human partner at some critical segments. It should be designed to stimulate the thoughts of the human translator and, in turn, understand human inputs in order to generate the next round of advice. At the same time, this design task is the hardest among all.

3.5   Discussion

A good translator does not want a machine translation engine that can produce translation results on its own and let the human translators edit the results afterwards. What is ideal for them is instead an AI-based translation agent that can serve the role of a real-time partner.

Even though it is important for this intelligent assistant to be able to produce some auto-translated contents on the fly, the assistant should also behave like a human partner (e.g. confirm good translation results or point out major problems with explanations and reasoning); have domain and linguistic knowledge similar to a human expert; have superior cognitive capability and unique analytic perspective to complement human deficiencies; have the ability to perform quick information search and retrieval to support real-time interaction; and have the ability to adapt to different characteristics of the human translator it works with (e.g. native/non-native speaker of certain language; level of knowledge in certain domain). Consequently, the assistant can help the human translator to understand the source content better and deliver better target expressions.

Leveraging machine understanding to complement human understanding and using human inputs to guide machine understanding are key building components for developing an AI-based machine translation agent.

Another challenging—but potentially rewarding—topic is how to facilitate in-depth constructive dialogs between a human translator and the machine partner. The goal is to stimulate each other and push the understanding forward through a conversation, this is the ideal symbiosis scenario between human understanding and machine understanding.

4 Conclusion

The objective of this study is to define a Human-Machine Teaming (HMT) model for AI-powered human-centered machine translation systems by learning from human-human group discussion. For this purpose, we used a data set collected from an online translation study group composed of expert and experienced translators. The data set had 10 translation pieces (five of them were English → Chinese translation pieces and the other five were Chinese → English translation pieces) and we analyzed 292 dialogs within which group members discussed the translation results on these pieces. We studied dialog categories and dialog moves. For dialog categories, word-level comments dominated the discussion (>50%), and the next three largest categories are *confirmation of good translation, source misunderstanding, poor target expression delivery* at both the sentence and above level and at the word level. For dialog moves, *simple but effective* dialog move seems to the dominant dialog move type. *Constructive* dialog moves, such as argumentative moves (indirect check, challenge, and counter-arguments) and constructive moves (adding information, explaining information, evaluating information, transforming information, summarizing information, etc.), happened sometimes but not very frequent. Based on these findings, we derive the HCI/HMT design implications for an AI-based agent: provide better capability beyond the word/phrase level to complement human deficiencies; focus on building algorithms to support better source understanding and target expression delivery; provide quick information search and retrieval to support real-time interaction; provide confirmation to a human partner's good translation with reasons and explanations; provide help regarding source understanding and target language delivery based on the native language of the human partner; act in the role of a "lead translator" who has better domain and linguistic knowledge, superior cognitive capability, and unique analytic perspective to complement human deficiencies; and perform in-depth constructive dialogs with human partners by stimulating thoughts from each other.

References

1. ISO 18587:2017: Translation services—Post-editing of machine translation output—Requirements. https://www.iso.org/standard/62970.html
2. Moorkens, J., O'Brien, S.: Post-editing evaluations: trade-offs between novice and professional participants. In: Proceedings of the 18th Annual Conference of the European Association for Machine Translation, EAMT 2015, pp. 75–81 (2015)
3. Green, S.: Beyond post-editing: advances in interactive translation environments (2016). https://www.ata-chronicle.online/featured/beyond-post-editing-advances-in-interactive-translation-environments/
4. Stephanidis, C.C., et al.: Seven HCI grand challenges. Int. J. Hum. Comput. Interact. 35(14), 1229–1269 (2019). https://doi.org/10.1080/10447318.2019.1619259
5. Lombrozo, T.: The structure and function of explanations. Trends Cogn. Sci. 10(10), 464–470 (2006)

Rethinking Personas for Fairness: Algorithmic Transparency and Accountability in Data-Driven Personas

Joni Salminen[1,2(✉)], Soon-gyo Jung[1], Shammur A. Chowdhury[1], and Bernard J. Jansen[1]

[1] Qatar Computing Research Institute,
Hamad Bin Khalifa University, Doha, Qatar
jsalminen@hbku.edu.qa
[2] University of Turku, Turku, Finland

Abstract. Algorithmic fairness criteria for machine learning models are gathering widespread research interest. They are also relevant in the context of data-driven personas that rely on online user data and opaque algorithmic processes. Overall, while technology provides lucrative opportunities for the persona design practice, several ethical concerns need to be addressed to adhere to ethical standards and to achieve end user trust. In this research, we outline the key ethical concerns in data-driven persona generation and provide design implications to overcome these ethical concerns. Good practices of data-driven persona development include (a) creating personas also from outliers (not only majority groups), (b) using data to demonstrate diversity within a persona, (c) explaining the methods and their limitations as a form of transparency, and (d) triangulating the persona information to increase truthfulness.

Keywords: Personas · Data · Fairness · Algorithms · Transparency · Ethics

1 Introduction

Personas are a user-centric design technique made popular by Cooper [1] in software development and in Human-Computer Interaction (HCI). Personas are defined as profiles of people that fictive but realistic [2]. They embody central aspects of the user or customer segments they describe, giving "faces" to user data [3] and summarizing diverse and complex audiences into a few archetypes [4, 5].

A persona profile typically includes a name, a picture, and a description detailing the attitudes and behaviors of the user segment the persona portrays [6]. Personas have consistently been used in a variety of fields, including software development and design [7], marketing [8], and health informatics [9].

Data-driven personas (DDPs) are created using digital user data and quantitative methods. DDPs are usually evaluated for aspects of usability, user experience, and value [10], but these evaluations often tend to overlook ethical aspects, e.g., fairness, privacy, transparency, and trust [11]. These ethical considerations have been

© Springer Nature Switzerland AG 2020
H. Degen and L. Reinerman-Jones (Eds.): HCII 2020, LNCS 12217, pp. 82–100, 2020.
https://doi.org/10.1007/978-3-030-50334-5_6

acknowledged as essential for algorithmic decision-making systems [11–14] and have been explored in the broader persona literature [15–17] but not for DDPs specifically.

The consensus of research in tangential fields of computer science and HCI has shown that algorithmic systems, and machine learning (ML) in general, involve various ethical issues. As ML and automation are becoming more widely used for persona creation [3, 18, 19], these ethical considerations warrant an inquiry in the context of DDPs. Yet, thus far authors have evaluated personas as quantitative information [20], not as products embedded in ethical and political contexts (i.e., the real world). The tangential research in related fields on algorithmic fairness [21, 22] makes it strikingly obvious that researchers and practitioners should acknowledge ethical guidelines when creating personas using algorithms. The lack of such guidelines forms a critical research gap that we begin to address in this manuscript.

The HCI community is becoming increasingly aware of algorithmic biases. For DDPs, this means that data and algorithms may introduce undesired generalizations or preconceptions into the personas. Relying solely on quantitative data might, e.g., lead to ignoring minority groups and inclusivity, as statistical methods tend to "favor" majority groups and obscure the outliers and deviations within user groups. By implicitly assuming information of certain segments of a population, the use of DDPs may reinforce existing patterns of social advantage or produce new ones [23].

To this end, there is a need to investigate how ethical considerations appear in the design practice of DDPs (i.e., those using automatic data collection means and opaque algorithmic processes to output personas that are based on behavioral and demographic data about users). For this, we pose the following research questions (RQs):

RQ1: What does fairness mean in the context of data-driven persona development?
RQ2: What guidelines should researchers and practitioners follow to create fair data-driven personas?

Our conceptual analysis is inspired by the principles for *Algorithmic Transparency and Accountability* introduced by ACM in 2017[1]. These include (1) awareness, (2) access, (3) accountability, (4) explanation, (5) data provenance, (6) auditability, and (7) validation and testing [24]. While there are several fairness criteria, e.g., those by Green and Chen [11] (i.e., accuracy, reliability, fairness), the ACM criteria are comprehensive and capture the ethical dimensions appearing in other frameworks. Regarding the practical implications of our analysis, we propose *four ethical data-driven persona guidelines* that cover the ethical concerns throughout the lifecycle of data-driven personas, including data collection, persona creation, and the application of data-driven personas for decision making within organizations. We also pose *nine ethical questions (EQs) for persona creation.*

---

[1] https://www.acm.org/binaries/content/assets/public-policy/2017_joint_statement_algorithms.pdf.

2 Data and Algorithms in Persona Generation

2.1 The Promise of Data

Persona creation has experienced dramatic changes in recent times. Quantitative methods have been leveraged to complement qualitative, interpretative methods in persona creation. Due to rapid development of data science algorithms, quantitative persona creation has been the topic in an increasing number of research articles [25–28]. Quantification of personas is contributing to the broader goal of creating more accurate and more compelling user archetypes from real data.

Moreover, it is seen that quantification can increase the scientific verifiability and credibility of personas, as quantitative methods have the clout of objectivity [29]. Statistical metrics can be used for interpreting how well a specific method creates personas [29, 30], which increases convenience for researchers.

Quantification of personas is also driven by the increasing availability of online user data [18]. When personas were first introduced in the 1990s, the Internet was still an emerging technology, and the tools to collect and process large amounts of user data were scarce. Since then, there has been tremendous progress in automatic collection of data via application programming interfaces (APIs) as well machine learning libraries (e.g., *scikit-learn*[2]) for automating the persona creation pipelines [31, 32], and automatic updating of the personas when the underlying data changes [33].

Simultaneously, data science techniques and algorithms have greatly evolved, including making a variety of statistical and computational approaches accessible for persona creation. For example, natural language processing (NLP) provides multiple methods for persona creation from textual data [34], and numerical data can be used for persona creation with the help of data dimensionality reduction algorithms such as factor analysis, clustering, and matrix factorization [18, 25, 35].

These developments have dramatically increased the feasibility of quantitative persona creation in online settings where personified big data about users or customers can be collected through social media and online analytics platforms (e.g., the APIs of Google, Facebook, and Twitter). Mijač et al. [36] argue that this constitutes a *"shift from using qualitative data towards using quantitative data for persona development"* [36] (p. 1427). In reality, mixed-method personas remain highly popular, with additional enrichment and validation afforded by qualitative analysis [37].

2.2 The Dangers of Data

Nonetheless, thus far, the ethical ramifications and impact of these profound changes in quantitative personas have been overlooked, with the majority of conceptual analyses focused on the role of personas amidst online analytics [8] or the research roadmap for fully automated persona creation [10, 38].

In contrast, only a few studies mention ethical considerations such as data privacy, algorithmic transparency, and risk of creating personas that represent averages or

---

[2] https://scikit-learn.org/stable/.

majority groups rather than diversity. Data privacy is mentioned by Wöckl [39] arguing that online datasets are typically aggregated, thus preserving the privacy of individual users. Even so, using social media data collected "in the wild" might involve issues of informed consent [40]. Moreover, using social media data presents confidentiality risks for participants, as users can be directly identified through profile characteristics or quotes.

We could locate only two previous studies specifically investigating *ethics and DDPs*. We note that the situation is different in the "mainstream" of persona research – this mainstream research, often qualitatively emphasized, has long recognized ethical issues such as inclusivity, stereotyping, and politics [15, 16, 41]. For example, Turner and Turner [41] provide an interesting conceptual analysis of stereotyping in personas, arguing that stereotyping might be inevitable, as personas always collate information from more detailed to less detailed – thus, naturally collapsing into large groups, common behaviors and tendencies, and the average. The rationale is similar to that of many algorithms of quantitative analysis – statistically speaking, concepts such as "regression to mean", "central limit theorem", "sampling", etc., all deal with representing and/or approaching the central tendency in the data [42]. Statistical methods, generally speaking, rely on means and modes that represent averages, not exceptions. A deviation from this rule can be found in methods of outlier detection [43] that specifically focus on discovering anomalies (i.e., deviations from the mean) in the data. However, outlier detection methods are not typically applied for persona creation, but the methods tend to rely on statistical generalization [37].

Of the studies discussing ethics of using algorithms and data for persona creation, the first one we located focuses only on demographic bias in DDPs [44], with the finding that DDPs inherit demographic imbalances from the source data, thus encouraging persona creators to consider the class balance in their datasets.

The second one analyzed inclusivity via quantitative personas [45], by combining exclusion assessment with DDPs. The findings of this proof-of-concept study show promise for analyzing disadvantaged groups via personas. These studies, although valuable, provide only a limited look into ethics in DDPs, which entails more issues of demographic bias and inclusivity. To this end, the study at hand is geared towards providing a more in-depth analysis of ethics in DDPs.

3 Ethics in Algorithmic Systems

There is a tremendous amount of research about the ethical aspects of computer science. Many aspects are, in fact, not novel but have been discussed over several decades. For example, the morality of computing systems was already discussed by Chorafas in 1966 [46] and Hamming in his 1969 essay in the Journal of the ACM [47]. Nonetheless, in the past few years, ethical themes have re-emerged as a trending topic in computer science and HCI, with an increasing research volume [23, 40, 48–51].

Ananny [48] places the ethics of algorithms within the broader framework of media ethics. He argues that algorithms should be understood beyond computer science's "purely mathematical, mechanistic focus". According to this view, algorithms exist within a complicated assemblage of "computational code, design assumptions, institutional contexts, folk theories [and] user models" [48] to form "Networked Information Algorithm" (NIA). As an NIA or unit of ethical analysis, DDPs describe not only an algorithmic system or merely the human interaction with that system, but "an intersection of technologies and people that makes some associations, similarities, and actions more likely than others" [48]. This embeddedness of algorithms within broader networks of human action forms the basis for understanding the normative and ethical dimensions of algorithmic systems. Gillespie proses that these ramifications may be traced along six ethical dimensions (EDs) [52]:

- *Patterns of inclusion*: the choices behind what makes it into an index in the first place, what is excluded, and how data is made algorithm ready.
- *Cycles of anticipation*: the implications of algorithm providers' attempts to thoroughly know and predict their users, and how the conclusions they draw can matter.
- *The evaluation of relevance*: the criteria by which algorithms determine what is relevant, how those criteria are obscured from us, and how they enact political choices about appropriate and legitimate knowledge.
- *The promise of algorithmic objectivity*: the way the technical character of the algorithm is positioned as an assurance of impartiality, and how that claim is maintained in the face of controversy.
- *Entanglement with practice*: how users reshape their practices to suit the algorithms they depend on, and how they can turn algorithms into terrains for political contest, sometimes even to interrogate the politics of the algorithm itself.
- *The production of calculated publics*: how the algorithmic presentation of publics back to themselves shape a public's sense of itself, and who is best positioned to benefit from that knowledge.

These EDs represent themes that reoccur across the various ethical frameworks in the field. Notions are also widely borrowed from ethical treatises in philosophy. For example, approaches that emphasize *procedural fairness* are based on the idea that algorithmic decision-making should be fair at every step and that algorithms should not be "forgiven" for making unfair decisions during the training process [6]. Adopting the idea of procedural justice, fairness in DDPs can best be assured when considering the normative dimensions of every step in the persona-creation process.

Procedural justice [10] requires that every step of the decision-making process is accurate, fair, consistent, correctable, and ethical [5, 6]. Each step in the creation *and* application of DDPs, therefore, has a normative dimension. An ethical inquiry into the DDPs will consider not only the fairness of the outcome of personas, but every step in the creation of DDPs, the human-algorithmic interface at each step (e.g., the algorithm's hyperparameters set by persona developers), the presentation of personas via the medium of choice, as well as the decision making processes relying on or influenced by DDPs. Each of these "links in chain" is a site for ethical inquiry.

Another concept is *equal opportunity*, referring to the notion that all groups should be treated equally fair. Adopted to the design of DDPs, this could be considered via the concept of *demographic parity*, in that no age, race, or gender is put in a disadvantaged position when the algorithm creates the personas. Since this can be difficult within the constraints of statistical generalization, researchers have created algorithms that specifically encode protected attributes or classes [54]. However, these are yet to be incorporated in DDPs methodologies.

The above approaches focus on *distributive fairness* of ML with the goal of achieving parity of decision outcomes. Attempts have also been made to encode Rawlsian fairness – i.e., the principle of equal opportunity of *individuals* as opposed to *groups* – to combat algorithmic bias, while not mitigating the predictive accuracy [53].

4 Algorithmic Transparency and Accountability in DDPs

4.1 Conceptual Framework

Our conceptual analysis adopts the principles for *Algorithmic Transparency and Accountability* by ACM [24] that include (1) awareness, (2) access, (3) accountability, (4) explanation, (5) data provenance, (6) auditability, and (7) validation and testing. This framework is chosen for two reasons: first, it is comprehensive, covering the main aspects of ethics in algorithmic systems. Second, it is released by ACM and thus provides legitimacy when evaluation systems, especially those that are applied in nature. Personas, as a technique, are highly applied for which warranted to analyze them using a generalizable framework such as the ACM guidelines.

Overarchingly, DDPs may be thought of as an attempt to disaggregate the aggregated data. The most salient normative issues, therefore, concern the ethics of categorization, bias, and discrimination, and the question of algorithmic transparency. Thus, we expand the ACM framework to include these dimensions. The outcome is a conceptual analysis framework with ten "pillars" (see Fig. 1).

	Awareness	Access	Accountability	Explanation	Data provenance	Auditability	Validation and testing
Persona developers	??	??	??	??	??	??	??
Algorithms	??	??	??	??	??	??	??
Inspiration users	??	??	??	??	??	??	??
Decision makers	??	??	??	??	??	??	??
Decision targets	??	??	??	??	??	??	??

Fig. 1. Conceptual framework for analyzing ethical issues of DDPs

It is important to acknowledge that various roles are involved in ethical considerations revolving around DDPs (Fig. 1). These include at least:

- *Persona developers* – these are the creators of personas. The creators have major agency in the chain of ethical DDPs, as they make critical decisions about data collection, choice of algorithms, setting of hyperparameters (e.g., the number of generated personas), and so on.

- *Algorithms* – these are models, algorithms and computational techniques used when creating the personas and presenting them to decision makers.
- *Inspiration users* – these are the users whose data is used for persona creation (e.g., interviewees, respondents, social media users, website visitors, customers in the company's database…).
- *Decision makers* – these are the end-users that "use" personas, meaning they make decisions based on personas and/or refer to personas in their thinking about the users and in communication with other stakeholders in user-centric actions.
- *Decision targets* – these are the users that are facing the consequences of decisions made based on persona information.

Therefore, ethical issues are not isolated in only the confined chambers of researchers creating them, but rather cover the entire persona lifecycle [55], from their creation of exploitation. For example, decision makers can make "bad" or ethically unquestionable decisions (e.g., discriminate, enforce existing stereotypes) based on personas. If the decisions were based on inaccurate persona information, then we should emphasize the responsibility of persona developers. However, if the information was accurate and the decisions were still wrong, the emphasis of responsibility should be on the decision makers. This goes to show that persona creation and application are intertwined in a complex, and often intractable relationship, which requires any analysis on this topic to consider multiple stakeholder perspectives.

Moreover, algorithms, although not people or legal subjects, have agency (i.e., power) over the decisions. Algorithms are amoral (i.e., they do not recognize moral guidelines unless imposed as formal rules), but they can still behave immorally from a human perspective [56]. This can take place via statistical selection processes (i.e., "algorithmic decision making" [57]), but also in the choice of the medium for presenting the personas (e.g., certain persona information can be presented more saliently than other information in a persona UI). Even a seemingly simple issue such as selection of persona pictures can form a major ethical choice, as the picture can evoke gender [15] and racial [58] stereotypes. These issues cannot be neglected, as argued by Salminen et al. [58], as personas forcefully have a specific gender and race.

4.2 Analysis

In this section, we apply the ACM framework to discuss the ethical aspects of DDPs. In each subsection, we present important EQs for persona developers to address.

Awareness. Definition [24]: *"Owners, designers, builders, users, and other stakeholders of analytic systems should be aware of the possible biases involved in their design, implementation, and use and the potential harm that biases can cause to individuals and society."*

A literature review on quantitative persona generation [37] reveals there is, in general, little consideration to ethical matters in quantitative persona articles. Instead, the papers tend to focus on technical justification and evaluation of personas as information. The focus differs from the conceptually oriented persona research, with repeated studies on ethical matters, especially focused on stereotypes [16, 41], and inclusivity [15, 45]. Thus, the awareness aspect shows there is "work to do" to activate quantitatively oriented persona researchers to consider ethical aspects of DDPs.

To this end, the EQs include:

EQ1: How can creators of DDPs be made more aware of ethical concerns relating to DDPs?

EQ2: How can persona users be made aware of potential bias in DDPs?

Siegel [29] refers to the "mystique of numbers" that in their case manifested in company stakeholders not questioning the user segments because these were based on data and algorithms. Thus, there may be a fallacy of objectivity, in that decision makers in some cases are not questioning DDPs because they are seen as objective representations of real user data. Coincidentally, this line of thinking would actually be preferred by creators of DDPs in certain sense, as DDP methodologies are partly created to address the lack of credibility of personas, which has been found a real concern in empirical user studies [59, 60] as well as conceptual treatise of personas [30]. The empirical user studies of DDPs, in turn, provide evidence that decision makers remain critical to DDPs, questioning the data and the details of how the personas were created [58, 61]. Data resistance can be an issue, especially when personas are not believed because they contain information that contradicts the user's existing biases. Based on these slightly conflicting empirical findings, persona users can perhaps be divided into two main groups based on their trusting attitudes: those that accept the persona information as facts without questioning [29], and those that are skeptical and require further explanations to "believe" the persona is real [61].

Access and Redress. Definition [24]: *"Regulators should encourage the adoption of mechanisms that enable questioning and redress for individuals and groups that are adversely affected by algorithmically informed decisions."*

This aspect concerns especially the individuals facing the consequences of decisions made based on DDPs. For example, organizations such as crime fighting agencies or insurance companies create "thug personas", "criminal personas", "diabetes personas", or "risk personas" that either over-generalize and thus provide basis for discriminatory decision making, or are accurate (e.g., capturing a person's higher risk of getting diabetes) and, therefore, make it possible to provide unfair terms for individuals at large. We can thus infer that providing free access to automatic persona generation systems can result in ethical vulnerabilities – the efficient use of personas can be unethical in nature.

The question hinges on an ethical understanding of algorithmic categories and probable similarity. As Gillespie [52] notes, categorization is a powerful political and semantic tool, particularly in the context of ML. Categories create order out of disparate information and present information in a fixed way that discourages alternatives. Minority groups can be especially vulnerable to being misinterpreted or having a lack of representation in DDPs, as data science algorithms tend to focus on averages and patterns and tendencies that reflect behaviors and traits of the majority subsets in the dataset. Thus, special consideration is needed to capture the diversity of user communities. While this can potentially be done within one generation of personas (depending on the correction methods available for a given algorithm), another option is to run algorithms several times: e.g., one set of personas from the full dataset and another set of "minority personas", identified by exploratory data analysis.

The matter of access is not only a question of obligation but can provide tangible benefits for decision makers. This is because useful insights for design of usability and user experience can often be found in outliers and minority segments (e.g., accessibility). Thus, DDPs can quantify issues of fairness and accessibility. For this, one of the central questions is:

EQ3: How can it be ensured that DDPs does not highlight marginalized, vulnerable, or otherwise disadvantaged populations in a harmful way?

Accountability. Definition [24] *"Institutions should be held responsible for decisions made by the algorithms that they use, even if it is not feasible to explain in detail how the algorithms produce their results."*

Algorithms and ML are increasingly understood as agential; as operating in terms that are becoming progressively unknowable and indecipherable to humans [62]. Holding algorithms accountable for potentially unethical DDPs is hampered by the opaqueness and lack of transparency of algorithms in general [50]. Thus, accountability of algorithms, therefore, relates closely to algorithmic transparency: the more is known about algorithmic decision-making, the better it can be evaluated for fairness. In most (but not all) cases, transparency of algorithmic decision-making leads to increased fairness [63, 64].

Clearly, the responsibility for the ethicality is shared by humans (persona creators and users) and algorithms. To be accountable, the humans involved in DDP projects need to understand the potential consequences of personas in the real world. This aspect of *actionability* is also noted by Gillespie. "What we need," notes Gillespie, "is an interrogation of algorithms as a key feature of our information ecosystem, and of the cultural forms emerging in their shadows with close attention to where and in what ways the introduction of algorithms into human knowledge practices may have political ramifications" [7].

Furthermore, it has been shown that automated systems may diminish people's sense of accountability and moral agency [23]. In other words, responsibility is shifted to the algorithm. This is a dangerous road, given the various types of biases involved with personas. Research has shown that personas are still generated mostly from survey data rather than behavioral data sources [37]. However, even when analyzed quantitatively, survey data may include several issues of validity (e.g., social desirability bias [65]). In a similar vein, setting the number of personas, applying hyperparameters for algorithms and other steps that involve manual tuning are subject to human bias. Therefore, "quantitative" does not automatically mean "objective" or "truthful", which is a critical consideration for accountability.

On the other hand, when personas are true to the data, this decreases – in theory [1, 66] – the decision makers' tendency to rely on user stereotypes that are compatible with their own biases. The implication is that adopting the principles of good ML (e.g., proper treatment of class imbalance [9] is ethical ML.

Some of the striking questions involve:

EQ4: What is the chain of responsibility in persona lifecycle, ranging from creation to application?

EQ5: Who is responsible for unethical choices based on personas; their creators or stakeholders applying them, and when?

Explanation. Definition [24]: *"Systems and institutions that use algorithmic decision-making are encouraged to produce explanations regarding both the procedures followed by the algorithm and the specific decisions that are made. This is particularly important in public policy contexts."*

Research suggests that people struggle to interpret and evaluate ML outcomes [67]. This also applies to personas that have been perceived as abstract [59], unrealistic [30], and confusing [68, 69]. Not only do people use algorithmic outcomes in unexpected and biased ways, but they are influenced by irrelevant information and display poor judgment in gauging the accuracy of algorithms. While it is not clear whether this phenomenon is fundamental to HCI or the result of factors like interface design or training [67], explainability inarguably poses a critical design challenge for DDPs.

Transparency has been suggested as a solution to trust concerns regarding data use and algorithmic decision-making [13, 70]. It is argued that by understanding how systems and algorithms work, decision makers using those systems or algorithms will feel more comfortable and trusting with the results [71]. On the other hand, previous findings on how to improve human-algorithmic interactions show that providing explanations or feedback does not necessarily improve human performance [67].

Particularly, users of DDPs may question the information in persona profiles because they are unsure of how it was created [61]. This problem is especially vexing for data-driven personas because their creation is an opaque algorithmic process. The more information and data the persona profile contains, the more complex its cognitive processing may become [61]. Thus, there is a trade-off of increasing informativeness ("roundedness" [7]) of personas and their understandability.

The challenge of explanations is further enhanced by the fact that the creation mechanisms of DDPs are complicated to understand by laymen and, at times, even other researchers. Moreover, if decision makers only see the DDPs without any explanations, they may still consider data-driven personas as untrustworthy because they may be unsure how the information in the persona profiles was inferred [30, 58].

Salminen et al. [72] investigated technically oriented explanations of information in DDP profiles and found that higher transparency through explanations increased the perceived completeness and clarity of the personas among end users. They encourage creators of DDPs to consider "persona transparency" by including clear statements of where the data originates, how it was collected, and what were the analysis steps that resulted in the personas shown to the decision makers.

Data Provenance. Definition [24]: *"A description of the way in which the training data was collected should be maintained by the builders of the algorithms, accompanied by an exploration of the potential biases induced by the human or algorithmic data-gathering process. Public scrutiny of the data provides maximum opportunity for corrections. However, concerns over privacy, protecting trade secrets, or revelation of* *analytics that might allow malicious actors to game the system can justify restricting access to qualified and authorized individuals.*"

Using social media data may present confidentiality risks for participants, as participants can be directly identified through their profile characteristics or comments [40]. Therefore, privacy of individuals can be violated and/or their views misrepresented when automatically selecting social media quotes for persona profiles. In contrast, the aggregated and non-personally identifiable information regarding quantitative performance metrics such as click and view counts can be useful for safeguarding the privacy of individual users [3]. In this sense, the structured data afforded by many Web analytics and social media platforms can support the ethical creation of personas.

In contrast, the extant trend [54, 73] to remove sensitive classes such as race and gender from the data can be problematic for ethical persona creation. This is because it reduces the ability of persona creators to, firstly, specifically portray marginalized group – when data is not available, these personas cannot easily be created and therefore understanding these user groups using DDPs becomes hard, if not possible. Secondly, the lack of protected class attributes can make it harder to fix the biases in quantitative algorithms – for example, an attribute such as race can be proxied by other variables in the dataset (e.g., income, location). This can especially take place with algorithms that learn latent patterns not directly visible in the dataset [21]. As a result, the decisions may involve a sort of a representation of the latent variable even when it is removed. For these purposes, masking data is challenging for ethical DDPs.

Auditability. Definition [24]: *"Models, algorithms, data, and decisions should be recorded so that they can be audited in cases where harm is suspected."*

Although algorithms and ML influence human decision-making, how humans and algorithms interact to form decisions is not well understood [67]. This may hinder the scrutiny of DDPs, as it might not be clear for researchers or practitioners how to audit personas. One promising alternative is to provide so-called "full stack personas" (*forthcoming*), using a persona system through which decision makers can download the raw data of their personas (called "interaction matrix").

Another challenge is the trade-off of private vs. publicly available data. Naturally, for replication and scrutiny, data used for DDP creation would need to be available for other researchers. However, making the data available can, on one hand, violate the terms of service (TOS) in online analytics platforms – for example, Twitter disallows direct sharing of tweets (they can be shared using Tweet IDs). On the other hand, if persona creation data is made available, this can violate the privacy of individuals based on whose information the personas are created – thus, researchers should consider getting the users' consent while adhering to TOS' of online platforms. Because this adds the complexity and required effort, most DDP studies fail to share their data [37].

Auditability can also involve aspects of users' choice – relevant questions here include, for example:

EQ6: Can users see their corresponding personas?
EQ7: Can user correct misinformation/mismatches of personas?
EQ8: Can online users "opt out" of their data being used for persona creation?

Validation and Testing. Definition [24]: "*Institutions should use rigorous methods to validate their models and document those methods and results. In particular, they should routinely perform tests to assess and determine whether the model generates discriminatory harm. Institutions are encouraged to make the results of such tests public.*" Validation of persona ethics suffers from the lack of standards and metrics. What is the metric for an ethical persona? The issue can be demonstrated via the example of representativeness, which is understood very differently whether one comes from a statistical background or from an ethics background.

In many of studies developing DDPs, representativeness (or inclusivity) tends to be considered from the perspective of statistics [37], not from the perspective of fairness. The difference is such a representative persona set describes the main tendencies of the data via personas, whereas an inclusive persona set would include personas evenly for each defined class. The objective of the former is efficient representation of central data, while the objective of the latter is the maximization of diversity [45].

As these two approaches appear incommensurable, the outcome is real challenge for validation of DDPs – or, as Hill et al. [15] put it, "can we have it both ways?".

Testing and validating DDPs can, nonetheless, provide answers to ethical questions. For example, consider the trade-off regarding complexity vs. comprehension. In other words, when designing explanations for explainable DDPs, the outputs can easily become too complex [72], which defeats the purpose. This trade-off prompts persona developers to carry out empirical testing and validation towards the goal of finding the optimal "simplicity-informativeness" ratio.

EQ9: How can more detailed reporting of ethical aspects be promoted within DDP creation?

5   Discussion

5.1   The Good, the Bad, and the Ugly of Personas

The findings of the conceptual analysis indicate that personas cannot be created in "blind faith" with the assumption that the underlying data and applied algorithms would automatically yield "objective" outcomes; rather, the risks and biases need to be properly scrutinized for each DDP project. This is important to avoid biased decisions based on the personas by stakeholders that are using them. In other words, issues relating to the nature of data (i.e., measurement errors, imbalance, protected classes), as well as the statistical nature of algorithms (overgeneralization) need to be considered when applying automatic quantitative methods for persona creation.

Somewhat ironically, DDPs were originally introduced to address the issue of human bias and limited data when using qualitative persona creation [10, 19, 27, 36]. However, new sources of bias emerged, forcing the creators of DDPs to exit the curtain of (alleged) objectivity. These new sources involve both human and machine bias. The former is exemplified by selection of data and algorithms, as well as setting the hyperparameter values such as the number of personas. The latter is exemplified by tendency towards means, modes, and averages. The former should be addressed by explicating and justifying the manual choices in DDP creation process. The latter can be addressed using statistical methods such as dividing the data into even subsets and/or applying outlier detection. In ML studies, there are several approaches to class balancing [74, 75] that can help process the data for fairer personas.

Overall, the ethical concerns in DDPs stem from (a) the increase in the use of online user data (e.g., social media profiles), as well as from (b) the use of opaque algorithmic processes to generate the personas. The automated processing of user data to create artificial user profiles (i.e., personas) thus transcends ethical questions about the data itself (privacy, ownership) as well as the algorithms involved in manipulating the data (transparency, fairness). All these factors must be considered and be subject to further research and development of ethical DDP methodologies.

We would like to point out that not all matters in this space are gloomy "risks" or "threats". There are positive opportunities as well. One of these is correcting biases and stereotypes decision makers have about users – because DDPs are based on quantitative evidence, they might be more believable for (at least skeptical) stakeholders. Thus, personas could be actually used to correct biases and stereotypes.

Another aspect is using DDPs as tools to pinpoint underprivileged groups. For example, if certain demographics are missing from the data, then communicating the absence of these groups via personas could be a compelling method to show "who is missing". It is then not necessarily the personas that are biased but the social structures that yielded the data, and personas simply reflected these structures.

In many respects, DDPs may be seen as offering a solution to the inscrutability of big data analytics. By presenting big data in a persona format, DDPs aim to humanize algorithmic machine learning and to package this information into a representation that is understandable to human reasoning. However, because of the unpredictable nature of human decision-making, the normative dimension of the interface between DDPs and end-users should be of concern to persona designers.

5.2 Ethical Data-Driven Persona Guidelines

Persona creators should be aware that harm from online research can occur for classes of people and communities [49]. The ethically questionable practices to avoid for persona creation (and conversely to strive for) are proposed in Table 1.

Table 1. What to avoid and what to strive for when creating ethical data-driven personas

Bad way	Good way
Generating personas based on averages and majorities while overlooking deviant or minority personas (a concern for inclusivity [45])	Creating personas also from outliers and deviating behaviors. Using subsets of data that describe marginalized groups, or specifically acquiring such data
Reinforcing stereotypes as a consequence of the previous point (a concern for application) [41]	Increasing the number of personas created to cover more subsegments in data [33], and using data to demonstrate diversity within a persona, such as showing multiple pictures for gender diversity [15]
Creating personas that appear "objective" and "perfect" because they are created using numerical data and algorithms (the "mystique of numbers" [29]), without communicating the limitations that each method inevitably has to the end users of personas (a concern of transparency)	Being frank about the applied methods and their limitations, adding explanations and other forms of transparency in persona systems [72]
Not corroborating the DDPs using triangulation or qualitative insights [2], while relying on the black-box data from online platforms whose sources of error and bias remain unknown (a concern of truthfulness)	Creating "hybrid personas" that are based on quantitative and qualitative insights [5] as a form of triangulation, and using both text and numbers to describe the personas [76]

In the *worst ethical scenario*, stakeholders are presented with personas that represent only majority user segments, without explaining how the personas were created (persona transparency [72]) and what are the drawbacks of the methods applied, and without ensuring that the data upon which the personas are built is actually valid. In the *best ethical scenario*, the ethically ideal personas (a) capture the diversity of the user segments, are (b) transparent in the sense that their generation and information is well explained and understood by decision makers and replicable if needed, and are (c) corroborated by using methods of triangulation.

Persona developers also have a responsibility in verifying that the users really understand the limitations of each method. This is more complex than it seems, as users can easily argue they understand (e.g., non-verbally nodding), whereas in reality, they do not understand. Asking the users to explain the DDPs in their own words is one tactic for ensuring proper understanding.

Decision makers should not blindly believe the outputs of DDP creation algorithms. Additional steps, such as ensuring data quality and triangulating the results with other methods, such as traditional qualitative interviews, are necessary. This is not a novel recommendation, as persona scholars have consistently advocated mixed-method personas [1, 2, 5] – however, in the "hype of data science", this old wisdom can easily be forgotten. In practice, practitioners with limited knowledge about quantitative methods should "ask stupid questions" to avoid the "mystique of numbers" [29], including asking clarification about how the personas were created, what manual choices the creation process involved, and how the results were validated.

6 Conclusion

Our goal was to tie DDPs into the algorithmic fairness, accountability, and transparency discussion. Through this linkage, we provide guidelines for data-driven persona creation that include (a) creating personas also from outliers (not only majority groups), (b) using data to demonstrate diversity within a persona, (c) explaining the methods and their limitations as a form of transparency, and (d) triangulating the persona information to increase truthfulness. These recommendations provide a starting point for developing standards for ethical data-driven persona creation.

References

1. Cooper, A.: The Inmates Are Running the Asylum: Why High Tech Products Drive Us Crazy and How to Restore the Sanity. Sams - Pearson Education, Indianapolis (1999)
2. Pruitt, J., Grudin, J.: Personas: practice and theory. In: Proceedings of the 2003 Conference on Designing for User Experiences, San Francisco, California, USA, pp. 1–15. ACM (2003). https://doi.org/10.1145/997078.997089
3. An, J., Kwak, H., Salminen, J., Jung, S., Jansen, B.J.: Imaginary people representing real numbers: generating personas from online social media data. ACM Trans. Web (TWEB) 12 (4), 1–26 (2018)
4. Salminen, J., et al.: Generating cultural personas from social data: a perspective of middle eastern users. In: Proceedings of the Fourth International Symposium on Social Networks Analysis, Management and Security (SNAMS-2017), Prague, Czech Republic. IEEE (2017). https://doi.org/10.1109/FiCloudW.2017.97
5. Salminen, J., et al.: From 2,772 segments to five personas: summarizing a diverse online audience by generating culturally adapted personas. First Monday 23, 8415 (2018). https://doi.org/10.5210/fm.v23i6.8415
6. Nielsen, L., Hansen, K.S., Stage, J., Billestrup, J.: A template for design personas: analysis of 47 persona descriptions from Danish industries and organizations. Int. J. Sociotechnol. Knowl. Dev. 7, 45–61 (2015). https://doi.org/10.4018/ijskd.2015010104
7. Nielsen, L.: Personas - User Focused Design. Springer, New York (2019). https://doi.org/10.1007/978-1-4471-7427-1
8. Salminen, J., Jansen, B.J., An, J., Kwak, H., Jung, S.: Are personas done? Evaluating their usefulness in the age of digital analytics. Pers. Stud. 4, 47–65 (2018). https://doi.org/10.21153/psj2018vol4no2art737
9. Zhu, H., Wang, H., Carroll, J.M.: Creating persona skeletons from imbalanced datasets - a case study using U.S. older adults' health data. In: Proceedings of the 2019 on Designing Interactive Systems Conference, DIS 2019, San Diego, CA, USA, pp. 61–70. ACM (2019). https://doi.org/10.1145/3322276.3322285
10. Salminen, J., Jung, S., Jansen, B.J.: The future of data-driven personas: a marriage of online analytics numbers and human attributes. In: ICEIS 2019 - Proceedings of the 21st International Conference on Enterprise Information Systems, Heraklion, Greece, pp. 596–603. SciTePress (2019)

11. Green, B., Chen, Y.: The principles and limits of algorithm-in-the-loop decision making. In: Proceedings of the ACM on Human-Computer Interaction (CSCW), pp. 1–24 (2019). https://doi.org/10.1145/3359152
12. Chander, A.: The racist algorithm. Mich. L. Rev. **115**, 1023 (2016)
13. Diakopoulos, N., Koliska, M.: Algorithmic transparency in the news media. Digit. J. **5**, 809–828 (2017)
14. Eslami, M., Vaccaro, K., Karahalios, K., Hamilton, K.: "Be careful; things can be worse than they appear": understanding biased algorithms and users' behavior around them in rating platforms. In: Proceedings of the 11th International AAAI Conference on Web and Social Media (ICWSM), Montréal, Canada, pp. 62–71 (2017)
15. Hill, C.G., et al.: Gender-inclusiveness personas vs. stereotyping: can we have it both ways? In: Proceedings of the 2017 CHI Conference, pp. 6658–6671. ACM (2017). https://doi.org/10.1145/3025453.3025609
16. Marsden, N., Haag, M.: Stereotypes and politics: reflections on personas. In: Proceedings of the 2016 CHI Conference on Human Factors in Computing Systems, pp. 4017–4031. ACM, New York (2016). https://doi.org/10.1145/2858036.2858151
17. Pröbster, M., Haque, M.E., Marsden, N.: Perceptions of personas: the role of instructions. In: 2018 IEEE International Conference on Engineering, Technology and Innovation (ICE/ITMC), pp. 1–8 (2018). https://doi.org/10.1109/ICE.2018.8436339
18. An, J., Kwak, H., Jung, S., Salminen, J., Jansen, B.J.: Customer segmentation using online platforms: isolating behavioral and demographic segments for persona creation via aggregated user data. Soc. Netw. Anal. Min. **8**, 54 (2018). https://doi.org/10.1007/s13278-018-0531-0
19. Zhang, X., Brown, H.-F., Shankar, A.: Data-driven personas: constructing archetypal users with clickstreams and user telemetry. In: Proceedings of the 2016 CHI Conference on Human Factors in Computing Systems, pp. 5350–5359. ACM, New York (2016)
20. Chapman, C.N., Love, E., Milham, R.P., ElRif, P., Alford, J.L.: Quantitative evaluation of personas as information. In: Proceedings of the Human Factors and Ergonomics Society Annual Meeting, pp. 1107–1111 (2008). https://doi.org/10.1177/154193120805201602
21. Hajian, S., Bonchi, F., Castillo, C.: Algorithmic bias: from discrimination discovery to fairness-aware data mining. In: Proceedings of the 22nd ACM SIGKDD International Conference on Knowledge Discovery and Data Mining, pp. 2125–2126. ACM (2016)
22. Stoyanovich, J., Abiteboul, S., Miklau, G.: Data, responsibly: fairness, neutrality and transparency in data analysis. In: International Conference on Extending Database Technology, Bordeaux, France (2016)
23. Mittelstadt, B.D., Allo, P., Taddeo, M., Wachter, S., Floridi, L.: The ethics of algorithms: mapping the debate. Big Data Soc. **3** (2016). https://doi.org/10.1177/2053951716679679
24. Garfinkel, S., Matthews, J., Shapiro, S.S., Smith, J.M.: Toward algorithmic transparency and accountability. Commun. ACM **60**, 5 (2017). https://doi.org/10.1145/3125780
25. Brickey, J., Walczak, S., Burgess, T.: A comparative analysis of persona clustering methods. In: AMCIS 2010 Proceedings (2010)
26. Laporte, L., Slegers, K., De Grooff, D.: Using correspondence analysis to monitor the persona segmentation process. In: Proceedings of the 7th Nordic Conference on Human-Computer Interaction: Making Sense Through Design, pp. 265–274. ACM, New York (2012). https://doi.org/10.1145/2399016.2399058
27. McGinn, J.J., Kotamraju, N.: Data-driven persona development. In: Proceedings of the SIGCHI Conference on Human Factors in Computing Systems, Florence, Italy, pp. 1521–1524. ACM (2008). https://doi.org/10.1145/1357054.1357292

28. Miaskiewicz, T., Sumner, T., Kozar, K.A.: A latent semantic analysis methodology for the identification and creation of personas. In: Proceedings of the SIGCHI Conference on Human Factors in Computing Systems, pp. 1501–1510. ACM (2008)

29. Siegel, D.A.: The mystique of numbers: belief in quantitative approaches to segmentation and persona development. In: CHI 2010 Extended Abstracts on Human Factors in Computing Systems, pp. 4721–4732. ACM, New York (2010). https://doi.org/10.1145/1753846.1754221

30. Chapman, C.N., Milham, R.P.: The personas' new clothes: methodological and practical arguments against a popular method. In: Proceedings of the Human Factors and Ergonomics Society Annual Meeting, pp. 634–636 (2006). https://doi.org/10.1177/154193120605000503

31. Jung, S., Salminen, J., An, J., Kwak, H., Jansen, B.J.: Automatically conceptualizing social media analytics data via personas. In: Presented at the 12th International AAAI Conference on Web and Social Media (ICWSM 2018), San Francisco, California, USA, 25 June 2018 (2018)

32. Jung, S., Salminen, J., Kwak, H., An, J., Jansen, B.J.: Automatic Persona Generation (APG): a rationale and demonstration. In: Proceedings of the 2018 Conference on Human Information Interaction & Retrieval, New Brunswick, NJ, USA, pp. 321–324. ACM (2018). https://doi.org/10.1145/3176349.3176893

33. Jung, S., Salminen, J., Jansen, B.J.: Personas changing over time: analyzing variations of data-driven personas during a two-year period. In: Extended Abstracts of the 2019 CHI Conference on Human Factors in Computing Systems, Glasgow, UK, pp. LBW2714:1–LBW2714:6. ACM (2019). https://doi.org/10.1145/3290607.3312955

34. Li, J., Galley, M., Brockett, C., Spithourakis, G., Gao, J., Dolan, B.: A persona-based neural conversation model. In: Proceedings of the 54th Annual Meeting of the Association for Computational Linguistics (Volume 1: Long Papers), pp. 994–1003. Association for Computational Linguistics, Berlin (2016). https://doi.org/10.18653/v1/P16-1094

35. Kim, H.M., Wiggins, J.: A factor analysis approach to persona development using survey data. In: Proceedings of the 2016 Library Assessment Conference, p. 11 (2016)

36. Mijač, T., Jadrić, M., Ćukušić, M.: The potential and issues in data-driven development of web personas. In: 2018 41st International Convention on Information and Communication Technology, Electronics and Microelectronics (MIPRO), pp. 1237–1242 (2018). https://doi.org/10.23919/MIPRO.2018.8400224

37. Salminen, J., Guan, K., Jung, S.-G., Chowdhury, S.A., Jansen, B.J.: A literature review of quantitative persona creation. In: Proceedings of the ACM Conference of Human Factors in Computing Systems (CHI 2020), Honolulu, Hawaii, USA. ACM (2020)

38. Salminen, J., Jansen, B.J., An, J., Kwak, H., Jung, S.: Automatic persona generation for online content creators: conceptual rationale and a research agenda. In: Nielsen, L. (ed.) Personas - User Focused Design. HIS, pp. 135–160. Springer, London (2019). https://doi.org/10.1007/978-1-4471-7427-1_8

39. Wöckl, B., Yildizoglu, U., Buber, I., Aparicio Diaz, B., Kruijff, E., Tscheligi, M.: Basic senior personas: a representative design tool covering the spectrum of european older adults. In: Proceedings of the 14th International ACM SIGACCESS Conference on Computers and Accessibility, pp. 25–32. ACM, New York (2012). https://doi.org/10.1145/2384916.2384922

40. Fiesler, C., Proferes, N.: "Participant" perceptions of twitter research ethics. Soc. Media +Soc. **4**, 1–14 (2018). https://doi.org/10.1177/2056305118763366

41. Turner, P., Turner, S.: Is stereotyping inevitable when designing with personas? Des. Stud. **32**, 30–44 (2011)

42. Spiegel, M.R., Constable, R.L.: Theory and Problems of Statistics. Schaum, New York (1961)

43. Ben-Gal, I.: Outlier detection. In: Maimon, O., Rokach, L. (eds.) Data Mining and Knowledge Discovery Handbook, pp. 131–146. Springer, Boston (2005). https://doi.org/10. 1007/0-387-25465-X_7

44. Salminen, J., Jung, S., Jansen, B.J.: Detecting demographic bias in automatically generated personas. In: Extended Abstracts of the 2019 CHI Conference on Human Factors in Computing Systems, pp. LBW0122:1–LBW0122:6. ACM, New York (2019). https://doi. org/10.1145/3290607.3313034

45. Goodman-Deane, J., Waller, S., Demin, D., González-de-Heredia, A., Bradley, M., Clarkson, J.P.: Evaluating inclusivity using quantitative Personas. In: Presented at the Design Research Society Conference 2018, 28 June (2018). https://doi.org/10.21606/drs. 2018.400

46. Chorafas, D.N.: Control Systems Functions and Programming Approaches by Dimitris N Chorafas. Academic Press, New York (1966)

47. Hamming, R.W.: One man's view of computer science. J. ACM (JACM) 16, 3–12 (1969)

48. Ananny, M.: Toward an ethics of algorithms: convening, observation, probability, and timeliness. Sci. Technol. Hum. Values 41, 93–117 (2016)

49. Hoffmann, A.L., Jonas, A.: Recasting justice for internet and online industry research ethics. In: Zimmer, M., Kinder-Kuranda, K. (eds.) Internet Research Ethics for the Social Age: New Cases and Challenges. Peter Lang, Bern (2016)

50. Neyland, D.: Bearing accountable witness to the ethical algorithmic system. Sci. Technol. Hum. Values 41, 50–76 (2016)

51. Ullmann, S., Tomalin, M.: Quarantining online hate speech: technical and ethical perspectives. Ethics Inf. Technol. (2019). https://doi.org/10.1007/s10676-019-09516-z

52. Gillespie, T.: The relevance of algorithms. In: Gillespie, T., Boczkowski, P., Foot, K. (eds.) Media Technologies: Essays on Communication, Materiality, and Society, pp. 167–194. MIT Press, Cambridge (2014)

53. Joseph, M., Kearns, M., Morgenstern, J., Neel, S., Roth, A.: Rawlsian fairness for machine learning. arXiv preprint arXiv:1610.09559 (2016)

54. Zehlike, M., Bonchi, F., Castillo, C., Hajian, S., Megahed, M., Baeza-Yates, R.: FA*IR: a fair top-k ranking algorithm. In: Proceedings of the 2017 ACM on Conference on Information and Knowledge Management, pp. 1569–1578. ACM (2017)

55. Pruitt, J., Adlin, T.: The Persona Lifecycle: Keeping People in Mind Throughout Product Design. Morgan Kaufmann, Boston (2006)

56. Arsiwalla, X.D., Freire, I.T., Vouloutsi, V., Verschure, P.: Latent morality in algorithms and machines. In: Martinez-Hernandez, U., et al. (eds.) Living Machines 2019. LNCS (LNAI), vol. 11556, pp. 309–315. Springer, Cham (2019). https://doi.org/10.1007/978-3-030-24741-6_27

57. Rouse, W.B., Sheridan, T.B.: Computer-aided group decision making: theory and practice. Technol. Forecast. Soc. Change 7, 113–126 (1975)

58. Salminen, J., Nielsen, L., Jung, S., An, J., Kwak, H., Jansen, B.J.: "Is more better?": impact of multiple photos on perception of persona profiles. In: Proceedings of ACM CHI Conference on Human Factors in Computing Systems (CHI2018), Montréal, Canada (2018)

59. Matthews, T., Judge, T., Whittaker, S.: How do designers and user experience professionals actually perceive and use personas? In: Proceedings of the SIGCHI Conference on Human Factors in Computing Systems, Austin, Texas, USA, pp. 1219–1228. ACM (2012). https:// doi.org/10.1145/2207676.2208573

60. Rönkkö, K., Hellman, M., Kilander, B., Dittrich, Y.: Personas is not applicable: local remedies interpreted in a Wider context. In: Proceedings of the Eighth Conference on Participatory Design: Artful Integration: Interweaving Media, Materials and Practices, vol. 1, Toronto, Ontario, Canada, pp. 112–120. ACM (2004). https://doi.org/10.1145/1011870. 1011884

61. Salminen, J., Jung, S., An, J., Kwak, H., Nielsen, L., Jansen, B.J.: Confusion and information triggered by photos in persona profiles. Int. J. Hum. Comput. Stud. **129**, 1–14 (2019). https://doi.org/10.1016/j.ijhcs.2019.03.005
62. Ziewitz, M.: Governing algorithms: myth, mess, and methods. Sci. Technol. Hum. Values **41**, 3–16 (2016)
63. Lee, M.K., Jain, A., Cha, H., Ojha, S.: Procedural justice in algorithmic fairness: leveraging transparency and outcome control for fair algorithmic mediation. Psychology **3**, 14 (2019)
64. Zarsky, T.: The trouble with algorithmic decisions: an analytic road map to examine efficiency and fairness in automated and opaque decision making. Sci. Technol. Hum. Values **41**, 118–132 (2016)
65. Fisher, R.J.: Social desirability bias and the validity of indirect questioning. J. Consum. Res. **20**, 303–315 (1993)
66. Nielsen, L., Storgaard Hansen, K.: Personas is applicable: a study on the use of personas in Denmark. In: Proceedings of the SIGCHI Conference on Human Factors in Computing Systems, Toronto, Ontario, Canada, pp. 1665–1674. ACM (2014)
67. Green, B., Chen, Y.: The principles and limits of algorithm-in-the-loop decision making. Proc. ACM Hum. Comput. Interact. **3**, 50–74 (2019)
68. Salminen, J., Jung, S., An, J., Kwak, H., Jansen, B.J.: Findings of a user study of automatically generated personas. In: Extended Abstracts of the 2018 CHI Conference on Human Factors in Computing Systems, Montréal, Canada, pp. LBW097:1–LBW097:6. ACM (2018). https://doi.org/10.1145/3170427.3188470
69. Salminen, J., Sengun, S., Jung, S., Jansen, B.J.: Design issues in automatically generated persona profiles: a qualitative analysis from 38 think-aloud transcripts. In: Proceedings of the ACM SIGIR Conference on Human Information Interaction and Retrieval (CHIIR), Glasgow, UK, pp. 225–229. ACM (2019). https://doi.org/10.1145/3295750.3298942
70. Ananny, M., Crawford, K.: Seeing without knowing: limitations of the transparency ideal and its application to algorithmic accountability. New Media Soc. **20**, 973–989 (2018)
71. Kizilcec, R.F.: How much information?: effects of transparency on trust in an algorithmic interface. In: Proceedings of the 2016 CHI Conference on Human Factors in Computing Systems, San Jose, USA, pp. 2390–2395. ACM (2016)
72. Salminen, J., Santos, J.M., Jung, S., Eslami, M., Jansen, B.J.: Persona transparency: analyzing the impact of explanations on perceptions of data-driven personas. Int. J. Hum. Comput. Interact. **36**, 1–13 (2019). https://doi.org/10.1080/10447318.2019.1688946
73. Ajunwa, I., Friedler, S., Scheidegger, C.E., Venkatasubramanian, S.: Hiring by algorithm: predicting and preventing disparate impact. Available at SSRN (2016)
74. Chawla, N.V., Bowyer, K.W., Hall, L.O., Kegelmeyer, W.P.: SMOTE: synthetic minority over-sampling technique. J. Artif. Intell. Res. **16**, 321–357 (2002)
75. He, H., Bai, Y., Garcia, E.A., Li, S.: ADASYN: adaptive synthetic sampling approach for imbalanced learning. In: Presented at the 2018 IEEE International Joint Conference on Neural Networks, June 2008. https://doi.org/10.1109/IJCNN.2008.4633969
76. Salminen, J., Liu, Y.-H., Sengun, S., Santos, J.M., Jung, S., Jansen, B.J.: The Effect of numerical and textual information on visual engagement and perceptions of AI-Driven persona interfaces. In: Proceedings of the ACM Intelligent User Interfaces (IUI 2020), Cagliary, Italy. ACM (2020)

Enriching Social Media Personas with Personality Traits: A Deep Learning Approach Using the Big Five Classes

Joni Salminen[1,2(✉)], Rohan Gurunandan Rao[3], Soon-gyo Jung[1],
Shammur A. Chowdhury[1], and Bernard J. Jansen[1]

[1] Qatar Computing Research Institute,
Hamad Bin Khalifa University, Doha, Qatar
jsalminen@hbku.edu.qa
[2] University of Turku, Turku, Finland
[3] Indian Institute of Technology Madras, Tamil Nadu, India

Abstract. To predict personality traits of data-driven personas, we apply an automatic persona generation methodology to generate 15 personas from the social media data of an online news organization. After generating the personas, we aggregate each personas' YouTube comments and predict the "Big Five" personality traits of each persona from the comments pertaining to that persona. For this, we develop a deep learning classifier using three publicly available datasets. Results indicate an average performance increase of 4.84% in F1 scores relative to the baseline. We then analyze how the personas differ by their detected personality traits and discuss how personality traits could be implemented in data-driven persona profiles, as either scores or narratives.

Keywords: Personas · Design · Personality detection · Neutral networks

1 Introduction

A persona is defined as a fictitious person that describes user or customer segments of a software system, product, or service [1, 2]. Personas are widely used in many professional fields, including e.g. software development and design [3], marketing and advertising [4], health informatics [5], and so on. A persona simplifies user-centric numbers into an easy-to-understand representation - another human being [6]. Through this property, personas aim to facilitate the communication about users within an organization, so that user-centric decisions (e.g., product development, design, marketing) can be made keeping the end user in mind [7].

Persona design, in turn, deals with the design of persona profiles that support persona users' tasks and goals, while not distracting them [8]. To be useful, personas should contain all information decision makers need to better understand the group of users the persona portrays. This is known as the *rounded persona principle* [9]. A typical persona profile includes a name, a picture, and a description detailing attitudes, needs, wants, and behaviors of the persona [10]. Rounded persona profiles can also include personality traits [11, 12], such as the "Big Five" (BF) traits: *extroversion*

© Springer Nature Switzerland AG 2020
H. Degen and L. Reinerman-Jones (Eds.): HCII 2020, LNCS 12217, pp. 101–120, 2020.
https://doi.org/10.1007/978-3-030-50334-5_7

(EXT), *agreeableness (AGR)*, *openness (OPE)*, *conscientiousness (CON)*, and *neu-roticism (NEU)* [13]. Together, these traits are seen to reflect one's personality, defined as a fairly stable state of mind of an individual, where "state of mind" refers to how the individual approaches the world and interacts with others [14].

Personality traits can help predict user and customer behavior under different circumstances and use cases, including shopping behavior [15], problem solving patterns [16], task performance [17], voting behavior [18], and so on. Knowing the personality traits can also aid in targeting the users with tailored advertising messages [19]. These linkages between personality traits and behavior imply that including personality traits in persona profiles can be useful, as personas are used for *predicting* user behavior in different situations [1]. Therefore, there are multiple potential benefits to the inclusion of personality traits to personas as completing information.

A related development in computer science is the progress made in automatic personality detection (APD). Overall, the factors that positively contribute to on-going research efforts on APD are (1) the availability of textual data (i.e., social media posts such as tweets, Facebook updates, and YouTube (YT) comments), (2) the personal nature of that data, and (3) the increase of popularity in "sharing" one's thoughts and feelings via social media platforms. Interestingly, these drivers strongly overlap with the drivers of "quantified" or data-driven personas (DDPs) [20], defined as personas that represent social media and online analytics user data in the form of personas [21]. Thus, there is an opportunity to *combine APD and DDPs for more efficient, more complete, and more useful personas that enhance decision makers (e.g., software developers, designers, marketers, etc.) understanding about their users and customers.*

However, in our knowledge, no previous work on DDPs has incorporated personality traits into the personas. Rather, the DDP layouts have focused on containing other information, such as text description, topics of interest, and audience size (see Fig. 1). This is somewhat surprising since APD techniques have rapidly evolved [22–24]. In particular, using neural networks (NNs) to analyze social media texts has yielded positive results for ADP [24, 25]. As put by Carducci et al. [26], social media platforms provide a rich source of user-generated texts that reflect "many aspects of real life, including personality" (p. 127). The fact that users freely share their opinions, moods, and feelings makes these users prime candidates for personality detection, as the personal information they share can be analyzed for personality cues [24].

By definition, DDPs are created using both numerical online analytics data that describes user behavior in an aggregated fashion [27] *and* user-generated social media posts that describe the persona's attitudes [28]. Therefore, APD from a persona's social media content appears as a prominent research gap. In particular, three aspects support this: (1) personality information can support the understanding and use of personas to predict user behavior (i.e., there is both information needs of persona users, (2) textual social media data that can be used for *both* persona creation and APD is widely available, and (c) technology is granting opportunities for merging efficient creation of DDPs with an increasing accuracy of APD from user-generated social media texts.

Therefore, in this research, we combine APD and DDPs to design personas with personality traits that could be automatically generated using numerical and textual social media data. Our research questions are as follows:

Fig. 1. An example persona, containing text description, demographics, topical interests, quotes, viewed content, and representative audience size - but no personality traits

- How can APD be applied to infer the BF personality traits of DDPs from social media posts of the personas?
- How can the personality traits implemented in the DDP design?

To develop a NN classifier, we collect three publicly available datasets with ground truth on personality traits (see Sect. 3). We then develop the classifier based on inspiration from state-of-the-art models, including the code and data from Majumder et al. [24] that predicts the BF personality traits [13].

To predict personas' personality, we generate 15 personas by collecting social media data of an international online news and media company and applying an automatic DDP creation methodology [21]. After generating these 15 personas, we collect their social media posts (i.e., aggregate each personas' YT comments) and predict the BF personality traits of each persona from the social media posts pertaining to that persona. We then interpret the results by analyzing how the personas differ by their detected personality traits.

We choose the BF framework as it is the most commonly chosen framework in the APD literature [24], making it possible to compare our results against a baseline model. However, our main contribution is not the development of the APD classifier – rather, we apply established, previously working methods in the domain of APD towards the goal of enriching DDPs with information on the persona's personality traits. Our contribution, thus, is demonstrating how DDP and APD methods can be combined for richer persona profiles that more realistically reflect the user population.

The remainder of this work is organized as follows. Section 2 summarizes the state-of-the-art research in APD. Section 3 explains our methodology, i.e., how we incorporate the available techniques in our modeling approach, as well as how we collect the data and evaluate the results. Section 4 presents the results in comparison to a baseline model and predicts the personality traits of 15 personas generated automatically from social media data. We conclude by discussing the limitations of the approach, implications for research and practice, and future research avenues.

2 Related Literature

2.1 Automatic Personality Detection

The roots of APD from social media texts can be found in two main streams of research: (1) *affective computing and sentiment analysis* [29] and (2) *linguistic styles and psycholinguistic databases* [30, 31]. The joint hypothesis of these streams is that language (e.g., spoken, written) or words reveal one's inner thoughts and, therefore, a person's personality [32]. As stated by Xue et al. [33], the textual information widely shared on social network is "the most direct and reliable way for people to translate their internal thoughts and emotions into a form that others can understand." (p. 4239). Thus, social media texts can reveal aspects of one's personality.

For this, research use many analytical predictors, including linguistic cues, syntactic features, and manually and automatically built semantic lexicons [34–36]. In other words, the intuition is that *linguistic markers* reveal one's personality, so that the use of questionnaires such as the BF Inventory [37] is not needed. Rather, the personality is inferred from unstructured text "in the wild".

For APD, anonymity of social media has two main implications. First, it can mitigate the social desirability bias of expressing one's true feelings. In other words, anonymity can decrease filters imposed by the need for pleasing others or the general opinion [38], possibly revealing truthful information about a person's thinking tendencies. Second, when user IDs are not available, identifying the same users brings about challenges in constructing adequate corpora for personality prediction [39]. Thus, anonymity can both hamper and facilitate APD from text.

Several methods and datasets have been applied for APD. These include, at least, Logistic Regression (LR) [40], K-Nearest Neighbors (KNN) [41], Naïve Bayes (NB) [42], Support Vector Machines (SVM) [43], and, more recently, deep neural networks [33] with architectures such as Convolutional Neural Networks (CNN) [44] and Recurrent Neural Networks (RNN) [45], including Long Short-Term Memory (LSTM), a subtype of RNN [46]. Thus, algorithms and technical framing of APD vary greatly – often, different methods are applied in combination, such as combining CNN and RNN [44]. The features used include, e.g., n-grams, Bag of Words (BOW), Linguistic Inquiry and Word Count (LIWC), and word embeddings [47]. These aim to represent different linguistic aspects that would correlate with the target personality trait.

The prominent datasets are, e.g., the myPersonality (MPD) [48] that contains Facebook status updates, the YT personality dataset [49], and the Essays dataset that contains a stream-of-consciousness essays [30]. These datasets are described in Sect. 3.3. Overall, the state-of-the-art performance is achieved using deep NN architectures trained on multiple datasets and feature representations [24, 33, 44, 46]. This is also the approach we take in this research, as explained in Sect. 3.

2.2   Personality Traits in Personas

Personality traits can potentially enhance understanding of *who* the persona is [54], enhancing the empathetic benefits attributed to the persona technique in general [55]. The main motive for inclusion of personality traits is the creation of "holistic persona description" [12] (see also the "rounded persona" concept [9]) that includes multiple types of information: (1) personal details such as demographics and interests, (2) personality traits as captured by psychological models ("psychographics"), (3) intelligence and learning styles, (4) knowledge that describes the persona's expertise and experience in a specific domain, and (5) cognitive processes that describe how the persona processes information. Despite the assumption that personality traits can enhance user understanding, as with many persona benefits [56], the potential of personality traits for persona user experience has not been empirically verified.

In their review of 47 persona templates, Nielsen et al. [10] found that personality and psychographics had been incorporated in persona profiles using manual means, often without using professional psychologists [11, 12, 50–52]. However, automatic inference of personality traits for personas has not previously been accomplished, to our knowledge. For this reason, Salminen et al. [53] consider APD as one of the open opportunities in DDP creation.

In the following section, we explain how we combine APD with DDP creation.

3   Methodology

3.1   Data-Driven Persona Generation

We generated two DDPs using real data from an actual organization, a large international news and media company. For this, we used the YT viewer data of the said organization. The persona generation follows the methodology developed by An et al. [21, 27] and Jung et al. [57], in which data is collected and processed automatically from online analytics platforms.

For this research, we collected 206 K video views from 13 K videos published between January 1, 2016 and September 30, 2018 on the YT channel of Al Jazeera Media Network (AJ+[1]). For the data collection, we used the YT Analytics Application Programming Interface (API[2]) with the channel owner's permission. The use of an API enables automatic updating of the personas at set intervals [58, 59] The dataset includes all the channel's view counts divided by demographic groups (age group × gender × country), of which there are 1631 with at least one view during the data collection period.

---

[1]   https://www.youtube.com/channel/UCV3Nm3T-XAgVhKH9jT0ViRg.

[2]   https://developers.google.com/youtube/analytics/.

The DDP creation methodology executes the following steps [60]:

- **Step 1:** Create an interaction matrix with YT videos as columns, demographic user groups as rows, and view count of each group for each video as elements of the matrix
- **Step 2:** Apply non-negative matrix factorization (NMF) [61] to the interaction matrix to infer p latent video viewing behaviors, where p is the number of personas
- **Step 3:** Choose the representative demographic attributes for each behavior by using weights from the NMF computation
- **Step 4:** Create the personas by enriching the representative demographic groups for each p personas with information, e.g., name, picture, topics of interest, etc.

After obtaining a grouped interaction matrix, we apply NMF for identifying latent video viewing patterns. NMF is particularly intended for reducing the dimensionality of large datasets by discerning latent factors [61]. Figure 2 illustrates the matrix decomposition of NMF; the resulting patterns inferred from the matrix discriminate the user groups based on the variation of their content viewing patterns.

An example of automatically generated persona is provided in Fig. 1. For further technical reference, we refer the reader to the articles by An et al. [21, 27], as these report the technical details and validation of the method. This research focuses on adding personality traits to these automatically generated DDPs. We utilize the persona's quotes to predict the personality traits. The quotes are comments retrieved from the most viewed content of the persona.

3.2 Retrieving Social Media Comments for Each Persona

The process for retrieving the social media comments for the personas is as follows:

- **Step 1:** Generate 15 personas using the dataset described previously
- **Step 2:** Take the top 10 YT videos that each persona has viewed the most
- **Step 3:** Take all comments from these videos and save them in a data structure

Moreover, we ensure that these videos do not overlap, i.e., one persona's top videos do not contain any videos from another persona's top videos. The purpose of this is to ensure that the social media comments between the personas vary adequately to detect any linguistic patterns. The comments of each persona are then used to generate a score for each BF personality trait using the NN described in the following.

3.3 Data Collection for Model Development

We combine three publicly available[3] datasets: essays dataset [30], YouTube personality dataset [49], and MPD [48]. These datasets were selected for two reasons. First, they are commonly used in APD research (see, e.g., [22, 24, 34]. Second, they all use

---

[3] The MPD dataset was previously available on the Web (http://mypersonality.org), but at the time of writing it has been withdrawn. The YT dataset is available upon request (https://www.idiap.ch/dataset/youtube-personality), and the essays dataset can be readily downloaded (https://github.com/SenticNet/personality-detection/blob/master/essays.csv).

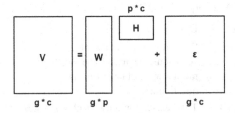

Fig. 2. Matrix decomposition carried out using NMF [21]. Matrix V is decomposed into W and H. g denotes demographic groups in the dataset, c denotes content (e.g., videos), and p is the number of latent interaction patterns that are used to create the personas. For this research, we set $p = 15$ to generate enough personas for comparison of their personality traits.

the same predicted classes, i.e., the BF personality traits. Because there are several personality trait taxonomies, it is important for model development that the textual data is associated with the same classes across the datasets used for training the model. The BF framework originates from the 1960s [62] and is continuously garnering research interest from psychologists and researchers in other fields to date [63–65].

In these datasets (see Table 1 for description), the BF traits form the five predicted classes. The definitions of the classes are, according to Agarwal [47] (p. 2):

- **OPE:** Artistic, curious, imaginative, curious, intelligent, and imaginative. Open individuals tend to be artistic and have sophisticated taste. They appreciate diverse views, ideas, and experiences.
- **CON:** Efficient, organized, responsible, organized, and persevering. Conscientious individuals tend to be reliable and focused on achieving, working hard, and planning for the future.
- **EXT:** Energetic, active, assertive, outgoing, amicable, assertive. These individuals are friendly and energetic, drawing inspiration from social situations.
- **AGR:** Compassionate, cooperative, cooperative, helpful, nurturing. Individuals that score high in agreeableness are peacekeepers. They are generally optimistic and trusting of others.
- **NEU:** Anxious, tense, self-pitying, anxious, insecure, sensitive. Neurotics are moody, tense, and easily tipped into experiencing negative emotions.

3.4   Strategy for Model Development

Each BF trait is modeled separately as a multiple binary classification task. We follow the approach taken by Majumder et al. [24] because of three reasons: (a) their method for personality detection is well documented in the related research article [24], (b) their code is publicly available in a GitHub repository[4] along with the training data, and (c) their model achieves good performance relative to other models in the field.

Thus, the GitHub code of Majumder et al. [24] served as a starting point for developing the classifier. Their results also form the baseline for benchmark

---

[4] https://github.com/senticnet/personality-detection.

Table 1. Description of the datasets used for model development

Name	Source	Description	Size (words)
Essays	Students	Students wrote stream-of-consciousness texts. The Big Five ratings were obtained using a questionnaire	2,467 essays (1,609,042)
myPersonality	Facebook	The dataset contains Facebook status posts as raw text, author information, and gold standard labels. The Big Five ratings were obtained using a questionnaire [47]	9,880 status updates (143,639)
YouTube personality	YouTube	The Big Five ratings were obtained from crowd raters predicting personality traits of vloggers "based on what they say in their YouTube videos." [49] (p. 1)	404 vlog transcripts (240,580)
			Total = 1,993,261 words

comparison. Due to practical reasons, our approach differs from Majumder et al. [24] in two main aspects. First, we were not able to replicate the process for obtaining the Mairesse features [36] used by Majumder et al. [24]. These features represent the linguistic cues of personality in text. Thus, we had to model the data without the Mairesse features, representing the text using word embeddings instead (see Sect. 3.5).

Second, we use two modeling choices from Sun et al. [66]: (a) an LSTM architecture and (b) multiple datasets. The reason of the former is that LSTM shows good performance in APD [66], while the intuition of the latter is that more data enables the model to train on more linguistic cues [22]. In addition, we use a CNN component, as combined processing steps in NN architectures have shown to increase performance [47]. The model architecture is described in Sect. 3.7.

3.5   Data Cleaning and Preprocessing

We followed the text cleaning and processing steps of Majumder et al. [24]. This included sentence splitting as well as data cleaning and unification, such as reduction to lower case. We then tokenized all the text. The words were then converted to fixed length vectors as in Majumder et al. [24], using the GoogleNews Word2Vec model, and using a fixed vector length of 300 dimensions. All sequences were set to a fixed maximum length, which was varied between 2,000 and 12,000 to identify the optimal length to model the data. Sequences longer than the maximum length were truncated, while those shorter than the maximum length were padded. We did not use any hand-picked features like word-count or Mairesse features; instead, we passed the entire data to the NN for feature learning.

3.6   Data Partitioning and Model Training

Having performed the preprocessing, we used 10-fold cross validation [67] for checking the accuracy of our model. We split the data during the training phase into ten folds (i.e., parts). Each time, a fold was isolated, and a model was trained on the remaining nine folds. Then, the validation accuracy was tested on the 10th fold. This was repeated ten times, keeping different folds aside for validation. We also trained different models for comparison of their predictive performance – this included comparing individually trained models with a combined model (i.e., five models that predict different traits individually vs. one that predicts all five traits simultaneously).

3.7   Neural Network Architecture

We developed a NN with two major sub-architectures: a single dimensional CNN since there is a spatial structure in the input text, and an LSTM network since there is also a temporal correlation between the words in the input text.

After training the model, the NN can identify the relationship between different words in the text and predict the personality trait to which it belongs. This is done by taking an arbitrary length input text, removing fillers, stop words, and foreign characters, tokenizing it, truncating or padding it to the maximum sequence length, then converting it into a matrix of shape (word embedding length = 300) by using the Word2Vec model [68]. The network transforms this matrix by passing it through a Convolution (32 filters of size 3 × 3) and Max Pooling (2 × 2 filters) layers to identify structural features in the text, then through a Spatial Dropout with a rate of 0.2. Then, the matrix is passed through a Bi-directional LSTM layer with 64 units to identify temporal features, and finally through the Dropout (rate of 0.5), Batch Normalization and Dense layers to predict the personalities. A Dense layer is where all neurons in the input layer are connected to all neurons in the output layer with the BF traits.

Max Pooling, Spatial Dropout, Dropout and Batch Normalization layers are added to prevent overfitting and control the number of parameters in the network. Note that a bidirectional LSTM can incorporate hidden states for both past and future information, and in cases where all the text is pre-specified, like for us, it enables better predictive performance. In turn, Batch Normalization transforms and normalizes the output of the network layer to stabilize and accelerate the training process.

3.8   Model Optimization

To optimize the model, we use binary cross-entropy loss, since the output for each personality trait is either 0 or 1. Cross-entropy loss measures the performance of a model that outputs probabilities between 0 and 1. The loss increases when the prediction diverges from the actual label, so the goal of the network is to learn weights that minimize the loss. We use the Adam optimizer [69] based on the stochastic gradient descent algorithm with adaptive learning rate. Adam uses two parameters in conjunction with the first and second moments of the gradient to increase speed of learning.

Similar to Majumder et al. [24], we use a learning rate of 0.001, clipping norm of 0.25 (this is the maximum absolute gradient value to prevent large spikes or updates of the function), and two beta parameters: $Beta_1$ of 0.70 (a parameter that controls the first moment of the gradient in the Adam optimizer) and $Beta_2$ of 0.99 (a parameter that controls the second moment of the gradient in the Adam optimizer).

These parameters lead the model to convergence with early stopping, meaning that the validation accuracy stopped improving. Epoch means a full model update run over the training data [70]. We took the results at the 10th epoch, since they did not improve from the 10th to the 15th epoch. Cross-validation was done with 80-10-10 split (train, development, test) and early stopping was done using the development dataset.

4 Results

4.1 Technical Performance

We use the F1 macro score for evaluating our model, as this metric considers both the precision (i.e., percentage of correct positive results) and recall (i.e., percentage of samples that are correctly identified as positive). The F1 score is the harmonic mean of precision and recall and reaches the best value of 1 with perfect precision and recall, and the worst at 0. This score was also available for the baseline are comparing with, hence allowing us to use it to compare fairly.

Results (see Table 2) show that our model trained combining the three datasets (i.e., Model 2) provides better scores than the baseline model for three personality traits: EXT (an increase of 26.1% in F1 score), OPE (18.1% increase), and AGR (24.1% increase). In contrast, our model loses to the baseline model in prediction of two traits: CON (a slight decrease of −1.8%) and NEU (a large decrease of −42.3%). The results indicate that our classifier achieves a good performance relative to the baseline (an increase of 4.84% in F1 scores on average). Yet, the mixed performance indicates the difficulty of correctly predicting all personality traits. The fact that Model 2 (trained with data from more sources) outperforms Model 1 indicates that using more sources increases the signal for the NN and, therefore, improves the results.

We also predicted each dataset separately to examine how well Model 2 performs by data source (see Table 3). In this, we ensure no data leakage takes place (i.e., separating training and prediction instances) by doing cross validation splits and training a model on the rest, then predicting the isolated fold.

The results in Table 3 show that EXT and OPE receive the highest scores on the YouTube dataset, suggesting that the network find the clearest signal for these traits in that social network. In turn, CON, AGR, and NEU are most easily detected in the essays dataset. Based on the results, personality traits are the hardest to infer from the Facebook status updates. Overall, the results support the application of the model on our DDPs, as their comments originate from YT and the model performs relatively best for YT.

Table 2. F1 scores for each BF trait using the essays dataset. Highest values bolded.

	EXT	OPE	CON	AGR	NEU
Baseline [9]	0.525	0.553	**0.553**	0.486	**0.575**
Model 1[*]	0.541	0.529	0.538	0.553	0.484
Model 2[**]	**0.662**	**0.653**	0.543	**0.603**	0.332

[*]trained   with   essays,   [**]trained   with essays + MPD + YouTube

Table 3. The F1 scores of Model 2 (trained with essays + MPD + YouTube data) on each dataset. Cross-validation with 10 folds and 80-10-10 split was applied. Highest values bolded.

	EXT	OPE	CON	AGR	NEU
Essays	0.662	0.653	**0.543**	**0.603**	0.332
MPD	0.681	0.576	0.406	0.559	0.357
YT	**0.719**	**0.686**	0.485	0.444	**0.403**

4.2   Personality Traits of Personas

As the comments from the same user are scarce (the dataset has typically only one comment per User ID), we predict the personas' personality traits from the aggregated comments of the users corresponding to a given persona. Thus, we group the collected comments (see Sect. 3.2) by persona and predict the personality traits of each grouped collection using Model 2 (e.g., "Persona 15" contains the combined comment texts of Persona 15). This yields a score for each personality trait of each persona, which can be used for enriching persona profiles with personality traits (see Fig. 3).

The results (Fig. 4) show that five personas (out of 15) score lower than average on EXT (P1-2, P4, P7-8), while six score higher (P5, P6, P12-15). Scoring lower on both EXT and NEU seems to be associated, as four personas out of the five that score low on EXT also score lower than average on NEU (P1-2, P4, P8). The personas that score higher than average for EXT and NEU tend to score lower than average on OPE and CON (e.g., P1-2). However, there are deviations from this, such as P7 that scores close to average on every trait. Four personas (P6, P9, P10, and P12) tend to score low on AGR. The observed variation indicates that the APD method applied produces variation in the detected personality traits among the personas, implying that the personas do differ by personality, at least to some degree. Future analyses are needed to understand comprehensively where these differences originate from (e.g., analyzing why the APD method gives these scores on the dataset).

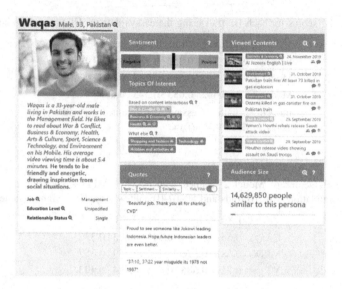

Fig. 3. An example of incorporating textual description of personality in data-driven personas. The bolded text "**He tends to be friendly and energetic, drawing inspiration from social situations.**" corresponds to the general description of high extroversion [47], reflected in the personas' comments based on automatic personality detection. The generic personality trait descriptions can be automatically inserted based on the personality scores obtained.

	cEXT	cNEU	cAGR	cCON	cOPN
Persona 1	-0.00594	-0.00513	0.001395	0.003455	0.004213
Persona 2	-0.00557	-0.00454	0.005118	0.003355	0.004117
Persona 3	0.000295	-0.00182	0.004562	0.001296	0.002204
Persona 4	-0.005	-0.00414	0.00739	0.00385	0.004828
Persona 5	0.004373	-0.00079	-0.00324	-0.00503	-0.00542
Persona 6	0.003649	-0.00219	-0.00448	0.00281	0.000664
Persona 7	-0.00254	0.003986	0.002426	-0.00141	-0.00211
Persona 8	-0.00321	-0.00439	-0.00188	0.000948	0.001926
Persona 9	0.000365	-0.00188	-0.00434	-0.0055	0.003846
Persona 10	0.000166	0.005008	-0.00406	0.000318	-0.00474
Persona 11	-0.00054	0.000358	0.00388	0.004834	0.001945
Persona 12	0.004527	0.000436	-0.00418	-0.00264	-0.00241
Persona 13	0.002657	0.008305	-0.00321	-0.00731	-0.00565
Persona 14	0.003993	0.002091	0.00112	0.000434	-0.00286
Persona 15	0.002775	0.004697	-0.00049	0.000593	-0.00055

Fig. 4. Personality scores (probability of a persona's aggregated comments reflecting a BF trait) of personas based on their aggregated social media comments. The cells show absolute differences from the mean score of the personality trait. Color coding indicates the size of the difference, with positive values in green and negative in red. (Color figure online)

5 Discussion

5.1 Contribution to Persona Research

Theoretically, the variability in the personality traits among the personas provides an interesting outlook of the "collective personality" of groups interested in the same online content. Perhaps this collective personality could be termed as *persona personality*, i.e., a grouped understanding of personality traits of a user segment. Traditionally, personality traits have been associated with *individuals*, not groups, in social psychology. Thus, the fact that persona can thus portray collective patterns of personality among different user segments is an interesting notion in the cross-section of HCI and social psychology. This notion could be empirically investigated by, e.g., analyzing the relationship between the persona's topical interests and personality. Perhaps certain groups are more drawn to some online content, and the topic of the content thus becomes a proxy measure for users' personality.

Conceptually, there are two challenges pertaining to the amalgamation of APD and DDPs. The first challenge is that a persona, by definition, consists of *several* individuals that are portrayed as *one* persona. However, individuals *within* that group may vary by personality traits. Thus, is it possible to construct "average" personality traits for a persona? How meaningful would this construction be?

Our exploratory results (Fig. 4) indicate that the APD methods can produce variability among the groups. For this method to work, it is required that the social media posts made by the users reveal observable trends toward a certain personality trait. It is also possible that, with other datasets, "averaging" the posts of many individuals would cancel out the individual personality differences.

Regarding the meaningfulness, this can be addressed by presenting the personality traits in "plain language", as demonstrated in Fig. 3.

The second challenge is the meaningfulness of the persona personality prediction altogether. In other words, does the endeavor have practical value? Theoretically, psychological information in persona profiles can enhance the understanding of persona users about the persona, and provide utility in various design/development tasks, as well as advertising purposes [19]. Thus, in terms of the possibility of inferring the personality traits, the *opportunity* of predicting a persona's personality is highly prominent. Yet, it is unclear if the personality traits are indeed needed or wanted by end users of personas. Rather, empirical results of these ideas are missing. This implies that user studies on how persona users engage with DDPs enriched with personality traits are direly needed.

Personality traits are not only potentially impactful information for persona profiles (as argued above) but analyzing the persona's behavior by personality traits opens a multitude of related research avenues. For example, can we find substantial personality differences between the personas? How do the personality traits of a persona correlate with the persona's online content consumption patterns? Addressing these questions would shed light on how personas are engaging (i.e., watching and commenting) with different online content and if this behavior differs by the personas' personality traits – in other words, enhancing user understanding.

5.2 Design Implications

There are at least two approaches that could be implemented for showing the personality traits in DDPs: (1) quantitatively inspired and (2) qualitatively inspired. In the former, the personality traits are shown as "scores" (see inspiration from previous research in Table 4A), while in the latter they are written in a form of a narrative to describe the persona (Table 4B).

Table 4. Examples of implementing persona information

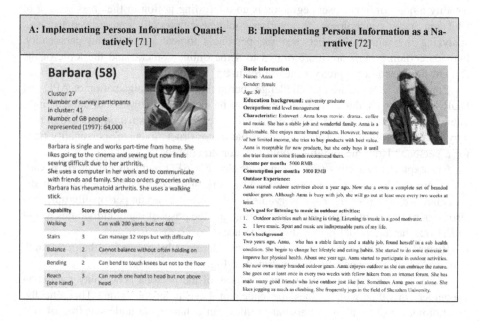

These ideas follow the division between different persona types, with the quantitative approach [71] resulting in a chart-like presentation of the details, with "scores" directly representing the quantitatively inferred information. In contrast, the qualitative approach [72] results in a persona layout enriched with more narrative-like, in-depth descriptions. The first option is supported by the fact that the scores of the personality traits are readily available following the application of the neural network.

The second option, in turn, is supported by the previous research that tends to infuse personality and psychographic information into a narrative format [11, 12, 50–52]. Writing the personality traits open might also be better for empathetic understanding of the persona – consider "Mary is an extrovert, enjoying discussions with new acquaintances" vs. "Extroversion$_{MARY}$ = 0.67". However, the disadvantage of the narratives is that their creation represents an additional step that seemingly requires manual effort. This would take us further from the overarching goal of fully automatic persona creation [73]. Yet, there are implementations of dynamic text templates [74] that could possibly be used for combining the narrative format and automation.

Previous research analyzing the role of text vs. numbers in persona profiles shows that this decision does not critically influence user perceptions of personas [75]. Nonetheless, more research is needed for testing which method of showing personality traits in personas, or combinations thereof, would provide the best option for optimal persona user experience. Moreover, the general question of "how does showing personality traits influence persona users' perceptions and/or actions?" requires an answer, to actually discover the impact of personality traits in personas. Thus, there are several open research questions that require empirical user studies.

5.3 Future Work on Improving Persona Personality Detection

The model we have used is quite simple relative to the state-of-the-art approaches in deep learning (see, e.g., [33, 44, 66]). We have assumed a relatively simple model because such a model is easily trainable without designing features and is computationally lightweight. Our results indicate that given sufficient data, a NN can be trained to predict personalities without hand-designed features being provided. At the same time, if hand-designed features are considered for a model like ours, it may be possible to increase accuracy or train a smaller model with less data and achieve similar results. Overall, while for the purpose of this research (i.e., demonstrating the APD for DDPs), the NN's performance is seen as adequate, results should be revisited as new algorithms and feature presentations for APD become available.

5.4 Ethical Considerations

APG preserves the privacy of individual users when generating the personas [28], because the information is collected as aggregated user statistics. For example, we can see information such as women aged 25–34, from New York, have *in aggregate* viewed Video X in total of Y times. This information, even though used for persona generation, does not violate the privacy of individual users, as it contains no personally identifiable information. The comments do contain User ID, but this ID tends to be in the form of a pseudonym, and the comments are further anonymized by removing the User IDs from the generated personas [21].

Regarding the ability of DDPs to represent minority groups (so-called "fringe personas" [71]), previous research has shown that the method applied here accurately replicates demographic characteristics of the data [76]. Thus, the choice of dataset dictates the characteristic of the output personas. A selection of an underrepresented subset of data, for example, would yield personas only from underprivileged subjects in the data. In this study, we generated personas using the whole dataset, as we were interested in average or typical users rather than minority subsets. However, future studies could use DDP techniques to generate "minority personas".

The use of personas enhanced with psychological traits comes with added responsibility. There may be a risk of manipulation. However, the story is not black-and-white, as there is a strong argument that people are not as easily gullible based on their psychologic profiles as is commonly presumed in the popular press [77]. As with most tools and applications of HCI, personas can be used "for good" and "for bad" – the final responsibility falls for the person wielding the tool.

6 Conclusion

Enriching personas with personality traits can enhance decision makers' understanding about users. Thus far, personality traits in personas have been based on manual data analysis. To provide a more efficient solution, we demonstrate how user-generated social media texts can be used to automatically assign Big Five personality traits to data-driven personas using a neural network classifier. The classifier trained on pre-existing datasets and achieved a good technical performance. In addition, the results show variation among personas in the detected personality traits.

Acknowledgments. We thank Dr. Lene Nielsen for discussions and inspiration on how to potentially display the automatically inferred personality traits in data-driven personas. We thank Al Jazeera Media Network for sharing the data that made this research possible.

References

1. Cooper, A.: The Inmates Are Running the Asylum: Why High Tech Products Drive Us Crazy and How to Restore the Sanity. Sams - Pearson Education, Indianapolis (1999)
2. Pruitt, J., Grudin, J.: Personas: practice and theory. In: Proceedings of the 2003 Conference on Designing for User Experiences, pp. 1–15. ACM, New York (2003). https://doi.org/10.1145/997078.997089
3. Nielsen, L.: Personas - User Focused Design. Springer, London (2013)
4. Salminen, J., Jansen, B.J., An, J., Kwak, H., Jung, S.: Are personas done? Evaluating their usefulness in the age of digital analytics. Persona Stud. **4**, 47–65 (2018). https://doi.org/10.21153/psj2018vol4no2art737
5. LeRouge, C., Ma, J., Sneha, S., Tolle, K.: User profiles and personas in the design and development of consumer health technologies. Int. J. Med. Inform. **82**, e251–e268 (2013). https://doi.org/10.1016/j.ijmedinf.2011.03.006
6. Pruitt, J., Adlin, T.: The Persona Lifecycle: Keeping People in Mind Throughout Product Design. Morgan Kaufmann, Boston (2006)
7. Nielsen, L., Storgaard Hansen, K.: Personas is applicable: a study on the use of personas in Denmark. In: Proceedings of the SIGCHI Conference on Human Factors in Computing Systems. pp. 1665–1674. ACM (2014)
8. Salminen, J., Jung, S., An, J., Kwak, H., Nielsen, L., Jansen, B.J.: Confusion and information triggered by photos in persona profiles. Int. J. Hum.-Comput. Stud. **129**, 1–14 (2019). https://doi.org/10.1016/j.ijhcs.2019.03.005
9. Nielsen, L.: Personas - User Focused Design. Springer, New York (2019). https://doi.org/10.1007/978-1-4471-4084-9
10. Nielsen, L., Hansen, K.S., Stage, J., Billestrup, J.: A template for design personas: analysis of 47 persona descriptions from Danish industries and organizations. Int. J. Sociotechnol. Knowl. Dev. **7**, 45–61 (2015). https://doi.org/10.4018/ijskd.2015010104

11. Anvari, F., Richards, D., Hitchens, M., Babar, M.A.: Effectiveness of persona with personality traits on conceptual design. In: Proceedings of the 37th International Conference on Software Engineering, vol. 2, Piscataway, NJ, USA, pp. 263–272. IEEE Press (2015)

12. Anvari, F., Richards, D., Hitchens, M., Babar, M.A., Tran, H.M.T., Busch, P.: An empirical investigation of the influence of persona with personality traits on conceptual design. J. Syst. Softw. **134**, 324–339 (2017). https://doi.org/10.1016/j.jss.2017.09.020

13. Gosling, S.D., Rentfrow, P.J., Swann, W.B.: A very brief measure of the Big-Five personality domains. J. Res. Pers. **37**, 504–528 (2003)

14. Ardelt, M.: Still stable after all these years? Personality stability theory revisited. Soc. Psychol. Q. 392–405 (2000)

15. Leong, L.-Y., Jaafar, N.I., Sulaiman, A.: Understanding impulse purchase in Facebook commerce: does Big Five matter? Internet Res. **27**, 786–818 (2017)

16. Hoffman, L.R.: Homogeneity of member personality and its effect on group problem-solving. J. Abnorm. Soc. Psychol. **58**, 27 (1959)

17. Barrick, M.R., Mount, M.K.: The Big Five personality dimensions and job performance: a meta-analysis. Personnel Psychol. **44**, 1–26 (1991)

18. Schoen, H., Schumann, S.: Personality traits, partisan attitudes, and voting behavior. Evidence from Germany. Polit. Psychol. **28**, 471–498 (2007)

19. Haugtvedt, C.P., Petty, R.E., Cacioppo, J.T.: Need for cognition and advertising: understanding the role of personality variables in consumer behavior. J. Consum. Psychol. **1**, 239–260 (1992)

20. Salminen, J., Guan, K., Jung, S.-G., Chowdhury, S.A., Jansen, B.J.: A literature review of quantitative persona creation. In: Proceedings of the ACM Conference of Human Factors in Computing Systems (CHI 2020), Honolulu, Hawaii, USA. ACM (2020)

21. An, J., Kwak, H., Salminen, J., Jung, S., Jansen, B.J.: Imaginary people representing real numbers: generating personas from online social media data. ACM Trans. Web (TWEB) **12**, 1–26 (2018)

22. Alam, F., Riccardi, G.: Predicting personality traits using multimodal information. In: Proceedings of the 2014 ACM Multi Media on Workshop on Computational Personality Recognition, pp. 15–18. ACM (2014)

23. Bleidorn, W., Hopwood, C.J.: Using machine learning to advance personality assessment and theory. Pers. Soc. Psychol. Rev. 1088868318772990 (2018)

24. Majumder, N., Poria, S., Gelbukh, A., Cambria, E.: Deep learning-based document modeling for personality detection from text. IEEE Intell. Syst. **32**, 74–79 (2017). https://doi.org/10.1109/MIS.2017.23

25. Kim, J.H., Kim, Y.: Instagram user characteristics and the color of their photos: colorfulness, color diversity, and color harmony. Inf. Process. Manag. **56**, 1494–1505 (2019). https://doi.org/10.1016/j.ipm.2018.10.018

26. Carducci, G., Rizzo, G., Monti, D., Palumbo, E., Morisio, M.: TwitPersonality: computing personality traits from tweets using word embeddings and supervised learning. Information **9**, 127 (2018)

27. An, J., Kwak, H., Jung, S., Salminen, J., Jansen, B.J.: Customer segmentation using online platforms: isolating behavioral and demographic segments for persona creation via aggregated user data. Soc. Netw. Anal. Min. **8** (2018). https://doi.org/10.1007/s13278-018-0531-0

28. Salminen, J., et al.: From 2,772 segments to five personas: summarizing a diverse online audience by generating culturally adapted personas. First Monday **23** (2018). https://doi.org/10.5210/fm.v23i6.8415

29. Cambria, E.: Affective computing and sentiment analysis. IEEE Intell. Syst. **31**, 102–107 (2016)

30. Pennebaker, J.W., King, L.A.: Linguistic styles: language use as an individual difference. J. Pers. Soc. Psychol. **77**, 1296 (1999)

31. Tausczik, Y.R., Pennebaker, J.W.: The psychological meaning of words: LIWC and computerized text analysis methods. J. Lang. Soc. Psychol. **29**, 24–54 (2010). https://doi.org/10.1177/0261927X09351676

32. Tskhay, K.O., Rule, N.O.: Perceptions of personality in text-based media and OSN: a meta-analysis. J. Res. Personal. **49**, 25–30 (2014)

33. Xue, D., et al.: Deep learning-based personality recognition from text posts of online social networks. Appl. Intell. **48**, 4232–4246 (2018). https://doi.org/10.1007/s10489-018-1212-4

34. Howlader, P., Pal, K.K., Cuzzocrea, A., Kumar, S.D.: Predicting Facebook-users' personality based on status and linguistic features via flexible regression analysis techniques. In: Proceedings of the 33rd Annual ACM Symposium on Applied Computing, pp. 339–345. ACM (2018)

35. Luyckx, K., Daelemans, W.: Using syntactic features to predict author personality from text. Proc. Digital Human. **2008**, 146–149 (2008)

36. Mairesse, F., Walker, M.A., Mehl, M.R., Moore, R.K.: Using linguistic cues for the automatic recognition of personality in conversation and text. J. Artif. Intell. Res. **30**, 457–500 (2007)

37. Rammstedt, B., John, O.P.: Measuring personality in one minute or less: a 10-item short version of the Big Five inventory in English and German. J. Res. Pers. **41**, 203–212 (2007)

38. Fang, J., Wen, C., Prybutok, V.: An assessment of equivalence between paper and social media surveys: the role of social desirability and satisficing. Comput. Hum. Behav. **30**, 335–343 (2014)

39. Kozinets, R.V., Dolbec, P.-Y., Earley, A.: Netnographic analysis: understanding culture through social media data. The SAGE Handbook of Qualitative Data Analysis, pp. 262–276 (2014)

40. Plank, B., Hovy, D.: Personality traits on Twitter—or—how to get 1,500 personality tests in a week. In: Proceedings of the 6th Workshop on Computational Approaches to Subjectivity, Sentiment and Social Media Analysis, pp. 92–98 (2015)

41. Pratama, B.Y., Sarno, R.: Personality classification based on Twitter text using Naive Bayes, KNN and SVM. In: 2015 International Conference on Data and Software Engineering (ICoDSE), pp. 170–174 (2015). https://doi.org/10.1109/ICODSE.2015.7436992

42. Sewwandi, D., Perera, K., Sandaruwan, S., Lakchani, O., Nugaliyadde, A., Thelijjagoda, S.: Linguistic features based personality recognition using social media data. In: 2017 6th National Conference on Technology and Management (NCTM), pp. 63–68. IEEE (2017)

43. Mitrou, L., Kandias, M., Stavrou, V., Gritzalis, D.: Social media profiling: a Panopticon or Omniopticon tool? In: Proceedings of the 6th Conference of the Surveillance Studies Network, Barcelona, Spain (2014)

44. Darliansyah, A., Naeem, M.A., Mirza, F., Pears, R.: SENTIPEDE: a smart system for sentiment-based personality detection from short texts. J. Univ. Comput. Sci. **25**, 1323–1352 (2019)

45. Tandera, T., Suhartono, D., Wongso, R., Prasetio, Y.L.: Personality prediction system from Facebook users. Procedia Comput. Sci. **116**, 604–611 (2017)

46. Yılmaz, T., Ergil, A., İlgen, B.: Deep learning-based document modeling for personality detection from Turkish texts. In: Arai, K., Bhatia, R., Kapoor, S. (eds.) FTC 2019. AISC, vol. 1069, pp. 729–736. Springer, Cham (2020). https://doi.org/10.1007/978-3-030-32520-6_53

47. Agarwal, B.: Personality detection from text: a review. Int. J. Comput. Syst. **1**, 1–4 (2014)

48. Stillwell, D.J., Kosinski, M.: myPersonality project: example of successful utilization of online social networks for large-scale social research. Presented at the International Conference on Mobile Systems (MobiSys) (2012)

49. Biel, J.-I., Gatica-Perez, D., Dines, J., Tsminiaki, V.: Hi YouTube! personality impressions and verbal content in social video. https://infoscience.epfl.ch/record/196978. https://doi.org/10.1145/2522848.2522877. Accessed 07 Jan 2020

50. Jones, M., Marsden, G.: Mobile Interaction Design. Wiley (2006)

51. Negru, S., Buraga, S.: A knowledge-based approach to the user-centered design process. In: Fred, A., Dietz, Jan L.G., Liu, K., Filipe, J. (eds.) IC3K 2012. CCIS, vol. 415, pp. 165–178. Springer, Heidelberg (2013). https://doi.org/10.1007/978-3-642-54105-6_11

52. Pichler, R.: A template for writing great personas (2012)

53. Salminen, J., Jansen, B.J., An, J., Kwak, H., Jung, S.-G.: Automatic persona generation for online content creators: conceptual rationale and a research agenda. Personas - User Focused Design. HIS, pp. 135–160. Springer, London (2019). https://doi.org/10.1007/978-1-4471-7427-1_8

54. Anvari, F., Tran, H.M.T.: Persona ontology for user centred design professionals. In: The ICIME 4th International Conference on Information Management and Evaluation, Ho Chi Minh City, Vietnam, pp. 35–44 (2013)

55. Câmara, M., Signoretti, A., Costa, C., Soares, S.C.: Business Affective Persona (BAP): a methodology to create personas to enhance customer relationship with trust and empathy. Revista Turismo Desenvolvimento, pp. 85–97 (2018)

56. Salminen, J., Jung, S., Chowdhury, S.A., Sengün, S., Jansen, B.J.: Personas and analytics: a comparative user study of efficiency and effectiveness for a user identification task. In: Proceedings of the ACM Conference of Human Factors in Computing Systems (CHI 2020), Honolulu, Hawaii, USA. ACM (2020). https://doi.org/10.1145/3313831.3376770

57. Jung, S., Salminen, J., Kwak, H., An, J., Jansen, B.J.: Automatic Persona Generation (APG): a rationale and demonstration. In: Proceedings of the 2018 Conference on Human Information Interaction & Retrieval, New Brunswick, NJ, USA, pp. 321–324. ACM (2018). https://doi.org/10.1145/3176349.3176893

58. Jung, S., Salminen, J., An, J., Kwak, H., Jansen, B.J.: Automatically conceptualizing social media analytics data via personas. Presented at the International AAAI Conference on Web and Social Media (ICWSM 2018), San Francisco, California, USA, 25 June 2018 (2018)

59. Jung, S., Salminen, J., Jansen, B.J.: Personas Changing over time: analyzing variations of data-driven personas during a two-year period. In: Extended Abstracts of the 2019 CHI Conference on Human Factors in Computing Systems, New York, NY, USA, pp. LBW2714:1–LBW2714:6. ACM (2019). https://doi.org/10.1145/3290607.3312955

60. Salminen, J., et al.: Generating cultural personas from social data: a perspective of middle eastern users. In: Proceedings of the Fourth International Symposium on Social Networks Analysis, Management and Security (SNAMS-2017), Prague, Czech Republic. IEEE (2017). https://doi.org/10.1109/FiCloudW.2017.97

61. Lee, D.D., Seung, S.H.: Learning the parts of objects by non-negative matrix factorization. Nature **401**, 788–791 (1999)

62. Norman, W.T.: Toward an adequate taxonomy of personality attributes: replicated factor structure in peer nomination personality ratings. J. Abnorm. Soc. Psychol. **66**, 574 (1963)

63. Ashton, M.C., Lee, K.: How well do Big Five measures capture HEXACO scale variance? J. Pers. Assess. **101**, 567–573 (2019)

64. Goldberg, L.R.: The development of markers for the Big-Five factor structure. Psychol. Assess. **4**, 26 (1992)

65. Yin, C., Zhang, X., Liu, L.: Reposting negative information on microblogs: do personality traits matter? Inf. Process. Manag. **57**, 102106 (2020). https://doi.org/10.1016/j.ipm.2019.102106
66. Sun, X., Liu, B., Cao, J., Luo, J., Shen, X.: Who am I? Personality detection based on deep learning for texts. In: 2018 IEEE International Conference on Communications (ICC), pp. 1–6 (2018). https://doi.org/10.1109/ICC.2018.8422105
67. Cawley, G.C., Talbot, N.L.: Efficient leave-one-out cross-validation of kernel fisher discriminant classifiers. Pattern Recogn. **36**, 2585–2592 (2003)
68. Le, Q., Mikolov, T.: Distributed representations of sentences and documents. In: Proceedings of the 31st International Conference on Machine Learning (ICML 2014), pp. 1188–1196 (2014)
69. Kingma, D.P., Ba, J.: Adam: a method for stochastic optimization. arXiv preprint arXiv:1412.6980 (2014)
70. LeCun, Y., Bengio, Y., Hinton, G.: Deep learning. Nature **521**, 436 (2015)
71. Goodman-Deane, J., Waller, S., Demin, D., González-de-Heredia, A., Bradley, M., Clarkson, J.P.: Evaluating inclusivity using quantitative personas. Presented at the Design Research Society Conference, 28 June 2018 (2018). https://doi.org/10.21606/drs.2018.400
72. Tu, N., et al.: Combine qualitative and quantitative methods to create persona. In: 2010 3rd International Conference on Information Management, Innovation Management and Industrial Engineering, pp. 597–603 (2010). https://doi.org/10.1109/ICIII.2010.463
73. Salminen, J., Jung, S.G., Jansen, B.J.: The future of data-driven personas: a marriage of online analytics numbers and human attributes. In: ICEIS 2019 - Proceedings of the 21st International Conference on Enterprise Information Systems, Heraklion, Greece, pp. 596–603. SciTePress (2019)
74. Jung, S., An, J., Kwak, H., Ahmad, M., Nielsen, L., Jansen, B.J.: Persona generation from aggregated social media data. In: Proceedings of the 2017 CHI Conference Extended Abstracts on Human Factors in Computing Systems, Denver, Colorado, USA, pp. 1748–1755. ACM (2017)
75. Salminen, J., Liu, Y.-H., Sengun, S., Santos, J.M., Jung, S.-G., Jansen, B.J.: The effect of numerical and textual information on visual engagement and perceptions of ai-driven persona interfaces. In: Proceedings of the ACM Intelligent User Interfaces (IUI 2020), Cagliary, Italy. ACM (2020)
76. Salminen, J., Jung, S.-G., Jansen, B.J.: Detecting demographic bias in automatically generated personas. In: Extended Abstracts of the 2019 CHI Conference on Human Factors in Computing Systems, pp. LBW0122:1–LBW0122:6. ACM, New York (2019). https://doi.org/10.1145/3290607.3313034
77. Phillips, M.J.: Ethics and Manipulation in Advertising: Answering a Flawed Indictment. Greenwood Publishing Group (1997)

Color for Characters - Effects of Visual Explanations of AI on Trust and Observability

Tim Schrills[(✉)] and Thomas Franke

Universität zu Lübeck, Ratzeburger Allee 160, 23562 Lübeck, Germany
{schrills, franke}@imis.uni-luebeck.de

Abstract. The present study investigates the effects of prototypical visualization approaches aimed at increasing the explainability of machine learning systems in regard to perceived trustworthiness and observability. As the amount of processes automated by artificial intelligence (AI) increases, so does the need to investigate users' perception. Previous research on explainable AI (XAI) tends to focus on technological optimization. The limited amount of empirical user research leaves key questions unanswered, such as which XAI designs actually improve perceived trustworthiness and observability. We assessed three different visual explanation approaches, consisting of either only a table with classification scores used for classification, or, additionally, one of two different backtraced visual explanations. In a within-subjects design with N = 83 we examined the effects on trust and observability in an online experiment. While observability benefitted from visual explanations, information-rich explanations also led to decreased trust. Explanations can support human-AI interaction, but differentiated effects on trust and observability have to be expected. The suitability of different explanatory approaches for individual AI applications should be further examined to ensure a high level of trust and observability in e.g. automated image processing.

Keywords: Human-AI interaction · Explainable AI · Machine learning · Trust in Automation · Human-automation interaction

1 Introduction

A central problem with many artificial intelligence (AI) systems is that they typically do not explain to users how they calculate their results [1], which makes it difficult for users to trace back, understand and, finally, rely on the outcome. Hence, a rising demand regarding AI research is to focus on technological approaches to achieve explainable AI (XAI) systems [2]. XAI addresses this challenge by adding information on how AI generates classifications, e.g. by analyzing how changing input affects result [3]. Technology connected to XAI is particularly important in the field of machine learning (ML), because of deep neural networks (DNNs), where sub-symbolic procedures are performed. Accordingly, the present study refers to the use of DNNs as one key approach in ML.

While users and application contexts can differ with regard to what information is needed to explain the behavior of ML systems, a key question from the perspective of

© Springer Nature Switzerland AG 2020
H. Degen and L. Reinerman-Jones (Eds.): HCII 2020, LNCS 12217, pp. 121–135, 2020.
https://doi.org/10.1007/978-3-030-50334-5_8

human factors is: what is a good explanation? Moreover, how can the perceived quality of XAI approaches be measured? Here it is important to note that many AI systems can be viewed as automated inferences that were previously carried out by humans [4]. Research on automation has long demonstrated perceived trustworthiness as a key variable [4–6]. A good AI explanation should thus aim to establish trust in the system used. In addition, a key requirement in the field of AI is that errors can be detected with as little effort as possible [7]. This is because ML systems can change their rules at runtime and without communicating this explicitly, thus resulting in a changing or, at very least, opaque rule systems, thereby limiting transparency for users. Good AI explanations should therefore also target increased perceived observability of AI systems [8].

Currently, XAI research mostly focuses on developing explanations in order to optimize the classification algorithm (i.e., technical optimization) and does not examine how users perceive different forms of explanations, e.g. [9]. So far, the usefulness of an explanation is measured by its mere impact on optimizing the algorithm. In the case of an AI classification, for example, this could be done by calculating the extent to which a particular data element (e.g., image pixel, word) affects the classification [10]. Due to their high complexity and sheer amount of information, technically optimized explanations may differ from those that are optimized to users' needs [11]. Nevertheless, it is clear that in many contexts the human user will be responsible for evaluating and accepting the proposed decision alternatives or actions of AI systems [12]. However, there is currently a lack of research regarding how good existing XAI approaches perform to increase traceability, and therefore trust and observability.

Explainability plays a role in many AI application contexts, e.g. image processing or natural language processing [13]. Consequently, the type of artifact an explanation can consist of is also strongly context-dependent, e.g., textual, graphical; see also [14]. However, given the early stage of development of empirical human factors XAI research in this area, it is expedient to reduce the complexity of relevant application contexts and choose experimental tasks with a low level of complexity and high experimental control. In order to investigate how explanation-approaches differ with regard to their usefulness for users (in terms of perceived trustworthiness and observability), we therefore focus on a very basic character recognition AI system, providing explanations by presenting visualizations based on the input.

The objective of the present research was to investigate the effect of visual explanations in ML systems on perceived trustworthiness and observability. To this end, we focused on two prototypical XAI visualization approaches and studied the user-related effects.

2   Background

Currently, many technical XAI approaches are developed with the aim of increasing the reliability and observability of ML systems – especially with regard to the detection of classification errors in trained systems, e.g. [15]. Often, those are local explanations, focusing to explain a specific outcome, not the general, cf. [16]. Most DNNs also display a value about how e.g. secure the classification is: a classification score.

Without additional explanations, however, it is impossible for users to understand exactly how these values were generated. To address this, within the area of visual classification analyses, pixel-wise backtracing is used to generate visual explanations based on the original input. One aim of an explanation should be to have the highest possible fidelity, i.e. address the connection between input and output in the best possible way [17]. Thus, for visual explanations, it makes sense to rely on methods that use backtracing and generating e.g. pixel-based heat maps. For example, a frequently examined approach in this area is Sensitvity Analysis (SA) [18]. Here, a systematic change of the input stimulus is used to identify which image components are particularly important for the classification. While this approach can reveal insights into the machines' information processing and possible errors, it is one-dimensional, as well as unipolar, and therefore not recommended to enhance understanding of the processes [19]. One further, recently proposed, approach is Layer-wise Relevance Propagation (LRP), in which the results are traced back inside the network in order to more precisely identify which pixels contribute for and which against the calculated classification [20]. This results in two-dimensional data, allowing better representations of networkactivity.

Still, those XAI visualization approaches highlight the relevance of the stimulus components for the classification of every pixel and thus produces results very rich in data. This data contains information about the relevance of every pixel for the chosen classification and about every other classification not chosen. Hence, these can be labelled omni-explanations. Since the presented information can be very complex, this could result in information overload for users [21], may hindering the development of trust, cf. [22].

A proposed procedure to increase both trustworthiness and observability, without inflating the information complexity, is based on how humans understand explanations in general. [14] argues that explanations could substantially benefit from relying on counterfactual thinking. This refers to a concept where hypothetical pasts are constructed and their effects assessed, in order to assess the present situation more easily [23]. Counterfactual explanations [24] or contrast cases 23 work in a structurally similar way as counterfactual thinking. Counterfactual explanation means that a reason (e.g. for a classification) does not only answer why the classification is correct, but also why other (almost equally) probable classifications are not [24]. For example, why the handwritten letter i was classified as i and not as the next-most probable option, j. The advantage of counterfactual explanations is that the amount of irrelevant information is reduced, because all information that also speaks for other, similar explanations is filtered out. At the same time, the extent to which the information shown describes the functioning of the system remains high. Therefore, counterfactual explanations could particularly meet users' demand for information and increase trustworthiness and observability of ML systems. Still, counterfactual explanations may result in incomplete explanations, since only one alternative is compared to the given classification. [25] found incompleteness to negatively affect how users evaluate an explanation. However, in this case, completeness refers to the proportion of available information on different process variables, and not to the complexity of the comparison with other possible outcomes. First studies using counterfactual explanations in XAI have shown to be effective at the technical level [26].

While first studies found positive results when presenting explanations in AI systems, e.g. [25, 27], there are no studies specifically comparing the effects of structurally different prototypical visual explanation-approaches and, to the best of the authors' knowledge, no quantitative user studies have yet been carried out to evaluate this way of generating explanations empirically.

2.1   Trust in AI Systems

In order for additional explanations in AI systems to have a positive effect on the user, they must address crucial interaction variables. As introduced above, the requirements for a successful user-AI interaction are closely related to the creation of trust (i.e., users' perceived trustworthiness of a system), see also [28].

So far, empirical research on trust in ML systems is limited. First research indicates that trust in AI systems can have a decisive effect on the behavior of users and can influence the extent to which e.g. provided classifications are perceived as useful [29]. Further, recent studies found that the level of trust to be significantly influenced by information related to the processing of the input data, e.g. [27]. As explicated above, it remains important to present only relevant influencing variables in order to make it as easy as possible for users to gain knowledge about the processing path and not e.g. conflict with previous mental models [30]. This specific perspective on trust in processing is – besides the purpose of the system and aspects related to the concrete performance – an important focus of the field of applied ML [31].

2.2   Observability of AI Systems

Since systematic biases can occur in the training of neural networks due to various factors, e.g. data set or sequence of training, cf. [32], a decisive success factor in the cooperation between humans and AIs is whether detected failures can be correctly attributed to the system [33]. However, for this to be possible, users must be able to understand the state of the system when the failure occurs. In this sense, observability refers to the system property of how correct conclusions about a system state can be drawn from the given output [34]. Here, the state of a ML system also includes the current, exact way of processing inputs to outputs, e.g. classification. Ensuring observability is a prerequisite for the design of highly functional systems in the context of human-centered development [35, 36]. [37] showed that in systems that do not guarantee complete reliability, additional information is important for the inspection of the data; an explanation, for example, would be additional information. Considering that a major part of ML systems is still characterized by limited reliability, it is particularly important to investigate observability as a target variable of XAI. Finally, systems that have higher observability may also obtain higher understandability of classifications results.

3   Present Research

The objective of the present research was to examine how different prototypical visualizations that aim to explain AI results affect the perceived trustworthiness and observability of an image classification system. Specifically, we compare the effects of the presentation of classification-scores with the additional presentation of two different backtraced visual explanations, whereby one is based on counterfactual reasoning. First, we assume that information about the classification process increases perceived trustworthiness and observability. This leads to the following two hypotheses:

H1.1) Visual explanations of classifications based on the input stimulus lead to higher trust in the system.

H1.2) Visual explanations of classifications based on the input stimulus lead to higher observability of the system.

Second, we assume that counterfactual explanations lead to higher trust and observability compared to omni-explanations by reducing the risk of information overload, which is why the following hypotheses can be formulated:

H2.1) Counterfactual explanations lead to higher trust than omni-explanations.

H2.2) Counterfactual explanations lead to higher observability than omni-explanations.

Finally, higher observability can also be expected to have an effect on the general comprehensibility of AI systems, hence:

H2.3) Counterfactual explanations are rated as more understandable than omni-explanations.

To examine these hypotheses, we choose basic character classification task. Here, no user-evaluated machine-learning systems, generating a backtraced visual explanation, exist. The low complexity of this task contributes to the fact that the resulting effects of the visualization can be clearly evaluated on basis of the input and are not significantly influenced by other variables, resulting in an ambiguous estimation. Thus, in tasks where the user has to make a greater effort to evaluate the results of the AI, the willingness to do so could adversely affect the experiment.

4   Method

4.1   Experimental Procedure

The invitation to participate in the study was distributed over e-mail and social networks. All participants were offered to enter a prize draw for a gift coupon. Psychology students of the local university were also offered course credit for taking part in the study. This research complied with the American Psychological Association Code of Ethics. Informed consent was obtained from each participant. The N = 83 users who completed the study had an average age of 25.4 years (SD = 8.1), 71% were female, 27% male and 1 person did not indicate gender. Participants generally had a rather low level of previous knowledge on AI systems (Mdn = 1.75, IQR = 1.25 – 2.75, possible score values 1-6 with a label of both poles as "true" and "false", score based on 4 items depicted in Table 1, Cronbach's alpha = .76) and an affinity for technology interaction score ($M = 3.43$, $SD = 1.17$) close to average value in the general population (3.5, see [38]).

Table 1. Translated texts of newly constructed items to assess previous AI knowledge; presented at the beginning of the study.

Please indicate to what extent you agree with the following statements	
01	I have already dealt with machine learning in the AI field
02	I understand how data is processed in neural networks.
03	I know technical approaches to increase the explainability in the field of machine learning
04	I have already dealt with the topic of AI

4.2 XAI Visualization Approaches

The study material was created using a public platform provided on the basis of [19]. The platform consists, among other things, of a neural network for number recognition, which was trained based on MNIST data records [39]. In addition, LRP [19] for the given input stimuli was calculated and provided. LRP Formula LRP Epsilon was selected and the beta value was set to 1.

In addition to the result of the classification, a classification-score overview was provided, in which a classification value is displayed for each potential digit. These represent the calculated probability for each possible category based on output-layer values of the DNN. Furthermore, heat map visualizations were provided for each input, as shown on the left in Fig. 1. The middle depiction – the LRP based visualization – is a manipulation of the actual input stimulus depicted on the left. In the present experiment, LRP-based images are used for the omni-explanation, since in LRP the value of each pixel for or against the classification is visualized. Stronger red hues indicate a higher relevance for the classification and stronger blue hues against the classification. If the respective pixel has no or very little influence, it is displayed in white.

The calculation of the stimuli for the counterfactual representation was based on the omni-visualization. The aim here is to mark the areas of the image that speak for the classification, but not for the next likely classification. To achieve this, in addition to calculating the omni-visualization of the assumed classification, the omni-visualization of the second most probable classification (e.g. not 3 but 0) was calculated. In the following step, the color values were modified so that: 1) one pixel, which had the same color in both images, was displayed as white and 2) a pixel, which in the selected classification was maximally red and – in the alternative classification – was maximally blue, received the darkest color. Smaller color distances result in a less intense color tone. Pixels within which the selected classification was blue (negative) and the alternative classification was red (positive) were also displayed in white. The results of the calculation of the counterfactual visualizations are generally colorless, i.e. in gray scales. A yellow overlay was used to increase similarity between omni- and

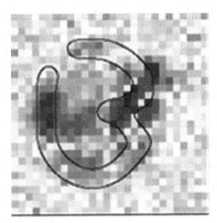

Fig. 1. Example of a Visualization for the omni-condition (left) and for the counter-condition (right).

counter-condition resulting in higher comparability with the colored images of the omni-condition while safeguarding clear discriminability of the two visualization approaches for the participants.

For this experiment, the stimuli set consisted of twenty different characters, which were manipulated for each condition, resulting in 60 different images. These were created before the experiment and represent the characters 0–9, as well as other partly ambiguous symbols. For each digit, a scoring overview (for all conditions), an omni-visualization as well as a counterfactual visualization were created.

4.3   Design and Procedure

The present study was set up as an online experiment in the German language. Three different conditions were defined that presented different information visualizations: in the first, the participants were only shown the input image, the AI classification and the classification scoring, but no additional visual or backtraced explanations (baseline-condition). In the second condition, the omni-visualization was additionally shown (omni-condition). In the third condition, the counterfactual visualization was shown, and the bar of the alternative number was marked in the scoring overview (counter-condition). In the course of the experiment, demographic data was first collected; then the three different conditions were explained in randomized order. Users were asked to perform the study only on sufficiently large screens. Examples for the different conditions are depicted in Fig. 1. Users were shown 20 randomly selected stimuli.

4.4   Scales and Measures

Trust was measured after each stimulus using the 5-item facets of system trustworthiness (FOST) scale [40]; see translated items 1–5 in Table 2. This allowed the assessment of key subfacets of trust for each trial (i.e., maximum scale length deemed acceptable for 20 presentations). The averages were calculated within each condition as one single value per condition for each participant, independent of the actual presented stimuli. Finally, the comprehensive Trust in Automation scale [41] was assessed at the end of the survey for each of the 3 experimental conditions, together with another FOST assessment in order to check the validity of the FOST scale in the context of the present study. As in previous research [40], both scales converged (with $r = .59$ for baseline-condition, $r = .57$ for omni-condition and $r = .69$ for counter-condition, all $p < .001$).

Table 2. Translated item texts of the Facets of System Trustworthiness (FOST) scale and all newly constructed scales. Reversed Items have been marked with "r" behind the number.

	Please indicate to what extent you agree with the following statements
01	The system's classification is reliable
02	The system's classification is precise
03	The system's classification is traceable
04	I can trust the system's classification
05r	I cannot depend on the system's classification
06	With the help of the visualization I am able to identify wrong mechanisms of the AI
07	I agree with the classification
08	The visualization provides a good explanation for the classification

Unfortunately, there is no generally accepted procedure to assess the observability of AI systems. Hence, we developed a single-item measure focusing on the key aspects of observability of enabling users to deduce systems states and detect failures. Item 6 in Table 2 shows the translated item text. To also operationalize the understandability of given explanations, we also added another item (see Item 8 in Table 2 for translated item text). Furthermore, for each stimulus, the level of agreement with the classification was measured in order to be able to identify effects of agreement related to trust and observability or vice versa; the translated text can be found in Item 7 of Table 2. For all additional items, we used the same Likert scale as for the FOST scale (see Table 2) coded as 1–6. The response scale had gradual formulations from "completely disagree" to "completely agree". The Trust in Automation scale was measured using a 7-point Likert scale. Reliability was good for all multi-item scales (see Table 3).

5 Results

In order to test the hypotheses, the data was analyzed with repeated measures ANOVA containing the three conditions. The violation of the sphericity assumption was controlled according to Mauchly's method [42], and in the case of a significant result, the correction supposed by [43] was performed. If the results were significant, additional post-hoc comparisons between the individual conditions were carried out; these were each carried out on the basis of a familywise performed Bonferroni correction [44]. The evaluation of the statistical power was based on the recommendation given by Cohen [45]. The Alpha level for all test to be rated as significant was $p < .05$.

Table 3. Reliability analysis and descriptive statistics for used multi-item scales and descriptive statistics for used single-item scales.

Scale	Cronbach's alpha	*Mean*	*SD*
Trust in automation	.82	4.37	0.85
FOST baseline-condition	.93	4.43	0.79
FOST omni-condition	.86	4.18	0.73
FOST counter-condition	.90	4.86	0.71
Observability baseline-condition	–	3.47	1.21
Observability omni-condition	–	3.83	1.08
Observability counter-condition	–	3.95	1.04
Understandability baseline-condition	–	3.84	1.22
Understandability omni-condition	–	4.17	1.00
Understandability counter-condition	–	3.95	1.20
Agreement baseline-condition	–	4.84	0.71
Agreement omni-condition	–	4.67	0.79
Agreement counter-condition	–	4.86	0.63

5.1 Hypotheses Testing

Descriptive statistics for all tested variables can be found in Table 3. The FOST scale was used to examine hypotheses H1.1 and H2.1, i.e. to determine trust in each condition. Although the ANOVA performed revealed a significant result, as expected, with $F(2, 164) = 10.06$, $p < .001$, $\eta^2 = .109$), post-hoc tests revealed (see Table 4) that the difference between the baseline-condition and the two experimental conditions was not as expected, as the baseline- and counter-conditions was not found to be significantly different. On this basis, H1.1 needs to be rejected. Only the omni-condition was significantly below both the baseline- and the counter-condition in the assessment of trust. Accordingly, this supports H2.1.

Table 4. Post-hoc performed pairwise t-test for Hypothesis 1.1 and 2.1. N = 83 for all tests. P-values are two-tailed. Familywise Bonferroni-Correction has been applied. Cohens'd has been calculated following [46].

Post-hoc tested groups FOST	t	p	*Cohen's d*
FOST baseline – FOST omni	3.24	.006	0.32
FOST baseline – FOST counter	0.76	>.999	0.07
FOST omni – FOST counter	−4.35	<.001	0.42

To test hypothesis H1.2 and H2.2, the values of the item to assess observability were examined (see Table 5). Significant results were also found here with $F(2, 164) = 7.25$ $p < .001$, $\eta^2 = .109$). Post-hoc tests showed that, as expected, the omni-condition and the counter-condition received better evaluations than the baseline-condition (i.e. without a visual explanation of the procedure). While H1.2 was confirmed by this, there was no difference between the omni-condition and the counter-condition, which is why H2.2. was rejected. The examination of hypothesis H2.3 did not reveal a significant result with $t(82) = 1.64$, $p = .106$, $d = 0.20$, both conditions showed almost equal ratings (see Table 3).

Table 5. Post-hoc performed pairwise t-test for Hypothesis 1.2 and 2.2. $N = 83$ for all tests. P-values are two-tailed. Familywise Bonferroni-Correction has been applied. Cohens'd has been calculated following [46].

Post-hoc tested groups	t	p	Cohen's d
Observability baseline - Observability omni	−2.95	.012	0.31
Observability baseline - Observability counter	−3.36	.003	0.42
Observability omni - Observability counter	−0.94	>.999	0.11

5.2 Exploratory Analysis

We further evaluated the correlations of level of agreement, and trust and observability for each condition. For trust, all correlations were significant, while this was only true for observability in the counter-condition (see Table 6).

Table 6. Descriptive statistics for agreement and correlation with trust and observability $N = 83$ for all tests. P-values are two-tailed. Familywise Bonferroni-Correction has been applied. Cohens'd has been calculated following [46].

Condition	Mean	SD	Pearson's r for [Condition] Trust	Pearson's r for [Condition] Observability
Agreement baseline-condition	4.84	0.71	.70*	.08
Agreement omni-condition	4.67	0.79	.70**	.04
Agreement counter-condition	4.86	0.63	.67**	.30*

* indicates $p < .05$ and ** indicates $p < .01$

6 Discussion

6.1 Summary of Results

The objective of the present research was to examine how different prototypical visualizations that aim to explain AI results affect the perceived trustworthiness and observability of a ML system. Overall, we found a mixed pattern of results regarding our hypotheses, indicating that relationships between variables may – in part – be more complex than expected.

The assumption, that additional information about the classification process based on the input material generally contributes to an increase of trust (H1.1), could not be confirmed; the representation of the omni-condition led to lower values than the baseline-condition. However, the assumption that an explanation based on the approach of counterfactual explanations achieves better values than the omni-condition was confirmed (H2.1, small significant effects).

The hypotheses on observability showed the opposite pattern. Here, results showed that the support by visual information increased the perceived observability (H1.2), but contrary to hypothesis H2.2, the two examined XAI visualization approaches did not differ with regard to the observability rating (only very weak and insignificant advantage of counter-condition compared to omni-condition). The examination of the hypothesis for the understandability of explanations (H2.3) did not show significant results and the effect size was too small to be further considered. Finally, we found strong and significant correlations between agreements to classification and perceived trust (see Table 6).

6.2   Implications

Results of the present study show that the visualization of the process of automated AI classifications can have an influence on how the system is evaluated in terms of trust and observability. However, this influence must be evaluated in a non-linear way – trust in AI can also decrease by adding additional information [30]. In line with previous research, we assume the poor performance of the omni-condition to be because information overload occurred and users were not able to build up additional trust [47]. As expected, this effect did not occur within the counter-condition (H2.1).

We further suspect that the result regarding the explanations' understandability to possibly be based on information overload too – the users may have relied on a heuristic process to judge the explanation due to the high amount of information the system generated, similar to the effort heuristic [11]. Yet, this remains speculative and needs further research before allowing to draw firm conclusions. Furthermore, the strong correlation between agreement and perceived trust needs to be further examined. Previous research has already shown that trust is depended on the predictability of a system [48]. Accordingly, we assume that trust in the context of AI also depends on whether expectations regarding the classification (i.e. based on the input) are violated. This especially applies to systems, where users need only little effort to build and verify expectations.

With regard to the observability of the system, the data indicated that the examined XAI visualizations were helpful for users. This lends support to previous notions [49], that a system's observability is therefore crucial for cooperation between humans and AI. This is also in line with our expectations, since without additional information about the process (as in the baseline-condition), conclusions about the actual functioning of the system can only be drawn with considerable additional effort and only to a lesser extent. Hence, it seems inevitable to address this issue more strongly in further research on the cooperation between AI and humans.

Concerning both primary variables examined, trust and observability, it can be seen that overall the counterfactual explanations proposed by [14] showed a positive tendency to be effective.

6.3 Limitations and Further Research

Some limitations and reveals many interesting open questions for future investigations. First, the dependent constructs (perceived trust and observability) need to be addressed more specifically in isolated tasks. Additionally, a more selective definition of measurable and distinguishable facets of explanations, as suggested by [17] could be helpful.

The task carried out in this experiment was kept as simple as possible. The aim was not to add any further possibly disturbing variables induced by a higher complexity of the task, and to present an AI system that functions as reliably and correctly as possible. Future studies should further control and specifically investigate the agreement of users with the AI's classification. On top of that, more complex tasks, e.g. the extraction of sentiment from texts, need to be examined, because the cooperation between human and intelligent system is necessary. However, future research has to consider tasks humans cannot evaluate without additional effort.

Ultimately, we focused on quantitative data in the present investigation to examine our hypotheses. Yet given the potential complexity of users' cognitive processing of different XAI visualization approaches, further research should also more closely examine aspects like visualization comprehension and the development of mental models of AI systems with qualitative methods. Detailed empirical quantitative investigations of cognitive processes involved in the processing of counterfactual explanations and other explanatory approaches should follow these qualitative studies to further advance the effectiveness of XAI in human-machine interaction [50, 51].

References

1. Adadi, A., Berrada, M.: Peeking inside the black-box: a survey on explainable artificial intelligence (XAI). IEEE Access. **6**, 52138–52160 (2018). https://doi.org/10.1109/ACCESS.2018.2870052
2. Weld, D.S., Bansal, G.: The Challenge of Crafting Intelligible Intelligence. ArXiv180304263 Cs. (2018)
3. Ancona, M., Ceolini, E., Öztireli, C., Gross, M.: Towards better understanding of gradient-based attribution methods for Deep Neural Networks. ArXiv171106104 Cs Stat. (2017)
4. Lee, J.D., See, K.A.: Trust in automation: designing for appropriate reliance. Hum. Factors **46**, 50–80 (2004)
5. Lee, J., Moray, N.: Trust, control strategies and allocation of function in human-machine systems. Ergonomics **35**, 1243–1270 (1992). https://doi.org/10.1080/00140139208967392
6. Muir, B.M., Moray, N.: Trust in automation. Part II experimental studies of trust and human intervention in a process control simulation. Ergonomics. **39**, 429–460 (1996). https://doi.org/10.1080/00140139608964474

7. Nushi, B., Kamar, E., Horvitz, E.: Towards Accountable AI: Hybrid Human-Machine Analyses for Characterizing System Failure. ArXiv180907424 Cs Stat. (2018)
8. Lim, B.Y., Dey, A.K.: Assessing demand for intelligibility in context-aware applications. In: Proceedings of the 11th international conference on Ubiquitous computing (Ubicomp 2009). p. 195. ACM Press, Orlando (2009). https://doi.org/10.1145/1620545.1620576
9. Montavon, G., Samek, W., Müller, K.-R.: Methods for interpreting and understanding deep neural networks. Digit. Signal Process. **73**, 1–15 (2018). https://doi.org/10.1016/j.dsp.2017. 10.011
10. Ribeiro, M.T., Singh, S., Guestrin, C.: "Why Should I Trust You?": Explaining the Predictions of Any Classifier. ArXiv160204938 Cs Stat. (2016)
11. Kruger, J., Wirtz, D., Van Boven, L., Altermatt, T.W.: The effort heuristic. J. Exp. Soc. Psychol. **40**, 91–98 (2004). https://doi.org/10.1016/S0022-1031(03)00065-9
12. Abdul, A., Vermeulen, J., Wang, D., Lim, B.Y., Kankanhalli, M.: Trends and trajectories for explainable, accountable and intelligible systems: an HCI research agenda. In: Proceedings of the 2018 CHI Conference on Human Factors in Computing Systems (CHI 2018), pp. 1– 18. ACM Press, Montreal QC (2018). https://doi.org/10.1145/3173574.3174156
13. Amershi, S., et al.: Guidelines for human-AI interaction. In: Proceedings of the 2019 CHI Conference on Human Factors in Computing Systems (CHI 2019), pp. 1–13. ACM Press, Glasgow (2019). https://doi.org/10.1145/3290605.3300233
14. Miller, T.: Explanation in Artificial Intelligence: Insights from the Social Sciences. ArXiv170607269 Cs. (2017)
15. Lapuschkin, S., Binder, A., Montavon, G., Müller, K.-R., Samek, W.: The LRP toolbox for artificial neural networks. J. Mach. Learn. Res. **17**(1), 3938–3942 (2016)
16. Hoffman, R.R., Mueller, S.T., Klein, G., Litman, J.: Metrics for explainable AI: Challenges and prospects. ArXiv Prepr. ArXiv181204608. (2018)
17. Ras, G., van Gerven, M., Haselager, P.: Explanation Methods in Deep Learning: Users, Values, Concerns and Challenges. ArXiv180307517 Cs Stat. (2018)
18. Selvaraju, R.R., Cogswell, M., Das, A., Vedantam, R., Parikh, D., Batra, D.: Grad-CAM: visual explanations from deep networks via gradient-based localization. In: 2017 IEEE International Conference on Computer Vision (ICCV), pp. 618–626. IEEE, Venice (2017). https://doi.org/10.1109/ICCV.2017.74
19. Samek, W., Wiegand, T., Müller, K.-R.: Explainable Artificial Intelligence: Understanding, Visualizing and Interpreting Deep Learning Models. ArXiv170808296 Cs Stat. (2017)
20. Binder, A., Bach, S., Montavon, G., Müller, K.-R., Samek, W.: Layer-Wise Relevance Propagation for Deep Neural Network Architectures. Information Science and Applications (ICISA) 2016. LNEE, vol. 376, pp. 913–922. Springer, Singapore (2016). https://doi.org/10. 1007/978-981-10-0557-2_87
21. Timmermans, D.: The impact of task complexity on information use in multi-attribute decision making. J. Behav. Decis. Mak. **6**, 95–111 (1993). https://doi.org/10.1002/bdm. 3960060203
22. Furner, C.P., Zinko, R.A.: The influence of information overload on the development of trust and purchase intention based on online product reviews in a mobile vs. web environment: an empirical investigation. Electron. Mark. **27**, 211–224 (2017). https://doi.org/10.1007/ s12525-016-0233-2
23. Roese, N.J., Morrison, M.: The psychology of counterfactual thinking. Hist. Soc. Res. Sozialforschung 16–26 (2009)
24. Sokol, K., Flach, P.: Glass-Box: explaining AI decisions with counterfactual statements through conversation with a voice-enabled virtual assistant. In: Proceedings of the Twenty-Seventh International Joint Conference on Artificial Intelligence Organization, Stockholm, Sweden, pp. 5868–5870 (2018). https://doi.org/10.24963/ijcai.2018/865

25. Kulesza, T., Stumpf, S., Burnett, M., Kwan, I.: Tell me more? The effects of mental model soundness on personalizing an intelligent agent. In: Proceedings of the 2012 ACM annual conference on Human Factors in Computing Systems (CHI 2012), p. 1. ACM Press, Austin (2012). https://doi.org/10.1145/2207676.2207678

26. Goyal, Y., Wu, Z., Ernst, J., Batra, D., Parikh, D., Lee, S.: Counterfactual Visual Explanations. ArXiv190407451 Cs Stat. (2019)

27. Bigras, E., et al.: In AI we trust: characteristics influencing assortment planners' perceptions of AI based recommendation agents. In: Nah, F.F.-H., Xiao, B.S. (eds.) HCIBGO 2018. LNCS, vol. 10923, pp. 3–16. Springer, Cham (2018). https://doi.org/10.1007/978-3-319-91716-0_1

28. Breuer, C., Hüffmeier, J., Hibben, F., Hertel, G.: Trust in teams: a taxonomy of perceived trustworthiness factors and risk-taking behaviors in face-to-face and virtual teams. Hum. Relat. (2019). https://doi.org/10.1177/0018726718818721

29. Zanker, M.: The influence of knowledgeable explanations on users' perception of a recommender system. In: Proceedings of the sixth ACM conference on Recommender systems (RecSys 2012), p. 269. ACM Press, Dublin (2012). https://doi.org/10.1145/2365952.2366011

30. Springer, A., Whittaker, S.: "I had a solid theory before but it's falling apart": polarizing effects of algorithmic transparency. arXiv preprint arXiv:1811.02163 (2018)

31. Hengstler, M., Enkel, E., Duelli, S.: Applied artificial intelligence and trust—The case of autonomous vehicles and medical assistance devices. Technol. Forecast. Soc. Change. **105**, 105–120 (2016). https://doi.org/10.1016/j.techfore.2015.12.014

32. Caruana, R., Lou, Y., Gehrke, J., Koch, P., Sturm, M., Elhadad, N.: Intelligible models for healthcare: predicting pneumonia risk and hospital 30-day readmission. In: Proceedings of the 21th ACM SIGKDD International Conference on Knowledge Discovery and Data Mining (KDD 2015), pp. 1721–1730. ACM Press, Sydney (2015). https://doi.org/10.1145/2783258.2788613

33. Krause, J., Perer, A., Bertini, E.: A user study on the effect of aggregating explanations for interpreting machine learning models. In: ACM KDD Workshop on Interactive Data Exploration and Analytics (2018)

34. Kalman, R.E.: A new approach to linear filtering and prediction problems. J. Basic Eng. **82**, 35–45 (1960)

35. Billings, C.E.: Human-centered aviation automation: principles and guidelines (1996)

36. Johnson, M., Bradshaw, J.M., Feltovich, P.J.: Tomorrow's human–machine design tools: from levels of automation to interdependencies. J. Cogn. Eng. Decis. Mak. **12**, 77–82 (2018). https://doi.org/10.1177/1555343417736462

37. Rovira, E., McGarry, K., Parasuraman, R.: Effects of imperfect automation on decision making in a simulated command and control task. Hum. Factors J. Hum. Factors Ergon. Soc. **49**, 76–87 (2007). https://doi.org/10.1518/001872007779598082

38. Franke, T., Attig, C., Wessel, D.: A personal resource for technology interaction development and validation of the affinity for technology interaction (ATI) Scale. Int. J. Hum.-Comput. Inter. **35**, 456–467 (2019). https://doi.org/10.1080/10447318.2018.1456150

39. Deng, L.: The MNIST database of handwritten digit images for machine learning research [best of the web]. IEEE Signal Process. Mag. **29**, 141–142 (2012). https://doi.org/10.1109/MSP.2012.2211477

40. Franke, T., Trantow, M., Günther, M., Krems, J.F., Zott, V., Keinath, A.: Advancing electric vehicle range displays for enhanced user experience: the relevance of trust and adaptability. In: Proceedings of the 7th International Conference on Automotive User Interfaces and Interactive Vehicular Applications (AutomotiveUI 2015). pp. 249–256. ACM Press, Nottingham (2015). https://doi.org/10.1145/2799250.2799283

41. Jian, J.-Y., Bisantz, A.M., Drury, C.G.: Foundations for an empirically determined scale of trust in automated systems. Int. J. Cogn. Ergon. **4**, 53–71 (2000). https://doi.org/10.1207/S15327566IJCE0401_04

42. Mauchly, J.W.: Significance test for sphericity of a normal n-Variate distribution. Ann. Math. Stat. **11**, 204–209 (1940). https://doi.org/10.1214/aoms/1177731915

43. Greenhouse, S.W., Geisser, S.: On methods in the analysis of profile data. Psychometrika **24**, 95–112 (1959). https://doi.org/10.1007/BF02289823

44. Holm, S.: A simple sequentially rejective multiple test procedure. Scand. J. Stat. **6**, 65–70 (1979)

45. Cohen, J.: A power primer. Psychol. Bull. **112**, 155–159 (1992). https://doi.org/10.1037/0033-2909.112.1.155

46. Dunlap, W.P., Cortina, J.M., Vaslow, J.B., Burke, M.J.: Meta-analysis of experiments with matched groups or repeated measures designs. Psychol. Methods **1**(2), 170 (1996)

47. Kizilcec, R.F.: How much information? Effects of transparency on trust in an algorithmic interface. In: Proceedings of the 2016 CHI Conference on Human Factors in Computing Systems (CHI 2016). pp. 2390–2395. ACM Press, Santa Clara (2016). https://doi.org/10.1145/2858036.2858402

48. Biros, D.P., Fields, G., Gunsch, G.: The effect of external safeguards on human-information system trust in an information warfare environment. In: Proceedings of the 36th Annual Hawaii International Conference on System Sciences 2003, p. 10. IEEE, Big Island (2003). https://doi.org/10.1109/HICSS.2003.1173894

49. Christoffersen, K., Woods, D.: How to make automated systems team players. Adv. Hum. Perform. Cogn. Eng. Res. pp. 1–12 (2002). https://doi.org/10.1016/S1479-3601(02)02003-9

50. Mueller, S.T., Hoffman, R.R., Clancey, W., Emrey, A., Klein, G.: Explanation in human-AI systems: a literature meta-review, synopsis of key ideas and publications, and bibliography for explainable AI. arXiv preprint arXiv:1902.01876 (2019)

51. Hoffman, R.R., Klein, G., Mueller, S.T.: Explaining explanation for "Explainable Ai". Proc. Hum. Factors Ergon. Soc. Annu. Meet. **62**, 197–201 (2018). https://doi.org/10.1177/1541931218621047

Human-in-the-Loop Design Cycles – A Process Framework that Integrates Design Sprints, Agile Processes, and Machine Learning with Humans

Chaehan So[✉]

Information and Interaction Design,
Humanities, Arts and Social Sciences Division,
Yonsei University, 03722 Seoul, South Korea
cso@yonsei.ac.kr

Abstract. Demands on more transparency of the backbox nature of machine learning models have led to the recent rise of *human-in-the-loop* in machine learning, i.e. processes that integrate humans in the training and application of machine learning models. The present work argues that this process requirement does not represent an obstacle but an opportunity to optimize the design process. Hence, this work proposes a new process framework, Human-in-the-loop Design Cycles – a design process that integrates the structural elements of agile and design thinking process, and controls the training of a machine learning model by the human in the loop.

The Human-in-the-loop Design Cycles process replaces the qualitative user testing by a quantitative psychometric measurement instrument for design perception. The generated user feedback serves to train a machine learning model and to instruct the subsequent design cycle along four design dimensions (novelty, energy, simplicity, tool).

Mapping the four-dimensional user feedback into user stories and priorities, the design sprint thus transforms the user feedback directly into the implementation process. The human in the loop is a quality engineer who scrutinizes the collected user feedback to prevent invalid data to enter machine learning model training.

Keywords: Human-in-the-loop · Design thinking · Design process · Agile process · Agile methodology · User feedback · Machine learning

1 Introduction

Design Thinking has established itself as a proven process to create innovative products from the end user perspective [1], commonly denoted as user-centered design [2] or human-centered design [3]. Despite the uncontested merits of design thinking for innovation [4], many online companies do not follow this methodology yet. In their view, it is incompatible with their product development process or machine learning system. The present work aims to propose a process framework for such companies that integrates design thinking with a development process that incorporates the human in the loop.

© Springer Nature Switzerland AG 2020
H. Degen and L. Reinerman-Jones (Eds.): HCII 2020, LNCS 12217, pp. 136–145, 2020.
https://doi.org/10.1007/978-3-030-50334-5_9

Why has it become essential in 2020 to re-integrate the human in the loop in machine learning systems? The underlying reason is that in recent years, the explosive growth of AI research results also led to increasing doubts on the validity of these findings. Apart from the concerns on *reproducibility* and *interpretability* [5], a new concern is on *controllability*, i.e. the demand for integrating humans in any process that relies on the outcome of machine learning, now referred to as *humans-in-the-loop* [6].

Two of the most crucial questions, about how humans in the loop should affect machine learning conceptually, were asked in a workshop on human-centered machine learning at the CHI 2016 conference by Gillies and colleagues [7]:

1. What is the role of humans in existing machine learning systems?
2. How does a human-centered approach change the way machine learning is done?

The present work suggests as an answer to the preceding questions to shift part of the learning process from machine learning to conventional psychological methodology. This shift allows not only for controlling the machine learning process but also speed up the human learning loop by more active involvement.

The proposed framework applies psychometrics to understand users' design perception to generate feedback for the subsequent design cycle, and to incrementally update a machine learning model to accommodate the fast-changing nature of user preferences in the online world. These elements are enabled by merging design thinking methodology with an agile process.

The inherent reason why online companies cannot implement design thinking methodology may lie in misunderstandings of its process. For example, the Stanford d. school design thinking process, introduced by IDEO in 2007 [8], specifies a cycle of five process phases from emphasize, define, ideate, prototype, and test. The first misunderstanding of many companies is to disregard the cyclical nature and instead implement a one-time execution of the five phases. The final test phase thus does not feed a subsequent learning cycle but merely serves as an end-to-end system test. Nevertheless, the cyclical nature can easily be implemented by an *agile process* [9], i.e. an iterative and incremental development process. The second misunderstanding occurs when businesses do not implement design thinking as an iterative learning cycle. Design thinking methods usually specify the sample size of a qualitative user test between five to ten people. As the testing phase is only performed once, the small sample size results in feedback that is not representative and thus risky to base product decisions on. The user feedback obtained in such a small qualitative workshop is prone to positive distortion as the participants tend to give feedback that pleases the makers of the presented prototypes. In conclusion, innovative companies have an understandable need for representative user feedback that is informative, i.e. provide directions for the implementation process.

Taken together, the preceding considerations lead to the following research question:

How can humans in the loop integrate into an agile process with design thinking and machine learning methodology?

2 Building Blocks

2.1 Psychometrics

In psychological studies, people's behaviors and perceptions are analyzed by qualitative [10] and quantitative research methodology [11]. The qualitative methodology is largely overlapping with design research [12], e.g. anthropological methods of investigating user contexts, or qualitative structured and semi-structured user interviews [10]. One major disadvantage of qualitative methods is their vulnerability to various cognitive and emotional bias effects. One such frequently encountered bias is *confirmation bias* [13], i.e. the tendency to ignore facts contradictory to prior judgment. Researchers exert confirmation bias e.g. when they ask *leading questions* [14].

Quantitative psychological research methodology aimed to reduce biases by a range of statistical tools summarized under the term *psychometrics* [15], the science of psychological measurement. One of its focus areas is the analysis of surveys from self-reported user perceptions [16]. E.g. it specifies how to find an underlying pattern of psychological factors in survey responses by *explorative factor analysis* [17].

2.2 Psychometric Measurement Instrument for Design Perception

The proposed framework is based on the author's prior work [8] that developed a measurement instrument for design perception from 1955 design works evaluations. It consists of 12 items in four design dimensions extracted by principal factor analysis.

The development of this measurement instrument followed psychometric scale construction methodology. This entailed that the initial item pool, generated by qualitative methodology, was systematically reduced by analyzing the factor structure by explorative factor analysis. The latter method investigates the items (survey questions) to detect statistical patterns that could correspond to underlying psychological factors [11]. The items displayed a so-called *simple structure* [15], i.e. the factor structure revealed that all items show high *convergent validity* (items for one construct load on the same component) as well as *discriminant validity* (items for different constructs load on different components).

For each of the four factors, a plausible interpretation could be found (*novelty, energy, simplicity,* and *tool*). Furthermore, when analyzed as a separate scale, each of these factors showed high reliability according to the convention by Cohen [18] with Cronbach alpha coefficients around 0.80. Together, these factors explain most of the variance in the survey responses (74%). The items are displayed in Table 1.

Table 1. Design dimensions – items

Novelty	Energy	Simplicity	Tool
Exciting	Powerful	Simple	Practical
Unique	Clever	Clear	Functional
Creative	Intuitive	Minimalistic	Useful

2.3   The Human in the Loop

Nushi and colleagues from ETH Zurich and Microsoft Research [19] disentangle machine learning systems into components that allow their troubleshooting methodology to locate the component responsible for failure to enable targeted fixes of that component. Their framework incorporates humans in the loop to simulate component fixes and evaluate the machine learning system before and after the fixes to reach a higher level of control. According to the authors, the preconditions for such a concept are the modularity of a machine learning system and the interpretability of its components.

Xin and colleagues [20] from University of Illinois, Urbana-Champaign, presented a concept for tackling the "tedious process of iterative experimentation" at a workshop at the Data Management for End-To-End Machine Learning (DEEM) 2018 conference. They point to several inefficient aspects of current machine learning systems that do not cater to human-in-the-loop in the iterative development process. Their framework caters to the developers' need for reusing intermediate results as opposed to rerunning the whole workflow. In particular, developers need to understand the impact of their code changes early as opposed to waiting until the computation is fully finished. Taken together, if a machine learning system integrates its developers, the humans in the loop, better by providing them with "rapid, approximate feedback", it will result in a significant speedup of the end-to-end process.

Taken together, machine learning should only be trained if humans in the loop have verified the validity of the input data, and learned from the model training by early approximate feedback. The approximate feedback generation may also allow for discarding older input data which may have become obsolete.

2.4   Agile Process

An agile process is mainly characterized by an iterative and incremental approach to development [21, 22]. This means that the product development process is not defined by a series of long, subsequent phases like in the waterfall model, but as a series of short temporal cycles called iterations [23]. Scrum, the most common agile method, calls these iterations *sprints* [24]. Google developed its design thinking method based on agile processes and thus called it *design sprint* [25].

One essential process aspect, *time-boxing* [26], is frequently misunderstood and thus incorrectly implemented. *Time-boxing* [27] specifies that the iteration duration is strictly fixed. In the real world, this means that the implementation team is not allowed to delay the iteration finish date despite the pressuring demands by project managers and business teams to obtain a planned scope at the end of an iteration. Instead of fixing the scope to be delivered, time-boxing allows for adjusting the scope to keep the timeline.

Scrum and the Google design sprint describe the iteration planning in a workshop called *sprint planning*. In this planning workshop, the implementation team defines the scope of the current sprint based on the customer feedback for the last sprint results. The new scope is fleshed out into *user stories*, i.e. requirements formulated from the user perspective [28]. All user stories are prioritized according to customer feedback.

3 Proposed Process Framework

This work proposes a process framework, as depicted in Fig. 1, that consists of a design thinking process, merged into an agile development process, that replaces the qualitative user test by quantitative measurement of user feedback. This replacement allows to generate scalable and instructional feedback for the subsequent learning cycle which is implemented as a design sprint.

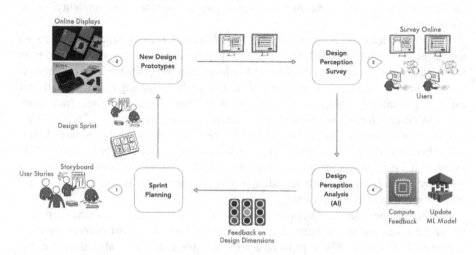

Fig. 1. Process framework: human-in-the-loop integration of end users into a machine learning-based analysis process

3.1 User Testing – by Design Perception Survey

For the user testing, the team acquires a pool of the company's real end users, and invites a portion of this user pool to answer an online survey at the design sprint end. This online survey displays the new prototypes which were produced in the preceding design sprint (see Fig. 2). The invited survey participants asses the 12 items of the design perception measurement instrument [29] about the displayed new prototypes. Additionally, the survey solicits qualitative feedback such as new feature requests or questions about functionality details.

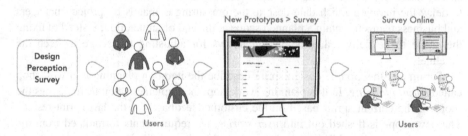

Fig. 2. User testing by design perception survey

3.2 Feedback Computation and Machine Learning Model Update – by Design Perception Analysis

The responses to the design perception survey are analyzed in the following manner. The users' scale responses are grouped according to the four design dimensions, e.g. exciting, unique, creative to novelty. For each design dimension scale, the composite scores are calculated. These composite scores represent the scale scores from each user and can be displayed by boxplots which provide visualized feedback to the implementation team (Fig. 3).

The human-in-the-loop aspect is realized by a human quality engineer who scrutinizes the received user responses in data quality, and discards invalid data like outliers or responses containing strong acquiescence bias. This data cleaning procedure is essential to retain only valid new data to add to the dataset on which the machine learning model is trained. The resulting model can serve as a pretrained model for quick simulations to support prototyping decisions.

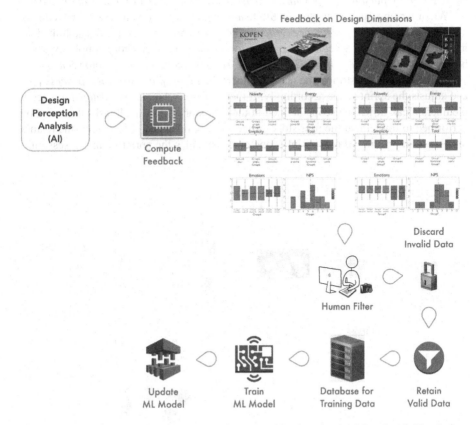

Fig. 3. Design dimensions feedback generation & machine learning model update fed by design perception analysis

3.3   Sprint Planning – by Design Dimensions Feedback

The sprint planning process is structured by the four design dimensions such that each design dimension corresponds to a category in the sprint storyboard (see Fig. 4).

The category (e.g. simplicity) refers to a high-level abstraction of scope or business requirements respectively. The team assigns the priority of each category according to the design dimensions' composite score in the computed feedback – the lowest score translates into the highest priority because it uncovers the strongest deficiency.

In descending priority of the design dimensions, the team decides which design dimensions shall be addressed in the upcoming sprint. For this decision, the team does not have to consider the ease or difficulty of implementation because the latter is reflected in the later effort estimation process. This means that user stories that are easier to implement will get less effort estimation units and will consequently be more likely implemented.

The team writes user stories for the selected design dimensions. For example, a user story in category simplicity could be formulated as *"As a frontend web user, I want to navigate to my personal page with the least possible number of navigational steps"*.

When writing such user stories, the team integrates the qualitative user feedback into the user stories' *acceptance criteria*. For example, if user feedback hinted to inconsistent colors, an acceptance criterion for a user story in category simplicity could be formulated as *"Check if all UI elements originate from the same color scheme"*.

Based on the user stories, the team conducts the *agile effort estimation process* [30] and adjusts the sprint scope accordingly. It then performs the *task breakdown*, i.e. team members break down the scope defined in the user stories into small tasks that must be performed to implement the user story. After the task breakdown, it reviews the team's understanding of the current sprint scope and concludes the sprint planning session.

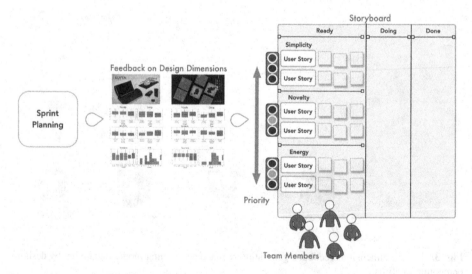

Fig. 4. Sprint planning by design dimension feedback

3.4   New Design Prototypes – by Design Sprints

The team executes the design sprint as a normal agile iteration as a self-organized team.

At the end of this process (see Fig. 5), the team applies special care to present its results in the subsequent survey because the users must be able to grasp the new functionality and from the online display. This care entails additional activities, like taking photos or producing renderings from different view angles, until users can grasp the gist of the new prototypes in their online survey displays (see Fig. 5, prototype displayed in the middle of Fig. 5).

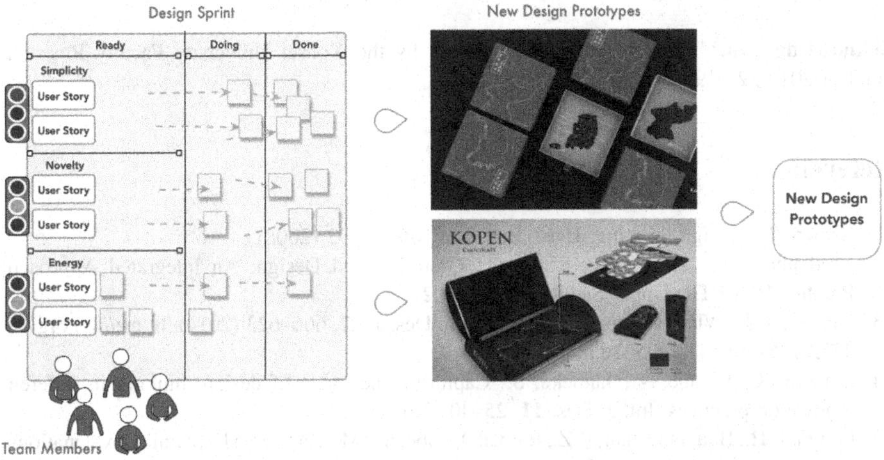

Fig. 5. New design prototypes by design sprints

4   Discussion

Many companies of online products or services that rely on a machine learning system do not know how to integrate humans in the loop and often assume that this would decrease efficiency. Likewise, companies that follow an agile product development process have difficulty integrating this process with design thinking methodology. The present work provides a solution for both these practical problems by proposing a new process framework, the Human-in-the-loop Design Cycles.

Several of its process elements go hand in hand to create synergic effects:

1. The design prototypes are used in online surveys. This enables high scalability of the user testing despite the collection of qualitative feedback by the same survey. Moreover, it allows collecting other user data which are used for the machine learning training.
2. The user test results are analyzed with a psychometric measurement instrument that generates quantitative feedback. The quantitative nature allows to directly use it in machine learning model training. Furthermore, this feedback is on a summarized,

structured level that is informative for the next design sprint because it provides directions by clear scores on design dimensions.

3. The quality engineer who reviews the generated feedback caters both for data quality improvement as well as for early detection of trends, e.g. changing user preferences.
4. The machine learning model is updated in each design sprint. Therefore, decision makers can always rely on the most recent user data and do not have to wait for the completion of a long training period [20].

The Human-in-the-loop Design Cycles merge the design thinking method into an agile process, and leverage the user feedback with the human in the loop for machine learning model training and directions for the design sprint.

Acknowledgment. This research was supported by the Yonsei University Faculty Research Fund of 2019-22-0199.

References

1. Brown, T.: Design thinking. Harv. Bus. Rev. **86**, 85–92 (2008)
2. Vredenburg, K., Isensee, S., Righi, C.: User-Centered Design: An Integrated Approach. Prentice Hall PTR, Upper Saddle River (2002)
3. Giacomin, J.: What is human centred design. Des. J. **17**, 606–623 (2014). https://doi.org/10. 2752/175630614X14056185480186
4. Maaike, K., Rianne, V., Janneke, S.: Capturing the value of design thinking in different innovation practices. Int. J. Des. **11**, 25–40 (2017)
5. Gilpin, L.H., Bau, D., Yuan, B.Z., Bajwa, A., Specter, M., Kagal, L.: Explaining explanations: an overview of interpretability of machine learning. In: Proceedings - 2018 IEEE 5th International Conference on Data Science and Advanced Analytics DSAA 2018, pp. 80–89 (2019). https://doi.org/10.1109/DSAA.2018.00018
6. Zanzotto, F.M.: Viewpoint: human-in-the-loop artificial intelligence. J. Artif. Intell. Res. **64**, 243–253 (2019). https://doi.org/10.1613/jair.1.11345
7. Gillies, M., et al.: Human-centered machine learning. In: Conference on Human Factors Computer System – Proceedings, 07–12 May 2016, pp. 3558–3565 (2016). https://doi.org/ 10.1145/2851581.2856492
8. IDEO: IDEO Human-Centered Design Toolkit, 2nd edn. (2008). https://doi.org/10.1002/ ejoc.201200111
9. Beck, K., et al.: Manifesto for Agile Software Development (2001)
10. Mason, J.: Qualitative Researching. Sage Publications, Thousand Oaks/New Delhi (2002). https://doi.org/10.1159/000105503
11. Giles, D.C.: Advanced Research Methods in Psychology. Routledge, East Sussex (2002)
12. Bayazit, N.: Investigating design: a review of forty years of design research. Des. Issues **20**, 16–29 (2004). https://doi.org/10.1162/074793604772933739
13. Nickerson, R.S.: Confirmation bias: a ubiquitous phenomenon in many guises. Rev. Gen. Psychol. **2**, 175–220 (1998)
14. Powell, M.B., Hughes-Scholes, C.H., Sharman, S.J.: Skill in interviewing reduces confirmation bias. J. Invest. Psychol. Offender Profiling **9**, 126–134 (2012). https://doi.org/ 10.1002/jip.1357

15. Kline, P.: The New Psychometrics: Science, Psychology, and Measurement. Routledge (1998)
16. Price, P.C.: Psychology Research Methods: Core Skills and Concepts v. 1.0. Psychology, pp. 215–260 (2012). https://doi.org/10.24926/8668.2201
17. Tabachnick, B.G., Fidell, L.S.: Using Multivariate Statistics. Pearson, Boston (2019)
18. Cohen, P.: Statistical Power Analysis for the Behavioral Sciences. Academic Press, New York (1977)
19. Nushi, B., Kamar, E., Horvitz, E., Kossmann, D.: On human intellect and machine failures: Troubleshooting integrative machine learning systems. In: 31st AAAI Conference on Artificial Intelligence, AAAI 2017, pp. 1017–1025 (2017)
20. Xin, D.D., Ma, L.L., Liu, J.J., Macke, S.S., Song, S.S., Parameswaran, A.A.: Accelerating human-in-the-loop machine learning: challenges and opportunities. In: Proceedings of 2nd Workshop on Data Management for End-to-End Machine Learning, DEEM 2018 - Conjunction with 2018 ACM SIGMOD/PODS Conference (2018). https://doi.org/10.1145/3209889.3209896
21. Cockburn, A.: Agile Software Development: Software Through People. Addison-Wesley (2001)
22. Fowler, M.: The New Methodology (2000)
23. Beck, K., Andres, C.: Extreme Programming Explained: Embrace Change. Addison-Wesley Longman, Amsterdam (2000)
24. Schwaber, K., Beedle, M.: Agile Software Development with Scrum. Prentice Hall (2002)
25. Knapp, J., Zeratsky, J., Kowitz, B.: Sprint: How to Solve Big Problems and Test New Ideas in Just Five Days. Simon & Schuster (2016)
26. Jalote, P.: Timeboxing: a process model for iterative software development. J. Syst. Softw. **70**, 117–127 (2003)
27. Bittner, K., Spence, I.: Managing Iterative Software Development Projects. Addison-Wesley (2006)
28. Cohn, M.: User Stories Applied: For Agile Software Development. Addison Wesley Longman Publishing Co., Inc., Redwood City (2004)
29. So, C.: What makes good design? Revealing the predictive power of emotions and design dimensions in non-expert design vocabulary. Des. J. **22**, 325–349 (2019). https://doi.org/10.1080/14606925.2019.1589204
30. Beck, K., Fowler, M.: Planning Extreme Programming. Addison-Wesley (2000)

Beyond the Buzzwords: On the Perspective of AI in UX and Vice Versa

Dieter P. Wallach$^{(\boxtimes)}$ (ID), Lukas A. Flohr (ID), and Annika Kaltenhauser (ID)

Ergosign GmbH, Europaallee 20a, 66113 Saarbrücken, Germany
dieter.wallach@ergosign.de
https://www.ergosign.de/de/

Abstract. Integrating Artificial Intelligence (AI) technologies promises to open new possibilities for the development of smart systems and the creation of positive user experiences. While the acronym «AI» has often been used inflationary in recent marketese advertisements, the goal of the paper is to explore the relationship of AI and UX in concrete detail by referring to three case studies from our lab. The first case study is taken from a project targeted at the development of a clinical decision support system, while the second study focuses on the development of an autonomous mobility-on-demand system. The final project explores an innovative, AI-injected prototyping tool. We discuss challenges and the application of available guidelines when designing AI-based systems and provide insights into our learnings from the presented case studies.

Keywords: User experience · Artificial Intelligence · AI and UX · Human-AI Interaction · Human factors · Design · Case studies · Predictive prototyping · ACT-R · Clinical decision support systems · Intensive care · Autonomous mobility-on-demand · Autonomous vehicles

1 Introduction

Trying to escape from the seemingly omnipresent acronym «AI» is almost impossible these days. Whether we look at bold promises of machine learning-based systems that pretend to match all our business needs, over AI-powered predictive maintenance tools that optimize servicing, to smart recruitment applications that claim to find the best candidates out of gazillions of applicants, to self-driving cars pledging to enhance safety and convenience, or AI-driven filters that allow intelligent replacements of skies to create truly dramatic (fake) photos – AI has become an irreplaceable buzzword to describe the impressive achievements stemming from recent advances in the development of smart machines. This marketese speech is, without doubt, not unfounded: in the past few years we have witnessed various impactful demonstrations of AI-injected systems [1] that nurtured brave expectations about future capabilities of intelligent tools. AI is currently undergoing another hype phase—and is experiencing at least its

© Springer Nature Switzerland AG 2020
H. Degen and L. Reinerman-Jones (Eds.): HCII 2020, LNCS 12217, pp. 146–166, 2020.
https://doi.org/10.1007/978-3-030-50334-5_10

third hype wave since the foundation of Artificial Intelligence as a scientific discipline at the famous Dartmouth conference in 1956. Hypes naturally come with valleys of disillusion and the course of AI is no exception.

The term *AI winter* was coined to describe a phase in which research funding and industry investment in AI declines, mostly due to disappointments in the light of excessive promises. The history of AI has counted two of such winters: the Lighthill report [2] heralded the first period of drought in the 1970s by pointing out the limitations of the then current technology to meet the grand plans of early AI approaches. Initial successes of so-called Expert systems in the 1980s helped to raise interest (and funding) in AI in a second wave, but the brittleness of resulting systems—aside from their often very narrow domains—led to another decline and, subsequently, to a second AI winter. It is fair to denominate the vast majority of systems developed in these earlier periods of AI history as being research demonstrators that illustrated the state of the art at that time. Applications flourishing in the current AI summer, however, clearly left the protective walls of research labs, but have long found their ways into commercial products. Speech-based systems, including Alexa and Siri, have conquered our living rooms and kitchens while machine learning approaches are now comprehensively used to analyze big data bodies in cloud-based computing to derive patterns and support decision making. AI is now described as a key technology of the millennium [3]. The unbridled blossoming of AI in its present third summer is facilitated by national-level research funding and gigantic industry budgets.

The broad commercial success of recent AI-injected systems comes, as a consequence, with a wide diversification in their user base. New functionalities of AI systems lead to questions of how these can be used to address relevant user needs. Taming the complexity of AI applications requires appropriate interfaces for Human-AI interaction. Evaluating these systems asks for innovative approaches to understand how we can identify barriers and improve a user's experience with AI systems using formative evaluation methods. The aforementioned considerations are of course just selected, non-exhaustive examples, but they point to a pool of critical questions for the future success of AI-based systems. In this paper, we argue that User Experience (UX) Design - as a human-centered discipline that is able to balance (potentially conflicting) requirements from users, technologies and businesses - provides a structured framework of methods to support the development of AI-based systems. To explore the relationship of AI and UX, we present three case studies from our lab and discuss respective learnings from these projects. Other authors have already ascertained that the "field—where UX meets AI—is full of tensions" [4], and we can only agree. While it is generally approved that a positive user experience is a core ingredient for the acceptance of a product or service (e.g. [5]), a discussion of the role of UX methods for the development of AI-injected systems has only recently seen several calls to action and participation from both researchers and major journals, e.g. [4,6,7].

2   UX and AI

A tremendous number of attempts aiming to arrive at a universal definition of the term «Artificial Intelligence» can be found in the literature—with not too much consensus in their core conclusions. We certainly do not intend to add another facet to these attempts, but will use Nilsson's description (1998) as a working definition for the remainder of this paper: "Artificial Intelligence (AI), broadly (and somewhat circularly) defined, is concerned with intelligence behavior in artifacts. Intelligence behavior, in turn, involves perception, reasoning, learning communicating, and acting in complex environments. AI has one of its long-term goals in the development of machines that can do these things as well as humans can, or possibly even better" [1,8].

Today's AI systems—with the possible exception of very sophisticated robots—mostly do not comprehensively match all aspects of Nilsson's intelligence behavior, but typically focus on a selection of these. With regard to commercial systems, some that use the attribute «AI» in advertisement may even just refer to single "AI-powered tools", like Luminar's "AI Sky replacement" or "AI skin enhancer" in photo processing. Note that Nilsson's definition also does not require any similarity to (postulated) underlying human structures or processes when generating intelligent behavior, but is taking an engineering perspective. With regard to the case studies reported in this article, the same stance is taken—with the exception of the ANTETYPE project (see section Sect. 5.3) where the goal is explicitly targeted towards a simulation of human behavior based on a theory about the human Cognitive Architecture [9]. It is worth to emphasize that Nilsson's definition clearly surpasses a purely Machine Learning (ML) approach, which is sometimes illegitimately equated with AI (see [10]).

Although several different definitions of «User Experience» are used in the literature, they mostly converge in their core meaning. For the purpose of the paper, we render the widely used definition put forward in [7,11] adequate: User experience (UX) can be described as a "person's perceptions and responses resulting from the use and/or anticipated use of a product, system or service [... It] includes all the users' emotions, beliefs, preferences, perceptions, physical and psychological responses, behaviors and accomplishments that occur before, during and after use". This definition importantly emphasizes a temporal aspect of the concept of user experience: the expectations and anticipations of a prospective user contributes to the total of a user's experience with a system, just as her experience during the actual usage situation and her retrospective considerations after use do.

3   Challenges in Human-AI Interaction

Intelligent, AI-injected systems perform more and more tasks previously carried out by humans. This achievement fulfills the last part of the above cited definition of AI by Nilsson: "machines that can do these things as well as humans can, or possibly even better" [1,8]. If we consider this part from a broader, human factors-oriented perspective, we can describe this process as automation [12, 13]. Following the steps of human information processing, Parasuraman, Sheridan and Wickens [13] describe four corresponding functions that can be automated: information acquisition (sensory data gathering), information analysis (processing of acquired information), decision selection (choosing an option) and action implementation (execution of selected decision). To differentiate automation levels, i.e. the degree to which tasks are performed by a machine, Flemisch et al. [14] propose an automation spectrum with five levels (manual - assisted - semi automated - highly automated - autonomous/fully automated). While advantages and benefits such as increases in effectiveness and efficiency are obviously prevalent throughout all of these levels, automation in general comes with a batch of well-known human factor challenges. Bibby et al. [15] argues that automated systems will always remain human-machine systems, no matter how advanced the technology gets. Bainbridge [16] concludes an "irony of automation" in the sense, that the role of a human operator becomes even more crucial the more advanced a system becomes. In today's cars, for example, systems like Adaptive Cruise Control and Lane Keeping Assistance are able to take over (parts of) the driving task. However, if a system limit is reached or an error occurs, the driver, i.e. the human operator, needs to understand what happened (or what is about to happen) in order to be able to take over control in potentially critical situations.

The driving situation outlined above evokes automation problems that can be allocated to three main reasons [17]: 1) Inappropriate trust, 2) Loss of manual skills and 3) Insufficient situation awareness. For the scope of this paper, we focus on these reasons, but want to point out that - depending on context and scope of an application - there might be other, more specific challenges prevailing, e.g. in terms of reliability, performance, expectancy, ethics, security (perception) or data privacy (see e.g. [18]).

3.1 Trust

Trust can be described as "a belief that something is expected to be reliable, good and effective" and as the mental state people have based on their expectations and perceptions [19]. With regard to the definition of User Experience in Sect. 2 of this paper, inappropriate trust can thus be either (a) the outcome of (positive or negative) expectations that precede actual driving and/or (b) are established as a result of an earlier or the current driving experience. The level of trust towards a system depends on its reliability, its perceived usefulness and transparency [20], i.e. the degree of its comprehensibility. For the use of intelligent systems it is essential, that the level of trust people have is appropriate. Neither "overtrust" nor "distrust" is desired [21] as it might eventually result in "misuse" or "disuse" [12, 13]. With increasing system experience people calibrate their level of trust [22], i.e. they adjust their trust level to match system capabilities, which eventually leads to appropriate use [21]. Besides perceived usefulness and perceived ease of use [23], trust has a major influence on the (public and personal) acceptance of systems (e.g. [24]).

3.2 Loss of Skills

We can observe a change of humans' role from active operating tasks to passive monitoring tasks in automated and AI-injected systems [25]. As a result, operators loose experience, training time and associated motor and cognitive skills [17]. Since automation often takes over the 'standard case', but might eventually fail in critical situations, Bainbridge's [16] irony becomes even more paradox.

3.3 Insufficient Situation Awareness

Situation awareness describes "a person's state of knowledge about a dynamic environment" [26, p. 60]. It includes the perception and comprehension of elements that are part of this environment, as well as the respective projection of future states based on this understanding [26]. In dynamic systems control, situation awareness is a prerequisite for making adequate decisions. If situational awareness is insufficient, it is more likely that humans make wrong decision. Human factors literature describes this adverse state also as «out-of-the-loop unfamiliarity», illustrating a situation in which the operator/user takes unnecessary much time to get back into the control 'loop' [27].

4 Design Guidelines

Besides general design processes and guidelines, e.g. [11,28,29], there are several attempts to provide specific guidance for designing Human-AV interactions. Recent collections, e.g. [1,30], focus on adapting approved general guidelines featuring a human-centred perspective. For instance, the People+AI Guidebook by Google [30] emphasizes an explicit focus on solving an actual problem where the strengths of AI can be used to support user needs. It is mandatory to find the right balance between augmenting and automating tasks - instead of simply adding AI functions on top of existing products just because of their technological feasibility or for marketese advertisements. Furthermore,'reward functions' of AI systems determining how AI defines successes and failures need to be designed and evaluated considering various perspectives and - if possible - be communicated to users [30]. In the same spirit, Amershi et al. (Microsoft) [1] put forward to "Make [the user] clear what the system can do" and how well it can do that. Building on the work of Horvitz [31], they propose 18 *AI usability guidelines* (see Table 1 for an excerpt), each complemented with a description and detailed examples. The set is split up in 4 categories: *initially* (G1–G2), *during interaction* (G3–G6), *when wrong* (G7–G11) and *over time* (G12–G18). While Amershi et al. [1] introduce the set as generally applicable, they also note an inherent trade-off in terms of its validity for specific applications.

Table 1. AI design guidelines by Amershi et al. (Microsoft) [1].

AI Design Guidelines	
G1	Make clear what the system can do
G2	Make clear how well the system can do what it can do
G3	Time services based on context
G4	Show contextually relevant information
G5	Match relevant social norms
G6	Mitigate social biases.
G7	Support efficient invocation
G8	Support efficient dismissal
G9	Support efficient correction
G10	Scope services when in doubt
G11	Make clear why the system did what it did
G12	Remember recent interactions
G13	Learn from user behavior
G14	Update and adapt cautiously
G15	Encourage granular feedback
G16	Convey the consequences of user actions
G17	Provide global controls
G18	Notify users about changes

5   Case Studies

In this section, we present three case studies that exemplify the design of AI-injected systems in different domains, discuss respective underlying interaction types and carve out some of the learnings we gathered. During the description of the projects, we also refer to the guidelines summarized in Table 1 to point to their usefulness. Using the model by Parasuraman, Sheridan and Wickens [13], Fig. 1 provides an overview of the studies by classifying their automation level along a continuum from low (fully manual performance) to high (full automation) in four functions: information acquisition, information analysis, decision selection and action implementation. The first case study, IMEDALytics (Sect. 5.1), is taken from a project targeted at the development of a decision-support system (DSS) for individualized medical risk assessment, monitoring, and therapy management in intensive care medicine. The second project, APEROL (Sect. 5.2), focuses on the development of autonomous mobility-on-demand public buses and the required services for their operation. The final case study, Predictive prototyping (Sect. 5.3), introduces ANTETYPE, a state-of-the-art user interface prototyping tool that we combined with the ACT-R Cognitive Architecture (see [9]) to support the prediction of human behavior based on synthetic cognitive models. We selected these examples from the pool of our current research projects to not only present cases from different domains, but also to consider different types of Human-AI interaction. While the interaction type «guardian angel» (see [32]) – resembling an automatic machine with a 'protective' character – prevails in the APEROL case, interaction in IMEDALytics can be adequately characterized as type of «colleague». Similar to that, users of the ANTETYPE prototyping tool interact with the respective AI-enhanced prediction module in a «best friend» style, where the tool acts as a partner who assists with delivering requested results.

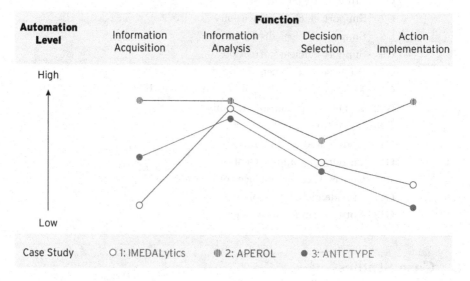

Fig. 1. Description of our case studies using an adaptation of the model by Parasuraman, Sheridan, and Wickens [13].

5.1   IMEDALytics: Clinical DSS for Intensive Care

Personalized medicine is a research field that unites many disciplines. The mutual aim of personal medicine is to treat patients based on their individual parameters, including their physiological constitution, gender-specific characteristics, or the results of an analysis of their genetic codes. Even highly skilled professionals are unable to recognize the complex statistical interrelations between all these parameters. Algorithmic analyses, however, can successfully rise to that challenge and detect meaningful patterns in complex data sets. It is paramount to present the ramified information—and possible identified patterns—to physicians in an unambiguous and understandable way, classifying the task as a problem of Explainable AI (XAI, see [33]). On the one hand, the healthcare staff's requirement to act rapidly under time pressure needs to be met. Simultaneously, the system needs to offer enough informational depth to persuade physicians and nurses to even consider the information in the first place.

In IMEDALytics, an ongoing applied research project, we are designing an AI-based system to support high-consequence clinical decision-making in intensive care units (ICU). This type of system belongs to the category of clinical decision support systems (CDSS). With the adoption of electronic patient records and significant advances in AI technology, CDSSs have the potential - from a technical perspective - to provide complementary insights into medical prediction, diagnosis and/or treatment choice [34–40]. Although CDSS can potentially enhance the quality of care, it is noteworthy that many CDSS—despite considerable progress in AI technology—still fail to be adopted into clinical practice [41,42]. An insufficient understanding of user needs due to lacking user research, as well as deficient considerations of HCI guidelines in system design are claimed to be main causes for the failure of adoption [43–47]. Results of Khairat et al. [45] indicate, based on a critical review of CDSS papers focusing on user acceptance, that poor workflow integration, questionable validity of systems, excessive interference by the systems and efficiency issues are often related to lower user acceptance.

Within a qualitative field study, Yang et al. [42] investigated a particular use case of a prognostic CDSS: the medical decision-making process for a ventricular assist device to partially replace heart functions. The authors likewise identified a lack of trust in the capabilities of an AI-injected CDSS to assist in difficult cases. Beyond this finding, they failed to observe the need for such support as the observed clinicians felt that they "knew how to effectively factor patient conditions into clinical decisions" [42]. In sum, Yang et al. argued for the necessity to carefully consider the social context. There is an urgent need for designers to gain a deeper understanding of CDSSs, their (future) users and their particular contexts of use to maximize opportunities for CDSSs.

While research within the fields of Medicine, Medical Informatics, and AI has until today mainly focused on supporting decisions for arriving at the correct diagnosis or the prediction of a deterioration of a patient's state [36–40], our case study focuses on supporting continuous decisions for optimal therapy, more precisely volume therapy. Volume therapy is defined as infusion therapy that serves to compensate for a volume deficit inside blood vessels. The particular challenge for treating ICU physicians is to determine the optimal, individualized indication for each patient based on medical guidelines and to administer the correct dose and the most suitable infusion solution. Incorrect therapy can result in undesired long-term consequences such as the need for long-term care or long-term ventilation. In IMEDALytics we focus on assisting physicians in individualized medical risk assessment, monitoring, and therapy management for volume therapy.

We argue, that in order to holistically support decision-making processes in intensive medicine, a change of perspective from classical problem solving through technology to the design of experience potentials is essential. Questions with which we were faced during project work ranged from general questions regarding the creation of positive Human-AI-Interaction to specific questions on data visualization techniques:

1. How can we combine the human abilities of healthcare professionals - such as their general understanding, their previous experiences, their flexibility and creativity in the decision-making process - with the powerful possibilities of an AI-based system?
2. How can we make the diagnosis and therapy suggestions provided by the system accessible to healthcare professionals without depriving their self-efficacy?
3. Which design processes are needed to design an interactive interface that leads to a long-term positive UX?
4. Which influence has (the type of) presented information - e.g. in the form of information visualizations - on the perceived transparency or even trust in a CDSS?

Understanding UX in Volume Therapy. To gradually address these questions and to derive solutions from the aforementioned perspective "experiences before functionality (technologies)", we chose an experience design approach as proposed by Hassenzahl [48]. This approach focuses on the user and concentrates first on his or her experience. Experiences are analyzed by using psychological needs to identify why an experience is considered positive.

In the very beginning of our project, our goal was to gain a detailed understanding of how physicians and nurses work together to make decisions around volume therapy and how CDSSs can be integrated into their daily clinical work. In particular, we wanted to understand decision-making within the specific organizational framework of an ICU and within a heterogeneous team. To gain insights into these experiences, we conducted contextual inquiries (observations and semi-structured interviews) [49] in three German ICUs [50]. We transferred and visualized our findings on workflows, situations, actions, emotions, context, and interactions that a (future) user may experience during a typical day along a time axis into a user experience map [51], thereby blending well-established UX methods and service design techniques. We modified conventional user experience maps to emphasize collaboration by including two users instead of one against the background of the ICU context. The goal of working with a user experience map was to aid discovery of experience opportunities that a CDSS for volume therapy might bring. Our findings show that adapting a system's interface to both, context and users, facilitates collaboration and embraces interactions with a CDSS to combine human and machine intelligence [50].

Subsequent to this ethnographic approach, we chose to complement our insights with additional interviews to validate gathered findings and to discuss initial design concepts derived from these findings with nurses and physicians. Therefore, we are applying a method inspired by Séguin et al.'s proposed *Triptech* approach [52] featuring storyboards to collect prospective users' reactions (likes/dislikes/potential use cases/questions/concerns) to early design concepts. In contrast to the Triptech approach that is used in focus groups, we are using the storyboards in individual interviews (Fig. 2). In a first step, interviewees assess the extent to which psychological needs (see [53], e.g., autonomy, competence, security) in volume therapy are currently met. This enables us to place an increased focus on the psychological needs according to Hassenzahl et al. [53] within the volume therapy and use psychological need statements as an impulse for the presentation of first concept drafts (second step). To gather user feedback, we present three to five design concepts in this second step that address the psychological needs that the interviewee prioritized in the initial step. The design concepts consist of storyboards (see Fig. 2) and help us to discuss design concepts with a focus on interviewees' experiences. Using storyboards, we enable prospective users to better imagine situations where CDSS support is desirable. Particularly, we intent to gather information on how to provide proper granular feedback (G15) and on how to clearly communicate users why the system did what it did (G11).

Fig. 2. Example storyboard for collecting first reactions to early design concepts for volume therapy CDSS.

As AI in the IMEDALytics case takes over the role of a 'colleague' (see [32]) supporting nurses and physicians particularly in their decision selection, considering this aspect is crucial to set the appropriate tone in the communication with users. I.e. system design has to carefully take the needs and user requirements into account to satisfy the mentioned guidelines by [1]. This in turn provides the preconditions to arrive at an appropriate level of trust and to facilitate system acceptance. In contrast to the 'colleague' metaphor, the AI-based system in APEROL, our second case study, can be described as an automatic 'guardian angle'.

5.2   APEROL: Autonomous Mobility-on-Demand

In autonomous mobility-on-demand systems, passengers are transported by robotic, self-driving cars [54], i.e. by vehicles with high or full driving automation (SAE levels 4 or 5 [55]). Due to the rapid progresses in vehicle automation, such AI-driven autonomous vehicles (AVs) will soon be introduced to the public. As a result, the use of public, demand-oriented transport systems and autonomous ride sharing will become reality in our daily commuting. Since AMoD services will be always available and neither rely on scheduled timetables nor on fixed stops, they will provide spatial and temporal flexibility to passengers while increasing efficiency and sustainability of transport systems [54,56]. Consequently, fewer vehicles will then be on our roads in terms of both riding and parking. AMoD offers great potential to solve major challenges of today's public transport systems, e.g. regarding congestion prevention, accessibility and first/last mile problems [54,56–58]. Traffic simulations on the integration of AMoD systems in major metropolises - e.g. New York City and Singapore [54] - support this promising conclusion and provide evidence for their effectiveness and efficiency. In addition, gained free time (due to not being engaged with the driving task) might increase our productivity or can be used for communication and relaxation [59], resulting in overall societal benefits.

Despite achieving technical maturity, AVs face major challenges with regard to public adoption. Adoption barriers include (inappropriate) user expectations, concerns about the technology's reliability, performance and security, as well as privacy considerations—and most important of all: trust issues [18]. To counteract these challenges, a precise understanding of people, systems, and their respective environment is essential [19]. A clear comprehension of a user's experience journey using an AMoD system enables the thorough design of corresponding touch points (i.e. HMIs) and Human-AV (i.e. Human-AI) interactions. Touch point design is a vital part of our publicly funded project APEROL (Autonomous, Personal Organization of Road Traffic and Digital Logistics; [60]). After having gathered a thorough understanding of the context of use through extensive user research in this project, we now focus on two main questions:

1. How can we create an enjoyable UX for (future) passengers when interacting with AVs before, during and after use?
2. How can we efficiently evaluate design concepts for the required interfaces at the respective touch points - especially in very early phases of the development?

In the next sections we provide insights on how we are tackling the aforementioned questions within the project APEROL.

Understanding UX in AMoD. In contrast to lower levels of driving automation, all occupants of AVs (SAE levels 4 and 5 [55]) are passengers that do not need to take care of the vehicle's driving at all. This situation can roughly be compared to taking a taxi. A main difference is, however, that no (human) driver, who controls the vehicle or can communicate with passengers, is present in AVs. Thus, there is no driver asking passengers where they want to go or notifying them when there is a traffic jam ahead. Instead, AI has to take over both responsibilities. The AI-powered system conducts primary driving tasks, i.e. navigating, steering and stabilization (see [61] for further elaboration), as well as secondary driving tasks (e.g. light control). To do this, environmental data from multiple sensor inputs (e.g. from stereo cameras, lidar and radar) is collected and analyzed in real-time, applying AI-based and stochastic algorithms for object detection and tracking. The algorithms use - for instance - artificial neural networks to recognize roads, other vehicles and infrastructure (e.g. [62]) or to predict the path of pedestrians and cyclists (e.g. [63]). Combining the sensor information with HD maps and GNSS data enables the AV to plan its movements through complex traffic environments. Even for sophisticated researchers such AI systems typically remain - at least to some extent - "black boxes" [64]. Ordinary passengers, not having knowledge about their capabilities, can experience a loss of control and a corresponding feeling of insecurity, making it difficult to establish an appropriate level of trust. However, trust is considered to be an essential prerequisite for technology acceptance (e.g. [24]). By providing passengers with appropriate information and feedback about the AV's current state, its activities and its intentions we intend to support trust calibration and aim to compensate the absence of a human driver.

To foster a comprehensive understanding of future AMoD users, their needs and requirements, prospective users need to be continuously integrated into the development process [65] from early phases on. Within the APEROL project, we co-conducted a citizens' dialogue on autonomous driving with a representative sample of 76 prospective users of an AMoD service [66]. The findings of this dialogue supported the challenges of Human-AI interaction mentioned above and served as a foundation for design considerations and decisions.

Designing Human-AV Interactions. Strengthened by insights from our user research activities we consider well-designed and trustworthy systems with an enjoyable UX as crucial to counteract the hurdles of AMoD adoption. Such systems inform and enable passengers (1) to understand the signals, intentions and actions of (AI-controlled) AVs, (2) communicate their own intents and needs, and (3) to foster an adequate level of trust towards the technology. Based on our research results and its synthesis with AI design guidelines (Sect. 4) we developed two conceptual design proposals for Human-AV interaction: an in-vehicle passenger information display and a smartphone travel app. The interface proposals are still in early concept phases and are currently evaluated in a study involving a representative user sample. By presenting these initial interface drafts we, nevertheless, hope to contribute to a discussion on the creation of efficient and enjoyable UX for future AMoD systems.

Smartphone App. Since there are no driving-related controls (e.g. steering wheel, gas pedal) available in AVs, the main user interface in AMoD systems will probably be a (smartphone) app. Particularly following AI Design Guidelines G1, G3, G4, G17 and G18 (Table 1), our app concept focuses on providing users with adequate information to arrive at a profound level of situation awareness, as well as on offering control functionalities while taking a ride in a (shared) AV.

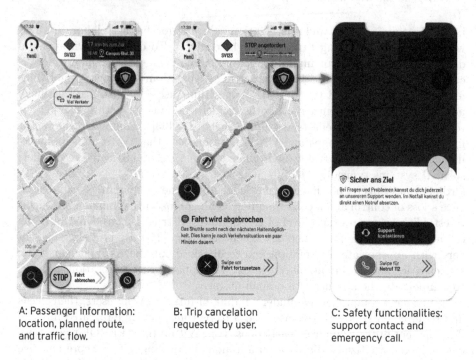

A: Passenger information: location, planned route, and traffic flow.

B: Trip cancelation requested by user.

C: Safety functionalities: support contact and emergency call.

Fig. 3. Conceptual design screens for a AMoD smartphone app. Created as part of the *APEROL* project.

Figure 3 shows three different states of the app concept's main screen during a ride. The app displays the AV's location, its planned route and traffic information in the map (Fig. 3: A) and provides - similar to hardware buttons in public busses - a "STOP" functionality (Fig. 3: B) to support efficient correction (G9; Table 1). In addition, an emergency button (see also [67]) provides direct access to customer support and emergency functionalities (Fig. 3: C).

In-Vehicle Passenger Information Display. Passenger information systems promise to increase user acceptance and customer comfort of public transport systems [68]. Similar to the smartphone app, our in-vehicle HMI concept for a shared AV encompasses a map displaying current location, route, planned stops as well as traffic conditions (Fig. 4: A, B, D). Furthermore, personal ticket IDs (Fig. 4: C) are displayed in a 'stop list' to anonymously communicate drop-off stops to respective passengers. When booking a ride, passengers receive the ticket ID which then functions as an (anonymous) allocator for individual passenger information. The in-vehicle HMI enables the passengers to get all required information without having to constantly monitor their smartphone, while at the same time protecting their privacy requirements.

Evaluating Human-AV Interactions. Since "autonomous ridesharing is still a theoretical subject [...,] users still lack the hands-on experience" [69] and field

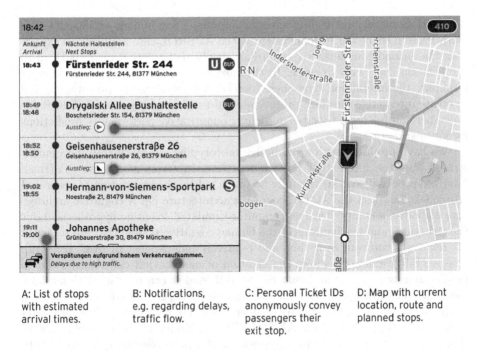

A: List of stops with estimated arrival times.

B: Notifications, e.g. regarding delays, traffic flow.

C: Personal Ticket IDs anonymously convey passengers their exit stop.

D: Map with current location, route and planned stops.

Fig. 4. Conceptual design of an in-vehicle passenger information display for AMoD. Created as part of the *APEROL* project.

studies with AVs are only practicable within tight boundaries impairing the results, adequate methods and tools are needed for exploration, prototyping and evaluation (see also [7]). Such methods are, however, necessary to enable continuous and iterative evaluations of interface and service concepts. For expert-based evaluation, guidelines (e.g. [1] are good starting points. Generally, the interaction with AVs and AMoD systems is highly context-sensitive, making the actual usage situation an essential aspect of evaluation setups. Context-based prototyping and empirical simulation studies are needed to conduct proper user experience evaluations. To meet these requirements, we constructed a simple video-based AV simulator with a CAVE-like environment. Placed in a standard office room, our AV simulator enables stakeholders and users to experience a simulated (shared) ride in an AV (see [70] for further elaboration). Initial user studies incorporating the setup [70] show promising results regarding both presence perception and its suitability for valid and context-sensitive usability testing.

5.3   AI-Based Predictive Prototyping

In the IMEDALytics case study we presented an AI-based clinical decision support system that will assists physicians in individualized medical risk assessment, monitoring, and therapy management in the—clearly circumscribed—domain of volume therapy. The assumed interaction type with the system can be characterized as physicians dealing with a competent, non-human «colleague» (see [32]). Passengers of the AMoD system in the APEROL case are likely to experience the autonomous bus as a «guardian angel» that safely transports them to the location they wish to reach. In the case study discussed in this section we exemplify the interaction type «best friend»: A designer uses a prototyping tool to create interactive interface prototypes and asks an AI-injected module of the tool—her helpful «best friend»—to deliver quantitative performance predictions for given scenarios.

We have proposed such a predictive prototyping approach [71] and demonstrated how the interaction performance (e.g. in terms of efficiency) of user interface proposals can successfully be predicted by the integration of generated AI-models based on the ACT-R cognitive architecture [9]. A cognitive architecture embodies a comprehensive, computer-simulated scientific hypothesis about the structures and mechanisms of the human cognitive system that are regarded "as relatively constant over time and relatively independent of task" [72, 312]. The ACT-R framework allows the creation of models that can then be run to predict and explain human behavior. ACT-R models can interact with an environment and learn (on a symbolic and sub-symbolic, neurally-inspired level) to adapt the behavior to the statistical structure of an environment. We have integrated ACT-R as a module in ANTETYPE, a commercial design tool to create sophisticated, responsive UI prototypes for desktop, mobile and web-based applications [73]. ANTETYPE was designed to support a seamless transition from the development of early wireframes defining the layout of an interface, over the creation of visual design alternatives to the creation of complex, responsive, interactive prototypes without switching between different software tools.

An ACT-R model is derived automatically using ANTETYPE's *monitoring mode* from observing a designer demonstrating the interactions to complete a relevant key scenario with an interface prototype. If interactions depend on the setting of specific values shown in the interface, (simulated) user actions can alternatively be described using a graphical inspector interface in ANTETYPE's *instruction mode*. To run simulated users on a prototype, a designer simply (1) demonstrates the necessary steps to complete a task scenario, and (if necessary) (2) instructs the model using ANTETYPE's instruction mode. After a designer has finished task demonstration, an ACT-R model is automatically generated by mechanisms described in detail in [71]. The model is then run on the scenario to create a distribution of performance times for a number of trials using the respective interface prototype. In this setting, the designer interacts with the prediction module by asking a «best friend» for performance predictions: the AI-based friend then delivers the results just like a friend would do after running a study. In our case, however, the participants are generated, synthetic users and the study is run automatically for an arbitrary number of trials. Figure 5 shows an example of using predictive prototyping to comparatively predict the performances of using three different interfaces for a given scenario (listening to a playlist on mobile music players, e.g. Spotify, QQMusic and a revised version of Spotify).

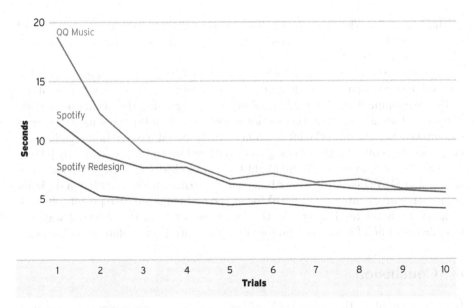

Fig. 5. Performance predictions for three different music player interfaces. Created as part of the *ANTETYPE* project.

The outlined predictive prototyping method illustrates how quantitative performance predictions (like time-on task, initial learning to skilled behavior) can support designers by providing quick and valid analyses of the performance consequences of design variants. Alternative design proposals can be compared with regard to defined quantitative performance metrics without the need to conduct effortful empirical usability evaluations. Predictive prototyping thus allows iteration cycles to be accelerated. It is, of course, not our goal to replace empirical usability tests. They remain an irreplaceable method to identify conceptual usability barriers or receive qualitative information about a user's experience with a system. In fact, predictive prototyping is in some sense complementary to empirical studies since it provides a promising approach to gather quantitative performance data that is beyond the (practical) scope of usability tests in a lab. We argue, that quantitative performance predictions cannot reliably be derived from empirical usability tests because (1) participants are typically not repeatedly exposed to a given test task: skilled performance—and learning—are, however, a function of the number of practice trials; (2) thinking-aloud, as a standard requirement for participants during usability test, interferes with the primary process of working on a task (see [74]); (3) most instructions in usability tests do not even require participants "to work as fast as possible" and (4) participants are aware of being recorded during usability tests and might thus focus on avoiding errors instead of working as efficient as possible on a (new) given task. By providing a solution to these objections, AI-based predictive modeling opens up new possibilities for interface designers. Initial applications of the method in real-world projects and encouraging goodness-of-fit comparisons of predicted and empirically observed user data provided evidence for the validity of the approach (see [71]).

The first and second case study reported in this paper emphasize how the methodological apparatus of human-centered design approaches can contribute to the development of better AI-based systems, increasing the likelihood of their adoption. The case study in this section shows how prototyping of user interfaces can directly benefit from the integration of an AI-based module that significantly enhances the scope of a prototyping tool. With regard to the guidelines by [1] (see Sect. 4), we want to especially highlight G2 (Make clear why the system did what it did) and G13 (Learn from user behavior). Learning from users (i.e. a designer demonstrating an interaction path) forms the basis of predictive prototyping. To support an understanding of *why* the model performs in the observed way, the module offers helpful visualization and tracing option to explain its behavior.

6   Conclusion

In order to explore the relationship of humans and AI, we presented three case studies for Human-AI interaction from our lab . These studies can, of course, only cover a small portion of the wide and 'tension-full' field where AI meets UX. The discussed challenges, guidelines, ideas and learnings might, however, be useful for further reference and exploration in other domains.

We illustrated the necessity to design understandable and trustworthy systems and the need to carefully consider contextual factors. CDSS, for example, still lack adoption in clinical practice, although their performance and capabilities have intensively improved over the last years due to the progress in AI technology [41,42]. We claim that a core reason for this can be traced back to a lack of acceptance that is due to negligence of considering user requirements and context during the design process. As Lacher et al. [19] point out, it is crucial to understand people, systems and context in order to counteract respective challenges—and this might be of particular importance when designing dynamic, machine learning-based systems.

We appreciate the rich value of AI capabilities for UX and contemplate AI as an enabler of new (product) experiences, while at the same tine emphasising the eminent role of UX methods and frameworks for envisioning and creating positive interactions between humans and AI. Established UX methods and service design techniques need to be applied and, where necessary, adapted to tackle the challenges of AI-based automation. We thus consider the relationship of UX and AI as mutually beneficial.

Acknowledgements. This work has been funded by the German Federal Ministry of Education and Research (BMBF) under the grant numbers 13GW0280B and 02L15A212 as well as by the German Federal Ministry of Transport and Digital Infrastructure (BMVI) under the grant number 16AVF2134A.

References

1. Amershi, S., et al.: Guidelines for Human-AI interaction. In: Proceedings of the 2019 CHI Conference on Human Factors in Computing Systems. ACM Glasgow (2019)
2. Lighthill, J.: Artificial intelligence: a general survey. In: Artificial Intelligence: a Paper Symposium (1973)
3. Glenn, J.C., Millennium Project Team: Work/Technology 2050: Scenarios and Actions, technical report, The Millennium Project, Washington (2019)
4. Cramer, H., Kim, J.: Confronting the tensions where UX meets AI. Interactions 26(6), 69–71 (2019)
5. Eden, G.: Transforming cars into computers: interdisciplinary opportunities for HCI. In: Proceedings of the 32nd International BCS Human Computer Interaction Conference (HCI 2018), no. July (2018)
6. Loi, D., Wolf, C.T., Blomberg, J.L., Arar, R., Brereton, M.: Co-designing AI futures: integrating AI ethics, social computing, and design. In: DIS 2019 Companion - Companion Publication of the 2019 ACM Designing Interactive Systems Conference, no. Ml, pp. 381–384 (2019)
7. Churchill, E.F., Van Allen, P., Kuniavsky, M.: Designing AI. Interactions 25(6), 35–37 (2018)
8. Nilsson, N.J.: Artificial Intelligence: A New Synthesis. Morgan Kaufmann Publishers Inc., San Francisco (1998)
9. Anderson, J.R., Bothell, D., Byrne, M.D., Douglass, S., Lebiere, C., Qin, Y.: An integrated theory of the mind. Psychol. Rev. 111(4), 1036–1060 (2004)
10. Vajapey, K.: What's the Difference Between AI, ML, Deep Learning, and Active Learning? (2019)
11. DIN Deutsches Institut für Normung e, V.: Ergonomics of human-system interaction - Part 210: Human-centred design for interactive systems (ISO 9241–210:2010) English translation of DIN EN ISO 9241–210:2011–01 (2011)
12. Parasuraman, R., Riley, V.: Humans and automation: use, misuse, disuse, abuse. Hum. Factors: J. Hum. Factors Ergon. Soc. 39(2), 230–253 (1997)
13. Parasuraman, R., Sheridan, T.B., Wickens, C.D.: A model for types and levels of human interaction with automation. IEEE Trans. Syst. Man Cybern.-Part A: Syst. Hum. 30(3), 286–297 (2000)
14. Flemisch, F., Kelsch, J., Löper, C., Schieben, A., Schindler, J.: Automation spectrum, inner/outer compatibility and other potentially useful human factors concepts for assistance and automation. Hum. Factors Assist. Autom. 2008, 1–16 (2008)
15. Bibby, K.S., Margulies, F., Rijnsdorp, J.E., Withers, R.M.J., Makarov, I.M.: Man's role in control systems. In: 6th IFAC Congress Boston (1975)
16. Bainbridge, L.: Ironies of automation. Automatica 19(6), 775–779 (1983)
17. Manzey, D.: Systemgestaltung und Automatisierung. In: Badke-Schaub, P., Hofinger, G., Lauche, K. (eds.) Human Factors, 2nd edn, pp. 333–352. Springer, Berlin, Heidelberg (2012). https://doi.org/10.1007/978-3-642-19886-1_19. Chapter 19
18. Kaur, K., Rampersad, G.: Trust in driverless cars: investigating key factors influencing the adoption of driverless cars. J. Eng. Technol. Manage. 48, 87–96 (2018)
19. Lacher, A., Grabowski, R., Cook, S.: Autonomy, trust, and transportation. In: Proceedings of the 2014 AAAI Spring Symposium, pp. 42–49 (2014)
20. Wolf, I.: Wechselwirkung Mensch und autonomer agent. In: Maurer, M., Gerdes, J.C., Lenz, B., Winner, H. (eds.) Autonomes Fahren, pp. 103–125. Springer, Heidelberg (2015). https://doi.org/10.1007/978-3-662-45854-9_6
21. Lee, J.D., See, K.A.: Trust in automation: designing for appropriate reliance. Hum. factors 46(1), 50–80 (2004)

22. Muir, B.M.: Trust in automation: Part I. theoretical issues in the study of trust and human intervention in automated systems. Ergonomics **37**(11), 1905–1922 (1994)
23. Davis, F.D., Bagozzi, R.P., Warshaw, P.R.: User acceptance of computer technology: a comparison of two theoretical models. Manage. Sci. **35**(8), 982–1003 (1989)
24. Carsten, O., Martens, M.H.: How can humans understand their automated cars? HMI principles, problems and solutions. Cognit. Technol. Work **21**(1), 3–20 (2018). https://doi.org/10.1007/s10111-018-0484-0
25. Bubb, H.: Das Regelkreisparadigma der Ergonomie. Automobilergonomie. A, pp. 27–65. Springer, Wiesbaden (2015). https://doi.org/10.1007/978-3-8348-2297-0_2
26. Endsley, M.R., Kiris, E.O.: The out-of-the-loop performance problem and level of control in automation. Hum. Factors: J. Hum. Factors Ergon. Soc. **37**(2), 381–394 (1995)
27. Wickens, C.D.: Designing for situation awareness and trust in automation. IFAC Proc. Vol. **28**(23), 365–370 (1994)
28. DIN Deutsches Institut für Normung e, V.: DIN EN ISO 9241–110:2008–09 Ergonomics Of Human-System Interaction - Part 110: Dialogue Principles (ISO 9241–110:2006) English Version Of DIN EN ISO 9241–110:2008–09 (2008)
29. Nielsen, J.: Heuristic evaluation. In: Nielsen, J., Mack, R. (eds.) Usability Inspection Methods, ch. 2, pp. 25–62. John Wiley, New York (1994)
30. Google: People + AI Guidebook: User Needs + Defining Success (2020)
31. Horvitz, E.: Proceedings of the SIGCHI conference on human factors in computing systems the CHI is the limit - CHI 1999, In: Proceedings of the SIGCHI Conference on Human Factors in Computing Systems, no. May, pp. 159–166 (1999)
32. Alan, Y., Urbach, N., Hinsen, S., Jöhnk, J., Beisel, P., Weißert, M.: Think beyond tomorrow - KI, mein Freund und Helfer - Herausforderungen und Implikationen für die Mensch-KI-Interaktion, technical report, EY & Fraunhofer FIT, Bayreuth (2019)
33. Samek, W., Wiegand, T., Müller, K.-R.: Explainable Artificial Intelligence: Understanding, Visualizing and Interpreting Deep Learning Models (2017)
34. McKinney, S.M., et al.: International evaluation of an AI system for breast cancer screening. Nature **577**(7788), 89–94 (2020)
35. Gulshan, V., et al.: Performance of a deep-learning algorithm vs manual grading for detecting diabetic retinopathy in India. JAMA Ophthalmol. **137**(9), 987–993 (2019)
36. Komorowski, M., Celi, L.A., Badawi, O., Gordon, A., Faisal, A.: The artificial intelligence clinician learns optimal treatment strategies for sepsis in intensive care. Nat. Med. **24**, 11 (2018)
37. Krishnan, G.S., Sowmya Kamath, S.: A supervised learning approach for ICU mortality prediction based on unstructured electrocardiogram text reports. In: Silberztein, M., Atigui, F., Kornyshova, E., Métais, E., Meziane, F. (eds.) NLDB 2018. LNCS, vol. 10859, pp. 126–134. Springer, Cham (2018). https://doi.org/10.1007/978-3-319-91947-8_13
38. Ettori, F., et al.: Impact of a computer-assisted decision support system (CDSS) on nutrition management in critically ill hematology patients: the nutchoco study (nutritional care in hematology oncologic patients and critical outcome). Ann. Intensive Care **9**(1), 53 (2019)
39. Tafelski, S., et al.: Supporting antibiotic therapy in German ICUS - analysis of user friendliness and satisfaction with a computer-assisted stewardship programme. Anasthesiologie und Intensivmedizin **57**, 174–181 (2016)
40. Saeed, M., Lieu, C., Raber, G., Mark, R.G.: Mimic ii: a massive temporal ICU patient database to support research in intelligent patient monitoring. In: Computers in Cardiology, pp. 641–644, September 2002

41. Belard, A., et al.: Precision diagnosis: a view of the clinical decision support systems (CDSS) landscape through the lens of critical care. J. Clin. Monitor. Comput. **31**, 02 (2016)
42. Yang, Q., Zimmerman, J., Steinfeld, A., Carey, L., Antaki, J.F.: Investigating the heart pump implant decision process: opportunities for decision support tools to help. In: Proceedings of the 2016 CHI Conference on Human Factors in Computing Systems, CHI 2016, New York, USA, pp. 4477–4488. ACM (2016)
43. McGinn, T.: Cds, UX, and system redesign - promising techniques and tools to bridge the evidence gap. In: EGEMS, Washington, DC, vol. 3, p. 1184, July 2015
44. Sittig, D.F., et al.: Grand challenges in clinical decision support. J. Biomed. Inform. **41**, 387–392 (2008)
45. Khairat, S., Marc, D., Crosby, W., Al Sanousi, A.: Reasons for physicians not adopting clinical decision support systems: critical analysis. JMIR Med. Inform. **6**(2), e24 (2018)
46. Horsky, J., Schiff, G.D., Johnston, D., Mercincavage, L., Bell, D., Middleton, B.: Interface design principles for usable decision support: a targeted review of best practices for clinical prescribing interventions. J. Biomed. Inform. **45**(6), 1202–1216 (2012)
47. Cai, C.J., Winter, S., Steiner, D., Wilcox, L. and Terry, M.: "Hello AI": uncovering the onboarding needs of medical practitioners for human-AI collaborative decision-making. In: Proceedings of ACM Human-Computer Interaction, vol. 3, November 2019
48. Hassenzahl, M.: Experience design: technology for all the right reasons. Synth. Lect. Hum.-Centered Inform. **3**(1), 01–95 (2010)
49. Beyer, H., Holtzblatt, K.: Contextual Design: Defining Customer-Centered Systems. Morgan Kaufmann Publishers Inc., San Francisco (1997)
50. Kaltenhauser, A., Rheinstädter, V., Butz, A., Wallach, D.: "You Have to Piece the Puzzle Together" - Designing for Decision Support in Intensive Care. In: Proceedings of the Designing Interactive Systems Conference 2020 (DIS 2020). Association for Computing Machinery, New York (2020). https://doi.org/10.1145/3357236.3395436
51. Kalbach, J.: Mapping Experiences: A Complete Guide to Creating Value Through Journeys, Blueprints, and Diagrams, 1st edn. O'Reilly Media Inc., Newton (2016)
52. Séguin, J.A., Scharff, A., Pedersen, K.: Triptech: a method for evaluating early design concepts. In: Extended Abstracts of the 2019 CHI Conference on Human Factors in Computing Systems, CHI EA 2019. NY, USA. Association for Computing Machinery, New York (2019)
53. Hassenzahl, M., Diefenbach, S., Göritz, A.: Needs, affect, and interactive products-Facets of user experience. Interact. Comput. **22**(5), 353–362 (2010)
54. Pavone, M.: Autonomous mobility-on-demand systems for future urban mobility. In: Maurer, M., Gerdes, J.C., Lenz, B., Winner, H. (eds.) Autonomes Fahren, pp. 399–416. Springer, Heidelberg (2015). https://doi.org/10.1007/978-3-662-45854-9_19
55. SAE International: J3016-JUN2018 - Surface Vehicle Recommend Practice: Taxonomy and Definitions for Terms Related to Driving Automation Systems for On-Road Motor Vehicles (2018)
56. Spieser, K., Treleaven, K., Zhang, R., Frazzoli, E., Morton, D., Pavone, M.: Toward a systematic approach to the design and evaluation of automated mobility-on-demand systems: a case study in Singapore. In: Meyer, G., Beiker, S. (eds.) Road Vehicle Automation. LNM, pp. 229–245. Springer, Cham (2014). https://doi.org/10.1007/978-3-319-05990-7_20

57. Chong, Z.J., et al.: Autonomy for mobility on demand. In: Proceedings of the 12th International Conference on Intelligent Autonomous Systems (IAS 2013), vol. 293, pp. 671–682, Springer, Heidelberg (2013). https://doi.org/10.1007/978-3-642-33926-4_64

58. Hinderer, H., Stegmuller, J., Schmidt, J., Sommer, J., Lucke, J.: Acceptance of autonomous vehicles in suburban public transport. In: Proceedings of the 2018 IEEE International Conference on Engineering, Technology and Innovation (ICE/ITMC 2018) (2018)

59. Fraunhofer IAO and Horváth & Partners: The Value of Time - Nutzerbezogene Service-Potenziale durch autonomes Fahren, technical report, Stuttgart (2016)

60. APEROL i.V. PSI Logistics GmbH. www.autonomousshuttle.de - APEROL - Autonome personenbezogene Organisation des Straßenverkehrs und digitale Logistik (2019)

61. Bubb, H., Bengler, K., Breuninger, J., Gold, C., Helmbrecht, M.: Systemergonomie des Fahrzeugs. Automobilergonomie. A, pp. 259–344. Springer, Wiesbaden (2015). https://doi.org/10.1007/978-3-8348-2297-0_6

62. Sun, Z., Bebis, G., Miller, R.: On-road vehicle detection: a review. IEEE Trans. Pattern Anal. Mach. Intell. **28**(5), 694–711 (2006)

63. Kooij, J.F., Flohr, F., Pool, E.A., Gavrila, D.M.: Context-based path prediction for targets with switching dynamics. Int. J. Comput. Vision **127**(3), 239–262 (2019)

64. Olden, J.D., Jackson, D.A.: Illuminating the "black box": a randomization approach for understanding variable contributions in artificial neural networks. Ecol. Model. **154**(1–2), 135–150 (2002)

65. Brell, T.: Aachener Bürgerdialog zum Thema autonome Mobilität (2019)

66. Brell, T., Philipsen, R., Ziefle, M.: Suspicious minds? - users' perceptions of autonomous and connected driving. Theor. Issues Ergon. Sci. **20**(3), 301–331 (2019)

67. Uber: Uber's Emergency Button (2019)

68. Beul-Leusmann, S., Jakobs, E.M., Ziefle, M.: User-centered design of passenger information systems. In: Proceedings of the IEEE International Professional Communication 2013 Conference (IPCC 2013) (2013)

69. Philipsen, R., Brell, T., Ziefle, M.: Carriage Without a driver – user requirements for intelligent autonomous mobility services. In: Stanton, N. (ed.) AHFE 2018. AISC, vol. 786, pp. 339–350. Springer, Cham (2019). https://doi.org/10.1007/978-3-319-93885-1_31

70. Flohr, L.A., Janetzko, D., Wallach, D.P., Scholz, S.C., Krüger, A.: Context-Based Interface Prototyping and Evaluation for (Shared) Autonomous Vehicles Using a Lightweight Immersive Video-Based Simulator. In: Proceedings of the Designing Interactive Systems Conference 2020 (DIS 2020). Association for Computing Machinery, New York (2020). https://doi.org/10.1145/3357236.3395468

71. Wallach, D.P., Fackert, S., Albach, V.: Predictive prototyping for real-world applications: a model-based evaluation approach based on the ACT-R cognitive architecture. In: DIS 2019 - Proceedings of the 2019 ACM Designing Interactive Systems Conference, pp. 1495–1502 (2019)

72. Howes, A., Young, R.M.: The role of cognitive architecture in modeling the user: soar's learning mechanism. Hum.-Comput. Interact. **12**(4), 311–343 (1997)

73. Ergosign GmbH: Antetype.com (2020)

74. Wallach, D., Scholz, S.: Thinking aloud: foundations, prospects and practical challenges. In: Klopp, J., Schneider, F., Stark, R. (eds.) Thinking Aloud - The Mind in Action. Weimar: Bertuch (2019)

A Paradigm Shift in Design Driven by AI

Qiong Wu[(⊠)] and Cun Jun Zhang

Tsinghua University, Beijing, People's Republic of China
`qiong-wu@tsinghua.edu.cn`

Abstract. The rapid development of artificial intelligence has brought many surprises and challenges to design. Its powerful computing intelligence, perceptual intelligence and cognitive intelligence can change or even replace many traditional designers' operations, especially those kinds of data-based and standardized work. AI already changed design method from design operations to computing logic, design object from objects to a complex adaptive system, and the goal of design also extended from solving problems to defining and solving problems. Based on the analysis of two cases we carried out, our understanding of artificial intelligence involved in the design process is summarized. Against the backdrop of artificial intelligence, the change of design tasks and methods, and how to give full play to the advantages of artificial intelligence to carry out the in-depth human-machine intelligent collaborative design in the future application are discussed.

Keywords: Artificial intelligence · Design method · Design evaluation

1 Introduction

In the recent two years, an increasing number of cases show that artificial intelligence technology is rapidly penetrating into the design and related industries. However, the mainstream thinking and methods of current designs are based on the traditional understanding of the relationship between human and product, thus it is difficult to solve the design problem of complex intelligent agents and the problem of human-machine deep collaboration in the design process.

In the era of artificial intelligence, the advanced intelligentization of "thing" itself changes the relationship between people and "thing", forming a complex relationship between man – intelligence (information system) – product/environment (physical system). Moreover, artificial intelligence also reconstructs every link from user research to design, user testing and evaluation, etc., forms a new demand for intelligence from macro to micro aspects, facilitates the emergence of new theories, new models, new methods, new products, new formats, and ultimately leads to a revolution in design paradigm.

With the support of super computing power and storage capacity of artificial intelligence, some design processes based on data and logic analysis can be efficiently completed by machines; those design methods and processes relying on observation, imagination, empathy and creativity are still the main tasks of designers. For a long time, human-machine deep collaboration is the major mode for the involvement of

H. Degen and L. Reinerman-Jones (Eds.): HCII 2020, LNCS 12217, pp. 167–176, 2020.
https://doi.org/10.1007/978-3-030-50334-5_11

artificial intelligence in the design process, including the use of data processing, knowledge graph, transfer learning and other methods, to assist in completing the design of specific forms and flow of things. The following will describe a case on teaching process of conceptual design based on artificial intelligence.

In addition, the in-depth research on the industrial standards and classification, abstraction and optimization methods of design specifications, the construction of design knowledge base and standards, the setting of rules for generation of forms and operation of flow of things, and the evaluation of the calculated results helped optimize the algorithm of artificial intelligence and better complete the design, these new works will become important parts of the design and bring about a paradigm shift. The following will describe a case on the research of image evaluation generated by artificial intelligence.

Based on the analysis of these two cases, our understanding of artificial intelligence involved in the design process is summarized. Against the backdrop of artificial intelligence, the change of design tasks and methods, and how to give full play to the advantages of artificial intelligence to carry out the in-depth human-machine intelligent collaborative design in the future application are discussed.

2 Research Project: Research on Computer-Generated Imagery Evaluation Standards

2.1 Project Overview

Computer-generated imagery is an important part of the application of artificial intelligence in the field of design. Currently, the evaluation method of the generated image is mainly qualitative evaluation, with no unified standard. This project aims to develop a set of universal criteria to measure the quality of computer-generated images, and to help algorithm researchers better evaluate their own work in the research, and modify and improve the algorithm based on the evaluation results. Meanwhile, the evaluation criteria can also be served to retrieve and sort the generated images. This project starts from the two perspectives of content and aesthetics. Through literature and user research, 21 high frequently mentioned image quality evaluation factors were summarized. The 21 factors were divided into two categories, subjective factors and objective factors, according to whether there were differences in the scoring of different people. Afterwards, the 8 objective factors are divided into specific evaluation criteria, and the quantitative calculation methods for these evaluation criteria are given.

2.2 Experimental Design

There is a total of 16 experimental subjects, ranging in age from 24 to 50 years old, and with the male and female ratio of 7:9. 6 of them have been exposed to art related education, and the eyesight of all subjects is normal or corrected without color weakness. The specific testing process is as follows: each subject was provided with 60 images (generated by StackGAN and BigGAN, there are 12 categories of objects, 5 for each category), in a jumbled order, and each image was rated by two people. The subjects were asked to complete three tasks, which respectively are rating the given several computer-generated images on a scale from 1 (completely dissatisfied) to 7 (very satisfied) from an overall perspective, from the perspective of image content, and from the perspective of image aesthetics. After the testing was completed, we also conducted interviews with the subjects, mainly to understand what aspects they would describe if they need to generate images. What factors in an image will affect satisfaction?

2.3 Experimental Results

Based on the above testing and interviews, we found that the main content and the feeling style are mentioned frequently in the user's description of the required image, and the factor that most easily affects the user's satisfaction with the specified generated image is whether it is consistent with the description. From the quantitative experimental analysis, it is found that the correlation coefficient between the score of content and the aesthetic is lower than that between the independent score and the total score, which proves that there is certain independence and a certain correlation. Meanwhile, we can know from the qualitative interview that the high-frequently mentioned factors, such as association, emotion, and the image with kinetic potential, will have an impact on the rating of aesthetic and content. In addition, 10 respondents pointed out that in addition to the content being completely illegible, if there is deformity or ambiguity, the aesthetic score will also be lower. Meanwhile, 9 respondents said that if an image is more likely to be regarded as a painting than a real photo, the tolerance for possible deformity or unreasonable elements in the image will be improved. Through the analysis of specific cases of high-frequently mentioned factors, we can find that all factors can be divided into two categories. Among all these factors, some factors, which are scored by two people with relatively consistent scores (the score difference is no more than 1) and similar descriptions, can be understood as objective factors that most people agree on. Other factors that show obvious differences in the scores of the two people (the difference score is more than 2), or show quite different description angles although showing the same score, can be regarded as more subjective factors that vary from person to person. We selected the influencing factors mentioned by more than 1/3 of total respondents as the basis of our specified evaluation criteria, and summarized and classified them based on the analysis results. The results are shown in the Fig. 1.

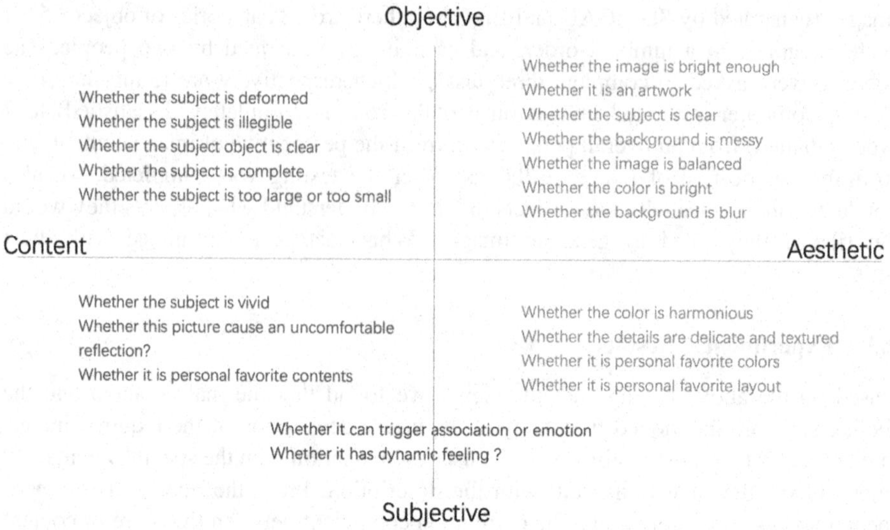

Objective

Whether the subject is deformed
Whether the subject is illegible
Whether the subject object is clear
Whether the subject is complete
Whether the subject is too large or too small

Whether the image is bright enough
Whether it is an artwork
Whether the subject is clear
Whether the background is messy
Whether the image is balanced
Whether the color is bright
Whether the background is blur

Content   Aesthetic

Whether the subject is vivid
Whether this picture cause an uncomfortable
reflection?
Whether it is personal favorite contents

Whether the color is harmonious
Whether the details are delicate and textured
Whether it is personal favorite colors
Whether it is personal favorite layout

Whether it can trigger association or emotion
Whether it has dynamic feeling ?

Subjective

Fig. 1. 21 high frequently mentioned image quality evaluation factors

Based on the factors summarized above, since subjective factors vary from person to person, it is difficult to form a unified criterion. Therefore, we took the objective factors as the basis of the evaluation criteria and formulated 8 evaluation criteria. Among them, the four criteria related to content are: the authenticity of the subject (factors for whether the subject is illegible or deformed), the moderate size of the subject (factors for whether the subject is too large or too small), the completeness of the subject (factors for whether the subject object is complete), the clarity of the subject (factors whether the subject object is clear). The four criteria related to aesthetics are: the brightness of the image (factors for whether the image is bright enough), the prominence of the subject (the three factors for whether the subject is clear, whether the background is messy and whether it is blurred), the degree of color brightness (factors for whether the color is bright or not), the degree of image balance (factors for whether the image is balanced).

2.4   Final Conclusion

we further explained the above 8 evaluation criteria in detail and the quantitative calculation was conducted by computer experts in the same group. The basic situation is as follows:

The Authenticity of the Subject
Criteria description:

- The object is completely unrecognizable, and it's impossible to guess what the content of the subject is.
- The intention of generation can be known by observation, but part of the subject object is deformed.
- The generated object is relatively real without obvious defects.

Quantitative method: the pretraining model of Glove Word Vector was introduced and used to calculate the respective word vector values of the predicted and expected categories, and to calculate the cosine similarity between the two values to complete the semantic similarity detection.

The Moderate Size of the Subject
Criteria description:

- Objects are too small and some components are too small to be clearly identified.
- Objects are of moderate size in the frame.
- The object size is too large and the image is too crowded.

Quantitative method: combining edge detection and semantic segmentation into this task and by taking a shortcut connection of deep subsurface to shallow subsurface, the semantic features of the high subsurface features can assist the shallow subsurface features to locate the significance area more accurately and adjust the irregular boundary position

The Completeness of the Subject
Criteria description:

- The object is very incomplete, with important parts not shown in the image.
- The object is more complete, but there are still some non-essential parts outside the image.
- The whole object is in the image, very complete.

Quantitative method: the above significance detection algorithm is used to extract the significance area and detect the length of the intersection line between the significance area and the boundary around the image.

The Clarity of the Subject
Criteria description:

- The object is very indistinct, and the species are barely distinguishable, but the parts are indistinguishable.
- The object is clear, but the details are a bit hard to see.
- The object is very clear and the details are relatively distinct.

Quantitative method: the significance detection algorithm is used to extract the detected foreground. Laplace operator is used to detect the space sharpness to indicate the clarity of the detected part.

The Brightness of the Image
Criteria description:

- The overall image is very dark, slightly affecting the recognition of the object.
- The overall image is relatively bright, but blurring, with insufficient contrast.
- The whole image is bright with obvious contrast between brightness and darkness.

Quantitative method: the RGB Value of each pixel is converted to HSV space, and the value of all pixels are detected.

The Prominence of the Subject

Criteria description:

- All objects in the image are similar in terms of the prominence degree, and it's unable to distinguish between the primary and secondary.
- The main objects can be identified in the image, but the background is more complex or interfering objects are more eye-catching.
- The subject in the image is very prominent, and the background is blurred to some extent.

Quantitative method: the significance detection algorithm is used to distinguish foreground objects from background. Laplace operator is used to detect the space sharpness of the foreground and background, and canny operator is used to calculate the marginal complexity of background.

The Degree of Color Brightness

Criteria description:

- With low color saturation, the image is overall pale or dark.
- Color saturation is OK, and the image is relatively harmonious.
- With high color saturation, the image appears very bright.

Quantitative method: the main five colors composition in the image are extracted by median segmentation, and the most important two colors are projected from the RGB space to the HSV space and their Saturation values are extracted.

The Degree of Image Balance

Criteria description:

- The image composition is very unbalanced and the focus of the image clearly deviates.
- The image focus is located near the center of the image and is relatively balanced. But it is rigid and lack of changes.
- The image is completely symmetrical or the center of the image is close to the golden section point, which is quite balanced.

Quantitative method: the symmetry of the image is mainly completed by comparing the brightness of the image. The RGB value of each pixel is converted to the HSV space, and the brightness value of all pixels are detected. The significance detection algorithm is used to extract the foreground.

Finally, we also validated the effectiveness of the criteria. Due to the complex factors affecting the satisfaction, it is difficult to find a highly correlated linear relationship between each standard score and user ratings. Finally, the correlation between standard scores and user ratings is quantitatively verified by means of distribution significance difference test, scatter diagram distribution observation and correlation evaluation.

3   Workshop: Human-Machine Intelligent Collaboration for the Design of Chair

3.1   Overview

Although artificial intelligence already has the ability to "generate new content," currently, and the process is only to extract rules from a large amount of data to generate new content which cannot form the truly innovative design. Just as the computer got involved in the design process as a design tool at the end of the last century, the introduction of artificial intelligence is of great significance to improving the efficiency of design and can promote the generation of new forms and assist people in innovative design to some extent. This workshop is designed to enable that students can master the current technology and methods of artificial intelligence generation, and make full use of the results of artificial intelligence calculation for innovative design. All the students involved in the project are graduate students majoring in design, with a total of 29 students which are divided into 6 groups, with 4 or 5 students in each group.

3.2 Specific Project Design

1) After the introduction of how to use AI to generate pictures of chairs, the students were provided thousands generated pictures of chairs, and almost 40,000 modeling and design pictures of chairs for training the artificial intelligence system (Fig. 2).

Fig. 2. Some generated pictures of chairs by AI

2) The learning of chairs by artificial intelligence is only limited to the morphological characteristics of the chairs, and thus their functional requirements can't be identified. From the results, some pictures have good effects, while some pictures cannot meet the form requirements of chairs.

3) The students were asked to analyze the form generated by artificial intelligence, and summarized the tips for designing new form to prepare for the conceptual design, and based on the results of artificial intelligence generation, the concept design of chairs is carried out. All these works should be finished in 20 min for each group.

3.3   Final Results

The designs and explanations of five groups are as following, one group failed to finish the task.

Group 1: They thought that they were inspired by the feeling obtained from the image, furry, soft-elastic, so they design a soft chair with spring legs.

Group 2: The image can't help in chair design because it has nothing to do with how the chair should be used. However, it was helpful for the design of certain partial shapes of chair.

Group 3: They thought that they were inspired by the form of the image, and they design a chair which like a seesaw.

Group 4: They thought that they were inspired by the feeling obtained from the image, warm, safe, so they design a way of stay-in, a "chair" without legs but with a shed.

Group 5: They thought that they were inspired by the form of the image, and they could design quite a lot in short times (Fig. 3).

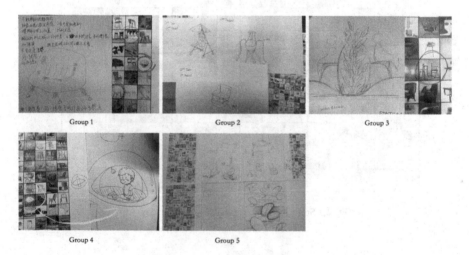

Fig. 3. The deliverables of 5 groups

3.4   Final Conclusion

In this project, the computer-generated imagery becomes a basic basis and reference for the design of form, and is an exploration of form without specific direction and broad significance, while it is still very helpful as an inspiration on form, structure, and even material design. On the other hand, if the images used for artificial intelligence training are classified and selected and input according to certain rules based on user research, the final generated form and outline will be more directional. Therefore, the use of artificial intelligence by designers should not only just be limited to using the results of the initial generation, but also by going deep into the process of how to train ai's solution setting. Only in this way, the function of artificial intelligence can be fully played, and the design of human-machine intelligence deep collaboration can be truly formed.

4   Conclusion

Now, innovations in emerging technologies are endless. Different from the previous period when behaviors carried out to solve a certain problem, the design should be made based on a deep understanding of social factors such as culture, economy and technology, and requires asking active questions, identifying problems across different fields, finding application scenarios, and defining the action scope of the design. The passive percipient of the new technology becomes the participant in its formation process, leading the original innovation of technology and realizing the new development of design, which is the expansion of design content and the core of the change of design paradigm.

The development of artificial intelligence is the result of the development of computer science, bionics, biology, psychology and other disciplines. In application, the integration of artificial intelligence and other technologies will bring more opportunities and challenges to design. For example, the future interaction design should make full use of automatic speech recognition, natural language processing, machine vision, big data analysis, emotional computing and other technologies, and integrate hearing, vision, smell, touch and other multi-channel interaction modes to form more natural and immersive user experience. Artificial intelligence can get involved in this complex process of calculation and judgment, and can choose the switching mode of different interaction channels for people based on the analysis of the situation.

The relationship between computing and design is getting deeper and deeper. Nowadays, computing is taken as not only the tool but also design object. In the near future, computing will become the intelligent subject in a collaborative design process with designers, and the design objects will include data, aesthetics, narration, interaction, interface, as well as algorithms, social system, and human perception. Designers need to have a broader and deeper understanding of society, culture, and technology, they should study the design methods based on data-driven, design knowledge base and standard system construction and generative design, and summarize the new thinking of design so as to better deal with the opportunities and challenges brought by the change of design paradigm in the era of artificial intelligence.

Acknowledgement. This research was supported by 2019 National Social Science Foundation Art Project "Interaction Design Method Research based on AI", the number is 19BG127. Dr. Feng Gao from Future Laboratory, Tsinghua University assisted in generating chair Images Based on Artificial Intelligence.

References

1. Jonanthan, F.: Design for Emerging Technologies. O'Reilly Media, Sebastopol (2015)
2. Halonen, R., Westman, S., Oittinen, P.: Naturalness and interestingness of test images for visual quality evaluation. In: Image Quality and System Performance VIII, vol. 7867, p. 78670Z. International Society for Optics and Photonics (2011)
3. Keelan, B.: Handbook of Image Quality: Characterization and Prediction. CRC Press, FL (2002)

AI Applications in HCI

Support Vector Machine Algorithm to Classify Instagram Users' Accounts Based on Users' Interests

Al-Batool Al-Ghamdi[✉], Ameenah Al-Sulami[✉],
Nouf Al-Jadani[✉], and Maha Aljohani[✉]

University of Jeddah, Jeddah, Saudi Arabia
{aalghamdi2633.stu,aalsulami0970.stu,
naljadani.stu,mmaljohani}@uj.edu.sa

Abstract. Instagram is an application on smartphones used to share photos and videos of users' life events. Instagram saves users' time to arrange a post based on users' interests. However, users still have a problem with some post appears that they don't want to see it because it's less important to them. Also, users spend a lot of time when searches for a particular account from the list of following. In this project, we proposed the classification of users' accounts and using content recommendation which aims to classify Instagram users' accounts based on users' interests. We use Support Vector Machine (SVM) algorithm as a particular class of machine learning to classify Instagram users' accounts. Then it used to sort the following list and rank the post. Also, we use content-based recommendation system to rank the post under each classification by analysis of the user's practice. We provided an improvement method suitable for users' interests that preserve time, effort and to make the users feel enjoyable when using Instagram.

Keywords: Instagram · Classification of users' accounts · Users' interests · Support Vector Machine · Rank the post · Content-based recommendation system · Analysis of the user practice

1 Introduction

Instagram is an application on smartphones used to share photos of users' life events. Users of Instagram mobile applications can take and manipulates photos using filters and frames and share them where other users can interact with them through likes and comments. Instagram was kick off in October 2010 and has seen tremendous growth. Based on statistical, Instagram has 20 billion photos posted with an average of 60 million photos per day for 200 million registered users [1]. According to these numbers, Instagram will treat as one of the most popular applications for sharing photos and for interacting with friends and worldwide brand [1].

Regardless of the popularity of Instagram [2]. Instagram worth concern from the research society like twitter and other social media. The importance of a deep understanding of Instagram lies in gaining deep insight into social issues about people's

© Springer Nature Switzerland AG 2020
H. Degen and L. Reinerman-Jones (Eds.): HCII 2020, LNCS 12217, pp. 179–196, 2020.
https://doi.org/10.1007/978-3-030-50334-5_12

activities [2]. For all those reasons, we choose Instagram for our research to classify the list of account based on the interest of the user by using machine learning.

Machine learning depends on statistical and computational principles and set of different approaches, but not restricted to statistics, probability theory and computational algorithms, it may be used in data mining, pattern recognition, processing of textual data and, audio-video files also it is used widely [3]. Machine learning divides into two types: supervised learning and unsupervised learning. Supervised learning defines desired outputs based on a prediction made on data with the inputs. Unsupervised learning defines to find the properties of the data with inputs [3].

In this paper, we proposed an algorithm which is (SVM) [4] to classify Instagram users' accounts. Then it used to sort the following list and rank the post. Also, we use a content-based recommendation system to rank the post under each classification by analysis of the user's practice. We provided an improvement method suitable for users' interests that preserve time, effort and to make the users feel enjoyable when using Instagram.

The remainder of the paper is organized as follows. Section 2 defines the problem. Section 3 defines the objectives of the research. Section 4 presents the related work on showing posts on Instagram. Section 5 describes the proposed system architecture. Section 6 presents the experiment and the result of our proposed. Section 7 presents our discussion and answer research questions. Finally, Sect. 8 concludes the paper and presents some of the future orientations.

2 Problem Definition

Instagram saves users' time to arrange the post based on users' interests, other users' interaction as well (e.g., number of likes) and other features (e.g., time of activity) [5]. However, users still have a problem with some post appears that they don't want to see it because it's less important to them. Another problem when the user searches for a particular account from the list of following, especially if the user has a lot of following, this makes the user spends a lot of time until to finds the account. Therefore, the user's challenges in sorting and organizing their accounts based on their interests are the research problem.

3 Research Objective

The study aims:

- To classify Instagram users' accounts based on users' interests using SVM.
- To design a method for analysis of the user's practice using a content-based recommendation system.
- To sort the following list after classification.
- To rank the post under each classification by analysis of the user's practice.

3.1 Research Questions

1 What is the benefit of classifying the list of following on Instagram?
2 What is the purpose of making a new method to classify the account on Instagram?

3.2 Research Hypothesis

1 The user who takes charge of sorting the account of the post rank method is better than the user who is using Instagram as it is.
2 Sorting the following list will save user time and effort.

4 Related Work

4.1 Classification

Instagram is a new form of communication where users can capture and share their photos or videos. Hu et al. [2] propose that their research was the first to conduct a deep analysis of photo content, user activities and types on Instagram. In their study, they use the computer vision technique to examine and describe local features in the photo. Based on computer vision technique, they identified the different types of active users on Instagram by used clustering. They obtained to get three results: First, they obtained eight different types of photo categories on Instagram by using the classical Scale Invariant Feature Transform (SIFT) algorithm. The eight types can be categorized based on their content which includes: self-portraits, friends, activities, captioned photos (pictures with embedded text), food, gadgets, fashion, and pets. Second, they discovered that there are five distinct types of users based on the photos they posted by used k-means clustering. The first group of users who love self-portraits. The second categorizes under users captioned photos whose embedded text mentions about quotes, mottos, poetries or even popular hashtags. The third group of users who focused on posting photos of food and they like to post other categories of photos as well. The users, in the fourth kind, are caring about their friends as seriously as caring about themselves and users posted activity and gadget. The users, in the fifth kind, are caring about activity and gadget. The study results show that there is not a direct relationship between the number of followers and the type of users characterized in terms of there shared photos, through statistical significance tests. They performed a two-tailed t-test and they obtained (p-value = 0.171). Therefore, the number of followers is independent of the type of users.

Nokwon and Soosun [6] introduce two experimental results from the classification of Instagram images, many applications use a convolutional neural network (CNN). Through this study, they tried some experiments to evaluate the competitiveness of the convolutional neural network. In the classification of images such as Instagram photos, more than one model was used in this experiment Alex Net model and ResNet50 model and the data Image Net 2012 set as training data set. The experiment showed the difference between the most popular social media sites Flickr and Instagram of the images searched by tag in terms of images with relatively higher resolution and refined tags. The experiment was in 12 categories and 20 images, and for the classification was used Alex Net model and ResNet50 model. The results showed that the classification using the Alex Net model has a higher error rate than the classification results using the ResNet50 model for 12 categories. Although the number of layers in the Alex Net model is eight compared to the number of layers in the ResNet50 model is 50. Therefore, they recognized that as a network became deeper the better results appeared. Another model of the convolutional neural network was used, called Inception v3 which is high performance compared to previous models especially the ResNet50 model with lower results in the previous experiment. The results showed that the classification using neural network model Inception v3 is more accurate than the neural network model ResNet50. The conclusion of this experiment is that classification using the convolutional neural network was effective, especially when using the neural network model Inception v3.

4.2   Classification Based on Image Caption

Kuncoro and Iswanto [7] ranked keywords of Instagram users' image caption that represented the description of the image by used Term-Frequency and Inverse Document Frequency (TF-IDF) method. TF-IDF method is a way to score the importance of words in a document based on the number of times they appear across multiple documents and it ranks from a certain user. Thus, the highest rank of keyword is indeed the main topic of a user. The aim of the experiment: The ranking keywords of Instagram users' image caption provided advanced research such as clustering, classification, and profiling of Instagram username. Second, the study developed Instagram data research with a different approach which is text mining. Third, the study was designed to retrieve significant words of the user automatically from the captions posted by the user.

Lahor et al. [8] worked another study about image caption to describe user-uploaded images. Keywords based on image comment data are arranged and ordered by using the TF-IDF method and Support Vector Machine Algorithm (SVM). The Support Vector Machine algorithm (SVM) is used to train keywords for comments and captions. The researchers created a customized social site based on the caption of images which will arrange the images based on the caption using the TF-IDF method. The TF-IDF method has been successfully used in this project and is an effective method of detecting and arranging keywords based on image captions. Uploaded images are trained by the Support Vector Machine algorithm (SVM) and keywords are calculated by TF-IDF Method. This system is suitable for Facebook and Instagram to arrange images based on the caption of images.

4.3   Classification Based on Hashtag

Heng and Wang [9] proposed system builds on Instagram to assist the user to rank pictures in priority order by improving the use of hashtags. The hashtags limited and can't satisfy users, where it is limited to the pictures for people who use the hashtags. Correlated pictures are expected to find for users from search, when the users search using keyword (e.g., "waterfall") on Instagram they not just expected pictures for a waterfall. The picture recommendation system is dividing into user-defined correlation (online phase) and system-defined correlation (offline phase). In the online phase, the users of Instagram can log in to the system and it gives the authentication to use the API Instagram and then they can to correlated pictures by keying in hashtags and the knowledge base is built. In the offline phase, the hashtags of pictures on Instagram are collated by the processor then refinery the information. Then, the relationship between the hashtags and synonyms is built by pointing free dictionary. Finally, the weights of all hashtags store in the knowledge base after estimate by the calculator.

4.4 Classification Based on User's Practices

Araújo et al. [1] investigated the users' practices on Instagram, they found that users tend to concentrate their posts during the weekend and at the end of the day. Also, people tend to endorse photos with many likes and comments, inducing the rich get richer phenomenon. Therefore, they analyzed the activity of users and interacted with the posts through like and comment activities. The dataset used in their analysis is 1, 265, 080 photographs or videos from 256, 398 popular and ordinary Instagram users with their features (Total number of posts, Website, Total number of followers list and Total number of the following list). Also, they collected post features (Identification number, Total number of likes, List of users who commented and liked the post, Total number of tags, List of tags, Time and Day and Filter). Data was collected using the Instagram Application Programming Interface (API). Conclusions emerge from their analysis: First, the users tend to concentrate their posts during the weekend and posts are shared during the afternoon and the evening, but a non-negligible number of posts are shared overnight. Second, the users prefer shared posts without a filter. Third, Worldwide brands used a tag in the caption when sharing the posts but to increase the probability of attracting the customer, worldwide brands cooperate with bloggers that tend to have a large number of followers, a large number of likes and comments, inducing the rich get richer phenomenon. Their findings can support future research to find new clustering algorithms such as clustering based on user practices in different social media networks.

4.5 Working of Instagram's Algorithm

Constine [5] presented a study on how Instagram's algorithm works which he said in July 2016, Instagram abandoned the reverse chronological algorithm because users lost 50% of their friend's posts and 70% of all posts. 800 million-plus users spending more time on the app and seeing 90% of their friends' posts because of relevancy sorting. Instagram feeds a unique rank for posts for everyone based on machine learning about the past behavior of the users. There are three main factors define what you see on Instagram, and it is as follows: (i) Interest: based on machine vision analyzing on actual of the post content and your past behavior on similar content the Instagram will predicate higher ranking for what matters to you; (ii) Recency: The priority for posts shared recently with posts over weeks-old ones, and (iii) Relationship: higher ranking for the people you've interacted with their posts by comment or like or tag.

Regardless of the main factors, there are additional signals impact on ranking are: (i) Frequency: Instagram shows you the last best posts since your last time visit the app; (ii) Following: Instagram will be selecting many people of your following if you follow a lot of people to avoid see a specific person all the time, and (iii) Usage: The time of using Instagram determines if you are just looking for the best post during a short session or spend more time for browsing.

Skrubbeltrang et al. [10] studied how the user commented on the Instagram announcement for algorithmic personalization. Social media has become the space for users when they disagree with certain organizational practices. This situation is especially disturbing when there are profound changes such as the announcement of Instagram for the algorithmic personalization. The starting point of this study is a collection of 3,913 tweets containing the hashtag #RIPINSTAGRAM Sent by 3378 users. Tweets were collected using Twitter Capture and Analysis Toolset (TCAT), the data was captured on March 17, 2016, two days after the Instagram announcement of algorithmic personalization. The main argument for the Instagram announcement about algorithmic personalization was to improve the user experience. The concept of algorithmic personalization relates to the creation of a valuable feed with useful content. However, Instagram users have a different view of this algorithm. This research aims to examine the feedback of users on the #RIPINSTAGRAM movement. Also, the emphasis was placed on examining user comments on algorithmic personalization implementation. About the examined data sample, it is important to note that only users from Twitter and Instagram were taken into account in this study. Therefore, the obvious implications of this study did not examine counter-narratives from the entire spectrum of Twitter and Instagram users but only from tweets and Instagram comments using the hashtag #RIPINSTAGRAM. Through this analysis, they found that users have concerns about algorithmic personalization. They found that many users feel oppressed by algorithms and as it's a hegemony that decides on their behalf. Therefore, users see the chronological order better for them and the implemented algorithm personalization aims to make a profit at the expense of user needs. This paper suggests that the user resists the organizational narrative of Instagram through some arguments that often include that Instagram makes a profit at the user's expense. Therefore, organizations must take account of user concerns and address them properly.

4.6   Comparison

(See Table 1).

Table 1. Similarity and difference between related work and our work.

Related work	Similarity	Differences
(Hu et al. 2014)	• Classification the account of user based on eight types (self-portraits, friends, activities, captioned photos (pictures with embedded text), food, gadgets, fashion, and pets)	• Classification the following list based on eight types rather than classification user account only
(Nokwon and Soosun 2017)	• Ranking of Images based on users' practice	• Classify images based on the users' interest to ranking the account rather than hashtags • Classify images based on (SVM) rather than Convolutional Neural Network (CNN)
(Kuncoro and Iswanto 2015)	• Ranking of Instagram users' image	• The method of ranking the images based on user interest rather than based on Instagram users' image caption
(Lahor et al. 2017)	• Ranking of Images using Support Vector Machine algorithm (SVM)	• Classify based on users' interest rather than classify based on captions • Ranking images method using (SVM) rather than using (TF-IDF) method to ranking image and (SVM) to training keywords
(Heng and Wang 2017)	• Ranking the images on priority order on the user's interest	• The method of ranking the images based on some criteria in ranking rather than using hashtags
(Araújo et al. 2014)	• Analysis of the users' activity and interact with the posts through like and comment activities	• First step, classification type of account. Second step, sorting the images into each classification by analysis of the users' practices rather than sorting based on user's practices without the first step that classification the user's account
(Constine 2018)	• Ranking the image on Instagram	• The users who take charge of ranking the images depend on classification type the account rather than ranking the images based on the user's past practice
(Skrubbeltranget al. 2017)	• Analysis of the user's comment about the concerns of the Instagram algorithm	• Classify the user account based on the type of account • Ranking the post in each classification based on analysis of the user's practice rather than using the personalizationa lgorithm

4.7   Summary of Related Work

We have presented several studies to arrange the user account in the application of Instagram, and these studies were based in the order on the analysis of images and analysis of the description of images, also through the classification of images using the convolution neural network and the order of images based on the caption using machine learning, the hashtag arrangement and the users' practices in Instagram. In addition, Instagram worked on a new way of sorting based on user interests and the recency of the post, and finally on the user's relationship with the people he interacts with by commenting or liking their posts. However, all previous studies did not involve that the user has a role in the ranking process. Also, no way has been suggested to sort the list of followers. This is what distinguishes our research that the user is responsible for the ranking of the posts and list of followers.

5   System Architecture

An analysis was conducted about the Instagram algorithm to identify how it works [5], which made us propose solutions to improve the algorithm suitable for users' interests by using the Support Vector Machine algorithm (SVM) [4].

As shown in Fig. 1, we added a new section in the setting page is called "account type," where the user can choose the account type from the drop list. We adopted eight account types based on the user interest to classify the user account; the types consist of (friends, self-portraits, activities, fashion, food, captioned photos, gadgets, and pets) [2]. Through classification, we can find who is similar to the user interest and who is different from the user interest. We use the classification to do two things, it used to sort the following list as categories, and it used to rank the post. Sorting the following list as categories depending on the classification only. But the ranking of the post depends on the classification of the user account and depends on the user practice. Therefore, we rank the post based on two steps. First, we classify the user account based on the account type. Then, we rank the post under each classification by analysis of the user practice. As shown in Fig. 2, the design methodology of the algorithm, for classification, we used SVM, and for ranking the post, we used content recommendation.

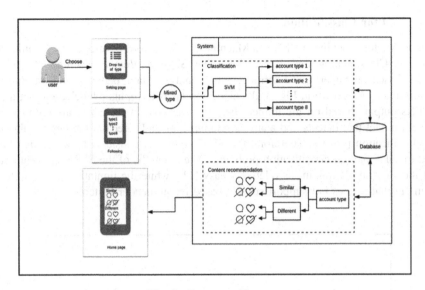

Fig. 1. System architecture.

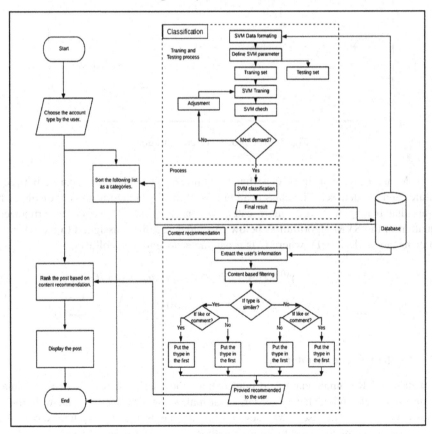

Fig. 2. The design methodology of the algorithm.

5.1   SVM for Classification

Support Vector Machine (SVM) is a Machine Learning Tool developed by Vapnik [4] used for Classification and Regression. The Support Vector Machine algorithm (SVM) based on Supervised Learning, which analyses data, patterns, and training to classify them. As shown in Fig. 3, the algorithm takes as inputs a labeled dataset then predicts outputs based on the trained data set. The goal of the SVM algorithm is to create a model that detects and analysis relationships and forecasts the target value in the classification process. Therefore, the SVM algorithm considered successful when used to solve pattern classification problems. The strengths of the SVM algorithm are that the algorithm's training is relatively easy [11], while the limitations of this algorithm are that it does not support content-based recommender systems.

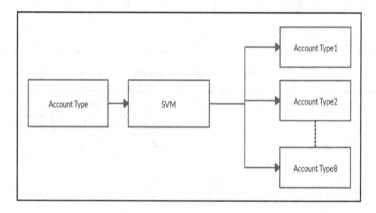

Fig. 3. The process of classification.

SVM algorithm is a linear classifier that finds a hyper plane to separate between features and the data set. The classification task in the SVM algorithm is to distinguish points that belong to two or more categories in a dataset. Therefore, a formalized Equation of the SVM algorithm as below. An input vector $x^{(i)}$ assigned to the positive (1) or negative class (-1), where C is a parameter to find y as follows:

$$y^{(i)} = (+1) \ if \ \theta^T x^{(i)} \geq 0 \ and \ (-1) \ if \ \theta^T x^{(i)} < 0.$$

$$min_\theta \ C \sum\nolimits_{i=1}^{m} \left[y^{(i)} cost_1 \left(\theta^T x^{(i)} \right) + \left(1 - y^{(i)} \right) cost_0 \left(\theta^T x^{(i)} \right) \right] + \frac{1}{2} \sum\nolimits_{i=1}^{n} \theta_j^2 \quad (1)$$

5.2   Content Recommendation

Content-based Recommendation System defines the user's interest in items by analyzing items description. It is a scenario that makes users to interact with web applications. Generally, the users will select from the items that the system shows the essence of the items to users, to interact with it, or to get specific detail [12].

The profile of the user's interests used by the recommendation system, where the profile consists of different types of information. Here, we conduct two types of information:

- Model of user's type: the type of account user (e.g., friends, self-portraits, activities, fashion, food, captioned photos, gadgets, and pets).
- The history of user interactions: this includes like, comment and saved posts.

Decision Tree (Iterative DiChaudomiser 3 Algorithm): ID3 developed by J. Ross Quinlan. It is based on Concept Learning System (CLS) algorithm. ID3 is a supervised algorithm from a fixed group of examples that build a decision tree. Resulting tree use for future classifies samples. Based on training examples, ID3 makes a decision tree and uses it to test classify data [13].

Formalized Equation of SVM algorithm as below, where it calculates the entropy of the set S. The result of entropy between zero and one, where zero is considered the best result and the worst result is one.

$$E(S) = -p + \log(p+) - p - \log(p-) \tag{2}$$

Therefore, we applied a model of decision tree, and the root of our decision tree is (similarity of account type). Figure 4 is an example of the decision tree for the training set of Table 2.

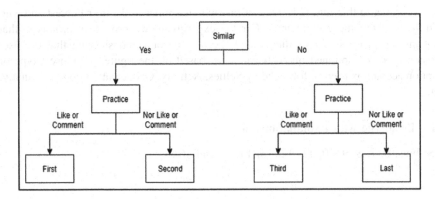

Fig. 4. Decision tree.

Table 2. Sample of training set.

Type	Similarity	Practice	Result
Type X	Yes	Like or comment	First
Type X	Yes	Not like or comment	Second
Type X	No	Like or comment	Third
Type X	No	Not like or comment	Last

6 Result and Experiment

Based on previous studies we showed before, where the user was not the core of the classification process. This study proposes a method for classification of Instagram user accounts based on the interests of the user by selecting the account type using the SVM algorithm, and content-based recommendation used to rank posts based on user practices and interactions. We adopted eight account types based on the user interest to classify the user account; the types consist of (friends, self-portraits, activities, fashion, food, captioned photos, gadgets, and pets) [2] as shown in Fig. 5.

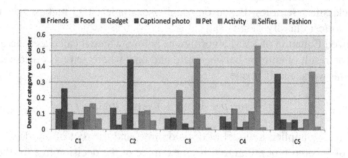

Fig. 5. Classification user's account based on account type [2].

According to this study [2], we can find who is similar to the user interest and who is different from the user interest. For the experiment, we provide a prototype that explains the process of classification of the user account, considering that the user account type is Captioned photo (C2). Thus, based on the figure, the closest type of Caption account is friends, followed by Selfies, Activity, Gadget, and Food, and finally, Pet.

6.1 Prototype with Explanations Steps

(See Figs. 6, 7, 8, 9, 10, 11, 12, 13, 14, 15 and 16).

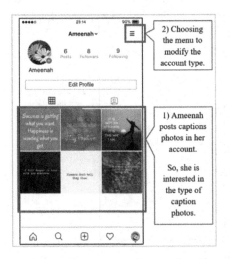

Fig. 6. User account profile.

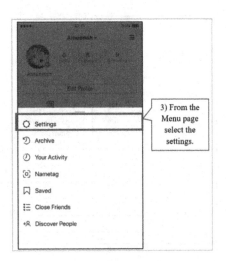

Fig. 7. User's menu page.

Fig. 8. User's setting page.

Fig. 9. Account page.

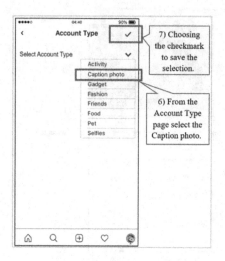

Fig. 10. Account type page.

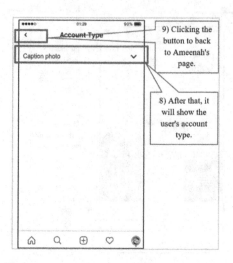

Fig. 11. Account type page after choose account type.

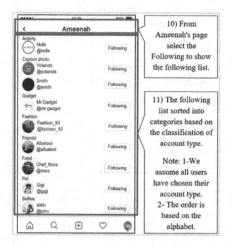

Fig. 12. Following list page.

Fig. 13. First post page.

Fig. 14. Second post page.

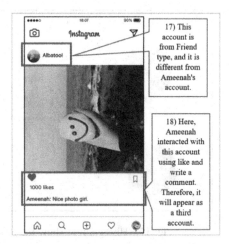

Fig. 15. Third post page.

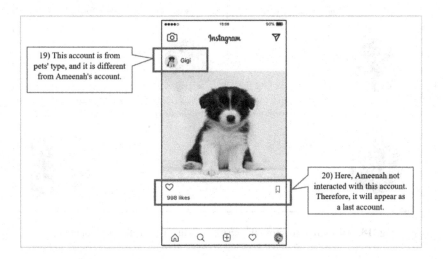

Fig. 16. Final post page.

6.2   Evaluation

The questionnaire contains two parts were used to collect feedback from participants. Part one of the questionnaire to collect the opinion of users for Instagram. After watching the video of our proposed prototype participants express their opinion. 23 participants were randomly selected, while 87% of participants take a long time to find a specific account of the following list and 91% of participants like sorting for the following list. The rate is widely ranged from one to five, where one very bad and five is very good. The range of satisfaction of participants in proposed solution higher. The results of the questionnaire as follows in Fig. 17 and 18.

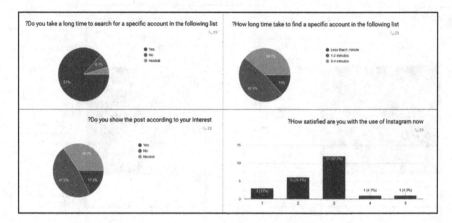

Fig. 17. Histogram to show the results of part one of the questionnaire.

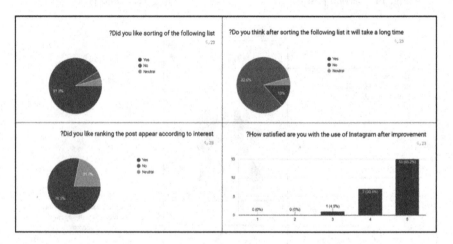

Fig. 18. Histogram to show the results of part two of the questionnaire.

7 Discussion

Based on the first question, the classification method allows users to control how an account is classified based on their interests by choosing the account type. Consequently, it depends primarily on the user and is an essential step in improving the way users use the application. Classifying the lists based on the type of user's account has a benefit. Where its reduction in the time of users in the process of searching for specific accounts. For the second question, the method makes the application very flexible and thus increases user satisfaction when using the app. Because when the users feel that, they control the account and the ranking of posts. It will lead to enjoy the application and organizing the time. We assume that when the user is the one who sorts the account, this will increase the satisfaction. Therefore, this classification process allows users to control the classification and ranking of their accounts and lists based on the account type. Thus, it makes the application flexible and efficient by saving time and effort for users. We offer an improvement algorithm that is suitable for users' interests to make them completely satisfied when using Instagram. The proposed idea will be applying through creating a prototype. The classification method adopted based on this study [2]. The prototype clarifies the classification process where we take eight account types based on the user interest to classify the user account, the types consist of (friends, self-portraits, activities, fashion, food, captioned photos, gadgets, and pets) [2].

8 Conclusion and Future Work

Instagram is the most popular social networking site, where it uses to share photos and videos. The Instagram algorithm based on anticipating user interests and interactions with the post. According to previous studies, that lacks a classified list of followers and posts based on the type of account. Therefore, Instagram users have trouble classifying and ranking their accounts based on their interests. In our research, we overcame the issue by proposing a new method for categorizing Instagram user accounts using the SVM algorithm. In addition, we are using the content-based recommendation to rank the posts. Therefore, the user can select the account type, and then classify the user account based on the custom account type. This method provides benefits to the user by saving time and effort and thus increasing the user satisfaction rate when using the application. A prototype has made to implement this idea and record the users' feedback. In recent times, the Instagram application policy has changed, which means the Instagram application is constantly evolving, and their policy may change from period to another period. Therefore, in the future, this work will be developing follow the Instagram policy.

References

1. Araujo, C.S., Correa, L.P.D., Da Silva, A.P.C., Prates, R.O., Meira, W.: It is not just a picture: revealing some user practices in Instagram. In: Proceedings - 9th Latin American Web Congress, LA-WEB 2014, pp. 19–23 (2014). https://doi.org/10.1109/LAWeb.2014.12
2. Hu, Y., Manikonda, L., Kambhampati, S.: What we Instagram: a first analysis of Instagram photo content and user types. In: Proceedings of the 8th International Conference on Weblogs Social Media, ICWSM 2014, pp. 595–598 (2014)
3. Jäderlund, M.: Wed 2.0: improving customer experience with wedding service providers through investigation of the ranking mechanism and sentiment analysis of user feedback on Instagram (2019)
4. Vapnik, V.N.: The Nature of Statistical Learning Theory. The Nature of Statistical Learning Theory. Springer, New York (1995). https://doi.org/10.1007/978-1-4757-2440-0
5. Constine, J.: How Instagram's algorithm works. Viitattu, 26 2018. https://techcrunch.com/2018/06/01/how-instagram-feed-works/. Accessed 01 Oct 2019
6. Jeong, N., Cho. S.: Instagram image classification with Deep Learning. 인터넷정보학회논문지 **18**, 61–67 (2017). https://doi.org/10.7472/jksii.2017.18.5.61

7. Kuncoro, B.A.: TF-IDF method in ranking keywords of Instagram users' image captions. In: 2015 International Conference on Information Technology Systems and Innovation, pp. 1–5 (2015). https://doi.org/10.1109/ICITSI.2015.7437705

8. Lahor, A., Kulkarni, A., Walunjkar, C., Shahapurkar, A.: Review paper on ranking of images based on caption on. Int. Res. J. Eng. Technol. **4**, 4–6 (2017)

9. Huang, Y., Wang, P.: Picture recommendation system built on Instagram. In: Proceedings of the 2017 International Conference on Artificial Intelligence, Automation and Control Technologies. ACM (2017)

10. Skrubbeltrang, M.M., Grunnet, J., Tarp, N.T.: #RIPINSTAGRAM: examining user's counter-narratives opposing the introduction of algorithmic personalization on Instagram. Monday **22**(4). https://doi.org/10.5210/fm.v22i4.7574. Accessed 03 Oct 2019

11. Cristianini, N., Shawe, T.J.: An Introduction to Support Vector Machines and Other Kernel-Based Learning Methods. Cambridge University Press (2000)

12. Hssina, B., Merbouha, A., Ezzikouri, H., Erritali, M.: A comparative study of decision tree ID3 and C4.5. Int. J. Adv. Comput. Sci. Appl. **4**, 13–19 (2014). https://doi.org/10.14569/specialissue.2014.040203

13. Pazzani, M.J., Billsus, D.: Content-based recommendation systems. In: Brusilovsky, P., Kobsa, A., Nejdl, W. (eds.) The Adaptive Web. LNCS, vol. 4321, pp. 325–341. Springer, Heidelberg (2007). https://doi.org/10.1007/978-3-540-72079-9_10

Customer Self-remediation of Proactive Network Issue Detection and Notification

Donald M. Allen[1(✉)] and Dmitry Goloubew[2]

[1] Cisco Systems, Colorado Springs, CO 80921, USA
donallen@cisco.com
[2] Cisco Systems, Diegem, Brabant 1831, Belgium
dgoloube@cisco.com

Abstract. Improving computer network availability has been a focus of researchers for the past 30 years and considerable investigation into the use of AI and Machine Learning, primarily in the operate space has been conducted. Previous efforts have been primarily reactive in nature, monitoring networks, developing base models, and trying to predict future failures based on those models. This approach has shown limited success due to the dynamic nature of network equipment and function. Cisco has been developing capabilities over the last decade to proactively analysis network devices and identify issues that could impact a networks availability. In the current approach issues are identified to the customer and it is the customer's responsibility to identify the issues that they determine need to be fixed. The capability has been trialed over the last 2 years and the research discussed in this paper is focused on the analysis of their actions. Machine Learning is applied to the issue consumption data set and observations made on the features that can be used to predict which issues will be fixed.

Keywords: Machine Learning · Proactive issue detection · Proactive issue remediation · Network management

1 Introduction

1.1 Artificial Intelligence and Machine Learning in Network Availability

Computer Networks have become a critical component in conducting business in a world economy that has become global. The need be a part of the globalization has led to a dramatic increase in the complexity of computer networks across all segments and they are growing more and more complex. The introduction of public cloud, private cloud, and hybrid cloud capabilities to an existing multi-vendor, multiple service corporate network have further complicated the operation and management. Research both in the public and private sector have turned to the use of Artificial Intelligence (AI) and Machine Learning (ML) to attempt to increase the manageability and availability of these networks although this application to this problem domain is not new.

There are two primary areas of research and development focus to address network availability and administrative complexity. Research in network availability has historically focused on using operational data to identify and predict future failure. Research in this area goes as far back as the 1990's where adaptive statistical systems

© Springer Nature Switzerland AG 2020
H. Degen and L. Reinerman-Jones (Eds.): HCII 2020, LNCS 12217, pp. 197–210, 2020.
https://doi.org/10.1007/978-3-030-50334-5_13

[1], expert systems [2], and probability based predictive modeling [3, 4] approaches which relied on identifying normal network operations and detecting deviations for expected behavior. Some of these approaches required the prior identification of conditions to detect (such as faults) which limited their effectiveness. These techniques were limited in their effectiveness due to the relative constant change in the network due to the rates of change in the network, the volume of data to be analyzed, the multidimensionality of the data and sources, and noisy data. As AI/ML capabilities have evolved these approaches have been replaced with more sophisticated methods that combine multiple ML capabilities into singular approaches that can model network operations and predict failures. Research in identifying and diagnosing network wide issues and hardware failure prediction has embraced anomaly detection using principal component analysis [5], Bayesian Networks [6], and broad spectrum of Machine Leaning techniques [7]. The use of anomaly detection techniques addresses the complexity, volume, and dirtiness of network operational data but at the same time makes identifying the cause of the anomaly more difficult. Changes in network configuration, application deployment and configuration, and traffic rerouting can change the types and nature of failures or performance degradation that can occur in networks, thus making modeling of failures more difficult and, in many cases, impractical.

Detecting and predicting network failure and performance issues can increase availability and reduce network downtime, however, most of these issues can be avoided by focusing on the source of these problems, mainly software failures. Software failures take many forms including the degradation of software with time as a function of the environment [8], security software vulnerabilities [9], software vulnerabilities [10], and user configuration error [11]. Tianyin and Zhou [12] noted that configuration errors are the dominant root cause for systems failures causing system outages and downtime. The complexity of configuring devices individually as well as in the larger network context, understanding the interdependencies, order of change, compatibilities, and methods for identifying root cause and remediation. In a study by Oppenheimer [12] failures at three large Internet service providers user configuration errors were identified as the most significant cause end-user visible service impact.

Researchers have proposed software systems that can automatically detect software configuration errors by identifying invariant configuration access rules [13] looking at user access and proposing a method for exposing misconfigurations and detecting error-prone configurations through developers identifying constraints that can be utilized to identify issues with bad code leading to system crashes, hangs, and silent failures in storage and open source server applications [14]. While demonstrating some success in the constrained environments, the limitations on such approaches is that the discovery of these rules to identify misconfigurations require service failures, the collection of contributing configurations, the codification of detection and prediction rules, and then the distribution of the logic to the points of application.

In typical service provider and large enterprise network environments composed of 10's of thousands of devices the resources, both compute and human, are extensive.

Determining what situations are worth the investment since not all misconfiguration or potential impacting conditions necessarily lead to outages or disruption in services is the focus of the research described in this paper.

1.2 Background

Cisco System's technical support organization handles over 2 million support cases annually where customers and partners have encountered a network operational issue, need assistance in configuration a device, etc. The cases addressed can be as simple questions about available software licenses to network-wide service outage that are causing significant loss of revenue or service disruption. The networks where Cisco products are deployed range from consumer home WIFI networks to web-scale service providers and represent a diverse set of deployment architectures and device uses. Network service quality and availability is a critical concern for all customers. The ability to ensure network availability is a combination of ensuring operational and network elements are functioning properly. Examples of operational factors are resource availability in devices, such as CPU and memory, perimeter security, and connectivity, such as network bandwidth. Network element issues are related to hardware and software quality and element configurations, both hardware and software. Network management systems have historically been focused on the operational monitoring of network element resources and identifying out-of-band conditions. These systems detect issues, raise alarms that are sent to a centralized console, and the alarms are addressed by human operators or automated systems. The application of Machine Learning (ML) to operational management has shown promise in automating an increasing number of operational issues particularly in large homogeneous deployment environments typically seen in web-scale networks [15].

The promise shown in the application of ML to operations management arena has not transferred to network element configuration management arena. Network outages and performance issues not related to resource availability are often the result of misconfigurations, software/hardware defects, security vulnerabilities, etc. The ability to detect network element specific issues and the impact that those issues have on network availability is challenging due to the features and options and their combinations across different deployments, the dependency that one network element has on the configuration of other elements in the network, and the services each provides. For example, the Cisco IOS software has over 16,000 commands mapped to routing, switching, internetworking and telecommunications functions. The possible configurations and the diversity of deployment environments that the same device/OS can be deployed, and the configuration and operational data needed to develop predictive models specific to each customer usage is impractical.

The need for technical assistance center support engineers (TAC engineers) to support customers with heterogeneous deployments, to reduce the time to providing customers with a root cause and remediation, and to reduce the number of repetitive tasks such as reviewing device log files or configuration files engineers began developing "scripts" they could use to look for issues programmatically during the early 2010's.

The goal was to develop automated capabilities to detect and facilitate the remediation of issues that machines are not capable due to the complexity of the problems. Initially the signature development were based on individual experiences based on case experience and evolved into a set of processes and methods to systematically through support case troubleshooting, lab testing, practical experience configuring devices, and the review of bugs and security vulnerabilities and working with software development teams to identify workarounds and fixes.

2   Proactive Network Issue Detection

Initially the issue detection capabilities, referred to as digitized intellectual capital or IC for short, was shared internally among TAC engineers using file shares and mailers. It evolved over time to be automated, running automatically on any files uploaded by a customer to a support case and adding the results to the case. The captured knowledge attempts to identify security, software defects and hardware issues, and misconfiguration issues.

In 2017 the decision was made to externalize the IC to customers for use proactively, the periodic analysis of customers devices to identify issues that have not yet resulted in a support case. Several efforts were needed in order enable this capability:

1) The detected issues had to be augmented to included customer consumable instructions on how to remediate a detected issue.
2) Detected issue severity, potential impact, and issue type had to be provided to customers so that they could decide which issues needed to be addressed on specific devices (based on business context).
3) A mechanism needed to be provided to customers so that they could verify that a change made in their environment fixed the problem.
4) A software capability was needed to connect customer's on-premise devices to the diagnostic engines within the Cisco cloud infrastructure. This capability would need to integrate with customers' existing network management capabilities (if available) to collect device output and integrate with the customers internal incident management system in order to support the seamless integration with their existing network operations (see Fig. 1).

The proactive capabilities were released in a product called Connected TAC [16] in early 2017, customers slowly began utilizing the capabilities in 2017 and most of the adoption occurred during 2018.

2.1   The Cisco Diagnostic Bridge

The Cisco Diagnostic Bridge was developed to provide the mechanism to collect customer device output data, pass that data to Cisco, and to consume the results of the device analysis. Device output collection is driven by the diagnostic engines in the Cisco Cloud.

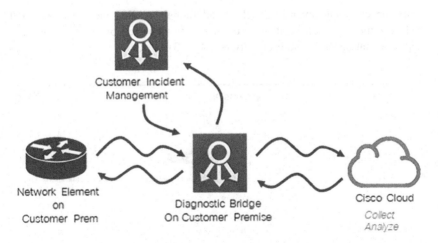

Fig. 1. Cisco Diagnostic Bridge deployment

The results of the device analysis are displayed in a Web-based user interface, shown in an inventory view (see Fig. 2) and a per device basis.

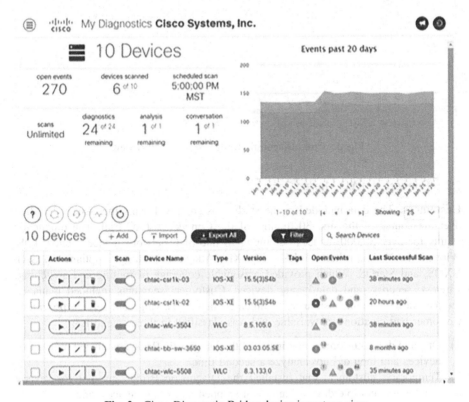

Fig. 2. Cisco Diagnostic Bridge device inventory view

Based on early customer feedback an additional "results' view was added that enabled customers to look at all devices that were impacted by the same issue and develop remediation plans more broadly (see Fig. 3).

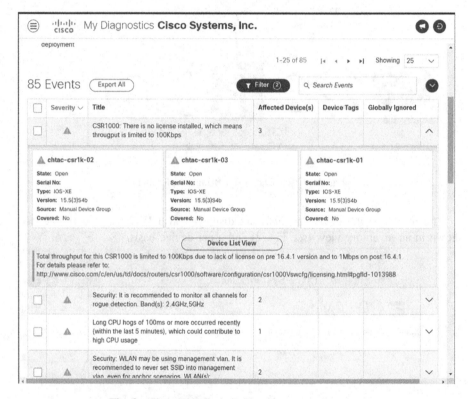

Fig. 3. Cisco Diagnostic Bridge issues (events) view

2.2   Connected TAC Market Trial

Customers. The data included in the study was compiled using the issues identified over the course of the first 30 months of the Connected TAC trial. The diagnostic results for over 30,000 devices belonging to one of 6 network device groups; IOS, Wireless LAN Controllers (WLC), IOS-XR, Adaptive Security Appliance (ASA), NXOS, and StarOS. Which provided reasonable coverage of routing and switching, wireless, security, and data center devices. Customers segments included managed service partners, retail, insurance, healthcare, finance/banking, and service providers. Customer participation was variable and was classified in three categories:

1) One and done, customers that installed the Diagnostic Bridge, analyzed one or two devices and then did not analyze a second time,
2) Temporary, customers that installed the Diagnostic Bridge, used it for several months for multiple devices, and then stopped analyzing devices, and

3) Active, customers that installed the bridge and were analyzing devices over several months preceding the construction of the data set.

Obviously, the participation characteristics of the customers will have an impact on the results, however, issues with data protection and anonymization have prevented us from distinguishing between the different types in the current data set.

User Interface Noise Reduction. Early customer utilization of the Connected TAC indicated that we were overwhelming customers with the issues being detected. In one early case where over 3800 devices were analyzed over 10,000 issues were identified (486 critical, 1350 warning, and 8337 informational). Irrespective of their impact that was an extreme number of issues for an organization to review, prioritize and fix. Several features were added to the application interface to enable a user to organize remediation plans. These included:

1) The ability for customers to "ignore" issues on a per device or global basis. Customers typically used this feature to ignore the operational issues (CPU high) and Cisco Best Practices that do not align with their operations approach (telnet port open).
2) An issue view that consolidated all the devices impacted by an issue under a single list item (see Fig. 4).
3) The ability to set a "remind me later" flag on an issue to temporarily hide the issue in the UI.
4) Integration with third-party business process automation tools that issues are sent to where the rules can be automatically applied to a result before it is percolated up to be addressed.
5) Filters were added in the UI (and persisted across use) to hide issues based on user context, and
6) A device grouping mechanism was added to enable customers to group "like" devices together and operate on them in a singular manner.

3 Consumption Data

The data included in the study was compiled using the issues identified over the course of the first 30 months of the Connected TAC trial. The diagnostic results for over 30,000 devices belonging to one of 6 network device groups; IOS, Wireless LAN Controllers (WLC), IOS-XR, Adaptive Security Appliance (ASA), and NXOS. Which provided diagnostic coverage of routing and switching, wireless, security, and data center devices.

The original data set consisted of over 1.6 billion records from the continuous monitoring of the issues detected and included all issues analyzed and included those that "passed" analysis and those that "failed". Since our research was focused on identifying those issues that customers remediated, we removed the "passed" items that were not preceded by a "failed" state during the analysis.

Fig. 4. Cisco Diagnostic Bridge issue view

3.1 Structure of the Data

A record used in the analysis took the form below:
<date/time><technology><module><module_labels><detection_type>
<issue_id ><issue_serverity>

> *date/time* – identifies when the issue was fixed
> *technology* – identifies the network device type the issue was detected against (IOS, WLC, IOS-XR, ASA, NXOS)
> *module* – identifies the diagnostic issue detection logic associated with the issue
> *module_labels* – identifies the set of tags associated with the module
> *detection_type* – indicates the type of issue being detected by the module (Availability, Capacity, Compatibility, Environment, Feature, Operational State, Performance, Security, Verification, and Unknown)
> *issue_id* – is a unique identifier for an issue detected for a specific device
> *issue_severity* – the potential impact the issue could have on a customer's device (critical, error, warning, notice, informational).

3.2 Demographics

Simple plots of the data looking at the all issues fixed across Technology and Detection Type did not provide any obvious patterns (see Fig. 5). Note that there are several items with an "unknown" detection type in the data set. This was a product of one of the diagnostic systems whose results were included had not classified their diagnostic modules, this classification is work in progress and we hope to include it in future analysis.

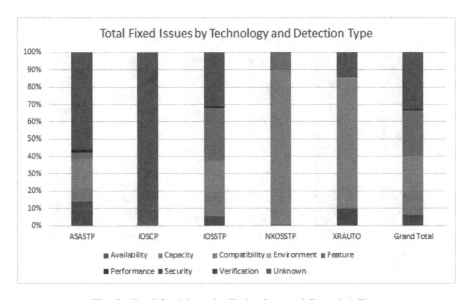

Fig. 5. Total fixed issue by Technology and Detection Type

A second plot containing just the unique Issues fixed across Technology and Detection Type resulted in similar but different patterns, indicating that certain Detection Types of IC were being fixed more frequently than others (see Fig. 6).

4 Machine Learning Consumption Analysis

4.1 Identifying Fixed Issues

When issue_severity changed from any severity value to "ok" for a given issue_id, we considered that issue_id to be 'fixed'. In our analysis of the data we found that there were a subset of modules reporting transient issues that would "fix" themselves as a function of when the analysis was conducted (issues like high CPU). Issue_id's from such module will likely have high ratio of being "fixed" based on the criteria used. Detecting whether issue_id was fixed by customer action or 'went away' because it was intermittent is outside of the scope current experiment and a subject of future study.

We conducted a series of experiments in applying machine learning in order to predict whether a given new issue would be fixed. Such prediction can be useful in 2 ways:

- For the IC curator it helps to understand what drives the customer decision to fix issues - insights on consumption would help focus on the IC that more customers find relevant to improving network availability.
- If an issue was found important by one customer, it may also be important to other "like" customers. The availability of this information would help customers focus their resources on issues that are considered by other customers.

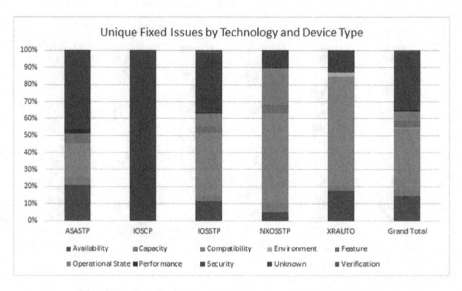

Fig. 6. Unique fixed issues by Technology and Detection Type

4.2 Analysis Experiments

The original historical data set was modified for the machine learning experiments using the method described above for identifying fixed issues and was composed from 3 parts:

- 1/3 of issues that were fixed (all fixed issues found in the data)
- 1/3 of issues that were not fixed, but occurred on devices where issues were fixed
- 1/3 of issues that were not fixed, but from modules that had other issues fixed

Data set has the following fields:
<time><technology><module><module_labels><issue_id><issue_severity><fixed y/n>

Note, the last column <fixed_y/n> is a label, its value is calculated using the method mentioned in the beginning. Unlike in the original data, each issue is only represented by 1 row in the new data set. The data is somewhat unbalanced (1/3 to 2/3) – this is intentionally done to reduce the risk of ML overfitting on device (i.e. assigning too much weight to particular devices) and on module (i.e. expecting that issues from certain modules will always be fixed).

Device_id was not shown to the ML as input, but has instead used as a fold (an input to split the dataset into training and testing, such that model will never see that same device in training and testing data) – this was intended to help the model generalize better. Using device id as part of input data can be studied in future experiments.

The H2O Driverless AI Machine learning product [17] was used to create models in below experiments. It evaluates multiple algorithms with different parameter settings to find the algorithm and settings performing best on a given data. The algorithm used by the models within H20 Driverless AI is GBM (Gradient Boosting Machine, [18]) which combines multiple, relatively simple models in a way that successive models rectify some of the weaknesses of the previous models. Figures in the Experiment sections below show model performance as Area under the curve (AUC, [19]) a method used to determine the performance of a binary classifier. In addition to a predictive model, a learning system generally produces a "feature importance" which is essentially the weight of each component of the input data in the decision of the model. This can be used evaluate the "usefulness" of various elements in the input and make improvements in data to enable building better models which would make more accurate predictions.

A number of the models were examined using ML interpretability feature of driverless AI in order to examine the patterns of inputs responsible for driving specific decisions.

Experiment 1. In this experiment we tried to predict whether an issue will be fixed (i.e. used <fixed y/n> as a label). All other data was used as input. issue_severity was identified as very strongly correlated with probability of fix and the model produced was able to make very accurate predictions. This finding was not surprising since one would naturally expect customers to fix issues with high severity, however it was comforting that the analysis produced this outcome. Subsequent experiments removed additional data (including severity) from input in order to see how prediction quality deteriorates if less information about each issue is available.

Experiment 2. In this experiment a model has been trained on all data except severity. The model still demonstrated good prediction performance at AUC 0.9176 which slightly below that of model using all data (see Fig. 7). Features based on module name and labels of the module were among the topmost useful features in predicting which issues would be fixed.

Fig. 7. Experiment 2 model less severity

Experiment 3. In this experiment the model was trained on all data except severity and module name. The model continued to demonstrate good prediction performance at AUC 0.91, slightly below that of model using all data except severity (see Fig. 8). Features based on the module labels were the top features.

Fig. 8. Experiment 3 model less severity and module name

Experiment 4. The final experiment removed the label information from the model. What remained was various module-related metadata. Without severity, module name, and module labels, the prediction quality of whether the issue would be fixed dropped significantly at AUC 0.7576 (Fig. 9).

Fig. 9. Experiment 4 model less severity, module name, and module labels

Top features were based on Detection Type metadata. It should be noted that unless all the device/module information was removed, Detection Type never appeared among the top features. It should be noted that Detection Type was not information presented to the user when they considered identified issues in the UI, the classification occurred independent from the Connected TAC market trial. It was included in this analysis to see if customers fixed issues of specific types based on their understanding of the issues identified. The analysis suggest that they do not.

These results suggest that exploring more regularized approaches with strong measures against overfit might be useful in further analysis of the data.

5 Conclusions

The results of the experiments conducted suggest that customers use issue_severity as the key driving factor in deciding whether to pursue fixing a detected issue. On the one hand this indicates that the efforts invested in setting severity are well served. On the other hand, it indicates that there aren't many other generally applicable tools for customers to sort through alerts, and allowing more ways to differentiate would possibly lead to better adoption, more fixes, and better network availability.

6 Next Steps

The data included in this analysis was constructed from several data repositories some of which had gone through different post-processes to address data protection and business reporting. In addition, some of the IC models have not yet been adequately classified (lack Detection Type). We continue to normalize the data set. In addition, only one year of the two and half years of available was included in the analysis leading to an inability to identify issues that we detected and resolved across calendar years. We are actively working on addressing these issues and plan to continue the analysis.

There was demonstrated value to providing customers will information to help them prioritize the problems they fix using available resources and network impact. However, there is opportunity to improve the tools and information that enable them to better sort through and differentiate the issues identified. Our research into how they consume issues is expected to accelerate future work in this area.

Finally, issue fixing is happening outside of the IC engine that detects and identifies issues, it is important to understand whether the customer has fixed the issue because of the alert from IC engine or if the issue was somehow externally found and fixed. To analyze this a future experiment will include duration prediction through the "staging" of results. One of the possible approaches could be to delay alerts for issues where 'time to fix' is reasonably predictable and track if the evidence of fix is also delayed. If the fix is seen without corresponding delay, it would be logical to believe that another approach was used to discover issues in question. On the other hand, if the fix was also delayed for a time, it would support the idea that alerts from the IC engine are used for locating issues.

References

1. Hood, C., Ji, C.: Proactive network-fault detection. IEEE Trans. Reliabil. **46**(3), 333–341 (1997)
2. Lazar, A., Wang, W., Dent, R.: Models and algorithms for network fault detection and identification: a review. In: Proceeding of the International Conference on Communication Systems, pp. 52–59, Singapore (1992)
3. Dawes, N., Altoft, J., Pagurek, B.: Network diagnosis by reasoning in uncertain nested evidence spaces. IEEE Trans. Commun. **43**(24), 466–476 (1995)

4. Deng, R., Lazar, A., Wang, W.: A probabilistic approach to fault diagnosis in linear lightwave networks. IEEE Sel. Areas Commun. **11**, 1438–1448 (1993)
5. Lakhina, A., Corvella, M., Diot, C.: Diagnosing network-wide traffic anomalies. ASC SIGCOMM Comput. Commun. Rev. **34**(4), 219–230 (2004)
6. Bashar, A., Parr, G., McClean, S., Scotney, B., Nauck, D.: Application of Bayesian networks for autonomic network management. J. Netw. Syst. Manag. **22**(2), 174–207 (2014)
7. Pitakrat, T., van Hoom, A., Grunske, L.: A Comparison of machine learning algorithms for proactive hard disk drive failure detection. In: Proceedings of the 4th International ACM Sigsoft Symposion on Architecting Critical Systems, pp. 1–10 (2013)
8. Castelli, R., Heidelberger, P., Hunter, S., Trivedi, K., Vaidyanathan, W., Zeggert, W.: Proactive management of software aging. IBM J. Res. Dev. **45**(2), 311–332 (2001)
9. Eschelbeck, G.: A proactive approach for computer security systems. J. Netw. Comput. Appl. **23**(2), 109–130 (2000)
10. Ramachandran, S., Ramachandran, A.: Rapid and proactive approach on exploration of vulnerabilities in cloud based operating systems. Int. J. Comput. Appl. **42**(3), 37–44 (2012)
11. Kycyman, E.: Discovering correctness constraints for self-management of system configuration. In: Proceedings of the International Conference on Autonomic Computing, pp. 28–35 (2004)
12. Oppenheimer, D., Ganapathi, A., Patterson, D.: Why do internet services fail, and what can be done about it? In: Proceedings of the with USENIX Symposium on Internet Technologies and Systems, Seattle, WA, pp. 1–16 (2003)
13. Yuan, D., Xie, Y., Panigraphy, R., Yang, J., Verbowski, C., Kumar, A.: Context-based online configuration-error detections. In: Proceedings of the 2011 USENIX Annual Technical Conference, pp. 619–634 (2011)
14. Xu, T., et al.: Do not blame users for misconfigurations. In: Proceedings of the 24th ACM Symposium on Operating Systems Principles, pp. 224–259 (2013)
15. Boutaba, R., et al.: A comprehensive survey on machine learning for networking: evolution, applications and research opportunities. J. Internet Serv. Appl. **9**, 16 (2018)
16. Connected TAC. http://www.cisco.com/c/en/us/support/services/connected-tac/index.html. Accessed 24 Jan 2020
17. H20 Driverless AI. https://www.h2o.ai/products/h2o-driverless-ai/. Accessed 29 Jan 2020
18. Gradient Boosting. https://en.wikipedia.org/wiki/Gradient_boosting. Accessed 29 Jan 2020
19. Area under the curve. https://en.wikipedia.org/wiki/Receiver_operating_characteristic#Area_under_the_curve. Accessed 19 Jan 2020

Cross-Scenario Performance Modelling for Big Data Ecosystems

Fatimah Alsayoud and Ali Miri[✉]

Department of Computer Science, Ryerson University, Toronto, Canada
{fatimah.alsayoud,Ali.Miri}@ryerson.ca

Abstract. Performance prediction is an essential aspect of several critical system design decisions, such as workload scheduling and resource planning. However, developing a model with higher prediction accuracy is a challenging task in big data systems due to the stack complexity and environmental heterogeneity. Workload modelling aims to simplify the connection between workloads factors and performance testing. Most of the workload models rely on a single scenario under test (SUT) method, where the trained and the evaluated data have the same distribution. However, a single SUT is not the ideal modelling method for big data workloads, as SUTs change frequently. Big data systems have a considerable amount of possible test scenarios that are generated from changing one or more elements in the testing environment, such as changing benchmarks, software versions, or cloud service types. To address this issue, we propose a cross-Scenario workload modelling method that aims to improve the workloads' performance classification accuracy. The proposed approach adopts the Transfer Learning concept for reusing models cross different but related scenarios. In this work, we evaluate the proposed approach on multi real-world scenarios in Hadoop which is an example of big data system. The empirical results showed that the proposed approach is more accurate than SUT method.

Keywords: Performance · Modelling · Transfer learning · Big data ecosystems

1 Introduction

Big data ecosystems have become the main element in today's technology. The ecosystems support big data sets and provide a variety of execution methods to meet system workload requirements. Big data ecosystems contain heterogeneous hardware and software, and they support a variety of data and workloads.

Designing optimal management policies and actions for big data ecosystems requires active monitoring and intelligent modeling. The model deign to test a particular objective like performance. Modeling for performance testing is one of the most successful management analyzing approaches. It can be used to measure the performance of a specific system object or a specific executing workload. In

© Springer Nature Switzerland AG 2020
H. Degen and L. Reinerman-Jones (Eds.): HCII 2020, LNCS 12217, pp. 211–228, 2020.
https://doi.org/10.1007/978-3-030-50334-5_14

both cases, the performance testing design is impacted by the characteristics of the running workloads. For example, a Hard Disk Drive (HDD) delivers its best performance when it serves sequential access workloads and not random access workloads. Another example is that the Hadoop ecosystem performs better with analytic workloads than Online Transaction Processing (OLTP) workloads.

Workload performance modeling provides an approach to examine performance on a particular Scenario Under Test (SUT), where the scenario can include the deployment solution, the software version or the benchmark setup of a particular Object Under Test (OUT). An example of OUT is Application Under Test (AUT). In general, the model result is a significant input element on many system decisions such as resource allocation. Therefore, it is crucial to design an accurate workload model as the performance test results reliability level is in line with the model accuracy.

Designing an accurate workload model for big data ecosystems is a challenging task due to ecosystem complexities and heterogeneity. There are several possible SUTs and lots of different case studies in big data ecosystems. For example, it is typical for the same ecosystem to have multi software versions, test workload performance with different benchmarking tools and to be executed on various deployment solutions [1].

Different SUTs produce dissimilar workload distributions. Many workload modeling approaches assume that trained and evaluated data has a similar distribution which is the same assumption as ML methods [2]. This assumption does not fit with big data ecosystem characteristics where the workload's distribution is changed with many possible SUTs. Constructing a model for each SUT from scratch is time-consuming and resource intensive. A similar distribution assumption does not work well in many real-life cases. For example, in computer vision, there is a need to recognize numbers either coming from handwritten data or from a picture where they have dissimilar distributions.

A number of deep learning related methods such as Transfer Learning (TL) are developed to deal with the distribution similarity constraint. TL provides a method to transfer knowledge between domains with a dissimilar distribution or dissimilar feature space to avoid building a fresh model every time the SUT is changed and to improve the model's accuracy. It is a well-used method in computer vision and natural language processing researchers. In this work, we will use TL to improve the performance model in a big data ecosystem.

1.1 Problem Statement and Motivation

The need for an accurate performance model remains even when the SUT or the executing workload is changed in a big data ecosystem. Designing an accurate model for a big data ecosystem such as Hadoop while considering SUT and workloads changing is a challenging task. Although there is a lot of Hadoop performance modelling work such as [3,4] and [5], most of it focuses on a single SUT. Only some consider multi SUT. For example, [6] provide a comprehensive analysis of how the workload behaviour, characteristic and distribution changes with SUTs change, and [7] designed a map task scheduling model for multi cloud service under test. However, none of the work considers improving the performance model for a particular SUT by utilizing another SUT model.

In practice, users typically change the setups to meet individual or application needs. For example, a big data ecosystem may be moved from on-premise to the cloud when there is a need for more storage. Another example is changing the benchmark measurement tool to analyze different SW elements. Although SUTs usually change frequently on a big data ecosystem, the scenarios modification factors have not been considered on the big data performance modelling yet.

In this paper, we investigate the accuracy of a big data ecosystem performance model with the proposed cross-scenario transfer approach. This approach builds a performance model based on a particular SUT ($Scenario_{src}$) and then transfers the source knowledge into another SUT ($Scenario_{tgt}$) to improve the target model's accuracy. A cross-scenario transfer approach adopts the inclusion method (multi scenarios) instead of the isolation (single scenario) method that is used by most existing performance modelling approaches. The inclusion method relaxes the sensitivity between model accuracy and the SUT characteristic. We demonstrate the approach with four scenarios: benchmarks, cloud service types, and Hadoop versions each with a couple of hypotheses. The experiential results show noticeable model accuracy improvement on the $Scenario_{tgt}$ with the proposed approach.

The paper is organized as follows. Sections 2 and 3 give a background of workload modelling and performance modelling challenges. The proposed approach overview is presented in Sect. 4. The evaluated case studies and the experimental result are discussed in Sect. 5. Finally, related work and the conclusion are presented in Sect. 6 and Sect. 7, respectively.

2   Workload Modelling

In general, modelling provides a foundational methodology to abstract and represent a particular aspect or relationship. Workload modelling establishes a connection between the workload characterization and the desired testing object. It helps to track how the workload and the corresponding testing object are changing. There are several possible algorithms for workload modelling such as predication, evolution, optimization and simulation. The algorithm is selected based on the model's objective. It is important to select the right design factors and define an accurate workload model. This is because many critical management decisions are using it as one of their fundamental elements.

Today's big data ecosystems serve a variety of workload types such as Online Transaction Processing (OLTP), Decision Support System (DSS), analytical and Machine Learning workloads. Each type has unique attributes and characterization. Moreover, the workload's pattern, behaviour and distributions change with the execution environment. Workload behaviours are very sensitive to execution environment components, setups and capability.

Workload modelling provides a method to simplify the relationship between workload characterization and behaviours with the desired testing object for a particular testing environment [8]. The testing object is the workload attributes that the model is designed to test it, such as performance, cost and resource utilization. The object measurement metric defined during the model construction is based on the final objective. For example, performance can be measured based on the workload's execution time or the throughput. Another essential aspect of workload modelling is the testing environment that affects workload behaviour and testing object values. In general, the model design is based on data from an environment with an aggregation of SWs and HWs. However, usually only one of the environmental elements is used to define the testing factors. For instance, in the application performance model, the application represents the testing environment and performance represents the testing object. Usually, the test application is called Application Under Test (AUT). The application performance model or workload model for performance testing investigates the relationship between application workloads and the corresponding performance.

Each aspect of the workload model should be designed and selected carefully since the accuracy of the design affects the accuracy of many management decisions and actions. The model can be used for descriptive, predictive and prescriptive analytics where the analytics output, for example, produces performance insight or predicts resource provisioning. The workload model can also be used for simulating workloads [9] and evaluating a system configuration [10]. Indeed, the workload-aware concept becomes a common aspect of different management architecture.

Workloads have different behaviours and patterns that change based on many factors like workload structure and the testing environment. For example, the behaviour of database workloads is different than the ML workloads. The last one is more complicated, requiring more resources and taking more time than the first one. The challenge occurs when a particular environment serves both types of workloads which is a normal situation in today's applications. The workload-aware concept is adopted on the system to serve each workload with its need, and define the management decision and action differently for each workload.

3   Big Data Performance Modelling Challenges

Modeling big data workloads for performance testing or in short performance modelling is a challenging task due to the ecosystem's complexity and the variability of the workload. It is challenging to design an accurate model for a big data ecosystem that has many interacting components and for workloads with very wide distributions. Traditional performance modelling assumes that data comes from a single SUT and has the same distribution. Both assumptions do not meet the need of big data ecosystems. Big data ecosystems have a complex architecture with several stages, multi-configuration parameters and multi SW elements. These ecosystems contain many highly interactive stages such as computing, resource management and a distributed file system which control how the workload is executed, how many resources are allocated to it and where it should be placed, respectively. Each of the controlling decisions impacts the workload's overall performance. Furthermore, the ecosystems have a massive amount of possible configuration parameters. Each of them has multiple possible values and each of the values affects the performance differently.

The SW elements in big data ecosystems are dependent on each other and some of the elements interact with elements from other ecosystems. For example, the Hadoop resource management element (YARN) [11] is used by many other systems such as Spark [12] and Storm [13]. Also, the Hadoop file system (HDFS) is used by OpenStack Swift and Amazon S3 [14]. The SW characteristics and the interaction have an implication on workload behaviour and therefore workload performance.

Each aspect of the big data ecosystem architecture impacts the performance of the workloads and can cause a change in workload distributions. It is hard to keep track of how each aspect of the ecosystem impacts performance. As written by [1] "we do not know much about real-life use cases of big data systems at all".

Two well-known modelling methods are used for simplifying big data ecosystem complexity: white box and black box methods. White box applies when the internal details are essential factors for decision making like considering configuration values for configuration tuning [15] or configuration optimization [16]. In contrast, the black box method does not consider the internal ecosystem details, and it is used by most work that focuses on the testing output instead of ecosystem details. Most of the black box methods and many of the white box methods follow the original modelling assumption of using a single SUT with the same distribution. Such assumptions would require building a considerable number of models from scratch to cover the possible big data scenarios. The proposed approach in this work benefits from the pre-built models on constructing a new one to improve model accuracy, and save model construction time and resources.

3.1   Scenario Under Test (SUT) Modelling

Most performance modelling approaches rely on a single SUT where data is collected from the same environment setups. For example, if the desired test object is an application, then the model is built based on collecting or simulating data from a particular application. Usually, the model built for a particular application cannot work as accurately for another application.

The performance modelling single SUT requirement is coming from the algorithm's restriction used on the model. The most used algorithms in performance modelling are analytic and Ml algorithms. Both types of algorithms require the trained data and the evaluated data to have the same distributions and feature space. To guarantee those requirements, the performance model expected data needs to come from a single SUT.

The issue is that most of today's case studies deal with changing the original scenario for different reasons. The model's accuracy cannot be guaranteed when any of the SUT factors are changed. For this reason, in most cases, the whole model has to be reconstructed when any change happens. A large number of models are needed to cover all of the possible scenarios.

Even though a single SUT method gets great attention from both industrial and academic communities, it has several limitations such as lack of supporting diverse scenarios. It requires contracting many models and isolating the built model from the other related models. It consumes time and resources, and is sensitive to workload distributions. A single SUT limitation motivates us to define the cross-scenario method that can support multi-scenarios in big data ecosystems and improve performance model accuracy.

4   Proposed Approach Overview

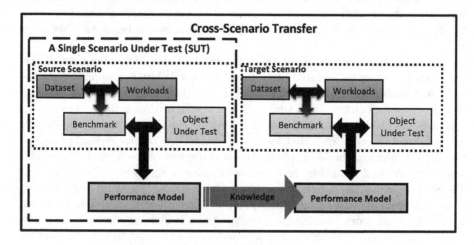

Fig. 1. Cross-Scenarios transfer performance modelling

The proposed approach overview is illustrated in Fig. 1 and the procedures are listed below:

- The examined dataset is Hadoop execution trace-data that is provided by the ALOJA open-access dataset [17]. The dataset has over 16.000 Hadoop executions with various setups like workload type, benchmark type, Hadoop versions, cloud service types and cloud providers.
- To provide the cross-scenarios transfer method with the correct data, both the Source $Scenario_{src}$ and Target $Scenario_{tgt}$ have to follow the same preparation process. For example, the process includes normalizing numeric data, coding categorical data and classifying the target output.
- Once the dataset is prepared, the $Scenario_{src}$ and the $Scenario_{tgt}$ are defined according to the desired hypothesis. For each examined hypothesis, the definition of the Source and Target scenarios are specified in Sect. 5.

- The Cross-Scenarios transfer method applies for each formulated hypothesis. The method contains three steps: build the source model according to $Scenario_{src}$, build the target model according to $Scenario_{tgt}$, and build the cross-scenarios transfer model according to the built source model and the $Scenario_{tgt}$.
- Source and Target models are constructed with Multi-Layer Perceptron (MLP).
- The built source model knowledge is used to build a cross-scenarios transfer model for the $Scenario_{tgt}$.
- The accuracy of results for the target (stand-alone) model and the target (cross- scenarios transfer) are analyzed for each hypothesis.
- We execute each hypothesis three times to calculate the average result of stand-alone and Transfer Learning models.
- To study the impact of sample size on the model's accuracy, we examined each hypothesis with six sample size $50, 150, 250, 350, 450$, and 500 that represents in the experiments as a ratio.

4.1   Methodology

Transfer learning is defined to relax distribution similarity constraints on trained and the evaluated data. TL assumes that the trained dataset and the validated dataset have different but related distributions. The TL method can be applied to almost all of the learning models such as classification, regression, and clustering. It provides a way to transfer knowledge between different learning tasks or between different domains. There are two types of domains: Source and Target. The Source domain is where the knowledge transfers from and the Target domain is where the knowledge transfers to.

5   Case Studies and Experimental Result

In order to evaluate the proposed approach, three different case studies are defined as Hadoop software versions, benchmark types and cloud service types. Each case study contains real-life scenarios that are used to determine the examined cross-scenario transfer.

5.1   Software Versions

Commercial and open-source software companies produce new software versions either to add new features or fix the software bugs. This can happen at any stage of the software life cycle. The frequency of producing new versions is in accordance with the software design model. In general, open-source software, such as big data ecosystems, release new minor and major versions more repeatedly than commercial software.

Versions have different configurations and therefore, the trace data that is produced is different in products. The trace-based method is the most used workload modelling method. Following how versions change is not a straightforward

Table 1. Experimental results: Hadoop versions hypothesis

Hypothesis	(Hadoop-1.0.3→ Hadoop-1.2.1)		(Hadoop 1→ Hadoop 2)		(Hadoop-1.2.1→ Hadoop-2.7.1)	
Sample ratio	Stand-alone	TL	Stand-alone	TL	Stand-alone	TL
10%	0.236 ± 0.043	0.371 ± 0.100	0.270 ± 0.040	0.391 ± 0.017	0.243 ± 0.070	0.278 ± 0.063
30%	0.310 ± 0.035	0.482 ± 0.122	0.310 ± 0.029	0.393 ± 0.017	0.344 ± 0.025	0.506 ± 0.122
50%	0.413 ± 0.057	0.485 ± 0.067	0.397 ± 0.041	0.509 ± 0.069	0.412 ± 0.022	0.573 ± 0.097
70%	0.232 ± 0.111	0.486 ± 0.113	0.445 ± 0.034	0.567 ± 0.151	0.451 ± 0.020	0.569 ± 0.077
90%	0.175 ± 0.041	0.388 ± 0.128	0.468 ± 0.017	0.572 ± 0.053	0.507 ± 0.018	0.636 ± 0.076
100%	0.120 ± 0.090	0.312 ± 0.227	0.500 ± 0.075	0.676 ± 0.055	0.526 ± 0.032	0.667 ± 0.025

task since several components are involved in the process. Although some work aims to simplify how versions are changed, for example model SW versions [18], it is still hard to predict how versions change and impact trace data behaviour [19].

Traditional workloads modelling assumes that trace data comes from a single Version Under Test (VUT) since trace data behaviours are relative to the software version. Such an assumption requires the model to rebuild as often as the software versions release.

In this section, we investigate how the new VUT performance model's accuracy improves when transferring knowledge from another VUT model. We evaluated three cross-HadoopVersion transfer hypotheses: Cross-MajorVersion transfer, Cross-MinorVersion transfer and Cross-Version transfer.

Cross-MajorVersion Transfer

We examine the model accuracy of Hadoop 2 when it uses knowledge from the Hadoop 1 designed model where $Scenario_{tgt} = Hadoop2$ and $Scenario_{src} = Hadoop1$. There is a significant component change between the two major versions. For example, while the MR framework takes the case of resource management on Hadoop1, Hadoop2 has a new resource management stage called YARN. Although changing the ecosystem architecture impacts trace data distribution and therefore performance mode, the version feature remains quite the same. Our results demonstrated that the Target scenario has by up to ∼45% more improvement than the stand-alone model.

Cross-MinorVersion Transfer

Each software major version has at least two minor versions. While the new major version contains the significant change, minor ones are usually developed to fix bugs or make a slight modification. This hypothesis tests two Hadoop1 minor versions 1.2.1 and 1.0.3 where $Scenario_{tgt} = Hadoop - 1.2.1$ and $Scenario_{src} = Hadoop - 1.0.3$. This hypothesis aims to evaluate the accuracy improvement when transferring knowledge between a pre-built model and a new one from the same major version but a different minor version. We expected the minor version to learn from each other better than the major versions since there are no huge changes between minor versions; most changes aim to fix bugs. The experiment showed that this hypothesis had an improvement between 17%–160%, where the accuracy improves as the sample size grows.

Cross-Versions Transfer

The last hypothesis tests model accuracy when both major and minor versions change. In this hypothesis, $Scenario_{tgt} = Hadoop - 1.2.1$ and $Scenario_{src} = Hadoop - Hadoop - 2.7.1$. This hypothesis had the same accuracy improvement as the major one reflected by up to ~47%.

The stand-alone and the transfer model accuracy of all cross-HadoopVersions transfer hypothesis are seen in Table 1 and Fig. 2.

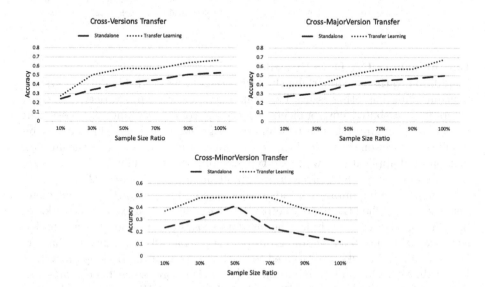

Fig. 2. Cross-HadoopVersions transfer hypothesis

5.2   Benchmark

Computer architecture contains many hardware and software components with different performances. Testing and comparing the performance of the components is an essential step for many further management actions. However, it is not easy to compare the performance of various components.

The benchmarking concept was defined to solve the testing difficulty. Benchmark is a measurement tool that provides a standard set of workloads with the corresponding dataset to test a particular goal like performance under a particular object like software. So, for example, vendors use a benchmark to compare their new product with the previous one. Besides, to provide testing standard suite, the benchmark can be used for simulation [20] and validating particular assumptions.

The traditional benchmarking method aims to test a particular object like SW or HW under a single benchmark [21]. Regardless of this method's usefulness, it has certain limitations like lack of supporting diversity objects, a small number of benchmarks and diversity accuracy.

Table 2. Experimental results: benchmarks hypothesis

Hypothesis	(TPC-H→ TPCH-hive)		(HiBench→ Hadoop-examples)		(HiBench→ HiBench2)	
Sample ratio	Stand-alone	TL	Stand-alone	TL	Stand-alone	TL
10%	0.344 ± 0.027	0.587 ± 0.310	0.213 ± 0.040	0.280 ± 0.143	0.262 ± 0.007	0.467 ± 0.093
30%	0.425 ± 0.060	0.462 ± 0.032	0.332 ± 0.015	0.379 ± 0.075	0.293 ± 0.043	0.380 ± 0.149
50%	0.500 ± 0.023	0.595 ± 0.100	0.429 ± 0.029	0.566 ± 0.081	0.335 ± 0.015	0.416 ± 0.075
70%	0.463 ± 0.060	0.535 ± 0.085	0.461 ± 0.011	0.577 ± 0.117	0.415 ± 0.050	0.476 ± 0.096
90%	0.564 ± 0.039	0.615 ± 0.011	0.451 ± 0.014	0.539 ± 0.030	0.393 ± 0.022	0.437 ± 0.088
100%	0.533 ± 0.027	0.585 ± 0.040	0.482 ± 0.054	0.603 ± 0.060	0.418 ± 0.028	0.507 ± 0.056

Benchmarking Big Data Systems

In addition to the benchmarking challenges seen in Sect. 3.1, big data ecosystem benchmarking has other issues like scalability, service types variety, use cases diversity, distributed environments, ecosystem complexity and the ecosystem repeatedly changing [1]. The benchmark design has many aspects that can be modified to meet one or more of the ecosystem characteristics such as the number of supported applications, workload types, a number of workloads, data set size, a number of workloads implementations and simulation support [22].

Defining the big data workloads model based on a single BUT cannot guarantee accuracy when the big data ecosystem case study changes. In this work, we use Hadoop as a case study for the big data ecosystem. Hadoop has a complex software stack and different configuration setups that affect workload behavior.

Several benchmarks are designed to meet the needs of the Hadoop ecosystem like evaluation [23] and assimilation [22]. Furthermore, some benchmarks are designed for Hadoop-related APIs such as HBase and Hive. The benchmarks can evaluate performance by measuring job running time or throughput that is calculated at the computing stage (MapReduce). The benchmark can also evaluate resource utilization through measuring CPU, memory and I/O that is calculated at the file system stage (HDFS). It is clear how complicated the benchmarking big data ecosystem is and how difficult it is to select the best benchmark suite. For these reasons, we aim to benefit from a previously built model with a particular benchmark when designing a new model with another benchmark through the cross-benchmark modelling method.

In this section, we investigate how the new BUT performance model's accuracy improves when transferring knowledge from another BUT. We evaluated three cross-Benchmark transfer hypotheses: Cross-BenchmarkType transfer, Cross-BenchmarkVersion transfer and Cross-BenchmarkExecutionAPI transfer.

Cross-BenchmarkType Transfer

Commonly, multi benchmarks are used to measure the same object. Trace data generated from different benchmarks may have a different distribution even when running on the same object. In this hypothesis, we examine HiBench [23] and Hadoop-Examples benchmarks. So, $Scenario_{tgt} = HiBench$ and $Scenario_{src} = Hadoop - Examples$. The HiBench benchmark contains the same fundamental read and write workloads on Hadoop-Examples and it also contains some ML workloads. This hypothesis focuses on evaluating model accuracy improvement when it reuses the built model from another benchmark type. The results of the correlational analysis show 32% improvement in the transfer model.

Cross-BenchmarkVersion Transfer

Usually, by the time, the same benchmark changes the tested workloads or the corresponding dataset to fix detected bugs, improve the benchmark or meet new requirements. In this hypothesis, we examine two versions of the HiBench benchmark, HiBench and HiBench2 where $Scenario_{tgt} = HiBench$ and $Scenario_{src} = HiBench2$. Our results demonstrated that the Target scenario has by up to ~78% more improvement than the stand-alone model.

Cross-ExecutionAPI Transfer

One of the most popular cases in big data ecosystems is executing the same workload from a different API. For example, a fundamental read workload can be executed directly in Hadoop or from the associated API such as Hive. In this hypothesis, we examine model accuracy when it builds based on data from the TPC-H benchmark [24] only and when it uses knowledge from the TPCH-hive benchmark. $Scenario_{tgt} = TPC - H$ and $Scenario_{src} = TPCH - hive$. The result shows that the transfer model has a 70% higher accuracy than the stand-alone model.

The stand-alone and the transfer model accuracy of all Cross-Benchmark type transfer hypotheses are shown in Table 2 and Fig. 3.

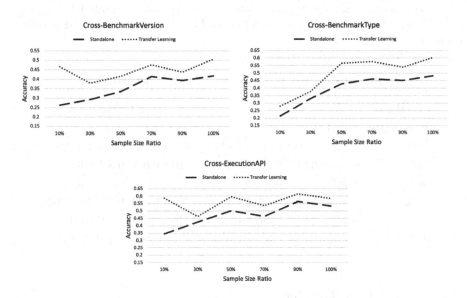

Fig. 3. Cross-Benchmark transfer hypothesis

5.3   Cloud Services

Cloud computing becomes an essential environment for individuals and big enterprises. At the same time, cloud is a very competitive area where new types and services are produced every day. It is very common that the user moves from one to another to satisfy their needs. As much as moving is required, sometimes it is difficult. For example, the user collects data and builds models based on their environment to achieve a particular objective. In most cases, when moving to a new environment, the objectives remain the same. However, the collected data and the built model cannot be reused in the new environment. It is time-consuming and causes resource exhaustion. The proposed method saves time, saves resources and improves accuracy.

The user moves to cloud or uses it as a solution for many things like getting higher performance or having more capacity. This work does not deal with comparing cloud and no cloud performance. It deals with taking advantage of the previously used method when using another one. In reality, users may move from cloud to on-premise or the opposite to meet their desired needs. The performance model is needed in both environments. The question is, does the user need to start a fresh performance model whenever moving from one solution to another? If yes, how long should the user wait to start collecting new data for building a new model?

In this section, we investigate how different cloud service types and cloud provider performance model accuracy improves when transferring knowledge from another service type or provider model. We evaluated two cross-CloudService transfer scenarios: cross-ServiceType transfer and cross-Providers transfer.

Table 3. Experimental results: cloud Service type hypothesis

Hypothesis	(IaaS→ SaaS)		(IaaS→ On-Premise)	
Sample ratio	Stand-alone	TL	Stand-alone	TL
10%	0.190 ± 0.01	0.269 ± 0.017	0.227 ± 0.010	0.266 ± 0.100
30%	0.231 ± 0.012	0.285 ± 0.084	0.316 ± 0.011	0.335 ± 0.076
50%	0.288 ± 0.02	0.358 ± 0.112	0.316 ± 0.009	0.409 ± 0.154
70%	0.272 ± 0.022	0.299 ± 0.1056	0.376 ± 0.039	0.413 ± -0.069
90%	0.294 ± 0.013	0.382 ± 0.023	0.448 ± 0.004	0.507 ± 0.150
100%	0.278 ± 0.020	0.319 ± 0.030	0.392 ± 0.026	0.450 ± 0.034

Cross-ServiceType Transfer

The big data ecosystem can deploy one of the cloud computing service type models such as IaaS (Infrastructure as a Service) or SaaS (Software as a Service), or it can deploy on-premise infrastructure. Each of the models has a unique environment and setup, and therefore, each produces different workload distributions.

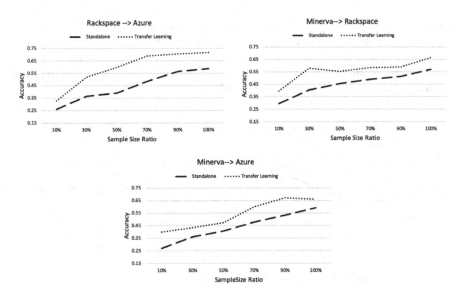

Fig. 4. Cross-Cloud provider transfer hypothesis

It is common for the user to move from one solution to another. The question is, can the user use the built model on one solution to help improve the accuracy of another one ? The result shows by up to ~30% improvement in the target model when the $Scenario_{tgt} = On - Premise$ and the $Scenario_{src} = SaaS$ and by up to ~42% when the $Scenario_{tgt} = IaaS$ and the $Scenario_{src} = SaaS$. It is clear that there is a benefit of using the previously built model in the cloud.

Table 4. Experimental results: Cloud provider hypothesis

Hypothesis	(Minerva→ Azure)		(Minerva→ Rackspace)		(Rackspace→ Azure)	
Sample ratio	Stand-alone	TL	Stand-alone	TL	Stand-alone	TL
10%	0.269 ± 0.023	0.399 ± 0.017	0.294 ± 0.030	0.396 ± 0.013	0.261 ± 0.037	0.329 ± 0.043
30%	0.361 ± 0.027	0.433 ± 0.067	0.406 ± 0.051	0.580 ± 0.140	0.365 ± 0.029	0.518 ± 0.173
50%	0.407 ± 0.016	0.473 ± 0.050	0.456 ± 0.040	0.552 ± 0.097	0.392 ± 0.030	0.597 ± 0.126
70%	0.477 ± 0.029	0.600 ± 0.154	0.488 ± 0.013	0.584 ± 0.109	0.484 ± 0.039	0.690 ± 0.042
90%	0.532 ± 0.023	0.671 ± 0.079	0.512 ± 0.014	0.588 ± 0.064	0.564 ± 0.013	0.704 ± 0.063
100%	0.591 ± 0.028	0.658 ± 0.040	0.569 ± 0.035	0.664 ± 0.042	0.588 ± 0.022	0.716 ± 0.069

Cross-Providers Transfer

There are hundreds of cloud providers in the market and all have different environments, loads and policies. The provider environment setup such as resource capability and amount of accept load impacts the behaviour and distribution of the workload. In this hypothesis, we evaluated the model with data generated from three providers: Azure, Rackspace and Minerva. The result shows by up to $\sim$48%, $\sim$43% and $\sim$53% where $Scenario_{tgt} = Minerva$ and $Scenario_{src} = Azure$, $Scenario_{tgt} = Minerva$ and $Scenario_{src} = Rackspace$, and $Scenario_{tgt} = Rackspace$ and $Scenario_{src} = Azure$ respectively.

The stand-alone and the transfer model accuracy of all Cross-CloudServices transfer hypothesis are seen in Table 3 and 4, and Fig. 5 and 4.

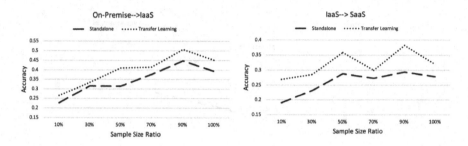

Fig. 5. Cross-Cloud Services type transfer hypothesis

6   Related Work

In this section, we discuss related work to performance modelling improvement in big data systems. Specifically, the discussion cover related approaches, methods and examined environments.

Model-driven [25] is one of the most commonly-used approaches in software design development. From the workload modelling perspective, the model can be designed to establish a relationship between workloads and certain aspects such as performance [8], resource utilization [26], cost [27] or power [28].

There have been numerous studies that employ model-driven on performance testing in big data system, specifically in Hadoop system, to gain insight information [3], establish features correlation [29], plan workload features [4] or to enhance the system [5].

Although several methods are reported in the literature to address performance modelling for big data systems, there is always room for improvement on such a complex system. For example, there is a wide choice of ML techniques available in the literature for performance modelling such as Supported Vector Machine(SVM), and tree-based regression have been respectively built upon time-series workloads [30], and [31] configuration tuning on Hadoop.

Previous big data performance modelling studies have almost exclusively focused on a single SUT method that is used as the model primary assumption. SUT method, as debated previously, does not fit the big data system needs. Therefore, the proposed approach adopts a cross-Scenarios modelling method instead of a single SUT. In order to address this design limitation, some literature starts to consider multi SUTs instead of a single SUT when designing the prediction model. Collaborate Mixture Density Networks (MDN), and feed-forward neural network is applied to improve resource usage prediction model for multi workload scenarios in the cloud environment [32] where the designed model is used to define optimal resource allocation policies. To support mix workload distribution on resources utilization estimation in the data centre [33] developed a feature extraction and model selection framework. Both designs intent on model resource utilization while we focus on performance. Besides, although the previous researches are applied ML methods to support multi SUTs, they did not examine transfer knowledge methods. They rely on a select concept for multi SUTs while the proposed approach relies on transfer concept for cross-Scenarios.

Transfer learning(TL) aims to improve model accuracy through sharing knowledge. Although the concept of transfer learning has gained attention since 1995 [2], it is most commonly used by only particular research areas like image recognition, and text classification more than other areas.

Over time, considerable literature has developed around applying TL for other research topics like dynamic resource provisioning [34], cloud configuration [35], software defect prediction [36] and software effort estimation [37]. More recently, a few work have been renewed interest in involving TL on improving performance modelling through considering different scenarios such as software configuration parameters [38] and hardware platforms [39]. The proposed approach has the same focus but considers big data system.

Although there are some deep learning related methods applied on Hadoop performance modelling such as a connected neural network (CNN)[5], currently, there is no work use transfer knowledge method on Hadoop system to support multi SUTs modelling. In addition, although there are many Hadoop performance modelling studies, the research on how a model accuracy can be improved through cross-Benchmark, cross-Cloud service types and cross-SoftwareVersions remains limited. For the first time, this paper addresses the need to understand how a new model construction can be improved by reusing a previously built model with cross-Scenarios in big data system.

7 Conclusions

Improving performance model accuracy is an essential step in big data ecosystems because it plays a critical role in many important management decisions and actions. Performance modelling's original assumption relies on a signal SUT that does not fit the big data ecosystem characteristic and causes low model accuracy. It is time-consuming and resource intensive. The proposed approach in this work provides the cross-scenarios transfer method that allows knowledge sharing between performance models with different but related scenarios. Transferring knowledge between models helps in improving target model accuracy. Big data ecosystems have many possible scenarios related to SW or HW changes. In this work, we explore the approach with four case studies: benchmarks, cloud service types, and Hadoop versions. Each of the examined case studies have several scenarios. We examine the cross-scenarios transfer method between the same case study scenarios to evaluate the target model's accuracy. Our result shows that the target performance model in the proposed approach is more accurate than SUT method. Such an improvement would make a significant change in management design decisions and actions and therefore, on the overall performance.

References

1. Chen, Y.: We don't know enough to make a big data benchmark suite-an academia-industry view. In: Proceedings of the WBDB, vol. 74 (2012)
2. Pan, S.J., Yang, Q.: A survey on transfer learning. IEEE Trans. Knowl. Data Eng. **22**(10), 1345–1359 (2009)
3. Yang, H., Luan, Z., Li, W., Qian, D.: MapReduce workload modeling with statistical approach. J. Grid Comput. **10**(2), 279–310 (2012)
4. Herodotou, H., Babu, S.: Profiling, what-if analysis, and cost-based optimization of mapreduce programs. Proc. VLDB Endow. **4**(11), 1111–1122 (2011)
5. Chen, C.-C., Hasio, Y.-T., Lin, C.-Y., Lu, S., Lu, H.-T., Chou, J.: Using deep learning to predict and optimize hadoop data analytic service in a cloud platform. In: Proceedings of the 15th International Conference on Dependable, Autonomic and Secure Computing (DASC), 15th International Conference on Pervasive Intelligence and Computing (PiCom), 3rd International Conference on Big Data Intelligence and Computing (DataCom) and Cyber Science and Technology Congress (CyberSciTech), pp. 909–916. IEEE (2017)
6. Chen, Y., Alspaugh, S., Katz, R.: Interactive analytical processing in big data systems: a cross-industry study of mapreduce workloads. Proc. VLDB Endow. **5**(12), 1802–1813 (2012)
7. Gouasmi, T., Louati, W., Kacem, A.H.: Optimal MapReduce job scheduling algorithm across cloud federation. In: Proceedings of the International Conference on Parallel and Distributed Processing Techniques and Applications (PDPTA), pp. 88–93 (2017)
8. Feitelson, D.G.: Workload modeling for performance evaluation. In: Calzarossa, M.C., Tucci, S. (eds.) Performance 2002. LNCS, vol. 2459, pp. 114–141. Springer, Heidelberg (2002). https://doi.org/10.1007/3-540-45798-4_6
9. Prats, D.B., Berral, J.L., Carrera, D.: Automatic generation of workload profiles using unsupervised learning pipelines. IEEE Trans. Netw. Serv. Manage. **15**(1), 142–155 (2017)
10. Ganapathi, A., Chen, Y., Fox, A., Katz, R., Patterson, D.: Statistics-driven workload modeling for the cloud. In: Proceedings of the 26th International Conference on Data Engineering Workshops (ICDEW), pp. 87–92. IEEE (2010)
11. Vavilapalli, V.K., et al.: Apache hadoop yarn: yet another resource negotiator. In: Proceedings of the 4th annual Symposium on Cloud Computing, p. 5. ACM (2013)
12. Apache Spark^{TM} - unified analytics engine for big data. https://spark.apache.org/
13. Apache Storm^{TM} - distributed dealtime computation system. https://storm.apache.org/
14. Apache Hadoop. https://hadoop.apache.org/docs/r2.9.0/
15. Zhu,Y., Liu, J., Guo, M., Ma, W., Bao, Y.: Acts in need: automatic configuration tuning with scalability guarantees. In: Proceedings of the 8th Asia-Pacific Workshop on Systems, pp. 1–8. ACM (2017)
16. Wang, K., Lin, X., Tang, W.: Predator–an experience guided configuration optimizer for Hadoop MapReduce. In: Proceedings of the 4th International Conference on Cloud Computing Technology and Science (CloudCom), pp. 419–426. IEEE (2012)

17. Berral, J.L., Poggi, N., Carrera, D., Call, A., Reinauer, R., Green, D.: Aloja: a framework for benchmarking and predictive analytics in hadoop deployments. IEEE Trans. Emerg. Top. Comput. **5**(4), 480–493 (2015)

18. Conradi, R., Westfechtel, B.: Version models for software configuration management. ACM Comput. Surv. (CSUR) **30**(2), 232–282 (1998)

19. Sharma, M.: Database environmental change impact prediction for human-driven tuning in real-time (DECIPHER), Ph.D. dissertation, Dakota State University (2013)

20. Mieścicki, J., Daszczuk, W.B.: Proposed benchmarks for PRT networks simulation, arXiv preprint arXiv:1710.05754 (2017)

21. Han, R., John, L.K., Zhan, J.: Benchmarking big data systems: a review. IEEE Trans. Serv. Comput. **11**(3), 580–597 (2018)

22. Han, R., et al.: BigDataBench-MT: a benchmark tool for generating realistic mixed data center workloads. In: Zhan, J., Han, R., Zicari, R.V. (eds.) BPOE 2015. LNCS, vol. 9495, pp. 10–21. Springer, Cham (2016). https://doi.org/10.1007/978-3-319-29006-5_2

23. Huang, S., Huang, J., Dai, J., Xie, T., Huang, B.: The HiBench benchmark suite: characterization of the mapreduce-based data analysis. In: Proceedings of the 26th International Conference on Data Engineering Workshops (ICDEW), pp. 41–51. IEEE (2010)

24. TPC Benchmarks. http://www.tpc.org/information/benchmarks.asp

25. Schmidt, D.C.: Model-driven engineering. Comput.-IEEE Comput. Soc. **39**(2), 25 (2006)

26. Harrison, P.G., Harrison, S., Patel, N.M., Zertal, S.: Storage workload modeling by hidden Markov models: application to flash memory. Perform. Eval. J. (PEVA) **69**(1), 17–40 (2012)

27. Yang, Z., Awasthi, M., Ghosh, M., Bhimani, J., Mi, N.: I/O workload management for all-flash datacenter storage systems based on total cost of ownership. IEEE Trans. Big Data (2018)

28. Tarsa, S.J., Kumar, A.P., Kung, H.: Workload prediction for adaptive power scaling using deep learning. In: Proceedings of the International Conference on IC Design & Technology, pp. 1–5. IEEE (201)

29. Yang, H., Luan, Z., Li, W., Qian, D., Guan, G.: Statistics-based workload modeling for mapreduce. In: Proceedings of the 26th International Parallel and Distributed Processing Symposium Workshops & Ph.D. Forum, pp. 2043–2051. IEEE (2012)

30. Lama, P., Zhou, X.: Aroma: automated resource allocation and configuration of mapreduce environment in the cloud. In: Proceedings of the 9th International Conference on Autonomic Computing, pp. 63–72 (2012)

31. Chen, C.-O., Zhuo, Y.-Q., Yeh, C.-C., Lin, C.-M., Liao, S.-W.: Machine learning-based configuration parameter tuning on hadoop system. In: Proceedings, IEEE International Congress on Big Data, IEEE 2015, pp. 386–392 (2015)

32. Khoshkbarforoushha, A., Ranjan, R., Gaire, R., Abbasnejad, E., Wang, L., Zomaya, A.Y.: Distribution based workload modelling of continuous queries in clouds. IEEE Trans. Emerg. Top. Comput. **5**(1), 120–133 (2016)

33. Iqbal, W., Berral, J.L., Erradi, A., Carrera, D.: Adaptive prediction models for data center resources utilization estimation. IEEE Trans. Netw. Serv. Manage. **16**(4), 1681–1693 (2019)

34. Zhu, Q., Agrawal, G.: Resource provisioning with budget constraints for adaptive applications in cloud environments. IEEE Trans. Serv. Comput. **5**(4), 497–511 (2012)

35. Hsu, C.-J., Nair, V., Menzies, T., Freeh, V.W.: Scout: An experienced guide to find the best cloud configuration, arXiv preprint arXiv:1803.01296 (2018)
36. Ma, Y., Luo, G., Zeng, X., Chen, A.: Transfer learning for cross-company software defect prediction. Inf. Softw. Technol. **54**(3), 248–256 (2012)
37. Kocaguneli, E., Menzies, T., Mendes, E.: Transfer learning in effort estimation. Empirical Softw. Eng. **20**(3), 813–843 (2014). https://doi.org/10.1007/s10664-014-9300-5
38. Jamshidi, P., Velez, M., Kästner, C., Siegmund, N., Kawthekar, P.: Transfer learning for improving model predictions in highly configurable software. In: Proceedings of the 12th International Symposium on Software Engineering for Adaptive and Self-managing Systems, pp. 31–41. IEEE (2017)
39. Valov, P., Petkovich, J.-C., Guo, J., Fischmeister, S., Czarnecki, K.: Transferring performance prediction models across different hardware platforms. In: Proceedings of the 8th ACM/SPEC on International Conference on Performance Engineering, pp. 39–50 (2017)

Interaction with the Soundscape: Exploring Emotional Audio Generation for Improved Individual Wellbeing

Alice Baird[1(✉)], Meishu Song[1], and Björn Schuller[1,2]

[1] Chair of Embedded Intelligence for Health Care and Wellbeing,
University of Augsburg, Augsburg, Germany
`alice.baird@informatik.uni-augsburg.de`
[2] GLAM – Group on Language, Audio, and Music, Imperial College London,
London, UK

Abstract. Our daily interaction with the soundscape is in flux, and complex natural sound combinations have shown to have adverse implications on user experience. A computational approach to stabilise the sonic environment, tailored to a user's current affective state may prove beneficial in a variety of scenarios, including workplace efficiency, and exercise. Herein, we present initial perception test results, from a rudimentary approach for soundscape augmentation utilising chromatic feature sonification. Results show that arousal and valance dimensions of emotion can be altered through augmentation of three classes of natural soundscape, namely 'mechanical', 'nature', and 'human'. Proceeding this we outline a possible approach for an affective audio-based recognition and generation system, in which users (either individually or as a group within a specific environment) are provided with an *augmentation* of their current soundscape, as a means of improving wellbeing.

Keywords: Audio generation · Wellbeing · Machine learning · Human Computer Interaction

1 Introduction

The soundscape is the combined audio components being heard at a given moment in time [52]. Involuntarily, we are continually interacting with the soundscape, as – unlike visual interaction – we cannot 'close our ears' to stop an audible input. With this in mind, uncontrolled audio environments, have shown to impact individual wellbeing, substantially heightening stress, and causing a long-term decline in workplace efficiency [31].

In regards to these topics, there are many more research efforts occurring in the fields of affective acoustic ecology [15], and general sound recognition [12],

This work is funded by the Bavarian State Ministry of Education, Science and the Arts in the framework of the Centre Digitisation.Bavaria (ZD.B).

© Springer Nature Switzerland AG 2020
H. Degen and L. Reinerman-Jones (Eds.): HCII 2020, LNCS 12217, pp. 229–242, 2020.
https://doi.org/10.1007/978-3-030-50334-5_15

with smart-device applications for aiding sleep, and meditative states now being much more common[1]. However, such apps do not yet personalise the audio in real-time manner.

Herein, we present background and initial findings to support the development of a system which does create a personalised interaction with sound. Showing through previous studies that multiple modalities can be used non-intrusively to gain an understanding of a user's current state [3], and that deep generative approaches show the ability to generate affective data [4].

This contribution is structured as follows; first we conduct a brief literature review of related work under the topics of sound and stress reduction, Human Computer Interaction (HCI) and affective audio, and computational audio generation approaches. We then perform a preliminary perception study, based on a rudimentary approach for soundscape augmentation, and discuss the results. Proceeding this we propose a state-of-the-art method for the application of affective soundscape audio augmentation. Finally, we conclude our results, and summaries our outlook for the next steps of this research area.

2   Related Work

2.1   Sound for Wellbeing

When discussing sound as a taxonomy, this extends across many branches, from environmental sounds to speech. Within the field of *sound healing*, there are many sound sources including; acoustic and synthetic, which show to have a variety of wellbeing benefits including stress reduction [50]. Previous studies have suggested that excessive sound levels can have an effect on the hospital working environment, having long-term implications for nursing staff [40].

Acoustic-based tools are used commonly by healing practitioners, e. g. tuning forks at 128 Hz for relieving tissue-based abnormalities [19], or ritual communal drumming, which has shown to improve wellbeing in young people [59]. Another sound-based practice aimed at the reduction of stress is Transcendental Meditation (TM) [27], partially utilising the spoken mantra[2]. Additionally, through the integration of both sound and breathing techniques, TM has shown to both physiologically and psychologically reduce stress, quantitatively showing a decreased average theta (θ) when monitoring via Electroencephalography (EEG) and increased alpha (α) [18].

As well as such vocal mantras, practitioners of TM integrate a series of acoustic instruments such as the Tibetan or crystal singing bowls. These bowls have a long history of use in mediation [24] and are played with a continuous oscillation around the circumference of the bowl, resulting in a full overtone sound which

---

[1] Popular applications currently available for the purpose of aiding sleep and reducing states of arousal include: Headspace, Noisli, Pzizz, Slumber, Calm, Sleep Cycle, etc.

[2] The spoken mantra, through the repetition of phrases such as 'has no meaning', would be personal to the individual and is selected due to the resonant and harmonising ability within the meditator.

sustains a prolonged resonation. The Tibetan singing bowl has been applied to many stress reducing scenarios – including as an aid to school teachers [9] – and has shown to increase feelings of spirituality, in turn relieving symptoms of stress including tension [20]. The Tibetan Singing bowl has also been integrated in a variety of mHealth stress reducing targeted apps [22].

In regards to synthetic-based sound tools, there have been a variety of studies which have shown stress reduction results, in various environments [31]. Synthetic music within a hospital has shown to have a strong impact on a patient's experience [61]. Similarly, the acoustic environment of a workplace benefits from artificial acoustic design [30], and through integration of synthetically designed audio environments the workplace experience also improves [25]. Synthetic audio generation has also been investigated in the realm of therapeutic applications, specifically exploring how synthetic sound might influence listeners experiences in psychological areas, such as creativity or self-perception [44].

There is also much research focused on how listeners perceive music and how emotions are brought on by music or what psychological mechanisms causes these emotions [26]. For example, music is often used to enhance the emotional impact of movies [7]. Unlike most other stimuli that evoke emotions, such as encounters with dangerous animals, threats or facial expressions, music has no obvious, intrinsic survival value [34]. Blood et al. presented a novel approach to the study of music and emotion, using positron emission tomography to measure cerebral correlates of affective and perceptual responses to musical dissonance [8].

2.2 HCI and the Use of Audio for Wellbeing Applications

Over the past two decades, researchers have increasingly realised the importance of recognising the emotional aspects which occur during human-computer interaction (HCI) [11]. For example, in many HCI scenarios a computer aided tutoring system is highly desirable and a response based on emotional or cognitive state of the human user may improve user experience [55]. During interaction humans provide emotion-based cues from physical gesture, facial expressions and also the voice [23]. Nowadays affective recognition systems are mainly developed through 2 key qualitative steps: understanding emotional response, adapting the development based on user experience.

One method for non-intrusively understanding a user's experience is through the voice, and there is an abundance of HCI applications specifically in the realm speech recognition, e. g. voice dialling [43]. Automated speech recognition systems are also integrated in language learning paradigms to improve pronunciation [51]. As well as his Voice-based user interfaces are becoming ubiquitously available, being embedded both into everyday mobility via smartphones, and into the life of the home via assistant devices [46].

As well as the voice, there has been an increased interest in the impact of in-game audio. Paterson et al. developed an audio design with a complex and immersive soundscape, which is emotionally engaging and supports the game narrative [45]. Similarly, Roden et al. proposed a framework for interactive narrative-based audio only adventure games [47], and Sliwinski et al. explored the development of an audio-visual game to induce wellbeing and mindfulness [56] Similarly, Rogers et al. discussed games which are considered relaxing and encourages research directions for exploring the role of game audio specifically, to improve player wellbeing, via stress reduction [48].

Thus, there is much research exploring the potential use of audio for wellbeing. Roger et al. identified the effect of music in games as a preventative measure against stress in everyday life by facilitation of relaxation [48]. In relation to health specifically, Willianmson et al. explored first-time mothers' breast-feeding difficulties through the use of audio-diaries [58], and Mirelman used audio-biofeedback for improving Parkinson's patients balance [38]. Additionally, Dijk et al. presented the concept of auditory–tactile stimulation for health and well-being through carefully selected audio–tactile stimuli causing a person's bodily, mental and emotional state to be altered [13].

2.3   Audio Generation

Although the scope of this study is focused largely on the generation of complex soundscapes, audio generation can refer to an array of audio-based fields, from speech synthesis to instrument modelling. In this regard, many of the methods mentioned will be found across all such domains, but are not limited to them. Conventional computational methods for audio generation would include a variety of digital signal processing approaches, such as Hidden Markov Models [53] or cellular automata [10]. These methods are still applied today, however the current state-of-the-art for the term audio generation would refer to a division within machine learning in which systems are largely data-driven [57].

An earlier deep approach for generating audio was Deep Minds WaveNet [57]. WaveNet is a progressive auto regressive generator, and is an audio adaptation of the PixelCNN [42], modelling features of raw audio which are represented as 8-bit audio files, with 256 possible values. During the training process, the model predicts values for waveforms (audio signals with a temporal resolution of at least 16 kHz samples per second) at each step comparing them to the true value, using cross-entropy as a loss function. In this way, the WaveNet architecture is applying a multi-class classification of 256-classes [35]. As a means of decreasing the computational time expense, that may be associated to such a classification task, WaveNet applies the method of stacked dilated casual convolutions, reducing the receptive field without any substantial loss in the resolution [60].

Although WaveNet has been showcased in the speech synthesis domain, the applications are broad. The original architecture showed promise for high fidelity in music with comparable human perception results [57]. Recently, an adaptation of the WaveNet framework is the NSynth (Neural Synthesizer) auto encoder specifically tailored towards synthesis of musical notes [16].

Another neural network approach, which was motivated by WaveNet , is SampleRNN [37]. This model is an unconditional end-to-end neural audio generation architecture that uses auto-regressive multilayer perceptron's and a Recurrent Neural Network (RNN), in a hierarchical structure, to capture temporal variance over large audio signal durations. Despite showing competitive human perception results against WaveNet, the SampleRNN suffers from unrealistic computation time and the perception results are not shown to be significant, rather tendencies [37]. However, the advantages of time dependent RNNs would be suitable for soundscape generation offline.

First proposed by Goodfellow et al. in 2014 [21], Generative Adversarial Networks (GANs) have found recent popularity within the data generation domain and are arguably becoming a fundamental approach for this type of task. Essentially, generating new samples of audio based on raw audio signals, GANs are a pair of unsupervised networks which compete against each other, *generating* new instances of data until the *discriminator*, can no longer reliably tell a difference.

As well as being applied for the task of unsupervised representation learning from audio spectrograms [1], GANs aimed specifically for use with audio generation were first introduced in 2018, with WaveGANs and SpecGANS [14]. Approaches typically applied in the vision domain, were explored by extracting spectrogram images and comparing the networks ability to generate audible spectrogram instances. This was followed by the Conditional WaveGAN [33], which specifically focused on waveform generation through a concatenation based conditioning approach. Despite WaveGAN showing strong results for what is described as *human audible* samples, post-processing for noise reduction and appropriate optimisation due to instability were required.

3   First Step Soundscape Augmentation Perception Study

To evaluate the efficacy of augmentation of the original soundscape to alter emotional perception, we conducted a short listening test with 10 individuals[3]. Listeners evaluated arousal and valence dimensions of emotion [49], for each audio file (listening in a randomised order, twice before giving their score), on a 5-point Likert scale (e. g. $0 =$ Low arousal/valence, $4 =$ High arousal/valence). All listeners used headphones for this study.

3.1   Preliminary Acoustic Analysis

As we have mentioned previously in Sect. 2.1, the singing bowl is a common acoustic instrument used by healing practitioner (including in Transcendental Meditation) for improving states of wellbeing. With this in mind, we have chosen to use its most similar synthetic signal – a Sine wave – for this first-step augmentation approach. A sine wave (also known as a sinusoid) is a continuous periodic oscillation. As a function of time (t), a sine wave can be expressed as:

$$y(t) = A sin(2\pi f t + \varphi)$$

where in this case A refers to amplitude from zero, f the frequency, i. e. the number of oscillations (cycles) occur over t, and φ is *phase* i. e. when the cycle of oscillation is $t = 0$.

---

[3] 5 Female and 5 Male. Nationalities: 2 British, 4 Chinese, 4 German.

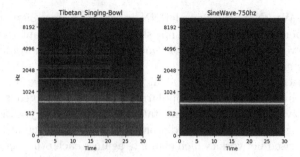

Fig. 1. Spectrogram representation of 30 s from a Tibetan Singing bowl recording (left), and a generated pure sine tone (right). Although similar in fundamental frequency, it should be noted, that overtones (as well as reverberation) which can be observed in the spectrogram representation of the singing bowl, may play a strong part in altering a listener's affective state.

We performed an initial acoustic analysis of multiple recordings from the singing bowl, taken from the Acoustics Sounds for Wellbeing Dataset [6], and compared this sine waves of matching frequency. Findings show that characteristics of the audio are similar (cf. Fig. 1, for spectrogram representation). For example, both are a continuous single frequency oscillation, and when monitoring pitch continuously the standard deviation came to 24.9 Hz, and 23.4 Hz for Tibetan and Sine, respectively. However, it is worth noting that aspects from the singing bowl such as resonance (and even human intervention) may play a deeper part in the improvement of wellbeing, and this is not replicated intrinsically through a single sine wave generator.

3.2   Audio Generation Approach

To summaries the rudimentary audio generation approach applied for this initial study, we utilised the Emo Soundscapes Database [17], and extracted Chroma features from 56 audio files (28 with lower rating of arousal and valence, and 28 with higher ratings of arousal and valence). Audio files were within the classes of 'Mechanical', 'Human', and 'Nature', and we then, sonified the corresponding chromatic notes (A-G#) as sine waves, overlaying this onto the original soundscapes.

To achieve this, we developed the first iteration of WELLSOUNDS[4] In this 'chromatic approach' we extract a 12 dimensional chromatic feature set from each trimmed (7 sec) audio file (prior to normalisation). At a given time-step based on the duration of the audio file. Features are then assigned to the corresponding Sine wave frequency (e. g. 65.4 Hz = C2, and 110.0 Hz = A2), and combined to make polyphonic (naive) chord combinations. The segments of audio are then concatenated to make a continuous 'augmentation' of the original audio file. The

---

[4] To apply the methods used in this study to new audio of fixed length visit the WELLSOUNDS Github: https://github.com/wellSounds/chromatic-approach.

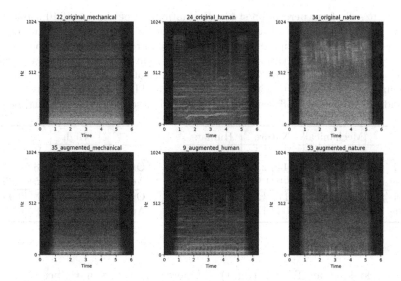

Fig. 2. Spectrogram representation of original audio and augmented audio. For each of the 3 classes – Mechanical, Human, and Nature. Through post processing of the original soundscapes it can be seen that the energy of noise is also reduced in the augmented soundscape, particularly prominent in the nature example.

resulting synthetic sine wave augmentation is then mixed onto the original audio file (proceeding a number of post-processing steps including equalisation and compression). A spectrogram representation of the WELLSOUNDS augmentation can be seen in Fig. 2[5].

3.3 Perception Study Results

Results from the study (based on the 3 classes), are shown in Table 1. To evaluate the significant (or not) difference between soundscape augmentation and original soundscape, we conduct a two-tailed T-test, rejecting the null-hypothesis at a significance level of $p < 0.05$ and below.

When observing the results from a class basis (cf. left of Table 1), of note we see there is a change in emotion perception across all classes, and particularly for the 'Nature' class a significant difference is shown between the augmented and original data types ($p = 0.001$, and 0.04 for valence and arousal, respectively). Although not necessarily a positive affect for the augmented soundscapes, this does show promise for the ability of such an augmentation approach to alter states of wellbeing. Additionally, from Fig. 3, we see that the standard deviation between listeners is quite wide, and therefore further studies with a larger group of listeners may give a more reliable trend.

---

[5] A selection of original and augmented soundscapes can be heard at the following link http://bit.ly/2T7uu4P.

Table 1. Results from perception study. Evaluating the perception of 10 listeners on a Likert scale of 0–4 for (V)alence and (A)rousal of the (Ori)ginal and (Aug)mented version of the soundscape. In the left table, results are presented based on the 3 soundscape classes (Mechanical, Nature, Human). In the right table, results are grouped by original ratings of (high) a (low) emotional dimensions of valence and arousal from the EmoSoundscape DB. Reporting Mean (μ) and Standard Deviation ($\pm$) across all listeners. * indicates significant difference, between (Ori)ginal soundscape, and (Aug)mented.

	Mechanical		Nature		Human	
	V	A	V	A	V	A
Ori (μ)	1.74	1.92	2.44	2.32	2.16	2.08
Aug (μ)	1.48*	2.05	1.88*	1.98*	1.55*	2.22
Ori ($\pm$)	0.93	1.11	1.17	1.09	0.92	1.03
Aug ($\pm$)	0.82	1.03	1.04	1.10	0.95	1.02

	High		Low	
	V	A	V	A
Ori (μ)	2.44	2.51	1.80	1.71
Aug (μ)	1.74	2.34	1.51	1.85
Ori ($\pm$)	1.18	1.04	0.81	0.99
Aug ($\pm$)	1.04	1.06	0.85	0.99

When looking at Table 1 (right) – where audio files have been grouped based on their original Emo Soundscapes DB emotion rating (i. e. High valence/arousal, and Low valence/arousal) – we see that although consistently different to the original source, High emotion does remain to higher than low emotional audio groups. Suggesting that trends in the audio files which are inherent to the emotion are left unchanged. However, this assumption requires further study.

Given this naive approach, further adaptation and audio choices based on emotional content may see further improvements in affective change. It is also worth noting that the audio applied here is extremely rudimentary, and further digital signal processing techniques, along with the use of more typically 'pleasing' audio may would be of value to explore.

4   A Deeper Approach for Soundscape Augmentation

Based on our initial findings, in this section we briefly outline a methodology for a soundscape augmentation, which is based on an individual's current state, and would be applied in further studies by the authors on this topic. An overview of this system is given in Fig. 3. Predominately an audio-based approach, we aim to utilise methodologies from the field of Speech Emotion Recognition (SER) [54], as well Generative Voice Conversion [28]. First in this section, we outline the feature extraction method for understanding and individuals state. Following this an *offline system*, in which the user would define a duration of listening, in a quiet space is defined. We also propose an *online system*, which in real-time 'augments' the natural soundscape, through sonification of audio features, generated based on emotional understanding of the user.

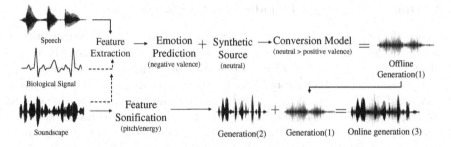

Fig. 3. Overview of the proposed affective soundscape generation system for wellbeing, via multimodal monitoring.

4.1 Feature Extraction and Emotional Prediction

From the user's input, a fusion of features known to the affective computing community (e. g., MFCCs, and spectral) [29], can be extracted from multiple modes (including the voice, as well as the current soundscape). Of note, in recent works we have found a correlation between biological signals, including hormone-based cortisol and speech features, during a stressful situation [3], suggesting that handcrafted features may be useful in this context to gain an understanding of a user state of lower wellbeing. As well this, if appropriate based on user-device, biological feature can also be utilised for understanding states of lower wellbeing [2].

Utilising deep, pre-trained neural networks, the tailored feature sets can then be classified for their emotionality (e. g., level of arousal and valence) [32]. The resulting, prediction are then used to define the current state of a user, as a condition for audio generation.

4.2 Offline Audio Generation

For the offline generation, perhaps in the scenario where a listener aims to reduce their affective state for short-term period, a pre-existing synthetic emotional source could be used. In this case, a dataset of synthetic audio could be applied, such as the richly annotated EmoSynth database [5]. From this, one-minute emotional samples can be created based on their emotional values; typically, this equates to aspects in audio such as, high arousal being equal to higher pitch and low arousal being equal lower pitch, with valence being a somewhat more complex aspect of emotion in terms of acoustic representation. As a means of obtaining varied (i. e. novel for each user interaction) audio outputs for each user, with more fine-grained differences, a generative adversarial strategy can be applied, such as 'StarGAN' [28]. In this scenario, a network can be trained on a selection of emotional classes. Following this depending on the given emotional prediction (or target) of the individuals state, a synthetic soundscape (the source) is then generated based on the target (user defined) emotion,e. g. if the user is in a state of high arousal, a low aroused soundscape is generated, for a (user-defined) given period of listening.

4.3 Online Generation Including Feature Sonification

For longer interaction periods, possibly even continual (i. e. for implementation in a chaotic working environment), we propose a method in which the offline audio generation is combined with a sonification of the features from the natural ongoing soundscape. To summarise this process, features such as, *chromatic, energy, and F0* can be extracted from the incoming soundscape signal, and reasoning be applied to sonify the Chroma and pitch-based features based on the energy of the signal at a given time-point. As well as this, the natural rhythm of the soundscape can be extracted and as an option, then applied to the resulting real-time generation. Rhythm is included, as a consistent rhythm has shown to have positive effects on wellbeing, producing a calming affect [36]. These two sonification approaches (feature-based and rhythm) are then applied to the offline generation process previously described, and the user is able to balance the level for each.

5 Conclusion and Outlook

In this contribution, we made preliminary user studies on the effect of augmenting natural soundscapes, as well as proposing a 'next-step' methodology for a personalised version of such a system. A series of *perception studies* [39] including those by the authors [5], support the initial assumption that specific combinations of audio can alter states of individual wellbeing - and initial results in this contribution also show similar trends. Thus, these findings support further development of the work described herein.

When *monitoring states* of poor wellbeing, there are many emotional states linked to this, prior work by the authors has focused on public-facing speech, as a marker of stress [3]. Findings have shown that through the use of a combination of conventional acoustic features, and machine learning algorithms, biological signals including skin conductance, blood volume pressure, and cortisol can be predicted during such states of lower wellbeing. Based on this, it would be of great interest to approach the development of a multimodal system, however with audio monitoring being non-intrusive and lower in resources, it may alone be the optimal modality.

In regards to audio generation, a deep auto regressive generative model such as WaveNet [41] has shown promise for generating affective data [4], and through the use of a generative adversarial network, the authors are currently experimenting with emotional data in a conversion paradigm, i.e., from one emotion to the other, e. g., happy to sad. Integrating such a generation method here, may allow for more variety in generation, however a naive training approach based on single emotions does also show promise for the desired outcome.

Acknowledgements. This work is funded by the Bavarian State Ministry of Education, Science and the Arts in the framework of the Centre Digitisation.Bavaria (ZD.B).

References

1. Amiriparian, S., Freitag, M., Cummins, N., Gerzcuk, M., Pugachevskiy, S., Schuller, B.W.: A fusion of deep convolutional generative adversarial networks and sequence to sequence autoencoders for acoustic scene classification. In: Proceedings of 26th European Signal Processing Conference (EUSIPCO), EURASIP, pp. 982–986. IEEE, Rome (2018)
2. Baird, A., Amiriparian, S., Berschneider, M., Schmitt, M., Schuller, B.: Predicting blood volume pulse and skin conductance from speech: introducing a novel database and results. In: Proceedings IEEE 21st International Workshop on Multimedia Signal Processing, MMSP 2019, 5 pages. IEEE, Kuala Lumpur, September 2019
3. Baird, A., et al.: Using speech to predict sequentially measured cortisol levels during a trier social stress test. In: Proceedings Interspeech 2019, pp. 534–538 (2019)
4. Baird, A., Amiriparian, S., Schuller, B.: Can deep generative audio be emotional? Towards an approach for personalised emotional audio generation. In: Proceedings IEEE 21st International Workshop on Multimedia Signal Processing, MMSP 2019, 5 pages. IEEE, Kuala Lumpur, September 2019
5. Baird, A., Parada-Cabaleiro, E., Fraser, C., Hantke, S., Schuller, B.: The perceived emotion of isolated synthetic audio: the emosynth dataset and results. In: Proceedings of the Audio Mostly 2018 on Sound in Immersion and Emotion, p. 7. ACM (2018)
6. Baird, A., Schuller, B.: Acoustic sounds for wellbeing: a novel dataset and baseline results (2019)
7. Baumgartner, T., Esslen, M., Jäncke, L.: From emotion perception to emotion experience: emotions evoked by pictures and classical music. Int. J. Psychophysiol. **60**(1), 34–43 (2006)
8. Blood, A.J., Zatorre, R.J., Bermudez, P., Evans, A.C.: Emotional responses to pleasant and unpleasant music correlate with activity in paralimbic brain regions. Nat. Neurosci. **2**(4), 382 (1999)
9. Brown, P.L.: In the classroom, a new focus on quieting the mind. https://www.nytimes.com/2007/06/16/us/16mindful.html. Accessed 2 Feb 2019
10. Burraston, D., Edmonds, E., Livingston, D., Miranda, E.R.: Cellular automata in midi based computer music. In: Proceedings of the 2004 International Computer Music Conference, p. no pagination. International Computer Music Association (2004)
11. Calvo, R.A., D'Mello, S., Gratch, J.M., Kappas, A.: The Oxford Handbook of Affective Computing. Oxford University Press, Oxford (2015)
12. Chu, S., Narayanan, S., Kuo, C.C.J.: Environmental sound recognition with time-frequency audio features. IEEE Trans. Audio, Speech Lang. Process. **17**(6), 1142–1158 (2009)
13. Dijk, E.O., Nijholt, A., Van Erp, J.B., Van Wolferen, G., Kuyper, E.: Audio-tactile stimulation: a tool to improve health and well-being? Int. J. Auton. Adap. Commun. Syst. **6**(4), 305–323 (2013)
14. Donahue, C., McAuley, J., Puckette, M.: Synthesizing audio with generative adversarial networks. CoRR abs/1802.04208 (2018)
15. Drossos, K., Floros, A., Kanellopoulos, N.G.: Affective acoustic ecology: towards emotionally enhanced sound events. In: Proceedings of the 7th Audio Mostly Conference: A Conference on Interaction with Sound, pp. 109–116. ACM (2012)

16. Engel, J., et al.: Neural audio synthesis of musical notes with wavenet autoencoders. In: Proceedings of the 34th International Conference on Machine Learning-Volume 70, pp. 1068–1077. JMLR. org (2017)

17. Fan, J., Thorogood, M., Pasquier, P.: Emo-soundscapes: A dataset for soundscape emotion recognition. In: 2017 Seventh International Conference on Affective Computing and Intelligent Interaction (ACII), pp. 196–201. IEEE (2017)

18. Fried, R.: Integrating music in breathing training and relaxation: II. applications. Biofeedback Self-regul. **15**(2), 936–943 (1990). (171–177)

19. Frigeni, B., et al.: Chemotherapy-induced peripheral neurotoxicity can be misdiagnosed by the national cancer institute common toxicity scale. J. Peripheral Nerv. Syst. **16**(3), 228–236 (2011)

20. Goldsby, T.L., Goldsby, M.E., McWalters, M., Mills, P.J.: Effects of singing bowl sound meditation on mood, tension, and well-being: an observational study. J. Evid.-Based Complement. Altern. Med. **22**(3), 401–406 (2017)

21. Goodfellow, I., et al.: Generative adversarial nets. In: Advances in Neural Information Processing Systems, pp. 2672–2680 (2014)

22. Handel, M.J.: mhealth (mobile health)–using apps for health and wellness. Explore **7**(4), 256–261 (2011)

23. Hartmann, K., Siegert, I., Philippou-Hübner, D., Wendemuth, A.: Emotion detection in HCI: from speech features to emotion space. IFAC Proc. Vol. **46**(15), 288–295 (2013)

24. Humphries, K.: Healing Sound: Contemporary Methods for Tibetan Singing Bowls. Ph.D. thesis, Loyola Marymount University, CA, US (2010)

25. Iyendo, T.O.: Exploring the effect of sound and music on health in hospital settings: a narrative review. Int. J. Nurs. Stud. **63**, 82–100 (2016)

26. Juslin, P.N., Västfjäll, D.: Emotional responses to music: the need to consider underlying mechanisms. Behav. Brain Sci. **31**(5), 559–575 (2008)

27. Kabat-Zinn, J., et al.: Effectiveness of a meditation-based stress reduction program. J. Psychiatry **149**(7), 936–943 (1992)

28. Kameoka, H., Kaneko, T., Tanaka, K., Hojo, N.: StarGAN-VC: non-parallel many-to-many voice conversion using star generative adversarial networks. In: 2018 IEEE Spoken Language Technology Workshop (SLT), pp. 266–273. IEEE (2018)

29. Kishore, K.K., Satish, P.K.: Emotion recognition in speech using MFCC and wavelet features. In: 2013 3rd IEEE International Advance Computing Conference (IACC), pp. 842–847. IEEE (2013)

30. Kortchmar, L., Vorländer, M., Slama, J.: Sound quality evaluation for the workplace: research on the influence of spatial sound distributions. Acta Acust. United Acust. **87**(4), 495–499 (2001)

31. Krichagin, V.: Health effects of noise exposure. J. Sound Vibr. **59**(1), 65–71 (1978)

32. Lalitha, S., Geyasruti, D., Narayanan, R., Shravani, M.: Emotion detection using MFCC and cepstrum features. Proc. Comput. Sci. **70**, 29–35 (2015)

33. Lee, C.Y., Toffy, A., Jung, G.J., Han, W.: Conditional wavegan. CoRR abs/1809.10636 (2018)

34. Lundqvist, L.O., Carlsson, F., Hilmersson, P., Juslin, P.N.: Emotional responses to music: experience, expression, and physiology. Psychol. Music **37**(1), 61–90 (2009)

35. Manzelli, R., Thakkar, V., Siahkamari, A., Kulis, B.: Conditioning deep generative raw audio models for structured automatic music. arXiv preprint arXiv:1806.09905 (2018)

36. Maurer, R.L., Kumar, V., Woodside, L., Pekala, R.J.: Phenomenological experience in response to monotonous drumming and hypnotizability. Am. J. Clin. Hypn. **40**(2), 130–145 (1997)

37. Mehri, S., et al.: Samplernn: An unconditional end-to-end neural audio generation model. arXiv preprint arXiv:1612.07837 (2016)

38. Mirelman, A., et al.: Audio-biofeedback training for posture and balance in patients with parkinson's disease. J. Neuroeng. Rehabil. **8**(1), 35 (2011)

39. Moscoso, P., Peck, M., Eldridge, A.: Systematic literature review on the association between soundscape and ecological/human wellbeing (2018)

40. Okcu, S., Ryherd, E.E., Zimring, C., Samuels, O.: Soundscape evaluations in two critical healthcare settings with different designs. J. Acoust. Soc. Am. **130**(3), 387–392 (2011)

41. van den Oord, A., et al.: Wavenet: A generative model for raw audio. CoRR abs/1609.03499, 4 (2016)

42. van den Oord, A., Kalchbrenner, N., Vinyals, O., Espeholt, L., Graves, A., Kavukcuoglu, K.: Conditional image generation with pixelcnn decoders. CoRR abs/1606.05328 (2016)

43. Panda, S.P.: Automated speech recognition system in advancement of human-computer interaction. In: 2017 International Conference on Computing Methodologies and Communication (ICCMC), pp. 302–306. IEEE (2017)

44. Parada-Cabaleiro, E., Baird, A.E., Cummins, N., Schuller, B.: Stimulation of psychological listener experiences by semi-automatically composed electroacoustic environments. In: Proceedings ICME 2017, pp. 1051–1056. IEEE, Hong Kong, July 2017

45. Paterson, N., Naliuka, K., Jensen, S.K., Carrigy, T., Haahr, M., Conway, F.: Design, implementation and evaluation of audio for a location aware augmented reality game. In: Proceedings of the 3rd International Conference on Fun and Games, pp. 149–156. ACM (2010)

46. Porcheron, M., Fischer, J.E., Reeves, S., Sharples, S.: Voice interfaces in everyday life. In: Proceedings of the 2018 CHI Conference on Human Factors in Computing Systems, pp. 1–12 (2018)

47. Roden, T., Parberry, I.: Designing a narrative-based audio only 3D game engine. In: Proceedings of the 2005 ACM SIGCHI International Conference on Advances in Computer Entertainment Technology, pp. 274–277. ACM (2005)

48. Rogers, K., Nacke, L.E.: Exploring the potential of game audio for wellbeing. In: PGW@ CHI PLAY (2017)

49. Russell, J.A.: A circumplex model of affect. J. Pers. Soc. Psychol. **39**(6), 1161 (1980)

50. Salamon, E., Kim, M., Beaulieu, J., Stefano, G.B.: Sound therapy induced relaxation: down regulating stress processes and pathologies. Med. Sci. Monitor **9**(5), 96–100 (2003)

51. Sanderson, P.: Cognitive work analysis and the analysis, design, and evaluation of human-computer interactive systems. In: Proceedings 1998 Australasian Computer Human Interaction Conference. OzCHI 1998 (Cat. No. 98EX234), pp. 220–227. IEEE (1998)

52. Schafer, R.M.: The Soundscape: Our Sonic Environment and the Tuning of the World. Inner Traditions Bear & Co., Vermont (1993)

53. Schirosa, M., Janer, J., Kersten, S., Roma, G.: A system for soundscape generation, composition and streaming. In: XVII CIM-Colloquium of Musical Informatics, p. no pagination (2010)

54. Schuller, B., Rigoll, G., Lang, M.: Hidden markov model-based speech emotion recognition. In: 2003 IEEE International Conference on Acoustics, Speech, and Signal Processing, 2003. Proceedings. (ICASSP 2003), vol. 2, pp. II-1. IEEE (2003)

55. Sebe, N., Cohen, I., Gevers, T., Huang, T.S.: Emotion recognition based on joint visual and audio cues. In: 18th International Conference on Pattern Recognition (ICPR 2006), vol. 1, pp. 1136–1139. IEEE (2006)

56. Sliwinski, J., Katsikitis, M., Jones, C.M.: Mindful gaming: how digital games can improve mindfulness. In: Abascal, J., Barbosa, S., Fetter, M., Gross, T., Palanque, P., Winckler, M. (eds.) INTERACT 2015. LNCS, vol. 9298, pp. 167–184. Springer, Cham (2015). https://doi.org/10.1007/978-3-319-22698-9_12

57. Van Den Oord, A., et al.: Wavenet: A generative model for raw audio. CoRR abs/1609.03499 (2016)

58. Williamson, I., Leeming, D., Lyttle, S., Johnson, S.: 'It should be the most natural thing in the world': exploring first-time mothers' breastfeeding difficulties in the UK using audio-diaries and interviews. Matern. Child Nutr. **8**(4), 434–447 (2012)

59. Wood, L., Ivery, P., Donovan, R., Lambin, E.: "To the beat of a different drum": improving the social and mental wellbeing of at-risk young people through drumming. J. Publ. Mental Health **12**(2), 70–79 (2013)

60. Yu, F., Koltun, V.: Multi-scale context aggregation by dilated convolutions. arXiv preprint arXiv:1511.07122 (2015)

61. Zheng, A., et al.: Effects of a low-frequency sound wave therapy programme on functional capacity, blood circulation and bone metabolism in frail old men and women. Clin. Rehabil. **23**(10), 897–908 (2009)

A Feature Importance Study in Ballet Pose Recognition with OpenPose

Margaux Fourie⬤ and Dustin van der Haar$^{(\boxtimes)}$⬤

University of Johannesburg, Kingsway Avenue and University Rds,
Auckland Park, Johannesburg, South Africa
{margauxf,dvanderhaar}@uj.ac.za

Abstract. Movements of the human body can finally be recognised and analysed using computer vision technology. Ballet is an activity that involves various movements and specific poses of the body, making it an attractive candidate for computer vision applications. This paper proposes a feature importance study for determining which body parts play the most significant role in ballet pose recognition. The study is based on the use of OpenPose for feature extraction together with Support Vector Machine, Random Forest and Gradient Boosted Tree classifiers. Recognition accuracies above 95% suggest that the methods are not only feasible but exhibit excellent results. The results also indicate that the body parts that were the most significant for the classification of ballet poses were those situated at the extremities of the body such as the wrists and feet. The study addresses challenges within the ballet domain as it relates to both training and choreography. Furthermore, the study confirms that as technology expands into all areas of life, it is worthwhile to explore the possibilities within artistic fields.

Keywords: Computer vision · Feature importance · Ballet · OpenPose

1 Introduction

An ever-increasing amount of application fields are using computer vision to assist and enhance activities within those domains. Human body movements and poses can accurately be recognised using recent advancements in graphics processing technologies and computer vision algorithms [1,2]. Ballet is a human activity that is especially attractive for computer vision due to the well-codified poses and the limited automated approaches that exist in the environment. The automatic identification of body parts that are significant for the recognition of different ballet poses becomes a relevant research problem considering the challenges that are present in ballet training and choreography.

Ballet has developed over multiple centuries, and its various established poses have become foundational elements of the art form [3]. It is, therefore, a frequent task in a ballet training environment for teachers and students to recognise and correct the poses being performed. To avoid bad training habits and injuries,

© Springer Nature Switzerland AG 2020
H. Degen and L. Reinerman-Jones (Eds.): HCII 2020, LNCS 12217, pp. 243–254, 2020.
https://doi.org/10.1007/978-3-030-50334-5_16

dancers need to be aware of the proper placement of different parts of the body when performing ballet poses [4]. There is a need for additional forms of training critique to avoid the development of flawed technique, which often results in injuries [4].

Ballet choreography is another area within ballet where pose recognition is relevant. Choreographers are responsible for creating dance pieces that are constructed by using sequences of poses. There is a need for the most important poses and body parts used in a choreographed piece to be determined and documented to reproduce created works with future generations effectively [5]. Both the areas of training and choreography in ballet have the potential to benefit from technological solutions to assist in correct training and the proper documentation of ballet choreography.

This paper proposes an approach that is based on a previous study [6] that has been completed for ballet pose recognition. Once distinct poses are recognised using computer vision methods, it is possible to determine the most important features used during classification. In turn, the particular parts of the body that played the most prominent part for the classification of the pose can be identified. The paper first provides information on the problem background along with current related work. The experiment setup is presented next, followed by the model. The results are then provided, and the paper ends with a discussion on future work and a conclusion.

2   Problem Background

Ballet has a vibrant historical dimension that reaches back to the 16th century [7]. Every step in a ballet class is, therefore, ingrained with centuries of traditions and adaptations [8]. In addition, ballet has also formed the basis for many other forms of dance [9]. Due to the well-established technique that is prescribed in ballet, it is a relevant application area for computer vision.

Ballet technique is a term which is used to describe the essential ingredients that enable a dancer to achieve the aesthetic appearance of poses and movements. Technique in ballet is mainly concerned with the proper placement of the different parts of the body. It involves concepts such as turnout, which is the outward rotation of the legs for a more appealing view of the legs and feet [3,10]. Alignment is another aspect of technique that refers to the vertical and horizontal lines of the shoulders and hips. In addition, stretched legs and feet are always emphasized in the building of a strong ballet technique [3].

Ballet training usually takes place in a studio with a class of students that are instructed by a ballet teacher. Advancement in ballet training has always relied on the verbal passing on of expertise from teachers to younger generations [11]. However, the traditional classroom approach presents the challenge of a lack of one-on-one attention that the students receive from the teacher [12]. There is a need for guided one-on-one training and correction, which has the potential to help dancers improve their skills. Furthermore, additional forms of direct feedback may create a better awareness of correct placement and prevent injuries caused by incorrect technique [4].

Choreography is another aspect that plays an important role within the ballet domain. It involves the construction of dance sequences that consist of a series of codified poses and movements [13]. The challenge that choreographers face is the accurate documentation of created works in order to ensure its preservation [14]. There is, therefore, an opportunity within the choreographic domain to explore the most significant poses and body parts that are used in dance pieces.

Since ballet technique is largely concerned with the placement of different body parts, the automated approaches that exist in this environment focus on the extraction of key body information. The various related research efforts in the ballet and technological domain are discussed in the following section.

3 Related Work

A related area of technology that has been investigated as it applies to the ballet domain is wearable garments. An approach by Gupta et al. focused on the instruction of beginner adult ballet dancers who had a teacher demonstrate ballet movements wearing a full-body garment [15]. The garment would light up the essential body parts being used by a teacher during the demonstration. This study had the advantageous effect of enabling students to focus on the most important key-points instead of complex technicalities. Some of the limitations that this system had include the high cost of such a wearable garment and the restriction it placed on movements [15]. These limitations indicate that there is a gap for systems that are cost-effective and less restrictive.

Research has also been conducted in the area of ballet choreography by Dancs et al., which aimed to automate the recognition and recording of a choreographer's movement [16]. The study used Microsoft's Kinect sensor in order to detect the different joints of the body. Furthermore, the study used classification algorithms such as Nearest Neighbor as well as Support Vector Machine (SVM) methods, which produced promising results with over 90% for accuracy. The success of the approach by Dancs et al. indicates that it is worthwhile to explore how computer vision methods may contribute to addressing challenges in ballet choreography.

Related research that closely links to the work of this paper includes a fairly recent posture recognition system by Saha et al., which included 20 ballet poses as primitives [17]. The system made use of pre-processing methods involving skin color segmentation to arrive at minimised skeletons of the initial images. The mathematical Radon transform method was used to calculate line integral plots and ultimately match images to specific primitives for recognition. The system produced a promising recognition rate of 91.35%. Furthermore, Saha et al. indicated that the area of ballet pose recognition is fairly young with a variety of opportunities for future research [17]. There is, in particular, an opportunity to build on this work by looking at improved and recent ways to extract skeleton key-point features such as utilising an OpenPose approach [18].

This study further relates to the optimisation of classifiers. When it comes to image classification, techniques that are often used to tune hyper-parameters and ultimately improve accuracy include random search, grid search and Bayesian optimisation [19]. Feature selection is another method that is used to improve classifiers by identifying which features are the most relevant to a particular problem [20]. A feature importance study is, therefore, a valuable step towards better recognition accuracies.

4   Experiment Setup

The feature importance study proposed in this paper is based on previous research [6] completed by the authors on the recognition of ballet poses. The experiment setup for this paper, which is concerned with feature importances, is therefore similar to the setup that was used for the completed pose recognition study.

The study compiled a primary dataset containing thirty classically trained ballet dancers as subjects that were captured performing eight distinct ballet poses. These poses included Demi-Plié, Second Position, Tendu, Sussous, Retiré, Développé, Arabesque, and Penché. The dancers were captured using a Microsoft Kinect sensor and a GoPro camera, which enabled the collection of video, depth and image data.

The dataset for this study consisted of Microsoft Kinect images that were captured at a 640 by 480 resolution. The data of about 7200 images was split into a training set consisting of 80% of the images and a testing set containing 20% of the images. An even distribution among different classes was used in both the training and testing sets. The authors focused on using the collected image data for this work and will, therefore, utilise the depth and video data in future work.

The success of collecting quality data for this study required certain constraints to be in place. It was first important that capturing should occur in a dance studio with an appropriate dance surface such as ballet mats. Mirrors or any clutter in the capture space were to be removed to minimise noise in the background. Furthermore, the lighting had to be at a suitable level. Concerning the participants, a role constraint of the study included that they had to be advanced level dancers that could execute each of the poses with sound technique. Lastly, standard black ballet attire had to be worn by participants to avoid unnecessary variations in the gathered image data.

Once the data has been collected, it can be used to apply various computer vision methods. The next section will unpack the model, which makes use of the captured dataset as the starting point to achieve pose recognition and the determination of feature importances.

5   Model

The model of this study is shown as a pipeline in Fig. 1, which consists of four separate stages, namely capturing, feature extraction, classification and feature importance. Each of these phases involves a set of methods or actions that need to occur before moving on to the next stage.

The model has the captured dataset as a starting point from which features are extracted during the second stage. The feature extraction method used in this model is known as OpenPose [18]. OpenPose is a recent and useful feature extraction approach that uses a multi-stage Convolutional Neural Network (CNN) for extracting human skeleton key-point data from images.

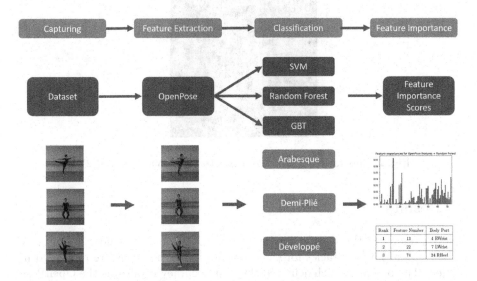

Fig. 1. Model for determining the most significant OpenPose features for different computer vision algorithms

The skeleton key-points can be seen in Fig. 2 with key body parts represented as numbers. Once the features have been extracted, different classification algorithms are utilised to perform training and testing on the dataset of ballet poses. The different classification methods that form a part of the model include Support Vector Machine (SVM), Random Forest (RF), as well as Gradient Boosted Tree (GBT). When training is completed, a feature importance study determines which OpenPose features played the most significant role in identifying particular poses. For the SVM model, the feature importances are determined by analysing the subsequent weights produced after training. For the RF and GBT classifiers, Gini importance is used, which computes how much each feature contributes to a decrease in node impurity. From the determined OpenPose key-point features, valuable insights are then derived by mapping the most important features to parts of the dancer's body.

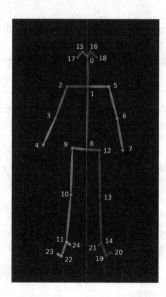

Fig. 2. Illustration of OpenPose skeleton key-point features [21]

6 Results

Before presenting the feature importance results from this study, a summary of the recognition accuracies for each of the relevant pipelines are presented in Table 1. The pipeline which achieved the best accuracy result was the OpenPose and Random Forest variation with a score of 99.375%.

Table 1. Summary of the results obtained by the pose recognition study as percentages.

Pipeline variation	Accuracy
OpenPose + Random Forest	**99.375**
OpenPose + Gradient Boosted Trees	99.305
OpenPose + Support Vector Machine	99.097

Based on the accuracy scores achieved by the pose recognition study, it is feasible to investigate how the OpenPose features impacted the identification of different poses. There are a total of 75 features extracted by OpenPose when an image is provided to the algorithm. The OpenPose features are based on 25 body parts which are represented in Fig. 2. The format in which the features are output by OpenPose are: (x-coordinate, y-coordinate, confidence score) for each of the 25 body parts which results in 75 features in total. It is therefore possible to determine, based on the feature number, what type of feature it is (x-coordinate, y-coordinate or confidence score) as well as what body part is associated with it. Table 2 shows the numbers and names associated with the OpenPose body parts.

Table 2. OpenPose body part numbers

Number	Body part	Number	Body part	Number	Body part
0	Nose	9	RHip	18	LEar
1	Neck	10	RKnee	19	LBigToe
2	RShoulder	11	RAnkle	20	LSmallToe
3	RElbow	12	LHip	21	LHeel
4	RWrist	13	LKnee	22	RBigToe
5	LShoulder	14	LAnkle	23	RSmallToe
6	LElbow	15	REye	24	RHeel
7	LWrist	16	LEye		
8	MidHip	17	REar		

For the extraction of meaningful information from the feature importance study, it is necessary to calculate a mapping between features and body parts. In order to determine which feature number is associated with which body part, the following algorithm has been constructed:

Input: f: feature number from 0 to 74
Output: b: the body part number that needs to be determined
Output: t: the feature type that needs to be determined
if $f \bmod 3 == 0$ **then**
$\quad b \leftarrow f \div 3$
$\quad t \leftarrow xCoordinate$
end
else if $f \bmod 3 == 1$ **then**
$\quad b \leftarrow (f - 1) \div 3$
$\quad t \leftarrow yCoordinate$
end
else if $f \bmod 3 == 2$ **then**
$\quad b \leftarrow (f - 2) \div 3$
$\quad t \leftarrow confidenceScore$
end

Algorithm 1: Mapping between features and body parts

6.1 Support Vector Machine Pipeline

The feature importances for the Support Vector Machine implementation is based on the feature weights that were produced and shown in Fig. 3. Valuable information can be extracted from the feature weight representation by making use of Table 2 and the algorithm presented earlier in this section. The results from applying the mapping calculation for the SVM variation are presented in Table 3.

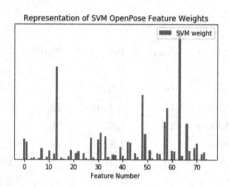

Fig. 3. Representation of feature weights for OpenPose + SVM

The top 10 most important body part features for the SVM pipeline are presented in Table 3. These results indicate that the three most significant body-parts for distinguishing between ballet poses using an SVM classifier are the left wrist, the right wrist and the left eye.

Table 3. Ranking for the top 10 important OpenPose features with SVM

Rank	Feature number	Body part	Feature type
1	63	21 LHeel	x-coordinate
2	13	4 RWrist	y-coordinate
3	48	16 LEye	x-coordinate
4	58	19 LBigToe	y-coordinate
5	57	19 LBigToe	x-coordinate
6	66	22 RBigToe	x-coordinate
7	31	10 RKnee	y-coordinate
8	49	16 LEye	y-coordinate
9	33	11 RAnkle	x-coordinate
10	27	9 RHip	x-coordinate

6.2 Random Forest Pipeline

The Random Forest Pipeline of this study made use of Gini importance to determine the most important features which are visible in Fig. 4. The most noteworthy body parts that have been calculated for this pipeline are presented in Table 4.

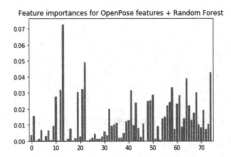

Fig. 4. Feature importance representation for OpenPose + Random Forest

From Table 4 the top three most important body parts that play a role in the recognition task of the Random Forest classifier were the right wrist, the left wrist and the right heel. Each of these body parts is situated towards the ends of the limbs, which may indicate that parts that are further away from the body are more crucial for identifying poses using a Random Forest.

Table 4. Ranking for the top 10 important OpenPose features with Random Forest

Rank	Feature number	Body part	Feature type
1	13	4 RWrist	y-coordinate
2	22	7 LWrist	y-coordinate
3	74	24 RHeel	confidence score
4	64	21 LHeel	y-coordinate
5	58	19 LBigToe	y-coordinate
6	21	7 LWrist	x-coordinate
7	12	4 RWrist	x-coordinate
8	41	13 LKnee	confidence score
9	19	6 LElbow	y-coordinate
10	68	22 RBigToe	confidence score

6.3   Gradient Boosted Tree Pipeline

The Gradient Boosted Tree classifier also made use of Gini importance to extract important features as shown in Fig. 5. The body parts that had the highest importance for this GBT pipeline are presented in Table 5.

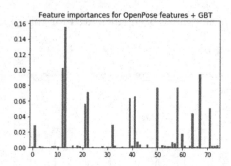

Fig. 5. Feature importance representation for OpenPose + GBT

From Table 5 it is clear that the right wrist as well as the right big toe had an important role to play in the distinction between ballet poses using a GBT classifier. This result gives an indication that body parts situated far away from the core of the body contribute the most when performing recognition using a GBT.

Table 5. Ranking for the top 10 important OpenPose features with GBT

Rank	Feature number	Body part	Feature type
1	13	4 RWrist	y-coordinate
2	12	4 RWrist	x-coordinate
3	67	22 RBigToe	y-coordinate
4	50	16 LEye	confidence score
5	58	19 LBigToe	y-coordinate
6	22	7 LWrist	y-coordinate
7	41	13 LKnee	confidence score
8	39	13 LKnee	x-coordinate
9	21	7 LWrist	x-coordinate
10	71	23 RSmallToe	confidence score

The results of the study indicate that the objective of determining the most significant body parts for recognising ballet poses with computer vision has been achieved. Generally, the skeleton points that had higher overall importance for distinguishing between different poses included the wrists as well as points situated in the feet or head. There is value in knowing which parts of the body carry a higher weight in determining how ballet poses may be classified as technology expands into this domain. It is especially relevant for ballet training where body parts with a higher feature importance score may need more emphasis during training to ensure the correct and improved execution of relevant poses.

For choreographers, a feature importance study has the potential to provide insight into which body parts play the most significant part in making the used poses and movements distinct from one another.

7   Future Work and Conclusion

This study has shown that it is possible to derive meaningful information from feature importance data gathered on different classifiers. The use of OpenPose key-point data contributed to effectively determine which parts of the body play a noteworthy role in the recognition of the poses chosen for this study. Some key findings in this paper indicated that the body parts situated further away from the centre of the body played a more significant role in the identification of different poses.

Future work for this study has the potential to contribute further to both the training and choreographic areas of ballet. For the ballet training environment, it would be valuable to build on the current study and consider the automatic correction of poses. On the choreographic side, this research may work towards the automated recording of dance sequences. Other computer vision techniques that are of interest for future work include various Convolutional Neural Network approaches, N-shot learning as well as Recurrent Neural Networks. Future work may also make use of video data in order to expand from static pose recognition to movement-based tracking and recognition.

The ballet field, with its deep historical roots and artistic associations, may seem to be in direct contrast with the modern, ever-growing field of technology. Despite the differences between the two fields, ballet's concrete underlying structure in terms of poses make it an ideal field to explore in conjunction with today's technological advancements [22]. Furthermore, technology enables the automation of tasks that were previously only performed by humans and it enables the discovery of new insights into the ballet art form. The field of ballet may, therefore, find value in the growth of automation through technology as it has the potential to serve as an enhancement tool for the improvement of current practices.

Acknowledgements. This research benefitted, in part, from support from the Faculty of Science at the University of Johannesburg.

References

1. Nishani, E., Çiço, B.: Computer vision approaches based on deep learning and neural networks: Deep neural networks for video analysis of human pose estimation. In: 2017 6th Mediterranean Conference on Embedded Computing (MECO), pp. 1–4. IEEE (2017)
2. Yao, B., Hagras, H., Alhaddad, M.J., Alghazzawi, D.: A fuzzy logic-based system for the automation of human behavior recognition using machine vision in intelligent environments. Soft Comput. **19**(2), 499–506 (2014). https://doi.org/10.1007/s00500-014-1270-4

3. Royal Academy of Dancing. The Foundations of Classical Ballet Technique. Royal Academy of Dancing (1997)

4. Bronner, S., Ojofeitimi, S., Spriggs, J.: Occupational musculoskeletal disorders in dancers. Phys. Ther. Rev. **8**(2), 57–68 (2003)

5. Sperling, J.: How do you write down choreography?—jody sperling dance blog (2010)

6. Fourie, M., van der Haar, D.: Computer vision for the ballet industry: a comparative study of methods for pose recognition (2020)

7. Di Orio, L.: Ballet: Method to method. Dance Informa American Edition (2013)

8. Butterworth, J.: Dance Studies: The Basics. Routledge, Abingdon (2011)

9. New York Film Academy. Ballet and modern dance: Using ballet as the basis for other dance techniques (2014)

10. Kassing, G., Jay, D.M.: Teaching beginning ballet technique. Human Kinetics (1998)

11. Trajkova, M., Cafaro, F.: E-ballet: designing for remote ballet learning. In: Proceedings of the 2016 ACM International Joint Conference on Pervasive and Ubiquitous Computing Adjunct - UbiComp 2016, pp. 213–216 (2016)

12. Dance Spirit. Working one-on-one: What to expect from private lessons (2014)

13. Speck, S., Cisneros, E.: Ballet for Dummies. Wiley, Hoboken (2003)

14. Snyder, A.F.: Securing Our Dance Heritage: Issues in the Documentation and Preservation of Dance. Council on Library and Information Resources, Washington DC (1999)

15. Gupta, M., Hallam, J., Keen, E., Lee, C., McKenna, A.: Ballet hero: building a garment for memetic embodiment in dance learning. In: Proceedings of the 2014 ACM International Symposium on Wearable Computers Adjunct Program - ISWC 2014 Adjunct, pp. 49–54 (2014)

16. Dancs, J., Sivalingam, R., Somasundaram, G., Morellas, V., Papanikolopoulos, N.: Recognition of ballet micro-movements for use in choreography. In: 2013 IEEE/RSJ International Conference on Intelligent Robots and Systems, pp. 1162–1167 (2013)

17. Saha, S., Konar, A.: Topomorphological approach to automatic posture recognition in ballet dance. IET Image Proc. **9**(11), 1002–1011 (2015)

18. Cao, Z., Hidalgo, G., Simon, T., Wei, S.-E., Sheikh, Y.: OpenPose: real-time multi-person 2D pose estimation using part affinity fields. arXiv preprint arXiv:1812.08008 (2018)

19. Bergstra, J., Bengio, Y.: Random search for hyper-parameter optimization. J. Mach. Learn. Res. **13**(Feb), 281–305 (2012)

20. Kuo, B.-C., Ho, H.-H., Li, C.-H., Hung, C.-C., Taur, J.-S.: A kernel-based feature selection method for SVM with RBF kernel for hyperspectral image classification. IEEE J. Sel. Top. Appl. Earth Obs. Remote Sens. **7**(1), 317–326 (2013)

21. Zhe, C., Hidalgo, G., Simon, T., Wei, S.-E., Sheikh, Y.: CMU-perceptual-computing-lab/openpose (2019)

22. LaViers, A., Chen, Y., Belta, C., Egerstedt, M.: Automatic sequencing of ballet poses. IEEE Robot. Autom. Mag. **18**(3), 87–95 (2011)

Educators in the Loop: Using Scenario Simulation as a Tool to Understand and Investigate Predictive Models of Student Dropout Risk in Distance Learning

Rômulo Freitas[✉] and Luciana Salgado[✉]

Universidade Federal Fluminense, Niterói, RJ 24210-310, Brazil
romuloponciano@id.uff.br, luciana@ic.uff.br

Abstract. Distance Learning suffers from a high dropout rate. Several works propose to use machine learning techniques to create predictive models that can identify students at risk of dropping out and, thus, reduce this index. However, predictive models can stop making accurate predictions over time and even contain cultural and prejudiced bias. Therefore, educators need to be included in the loop of modeling and simulating predictive models to identify problems and requirements that may not be easily identified by just accessing the outcomes. Our work proposes a prototype to simulate scenarios without changing the predictive model so that educators can evaluate the results of AI. After the development of the prototype and three different predictive models, educators carried out a formative evaluation on the prototype. The findings indicate that this type of scenario simulation can be useful for questioning the results of an AI, even with people without technical knowledge about predictive models.

Keywords: Distance Learning · Artificial Intelligence · HCI · Human in the loop

1 Introduction

Scientists discuss the use of technology in Distance Learning (DL) since the second generation [10,21,24]. However, only in recent decades, new generations of DL have gained more space thanks to several factors, such as the increased access to the Internet and personal computers, the lower economic cost in comparison with traditional learning, and the growing number of students who are unable to attend classroom lectures [5,22,29,30]. Another significant factor for greater adherence to distance learning was the development of Virtual Learning Environments (VLE) [28].

Nowadays, DL is present in 67.9% of China's universities [5], 74% of people who have some academic training on the African continent [13,29], 65% of courses offered by Open University in the United Kingdom [4,9], and 36% of

© Springer Nature Switzerland AG 2020
H. Degen and L. Reinerman-Jones (Eds.): HCII 2020, LNCS 12217, pp. 255–272, 2020.
https://doi.org/10.1007/978-3-030-50334-5_17

institutions in the United States [22,30]. In Brazil, in 2018, 40% of all students are enrolled in higher education offered by DL modality [12].

Despite this high growth in different parts of the world, DL still suffers from a significant problem: the high number of dropouts [5,22,29,30]. In Brazil, only 21.7% of all students enrolled in higher education distance courses finish their courses in 2018 [12]. Jordan [15] presented a study of 2014, demonstrating a completion rate in Massive Open Online Courses (MOOCs) of less than 10% on a global scale.

A proposed approach to solve this problem is to use intelligent models to predict students at risk of dropout [18,25,31]. These proposals emerged due to the massive data collection in several spheres, together with a higher computational power [31].

However, as demonstrated by Joh [14], the data used for model training can contain cultural bias and thus lead the model to make decisions based on prejudices or contexts that do not reflect the reality where the model is applied. Besides, laws such as the General Data Protection Regulation (GDPR) [7] and the Brazilian General Personal Data Protection Law 13.709 (GPDPL) [17] imply that users must make the final decisions behind the model's predictions [2]. So, these users need, somehow, understand and explore the results obtained through the models.

Therefore, our research investigated if simulating scenarios, based on a real prediction dropout, can be used to allow educators to understand and investigate the results of a predictive model. To achieve our goal, we have developed a Scenario Simulation Tool (SST) that allows users to interact with the model without changing the model itself. To evaluate the SST, we ran an empirical study with 3 educators who conducted a set of evaluations and commented on the experience. These evaluations occur in two models, one of which was a prejudiced model and the other a black-box model. In addition, it is important to note that this research was conducted as a formative evaluation.

The next sections follow with related works to the explanation of predictive models, even if the objective is to understand results or evaluate and to question results. In the third section, we describe the development of SST. Furthermore, we present a section to describe the formative evaluation and the results obtained during these evaluations. The last section contains our conclusions, limitations, and future works.

2   Related Works

Ortigosa and colleagues [26] researched the development of an Early Warning System (EWS) that focused on predicting evasion and passing this information to users of these systems (educators). For this, they developed an application made up of 4 components. The first was responsible for extract and pre-processed the input data. The second module was responsible for generating different predictive models with the data processed by the first component. The third module is to evaluate the predictive models and the most impacting attributes for the predictions of these models. Finally, a module responsible for presenting this data to users.

As the explanation behind the prediction was an important requirement for the authors, they chose to use only white-box models, claiming that these requirements prevented them from using other types of models. They made this choice even pointing out "black box" models with better results.

After analyzing the work, we see that the main advantages of the EWS proposed by the authors are the possibility of inserting manual notes that can affect the prediction and the information available to users, informing the most relevant attributes for the results. Despite showing an exciting result, the EWS does not allow the user to find out faulty predictions. So, when the contexts used to train the model no longer reflect the reality experienced, users of the application would not be able to perceive this gap in predictive models.

The research conducted by Wollf and collegues [32] is another work that is concerned with the prediction of students' dropout and to present these results to users. They used a combination of four models trained by three algorithms to perform the prediction. Two of these models used the k Nearest Neighbors algorithm (k-NN) and are used to group students with similar data in different sets. The authors used two k-NN because one of them only uses demographic data, while the other model only uses data from the virtual learning environment (VLE). The other two models use different algorithms. One algorithm consists of a Regression and Classification Tree (CART) and the other of a Bayesian Network. Both used to predict students, both with demographic data and VLE data. Then, all these models vote for the final decision on whether a student will evade.

A point worth mentioning about the authors' work is the use of the four predictive models to try to minimize errors. However, the authors do not present any statistical comparison between individual and "all-four model" results. So, we have been unable to determine whether this strategy is, in fact, effective. Still, even if there is a reduction in wrong predictions, eventually, errors will arise, and the models may stop to reflect the reality where the tool is applied. Users, however, have no way of evaluating these wrong results. In other words, it still suffers from the same problem found in the research by Ortigosa and collegues [26].

The main goal of the work of Kotsiantis and Pintelas [16] consists of a tool for predicting students at risk of dropping out of DL. The difference between his work and the others discussed earlier is that this tool does not have a predefined algorithm or model for prediction.

They built a tool that had different algorithms, and that was able to assist DL educators in chose which algorithm is best for training a predictive model. The tool is composed of 6 components: (1) a module with the machine learning algorithms and a guide to help the educator, (2) algorithms to perform association rules, (3) a component to perform and present statistics on the data, (4) an algorithm for selecting the best attributes from the informed database, (5) a set of methods to balance the database, if necessary and, finally, (6) another module to export the model trained on an educator use page.

The authors' research is more involved with the possibility of facilitating the creation of predictive models for end-users than understand and to question these results. After training, the educators had no choice but to use that model or try to create a new one.

Discussions about these works reinforce the need for solutions that empowers educators to question the results of predictive models. For this reason, unlike others, our research seeks to allow educators to be able to question and evaluate the results of predictions.

3   Scenario Simulation Tool

The tool that we propose in this research to assist educators in understanding the predictions of a dropout in DL, through predictive models, is composed of three modules: predictive model, scenario simulator, and interface module. In this section, we will discuss these modules and how they work together.

In summary, the predictive model component receives real data and makes its predictions. The interface module presents these real predictions to the users. For comparative purposes, the user can change a copy of the student's original data and make predictions with that changed data, generating different scenarios.

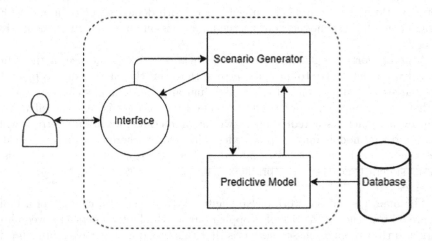

Fig. 1. SST components

Figure 1 shows the three modules in operation. The scenario generator will receive the input data, that is, the data extracted from the platform. Then the scenario generator will pass the original data to the predictive model, already trained, which will return with a result.

The interface module is responsible for receiving the data and presenting it intuitively so that educators can analyze it, clearly identifying the original scenario of the hypothetical scenarios. Finally, the interface module should still provide a way for educators to create and simulate their hypothetical scenarios until they are satisfied.

3.1 Module: Predictive Model

This module is responsible for making the original and scenario predictions. To build this module, we need to answer two requirements: (1) what data and (2) which algorithm we will use to train the model.

The first requirement, in the case of DL, can vary between two main types: personal data of students, such as race, location, and age, or data extracted from the VLE used. That is, how many times the student accessed the platform, what is the average time the student stays on the platform, how many video lessons the student watched in a given week, responses from forums, and others.

Dataset for Training: Our database has 432 different students, where 323 have abandoned their courses, and 109 have not. We cannot describe the details of this base due to ethical issues, as we extracted it from a real context. However, the database has data such as grades, access to the platform, discussion forums, and personal data such as race, age, family income, and sex.

Some attributes, such as age and family income, were discretized. The objective of this discretization is to represent the data in forms of categories so that their different numerical values, which can be close to each other, do not have different weights in the learning process [19].

For discretization, we use the simple method of distribution by the same size [6]. In this method, we divide the set of numerical values into equal parts, or as close as possible [6,19].

In addition to discretization, we normalize all numeric attributes. This process of normalizing numerical data consists of a technique for placing different numerical attributes in the same weight [8]. Thus, for example, the attributes for the quantity of access to the forum, which have values between 0 and 5000, would not impact wrongly the use of attributes such as grades, which have values between 0 and 10.

The method chosen for normalization was the min-max [8]. To normalize a xi value, take this value, subtract it from the lowest possible value of that attribute, and divide the result by subtracting the highest possible value from the attribute with the lowest possible value from the attribute [8].

We chose to use these methods of discretization and normalization due to our primary objective. As we do not seek to achieve the best accuracy or test different methods of prediction, we use the methods considered most straightforward.

Algorithms for Training: There are several algorithms to train classificatory predictive models [1,8]. This wide variety of algorithms can even make it difficult to choose which one to use for which purposes. However, as our goal is to investigate if the use of scenario simulations allows educators to investigate and question the results of the models, then we chose to carry out the training of three models, with three different algorithms: k-NN, Decision Tree and Network Neural.

To test all three algorithms, we used the K-fold Cross-Validation technique. This technique divides the dataset into a set for training and a set for post-training tests [8,23,27]. The method divided the dataset into k parts. Then, it removes x% of the data from each of these parts. The training process occurs with the remaining dataset, and the test occurs with the removed parts. In general, the recommendation is to use 30% of the database as a test and a k with a value of 10 [27]. Also, after checking the accuracy, we performed a new training of the models with all the base data.

We use Python[1] in all pre-processing, division of the base, tests, and training process with the help of the Sklearn library[2]. We chose this language and library because they are considered stable and widely used.

K-NN. The k-nearest neighbors algorithm (k-NN) is a pattern recognition algorithm used in clustering and classification models [3,8]. To classify a particular entry, it checks which other entries (those used in training) are closest to this new entry. Then, a vote on the nearest k entries decides the class [3,8].

To find the best k, we write an algorithm that evaluates the training of k-NN models with k's ranging from 1 to 29. Then the algorithm store in different vectors the results of each accuracy and their averages. After that, we insert these results in a graph, shown in Fig. 2.

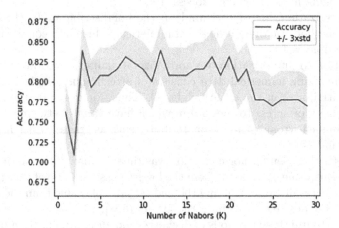

Fig. 2. Results to find the better k

If the graph showed an increasing result of the accuracy, in its final values, we would extend the limit value for our best k test. However, after k 20, the

---

[1] https://www.python.org/.
[2] https://scikit-learn.org/stable/.

accuracy value started to drop. Thus, the best value of k for our database is the value 12.

It is important to highlight that we train this model intending to use it to instruct educators about the tool. For more information on this instruction, see the section of tests, where we describe the tests with the SST. The final accuracy of the model was 0.8384615384615385.

Decision Tree. The Decision Tree is an algorithm used for classification, based on attribute relationships that the algorithm considers most important, hierarchically [8,20]. To assemble these relations, the algorithm divides the base and recursively attributes the entropy of the attributes until it assembles a tree, with a parent node that, based on different conditions, decides the next child. The algorithm repeats this process until reaching a leaf, which represents one of the possible classes of the trained model [8,20].

We chose a model based on the Decision Tree, as it is a model that is easy to interpret. We can extract its resulting tree and fully understand how the model arrives in its decisions. Therefore, to train this model, we made a copy of the original dataset and changed it so that the data was prejudiced. Thus, all students who were of the black race had their dropout class changed to yes, otherwise the dropout class was changed to no. Therefore, we will use this model to see if educators will be able to find this racism in the predictions of the Decision Tree.

Then, with this racist dataset, we trained the model and extracted the tree shown in Fig. 3. This tree shows that the model is, in fact, racist.

As the training converts the categories into numbers, the category of races was as follows: white = 0; indigenous = 1; black = 2; other = 3; mestiza = 4. Looking at Fig. 3, we see that the tree will point to class 0 (non-dropout) for any entry where the race is less than or equal to 1.5 and greater than or equal to 2.5. That is, only cases where race is equal to 2 will be classifiers with class 1 (with dropout). Due to overfitting, the accuracy of the model was 1.0. However, we already expect it due to our changes.

Neural Network. We train our Neural Network with a Multilayer Perceptron (MLP). This algorithm consists of creating layers and neurons that are activated or not. Each layer is lined up, and the output from one layer becomes the input to the other until it reaches its last layer and presents the final class [11].

The MLP is considered a black-box model. Therefore, we cannot extract accurate information, such as the Decision Tree, to understand how the model reaches its decisions [11]. Thus, it is the model we use to investigate if educators will be able to understand and question their results through simulations.

To train the model, we need to define some parameters. Since our main objective is not the accuracy, we, therefore, consider the standard values of the Sklearn library. The parameters we changed were: the number of layers, the number of neurons in each layer, the method for weight optimization, and the maximum number of iterations.

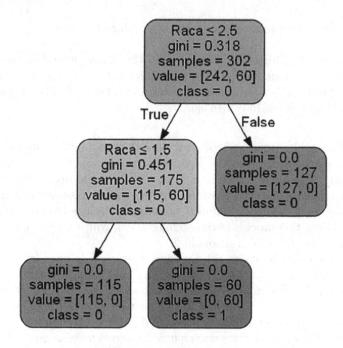

Fig. 3. Racist decision tree

To define the best number of layers and neurons, we made a small algorithm to test all possible combinations of 3 to 27 layers and neurons. The algorithm store the results of each accuracy in a vector. Another vector contains the number of layers and neurons used in that combination.

We also performed tests with this same script, switching the optimization method to Limited-memory Broyden–Fletcher–Goldfarb–Shanno (LBFGS), Stochastic Gradient Descent (SGD) and Adaptive Moment Estimation (Adam). These were our choices because they are the algorithms present in the library we use.

With the values present in the vectors, we were able to generate a table ordered by the best accuracy and, thus, visualize the best results with their quantities of layers and neurons. In Table 1 we present the best results in each optimization method for comparison.

Table 1. Comparison between weight optimization methods with layers and neuron

Method	LayersXNeurons	Accuracy
LBFGS	[13 × 25]	0.876923
SGD	[5 × 23]	0.869231
ADAM	[5 × 9]	0.884615

As ADAM had the best result, we chose it as an optimization method for weights, in addition to values for layers and neurons. Its final accuracy, trained with all data, was 0.8846153846153846.

3.2   Module: Scenario Generator

The scenario generator is the central module of the tool. It is through it that the data arrives in the predictive model, and it is also responsible for sending the results to the interface. This module will be executed after a user interaction requesting the analysis of a student in the SST. The scenario generator must be able to generate a scenario with attributes entirely chosen by the user.

So, the user has three columns: the first one (column A) is the original data, which the user can not edit in anymay. The second one is a copy of the original data, which he can edit the values (column B of Fig. 4). After the edit, when the request for the prediction of this data happens, this edited scenario is saved and made available to the user, as shown in Fig. 4 (column C).

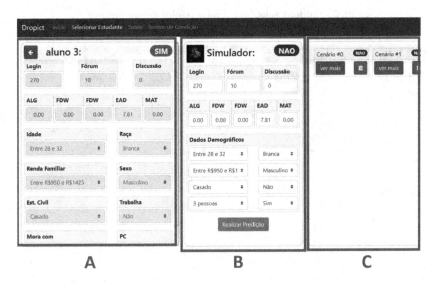

Fig. 4. Columns for view original and generated scenarios

3.3   Module: Interface

The interface is an essential component for the tool, as it is through it that the user will perform all interaction with the scenarios, also, to observe the results. As shown in Fig. 5, after selecting the AI model, the tool should provide a list of students (A) with their predictions of dropout, yes (red) or no (black). When selecting a student, the interface will present the basic information of the student (B) and the option to perform simulations and predictions with the selected student (blue button inside B).

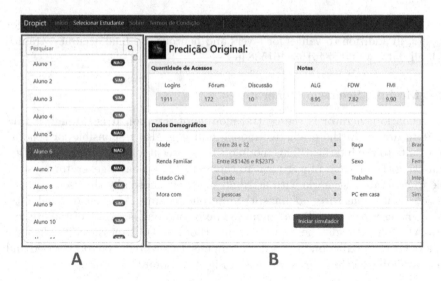

Fig. 5. Student selection screen (Color figure online)

Fig. 6. Comparison between scenarios

At this point, the user will be able to view any of the scenarios by clicking on them. Besides, as shown in Fig. 6, the interface must allow the user to be able to view more than one scenario at a time. With it, the user will be able to compare, in a single visualization, the real prediction with other scenarios.

4   Formative Evaluation

In order to evaluate weather scenarios can help DL educators to understand and question the results of AIs, we have trained the three models that we described earlier: k-NN, Decision Tree, and Neural Network. We use the first model to demonstrate in a video[3] tutorial how to use the tool. The Decision Tree and the Neural Network are, in fact, the models for educators to evaluate.

As our objective also involves checking if we can use scenarios to question the results, we decided to train a racist Decision Tree. We changed the data for DT training so that all students of the black race were with dropouts and everyone else with no dropout. This way, DT was biased and racist, as discussed in the section about its training.

As the main idea of these evaluations was to investigate if the educators would be able to identify the bias and racism of the Decision Tree and the educators' view of the Neural Network, after using the scenarios, we made available the tool described above through the address https://dropict.com.br/. Thus, educators can evaluate remotely. We chose to do it this way to try to encourage educators to try simulations without looking like a pressure to get some right prediction.

4.1   Participants

The participants in this study are teachers, mediators, or tutors who have at least one year of experience in Distance Learning in higher education courses. It is not a requirement that they have prior knowledge about predictive models or not. However, it is essential to know about VLEs because three attributes have a direct relationship with these environments.

4.2   Procedures

The first step was sending the invitations and consent form, via email, to participate in the study. Those who got in touch, demonstrating interest, received the evaluation context.

This evaluation context is a file that contains a usage scenario for educators to get involved and better understand the context and objectives. During this scenario, educators should answer three questionnaires at different times. The educators were then introduced to the following script:

> Before you start, please answer this questionnaire about your experience in Distance Learning and the use of Artificial Intelligence applications: https://forms.gle/NUL7fwz55ZpuzQUC9
> Study scenario: João, a distance mediator at Universidade Resgate, works to assist students in distance courses at his University. He always observed a high dropout rate and, several times, evaluate solutions with the Institution to try to solve this problem.

---

[3] https://www.youtube.com/watch?v=vyAbM74jZAE.

Now, the University where he works hired a company to develop an Artificial Intelligence (AI) capable of predicting students who are at risk of dropout. However, João, who had already read about AIs that learn wrongly and make wrong decisions with cultural biases, warned the University. As the Institution trusts its work, they asked João to evaluate whether these AIs work correctly.

The company developed a prototype to evaluate through simulations and a video tutorial for the University. The University secretary contacted João and other professors who volunteered and gave the following guidelines for the evaluations:

(Put yourself in João's place and follow the same steps)

1. Watch the tutorial video about the tool:
   https://www.youtube.com/watch?v=vyAbM74jZAE
2. Access the tool's website:
   https://dropict.com.br/
3. Choose the Decision Tree AI and a student with "Yes" prediction. Use the simulator to change your data so that your prediction changes.
4. Go back, select a student with "No" prediction and run simulations to change your result.
5. If you wish, feel free to take further evaluations with other students using the AI Decision Tree
6. After evaluating the Decision Tree, complete this questionnaire:
   https://forms.gle/RqT5zfxZed9xSThe9 Go back to the beginning of the site, choose the AI Neural Network and a student with a "Yes" prediction. Use the simulator to change your data so that your prediction changes.
7. Go back, select a student with "No" prediction and run simulations to change your result.
8. If you wish, feel free to take further evaluations with other students using the AI Neural Network
9. After evaluating the Neural Network, complete this questionnaire:
   https://forms.gle/q2qnzbsLmxu3WhSH9

So each educator answered three questionnaires. The first is related to his personal experience with DL and the use of AIs. The other two questionnaires were related to the evaluations made using the Decision Tree and the Neural Network.

We design the first questionnaire to investigate the profile of the participants. They should answer some questions about the DL experience and to which courses and Universities they belonged. We also asked about the contact they had with AIs, such as Google Maps, Spotify, and Netflix, and what they thought of the results and recommendations of these AIs.

The second and third questionnaires related to the evaluations with the two different models. It had closed questions, in general, for users to mark in options on the Likert scale or just "yes"/"no". Each question also had another field so that educators could comment on their previous responses. The purpose of these questionnaires was to investigate educators' opinions about the use of the simulator. We also wanted to know if they approved the results of the models.

In total, three educators did the evaluations. Next, we discuss the results obtained.

4.3 Analysis

After the evaluations, we collected empirical data from the questionnaire answers. We performed an analysis of each of these answers, and we did an initial analysis to check whether educators reached the same conclusion in closed questions, such as, for instance, agree with the results of the models. After this analyze, we review the answers of each educator, including the comments that they made on their choices.

Analysis of participants: The educators who took the entire process represents four courses and three different Brazilian universities: Administration - Universidade Federal Rural do Rio de Janeiro (UFRRJ); Computing - Universidade Federal Fluminense (UFF); Goografia - Universidade do Estado do Rio de Janeiro (UERJ); Pedagogy - Universidade Federal Rural do Rio de Janeiro (UFRRJ). Their experiences with distance education ranged between 3, 4, and 6 years.

Everyone was satisfied with the answers given by the AIs that they have experience. However, when asked about the confidence in the answers, we had three different answers. Two of the three educators trust in the IAs that they use. However, one person said he had little confidence and, when describing the reason for the lack of confidence, commented:

> P3: I trust in an objective way. For instance, I want to reach a particular place using Google Maps. When I am approaching the place, the App tells me a place to have lunch, and I do not trust the indication of the App. I do know that exists a variety of factors that I do not control in its decision.

These different responses from the courses, universities to which they belong, and even in the experience with AIs, show to us that the evaluations were carried out by profiles with different visions and experiences. To top it off, we still had a person who has already identified biases in the AI responses, commenting on a Google Maps instance, so that he would not get in the way of a poor community:

> P3: Again, Google Maps. I was going to a particular location, in which I knew the most viable route (fast and safe), but I did not know precisely the number of the location, so use the App, which suggested that I take a route further away from that I would do. I realized that the App made a path around a peripheral community, in which I would have passed through.

Analysis of the Decision Tree Predictive Model: When using the model built with the Decision Tree algorithm, we would like to see if educators would find the racism that existed in the model. At first, as the first question was to say whether the educator agrees or not with the model's responses, everyone said they did not agree. In this response, we had two comments.

> P3: I do not agree with the logic that defines the student's situation. I do think the scheme reproduces a racial prediction. For example, in the simulation with student 28, just because I did change the race from black to white, it left the condition of potential for dropout. The same happened with student 3, in which I did change the race from white to black, and it became a student with confirmed dropout potential. Thus, in both situations, although the students are in the same conditions, only the difference between white and black race defines the condition of evasion.
>
> P2: One student with excellent grades and many interactions on the platform have prediction set to yes for dropout.

P3 started by describing the whole problem that he found in the predictions and pointed out the identification of the racism present in the model. However, P2 seems not to have agreed because he was unable to change the prediction with the attributes he considered important.

The next questions only reinforced these inferences. P3 identified two attributes used for the prediction: family income and race. P1 and P2 did not answer, but P2 explained the reason.

> P2:I didn't find anything that changed the prediction. I made inverse choices, and it didn't change.

P2 failed to identify racism. Apparently, due to attempts to change only the grades and access attributes. As P1 did not comment or answer anything, we do not know where the difficulty was. However, it is worth remembering that P1 also answered the first question, disagreeing with the model's results.

Finally, when asked if the use of simulations and scenarios was useful for understanding and questioning the results, P2 and P3 replied that it helped a lot, while P1 responded indifference. We still had a comment from P3 justifying his choice in this regard.

> P3: They contributed to my understanding that, although the variables or categories used have some relationship with the result that is being sought, these social and economic variables, considered in isolation, in a quantitative way, do not present concrete results of reality.

Analysis of the Neural Network Predictive Model: When using the model built with the MLP algorithm, we would like to see if educators would identify and be able to question the results of the Neural Network. As we do not know how the model arrives in its conclusions, we are more interested if educators would be able to evaluate these results in any way. In the beginning, as the first question was to say whether the educator agrees or not with the model's responses, we had a different answer for each educator.

P1 agree and explained the reason. In other words, the educator agrees because it is based on attributes that P1 considers to have a real impact on DL dropout. P3 said precisely the opposite.

P1: The predictions of the Neural Network regarding the student "Yes" was based on the amount of access, and grade. Students with "No" prediction was based on the grade.

P3: I do believe that the prediction of data does not correspond to the real situations that define the motivation for dropout

When we ask educators about the attributes they found to be important for the results, P1 and P2 marked the amount of access to the platform and the discussion forums. P1 also checked grades and family income. However, P2 and P3 did not mark other attributes.

These results may indicate confusion among educators, contrary to what we would expect. However, all agreed on the usefulness of the scenarios for questioning the AI, although P3 disagreed with the results.

5   Findings

5.1   Were Users Able to Identify Prejudices in the Use of the Decision Tree?

When we discuss the results of the evaluations in the Decision Tree, we see that there may be potential in the use of simulations and scenarios for the identification of prejudices in IAs. However, for this to occur effectively, it would be necessary to study other ways to make these simulations.

We can say it because we had a successful case where the educator found prejudice. However, he only found it due to his own experience with the use of other AIs, where he had already identified prejudices. Then, from his experience, the educator performed simulations with the attribute where there was racism.

In the case of other educators, they identify wrong predictions. However, they were unable to identify racism. In one of the comments, it was clear that the educator was unable to identify the attributes that affected the Decision Tree predictions.

5.2   Were Users Able to Question the Results of the Predictive Models (Neural Network and Decision Tree)?

When we analyze, not only the results of the evaluations in the Neural Network but also in the Decision Tree, we can see clear alerts raised by the educators, in all cases. One of the educators stated that the predictions were wrong because when he changed attributes that he considers important, the AI did not make different predictions. Another one said that the results were wrong due to a change in socio-economic attributes that resulted in a different prediction, arguing that these attributes should not be considered, although these alerts vary according to the experience and vision of each educator.

Besides, the educators agreed that the use of simulations brought reflections and allowed for questioning. Despite this, it was also clear that educators failed to understand the causes related to the Neural Network predictions.

5.3 Conclusion

Recent works [14] confirms that we are living, right now, with AI solutions that make decisions and show culturally biased results (for example, due to the prejudice about what defines racism in predictions that point black people as people at risk of evasion, just because they are black). Thus, we increasingly need ways to question the results of these models. For this reason, we present a research that investigated the use of scenario simulations to allow educators, without technical knowledge about AI, to question the results of predicted models.

The main findings suggests that the use of these simulations can work for this questioning. Educators were able to agree and disagree with the results. In one case, an educator was able to find a correct prejudice in the DT model. However, it is still necessary to do a deeper analysis to find whether these findings remain with a more significant number of educators and with a greater cultural variety.

In addition to this deeper analysis, we also need to carry out studies that identify disruptions and help educators in their simulations. For example, can we guide educators to evaluate specific attributes? What would be the best way to do this? If we have a better interaction and guidance, could it be used to understand the results of a Neural Network?

So, from what we have learned so far, we conclude that simulations can have the potential to question results and even to identify prejudices. However, further investigation is needed to see if the use of these simulations proves to be truly useful with a significant number of users.

Acknowledgement. The authors want to thank the Brazilian funding agencies that support this project in different ways: CAPES, CNPq and FAPERJ. They would also like to express their gratitude to the volunteers who participated in the study.

References

1. Akoka, J., Isabelle, C., Nabil, L.: Research on big data-a systematic mapping study. Comput. Stand. Interfaces **54**, 105–115 (2017)
2. Albrecht, J.: How the GDPR will change the world. Eur. Data Prot. Law Rev. **2**, 287–289 (2016)
3. Altman, N.: An introduction to kernel and nearest-neighbor nonparametric regression. Am. Stat. **46**, 175–185 (1992)
4. Baxter, J.: Who am I and what keeps me going? Profiling the distance learning student in higher education. Int. Rev. Res. Open Distrib. Learn. **13**(4), 107–129 (2012)
5. Cai, Y., Guo, W.: Responses of Chinese higher education to the information society. E-Learn. Digit. Media **3**(3), 353–360 (2006)

6. Chmielewski, M., Grzymala-Busse, J.: Global discretization of continuous attributes as preprocessing for machine learning. Int. J. Approximate Reasoning **15**, 319–331 (1996)
7. General Data Protection Regulation. https://gdpr-info.eu/. Accessed 24 Feb 2020
8. Han, J., Kamber, M.: Data Mining: Concepts and Techniques, 2nd edn. Morgan Kaufmann, Burlington (2006)
9. Hanson, J.: Displaced but not replaced: the impact of E-learning on academic identities in higher education. Teach. High. Educ. **14**, 553–564 (2009)
10. Harasim, L.: Shift happens: online education as a new paradigm in learning. Internet High. Educ. **3**(1–2), 41–61 (2000)
11. Hastie, T., Tibshirani, R., Friedman, J.: The Elements of Statistical Learning: Data Mining, Inference, and Prediction. SSS, 2nd edn. Springer, New York (2009). https://doi.org/10.1007/978-0-387-84858-7
12. INEP. Censo da Educação Superior: Notas Estatísticas (2018). http://tiny.cc/crufkz. Accessed 24 Feb 2020
13. Isaacs, S.: The eLearning Africa Report 2013 (2014)
14. Joh, E.: The new surveillance discretion: automated suspicion, big data, and policing. Harv. L. Pol'y Rev. **10**, 15 (2016)
15. Jordan, K.: Initial trends in enrolment and completion of massive open online courses. Int. Rev. Res. Open Distrib. Learn. **15**(1), 133–160 (2014)
16. Kotsiantis, S., Pintelas, P.: A decision support prototype tool for predicting student performance in an ODL environment. Interact. Technol. Smart Educ. **1**, 253–264 (2004)
17. Lei Geral de Proteção de Dados Pessoais. http://tiny.cc/ulvfkz. Accessed 24 Feb 2020
18. Liang, J., Li, C., Zheng, L.: Machine learning application in MOOCs: dropout prediction. In: 11th International Conference on Computer Science & Education (ICCSE), pp. 52–57. IEEE (2016)
19. Liu H., Rudy S.: Chi2: feature selection and discretization of numeric attributes. In: 7th IEEE International Conference on Tools with Artificial Intelligence. IEEE (1995)
20. Maimon, O.: Data Mining with Decision Trees: Theory and Applications. World Scientific, Singapore (2008)
21. Mayer, R.: Multimedia learning. In: Psychology of Learning and Motivation, pp. 85–139. Academic Press (2002)
22. Means, B., Toyama, Y., Murphy, R., Bakia, M., Jones, K.: Evaluation of evidence-based practices in online learning: a meta-analysis and review of online learning studies (2009)
23. Mitchell, T.: Machine learning and data mining. Commun. ACM **42**(11), 30–36 (1999)
24. Moore, J., Dickson-Deane, C., Galyen, K.: e-Learning, online learning, and distance learning environments: are they the same? Internet High. Educ. **14**(2), 129–135 (2011)
25. Niemi, D., Gitin, E.: Using big data to predict student dropouts: technology affordances for research. International Association for Development of the Information Society (2012)
26. Ortigosa, A., Carro, R., Bravo-Agapito, J., Lizcano, D., Alcolea, J., Blanco, O.: From lab to production: lessons learnt and real-life challenges of an early student-dropout prevention system. IEEE Trans. Learn. Technol. **12**, 264–277 (2019)
27. Reitermanova, Z.: Data splitting. In: WDS, vol. 10 (2010)

28. Ribeiro, E., Mendonça, G., Mendonça, A.: A importância dos ambientes virtuais de aprendizagem na busca de novos domínios da EAD. In: Anais do 13° Congresso Internacional de Educação a Distância, Curitiba, Brasil (2007)
29. Sesabo, J., Mfaume, R., Msabila, D.: Opportunities and challenges in implementing distance learning and e-learning: a case study. In: Handbook of Research on Educational Technology Integration and Active Learning, pp. 329–345. IGI Global (2015)
30. Snyder, T., Dillow, S.: Digest of education statistics, 2008. Government Printing Office, US Department of Health, Education, and Welfare (2009)
31. Vitiello, M., Walk, S., Chang, V., Hernandez, R., Helic, D., Guetl, C.: MOOC dropouts: a multi-system classifier. In: Lavoué, É., Drachsler, H., Verbert, K., Broisin, J., Pérez-Sanagustín, M. (eds.) EC-TEL 2017. LNCS, vol. 10474, pp. 300–314. Springer, Cham (2017). https://doi.org/10.1007/978-3-319-66610-5_22
32. Wolff, A., Zdrahal, Z., Herrmannova, D., Kuzilek, J., Hlosta, M.: Developing predictive models for early detection of at-risk students on distance learning modules. In: Machine Learning and Learning Analytics Workshop at The 4th International Conference on Learning Analytics and Knowledge (LAK14), Indiana, USA, 24–28 Mar 2014 (2014)

Is My Home Smart or Just Connected?

Susanne Furman and Julie Haney[(✉)]

National Institute of Standards and Technology, Gaithersburg, MD, USA
{Susanne.Furman, Julie.Haney}@nist.gov

Abstract. The smart home market will approach 40 billion USD (United States dollars) by 2020 and household penetration to reach 47.40% in 2023. Experts say that we will move from turning lights on and off by giving a voice assistant commands to a smart home that collects, analyzes and acts upon information, turning our smart devices into intelligent homes. As homes become more intelligent with the use of artificial intelligence (AI), will the inhabitants understand what that might mean and what makes a device or home smart? Between February and June of 2019, we conducted semi-structured interviews of 40 smart home consumers to understand their perceptions of smart homes. During the interview we asked them what the Internet of Things (IoT) meant, what makes a smart device, what makes a smart home. Overall, participants were unfamiliar with the term IoT. We coded the responses with major codes. Reasons that participants said made devices smart: they were connected to the internet, were programmable, and had some type of learning component (e.g., natural language processing, machine learning, learn over time). Participants said the following made homes smart: have smart devices, connected, made life easier, were programmable and they could control devices in the home. Only a few participants included learning into their descriptions of smart homes. As smart devices and smart homes mature into an intelligent home driven by artificial intelligence, it is critical for consumers to understand the implications of use.

Keywords: Smart home · Artificial intelligence · Connected home · Internet of Things (IoT)

1   Introduction

You get up and go into your smart bathroom to take a shower. Your shower is programmed to remember your shower habits, so you hop in and the water temperature, spray and lighting are just the way you programmed it. A smart home is defined as one that is connected, automated, and remote-controlled by the use of internet and mobile devices to help you control different features in your home [1].

If it were truly an intelligent home (i.e., AI-powered), when your alarm clock goes off in the morning, it would have scanned your schedule and turned the shower on to your preferred spray, lighting and temperature of 103 °F. You haven't been feeling all that great today, so when you get home there's a package delivered by drone and you open it to find cold medicine. Your health sensors embedded in your bathroom detected

H. Degen and L. Reinerman-Jones (Eds.): HCII 2020, LNCS 12217, pp. 273–287, 2020.
https://doi.org/10.1007/978-3-030-50334-5_18

signs of an illness and placed the order for you so it would be there when you got home.

The smart home market will approach 40 billion USD by 2020 [2] with household penetration expected to grow from 27.50% in 2019 to 47.40% in 2023 [3]. But connected smart home devices are only the beginning when it comes to smart home technology as the popularity grows and the technology is driven by artificial intelligence (AI).

Experts say that we will move from turning lights on and off by giving voice assistants commands to an intelligent home. Robotics will give us machines that offer a helping hand with cleaning, cooking and more. Central to this will be the data that the smart home collects, analyzes and acts upon, turning our gadgets into intelligent homes. Currently, AI-powered gadgets are voice assistants that get the latest news, weather forecast, or turn on our lights when we tell it to [4]. Even though these are "AI" systems they still continue to rely on human initiative because we tell them what to do or schedule them to do what we want [5].

Yet smart devices and homes come with well-described privacy and security issues. As homes become more intelligent or adaptive [6] in which the home seeks to adapt to its inhabitants and respond to their informational and comfort needs, do the inhabitants understand what that means or what makes a device or home smart?

Between February and June of 2019, we conducted semi-structured interviews of 40 smart home consumers to understand their perceptions of smart homes. We asked them questions about what makes devices and homes smart, purchase and general use questions, installation and troubleshooting questions, privacy and security questions, and safety questions (see Appendix A). For this study we were interested in what participants said makes the devices smart and what they said it means to have a smart home. This paper describes a subset of collected data centered on what participants thought the IoT means and makes a device and a home smart.

2   Background

For our AI assistants to assist us and make our decisions, machine learning technology enters into the picture. According to Forbes [6], machine learning is an application of AI that enables a smart device to learn and improve based on its experience as well as data it collects and analyzes. In the context of our research we consider artificial intelligence as the development of computer systems able to perform tasks that normally require human intelligence and it is the ability of computer programs to think and learn. Our devices can do a lot for us and, in the future, they will have the ability to adapt to our needs and goals. But do consumers of smart home devices understand what makes a smart home smart or do they confuse smart with connected?

Just what is a smart home anyway? According to Consumer News and Business Channel (CNBC), a smart home is defined "as a home that is equipped with network-connected products for controlling, automating and optimizing functions such as temperature, lighting, security, safety or entertainment either remotely by a phone, tablet, computer or a separate system within the home itself" [7].

The first 'wired homes' (i.e., homes with interactive technology) were actually built by hobbyists in the early 1960s [8]. What makes a home smart is the interactive technologies that it contains. According to Aldrich [1] a "smart home" is defined as a residence that is equipped with computing and information technology that anticipates and responds to occupant's needs, promoting comfort, convenience, security, and entertainment managed by technology with the home and connections to the world beyond.

In the homes of the future, computer software will play the role of an intelligent agent that perceives the state of the physical environment and residents using sensors and artificial intelligence techniques that will take actions to achieve specific goals for the people living in the home (e.g., minimizing the consumption of resources, or maintaining the health and safety of the home and residents) [9].

But little is known about what consumers believe makes a device or a home smart. PricewaterhouseCoopers (PwC) hired a global research firm to conduct a survey of 1000 respondents in October 2016 to understand consumers attitudes and experiences with the connected home, i.e., smart homes [10]. One of the questions they focused on was "to what degree do consumers understand the concept of IoT and the smart home?" Results showed that the term "internet of things" was largely unfamiliar, yet the idea of devices being smart is a concept most respondents understood. What is smart according to respondents is: the ability to collect/monitor data and project future usage for efficiency, ability to connect to other devices, or something that helps out with everyday life and makes it simpler.

Smart homes are still in their infancy and react mostly to commands, but the smart homes of the future will make intelligent decisions for us as they run our lives in our home environment. There are big differences and many implications between smart device consumers adopting individual devices and signing up for a smart home life.

3   Methodology

Between February and June of 2019, we conducted a semi-structured interview study to understand end users' perceptions of, and experiences with, smart home devices from purchase decision to implementation to everyday usage (see Appendix A). This paper describes a subset of collected data centered on what is the IoT and what makes a device and a home smart.

3.1   Participant Recruitment

We hired a consumer research company to recruit general public consumers who had two or more different smart home devices. To determine eligibility, potential participants completed an online screening survey about their smart home devices, basic demographics, role with devices (e.g., purchaser, installer, troubleshooter, user), and number of household members. We reviewed the screening information and selected participants who met the minimal requirements. General public participants received a $75 prepaid gift card as compensation. Thirty-three general public consumers completed the interview and we identified seven participants from federal employment.

The study was approved by the National Institute of Standards and Technology (NIST) Human Subjects Protections Office (HSPO). Prior to data collection, participants were informed of the study purpose and how their data would be protected. Data were recorded without personal identifiers (instead using generic identifiers. e.g. P1, P2…) and not linked back to individuals.

3.2 Data Collection

We collected data from 40 semi-structured interviews that lasted 41 min on average as well as demographic information. The in-depth interviews afforded a greater richness of data, the ability to ask follow-up questions to explore, and the opportunity for participants to provide other relevant information not explicitly targeted by the interview protocol.

We piloted the interview protocol with four individuals to determine the face validity of the questions and language. We made minor adjustments to the interview instrument based on feedback from the pilot. We audio recorded all interviews and hired a transcription company to transcribe them. Interview questions addressed several areas in the following order: understanding of smart home terminology; purchase and general use; installation and troubleshooting; privacy; security; and safety. For this paper, we are focusing on the questions about what is the "Internet of Things", what makes devices and what makes homes smart.

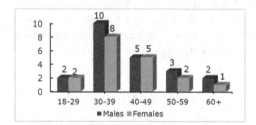

Fig. 1. Males & females by age category

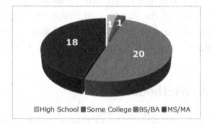

Fig. 2. Education

3.3 Participant Demographics and Devices

Twenty-two males (55%) and 18 females (45%) completed the study. The majority were between the ages of 30–49 (see Fig. 1). Participants were highly educated with 18 (45%) having a master's degree or above and 20 (50%) with a bachelors' (i.e., BA/BS) degree. (see Fig. 2). Of the 40 participants, 32 (80%) had installed and administered the devices, while eight (20%) were general device users. Participant occupations included diverse occupations from assistant principal to community arts specialist. Six participants had occupations in computer science or IT fields. Table 1 shows the participant occupations.

Table 1. Occupations

Participant occupations		
Accountant	Events coordinator	Professor
Administrator	Events manager	Program Coordinator
Administrative assistant	Event planner	Program mgt analyst
Analyst	Executive Admin Assistant	Project manager
Assistant principal	Federal employee	Research chief
Business consultant	Financial analyst	Retail services specialist
Cognitive scientist	Health educator	Retired (N = 2)
Community arts specialist	Human resources manager	Security
Computer scientist (N = 2)	Information specialist	Senior tech analyst
Consultant	Lead engineer	Software engineer
Customer service rep	Liaison	Special educator
Educationist	Lobbyist	Systems engineer
Electrical engineer	Operational safety analyst	

Smart devices in participant's homes included: security cameras, motion detectors, door locks, and water-leak detectors. Smart entertainment devices included: smart televisions, speakers, streaming devices, and other connected media. Devices in the home environment category included: energy-saving technologies (e.g., smart plugs), lighting thermostats, and temperature sensors, smoke detectors, and air quality sensors. Smart appliances included: large and small connected appliances (e.g., refrigerators, coffee pots, robot vacuums). Virtual assistants included voice-controlled devices such as Amazon Alexa and Google home. See Fig. 3 for the general categories of devices.

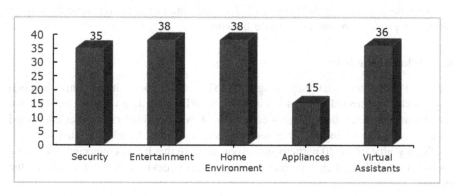

Fig. 3. Types of smart home devices

3.4 Qualitative Analyses

We conducted semi-structured interviews of 40 smart devices consumers to understand their perceptions of and experiences with smart home devices. Three NIST researchers initially coded a subset of four interviews and then met to develop and operationalize a codebook to identify concepts within the data. Based on the codebook, we performed iterative coding on the transcripts. We met and discussed the codes and progressed to the recognition of relationships among the codes as we examined patterns and categories to identify themes in our data.

We were interested in a subset of the questions in the in-depth interview to study whether the consumers in our study understood what IoT was and what made devices and homes smart. We focused this paper on the following research questions:

- What do smart device consumers think the Internet of Things (IoT) is?
- What do smart home consumers think make devices "smart"?
- What do smart home consumers think it means to have a "smart" home?

To answer our research questions, we coded the transcripts using the terms that we developed in our code book using a widely accepted grounded theory qualitative data analysis method [11]. We used two codes for what is the Internet of Things: connected by internet or WIFI (i.e., wireless fidelity) and the second code of: don't know. For smart devices, we coded responses with the following codes: learn/machine learning; programmable, connected, automated, and collects information and acts. For smart homes, we coded responses using the following codes: programmable, connected, controllable, home has smart devices, automated, makes life easier, and learns over time.

4   Results

We asked participants a series of questions about their experience of smart home devices in their homes. For this part of the study, we were interested in what participants thought about: what IoT is, what made a device smart, what made a home smart, and what the relationship is between the IoT and smart devices. Example participant quotes are provided below to illustrate the concept.

4.1   What Is the IoT

We asked participants what they thought the IoT was. We coded the responses into two major codes: connected devices by internet or WIFI and didn't know. Most of the participants answered that it was a collection of WIFI-enabled or internet connected devices and a few saying that they were not sure or hadn't heard of the IoT.

Twenty-nine of the 40 participants responses were that it was connected devices by internet or WIFI. Participants said it was basically devices that connected to the internet.

P10: *My thought about what the internet of things is, basically a bunch of networked single maybe double purpose devices, micro appliances just connected to a network and they kind of work with each other.*

P11: *I consider the internet of things to be essentially devices that are connected to the internet and specifically in many cases, devices that may connect to cloud services, devices that produce data, or that data is aggregated and collected, and then potentially used to make decisions.*

Nine participants had never heard of the IoT or didn't know what it meant. Participants thought it was more of a technical term that they wouldn't use day to day or had never heard of it.

P2: *The Internet of Things. I haven't really used that word too much to be honest. I feel like that's more of a maybe more technology term for … I don't think it's a colloquial term that people use day-to-day.*

P31: *I don't know that I've heard that term, actually, and I'm kind of someone that should, I feel. I would assume it's just kind of a generalized term of how the internet affects our lives, but I don't know that I'm remotely close to the answer.*

4.2   What Participants Think Makes a Device Smart

We asked participants what they thought made a device smart. We coded the transcripts using the terms from previous research used to define smart devices: learn/machine learning; programmable, connected, automated, and collects information and acts. Most of the responses fell into three code categories: learn/machine learning, programmable, and connected.

Participants mentioned that to be smart the device needed to learn over time from the commands the owner issued, that there was some natural language processing, some type of machine learning, or that the device could think for itself. For example, P1 said: *"I guess it would be something like a Nest that over time it figured it… it knows when you leave, so it can turn things down."* P7 talked about machine learning: *"Maybe some machine learning involved so we can just evolve over time, they get smarter over time."* P14 talked about the device thinking for itself: *"What makes a device smart? One would think if they can think for themselves or perform an action."* P8 provided an elaborate response:

"So, smart devices, in general, they … I would guess would you say they have a Learning component, but I guess they also share an Internet platform where they are able to be updated, they are able to be networked, and they think… I don't want to say machine learning. I don't want to go that far. Basically, they adapt, I'm going to use my Nest thermostat, for example. It adapts to your usage.… Then I think it uses an algorithm or machine learning, in some way, shape or form, to then better configure itself to you needs."

Twelve participants responded by saying that the because the devices were connected (i.e., internet or WIFI) that they were smart. P11 answered this way, *"These are devices that don't fully function purely on their own but need some sort of network connectivity to basically report information or to make decisions."* P18 put it simply, *"Your ability to interface on the internet."* P27 mentioned Bluetooth connectivity, *"I think it's that they can be used outside the home or they can be used without having to press a button. It's more you can use it via Bluetooth or whatever."*

Eleven of the 40 participants mentioned that the device was programmable and that is what made it smart. P5 expressed it this way, *"I guess they're programmable that you can instruct them to do things according to your wishes…"* P13 talked about not only can the devices be remotely controlled but they could also be programmed, *"They can be remotely controlled, but also can be programmed to react to external stimuli on their own."* P19 said that he is what made them smart, *"..it's myself that makes them smart... I guess what makes them smart is the programmable decision points that are programmed into the interface."* P28 responded that you can program them remotely, *"You can program them, you can schedule a smart device in your home. You can remotely program them when you're away from home."*

A few participants mentioned automated, ease of interaction, or electronics/ technology as the reason why devices are smart. P10 said, *"A device that is smart is one that functions without any human interaction or can function based off of sensors or timing or some kind of automated schedule."* P35 mentioned ease of interaction, *"The ease of interaction with them."* P31 said technology made them smart, *"I think that devices are smart because they utilize technology to do things that were once low tech."*

4.3   What Participants Said Makes a Home Smart

We asked participants what they thought made a home smart. We coded the transcripts using terms that were used in previous research to define a smart home. Codes included:

Programmable, connected (internet, WIFI), ability to control devices, home with smart devices, and a home that makes life easier.

Approximately half of the participants thought that a smart home was one that was connected (i.e., internet or WIFI connected). As P11 explained it, *"I look at a smart home as a home that has some sort of network, ether wired or most likely nowadays, wireless that is most likely internet connected...".* P28 talked about the home being all wired up. P28 described it this way, *"It means it's all wired up. It's connected to the Internet. You have smart devices. Everything's interconnected".*

About a fourth of participants said a home was smart because it had a number of smart devices. As P4 simply put it, *"A home that has some of these devices, to me would be smart or smarter home."* P10 said a smart home needs a certain number of devices, *"I don't consider my home a smart home. It has a lot of smart things in it, but I don't think it's smart enough to call a smart home. So, I think you have to have a number of smart devices in your house to qualify for that."* P15 thought it would be a home with just one smart device, *"Well again, I'd say that's simply a home that has any smart device in it, would probably qualify as a smart home."* P35 wasn't sure but added, *"I don't know. A smart device in your home."*

Another 25% said that a smart home was programmable, responds to our commands or is controllable. P1 talked about the device responding to a command, *"You could say, what's the weather? And it tells you."* P40 talked about controlling the home, *"Actually to myself it means more control over the home itself, especially when I am not there."* P1 described a smart home as one that is programmable, *"It might turn the lights off after you go to bed, or it's set up at a schedule so that people know that you're still at home even thought you might be away."*

Some participants said that a smart home simply makes life easier. P31 expressed it this way, *"Well, for me, it's just having those devices in my home that are meant to make life a little bit easier, but also maybe even make my home a little bit more secure."* P41 talked about quality of life, *"A home that's connected to electronic devices that would make life easier, quality of life easier."*

Only two participants mentioned anything about learning. P12 said, *"A smart home would be it knows to lock the doors when you open up the door and then close it behind you, setting room temperatures for you when you're inside of the house of outside of the house, setting your refrigerator at a certain temperature or freezer at a certain temperature."* P29 talked about a home that anticipates his needs, *"I think it's a combination of a home that works well for me and also one that anticipates my needs, but also kind of runs itself efficiently."*

5   Discussion

In this paper we describe a subset of data we collected in a semi-structured interview study on what the IoT is, makes a device and what makes a home smart. We wanted to understand if participants understood what made devices and homes smart.

As PwC [11] found previously, participants were largely unfamiliar with the term "internet of things". Similarly, the majority of our 40 participants heard of the term, and only nine said that they had never heard the term or didn't know what it meant.

The majority of the PwC participants (81%) were familiar with the concept of a smart home device and used terms like connected devices, makes life simpler, and collected and monitored data to increase efficiency. Possibly because our participants were all smart device consumers, they were a bit more experienced with smart devices. They described what made a device smart by talking about machine learning and natural language processing, connected devices, automation, and programmable.

Participants also used similar words to describe what made a smart home. About half of our participants said a smart home was one that was connected, about a fourth of participants said that it was a home with a number of smart devices, another fourth said it was smart because it could be programmed, and a few said a smart home made life easier. Only two participants mentioned that some learning component made a home smart.

Makridakis (2017) argues that within the next decade, the AI revolution will have an even greater impact than both the Industrial and Digital Revolutions [12]. Pessimists worry that as AI machines become smarter than humans are, that they will be making our decisions for us. Others are concerned about increased unemployment that may change drastically with the widespread introduction of AI technologies leading to massive job reductions [13]. Scientists like Etzioni (2016) do not believe that AI is a threat to humanity [14]. But there is little doubt that during the next decade that AI technologies will greatly impact our societies and lives in general.

In the next decade of smart homes, more and more AI will be driving these intelligent devices and homes that integrate these devices. No doubt, this could potentially impact the privacy and security of homeowners as well as trust they have in the devices when these devices begin making decisions for us and control not only homes but our lives as well. As Stephen Hawking has warned that the creation of powerful artificial intelligence will be "either the best, or worst thing, even to happen to humanity" [15].

6 Limitations

Our study may be limited in generalizability because of the limitations of in-depth interview studies (e.g., recall and social desirability biases). The participants were well-educated individuals living in a high-income metropolitan area and may not be representative of the U.S. smart home device consumer population. Our study also does not capture the perceptions of consumers who do not have or choose not to have smart devices in their homes. We realize that non-adopters may have different perceptions of AI and smart home devices. However, there is a lack of research in this area and even with these limitations, our exploratory study does shed some light on what smart home device consumers think the IoT is, what makes devices smart and what makes a home smart. Subsequent surveys of a broader population and specifically about these research questions would be of benefit.

7 Conclusion

Let's imagine that it is nearer the end of this decade and AI has been introduced in most if not all smart homes and devices. Your intelligent home knows that you want to awake to new music on your music channel, so it wakes you up to a song on your list. But you never set an alarm because your intelligent home knows you have a spin class this morning because it checked out your workout goals. Your intelligent home checked the availability for a class at the local cycle gym, and when it found a suitable class, it scheduled you and paid for it as well. The home calculated your travel time and set your alarm appropriately the night before.

You get out of bed with your eyes barely open and you can smell the coffee brewing downstairs in the kitchen. Your refrigerator made sure that you had your favorite yogurt, and had it delivered earlier in the week. Your home knows that you have gained some extra weight, so it cuts down the portions and alerts your doctor that your cholesterol levels were elevated. You head to work after your spin class.

After a long day at work it's time to return to your intelligent home. Your car alerts you home that you are on your way and your ETA is 34 min. Your intelligent home knows exactly what music to play and the temperature that you enjoy. You pull into the driveway and walk up to your door and your home scans your retinas and determines that indeed it is you. Your intelligent home decides that you should have salmon with steamed vegetables this evening to meet your health goals. After dinner you retire to your den to watch your favorite show. Oh, and by the way, you don't have to clean up because your home robot will clean up after you go to bed.

Are you comfortable with your intelligent home recording your every move and making decisions for you? Currently there is little research exploring what consumers think is the Internet of Things, what makes a device smart and what makes a home smart, or concerns consumers have about their homes recording their homes, lives, and making decisions for them. More research is needed to understand how consumers perceive artificially intelligent homes and what concerns consumers may have with AI embedded devices.

Disclaimer

Certain commercial companies or products are identified in this paper to foster understanding. Such identification does not imply recommendations or endorsement by the National Institute of Standards and Technology, nor does it imply that the companies or products identified are necessarily the best available for the purpose.

Appendix A Usability of IoT Interview Questions

SECTION A: Terminology

You may have heard the term "internet of things," or IoT for short. Can you talk a little about what you think the internet of things is?

What about devices makes them "smart?"

What does it mean to have a smart home?

What do you think is the relationship between internet of things and "smart" devices?

SECTION B: Purchase and General Use

For people with more than one smart device in their household:

You indicated that you have more than one smart home device. When answering the interview questions, please talk about your overall or general experiences with your devices. So, there's no need to answer a question separately for every device you own. However, if you had any particularly notable or different experiences with specific devices, please do mention those.

For Decision-makers:

Why did you decide to purchase the smart home devices?

[If participant doesn't mention sources of information:]   In general, how did you learn about the devices before you bought them?

What hesitations, if any, did you have about getting the devices?

For Everyone:

How do you use your smart home devices?

How do you access the devices – remotely with an app, while physically in the home, or both?

How do others in your household use the smart home devices?

- If you happen to know, how do they access the devices – remotely, while physically in the home, or both?

    What do you like most about the devices?

- What are the benefits, if any, of having these devices?

What do you like least or dislike about the devices?

How have your opinions or expectations of the devices changed, if at all, from the time you first used them until now?

In what ways, if any, have you changed your behaviors because of your smart home devices?

- Positive behavior changes? Negative behavior changes?
- In what ways, if any, have you become reliant on your smart home devices?

What concerns, if any, do you have about the devices?

- *[Depending on whether they access the devices remotely or physically:]*

How might the concerns be different depending on how you access the device, for example if you access it remotely through a mobile app or if you have to be physically present to access the device?
What do the other members of your household think about the smart home devices?
Have you had visitors to the home who have had to use the smart home devices?

- *[If yes:]* How did they use the devices?
- What did they think?

What smart home devices, if any, have you had in the past, but are no longer using?

- What are the reasons for no longer using this device?

What devices would you like to get in the future? Why?

SECTION C: Installation and Troubleshooting
Who installed the smart home devices?
Who administers (configures or maintains) the smart home devices?
For Installers: In general, what was your experience with the installation of the devices?

- What went well?
- What didn't go as well?
- How did you determine that the installation was successfully completed?
- Have you ever had to reinstall a device? If so, what were the reasons for the reinstallation?

[If have more than one device:] What has been your experience adding additional devices to the home?
For DIYers:
In the screening questionnaire you indicated that you build your own smart home devices or platforms or that you create custom extensions for your devices.
Can you tell me more about what you've done?
For Administrators:
What configuration changes, if any, have you made to the devices since installation?

- *[If participant makes configuration changes:]* How often do you make changes?

Let's now talk about manufacturer updates to your devices. These could be updates that fix known issues or updates to the next version of software or firmware. How do you know that updates are available or needed?

- How are updates done on your device - automatically or do you have to initiate them?

[If manual initiation:]

- How often do you check for updates?
- How do you decide whether to update or not update?

What things, if any, would you like to be able to do with the devices, but haven't? Why?

For Everyone:
How do you try to figure out how to do something with your devices?

- What sources do you consult or use?

What kinds of problems, if any, have you encountered while using your smart home devices?

- How did you go about trying to resolve those problems?

SECTION D: Privacy

What type of information, if any, do you think the devices are collecting?
How do you know that? [If not sure how to answer:] For example, are you making an educated guess based on past experiences, did you read a privacy policy for the device, or did you read about this somewhere?
[Skip rest of questions in this section if the participant thinks the devices don't collect any information.]
Where do you think that information goes?
Which of this information, if any, would you consider to be personal?
What are your concerns, if any, about how information is collected, stored, and used?

- In what ways, if any, have you acted to minimize or alleviate some of those concerns?
- What kinds of actions would you like to be able to take to address your concerns, but haven't, don't know how, or are not sure that you can?

What are your concerns, if any, about who can see your information or monitor your usage patterns with the devices? *[if YES ask for clarification: for example, employees of companies/manufacturers, other household members, hackers].*
In what ways, if any, does your device or the device manufacturer provide a means to control or manage what information is collected and how it is shared?
Who do you think is responsible for protecting the privacy of information collected by your smart home device?

- What are the reasons you think they are responsible?

SECTION E: Security

For this next set of questions, when I am talking about security, I don't mean physical security like someone breaking into your home. Rather, I'm referring to how the devices protect your information from people who might try to access your devices without your permission or even someone in your household who might do something purposefully or accidentally.
What are your concerns, if any, about the security of your devices?

- In what ways, if any, have you acted to minimize or alleviate some of those concerns?
- What kinds of actions would you like to be able to take to address your concerns, but haven't, don't know how, or are not sure that you can?

Who do you think is responsible for the security of your smart home devices? Why? What restrictions, if any, are placed on who in your household can use the devices and what they can do?
How do you authenticate to or get into any apps associated with the device? *[If not sure how to answer:]* for example, password, PIN, fingerprint, face recognition.

- What issues or problems, if any, have you experienced with authentication?

Does more than one person in your household use an app to access the same device?

- What concerns, if any, do you have with multiple people having access to the app?
- Does more than one person use the same account and authentication (like a pass word or PIN) to access the app?
  - *[If yes:]* What concerns, if any, do you have with sharing the same account and authentication information?

SECTION F: SAFETY
For the next two questions, when I talk about safety, I'm referring to the physical safety and well-being of the people and items in your household.
In what ways, if any, do you think the devices contribute to safety?
In what ways, if any, do you think the devices might pose a safety risk?

SECTION G: Conclusion
Is there anything else you'd like to add related to anything we've talked about?

References

1. Harper, R.: Inside the smart home: ideas, possibilities and methods. In: Harper, R. (ed.) Inside the smart home, pp. 1–13. Springer, London (2003). https://doi.org/10.1007/1-85233-854-7_1
2. Smart Home Statistics, Alarms.Org. https://www.alarms.org/smart-home-statistics/
3. Smart Home, Statista. https://www.statista.com/outlook/279/109/smart-home/united-states
4. What Will Smart Homes Look Like 10 Years From Now? Time – Patrick Lucas Austin, 25 July 2019. https://time.com/5634791/smart-homes-future/
5. How AI Technology Has Transformed Smart Homes, HomeSelfe. https://www.homeselfe.com/how-ai-technology-has-transformed-smart-homes/
6. Marr, B.: What is the difference between artificial intelligence and machine learning? Forbes (2016). https://www.forbes.com/sites/bernardmarr/2016/12/06/what-is-the-difference-between-artificial-intelligence-and-machine-learning/#8dc818a2742b
7. Weiser, M.: The computer for the 21st century. Sci. Am. **265**(3), 94–104 (1991)
8. Just what is a 'smart home' anyway? Diana Olick, CNBC, 10 May 2016. https://www.cnbc.com/2016/05/09/just-what-is-a-smart-home-anyway.html

9. Aldrich, F.K.: Smart homes: past, present and future. In: Harper, R. (ed.) Inside the Smart Home, pp. 17–39. Springer, London (2003). https://doi.org/10.1007/1-85233-854-7_2

10. Cook, D.J.: How smart is your home? Science **335**(6076), 1579–1581 (2012)

11. PwC Consumer Intelligence Series: Smart home, seamless life Unlocking a culture of convenience, January 2017. https://www.pwc.fr/fr/assets/files/pdf/2017/01/pwc-consumer-intelligence-series-iot-connected-home.pdf

12. Glaser, B.G., Strauss, A.L.: Discovery of Grounded Theory: Strategies for Qualitative Research. Routledge, Abingdon (2017)

13. Makridakis, S.: The forthcoming information revolution: Its impact on society and firms. Futures **27**(8), 799–821 (1995)

14. Stewart, I., Debrapratim, D., Cole, A.: Deloitte (2015). https://www2.deloitte.com/content/dam/Deloitte/uk/Documents/finance/deloitte-uk-technology-and-people.pdf

15. Etzioni, O.: No, the experts don't think superintelligent AI is a threat to humanity. MIT Technol. Rev. (2016). https://www.technologyreview.com/s/602410/no-the-experts-dont-think-superintelligent-ai-is-a-threat-to-humanity/

16. Herm, A.: Stephen Hawking: AI will be 'either best or worst thing' for humanity. Guardian, 16 October 2016. . https://www.theguardian.com/science/2016/oct/19/stephen-hawking-ai-best-or-worst-thing-for-humanity-cambridge

Design Intelligence - Pitfalls and Challenges When Designing AI Algorithms in B2B Factory Automation

Jennifer Heier[1(✉)], Jan Willmann[1], and Karsten Wendland[2]

[1] Bauhaus Universität Weimar, 99423 Weimar, Germany
{jennifer.heier,jan.willmann}@uni-weimar.de
[2] Hochschule Aalen, 73430 Aalen, Germany
karsten.wendland@hs-aalen.de

Abstract. This paper presents results from the on-going research in industrial AI, namely a use case from Business-to-Business (B2B) factory automation, focusing on Artificial Intelligence (AI) technology to predict specific time series for factory planning. This research wants to shed light on the progress in industrial AI applications and, most importantly, the respective design and development process. Assuming that a lack of human-centered-design is a key source for considerable pains of the users, e.g. to trust in the system, and problems for stakeholders involved, e.g. exaggerated expectations [1, 2]. The paper outlines a) a B2B-factory planning case study, including setup and implementation, b) the validation of the process and its results through interviews, and c) the pitfalls and challenges of designing AI algorithms in the given context. Of particular importance are 14 themes that have been developed from analysis of a qualitative study with the development team, users and stakeholders involved. Some of the themes are relevant to other use cases and domains as well, some are use case specific and some derive from the focus of the design perspective. Those insights serve as a basis for further steps of investigation and, ultimately, foster a (cross-disciplinary) transfer of knowledge towards other domains.

Keywords: Machine learning · UX · Factory automation

1 Introduction

Due to the unprecedented advancement in technology and availability of Big Data, Artificial Intelligence (AI) has become a major factor in business development and optimization, including for example predictive maintenance for machinery, or AI-driven marketing campaigns with customized content for the user [3, 4]. Whereas the use of AI in commercial applications is constantly progressing and research is becoming widely accessible and documented, the world of industrial AI applications and AI agents is a white spot [5]. In the commercial domain, the creative community - such as User Experience (UX) design - already discusses and develops novel B2C applications, and thus pointing to opportunities, as well as challenges of design in the age of AI [6–10]. In fact, design innovation and diversity are considerably lacking in

© Springer Nature Switzerland AG 2020
H. Degen and L. Reinerman-Jones (Eds.): HCII 2020, LNCS 12217, pp. 288–297, 2020.
https://doi.org/10.1007/978-3-030-50334-5_19

the domain of data science and machine learning community [11, 12], either in B2C, even more in the industrial sector. This paper therefore describes key paradigms of designing with AI and analyzes a specific use case in the domain of B2B factory automation. It provides an outlook to further points of investigation, as well as a starting point for solutions to the given challenges.

2 Context

The portfolio of the respective company focuses on the B2B industrial automation market. Customer services, software, logistics, and hardware are the focus areas. The described use case is based in the hardware unit and its goal is to improve and optimize the factory planning process of a production site for industrial controls in Germany [13]. The current factory planning process is done manually by a group of human planners. Each planner is responsible for a certain number of products, 1700 in total. Information and data from sales, material procurement, capacity of the factory and customer delivery wish dates need to be taken into consideration and influence the process. Their plan is conducted 52 weeks into the future, in order to plan how many pieces of each product need to be produced in order to keep the customer wish date. For the advancement of production, time series prediction with neural networks has been chosen and presents the given technology for the use case [14]. In this, a data model is trained with historic data (consisting of actual pieces sold in the past), tested and validated. If a model has a certain output quality according to the training and testing data it is used to predict 52 weeks into the future, resulting in so called 'predictive demand planning' (Fig. 1).

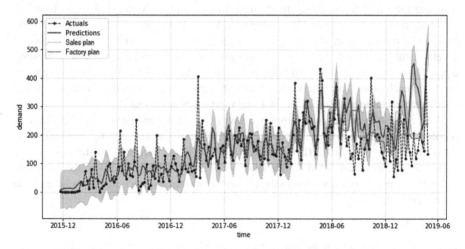

Fig. 1. Visual plot of the training (2015-12–2018-06) and validation (2018-06–2019-05) of a neural network for one specific product; x-axis is time and the y-axis are the demand in pieces.

In order to understand and analyze the development process of the described use case, qualitative research methods were used. The qualitative approach is necessary not only to understand why circumstances have been perceived in a certain way, but also to detect unknown topics. In addition, human-centered-design research follows the principle of a divergent way of thinking [15]. As such, 8 one to one (semi-) structured interviews were conducted. Their duration was ranging from 60 min up to 90 min, mainly in person with the respective project team members. The different roles of the interviewees ranged from development team, users and other stakeholders involved. The structure of the interviews was divided in three main parts. First, a section with general questions about the overall target of the project, the role of each interviewee, as well as the AI expertise, second a process- based part with a focus on each step of the development and implementation process, including related issues and challenges, as well as room for future improvement, and third a section on lessons learnt and the underlying role of design in the overall process. Additional knowledge about the design perspective is drawn by the fact that the researcher was a part of the development team as well. The roles of the different disciplines represented by the team members vary from data scientists (with a heavy background in statistics and Machine Learning), a data analyst, a machine learning engineer, a UX designer, a finance specialist, the business domain experts on the clients' side, as well as the production planners and their managers.

3 Results

Analyzing the interviews by going through the transcripts and looking for aspects that were important to a majority of the interviewees revealed some initial topics. By grouping the insights and compare them to the overall issues and challenges found in literature review the interviews resulted in 14 clusters. Those 14 clusters can be grouped by their relation a) to the given use case, b) their relevance for AI projects and development in general, and c) to the design expertise (see Table 1). An interesting aspect found, was the fact that all interviewees described a different process, some more similar to each other than others. However, it became obvious that it is difficult to find a common process model for all project team members involved.

The order of the following topics derives from the importance for the different people interviewed. Starting with those which were worth mentioning from all interviewees; development team (DT), users (U), as well as other stakeholders (S), to the ones that were more important to a smaller set of the participants. This is also indicated in detail by the letters associated to the cluster, as well as a choice of quotes taken from the interview transcripts.

01 AI-expertise (DT, U, S)

"Compared to the beginning of the project, I gained a lot of knowledge about the technology."

Quote 1. A participant related to the user group
The participants were asked to rate their own AI expertise on a scale from 0 (low) to 10 (high). The reference was up to themselves. Interestingly, nobody rated her-/himself

a 0 or 10. Whereas the data scientists compared themselves towards experts in the field of AI or machine learning and therefore scored around 7 or 8, the business domain experts surprisingly scored themselves alike. Due to the fact, that they compared their expertise from the beginning of the project to the steep learning curve they made towards the point of the interview. The data scientists agreed that a certain level of knowledge is helpful and a key requirement to realize a successful project in the AI-B2B context (including, for example, used technical terminologies, the expertise to rate and evaluate the quality of the AI algorithm, expectations and prioritization of specific agent functionalities).

02 Iterative working mode (DT, U, S)

"To keep the sprints and present results on a regular basis was key for the success of this project."

Quote 2. A participant related to the development team

Due to the complexity and scale of such an industrial AI project, an iterative approach to develop and implement an AI algorithm is necessary. In the interviews, all participants agreed on this factor. However, while at this stage it is not of key importance which specific iterative method is used (e.g. SCRUM), all involved members and stakeholders agree on the iterative approach. Regular meetings to present interim results and discuss next steps are crucial for the process. And again, if the iterative working method is known to all team members, the more efficient the project.

03 Feedback structure, structured feedback (DT, U, S)

A very important aspect around the success of implementing an AI algorithm is the possibility to give feedback and to decide whether to use the data from the AI forecast or not. In the given use case, the business domain expert asked the planners and users for their direct feedback. Since this feedback had no specific structure or format, it was difficult to be considered by the technical development team. Also, an automated approach to include the feedback into the AI forecast was missing and therefore feedback from the planners and users meant extra effort with no significant impact on the AI system and its further development. Quite logically, this caused frustration and a lack of motivation to provide feedback on the planners and user side.

04 Definition of Design (DT, U, S)

"To me design is the look and feel of a product ... But I know this is not what you as a UX person do."

Quote 3. A participant related to the development team

One question in the interview was targeted towards the interpretation and definition of design. It became quite clear, that in the given cultural setting (Germany), design is perceived as making things look nice and aesthetic. This might be different in the English-speaking world. Rephrasing the question was necessary. Human-Centered-Design and UX as a concept served the purpose better. It evokes the idea of the human as a focus for any step in the process. Need-driven development, instead of primarily technology-driven aspects were perceptions in that context. This clarification and course correction served as a basis for further investigations.

05 Visualization (DT, U, S)

Another aspect that plays an important role is visualizing data and output of the AI system. In the given use case line charts and different dashboards in tableau [16] were used. Primarily to communicate the results among all stakeholders involved. Internally the tech team (data scientist, engineers and analyst) also used it to understand the raw data and to evaluate the models. The tool was not used by the planners and users, due to the fact, that the graphics are not helpful for the planning process and the manufacturing site needs numbers. It was an additional tool in their process they refused to use. The value add of a visual representation of the results was not clearly communicated or understood by all stakeholders involved.

06 Planning process (DT, U, S)

Process analysis of the current manual planning was conducted. It became quite clear that the current process is one source for the low-quality planning outcome, because it is influenced by subjective human behavior and bias. The development team was lacking the expertise to also address this issue. On top it was not perceived as an important aspect or step by the management. So, the process was left as given and the AI forecast had to fit into the given process. The result is an extra line with a figure the users and planners must evaluate and take into consideration for the factory plan. It is perceived as an extra effort, not as an optimization of the workflow.

07 Culture and mindset (DT, U, S)

"It is really challenging to implement a new technology into old structures. The users need space and time to adapt to the new way of working."

Quote 4. A participant related to the development team
The exchange with the planners and users was very hard. Due to different aspect of the project set up, but also due to the fact that the AI solution had to fit in the given company structures and work culture. On the long run, AI implementations will perform best, when not only a solution is produced and added to the given infrastructure, but also the structures need to change. Implementing AI needs a change in company culture and people mindset.

08 Expectations (U, S)

"I expect 90% accuracy by the AI prediction, compared to the manual factory plan."

Quote 5. A participant related to the stakeholder group
When it comes to the evaluation of the AI output (time series prediction), the business domain experts expect a very high accuracy regarding the predictions of the AI algorithm, clearly outperforming the human planner. From a statistics perspective, however, this expectation is unrealistic. The models are trained on historic data. This data is deliberately cleaned from so called 'outliers' (meaning data that is unusual, like a big amount of orders that one client made due to some unknown reasons is eliminated from the data set). In turn, if those outliers would be integrated in the predictive model as a pattern, wrong forecasts would be generated, and as a consequence, such data sets are smoothed out in practice. Nevertheless, research showed that the business domain experts expect the AI algorithm to detect those special orders in advance. This is

impossible. Especially time series predictions are very hard to evaluate in advance, therefore a realistic expectation management is a very important aspect. Some products with a high number in orders are easier to predict than products with a small volume or even customized configurations. AI forecasts serve as a value add, especially because it is based on data and not on explicit or implicit human intervention but will not independently decide which number of products to plan.

09 Starting point (U, S)

The project was initiated by upper management which wanted to improve the outcome of the factory planning process. Without directly involving the planners a first technical study was created as a Proof-of-Concept (PoC). However, since planners and users were not integrated from the beginning the PoC had not comprehensive value and its significance has been fairly limited. This is not an AI specific challenge and represents a well-known problem for any project set up. In the described use case, however, it added additional problems, for example, when it came to trust into the output of the AI algorithm and its representative validity.

10 Trust in the output (U, S)

Although expectations for the functionality of the developed AI algorithm are high, it doesn't necessarily mean that humans trust the outcome. For instance, fear of losing job and power are involved, as well as traceability of one's own activities and the unknown mechanisms behind the technology. A testing phase, where manual figures and the AI forecast were used in parallel, helped to ensure validity and trust into the overall approach in the given use case. Unfortunately, there was no structure in place to explain the AI algorithm to the planners and users, which would have supported the acceptance in addition.

11 Biased presentations (DT, S)

"In hindsight, I think we preferred to show the line charts of the products where the AI predictions performed really well."

Quote 6. A participant related to the development team

The data scientist perspective revealed another very important aspect. When asked in the interviews for the means and frequency of the regular interim presentations, data scientists realized that they showcased the positive outcomes over the negative ones, which led to considerably biased presentations. They justified this 'mechanism' by the fact that business puts pressure on the outcome and hence 'data victory' is rated over failure in such AI projects. At the same time, they realized that this behavior strikes back, for example, when it comes to meeting and managing the expectations of the business domain experts. As provided by the interviews, there seems to be a fine line between implementing AI into such (industrial) contexts and the choice of the right use case combined with the data interpretation which justifies this means the most.

12 Gap between prototype and implementation (DT, S)

"We had to put a lot of effort and time in the migration of the PoC into a stable productive system."

Quote 7. A participant related to the development team
In the given use case, the first PoC was a selected set of initial 25 products (out of 1700) to test the time series prediction performance. The selection was made by the business domain expert and aligned with the data scientist. As described above, data was cleaned and a first set of models was trained, tested and evaluated. The outcome was surprisingly accurate and thus had been decided to develop and to use the technology for the overall factory automation planning process. In the course of the project, it became clear that the given infrastructure (cloud environment, data security) of the previous PoC was not sufficient and thus a new infrastructure was set up. The new setting didn't perform as well, as the initial experimental environment. A lot of time and capacity was allocated to create a productive setting within the given constraints of data security and company structures. The interviews revealed that this was a pain for all team members involved and extended the final implementation of the project.

13 Orient, manage, prioritize, eliminate (DT, S)

UX in the AI project is seen as a way to guide activities in a way that the outcome is the best solution for all stakeholders involved. Although it is clear that not everyone will be satisfied it can also be used as a vehicle to communicate certain decisions, based on needs and not on personal preferences. It was very obvious from the interviews that UX should also help to focus on the most important features, meaning that it should also eliminate wishes and features that are not necessarily needed.

14 UX and timing (DT, S)

"UX really is about the right timing... if it comes too late in the process it cannot influence the direction anymore."

Quote 8. A participant related to the stakeholder group
The timing for any design or user research activities is very important. All team members agreed on the importance to do the user research at the very beginning of the project, or latest after the successful first technical feasibility study (PoC, Prototype). Only at the end of the project this value add was seen. In the case of early adoption, it could help to support prioritizing the backlog, write user stories and understand the overall process better. It is also clear, that due to the complexity and unforeseen challenges along the way, research is an ongoing process and cannot evaluate all features and needs of the planners and users firsthand. It is perceived as a negative aspect when introduced late in the process, when the team had decided on a way to go already.

Table 1. Overview of the 14 themes and their classification into their relevance to the a) use case, b) AI overall, c) design.

Relevance	Clusters
Use case specific	05, 06, 09, 11, (12)
Overall AI relevant	01, 02, 03, 07, 08, (09), 10, 12
Design specific	04, 13, 14

4   Discussion of Results

The results above clearly show that there are significant challenges when it comes to the development of AI algorithms in the context of industrial applications. Some of them are not necessarily design-specific and/or B2B-use case specific but need first of all a) to be acknowledged b) to be validated and c) to be addressed in further steps of development and future projects.

The qualitative approach was very helpful to discover the range of different challenges. It opened up the perspective of purely design specific issues. This is also clearly represented by the 14 themes that show a wide spread of relevant aspects to take into consideration while designing AI algorithms. Since the data sample was limited to the given use case and respective development team, it needs to be further elaborated if the 14 themes are sufficient or will be enriched in number and size with further research. Some of the found issues were expected outcomes of the interviews, since the literature review already revealed some overall relevant AI specific challenges. The insight, that there seemed to be not one single process set-up that was valid for all interviewed participants, was unexpected. Furthermore, this shows how important the study of the overall development and implementation process of AI algorithms in the industrial domain really is.

5   Conclusion

The insights derived from the research show that some of the challenges are also relevant in other projects, meaning not use case specific [3]. It seems that some issues around AI have an overall validity not based on domain or use case. Expectation management is often an issue when it comes to the impact of AI for example [1, 2] (others see Table 1).

Therefore, this research contributes to the scientific discourse and community by demonstrating that some of the already discussed issues around AI are also valid in industrial AI applications and contexts. That implies, possibly adopting models and techniques in order to address the mentioned challenges, as well as transferring them from this research to other domains.

Other themes are more specific for the given use case, which can be due to the fact, that the domain is industrial AI and not much research is published so far. It also shows that developed design principles or any form of design solution needs to be implemented in a specific context. Here, forms of conceptualizing or generic abstraction miss the specific problem (while being difficult to transfer to other domains and use cases). Thus, the State-of-the-Art has been extended through the focus of this paper into the given domain. Starting to provide insight into the processes and current status of the industrial AI landscape.

The research and conducted interviews show also that some topics are design specific and it needs to be clarified how designers can add value to this process. An evaluation on which ones are the most design specific tasks can be a next step of research. Additionally, investigations into other very similar use cases will be pursued, elucidating how other teams have fostered solutions. This research will address the question how others solved those challenges or even expand the problem definition.

Based on the 14 themes some initial ideas for improvements have been derived. Taking the AI-expertise as an example, the project team came up with a concept for a personal training. The value add of such an activity would be the attempt to start the project with a certain level of AI-expertise from all team members involved. Also addressing other issues, like the expectation management for example, as well as the possibility to give every team member a certain role and task to be represented in the training, making the training a cross-disciplinary effort and unified approach. Whereas the overall concept of the training could easily be transferred to other domains and target groups, the specific content of the trainings needs to be very use case specific. This means, in turn, that the data used for presenting certain characteristics and features needs to be very similar to the ones the training participants are used to. In the case of factory planning and demand forecasting, historic data from actual orders are needed. Additionally, talking about time series predictions, doesn't necessarily mean to introduce all machine learning approaches, such as image or voice recognition, because it is not used and necessary in the given context. Further exploration on possible solutions for the development of AI applications in industrial AI needs to be done.

To sum up, understanding and analyzing the initial pitfalls and key challenges of the development of AI agents for predictive demand planning in factory automation offers a strategic and productive starting point for the development and, at the same time, to bring forward a robust method to improve the set up and implementation of similar use cases.

As a next step, the research from other, but very similar, factory automation site activities will be analyzed. Based on the most relevant aspects further research with other, also external experts, will be conducted. Parallel to this, a comprehensive investigation into already given principles and tools from other domains will help to address relevant design and development steps towards future solutions in the B2B factory automation context. This dialogue is so important, because AI algorithms enter every aspect of human life and with this comes great responsibility and power that shouldn't be left to a limited group of people in society.

References

1. Amershi, S., et al.: Guidelines-for-human-AI-interaction. In: CHI 2019, Glasgow, Scotland, UK (2019)
2. Google. People AI Guidebook. https://pair.withgoogle.com. Accessed 24 Feb 2020
3. Chui, M., et al.: McKinsey Global Institute: Notes from the AI Frontier, discussion paper (2018). https://www.mckinsey.com/~/media/mckinsey/featured%20insights/artificial%20in telligence/notes%20from%20the%20ai%20frontier%20applications%20and%20value%20of %20deep%20learning/mgi_notes-from-ai-frontier_discussion-paper.ashx. Accessed 24 Feb 2020
4. Kureishy, A., et al., Achieving Real Business Outcomes. O'Reilly Media (2019)
5. Dunning, T., et al.: AI and Analytics in Production. O'Reilly Media (2018)

6. Clark, J.: Design in the Era of the Algorithm (2017). https://bigmedium.com/speaking/design-in-the-era-of-the-algorithm.html. Accessed 24 Feb 2020
7. Hebron, P.: Machine Learning for Designers. O'Reilly Media (2016). https://www.oreilly.com/library/view/machine-learning-for/9781491971444/copyright-page01.html.   Accessed 24 Feb 2020
8. Noessel, C.: Designing Agentive Technology: AI That Works for People. Rosenfeld Media, New York (2017)
9. Lovejoy, J., Holbrook, J.: Human-Centered Machine Learning (2017). https://medium.com/google-design/human-centered-machine-learning-a770d10562cd. Accessed 24 Feb 2020
10. Taschdjian, Z.: UX design in the age of machine learning (2018). https://uxdesign.cc/ux-design-in-the-age-of-machine-learning-2fcd8b538d67. Accessed 24 Feb 2020
11. Li, F.: Put humans at the center of AI. MIT Technol. Rev. **120**(6), 26 (2017)
12. Yang, Q.: The role of design in creating machine-learning-enhanced user experience. In: The AAAI 2017 Spring Symposium on Designing the User Experience of Machine Learning Systems (2017)
13. Siemens AG. Industrial Controls - SIRIUS. https://new.siemens.com/global/en/products/automation/industrial-controls/sirius.html. Accessed 24 Feb 2020
14. Nielsen, A.: Practical Time Series Analysis: Predictions with Statistics and Machine Learning. O'Reilly Media, Sebastopol (2019)
15. Design Council. Framework for Innovation (2019). https://www.designcouncil.org.uk/news-opinion/what-framework-innovation-design-councils-evolved-double-diamond. Accessed 24 Feb 2020
16. Tableau Software. https://www.tableau.com. Accessed 24 Feb 2020

Socio-Technical Design of Hybrid Intelligence Systems – The Case of Predictive Maintenance

Thomas Herrmann[✉][iD]

Ruhr-University of Bochum (IAW, IMTM), Bochum, Germany
thomas.herrmann@rub.de

Abstract. This paper focuses on hybrid intelligence systems since this approach appears as most advanced to deal with the socio-technical challenges of Machine Learning. The analysis starts with a taxonomy being derived from literature that characterizes hybrid intelligence. This taxonomy is contrasted with the application area of predictive maintenance where machine learning could be used to derive warnings from the sensor data of a production plant. Thus, AI would replace the effort of deriving hypotheses based on the experience of the plant operators. The case study on Predictive Maintenance reveals a series of challenges that require keeping the organization and the human and in the loop. To achieve this goal, we derive appropriate design recommendations such as integrated support of communication and coordination, possibilities for intervention.

Keywords: Machine Learning · Hybrid intelligence · Predictive maintenance · Socio-technical design

1 Introduction

There is an ongoing discussion of how the advance of Artificial Intelligence, especially Machine Learning, will change the work of people [1, 2], There are serious concerns about people losing their jobs, and society or companies may lose the essential contributions people can accomplish based on human intelligence and creativity.

The analysis of this paper focusses on "hybrid intelligence systems" since it appears as most advanced for dealing with these concerns from a socio-technical perspective. It origins from a discussion about the insufficiency of AI [3] but is put into the context of a human-centered, socio-technical design. Dellermann et al. point towards the following elements of a definition of hybrid intelligence [4]:

- socio-technical ensembles and its human and AI parts can co-evolve to improve over time,
- using the complementary strengths of human and AI,
- the ability to collectively achieve better results than each of either human beings or AI could have done in separation,
- continuous improvement by learning from each other.

Apparently, achieving hybrid intelligence requires certain types of socio-technical arrangements with appropriate features of human-computer interaction. This paper

H. Degen and L. Reinerman-Jones (Eds.): HCII 2020, LNCS 12217, pp. 298–309, 2020.
https://doi.org/10.1007/978-3-030-50334-5_20

investigates the following questions: Which factors influence this combination and what are the options to design the appropriate H-C-I-features.

By reviewing the literature, Dellermann et al. [4] provide a taxonomy referring to tasks' characteristics, learning paradigms, and types of interaction. However, this taxonomy pursues a high level of abstraction and requires further concretization in order to provide meaningful insights that could support socio-technical design of hybrid intelligence systems. Therefore, we relate the concept of hybrid intelligence to a concrete practical case: Predictive maintenance in a car manufacturer's body assembly where malfunctions lead to plant downtimes and must be resolved as quickly as possible. To handle these problems is the responsibility of the plant operator.

By referring to this case, we can derive examples and generalized suggestions of how hybrid intelligence can be achieved:

- Characterization of concrete tasks and their combination into jobs that enable people to apply and develop complementary strengths compared to AI.
- Going beyond the interaction modes described by Dellerman et al. [4] by emphasizing a variety of possibilities of adaptation and re-configuration. That includes possibilities of experimental exploration as well as supporting the negotiation between staff members whether a certain adaptation should be sustainably implemented.
- The role of intervention as interaction paradigm [5] in the context of exploration and re-configuration to support evolution [see Fig. 2].

2   Literature Background: Hybrid Intelligence

There is a long lasting discussion about combining and intertwining human strengths and AI effectively to achieve better results than each of them separately. For example, Herrmann and Just [6] propose expert systems to be designed as experts' systems that help them to improve their work and their competences.

Amershi et al. [7] explore new ways for designing Machine Learning (ML) systems that emphasize the interaction with their users. Accordingly, a recognition of human work within the machine learning workflow is needed that acknowledges human work practice and allow for reciprocal adaption between human and ML-system. This kind of approaches go beyond the tendency to focus on either optimizing the human or the technical component separately (cf. Behymer & Flach [8]). Beyhmer and Flach propose a seamless socio-technical integration of the technical and the human side that also consider team processes. Furthermore, we suggest from our experience with predictive maintenance that such a human-centered ML-workflow includes cycles of adaptation even after an organization has implemented the system and employs it regularly.

This suggestion is also pursued by Kamar [3] who argues that human strength should be included via crowdsourcing to complement the performance of a running AI-system. With the term "hybrid intelligence system", he refers to a kind of workflow where the system asks people to verify or correct its results. This term should not be confused with "hybrid intelligent systems" (cf. [9]) that refers to the combination of intelligent techniques with conventional software systems such as spreadsheet or databases. By contrast, Karma's concept [3] is meant as strategy of how people can be automatically involved to overcome the weaknesses of an AI-system. Here, the main idea is that the system asks for help based on models of human expertise and potential whenever human abilities might contribute to the improvement of AI-results.

Similarly, Cai et al. [10] argue for offering light way possibilities with which humans can interactively refine AI-results, by exploring the space of possible solutions and pursuing hypothesis-testing. This is proposed as a way to augment human experts instead of replacing them (as proposed by Herrmann and Just [6] in the case of expert systems). These kind of approaches require explainability to help the user understand the background of results and decisions that are proposed by ML-systems [11]. Explainability is a crucial prerequisite to allow for users' building trust into the abilities and appropriateness of an AI-system.

Dellerman et al. [4] seek to provide an overview over these different approaches by extracting a taxonomy from the literature. They try to understand the relevant factors that contribute to hybrid intelligence aiming at the combination of the complementary strengths of human and AI to achieve more intelligent behavior than each of the two can do separately. Their findings identify tasks for hybrid intelligence on a very abstract level of internal cognitive processes: recognition, prediction, and reasoning. All kind of behavior that changes the surrounding world is referred to by the term "action". Most important are the types of interaction that Dellerman et al. [4] found in the literature. The authors mainly consider the question what is entered to the system by humans and how, and which output AI delivers, such as queries given to humans or feedback. Feedback covers suggestions and predictions as well as proposals for clustering of data and for optimizing the handling of a task. Most important – with respect to our understanding of hybrid intelligence – is output that supports interpretability of what is going on inside of the ML-black box. The authors found that not only the integration of AI-experts but also of domain experts should be addressed by these modes of interaction. However, all these considerations of different interaction modes neglect the interactions of users that are going beyond the direct man-ML-interaction by emphasizing the involvement of communication with other people in the context of somebody's ML-supported tasks. In addition, an important question remains open as to how to promote the adaptation and improvement of the ML system during use in response to the acceptance of ML outcomes by the organization representing the system's context.

Considering this wider context means employing a socio-technical approach, which is actually proposed by Dellerman et al. who intend to go beyond a role of humans that is limited to the process of developing machine learning models. They argue that dealing with real world problems requires the perspective of collaboration within "socio-technological ensembles" ([4], p. 2).

In accordance with such a socio-technical perspective, Amershi et al. [7] argue that the role of practitioners should not be limited to the typical ML-workflow activities such as: collecting data, selecting features to represent the data, preprocessing and transforming the data, choosing a representation and learning algorithm to construct the model, tuning parameters of the algorithm, and finally assessing the quality of the resulting model. By contrast to this limitation, the distribution of activities between human and AI-components in the course of decision making [12] should take into account that humans have superior abilities when dealing with uncertainty and equivocality. While AI can extend humans' ability to handle complexity, people's strengths allow for communication and negotiation during decision making as well as offering a more holistic and intuitive approach. This means to keep the human in the loop not only for the developing of ML-models but also when the ML-model is employed in an organization to handle certain tasks.

Rahwan [13] goes beyond keeping the human in the loop (cf. Dellerman et al. [4]) by emphasizing the perspective of keeping the "society in the loop" e.g. by implementing mechanisms for negotiating the values of various stakeholders. We propose that this approach could also be applied to the level of an ML-system's direct context by offering socio-technical processes that keep the organization in the loop.

Consequently, ML-systems could become a subject of approaches that pursues a fluent transition between design for use and design in use to support an evolutionary growth of the system while being employed [14]. Lindvall et al. [15] – for example – propose an ongoing correction of the ML-model by the user in the sense of machine teaching that takes place after the ML-system is deployed. This needs specific interaction modes to be employed that allow also for collaboration between several users. This kind of interaction modes can be derived from concepts that pursue the prototyping of AI-solutions within cycles of evaluation and improvement [16]. Another approach could be to provide possibilities for users' interventions that finally lead to insights whether and how an AI-system should be re-configured [5].

In summary, the design and application of hybrid intelligence with in sociotechnical processes can be a subject of evolutionary growth and re-seeding as described by Fischer: The continuous growth would be driven by domain experts while reseeding evolutionary growth, reseeding means the delivery of a new version that is developed by AI-experts [17].

3   The Empirical Investigation of a Predictive Maintenance Case

Predictive Maintenance (PM) is a process in which the evaluation of sensor data is used to predict whether and where malfunctions can occur in the plant and when. In the PM-project that we have investigated, hypotheses were built to derive warnings for a car manufacturer's body assembly. The hypotheses are based on considering the fluctuations or outliers in the stream of sensor data. If certain thresholds are violated, a warning is issued. Succeeding (see Fig. 1), the plant operator will see the PM-warnings and will inspect the plant to decide whether they are relevant.

The pursued approach here was to use the available observations and experience of the staff to derive rules that were interpreted by the PM-Software. Thus, hypotheses were built that describe the conditions under which a malfunctioning might occur. It became obvious that a machine learning approach could replace this procedure of building and testing hypotheses. A precondition for employing machine learning is the availability of sufficient data sets that are based on fine grained sensor data. With such a data-driven approach it is possible to anticipate equipment failures and to schedule corrective maintenance to avoid unexpected equipment downtime [18]. PM aims at an anomaly detection based on discrete or continuous data (such as electricity flow or air pressure fluctuations) and helps to manage maintenance cycles [19].

The plant operator is the main addressee of the PM-messages. He either plans and supervises the handling of the maintenance, or he makes sure that the PM message is dealt with in a special meeting. In addition, s/he must assess each PM message for its relevance and reliability. The thresholds of parameter values, which trigger the PM message on the basis of hypotheses, must be adjusted if necessary. This is also the case if malfunctions occur for which there was no PM message before.

At the start of implementing such a PM-system, several problems can occur that require improvement. We interviewed four people being in various roles in the PM-project (for example plant operator, master craftsman, quality assurance). From the interviews, we developed a better understanding of the tasks to be carried out in the context of the PM-system and we identified 77 problems to be considered. A severe problem is that too many false positive messages are generated that give warnings that have no real basis. Possibly, the observed problems can be overcome, if machine learning will be employable to replace the building and modification of hypotheses and their underlying thresholds. However, a machine learning approach has to be based on a sufficient amount of training data. We will discuss how far at least at the beginning of an ML-based PM-system project, the plant operators will have to deal with similar tasks and problems as they occur in the case of a hypotheses-based PM. The descriptions of tasks and problems will help to derive insights about the necessities and possibilities of keeping the organization in the loop as well as the human when introducing AI-based PM, and how the implied challenges can be overcome by pursuing an approach of hybrid intelligence.

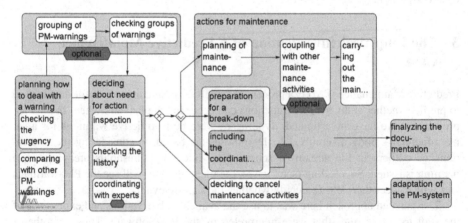

Fig. 1. Workflow of handling a PM-warnings

4   Tasks and Challenges of AI-Based Predictive Maintenance

Dealing with indicators for breakdowns and with fixing them is the task of several different roles. Mainly the plant operator but also the master craftsman who supervises the plant operators, the foreman who coordinate the workers and assign them their tasks, the specialized workshops that help in the case of extensive repairs, and the quality assurance team that proactively contributes to the avoidance of breakdowns.

In what follows we focus on the tasks of the plant operator since he interacts in the first place with the PM system and his tasks are of main interest to understand the human strengths that could be added into a hybrid intelligence constellation. The practice of plant operators covers all tasks of daily routines such as starting and stopping the plant, preparing the production of specific series, taking care of the supply of the incoming parts, doing inspections and replacing machine parts and caring for basic repair work. These tasks are interwoven with a variety of communication activities required for coordination or planning, for solving complex problems, for negotiating limited resources, for consulting or for the constant renewal of the relevant competences. With the advance of Predictive Maintenance, the setting up and maintaining of the machines is enhanced by a second level of tasks that are displayed in Fig. 1.

Each time a warning is issued, the plant operator is required to carry out an on-site inspection to check the relevance of the message. To make this step more efficient he might decide on a reasonable way of pooling the messages to reduce the frequency of doing an on-site inspection. Consequently, warnings have to be compared with each other and have to be prioritized with respect to their urgency. In a next step, the plant operator has to decide whether there is a need for further action. This decision includes the on-site inspection, checking the history of the parts being a subject of the warning, and, optionally, including the opinion of other experts. Depending on the decision, the warning is either ignored (maintenance activities are cancelled) or the maintenance activities are planned, coordinated and carried out. Further meeting can be necessary for coordination and instead of immediate maintenance, a preparation for a break-down-situation might take part (e.g. by getting replacement parts ready). All in all it is important, that all activities around dealing with a PM-message should be carefully documented. This documentation can serve as a knowledge base to deal with the next PM-warnings and can serve as an input to improve the ML-system

If the on-site check reveals that a warning was not appropriate, the plant operator – potentially together with his colleagues – decide whether the PM-system has to be adapted. Such an adaptation of the hypotheses or the underlying thresholds will also have to be taken into consideration, if a break-down occurs without a preceding warning.

In the context of these tasks, the interviews reveal a series of problems that are assumed by the interviewees based on their experience with plants and on their understanding of the PM-project in their department. We cluster the selected problems along the following categories:

4.1 Communication and Coordination

The possible adjustment of the thresholds will involve a considerable amount of discussion and coordination, which will hardly be manageable. This will be too extensive a task to be administered centrally. Additionally, different plant operators might disagree on how to determine a threshold. Furthermore, it seems to be unclear when a PM-messages should be a subject of discussion with other employees, e.g. the master craftsman or the specialized workshops. It turns out that the interviewees expect that the PM-system implies a lot of additional coordination and communication to deal with the PM-messages appropriately

4.2 Flexibility and Continuous Adaptation During Use Time

With respect to a continuous improvement of the PM-System, experience from one part of the plant (e.g. a robot) cannot necessarily be transferred to another part. A great deal of effort is therefore required to adjust the threshold values for every specific case. Configuration of PM then becomes a very comprehensive, possibly permanent task that has to be assigned to different roles of the workforce.

If a plant operator does not have the authority to configure the PM parameters, s/he cannot independently optimize the achievement of his goals – namely increasing the availability of the plant. It is a challenge to take the risk and responsibility for the consequences if changes in the thresholds and their effects can be studied experimentally. Based on these problem descriptions, we assume that a PM-system must be flexible enough to be continuously adapted and that organizational structures have to be established that coordinate the adaptation.

4.3 Support for Learning and Explainability

It is more difficult to understand why the system has not issued a warning about a fault that has occurred than to understand the accuracy or inadequacy of a given message. The PM-system itself cannot explain the background of messages, which people must therefore understand on the basis of their own experience and reasoning capabilities. In this context, employees may follow the PM messages schematically without checking their plausibility.

If the PM-system derives and display a new PM-message, it is unclear to what extent the history of similar PM-messages is also taken into account by the system.

It is most challenging to judge the fit between the time specifications of a PM message and reality, i.e. about when the anticipated break-down will actually occur.

The description of these problems suggests the conclusion that not only the ML- or rule-based system should help the user to understand the background of PM messages. Rather, the entire documentation of the handling of these messages or of the maintaining of the system must also help to find suitable explanations.

4.4   Efficiency, Stress and the Avoidance of Misuse

The employees expect that they have to react to an extremely large number of message, and they are afraid that too many incorrect messages do not lead to a win-win situation. For example, every PM notification involves the effort of an on-site inspection, although there may be nothing to be seen there. In this context, an interviewee thinks it is possible that some employees could manipulate PM-thresholds not aiming on the improvement of the PM-system but with the goal to reduce their workload. People could make improper threshold adjustments to reduce the frequency of notifications. Therefore, the access to the modification of thresholds should be restricted. However, the interviewees also assume that the adjustment of the PM thresholds cannot be done only by a few people, but must include several plant operators. Obviously, it is challenging to avoid misuse of the option to directly adapt the system on the one hand, and to allow a sufficient number of users to contribute directly to improving the PM system on the other.

4.5   Technical Quality

The employees assume that the current technical possibilities of the available sensor technology are not sufficient; data might be to coarse, e.g. only providing "yes" or "no" values instead of giving concrete numbers (e.g. indicating how many sealing caps are still in the magazine and not only whether it is empty or not). Furthermore, the interviewees assume that the PM-system does not take the history of a specific PM-message into account. For example, if the system displays a notification that a pipe might break with in the next three days, it should take into account whether past warnings about this pipe where appropriate. It seems to be desirable that this kind of history is also processed by the PM-system and that it is possible to extend the quality of sensor data after the system has already been implemented.

5   Design Recommendations: Interaction Principles for Hybrid Intelligence

Based on the tasks and problems described in Sect. 4, we can derive a series of design recommendations that are not only relevant for ML-based PM to contribute to a concept of hybrid intelligence that takes substantial competencies and strength of practitioners into account. We suggest that these recommendations also go beyond the scope of PM and are relevant in various fields of ML applications to support hybrid intelligence.

1. The assumed problems with communication and coordination point towards the requirement that features for communication support should be seamlessly integrated into the ML-system. The content of the communication belongs to the realm of human strength especially in the course of negotiation. The system can help to

distribute messages and to mediate communication. The training of the ML-system could also include aspects of coordination – e.g. the system could propose who should handle a specific PM-messages. The proposals could be derived from experiences of how a certain message was dealt with in the past. Integrating communication support features can help to keep not only single employees but the organization as a whole in the loop. To keep-the-organization-in-the-loop means including the interactions and processes between the relevant stakeholders who have possibly to deal with a PM-message and with maintaining the PM-system.

2. With respect to the problems of flexibility, the way of how a PM-system is designed and socio-technically implemented should allow for advancing the ML-system by its users. This covers the ML-workflow from data collection to constructing the model [7] as well as the time of using the ML-system. Mechanisms of reinforcement learning can be applied where the user labels the output of the ML-system whether it is correct or incorrect. When doing so, the users must be supported to realize whether this kind of their feedback has a solicited effect that is sufficient and timely. If the users' feedback does not directly lead to the intended results, it may be reasonable to offer the possibility to directly enter if-then-else-rules that overrule the derivation of inappropriate PM-messages. The users' activities of adapting the ML-system should be documented – possibly with a diary-like style – to allow for increased accountability. Furthermore, this kind of documentation can be designed to help to acknowledge the users' contributions to the improvement of the system, and to support the protection of their experiential [20] property. We use this term in analogy to intellectual property to refer to the competencies of workers that are based on their experience and represent the value of their contribution to the tasks of their organization.

3. The described problems reveal that modifications which the users carry out could imply a misuse and therefore should be restricted. A solution to this challenge can be provided by so-called intervention interfaces [5]. They allow for temporal changes of automated processes that interrupt the regular procedure. During this interruption the user can change the behavior of the system. For example, the PM-threshold-values can be temporarily adjusted, the exceeding of which triggers a warning. After a pre-defined period of time, the system automatically returns to the condition of regular usage (see Fig. 2) that represents its state before the intervention. If the same type of intervention happens more often, a direct reconfiguration could be triggered: either the system adapts automatically or the user carries out an adaptation by employing methods of end-user development (EUD) (see Fig. 2). To increase accountability, alternatively the reconfiguration can be a subject of negotiation or be executed by an authorized person.

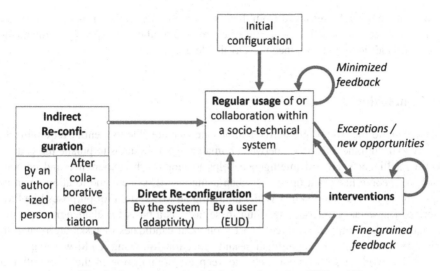

Fig. 2. Intervening usage and re-configuration ([21], p. 77)

4. To overcome deficits in explainability and in learning support, interventions can also help to explore the system and to research it with what-if-questions. It supports experimental investigation: Experienced users could change parameters, thresholds or even statistical methods to see the effects and whether these changes help to avoid false positive messages of false negatives (i.e. a malfunctioning that occurs without a previous warning). These kind of experiments should also refer to possible warnings that the PM-system has issued – or not issued – in the past: would an experimental change cause that a correct output of the PM-system – that it gave in the past – had been suppressed? That means that it might be of interest that interventions are also applied to events that took place in the history of a PM-system's behavior.

5. The availability of the history of a PM-system's warnings and the related adaptations may also contribute to support processes of human learning and to overcome efficiency problems. When a certain warning is issued, the workforce should be able to see whether the system had given similar warnings in the past, and if yes, how the organization has dealt with them. Consequently, not only the history of the systems behavior and its adaptation should be documented but also the history of the maintaining of the production plant to which the PM-system is related. That implies that the ML-system is intertwined with knowledge management features. For example, if a warning is issued and the plant operator cannot find any evidence that supports this warning, this has to be documented with a direct relation to the issued warning. The documentation of these cases can help to avoid unnecessary work.

6. The technical insufficiency of the sensor equipment that was indicated by the interviewees leads to the requirement that a ML-system must be able to adapt to changes in the context to which it is related. Thus, if a production plant is retrofitted with advanced sensor technology, the ML-based PM-system should be able to integrate

the data that can be retrieved from these sensors into its model of decision-making. The interface of the ML-system must be prepared to allow for specifying the handling of additional data that becomes available afterwards.

6 Conclusion

By referring to the case of predictive maintenance we are able to identify requirements of how to design the interaction between human and ML-systems to pursue the goal of hybrid intelligence. Hybrid intelligence helps to employ the experience and competencies of people like plant operators when using an ML-system and to allow them to apply and to develop their skills. With employing an ML-system for purposes like PM, a series of new tasks emerge. Handling these tasks is a basis for challenging specific strengths of the human workforce. Most prominent candidates of tasks are related to articulation work [22] for coordination and reflection following a PM-warning. This articulation work and its support helps to keep the organization in the loop within a more holistic approach of socio-technical design including the assignment of tasks between various roles [23].

We go beyond the interaction modes described by Dellerman et al. [4] by emphasizing a variety of possibilities of adaptation and re-configuration. That includes possibilities of experimental exploration as well as supporting the negotiation between staff members whether a certain adaptation should be sustainably implemented. Intervention as interaction paradigm [6] can be employed to support exploration and to prepare re-configuration and evolution of a ML-system (see Fig. 2) by temporarily changing the system and observing the effects.

In summary, a differentiation of interaction modes has to be provided that addresses different goals where the users and the organization can contribute their strengths such as improving efficiency or innovativeness, or increase their competencies. Further research has to focus the possibilities for continuous development of human competencies in dealing with ML-systems and protection of the "experiential property" of the people involved. This protection is an important motivational factor if users are expected to employ their skills for the further advancement of ML-systems.

Acknowledgements. The empirical work in the PM case was supported by Jan Nierhoff. Intensive discussions with Sabine Pfeiffer about the impact of AI on human work and organizations led to the concepts of "keeping-the-organization-in- the-loop" and "protection of experiential" property.

References

1. Brödner, P.: "Super-intelligent" machine: technological exuberance or the road to subjection. AI Soc. **33**, 335–346 (2018). https://doi.org/10.1007/s00146-017-0731-6
2. Brynjolfsson, E., Mitchell, T.: What can machine learning do? Workforce implications. Science **358**, 1530–1534 (2017)

3. Kamar, E.: Directions in hybrid intelligence: complementing AI systems with human intelligence. In: IJCAI, pp. 4070–4073 (2016)
4. Dellermann, D., Calma, A., Lipusch, N., Weber, T., Weigel, S., Ebel, P.A.: The future of human-AI collaboration: a taxonomy of design knowledge for hybrid intelligence systems. In: HICSS (2019)
5. Schmidt, A., Herrmann, T.: Intervention user interfaces: a new interaction paradigm for automated systems. Interactions **24**, 40–45 (2017)
6. Hermann, T., Just, K.: Experts' systems instead of expert systems. AI Soc. **9**, 321–355 (1995). https://doi.org/10.1007/BF01210586
7. Amershi, S., Cakmak, M., Knox, W.B., Kulesza, T.: Power to the people: the role of humans in interactive machine learning. Ai Mag. **35**, 105–120 (2014)
8. Behymer, K.J., Flach, J.M.: From autonomous systems to sociotechnical systems: Designing effective collaborations. She Ji: J. Des. Econ. Innov. **2**, 105–114 (2016)
9. Goonatilake, S., Khebbal, S.: Hybrid Intelligent Systems. Wiley, London (1994)
10. Cai, C.J., et al.: Human-centered tools for coping with imperfect algorithms during medical decision-making. In: Proceedings of the 2019 CHI Conference on Human Factors in Computing Systems, pp. 1–14 (2019)
11. Adadi, A., Berrada, M.: Peeking inside the black-box: a survey on explainable artificial intelligence (XAI). IEEE Access **6**, 52138–52160 (2018)
12. Jarrahi, M.H.: Artificial intelligence and the future of work: human-AI symbiosis in organizational decision making. Bus. Horiz. **61**, 577–586 (2018)
13. Rahwan, I.: Society-in-the-loop: programming the algorithmic social contract. Ethics Inf. Technol. **20**, 5–14 (2018). https://doi.org/10.1007/s10676-017-9430-8
14. Fischer, G., Herrmann, T.: Socio-technical systems: a meta-design perspective. Int. J. Sociotechnol. Knowl. Dev. IJSKD. **3**, 1–33 (2011)
15. Lindvall, M., Molin, J., Löwgren, J.: From machine learning to machine teaching: the importance of UX. Interactions **25**, 52–57 (2018)
16. van Allen, P.: Prototyping ways of prototyping AI. Interactions **25**, 46–51 (2018)
17. Fischer, G.: Seeding, evolutionary growth and reseeding: constructing, capturing and evolving knowledge in domain-oriented design environments. Autom. Softw. Eng. **5**, 447–464 (1998). https://doi.org/10.1023/A:1008657429810
18. Sipos, R., Fradkin, D., Moerchen, F., Wang, Z.: Log-based predictive maintenance. In: Proceedings of the 20th ACM SIGKDD International Conference on Knowledge Discovery and Data Mining, pp. 1867–1876 (2014)
19. Kroll, B., Schaffranek, D., Schriegel, S., Niggemann, O.: System modeling based on machine learning for anomaly detection and predictive maintenance in industrial plants. In: Proceedings of the 2014 IEEE Emerging Technology and Factory Automation (ETFA), pp. 1–7. IEEE (2014)
20. Kolb, D.A., Boyatzis, R.E., Mainemelis, C.: Experiential learning theory: previous research and new directions. Perspect. Think. Learn. Cogn. Styles **1**(8), 227–247 (2001)
21. Herrmann, T., Lentzsch, C., Degeling, M.: Intervention and EUD. In: Malizia, A., Valtolina, S., Morch, A., Serrano, A., Stratton, A. (eds.) IS-EUD 2019. LNCS, vol. 11553, pp. 67–82. Springer, Cham (2019). https://doi.org/10.1007/978-3-030-24781-2_5
22. Suchman, L.: Supporting articulation work. In: Computerization and Controversy: Value Conflicts and Social Choices, 2 edn., pp. 407–423 (1996)
23. Jahnke, I., Ritterskamp, C., Herrmann, T.: Sociotechnical roles for sociotechnical systems-A perspective from social and computer sciences. In: AAAi Fall Symposium Proceedings, vol. 8, pp. 68–75 (2005)

EasySketchDesign: Product Sketch Design Assisted with Interactive Sketch Retrieval

Yukun Hu[✉], Suihuai Yu, Jianjie Chu, Yichen Yang, Chen Chen,
and Fangmin Cheng

Northwestern Polytechnical University, Xi'an, People's Republic of China
huyukun0315@163.com

Abstract. We present EasySketchDesign, a sketch interface that integrates the sketch retrieval technique to search pictures related to current design form the image library quickly and exactly. The sketch drawn by the designer and the referential product data set are first transformed into a clear outline by means of edge detection, image dilation, etc. Then, the improved Recursive Cortical Network (RCN) is used to select the existing products similar to the sketch. Through such a design mode, the designer can be inspired by other people's work. Besides, they can know whether their work has the risk of being the same as the existing product to guarantee innovation. The evaluation study shows this system is easy to use and effective in transcending the creative potential of traditional sketching in Product conceptual design.

Keywords: Conceptual design · Product design · Sketch interface · Image retrieval

1 Introduction

Conceptual design is an essential stage of the product development process, where sketch plays an essential role to express design ideas. Before and during the sketch design process, designers usually need to browse lots of reference pictures, and some of the most-related pictures need to be reviewed over and over again. The lookup procedure can cost a substantial amount of time and effort, thus hindering the rapid iteration of product design processes. Moreover, it is difficult to identify and make use of local design elements of reference pictures such as lines. To solve the above problem, this paper tries to design a sketch assistant system based on the existing sketch retrieval technology. The system allows designers to get the existing products with only a few strokes on the sketch screen. In this way, the images of the existing products will appear on the interface of the design software, enabling designers to carry out iterative design with reference to these images.

The problems regarding picture retrieval of sketch have been under examination since 1990s. The purpose of Sketch based Image Retrieval is to retrieve the pictures relevant to the sketch provided by users [1]. However, in terms of the function of sketch retrieval, there is still plenty of scope for improvement.

© Springer Nature Switzerland AG 2020
H. Degen and L. Reinerman-Jones (Eds.): HCII 2020, LNCS 12217, pp. 310–320, 2020.
https://doi.org/10.1007/978-3-030-50334-5_21

We distill these synergistic insights into sketch-aider, a system that judiciously combines sketch retrieval technology and product conceptual design. A user study is carried out with the aim of evaluating our system under the assistance of professional designers. The hypothesized advantages of our hybrid workflow for conceptual design are verified.

In the remainder of the paper, Sect. 2 reviews Sketch-based Image Retrieval and related technologies. Section 3 elaborates on the motivation of developing the system. Section 4 explains the EasySketchDesign system and the related retrieval calculation, and introduces the user interface to achieve iterative sketch and refinement process. Section 5 presents a user study to demonstrate its effectiveness in terms of convenience and swiftness. We then discuss in Sect. 6 and conclude in Sect. 7, and then describe future work and limitations in Sect. 8.

A central idea of our work is the use of sketch retrieval to assist designers in conceptual design. This paper proposes a simpler and more practical auxiliary hand drawing interface. When the designer is doing hand drawing, it selects the existing product which bears most resemblance to the current sketch from the library by analyzing incomplete curves and presents it to the designer, which brings lots of conveniences. The design mode can not only save designers repetitive and unimaginative work, but also enhance the design efficiency. Moreover, the neural network based retrieval method we use is accurate in matching and can resist interference. The EasySketchDesign, in particular, can be used to detect conceptual designs which bear a strong resemblance to the existing products.

2 Related Work

Image retrieval technology based on sketch is a kind of technology used for retrieving image from database. This technology is a popular and effective method. Images can be retrieved from database by inputting rough sketches. Sketch-based image retrieval technology is applied to shapes identification, biometric security and other fields. Even if users are not skilled artists, their rough sketch will be sufficient enough to retrieve relevant images from the database [2]. A lot of research has been done to explore SBIR-related technology. Pedro Sousa et al. presented a new way to describe the spatial arrangements of visual elements by integrating spatial proximity in the topology graph, through the use of adjacency weights [3]. A. Del Bimbo et al. studied Elastic match, a reliable method for image retrieval based on contour-based techniques. In this way, similarities in shape between objects in the image and the sketch provided by the user are easily detected [4]. Besides, Contour-based techniques include grid and interest points, such as edge points [5].

In recent years, researchers have gradually applied machine learning algorithms to SBIR. Yang's article proposed a deep neural network architecture based on Alexnet for sketch recognition and discusses the differences in design between sketch-DNN and DNNs for photographic images [6]. Qi et al. introduced a novel convolutional neural network based on Siamese network for SBIR to gauge the compatibility between image edge and sketch [7]. Bui studied several triplet CNN architectures for measuring the similarity between sketches and photographs, exploring the ability of networks to generalize across different object classes from limited training data [8]. Wang et al. developed an efficient online triplet sampling method to learn the model with distributed asynchronized stochastic gradient, enabling us to learn deep ranking models from large amount of training data [9].

The traditional machine learning algorithm and deep learning algorithm are adequate for such tasks. However, we need large amount of data. In order to identify the required pictures through some hand drawn curves with a relatively small volume of data, we refer to a relatively novel machine learning algorithm called Recursive Cortical Network(RCN) [10]. We then improve the algorithm to complete the task. The algorithm models the contour and the surface of an object separately because the contour and the surface are represented by two independent and interacting mechanisms in human brains [11–13]. Therefore, the object is recognized after its contour and surface are identified separately and then combined [14]. In the process of recognition, Loopy Belief Propagation [15] in probability graph model is used to process the extracted contour and the object image to get the result.

3 Motivation: Interactive Sketch Retrieval for Product Conceptual Design

EasySketchDesign is motivated by ideas from multiple and complementary disciplines —the wealth of sketching practice and SBIR.

3.1 Interaction Between Sketch Retrieval and Product Conceptual Design

At present, sketch retrieval is only applicable to image retrieval. In terms of the function of sketch retrieval, there is still plenty of scope for improvement. In the process of product conceptual design, a very simple model is used to find reference pictures. It helps designers complete some tasks and builds a bridge between traditional industrial design and machine learning.

3.2 Auxiliary Product Conceptual Design

A central idea of our work is the use of sketch retrieval to assist designers in conceptual design. This paper proposes a more simple and practical auxiliary hand drawing algorithm. When the designer is employed in making line drawing, the algorithm selects the most similar existing products from the database through analyzing the incomplete curves drawn by the designer, which brings convenience to the subsequent iterative design. This algorithm is highly accurate in matching and resistant to interference. It not only saves designers of the repetitive and unimaginative work, but also improves design efficiency. In particular, the EasySketchDesign proposed in this paper can also be used to test whether the conceptual design is innovative.

4 System Overview and Setup

4.1 Workflow

In this section, we propose an innovative conceptual design workflow that combines sketch retrieval and conceptual design. The sketch image retrieval algorithm used in the EasySketchDesign consists of five main steps as follows.

Establishment of the Image Library. Users collect pictures to create a reference image library to browse before and during the design process. These pictures can be obtained from the web, or their previous design work.

Outline Detection. We use OpenCV to process images. All the images in the library are first converted to grey images, and then the Sobel operator is used to extract outlines.

Feature Extraction of the Data Set. A Gabor filter is used to extract the features of images in the library from its outlines. To simplify the procedure, advanced features are extracted and saved for future use. This is the learning process of the model, which is similar to the max pooling in image processing.

Backtracking of Advanced Features and Comparison with Test Features. In this stage, the advanced features are regenerated through a process similar to backtracking. At the same time, Loopy Belief Propagation is used to compare the generated image and the test data. Choose the image that best conforms to the inputted sketch image.

Output of Search Results. When the user sets the number of images to be returned, the system will display a set of retrieval results sorted by similarity from high to low.

4.2 Retrieval Algorithm

The overall system diagram of the retrieval algorithm is shown in Fig. 1.

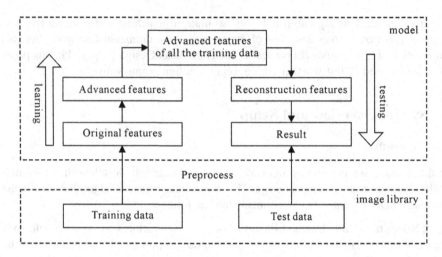

Fig. 1. System diagram of the retrieval algorithm

Step 1. Before the experiment, you need to establish the image library. After designers draw the curves, we need to help them find the existing products most similar to their image. The curves drawn by designers is used as the training image. Specific pictures are collected as test image.

Step 2. Preprocess the collected data and conduct feature extraction. Since the training image in the experiment is hand-drawn curves and the test image is pictures of real objects, their preprocessing process will be different. For the training data, only the feature extraction is needed before the experiment. For the test data, the traditional image processing technology is needed to extract the outline of the real image. Then the feature extraction should be under way. The first step of feature extraction is as follows.

$$Y = X * w \tag{1}$$

W is a set of convolution kernel used to extract features. X is the image whose feature should be extracted. Y is a set of results after convolution. $*$ represents convolution operation. Then the convolution result is processed by non maximum suppression and binarized to ± 1 to get the final result Z, which is called the extracted feature. At the same time, the dimension of feature is equal to that of convolution kernel.

Step 3. Use the improved RCN model to match the preprocessed curves with the preprocessed object image. Learn the features of the curves after processing. The learning process is as follows:

$$S = \{(r, c)|Z\{r - a : r + a + 1, c - a : c + a + 1\} = -1\} \tag{2}$$

r and c respectively represent the abscissa and ordinate of any number equal to +1 in Z. a is the suppression radius. S is the result of learning. We can see that the learning process is essentially a pooling process. By suppressing the area near +1 (the square area with a side length of *2a*) and keeping the value of the middle point position, the whole image can be learned. Then, select a small number of advanced features. The feature of a point represents the feature of an area. After the learning process, the results are backtracked on the test data set. In this way, the training image is regenerated, and different scores are given for different test images. The meaning of scores is as follows.

$$D = p(X^{'}|S^{'}) \tag{3}$$

$S^{'}$ represents the image obtained by de pooling. $X^{'}$ represents the test image. D represents the score. The formula above indicates that the test image with the highest conditional probability is the best matching image under the condition of retracing the trained image.

Step 4. Return the best matching results to the designer, analyze the results and complete the experiment.

4.3   User Interface

This paper fully exploits the advantages of Sketch-based Image Retrieval and product conceptual design to produce EasySketchDesign. It expands the application of Sketch-based Image Retrieval and assists designers in product conceptual design. The main interface of EasySketchDesign consists of four parts, including system operation, drawing board, drawing tools and result display, as shown in Fig. 2. The primary function of system operation is to control the operation process of the whole system, including screenshots, search, update, etc. The sketchpad is shaped like a rectangle. Users can draw directly on the sketchpad. The result display demonstrates the retrieval results of the system. The image list is arranged in descending order according to the similarity with the sketch. Figure 3 shows the overall workflow of our system.

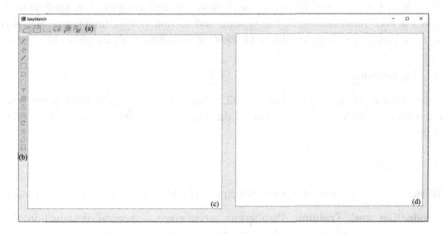

Fig. 2.   User interface. (a) System operation. (b) Drawing tool. (c) Drawing board. (d) Result display.

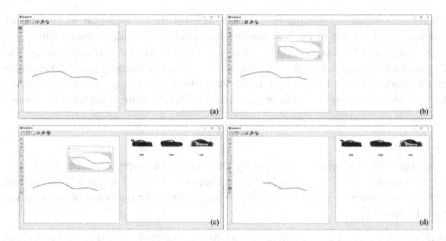

Fig. 3. System workflow. (a) Drawing. (b) Capture. (c) Update. (d) Modify figure.

4.4   Implementation

The user interface of EasySketchDesign is developed using C++ with Qt creator. We use a Wacom digital display with a stylus as input device. During the sketch design process, the user uses a screen snap tool integrated into the sketch interface to generate a sketch image. Next, the captured sketch image is automatically inputted to the background image retrieval procedure, which is developed using Python. Then the retrieval procedure compares the features with the inputted sketch image and output the similar images in the reference window of the Qt interface.

5   User Study

We evaluated our system with professional illustrators and designers. Our study aims to exam the core functionality of the system, and to find out its limitations. We also include a purely sketching condition to compare sketching with EasySketchDesign.

5.1   Participants

We recruited eight participants (age 24–32, 4 female) for our study. Participants were all experienced with sketching and Hand-drawn tools. Participants were compensated for their time.

5.2   Procedure

The study was conducted in our lab, which lasted a total of 50 min with three phases.

Introduction and Training. Participants were given a general introduction that explained the entire process and given time to get used to the EasySketchDesign.

Participants practiced using the EasySketchDesign until they felt confident. This phase lasted a total of 10 min.

Fixed Tasks. We designed fixed tasks to compare sketch with simple sketch. In order to eliminate learning effects, we balance the order of systems among participants. This phase lasted a total of 15 min.

The task involved drawing the left view of the car. There were two groups of participants. One group drew with EasySketchDesign. The other group drew in a normal way. In the process of drawing without EasySketchDesign, participants can refer to pictures in the local computer folder. Figure 4 shows the sketching of two participants (participant number P3 and P5).

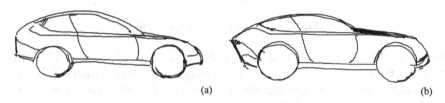

(a)   (b)

Fig. 4. (a) Sketch drawn by P3 with EasySketchDesign. (b) Sketch drawn by P5 without EasySketchDesign.

Freeform Design. Finally, in the third phase, participants were enabled to design whatever they wanted in the system. After the study, they needed to finish a questionnaire. This phase lasted a total of 25 min.

5.3   Results

Results for Fixed Tasks. For the fixed tasks, we used completion time to conduct quantitative measure. Then, we analyzed the time needed in the two different situations mentioned above.

The result shows that it took participants less time to complete the tasks when using EasySketchDesign. The completion time of each participant is shown in Appendix A. The average time of producing sketches by purely sketching (m = 623, σ = 38) was longer than that of producing sketches with EasySketchDesign (m = 535, σ = 30).

However, we should take these statistics into careful consideration, because our concentration was on qualitative measures, and the tasks were not carefully controlled. The study shows that two primary factors are behind such results. First, adapting to the EasySketchDesign costs more time and required more mental effort. However, so long as participants master the EasySketchDesign, they will draw designs with much ease and more efficiency.

Qualitative Feedback for Freeform Design. Participants successfully used EasySketchDesign to complete the design task. During the short design period, participants produced the sketch design of helmet, shampoo bottle, as shown in Fig. 5. In general, participants made positive response to EasySketchDesign. From participant 1's comments, it was clear that the system was "a good way to assist in conceptual design", but that "it was necessary to become familiar with the use of the system". Below, we report the partial feedback received for individual components.

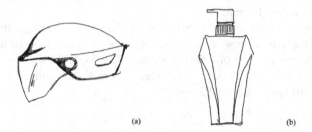

(a)

(b)

Fig. 5. (a) Helmet. (b) Shampoo bottle

Provide Picture Reference In real Time. Participants found this feature useful. They found that the accurate retrieval of the desired images in real time can not only improve the conceptual design but also help identify sketches that highly resemble the existing products. Participant 4 said, "Simply draw one or more lines based on your idea and quickly find an existing product image that fits your idea for reference. It makes me feel very happy."

Ability to Combine Concept Design and Image Retrieval In real Time. Tests show that EasySketchDesign can be used to find the desired images. It costs less time compared with participants looking for images in the local computer folder on their own. Participant 7 said, "It's very convenient. You don't have to go through a lot of pictures to find the right one. It takes very little time. However, it still took a while to wait for the retrieval results". "It consumes me less time so that I can spend more time in referring to models."

Participants also provided us with feedback on other aspects of the system. At present, content-based image retrieval is widely used. Whether it can be included in our system or not, this is an interesting and constructive suggestion for future work. In addition, some participants suggest referring to other kinds of products when drawing sketches. For instance, when drawing sketches of cars, we can not only refer to pictures of cars but also those of trucks and airplanes. Besides, some participants hope they can retrieve 3D models through sketches.

6 Discussion

Our evaluation indicated that our core ideas enjoyed popularity among the participants. They were enabled to use the system to create the designs they wanted. The sketch design completed by the participants shows the effectiveness of EasySketchDesign and creates a new interactive system for conceptual design. However, users' feedback demonstrates some limitations, which indicates that there is room for development in the future.

7   Conclusion

Through the improvement of a very novel machine learning model, this paper aims to combine product design sketch and sketch retrieval (SBIR), and increase their interaction. An interaction mode and a prototype system are developed, which benefit the design conception, expression and communication. Users' feedback proves that our system is useful and effective, and can address various design tasks. We hope this work can provide reference for researchers of industrial design and machine learning, and promote the combination of industrial design and machine learning.

8   Limitations and Future Work

There are some differences in users' cognition. Different users may have different understandings toward the same sketch [1]. These methods are usually combined with sketch retrieval algorithms to enhance the accuracy of retrieval results [16–18]. Therefore, we should consider the semantic information contained in the sketch and the image to be retrieved so as to enhance the accuracy of sketch retrieval results.

Further expand the data set to improve the system. The enlargement of the data set enables designers to refer to pictures of different kinds of products, giving them more inspiration. Besides, 3D model can be retrieved through sketches, providing more detailed reference for designers. However, this is a challenging task.

Although the method has achieved some results, it also has some limitations. Human beings usually have a focus of observation in the process of recognizing objects. However, there is no difference between the features in this paper's experiment. Therefore, in the following research, we can solve this problem by adding weight to different features so as to improve the stability of the model. This is what we need to study in the next stage.

Appendix A

Sketching with EasySketchDesign		Purely sketching	
P2	569	P1	634
P3	532	P4	601
P6	488	P5	580
P8	551	P7	680

References

1. Eitz, M., Hildebrand, K., Boubekeur, T., Alexa, M.: Sketch-Based image retrieval: benchmark and bag-of-features descriptors. IEEE Trans. Vis. Comput. Graph. 17(11), 1624–1636 (2010)
2. Paper, C., Cheng, M., Huang, X., Hu, S.: Global contrast based salient region detection. IEEE Trans. Pattern Anal. Mach. Intell. 37(3), 569–582 (2011). https://doi.org/10.1109/CVPR.2011.5995344
3. Sousa, P., Fonseca, M.J.: Sketch-based retrieval of drawings using spatial proximity. J. Vis. Lang. Comput. 21(2), 69–80 (2010)
4. Del Bimbo, A., Pala, P., Santini, S.: Visual image retrieval by elastic deformation of object sketches. In: Proceedings of 1994 IEEE Symposium on Visual Languages, pp. 216–223. IEEE (1994)
5. Chalechale, A., Naghdy, G., Mertins, A.: Sketch-based image matching using angular partitioning. IEEE Trans. Syst. Man Cybern.-Part A: Syst. Hum. 35(1), 28–41 (2004)
6. Yang, Y., Hospedales, T.M.: Deep Neural Networks for Sketch Recognition (2015)
7. Qi, Y., Zhang, H.: Sketch-Based Image Retrieval Via SIAMESE Convolutional Neural Network Yi-Zhe Song School of Information and Communication Engineering, BUPT, Beijing, China School of EECS, Queen Mary University of London, UK
8. Bui, T., Collomosse, J., Ribeiro, L., Ponti, M., Paulo, S.: Generalisation and Sharing in Triplet Convnets for Sketch based Visual Search (2016)
9. Wang, J., et al.: Learning fine-grained image similarity with deep ranking. In: Proceedings of the IEEE Conference on Computer Vision and Pattern Recognition, pp. 1386–1393 (2014)
10. George, D., George, D., Lehrach, W., et al.: A generative vision model that trains with high data efficiency and breaks text-based CAPTCHAs. Science 2612, 1–19 (2017)
11. Craft, E., et al.: A neural model of figure – ground organization. J. Neurophysiol. 97(6), 4310–4326 (2007)
12. Lamme, V.A.F., Rodriguez-rodriguez, V.: Separate processing dynamics for texture elements. Boundaries Surf. Primary Visual Cortex Macaque Monkey 1, 406–413 (1999)
13. Deyoe, E.A., Van Essen, D.C.: Concurrent processing streams in monkey visual cortex. Trends Neurosci. 11, 219–226 (1988)
14. Le, R., Heess, N.: Learning a generative model of images by factoring appearance and shape. Neural Comput. 23, 593–650 (2010)
15. Pearl, J.: Probabilistic reasoning in intelligent systems : networks of plausible inference (1988)
16. Datta, R., Joshi, D., Li, J.I.A., Wang, J.Z.: Image retrieval: ideas influences, and trends of the new age. ACM Comput. Surv. (Csur) 40, 1–60 (2008)
17. Sun, X.: Indexing Billions of Images for Sketch-based Retrieval, pp. 233–242 (2013)
18. Hu, R., Collomosse, J.: A performance evaluation of gradient field hog descriptor for sketch based image retrieval. Comput. Vis. and Image Understand. 117(7), 790–806 (2013)
19. The completion time of each participant (s)

Contextual Programming
of Collaborative Robots

Chien-Ming Huang[✉]

Johns Hopkins University, Baltimore, MD 21218, USA
cmhuang@cs.jhu.edu
http://www.cs.jhu.edu/~cmhuang

Abstract. Collaborative robots are envisioned to assist people in an increasing range of domains, from manufacturing to home care; however, due to the variable nature of these fields, such robots will inevitably face unfamiliar situations and unforeseen task requirements, and must be able to interact with users who possess diverse skill sets, backgrounds, and needs. Presently, robust, autonomous solutions for appropriately handling these vast possibilities and uncertainties are unattainable. *End-user robot programming* offers an alternative approach that lets end users provide task specifications and author robot skills to meet their own specific contextual constraints and custom task needs. Contextual information—such as task objects, environmental landmarks, and user preferences—is essential in realizing desirable, flexible, and reliable robot programs. However, most robot programming systems at present do not afford intuitive ways of specifying contextual information. In this paper, we draw on our prior work to illustrate the barriers to end-user robot programming when using a state-of-the-art programming interface. We then present two case studies that explore new approaches to providing a robot system with contextual information about the user, task, and environment, and how these methods can help improve task performance and user experience. We discuss our findings and future directions for building effective end-user programming tools to bring robotic assistance closer to everyday users.

Keywords: Human-robot interaction · Collaborative robotics · End-user robot programming · Programming by demonstration

1 Introduction

Collaborative robots hold great promise for augmenting human capabilities and providing assistance in various domains—from manufacturing to home care to search and rescue missions. The successful integration of robotic assistance into these types of task domains requires that robots work with people with diverse skill sets and needs, perform a variety of manipulation tasks, and operate in complex human environments that typically involve established physical infrastructures—all while being customizable to meet specific task

© Springer Nature Switzerland AG 2020
H. Degen and L. Reinerman-Jones (Eds.): HCII 2020, LNCS 12217, pp. 321–338, 2020.
https://doi.org/10.1007/978-3-030-50334-5_22

requirements and contextual constraints. At present, developing a robot that can autonomously and appropriately respond to every possible situation is an intractable problem. *End-user robot programming* offers an alternative approach that empowers end users to harness the full potential of programmable robots and facilitates the integration of collaborative robots into human environments in the short term.

Programming by demonstration (PbD)—also known as learning from demonstration (LfD) [6,7,9,30]—has emerged as a promising framework of end-user robot programming. It explores various abstraction methods, supporting tools, and authoring interfaces for robot programming, aiming to teach robot skills and adapt them to a variety of task configurations (e.g., [4,10,23,37,42]). PbD research has investigated how people may train robots in new skills through kinesthetic teaching [3,14], natural instructions with verbal and non-verbal behaviors [19,21,24,33,34,36], vision-based human demonstrations [10, 42], visual programming [5,12,17,26], embodied enactment [27], and teleoperative demonstrations in virtual reality [43] or via motion capture [8,16,31]. While still in its infancy, research on PbD has established its potential in training task concepts (e.g., [22]) and manipulation skills (e.g., [2]). Among the variations of PbD, kinesthetic teaching allows end users to program robots through direct action demonstration, while visual programming offers accessible interfaces to allow users to focus on programming the logic of a robot task. A hybrid use of kinesthetic teaching and visual programming has become a common implementation of robot programming by demonstration in both industry (e.g., Universal Robots, Elephant Robotics) and academia (e.g., [17,26]).

Although this hybrid approach has certainly lowered the barriers to entry for end-user robot programming, most people still have difficulties providing effective and efficient demonstrations. As we illustrate in our informative study [1] (Sect. 2), everyday users generally lack an accurate mental model of how high degrees-of-freedom robots operate (e.g., what their capabilities and limitations are) and are typically provided with unproductive programming interfaces to begin with. In particular, in most current PbD systems, there is no straightforward way of specifying pertinent contextual information—such as task-relevant objects, environmental constraints, and user preferences—to ensure that the resulting robot programs are correct and productive. We note that contextual information is critically important for collaborative robots, as they have direct access to and influence upon their surrounding environments and users. The necessary consideration of physical context sets PbD apart from end-user programming for typical computer programs [39], which usually do not involve real-time physical interactivity.

In this paper, we argue that straightforward methods of encoding contextual information via PbD are integral to an end user's production of effective and efficient robot programs that meet their task constraints and needs. We first describe an informative study that highlights key barriers to productive end-user robot programming [1]. We then present two case studies that illustrate new modalities for providing contextual information in robot programs and address a number of the previously identified barriers. The first case study focuses on enabling users to directly specify environmental contexts in situ using gestures and illustration tools (***programming by situated illustration***) [11], while the second study uses egocentric vision to capture user preferences for performing complex manipulative tasks (***programming by first-person demonstration***) [38]. We demonstrate that these modalities improve task performance and user experience for repetitive task specification [11] and dynamic human-robot collaboration [38]. We conclude this paper with a discussion of the resulting implications for designing effective end-user robot programming systems.

2   Barriers to End-User Robot Programming

2.1   Informative Study

To explore potential barriers to programming a collaborative robot, we conducted an informative study in which participants were asked to program a UR-5 robotic arm to complete four common manipulation tasks, including stacking, hanging, and pouring task objects such as blocks, cups, and towels [1] (Fig. 1). Participants were instructed to use kinesthetic teaching to program the robot and were free to use continuous trajectories, waypoints, or a combination of the two during the programming process [2]. After giving their informed consent, each participant was provided with a tutorial on how to use the state-of-the-art programming interface for the UR-5: the PolyScope on the teach pendant that supplements the robot. They were then given an opportunity to practice by programming a pick-and-place task. After completing the practice task, participants completed four manipulation tasks using the programming interface. They could correct the program as many times as they wanted until they were happy with the task result. Regardless of their progress, each participant was stopped fifteen minutes before the hour to complete an open-ended interview and a demographics questionnaire. The study was video-recorded and participants received $10 USD for study completion. Eight participants (6 females and 2 males) were recruited for the study, with ages ranging from 19 to 57 ($M = 31.13, SD = 16.22$). These participants came from various backgrounds and disciplines and had varying degrees of experience in programming and technology.

Fig. 1. Our informative study revealed that users face various difficulties in task planning and action demonstration when programming a collaborative robot [1].

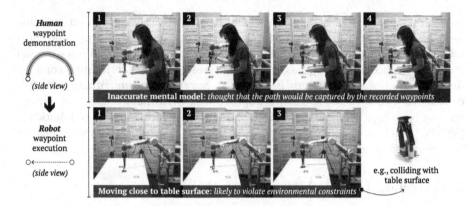

Fig. 2. A common error in robot programming by demonstration. The user mistakenly thought the robot would record trajectories between waypoints, which resulted in task failures and collisions.

2.2 Key Observations and Findings

Overall, we observed a number of user frustrations and challenges in specifying and editing robot programs, and found that participants generally did not have an accurate mental model of the robot's capabilities and limitations; a complete, accurate mental model allows users to learn about and interact with a system more effectively [18,41] and to predict and explain their interactions with that system [25]. In particular, our observations of the demonstration performances and interviews with the participants revealed these common difficulties in action demonstration during robot programming:

- *Trouble moving the robot into a desired configuration.* The unfamiliar kinematics of the robot hindered the participants' ability to provide direct demonstrations of task-relevant actions (Fig. 1).
- *Fatigue during kinesthetic teaching.* Three participants directly mentioned how difficult programming the robot could be when using kinesthetic teaching, while other participants conveyed this indirectly through expression of fatigue while programming or when they showed reluctance in—or even decided to forego—correcting their flawed programs.
- *Demonstrations resulting in suboptimal or unsmoothed action trajectories.* Participant fatigue during kinesthetic teaching resulted in extraneous movements and lag time (where no movement occurred) in most of the participants' programs that used continuous recording.
- *Confusing waypoint specification with path recording.* One participant thought that trajectories between waypoints were recorded and that they represented actual paths that the robot would later trace through (Fig. 2). Such inadequate understanding often led to task failures or unexpected collisions with obstacles.
- *High cognitive demand when tracking programming steps.* Two participants forgot to record a path during one of the tasks, illustrating how a complex

programming process can lead to high cognitive load—which consequently reduces the quality of the resulting user-specified robot programs.

– *Disconnect between specified program logics and contextual landmarks.* Some participants found the tab structure of the PolyScope interface confusing, since it separates robot action selection from robot action parameter specification. One participant suggested that it would be more intuitive for both command selection and program editing to be located in one central hub. Additionally, we observed participants make frequent switches between action demonstration (i.e., kinesthetic teaching) and program specification (i.e., using the visual programming interface); this disconnect may have contributed to the participants' insufficient mental models of their robot programs.

Overall, the user experiences that we observed reveal there is still significant room for improvement in current end-user programming interfaces, especially with respect to increasing usability and maximizing user productivity. Based on our observations and the feedback we received from participants, we identified several design opportunities for end-user programming interfaces; in particular, we sought to enable and streamline the process of providing contextual information in robot programming.

Next, we present two novel frameworks of robot programming: (1) programming by situated illustration—a framework that allows users to directly specify environmental contexts and task actions in situ, thus overcoming the disconnect between program specification and action demonstration and thereby reducing users' cognitive load—and (2) programming by first-person demonstration—a framework that allows users to demonstrate tasks from their own perspectives without worrying about the complex, unfamiliar kinematics of the robot.

3   Programming by Situated Illustration

Common PbD systems used in industrial settings (e.g., the PolyScope interface) involve little perception of the environment and rely primarily upon replaying demonstrated action trajectories or tracing through recorded key waypoints. This limited perception constrains the generalizability and scalability of PbD; however, perception of task-relevant objects and the environment usually requires specialized processes for training objects for visual recognition and robot manipulation (e.g., [17]), which consequently creates additional technical barriers for end users. To address these limitations, we explore the framework of *programming by situated illustration*, which seeks to facilitate programming robots to operate within flexible environments, in which objects and environmental landmarks are not predefined; this type of environment lies in direct contrast to automation scenarios with predefined procedures and task configurations.

Situated tangible robot programming [32] is an example of this framework; it allows users to specify task-relevant objects and provide annotation in the environment through the use of tangible blocks. However, tangible programming does not support 3D specification (e.g., labeling the height of an object), and its expressiveness is limited by the number of blocks used. Below, we describe an alternative implementation of situated programming enabled by projection-based augmentation.[1]

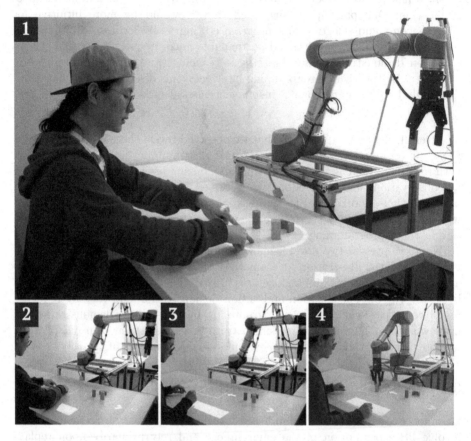

Fig. 3. PATI supports the augmented and situated specification of robot tasks, allowing users to teach their robots new tasks by directly referencing and interacting with the environment via virtual tools (e.g., shape tools) and common touch screen gestures, such as pinch, tap, and drag-and-drop. This figure illustrates a sequence of specifications for a simple pick-and-place task.

3.1   System Prototype

We developed a Projection-based Augmented Table-top Interface (PATI) for robot programming[2] (Fig. 3)—a prototype system designed to streamline the

---

[1] Please refer to [11] for a detailed description of our implementation and its evaluation.

[2] This project is available at https://intuitivecomputing.github.io/PATI.

processes of visual tracking, object referencing, and task specification in robot programming by enabling users to directly reference and annotate the environment through gestural illustration. The PATI system allows users to program a robot manipulator directly on a tabletop surface through an intuitive tangible interface. Our current implementation involves the use of a UR5 robot manipulator, a top-down projector, and a Kinect2 RGB-D camera mounted on the ceiling. Aside from the hardware setup, the PATI system consists of four software modules: *Visual Perception*, *Tangible User Interface (TUI)*, *Program Synthesis*, and *Robot Control*. The modules of Visual Perception, Program Synthesis, and Robot Control are implemented in the Robot Operating System (ROS) [29], while the TUI is implemented in Unity. The Visual Perception module detects and tracks objects in the environment—as well as a user's touch input—through the use of depth data and RGB color images from the Kinect2 camera. User input is then sent to the TUI module, in which different types of gestures are recognized. Once the user completes their program specification via the TUI, the Program Synthesis module translates the user's task-level specifications into a set of robot commands, including gripper actions and the waypoint specifications of intended trajectories. The commands are then forwarded to the Robot Control module, which subsequently generates corresponding motion plans for robot execution.

3.2 Empirical Evaluation

Below, we summarize a user study conducted to assess the effectiveness of PATI. Our evaluation focused on simple manipulation tasks (such as pick-and-place) that are fundamental to a variety of common functions which robots have been envisioned to assist people in performing. Our central hypotheses were that the PATI system would help participants achieve greater *task performance* and that it would offer higher *usability* to participants than the built-in PbD method for the UR5. We designed a within-participants study with two experimental conditions. In the control condition, participants used the UR5 programming interface (PolyScope), representing a state-of-the-art method for robot programming in industry. In the experimental condition, participants used our PATI system. We counterbalanced the order of the conditions presented to the participants. The study took approximately one hour to complete and participants were compensated with $10 USD.

We used a combination of objective and subjective measures to assess task performance and usability of the PATI and PolyScope interfaces. For task performance, we measured *task time* (how long it took to complete the task), *number of task mistakes*, and *number of questions asked*. For usability, we measured *practice time* (time users needed to be familiar with and comfortable using a new interface) and *task load* (an adapted version of the NASA TLX [13]).

We recruited 17 participants (9 females and 8 males) on a college campus for this study. They were aged 23.48 years on average ($SD = 4.81$) and reported having familiarity with robots ($M = 4.00, SD = 1.97$) and programming ($M = 4.18, SD = 1.88$) on 1-to-7 rating scales, with 7 being the most familiar. The participants also had a variety of educational backgrounds, including engineering, psychology, writing, and medicine.

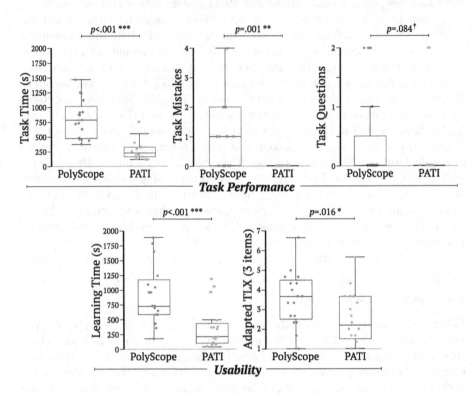

Fig. 4. Box and whisker plots of our data on the objective measures of task performance and the subjective measures of usability.

3.3   Main Findings

Our main findings are summarized in Fig. 4. We used non-parametric Wilcoxon signed-rank tests in accordance with the distribution of the analyzed data. With regard to task performance, we found that participants needed significantly less time to complete the experimental task ($Z = 3.62, p < .001$) when using the PATI system ($M = 276.28, SD = 167.94$) than they did when using the PolyScope interface ($M = 808.37, SD = 324.02$); the participants did not make any mistakes when using PATI ($M = 0.00, SD = 0.00$) while they made more than one mistake on average when using PolyScope ($M = 1.12, SD = 1.11$), $Z = 3.23, p = .001$; and the participants asked the experimenter marginally fewer questions ($Z = 1.73, p = .084$) during the task when using PATI ($M = 0.12, SD = 0.49$) than they did when using PolyScope ($M = 0.35, SD = 0.70$).

With regard to usability, we found that participants needed significantly less time before they were familiar with the programming interface and felt ready for the experimental task sooner ($Z = 3.34, p < .001$) when using PATI ($M = 384.21, SD = 366.08$) than they did when using the PolyScope interface ($M = 919.83, SD = 495.77$); we also found that participants experienced less task load ($Z = 2.41, p = .016$) when using our system ($M = 2.16, SD = 1.31$) than they did in the control condition ($M = 3.55, SD = 1.38$).

Overall, our results indicate the potential of *programming by situated illustration*; in particular, participants were able to learn how to use the system in a shorter period of time and achieved greater task efficiency with less task load when using PATI than they did when using a state-of-the-art PbD system.

4   Programming by First-Person Demonstration

While kinesthetic teaching allows users to directly provide action demonstrations by maneuvering a robot, our informative study revealed that most people have difficulty providing desirable demonstrations due to their unfamiliarity with

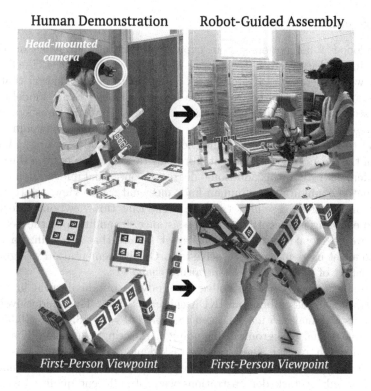

Fig. 5. We explore how first-person demonstrations capture natural behavioral preferences for task performance and how they can be utilized to enable user-centric robotic assistance in human-robot collaborative assembly tasks.

robot kinematics, which are admittedly unnatural to human users. Arguably, the most natural method of human task demonstration is simply performing the task. Prior research on robot *learning by watching* has explored how robots may learn new tasks by observing how humans perform the tasks either in situ [20] or through videos [40]. Contrary to prior research, the framework of *programming by first-person demonstration* explores methods of enabling robots to learn new skills from a human demonstrator's own first-person perspective (Fig. 5). We note that this type of first-person demonstration is different from showing a task to a learner via a teaching process, which requires consideration and estimation of the learner's perspective during the teaching of the task; the unique aspect of our approach is allowing a robot learner to channel directly into a human teacher's perspective. First-person vision provides a dynamic viewpoint representing the region of attention and offers the human teacher's perspective on task performance (e.g., how the hands interact with objects of interest). We argue that first-person demonstrations naturally capture human preferences for task performance and encapsulate unique, task-relevant contextual information critical to training robot manipulation skills. Below, we describe our exploration of first-person demonstration as an intuitive method of robot programming.[3]

4.1 System Prototype

We developed a perception system capable of parsing a first-person demonstration into a First-person Experience-based Assembly Tree (FEAsT) model (Fig. 6), which hierarchically stores task and contextual information that a collaborative robot can then use to assist a human user. A FEAsT model encodes (1) the sequential procedure of the task, (2) spatial configurations symbolizing how different task objects fit together, and (3) first-person viewpoints corresponding to the various task actions (i.e., connecting and screwing). A unique aspect of the FEAsT model is that it stores key task viewpoints from the original human demonstration; this additional degree of contextual information captures which spatial configuration a human finds most natural to view a part or set of parts from during an assembly task; we argue that this viewpoint information is key to enabling user-centric robotic assistance. In addition to the perception system, we developed an autonomous robot system that can utilize a FEAsT model to assist users in a collaborative task. Our implementation was grounded in the context of assembling a kit-furniture chair.

We first conducted a data collection study to obtain natural first-person demonstrations of assembling an IKEA children's chair. This study involved 12 participants (7 females, 5 males), aged 18 to 46 ($M = 28.58$, $SD = 10.55$), with various educational backgrounds, including engineering, education, finance, and neuroscience. On average, the assembly task demonstration length was 137.96 s ($SD = 26.52$ s). Overall, participants were able to complete the assembly task and their resulting task demonstrations were of sufficient quality to enable a

---

[3] Please refer to [38] for a detailed description of our implementation and its evaluation.

collaborative robot to provide user-centric assistance. We chose one of these demonstrations to populate the FEAsT model that was used in our evaluation study, described below.

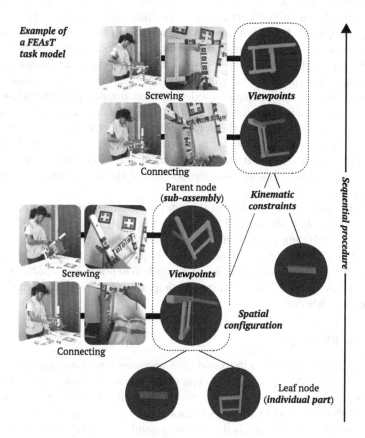

Fig. 6. The hierarchical structure of a FEAsT: leaf nodes are *parts*; parent nodes are *sub-assemblies*; edges are *kinematic constraints* between a parent node and its child nodes; and sub-assembly nodes contain relevant *first-person viewpoints*.

4.2 Empirical Evaluation

To explore the importance of egocentric views of task performance in authoring effective collaborative robot programs, our evaluation focused on assessing how user-centric robotic assistance may influence a user's behavior during a collaboration and affect their perception of their robot partner. We hypothesized that robotic assembly assistance based on a first-person demonstration would lead to better user experience than robotic assistance that did not consider first-person viewpoints.

Our user evaluation followed a within-participants design, with each participant working with the robot in either a *standard assistance* or *user-centric assistance* condition. We counterbalanced the order in which the conditions were presented to participants. In the *standard* condition, the robot fetched task parts and presented them to the participants matching the viewpoint shown on the cover page of the official IKEA assembly manual. In the *user-centric* condition, the robot fetched parts and presented them to users matching the first-person viewpoint extracted from one of our previously collected human demonstrations.

To assess participants' performance and user experience, we measured the number of times the participants used their non-dominant hands or switched between hands when performing screwing actions. We also measured the number of times participants dropped the screwdriver during the task *(tool drops)*. In addition, we measured participants' *perceived teamwork*, or how cooperative and how good of a teammate participants perceived the robot to be, and *perceived consideration*, or how considerate the robot was of the user's actions, tasks, and comfort during the interaction.

Our data analysis included a total of 20 participants (10 females, 10 males), aged 18 to 65 ($M = 27.70$, $SD = 13.86$), who had a variety of educational backgrounds, including engineering, applied math, biology, music, and international studies. Nineteen out of twenty participants reported themselves as right-handed, with the remaining participant being left-handed. Each participant was compensated with \$5 USD for their participation in the study, which lasted approximately 30 min.

4.3   Main Findings

Figure 7 summarizes our results based on a one-way repeated-measures analysis of variance (ANOVA), in which the type of assistance—either standard or user-centric—was set as a fixed effect, and the participant was set as a random effect.

Our results revealed that participants were more likely to use their non-dominant hand or switch hands during the assembly task ($F(1, 38) = 37.79, p < .001, \eta_p^2 = 0.499$) when working with the robot providing standard assistance ($M = 2.65, SD = 0.81$) than when working with the robot providing user-centric assistance ($M = 0.75, SD = 1.12$). We observed that the fixed—and sometimes awkward—presentation of the chair parts in the standard condition prompted participants to engage in unproductive hand use. In contrast, participants were more often able to use their dominant hand to carry out task actions when provided with user-centric assistance. Moreover, we observed that participants tended to drop the screwdriver more frequently ($F(1, 38) = 3.73, p = .061, \eta_p^2 = 0.089$) when provided with standard assistance ($M = 0.65, SD = 0.81$) than when provided with user-centric assistance ($M = 0.25, SD = 0.44$). While we were unable to identify a direct relationship between non-dominant hand use and tool drops, we speculate that these two behaviors are possibly associated and might have influenced each other.

Participants reported significantly greater perceived teamwork ($F(1, 38) = 4.88, p = .033, \eta_p^2 = 0.114$) with the user-centric robot ($M = 6.09, SD = 0.69$)

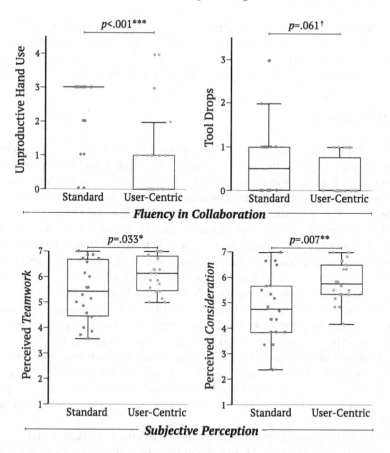

Fig. 7. Box and whisker plots of our data on the behavioral measures of unproductive behavior and the subjective measures of user experience.

than with the standard robot ($M = 5.42, SD = 1.15$). They also perceived the user-centric robot ($M = 5.83, SD = 0.80$) to be more considerate (F(1,38) = 8.27, $p = .007, \eta_p^2 = 0.179$) in terms of accommodating how they preferred to perform the task than compared to the standard robot ($M = 4.86, SD = 1.28$); for example, P15 commented, *"[The user-centric robot] could actually feel when I was uncomfortable—like I couldn't actually put the pieces together in a really comfortable way, so he just kind of helped me do that, and it was really nice because I felt like we were working together."* Additionally, participants agreed that the user-centric robotic assistance allowed them to align pieces and screw them together more easily than in the standard assistance condition, as described by P2: *"The [user-centric] robot did a slight, nice movement into the position where I was kind of facing it, so it was easier for me to screw."*

Overall, our results indicate the potential of *programming by first-person demonstration*; in particular, we demonstrate how first-person demonstration may be used to generate user-centric assistance in human-robot collaborative assembly. Our results show that, when working with the robot offering user-centric assistance, participants felt that the robot was a more considerate collaborator and were less likely to engage in unproductive behavior.

5 Discussion

Most robot programming systems in industrial settings have little contextual awareness of their surroundings and users, and simply replay human demonstrations (e.g., action trajectories). While effective in certain settings and applications that require repetitive task performance, this limited contextual awareness restricts the desirability, flexibility, and reliability of the resulting specified robot programs. We present two new modalities of authoring demonstrations that explicitly and implicitly represent contextual information regarding task objects, environmental landmarks, and user preferences. In particular, we explored a new way to streamline the specification of robot actions and environmental contexts (***programming by situated illustration***) and a new method of capturing subtle user preferences for task actions via the egocentric perspective (***programming by first-person demonstration***). Programming by situated illustration improves upon the current hybrid implementation of PbD systems, while programming by first-person demonstration allows for additional user context (e.g., how a user would like to perform a task), which is critically important in human-robot collaboration. Through empirical evaluations with naive participants, we illustrated how these two modalities may enhance task performance and user experience.

This research points to future directions in enriching the contextual programming of collaborative robots. First, techniques of computer vision and natural language processing should be leveraged to capture the rich contexts embedded in interactive demonstrations and the physical world. Our case studies, along with other prior research (e.g., [17,26]), illustrate how vision-augmented programming can aid end users in efficiently providing program specifications and generating flexible robot programs; for instance, the system may recognize a user's handedness and adjust the parameters of a demonstration accordingly. Second, as programming media mature and supporting tools (e.g., visual sensing) become more widely available, the scale and complexity of robot programs will grow exponentially. Furthermore, the situated interactivity that physically embodied robots afford adds an additional layer of complexity to their programs; the increasing complexity of robot programs necessitates that program outputs accurately reflect program specifications (e.g., [28]). Assured robot programs will help end users build trust in and adopt emergent robotic technologies over time. Third, as analogous to common metrics in human-robot interaction (e.g., [15,35]), in order to make productive progress in advancing end-user robot programming, we need to develop a common set of evaluation metrics for robot programming. Prior research has used various measures of efficiency in programming and debugging (e.g., [5]), task load (e.g., [11]), program accuracy, and custom scales of user experience (e.g., [38]); however, it is less clear how to quantify the generalizability, quality, and expressiveness of a program. Reliable, agreed-upon scales to probe different aspects of user experience will also be instrumental in catalyzing the advancement of end-user robot programming.

In addition to the research directions discussed above, future research on end-user robot programming should involve domain-specific end users, such as production workers and caregivers, all throughout the stages of design, development, and evaluation, following the principles of user-centered design. Working closely with real-life domain users will help develop more effective systems for potential users in those fields and ensure that the resulting systems can be more easily integrated into existing workflows and adopted by the intended users. In a similar vein, we must deepen our understanding of domain contexts and incorporate them when designing domain-specific programming tools. For instance, an ethnographic study on how production workers currently use state-of-the-art programming interfaces would provide invaluable insight into the challenges and barriers they face, contextualized in real-world settings and constraints.

6   Conclusion

We envision that robotic assistance will positively transform the future of work, care, and living, and believe that empowering end users to be able to intuitively author robot programs will improve the accessibility of robotic assistance while better meeting domain users' needs and constraints. Through empirical studies, we have determined that there still remains much room for improvement in current end-user programming interfaces with respect to increasing usability and maximizing user productivity, and that contextual information is key in creating effective task specifications and user-friendly robotic assistance. Advancing the contextual programming of collaborative robots will require further research on human-computer interaction, artificial intelligence, robotics, formal methods, and other related fields. Together, these efforts will help democratize robotic assistance for use by everyday people.

Acknowledgements. I would like to thank Gopika Ajaykumar, Yuxiang Gao, and Yeping Wang for helping with system implementation and user evaluation, and Jaimie Patterson for proofreading this paper. This work is partially supported by the National Science Foundation award #1840088.

References

1. Ajaykumar, G., Huang, C.M.: User needs and design opportunities in end-user robot programming. In: Proceedings of the 15th International Conference on Human-Robot Interaction (HRI), Late-Breaking Report. ACM (2020)
2. Akgun, B., Cakmak, M., Jiang, K., Thomaz, A.L.: Keyframe-based learning from demonstration. Int. J. Soc. Robot. 4(4), 343–355 (2012). https://doi.org/10.1007/s12369-012-0160-0

3. Akgun, B., Cakmak, M., Yoo, J.W., Thomaz, A.L.: Trajectories and keyframes for kinesthetic teaching: a human-robot interaction perspective. In: Proceedings of the Seventh Annual ACM/IEEE International Conference on Human-Robot Interaction, pp. 391–398. ACM (2012)
4. Aleotti, J., Caselli, S.: Robust trajectory learning and approximation for robot programming by demonstration. Robot. Auton. Syst. **54**(5), 409–413 (2006)
5. Alexandrova, S., Tatlock, Z., Cakmak, M.: RoboFlow: a flow-based visual programming language for mobile manipulation tasks. In: 2015 IEEE International Conference on Robotics and Automation (ICRA), pp. 5537–5544. IEEE (2015)
6. Argall, B.D., Chernova, S., Veloso, M., Browning, B.: A survey of robot learning from demonstration. Robot. Auton. Syst. **57**(5), 469–483 (2009)
7. Billard, A., Calinon, S., Dillmann, R., Schaal, S.: Robot programming by demonstration. In: Siciliano, B., Khatib, O. (eds.) Springer Handbook of Robotics, pp. 1371–1394. Springer, Heidelberg (2008). https://doi.org/10.1007/978-3-540-30301-5_60
8. Calinon, S., Billard, A.G.: What is the teacher's role in robot programming by demonstration?: toward benchmarks for improved learning. Interact. Stud. **8**(3), 441–464 (2007)
9. Chernova, S., Thomaz, A.L.: Robot learning from human teachers. Synth. Lect. Artif. Intell. Mach. Learn. **8**(3), 1–121 (2014)
10. Finn, C., Yu, T., Zhang, T., Abbeel, P., Levine, S.: One-shot visual imitation learning via meta-learning. arXiv preprint arXiv:1709.04905 (2017)
11. Gao, Y., Huang, C.M.: PATI: a projection-based augmented table-top interface for robot programming. In: Proceedings of the 24th International Conference on Intelligent User Interfaces, pp. 345–355. ACM (2019)
12. Glas, D.F., Kanda, T., Ishiguro, H.: Human-robot interaction design using interaction composer eight years of lessons learned. In: 2016 11th ACM/IEEE International Conference on Human-Robot Interaction (HRI), pp. 303–310. IEEE (2016)
13. Hart, S.G.: NASA-task load index (NASA-TLX); 20 years later. In: Proceedings of the Human Factors and Ergonomics Society Annual Meeting, vol. 50, pp. 904–908. Sage Publications, Los Angeles (2006)
14. Hersch, M., Guenter, F., Calinon, S., Billard, A.: Dynamical system modulation for robot learning via kinesthetic demonstrations. IEEE Trans. Rob. **24**(6), 1463–1467 (2008)
15. Hoffman, G.: Evaluating fluency in human-robot collaboration. IEEE Trans. Hum.-Mach. Syst. **49**(3), 209–218 (2019)
16. Hsiao, K., Lozano-Perez, T.: Imitation learning of whole-body grasps. In: 2006 IEEE/RSJ International Conference on Intelligent Robots and Systems, pp. 5657–5662. IEEE (2006)
17. Huang, J., Cakmak, M.: Code3: a system for end-to-end programming of mobile manipulator robots for novices and experts. In: Proceedings of the 2017 ACM/IEEE International Conference on Human-Robot Interaction, pp. 453–462. ACM (2017)
18. Kieras, D.E., Bovair, S.: The role of a mental model in learning to operate a device. Cogn. Sci. **8**(3), 255–273 (1984)
19. Kollar, T., Tellex, S., Roy, D., Roy, N.: Toward understanding natural language directions. In: Proceedings of the 5th ACM/IEEE International Conference on Human-Robot Interaction, pp. 259–266. IEEE Press (2010)
20. Kuniyoshi, Y., Inaba, M., Inoue, H.: Learning by watching: extracting reusable task knowledge from visual observation of human performance. IEEE Trans. Robot. Autom. **10**(6), 799–822 (1994)

21. Lauria, S., Bugmann, G., Kyriacou, T., Klein, E.: Mobile robot programming using natural language. Robot. Auton. Syst. **38**(3–4), 171–181 (2002)
22. Lázaro-Gredilla, M., Lin, D., Guntupalli, J.S., George, D.: Beyond imitation: zero-shot task transfer on robots by learning concepts as cognitive programs. arXiv preprint arXiv:1812.02788 (2018)
23. Lee, A.X., Lu, H., Gupta, A., Levine, S., Abbeel, P.: Learning force-based manipulation of deformable objects from multiple demonstrations. In: 2015 IEEE International Conference on Robotics and Automation (ICRA), pp. 177–184. IEEE (2015)
24. Matuszek, C., Bo, L., Zettlemoyer, L., Fox, D.: Learning from unscripted deictic gesture and language for human-robot interactions. In: AAAI, pp. 2556–2563 (2014)
25. Norman, D.A.: Some observations on mental models. In: Mental Models, pp. 15–22. Lawrence Erlbaum Associates, Inc., Hillsdale (1983)
26. Paxton, C., Hundt, A., Jonathan, F., Guerin, K., Hager, G.D.: CoSTAR: instructing collaborative robots with behavior trees and vision. In: 2017 IEEE International Conference on Robotics and Automation (ICRA), pp. 564–571. IEEE (2017)
27. Porfirio, D., Fisher, E., Sauppé, A., Albarghouthi, A., Mutlu, B.: Bodystorming human-robot interactions. In: Proceedings of the 32nd Annual ACM Symposium on User Interface Software and Technology, pp. 479–491 (2019)
28. Porfirio, D., Sauppé, A., Albarghouthi, A., Mutlu, B.: Authoring and verifying human-robot interactions. In: The 31st Annual ACM Symposium on User Interface Software and Technology, pp. 75–86. ACM (2018)
29. Quigley, M., et al.: ROS: an open-source robot operating system. In: ICRA Workshop on Open Source Software, Kobe, Japan, vol. 3, p. 5 (2009)
30. Ravichandar, H., Polydoros, A.S., Chernova, S., Billard, A.: Recent advances in robot learning from demonstration. Annu. Rev. Control Robot. Auton. Syst. **3**, 297–330 (2020)
31. Schaal, S., Ijspeert, A., Billard, A.: Computational approaches to motor learning by imitation. Philos. Trans. R. Soc. Lond. Ser. B: Biol. Sci. **358**(1431), 537–547 (2003)
32. Sefidgar, Y.S., Agarwal, P., Cakmak, M.: Situated tangible robot programming. In: Proceedings of the 2017 ACM/IEEE International Conference on Human-Robot Interaction, pp. 473–482. ACM (2017)
33. She, L., Cheng, Y., Chai, J.Y., Jia, Y., Yang, S., Xi, N.: Teaching robots new actions through natural language instructions. In: 2014 RO-MAN: The 23rd IEEE International Symposium on Robot and Human Interactive Communication, pp. 868–873. IEEE (2014)
34. She, L., Yang, S., Cheng, Y., Jia, Y., Chai, J., Xi, N.: Back to the blocks world: learning new actions through situated human-robot dialogue. In: Proceedings of the 15th Annual Meeting of the Special Interest Group on Discourse and Dialogue (SIGDIAL), pp. 89–97 (2014)
35. Steinfeld, A., et al.: Common metrics for human-robot interaction. In: Proceedings of the 1st ACM SIGCHI/SIGART Conference on Human-Robot Interaction, pp. 33–40 (2006)
36. Stenmark, M., Nugues, P.: Natural language programming of industrial robots. In: ISR, pp. 1–5. Citeseer (2013)
37. Sylvain, C.: Robot programming by demonstration: a probabilistic approach (2009)
38. Wang, Y., Ajaykumar, G., Huang, C.M.: See what i see: enabling user-centric robotic assistance using first-person demonstrations. In: Proceedings of the 15th International Conference on Human-Robot Interaction (HRI). ACM (2020)

39. Weintrop, D.: Block-based programming in computer science education. Commun. ACM **62**(8), 22–25 (2019). https://doi.org/10.1145/3341221
40. Yang, Y., Li, Y., Fermüller, C., Aloimonos, Y.: Robot learning manipulation action plans by "watching" unconstrained videos from the world wide web. In: AAAI, pp. 3686–3693 (2015)
41. Young, R.M.: The machine inside the machine: Users' models of pocket calculators. Int. J. Man-Mach. Stud. **15**(1), 51–85 (1981)
42. Yu, T., et al.: One-shot imitation from observing humans via domain-adaptive meta-learning. arXiv preprint arXiv:1802.01557 (2018)
43. Zhang, T., McCarthy, Z., Jow, O., Lee, D., Goldberg, K., Abbeel, P.: Deep imitation learning for complex manipulation tasks from virtual reality teleoperation. In: 2018 IEEE International Conference on on Robotics and Automation (ICRA) (2018)

AI Mobility Solutions for an Active Ageing Society. Introducing Aesthetic Affordances in the Design of Smart Wheelchairs

Setsu Ito[1(✉)], Shinobu Ito[1], and Irina Suteu[2]

[1] The University of Tokyo, Tokyo, Japan
setsuito@studioito.com
[2] Nuova Accademia di Belle Arti, Milan, Italy

Abstract. In the next paper we argue that user-centered product design can play an important role in the development of a new generation of smart wheelchairs that places an emphasis on the users' functional and aesthetical needs. We present the concept of "aesthetic affordance" [1] and propose interaction aesthetics and user scenarios as valid frameworks for designing AI mobility devices for elderly users. The term "affordance" in this specific case study is seen as bringing together the capability of a device to enable a specific action [2] and the possibility of that device to communicate a certain meaning [3]. We stress out how the smart wheelchairs, which successfully convey their actual mobility support function, can help the elderly people become more easily accepted as active citizens by the rest of the community. In this sense the aesthetics of the product have an equal importance to the innovative AI implementations. An initial review of the existent AI augmented wheelchairs revealed an overall lack of concern about the aesthetic functions of the mobility devices and more important the lack of consideration of how the person using it is perceived by the rest of the society.

To support this argument we present the different design and development phases of a new concept for the working prototype of a wheelchair created for a large Japanese company. Although the concept has received international acclaim from the design community, we suggest that the most important feature of the product, that of addressing the important ergonomic issue of aesthetic affordance, is still left implicit and needs further investigation.

Keywords: Elderly people · Smart wheelchairs · Artificial intelligence · Aesthetic affordances · User experience design

1 Introduction

One of the most significant trends of the 21st century is the increase in the ageing population and the impact of this change in all aspects of the daily life. According to a recent United Nations report, by 2050, one in six people in the world will be over age 65 (16%), up from one in 11 in 2019 (9%) [4] (UN, 2019). This demographic change is already affecting all sectors of society and has a strong impact in the way in which the role of the elderly people is perceived by their families and communities. Moreover,

© Springer Nature Switzerland AG 2020
H. Degen and L. Reinerman-Jones (Eds.): HCII 2020, LNCS 12217, pp. 339–352, 2020.
https://doi.org/10.1007/978-3-030-50334-5_23

starting from the extended presence in the labour market, to the active role elderly play in the family economy, the rising numbers of elderly people ask for important changes in the offer of healthcare support. These demographic shifts generated new policy tools such as "active ageing" which respond to the behavioural changes of the older generations. Concepts such as "successful aging, healthy ageing, productive ageing" [5] are gradually being assimilated in the shared vision of the contemporary societies.

At individual level, the changing elderly users' behaviour has triggered a new generation of technological solutions which addresses the contrast between the state of cognitive well being and the reduced mobility issues. The application of the artificial intelligences (AI) to mobility devices, and in particular to wheelchairs has been recognized as one of the most promising fields in the future of healthcare [6–9]. While many literatures have investigated the technological aspect of the application of the AI to wheelchairs, less attention has been placed to the human aspect of the interaction modalities between the users and the devices that they have to live with.

The paper is structured in 4 parts: **first part** we will present the hypothesis of the project and initial research on the user behaviour, **second part** will describe the ideation and development of a prototype developed from 2014 to 2015 by AISIN SEIKI Co., Ltd. Design Dept as a concept proposal model. In this part we will present the esthetical value of the mobility device as an important factor of social recognition and acceptance and explain how the concept of aesthetic affordance has been applied to the design of the prototype. In the **third part** we will discuss the results of the initial tests with the prototype, and propose several user scenarios for the future improvements of the smart wheelchair. We will explain how the user scenarios are based not only on the observations of the functional manipulation of the prototype, but most importantly on the perception and social acceptance of the individuals using the device by the other members of their community. In the fourth part we draw future directions in which the prototype can be developed, and explain how due to the fast pace of the advances in the development of the AI applications, the design of the smart mobility devices has to be seen as a "work in progress" process. Finally we draft future work in which the design of smart wheelchairs can integrate the aesthetic and emotional needs of the users and the most updated AI technologies.

2   Background. The Evolution of the "Silver Market Phenomenon" in Japan

The "silver market" or "mature market" phenomenon identifies the segment of elderly consumers that in the last decade have gained an increased importance in the economic landscape worldwide. Due to its large segment of elderly population, Japan is in this case the most important example of how demographics have shaped the consumer market. This phenomenon is due to the change in the financial autonomy of the elderly, their expenditure capability and their needs for products services and systems adapted to a longer life expectancy [10, 11]. At individual level, according to Usui, [12] some of main elements that trigger this behavioural change are the ability to economically support themselves as they grow old, and willing to pay more for long term care; this induces a change in the attitude towards spending money and emphasizes the importance given to the quality of services and products that will help them lead an independent life-style. In the same time, at community level the peer observation and the social acceptance by the same age groups pay an important factor in the self-esteem and wellbeing [quote]. More over, the evolution of the "silver market" is both an out breaking phenomenon and an important growth opportunity not only for the Japanese [13–15] but also for the European healthcare market [16, 17].

In this context the mobility systems presently available on the Japanese market are no longer satisfying the desires of elderly users who are reluctant to be identified as "old" and are striving for their active-ageing social status. The case study presented in this paper started from the observation of a group of users in the process of handling different mobility devices, their desire to fit into their own communities and their ability to adapt and transform daily objects into mobility supports, as a way to avoid the rigid functional aesthetics of a traditional wheelchair. These insights have helped AISIN, review their design strategy and team-up with the designers, authors of this paper, to generate a new smart mobility concept. The project was organized in 3 phases: **firstly** a benchmark research established the product target zone and the technical parameters for the future smart wheelchair, **secondly** the user behaviour research helped outline the user segments and **thirdly** a working prototype was developed. Two of the authors of the paper have been actively involved with their design studio[1] in all the steps of the process.

2.1   Overview of the Behavioural Trends in an Active Ageing Context

One of the main characteristics of the elderly citizens who are actively ageing and in good health is the discrepancy between the chronological age and the cognitive age [18]. This gap, as explained by Kohlbacher and Chéron [19], determines the difference between the actual birth age and the self perceived age and has been previously coined as "subjective age", or the age one individual sees her/himself as having. More importantly this has been recognized as an important insight in marketing research as a way to understand and frame the characteristics of the changes in the behavioural trends. To sustain this argument, a study done in one of the main commercial areas in Tokyo, revealed that silver shoppers feel 8 years younger than their actual age and tend to "avoid products associated with old-fashioned design or features that might make them appear old or reveal health problems (e.g. hearing aids)" [20].

In addition to the perceived age and efforts to present themselves as part of the active society, an important consumer trend of the silver users in Japan is their capability and curiosity to experiment with digital devices and robotics [21, 22]. Robots are an integrant part of the popular culture in Japan and the tendency to attach to robots an anthropomorphic meaning is a key in understanding the elderly users relation with AI robotics technologies [23]. Moreover, robots are intrinsically thought of and designed with AI capabilities and their social behaviour is a key motivation for elderly users to engage in interactive experiences [24].

---

[1] Studio Ito, Milan.

2.2 Benchmarking the Existent Smart Mobility Solutions in the Japanese Market

The afore-mentioned trends come in contrast with the present offer of wheelchairs and smart mobility solutions on the Japanese market. This contrast was individuated as an important business opportunity for AISIN, one of leading Japanese companies specialized in mobility solutions.

In order to structure the project brief the company engaged in a benchmark research, which helped frame an initial area in which the product will be inserted. As such starting from the 1st phase of benchmarking the company worked in close connection to the designers in order to establish a). the mobility limits and areas and b). the technological parameters of the future product.

The mobility factors have been then organized according to the *body features* – from active to passive elderly persons and the *movement distance* from home to neighbourhood and intercity transport (Fig. 1). The initial analysis of the mobility solutions has helped the team expand the target zone from traditional wheelchairs to electric wheelchairs, senior cars and electrical bikes. Including lightweight mobility devices such as electrical bicycles, which are not necessarily related to the healthcare mobility, played an important role in envisioning the structural features of the future device, and introduces the importance of the aesthetics affordances, which we will discuss later in the paper.

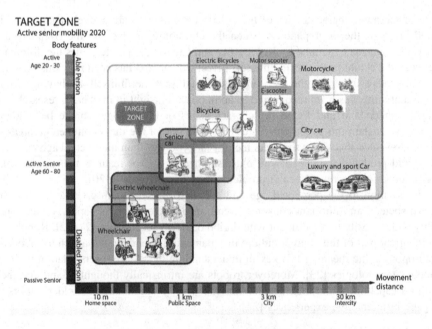

Fig. 1. Target zone – Body features/Movement distance

The second dimension which played an important role in the definition of the design requirements was the mapping of new and innovative mobility solutions with a futuristic look, linked in the consumers imagination with young, active and tech savvy users (Fig. 2). In this case the matrix expanded the first visualization and focused on two axes: light – heavy weight and active – passive citizens.

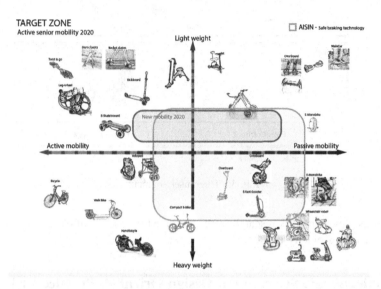

Fig. 2. Light/Heavy – Active/Passive

The area of intervention in Fig. 2 shows also the intersection between the new directions for the 2020 mobility trends and the area of products in which the AISIN braking technology will be applied. In this sense the new trends indicate the lightweight mobile solutions for active ageing and the shift from the medium to heavy weight mobility solutions for both active and reduced mobility users.

2.3   Identification of the Design Opportunities in 2 Ageing Phases: Pre-retirement, and Post-retirement

Having seen the initial mapping of the mobility, distance, and weight requirements the following step took into consideration a more detailed target user analysis. In this 2nd phase of the design process the designers and representatives of the company investigated the different products used by the silver market consumers in the pre-retirement age 50+ and post-retirement age 90+ phases. The three categories in which the products have been mapped are: "universal design" which includes products accessible to a wider market, "luxury and high quality design" which refers to the previously mentioned preferences for high quality products and services and "caregiver" which indicates users with reduced mobility and the need for assisted care (Fig. 3).

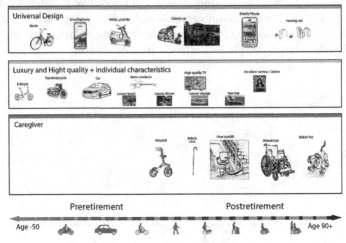

Fig. 3. Three user segments

The insights from desk research were completed by a series of observation sessions organized with 8 elderly users.

3 Methodology. Setting-up a Design Oriented, Practice Led Research

In order to address the needs of the individuated product zone, the research was therefore organized in a cycle of sessions of observation, reflection and design. Many literatures have recognized the practice based, approach as particularly relevant for the development of complex design systems. Schön [25] outlines the how "reflection on action" supports the practitioners/researchers expand their attention not only on the result of the project, but also on the creative process and the methods developed in action. In this concern as Nigel Cross suggests, design and reflection are too be seen as two intertwined, equally important processes [26, 27]; these processes, as Scrivener sustains, may bring "greater objectivity – or critical subjectivity – to the whole project" [28] and should be communicated as a intrinsic part of the project.

The initial benchmarking developed by AISIN in collaboration with the designers, pointed out to the following three main directions for the future product.

1. Organizing a series of participant observation sessions with elderly users in different environments.
2. Individuating the technological components that will shape the interactive functions of the future prototype.
3. Investigate the aesthetic features that will make the functions of the smart wheelchair more affordable for the active elders.

3.1 Participant Observation

In order to refine the initial research and benchmarking and generate the preliminary concept the designers involved in the project, organized a focus group with 8 senior citizens in two sessions: a 1 h observation session in which the participants were asked to use a "folding walker" mobility solution and second a 2 h session of un-structured interviews with the users. The group included 8 participants, and an equal no. of male and female between 69 and 84 years old. All participants were able to walk without wheelchairs. The conversations were centered on 3 main questions:

Q1: Do you find difficult walking?
R1: 6 on 8 participants indicated walking problems in particular due to and legs and back problems.
Q2: What kind of mobility aids you find more helpful?
R2: 3 participants – 2 m, 1f - use canes occasionally; 2 participants – 1 m 1f – use a wheeled shopping cart.
Q3: How should their future wheelchair look like?
R3: All participants focused on the way the wheelchair will make them be seen as "disabled" or no more capable of an active life and where concerned about their status in their local community.

3.2 Environment

Although the initial benchmarking pointed out to a target zone that included both indoors and outdoors usage, the observation sessions were placed outside. This was in part due to the Japanese cultural context in which the interior space in the family homes in the cities is particularly limited. During the session the participants were asked to walk with their own mobility devices and simulate different actions: sitting, standing up, leaning on it, pushing it, and in the case of collapsible devices folding it (Fig. 4).

Fig. 4. Participated observation of the user behaviour

3.3   Creating an Aesthetical Affordable Prototype

The observations and interviews with the elderly users have brought to attention several aspects that confirmed the initial hypothesis of the research and helped the designers and AISIN draft the most desired features of the future prototype. As such, the findings show two types of expectations from the part of the users:

- **1st** a series of aspects related to the **functionality** of the mobility device: the weight, height and comfort of the seating and backrest, the ease of interacting with the control buttons, speed and ease of maneuvering the chair.
- **2nd** several aspects related to the **form and meaning** of the mobility device: the quality and texture of the materials, the shape, color and communication of the wheelchair's function. Here it is important to mention the strong adversity of all the participants towards the "traditional" wheelchair look and their desire not to be seen as bounded to the mobility device. The social perception of their presence had to be in this sense *improved* by the display of the device and not *compromised* by it.

The challenge of the designers was therefore to convey the advanced smart system produced by the company in a product that can satisfy the above-mentioned desires of the target users.

For this reason the designers opted to introduce several materials used in the home furniture industry such as upholstered fabric, translucent polyurethane, and an internal RGB led system that lights-up when the chair is moving (Fig. 5).

In the mean time a keen attention was placed on the type of movement – controlled sliding instead of being wheeled by the user or by a caregiver, and the feedback – using light instead of sound.

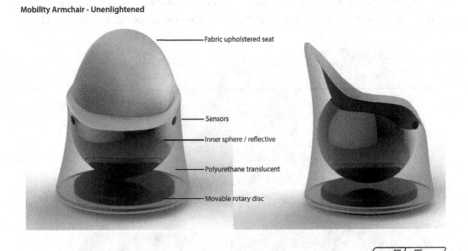

Fig. 5. Preliminary rendering of the concept

4   Discussion. Creating Aesthetically Affordable User Experiences

Considering the insights from the research in action process described above, in the following part we suggest that **aesthetic affordances** should be more thoroughly considered in the process of designing AI healthcare mobility systems. The concept of affordance has been widely recognized in the design and research as essential in the user-centered product design and defines the relational qualities of an object that make its functions intuitive and its use self explanatory [29]. Norman's research on affordances provided a useful tool for practitioner designers enabling them to link cognitive perception and actions [30–32]. More recent literatures have extended this framework to include new dimensions of the interactive and smart products affordances and outlined new methods to determine novel affordances [33].

This is due to the ubiquity of IT systems, the integration of digital and interfaces in the product design but also to the evolution and spread of game design applications, IOT systems and smart products. As Isbiter et al. emphasize the activity based design in games and outline to the term **social affordances** [34], furthermore, analyzing the user engagement and interaction with character user interfaces, Van Vugt advances the concept of **affective affordances** [35], and investigating the transfer of illustrated children's books into a digital app Schwebs makes reference to **aesthetic affordances** [36]. Setting up a wider theoretical framework for understanding the relation between affordances and aesthetics Xenakis and Arnellos explain how the term "aesthetics" is not limited to the formal aspect, they consider "aesthetic experience as a complex cognitive phenomenon that constitutes several processes that emerges through interaction" [1].

This perspective is also proposed by the authors of this paper as a viewfinder for the future development of the AI mobility systems in particular because intertwines relational, functional and formal aspects of the aesthetic experiences.

4.1   Drawing Usability Hints from the Tests with the Prototype

As mentioned in the previous part, the practice led research process has helped the interdisciplinary team of designers address both the users' practical and functional needs but most importantly their desire to be acknowledged as an active part of society. This was made possible by engaging into a two-folded investigation process in which the participated observation sessions were closely connected to the actual design sessions and development of the prototype. An essential factor in all the design cycle was the sensibility of the designers with concern to the emotional impact the aesthetics of the AI wheelchair, which made possible the anticipation of the elderly users desires. This aspect was perceived as a valuable input by the company and translated in the workflow of the team. In this sense rather then shaping the brief around the innovative technology solutions, the company decided to emphasize the usability aspects and the aesthetics of the product. This gave to the designers and authors of this paper the possibility to bring together three main concepts: affordances, aesthetics and emotional user experience in an aesthetically affordable AI wheelchair (Fig. 6).

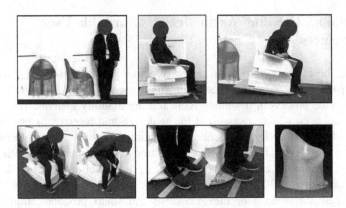

Fig. 6. Lab tests with the work in progress prototype

4.2   Understanding the Value of Aesthetic Affordances

One of the most important insights gathered from the literature search, the bench-marking of the existent products and the conversations with the users was their fear of being seen as incapable of moving and be judged not on their potential and vivacity but on the meaning conveyed by the use of the traditional wheelchair. In this concern the designers made an effort to change the metaphor attached to the product by introducing the characteristics of the *armchair* rather then a *wheelchair* (Fig. 7):

Ergonomic, functional features

- Height of the seat – was augmented with respect to the seat of the wheelchair.
- Possibility to lean with the armchair – was introduced in order to balance the augmented seat height.
- Height of the backrest – augmented in order to better support the posture of the user.
- Armrest – modeled to better support the forearms.

Sensors, controller, battery

- All the electronic components were imbedded in the body of the armchair.
- The control button is kept minimal, as a pad at the same level with the surface of the armrest, and follows the intuitive movement of the chair – left/right, forward/backward (i.e. putting more pressure on the left side of the control pad will make the chair move to the left).
- The armchair moves on a wheeled platform hidden underneath its structure, the user doesn't have to spin the wheels and the movement of the armchair is not obvious.

Aesthetic features

- The armchair has a futuristic, sculptural look emphasized by the white color chosen.
- The simplicity of the form is balanced by the inner RGB led system that lights-up when the chair is moving.
- The materials used to fabricate the armchair are usually used for indoor furniture and not in the healthcare.

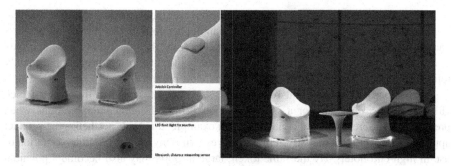

Fig. 7. Working prototype

All the above mentioned elements allow an increased aesthetic affordance of the product which communicates a meaning different from that of an mobility assistance device and gives the elderly a different identity. More importantly the futuristic, compact look of the product offers a sense of control and attractiveness that has the potential to reinforce the position of the elderly users in the community[2].

4.3   Drafting User Scenarios for Aesthetically Affordable AI Products

In the previous parts it was shown how the collaboration between the designers, AISIN and the insights from the user behaviour research have shaped an innovative smart mobility system that put forward the desires of social acceptance of the elderly users. While the argument of the paper focused on a unique product developed for a specific market we suggest that user scenarios for aesthetically affordable smart products are particularly useful for envisioning future developments of the product. Moreover given the complexity of the AI mobility systems the scenarios may support focusing on the specific tasks and the quality of interaction the users want to have with the smart mobility systems. In this concern we suggest that the starting elements in drafting future scenarios should anticipate the possibility of having a group of smart mobility systems users and include also the condition in which the user identifies with his/her smart mobility system.

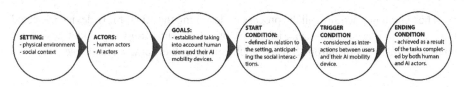

Fig. 8. User scenario framework to support the design of aesthetic affordances for AI mobility systems.

---

[2] The design won several international awards, among them Good Design Award 2015.

The user scenario framework presented above attempts to indicate the different steps in which the aesthetic affordances have an impact on both the identity of the users and their perceived state of well being especially from the community in which they live. Aesthetic affordances are not solely related to the form of the product but mainly refer to the integration of the 3 featured mentioned previously.

This is particularly relevant for the case study we presented in this paper which although it was designed for a specific market gained different interpretations when presented in different cultural contexts. As an example, due to its aesthetics the product appealed to hospitality industry representatives, who envisioned possible scenarios of use in high-end hotels. By the same token, large airports may also become a potential environment where the smart mobility devices can be successfully implemented.

5   Conclusion

In conclusion, the product development of a new concept for an AI mobility system for the Japanese market opened new considerations regarding the application of the aesthetic affordances concept to the quality of human machine interaction. The investigation of the Japanese "silver market" pointed out the emotional connection that the active elderly users have with their mobility systems, and the importance of the mobility aids in defining their identity. The success of the product developed was brought by several factors. Firstly by the close collaboration between AISIN and the designers, as well as the dedication of the group to investigate the potential of an aesthetically meaningful product; secondly by the close attention of the designers to the emotional bond of the elderly with their mobility devices and their fears on how starting using a mobility device may affect their place in their community. This led the authors to establish a reflection in action process of investigation that generated a two-folded outcome:

- A successful *product* – a functional prototype which shifted the stereotyped meaning attached to the AI wheelchairs, gave an enhanced quality to the interaction modalities offered by the smart mobility device and took into consideration the social perception of the elderly using the device.
- An innovative *process* – a creative collaboration focused primarily on the interaction aesthetics rather then emphasizing the advanced technology and functional performance of the smart product.

The experience acquired in the process of designing the AI mobility device indicated the need of drafting a user scenario framework (Fig. 8) to support product designer's innovative methods of introducing AI applications in their practice and research.

References

1. Xenakis, I., Argyris, A.: The relation between interaction aesthetics and affordances. Des. Stud. **34**(1), 57–73 (2013)
2. Norman, D.: The Design of Everyday Things: Revised and Expanded Edition. Basic books, New York (2013)

3. Overbeeke, K., Wensveen, S.: From perception to experience, from affordances to irresistibles. In: Proceedings of the 2003 international conference on Designing pleasurable products and interfaces. (2003)
4. http://www.oecd.org/economy/japan-economic-snapshot/. Accessed 30 Jan 2019
5. Lassen, A.J., Moreira, T.: Unmaking old age: political and cognitive formats of active ageing. J. Aging Stud. **30**, 33–46 (2014)
6. Matía, F., Sanz, R., Puente, E.A.: Increasing intelligence in autonomous wheelchairs. J. Intell. Rob. Syst. **22**(3–4), 211–232 (1998)
7. Lankenau, A., Rofer, T.: A versatile and safe mobility assistant. IEEE Robot. Autom. Mag. **8** (1), 29–37 (2001)
8. Pineau, J.: Designing intelligent wheelchairs: reintegrating AI. In: 2013 AAAI Spring Symposium Series (2013)
9. Leaman, J., La, H.M.: A comprehensive review of smart wheelchairs: past, present, and future. IEEE Trans. Hum.-Mach. Syst. **47**(4), 486–499 (2017)
10. Kohlbacher, F., Herstatt, C. (eds.): The Silver Market Phenomenon: Marketing and Innovation in the Aging Society. Springer Science & Business Media, Berlin (2010). https://doi.org/10.1007/978-3-642-14338-0
11. Wellner, K.: The Silver Market Phenomenon. User Innovators in the Silver Market, pp. 9–25. Springer Gabler, Wiesbaden (2015). https://doi.org/10.1007/978-3-658-09044-9
12. Usui, C.: Ageing society and the transformation of work in the post-fordist economy. In: The Demographic Challenge: A Handbook about Japan. Brill, pp. 163–178 (2008)
13. Kohlbacher, F., Gudorf, P., Herstatt, C.: Japan's growing silver market – an attractive business opportunity for foreign companies? In: Boppel, M., Boehm, S., Kunisch, S. (eds) From Grey to Silver, pp. 189–205. Springer, Heidelberg (2011). https://doi.org/10.1007/978-3-642-15594-9_17
14. Storz, C., Pascha, W.: 10. Japan's silver market: creating a new industry under uncertainty. In: Institutional variety in East Asia: Formal and informal patterns of coordination, p. 222 (2011)
15. Mertens, P., Russell, S., Steinke, I.: Silver markets and business customers: opportunities for industrial markets? In: Kohlbacher, F., Herstatt, C. (eds) The Silver Market Phenomenon, pp. 353–3370. Springer, Heidelberg (2008). https://doi.org/10.1007/978-3-540-75331-5_24
16. Gassmann, O., Keupp, M.M.: The Silver Market in Europe: Myth or Reality? Information and Communication Technologies for Active Aging—Opportunities and Challenges for the European Union. IOS Press, Amsterdam (2009)
17. Klimczuk, A.: Comparative analysis of national and regional models of the silver economy in the European Union. Models of the Silver Economy in the European Union. Int. J. Ageing Later Life **10**(2), 31–59 (2016)
18. Ibid 10, p. 244
19. Kohlbacher, F., Chéron, E.: Understanding "silver" consumers through cognitive age, health condition, financial status, and personal values: empirical evidence from the world's most mature market Japan. J. Consum. Behav. **11**(3), 179–188 (2012)
20. Ibid 19, p.186
21. Obi, T., Ishmatova, D., Iwasaki, N.: Promoting ICT innovations for the ageing population in Japan. Int. J. Med. Inform. **82**(4), 47–62 (2013)
22. Goeldner, M., Herstatt, C., Tietze, F.: The emergence of care robotics—a patent and publication analysis. Technol. Forecast. Soc. Change **92**, 115–131 (2015)
23. Usui, C.: Japan's population aging and silver industries. In: Kohlbacher, F., Herstatt, C. (eds.) The Silver Market Phenomenon, pp. 325–337. Springer, Heidelberg (2011). https://doi.org/10.1007/978-3-642-14338-0_24

24. Shiomi, M., et al.: Effectiveness of social behaviors for autonomous wheelchair robot to support elderly people in Japan. PLoS ONE **10**(5), e0128031 (2015)

25. Schön, D.A.: The Reflective Practitioner: How Professionals Think in Action. Routledge, Abingdon (2017)

26. Cross, N.: Design research: a disciplined conversation. Des. Issues **15**(2), 5–10 (1999)

27. Mäkelä, M.: Knowing through making: the role of the artefact in practice-led research. Knowl. Technol. Policy **20**(3), 157–163 (2007)

28. Scrivener, S.: Towards the operationalisation of design research as reflection in and on action and practice. In: Foundations for the future. Doctoral education in design: Proceedings of the Conference, La Clusaz, France (2000)

29. Gibson, J.: The concept of affordances. Perceiving Acting Knowing **1** (1977)

30. Norman, D.: Affordances and design (2004). http://www.jnd.org/dn.mss/affordances-and-design.html

31. Kaptelinin, V., Nardi, B.: Affordances in HCI: toward a mediated action perspective. In: Proceedings of the SIGCHI Conference on Human Factors in Computing Systems (2012)

32. Gaver, W.W.: Technology affordances. In: Proceedings of the SIGCHI conference on Human factors in computing systems (1991)

33. Shu, L.H., et al.: Three methods for identifying novel affordances. AI EDAM **29**(3), 267–279 (2015)

34. Isbister, K., Márquez Segura, E., Melcer, E.F.: Social affordances at play. Game design toward socio-technical innovation. Proceedings of the 2018 CHI Conference on Human Factors in Computing Systems (2018)

35. Van Vugt, H.C., et al.: Affective affordances: improving interface character engagement through interaction. Int. J. Hum Comput Stud. **64**(9), 874–888 (2006)

36. Schwebs, T.: Affordances of an app: a reading of the fantastic flying books of Mr. Morris Lessmore. Barnelitterært forskningstidsskrift **5**(1), 24169 (2014)

Prediction-Based Uncertainty Estimation for Adaptive Crowd Navigation

Kapil D. Katyal[1,2(✉)], Katie Popek[1], Gregory D. Hager[2], I-Jeng Wang[1,2], and Chien-Ming Huang[2]

[1] Johns Hopkins University Applied Physics Lab, Laurel, MD 20723, USA
Kapil.Katyal@jhuapl.edu
[2] Johns Hopkins University, Baltimore, MD 21218, USA

Abstract. Fast, collision-free motion through human environments remains a challenging problem for robotic systems. In these situations, the robot's ability to reason about its future motion and other agents is often severely limited. By contrast, biological systems routinely make decisions by taking into consideration what might exist in the future based on prior experience. In this paper, we present an approach that provides robotic systems the ability to make future predictions of the environment. We evaluate several deep network architectures, including purely generative and adversarial models for map prediction. We further extend this approach to predict future pedestrian motion. We show that prediction plays a key role in enabling an adaptive, risk-sensitive control policy. Our algorithms are able to generate future maps with a structural similarity index metric up to 0.899 compared to the ground truth map. Further, our adaptive crowd navigation algorithm is able to reduce the number of collisions by 43% in the presence of novel pedestrian motion not seen during training.

Keywords: Human robot interaction · Adaptive crowd navigation · Reinforcement learning · Prediction

1 Introduction

Humans and robots that co-exist in unstructured environments play a key role in bringing robotic assistance to the mainstream. We have seen unprecedented improvements in the field of autonomous mobile robot navigation in the presence of static and dynamic obstacles in the scene. This research has paved the way for industries, such as autonomous driving to move from proof-of-concept to field-able systems. While the progress has been significant, several challenges remain that provide unique opportunities to increase the reliability, safety and performance of autonomous mobile platforms to human level performance.

Here, we describe an approach centered around making predictions of the environment as a critical element for mobile robot navigation in highly dynamic and cluttered spaces. Our underlying assumption is that predictions of spatial

H. Degen and L. Reinerman-Jones (Eds.): HCII 2020, LNCS 12217, pp. 353–368, 2020.
https://doi.org/10.1007/978-3-030-50334-5_24

structures and other agents in the scene play a vital role for humans to successfully navigate in similarly highly dynamic and dense environments. Specifically, we believe prediction allows humans to plan trajectories that extend beyond their visual line-of-sight as well as anticipate the movement other humans in the environment. This suggests errors in prediction can capture 'surprise' events that enable humans to alter the risk of their own internal navigation policy.

Here, we summarize and extend the works presented in [1,2] by providing mobile agents with a version of predictive capabilities. We develop techniques that use generative neural networks that leverage spatial structures as a prior for making map predictions that extend beyond the robot's line-of-sight. We extend this to include map prediction with multiple hypotheses and an information-theoretic robot exploration algorithm. Finally, we extend prediction to include pedestrian motion and develop a risk sensitive control algorithm for navigating around humans. Our objective is to show prediction is a key enabler that leads to more efficient and robust mobile navigation policies.

The remainder of this paper is organized as follows. In Sect. 2, we provide a brief overview of existing work in prediction and robot navigation in human crowds. In Sect. 3, we compare and contrast several approaches to occupancy map prediction. In Sect. 4, we extend approaches to occupancy map prediction to include generation of multiple hypotheses for efficient robot exploration. In Sect. 5, we extend prediction to include pedestrians for adaptive crowd navigation.

2   Related Work

2.1   Deep Learning for Generative Models

Deep neural networks have been used in a number of promising ways to achieve high performance in domains such as vision, speech and more recently in robotics manipulation [3,4]. Oh et. al. used feedforward and recurrent neural networks to perform action-conditional video prediction using Atari games with promising results [5]. These have also been used in image completion, e.g., by Ulyanov et al. [6]. In addition, GANs have demonstrated a promising method for image generation [7]. Isola et al. proposed an approach for training conditional GANs which create one image from another image [8].

2.2   Deep Learning for Navigation

More recently, several papers have described approaches to combine elements of deep neural networks with autonomous navigation. These include using deep neural networks for model predictive control [3]. Tamar et al. proposed Value Iteration Networks, which embed a planner inside a deep neural net architecture [9]. Several papers investigate the use of deep reinforcement learning to develop collision-free planning without the need of an internal map, however, these are still restricted by the sensor's FOV [10,11].

2.3   Crowd Navigation

Crowd navigation has been studied extensively in recent literature (e.g., [12]) and can be classified into three general areas: (1) algorithms that react to moving obstacles in real time, (2) trajectory based approaches that plan paths by anticipating future motion of obstacles, and (3) reinforcement learning based approaches that learn a policy to navigate in crowded environments. Reaction based methods include works such as reciprocal velocity obstacles (RVO) [13] and optimal reciprocal collision avoidance (ORCA) [14]. Trajectory based approaches, such as [15,16], explicitly propagate estimates of future motion over time and perform trajectory optimization on those future states for collision avoidance. Additionally, several recent works use variations of reinforcement learning to learn policies capable of crowd navigation (e.g., [17–19]). Everett et al. [18] developed a decentralized approach to multiagent collision avoidance using a value network that estimates the time to goal for a given state transition. Chen et al. [19] further extended this work by adding an attention mechanism and a novel pooling method to handle a variable number of humans in the scene. Kahn et al. [20] investigates adaptive navigation polices based on uncertainty; however, they only considered environment uncertainty with static obstacles and not navigation in the presence of pedestrians.

3   Occupancy Map Prediction

A major limitation of existing robot navigation algorithms is the limited field-of-view of traditional sensors. This is in contrast with biological systems that routinely make predictions of their environment. For example, imagine walking through a hallway or corridor. Often, we can predict spaces around a corner because we have seen similar hallways and corridors in the past. This prediction allows us to generate trajectories that extend beyond our line-of-sight. In this section, we describe an approach that allows robot systems to generate predicted occupancy maps that extend beyond the sensor's line-of-sight. We evaluate several neural network architectures, loss functions and datasets to determine what approaches generate most accurate predicted occupancy maps. Formally, we are attempting to learn a function that maps an input occupancy map to an expanded occupancy map that extends beyond the FOV of the sensor.

$$f : x \rightarrow y_i$$

where x represents the state, in this case, the input occupancy map as an image, y_i represents the output occupancy map and $i \in \mathbb{R}$ represents percent increase of the expanded occupancy map. Components of the function f include an encoding function $f_{enc}(x) \rightarrow h \in \mathcal{H}$ which maps the state space, input occupancy maps to a hidden state and $f_{dec}(h) \rightarrow (y_i)$, which is a decoding function mapping the hidden state to an expanded, predicted occupancy map.

In our experiments, we compare several different neural network architectures including:

(A) a feedforward network based on a U-Net architecture (**unet_ff**)
(B) a feedforward network based on the ResNet architecture (**resnet_ff**)
(C) a GAN using the feedforward network from (a) as the generative network (**gan**)

3.1 U-Net Feedforward Model

The U-Net feedforward model is based on the network architecture defined by Ronneberger et al. [21] and consists of skip connections which allows a direct connection between layers i and $n - i$ enabling the option to bypass the bottleneck associated with the downsampling layers in order to perform an identity operation. Similar to [8], the encoder network consists of 8 convolution, batch normalization and ReLU layers where each convolution consists of a 4×4 filter and stride length of 2. The number of filters for the 8 layers in the encoder network are: (64, 128, 256, 512, 512, 512, 512, 512). The decoder network consists of 8 upsampling layers with the following number of filters: (512, 1024, 1024, 1024, 1024, 512, 256, 128).

3.2 ResNet Feedforward Model

The ResNet feedforward model is based on the work by Johnson et al. [22] which consists of 2 convolution layers with stride 2, 9 residual blocks as defined by [23] and two deconvolution layers with with a stride of $\frac{1}{2}$. A key reason this network was selected was based on the ability to learn identify functions, which is key to image translation as well as the success in image-to-image translation demonstrated by the CycleGAN network [24].

3.3 GAN Model

The GAN networks is based on the pix2pix architecture [8] which has demonstrated impressive results in general purpose image translation including generating street scenes, building facades and aerial images to maps. This network uses the U-Net Feedforward model defined in Sect. 3.1 and consists of a 6 layer discriminator network with filter sizes: (64, 128, 256, 512, 512, 512).

3.4 Occupancy Map Prediction Experiment and Results

Our approach to testing occupancy map prediction using the networks defined above first involved generating a dataset and then performing qualitative and quantitative analysis of the predicted images compared to the ground truth.

A dataset of approximately 6000 images of occupancy map subsets was created by simulating a non-holonomic robot moving through a two-dimensional map with a planar LIDAR sensor in C++ with ROS and the OctoMap library [25]. Two maps were created in Solidworks with the path width varying between

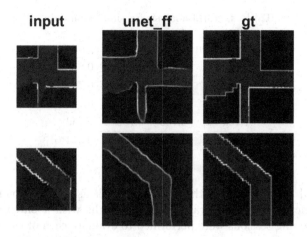

Fig. 1. This figure shows qualitative sample map predictions using the unet architecture compared to the ground truth map.

3.5 m to 10 m. These were converted into OctoMap's binary tree format using binvox [26,27] followed by OctoMap's binvox2bt tool. The result is an occupancy map with all unoccupied space set as free. We require space outside of the walls to be marked as unknown to provide a ground truth for our estimated maps. These ground truth maps were created by fully exploring the original occupancy maps (Fig. 1).

The robot is modeled as a Dubin's car, with a state vector $\mathbf{x} = [x, y, \theta]$ and inputs $\mathbf{u} = [v, \dot{\theta}]$ where (x, y) is the robot's position, v is the velocity, and θ and $\dot{\theta}$ are the heading angle and angular velocity, respectively. For simplicity, the robot is constrained to move at fixed forward velocity of 0.5 m/s. A planar LIDAR sensor with a scanning area of 270° and range of 20 m is used to simulate returns given the robot's current pose against the ground truth map. These simulated returns are used to create the "estimated" occupancy map. Path planning is done with nonlinear model-predictive control and direct transcription at 10 Hz. At each time step, a subset of the maps (both the estimated and ground truth) are saved. A 5 m by 5 m square centered around the robot's pose was chosen with a resolution of 0.05 m. At each time step, the robot's current state and action space are also logged. Occupancy maps are expanded over time, so our simulation performs a continuous trajectory and the data set is built consecutively instead of randomly sampling throughout a map. A total of six trajectories were simulated. Four paths were used for training data (5221 images) and two were used as a test set (1090 images). Ground truth datasets of the expanded occupancy maps were also generated. These expanded occupancy maps range from 1.10x to 2.00x expansion in increments of 0.10x, e.g., a 2.00x expansion results in a 10 m by 10 m square subset centered around the robot.

Table 1. SSIM analysis for simulation data

Expansion	unet_ff	resnet_ff	gan
1.10x	0.899	0.861	0.818
1.30x	0.818	0.780	0.790
1.50x	0.770	0.773	0.759
1.70x	0.760	0.752	0.736
2.00x	0.767	0.770	0.574

We trained each variant of the neural network using the expanded ground truth occupancy maps from scratch for 200 epochs with a batch size of 1. A total of 15 training sessions were performed to evaluate each of the three neural network architectures across five expansion increases (1.10x, 1.30x, 1.50x, 1.70x, and 2.00x). We use the Adam optimizer with an initial learning rate of 0.0002 and momentum parameters $\beta_1 = 0.5, \beta_2 = 0.999$. In the feedforward models, L1 loss was used as proposed in PatchGan [8] and in the GAN model L1+discriminator loss was used. The decoder layers of the network used a dropout rate of 0.50 and weights were initialized from a Normal distribution ($\mu = 0, \sigma = 0.2$). All models were implemented using PyTorch [28].

Table 1 provides the structural similarity index metric (SSIM) for each of the networks. Based on the SSIM metric, it can be seen that the U-Net feedforward model outperforms the other networks at 1.10x and 1.30x expansion confirming the qualitative assessment. The quality of the prediction generally decreases as the expansion percentage increases and with expansions 1.50x and above the three networks achieve similar performance. This leads us to believe skip connections across layers of an autoencoder network play a critical role in generating accurate predictions of future maps.

4   Uncertainty-Aware Occupancy Map Prediction

In the previous section, we explored properties of neural network architectures, loss functions and datasets used to validate the approach of occupancy map prediction. We now extend our neural network architectures to include generation of multiple hypotheses to measure the uncertainty of the predictions [2]. To capture this uncertainty, we modify the single hypothesis network to output multiple hypotheses predictions. We do this by branching N heads with each head capable of making its own prediction. The loss function is inspired by [29] to become a weighted sum, $1 - \epsilon$, of the best performing head loss and the weighted sum, $\epsilon/(N - 1)$, of the losses of the other heads. In our experiments, we set $\epsilon = 0.05$.

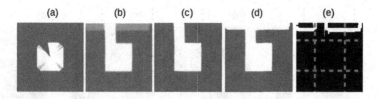

Fig. 2. (a) Input occupancy map based on lidar's FOV, (b) Prediction using single hypothesis resulting in blurred image, (c) and (d) 2 hypotheses generated using multiple hypotheses prediction, (e) Image representing variance between the multiple hypotheses

We show that measuring the uncertainty allows us to develop an information-theoretic exploration policy that drives the robot towards regions of high uncertainty. We modify the unet_ff architecture described in Sect. 3 to generate multiple hypotheses. By forming multiple hypotheses, we can compute the differences across the images to estimate regions of highest uncertainty. We first evaluate the benefits of making multiple predictions compared to single predictions using real world data sets provided by Google Cartographer [30] as described in Fig. 2. Here, even the average structural similarity index and peak signal to noise ratios improved when generating multiple predictions (Table 2).

Table 2. Quantitative analysis with multiple hypotheses prediction

Method	SSIM	PSNR	Speed (ms)
Our Method - Single Hypothesis	0.903	16.907	4.3
MHP-4 (avg)	0.911	17.204	16.1
MHP-8 (avg)	0.912	17.157	32.3
MHP-4 (best)	0.919	18.022	16.1
MHP-8 (best)	0.921	18.252	32.3

We next evaluate our information-theoretic exploration policy. We use the Gazebo simulation environment where the goal of the robot is to efficiently explore the environment to generate a map. Our approach is to drive the robot towards regions with highest uncertainty and compare to existing map exploration algorithms. As an example, in Fig. 2 (a), we show the input to our map prediction algorithm. In (b), we show that by only making a single prediction when multiple futures could exist results in a blurry image. In (c) and (d), we show that making multiple predictions allows our algorithm to represent the possible futures as distinct hypotheses. In (e), we show the difference in the hypotheses representing regions of high uncertainty.

We then cluster the image representing regions of high uncertainty and compute the region with highest variance across the hypotheses. We select this region as the next area to explore and compare with several alternative methods of robot

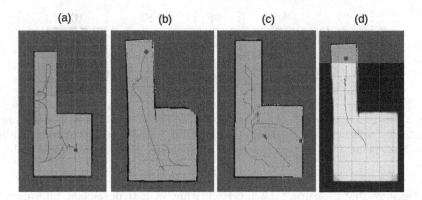

Fig. 3. Trajectory of robot during exploration using (a) Frontier Exploration [31], (b) Information-Theoretic Bayesian Optimization [32,33], (c) Frontier Exploration using Distance [34], (d) Our Method

Table 3. Total path length

Method	Path length
Frontier exploration [31]	28.17 m
Information-theoretic Bayesian optimization [32,33]	17.30 m
Frontier exploration using distance [34]	35.26 m
Our method	**10.05 m**

exploration. As seen in Fig. 3, and further summarized in Table 3, we show a significant reduction in overall path length needed to explore the space compared to the alternative approaches. This shows uncertainty-aware prediction of occupied space can play a critical role in efficient exploration of unknown spaces.

5   Adaptive Crowd Navigation

In this section, we extend our uncertainty-aware occupancy map prediction to include prediction of humans in the environment. Our underlying assumption is that enabling prediction of pedestrians can play a critical role in adaptive crowd navigation policies that will ultimately lead to fewer collisions. As illustrated in Fig. 4, our goal is to show errors in pedestrian prediction can serve as a measure of 'surprise' (i.e. policy uncertainty) to help detect novel pedestrian motion not seen during training. By detecting novel pedestrian motion, we can alter the risk of the robot's control policy thereby reducing the probability of collision.

5.1   Pedestrian Prediction

Our pedestrian prediction algorithm is summarized in Fig. 5. This architecture consists of a generator and a discriminator network. The generator network

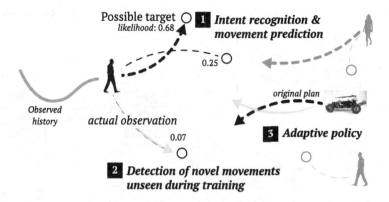

Fig. 4. Adaptive crowd navigation policy that uses pedestrian intent and prediction error to adjust the risk profile of a control policy.

includes a recurrent encoder network, a variational autoencoder, a recurrent decoder network, and an intent predictor. The discriminator network classifies samples representing either real or fake trajectories from the generator. Our main contribution lies in combining a probabilistic interpretation of the desired goal with embeddings learned from past trajectories. This approach allows us to make predictions of future pedestrian trajectories that meet or exceed state-of-the-art algorithms. The details of our pedestrian prediction approach are further presented in [1].

5.2 Crowd Navigation

For our adaptive crowd navigation algorithm, we leverage the CrowdSim simulation environment provided by [19]. CrowdSim supports a flexible interface that enables learning robot policies through simulated pedestrian motion. The pedestrian controller supports using an optimal reciprocal collision avoidance (ORCA) model to simulate pedestrian motion [14]. This model consists of parameters such as preferred velocity, the maximum distance and time to take into account neighboring agent behavior, pedestrian's radius, and maximum velocity. In addition, CrowdSim provides an OpenAI Gym like environment [35] to experiment with reinforcement learning based policies controlling a robot's actions to reach a target goal while avoiding obstacles.

We use a similar state space as described by [19,36] which consists of the following parameters with respect to the robot position as the origin and the x-axis pointing towards the goal: distance from robot position to goal, robot's preferred velocity, actual velocity and radius. For each pedestrian, the state includes position, velocity, radius, and distance between pedestrian and robot.

The action space consists of 3 discrete speeds and 6 discrete rotation angles for a total of 18 actions. The reward function encourages the robot to successfully reach the target while avoiding collisions with other pedestrians, and is defined similar to [18,19] as:

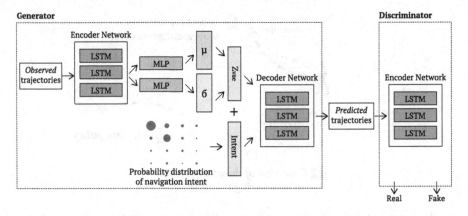

Fig. 5. Our pedestrian prediction network architecture. The generator network consists of a recurrent encoder network, a variational autoencoder, an intent prediction module and recurrent decoder network. The discriminator network consists of a recurrent encoder network to distinguish between real and fake trajectories.

$$
R(\mathbf{s}, \mathbf{a}) = \begin{cases} -0.25 & \text{if} \quad d_{min} < 0 \\ -0.1 - d_{min}/2 & \text{else if} \quad d_{min} < 0.2 \\ 1 & \text{else if} \quad \text{robot reached goal} \\ 0 & \text{o.w.} \end{cases}
$$

where d_{min} is the minimum distance separating the robot and the humans during the previous timestep.

To implement our adaptive crowd navigation policy, we train a risk averse and an aggressive policy. The aggressive policy consists of a preferred velocity of 2.0 m/s, and the risk averse policy is limited to 1.0 m/s. Our first set of experiments focuses on the performance of CADRL [36] and SARL [19] algorithms with pedestrian motion that is in-distribution of the training data and then outside of the distribution. We trained both algorithms with preferred robot velocities set to 2.0 m/s with a static pedestrian motion model. The starting and ending positions of the pedestrians were sampled uniformly inside a square of width 10 m. We followed this experiment with a series of tests where the adaptive control policy uses various methods of novelty detection of new pedestrian behaviors.

Our first evaluation compares SARL and CADRL with a one-class SVM with a radial basis kernel [37]. We train the one-class SVM algorithm based on the fixed pedestrian motion profile and evaluate its ability to detect novel distributions of pedestrian motion data. Our subsequent tests use deep learning based approaches for novelty detection including Social GAN [38] and our intent-aware pedestrian prediction algorithm. We trained both deep learning algorithms with the same fixed pedestrian motion profile that was used when training the original RL policies. We then tested pedestrian prediction with a changing distribution of pedestrian motion while allowing the robot to navigate towards the goal as described in Table 4. We compute an estimate of novelty by thresholding the prediction error, as measured using the final displacement error (FDE), by a value α. If the error exceeds α, the policy moves from an aggressive behavior to a risk averse policy with the goal of avoiding collisions. The value of α was chosen by computing the mean and standard deviation of the FDE in the training set. In our experiments, α was set to 3 standard deviations from the mean of the training set to eliminate outliers.

Table 4. ORCA model parameters

Parameters name	Min value	Max value
Preferred velocity	0.5	2.0
Radius	0.2	0.8
Neighbor distance	2.0	20.0
Time horizon	0.1	5.0

Our metrics to compare the relative performance of each algorithm consists of the number of successful trials, number of collisions, the average navigation time, the discomfort level, and the average reward. The discomfort level is defined as the frequency of the separating distance being less than the desired separation distance, in this case 0.2 m. The results after running 500 test cases are reported in Table 5. We use the notation $method - p$ where $method$ describes the method used (i.e. SVM, SARL, etc.) and p is the number of pedestrians in the scene.

The first two rows of Table 5 evaluate CADRL and SARL algorithms using pedestrian motion that is in-distribution of the training data. These algorithms generally performed well with SARL resulting in less collisions. Rows 3 and 4 then show the results of CADRL and SARL in the presence of out-of-distribution, novel pedestrian motion in which both algorithms have a significantly higher number of collision and discomfort rates. The one-class SVM algorithm to detect novel pedestrian motion was only able to show a modest improvement in reducing the number of collisions by 2 compared to the SARL algorithm.

The subsequent rows of Table 5 compare deep neural network approaches to detect novel pedestrian motion. Specifically, we compare our intent aware approach with that of Social GAN. Using Social GAN improved the one-class SVM by further reducing the number of collisions by 20. Our intent-aware pedestrian prediction algorithm provided the best performance across almost all of the metrics. We were able to further reduce the number of collisions by 5 compared to Social GAN and overall by 30 compared to the non-adaptive SARL policy. In addition to reducing the number of collisions, we also reduce overall discomfort rate and increase overall reward. Further, we show that these benefits scale as the number of pedestrians in the scene extend from 5 to 20.

Table 5. Quantitative analysis of collision avoidance

Method	Dist. shift	Succ.	Coll.	Nav. time	Disc. rate	Avg. rwd.
CADRL-5	N	455	45	4.48	2.02	0.349
SARL-5	N	490	5	4.61	0.99	0.389
CADRL-5	Y	420	80	**4.52**	3.53	0.296
SARL-5	Y	425	70	4.62	2.27	0.303
SVM-Adapt.-5	Y	426	68	5.34	2.14	0.331
SGAN-Adapt.-5	Y	445	45	6.31	2.03	0.386
Ours-Adapt-5	Y	**450**	**40**	6.74	**1.98**	**0.409**
SARL-10	Y	388	99	**5.21**	2.62	0.234
Ours-Adapt.-10	Y	**444**	**54**	8.49	**2.18**	**0.330**
SARL-15	Y	290	205	**5.30**	4.89	0.115
Ours-Adapt.-15	Y	**366**	**132**	8.69	**4.20**	**0.212**
SARL-20	Y	172	324	**5.27**	6.70	-0.017
Ours-Adapt.-20	Y	**262**	**237**	8.65	**6.29**	**0.066**

6 Hardware Prototype

We further assess the real world applicability of our algorithms by evaluating in a proof-of-concept physical test environment (Fig. 6). Our physical test bed consists of the MIT Rapid Autonomous Complex-Environment Competing Ackermann-steering Robot (RACECAR) navigating through several pedestrians. This platform consists of a Hokuyo UST-10LX LiDAR, Sparkfun IMU, the Traxxas 1/10-scale chassis and an onboard NVidia Jetson processor with GPU.

We use a leg detector algorithm based on an SVM classifier to detect pedestrians with respect to the camera frame and a custom SLAM library to generate maps and estimate robot position. Using the pose of the robot with respect to the global frame and the pedestrian with respect to the robot, we transform the pedestrians to a global coordinate frame allowing us to run our trained navigation policies directly from simulations without requiring further training on the physical hardware. As part of this hardware demonstration, we were able to verify that the trained policy can transfer from simulation to the physical robot, execute in real time, operate on noisy sensors and is able to successfully reach its goal while navigating around pedestrians to avoid collisions.

Fig. 6. Hardware demonstration using MIT Racecar navigating around moving pedestrians.

7   Conclusion

In this paper, we highlight the importance of integrating predictive capabilities to mobile robotic systems as we believe this is a critical capability needed to improve the robustness and efficiency of navigation policies. We first experiment with the ability to predict beyond the robot's line-of-sight using spatial structures as priors. We investigated several neural network architectures and evaluated the general trade-offs between performance and generation of high quality predictions. Next, we show extensions to occupancy map prediction by making multiple hypotheses. Using the multiple hypotheses, we compute regions of high uncertainty as a heuristic for efficient map exploration. We further extend this approach to include prediction of pedestrian motion. We show that by measuring the error between the predicted and observed trajectories, we can detect novel pedestrian motion. This enables a risk sensitive control policy resulting in significantly less collisions compared to alternative methods.

While the work present here show promising results, there are a number of possible extensions for further exploration. We can extend our map prediction algorithms to predict semantic information beyond occupied spaces. We can also improve information-theoretic exploration by using additional forms of uncertainty estimation including bootstrapping [39] and stochastic dropout [40,41]. For pedestrian prediction, we can incorporate semantic information, group and social dynamics and additional forms of intent estimation to generate better predictions. Finally, we can extend our adaptive, risk-sensitive navigation policy to continually learn in the presence of novel pedestrian motion.

Acknowledgements. This work is partially supported by the Johns Hopkins University (JHU) Institute for Assured Autonomy (IAA) Fund.

References

1. Katyal, K., Hager, G.D., Huang, C.-M.: Intent-aware pedestrian prediction for adaptive crowd navigation. In: 2020 International Conference on Robotics and Automation (ICRA) (2020)
2. Katyal, K., Popek, K., Paxton, C., Burlina, P., Hager, G.D.: Uncertainty-aware occupancy map prediction using generative networks for robot navigation. In: 2019 International Conference on Robotics and Automation (ICRA), pp. 5453–5459, May 2019
3. Finn, C., Levine, S.: Deep visual foresight for planning robot motion. In: 2017 IEEE International Conference on Robotics and Automation (ICRA), pp. 2786–2793. IEEE (2017)
4. Levine, S., Pastor, P., Krizhevsky, A., Quillen, D.: Learning hand-eye coordination for robotic grasping with deep learning and large-scale data collection. arXiv preprint arXiv:1603.02199 (2016)
5. Oh, J., Guo, X., Lee, H., Lewis, R.L., Singh, S.: Action-conditional video prediction using deep networks in Atari games. In: Cortes, C., Lawrence, N.D., Lee, D.D., Sugiyama, M., Garnett, R., Garnett, R. (eds.) Advances in Neural Information Processing Systems 28, pp. 2845–2853. Curran Associates Inc. (2015)
6. Ulyanov, D., Vedaldi, A., Lempitsky, V.S.: Deep image prior. CoRR, vol. abs/1711.10925 (2017). http://arxiv.org/abs/1711.10925
7. Goodfellow, I., et al.: Generative adversarial nets. In: Ghahramani, Z., Welling, M., Cortes, C., Lawrence, N.D., Weinberger, K.Q. (eds.) Advances in Neural Information Processing Systems 27, pp. 2672–2680. Curran Associates Inc. (2014). http://papers.nips.cc/paper/5423-generative-adversarial-nets.pdf
8. Isola, P., Zhu, J.-Y., Zhou, T., Efros, A.A.: Image-to-image translation with conditional adversarial networks. In: CVPR (2017)
9. Tamar, A., Wu, Y., Thomas, G., Levine, S., Abbeel, P.: Value iteration networks. In: Advances in Neural Information Processing Systems, pp. 2154–2162 (2016)
10. Tai, L., Paolo, G., Liu, M.: Virtual-to-real deep reinforcement learning: continuous control of mobile robots for mapless navigation. CoRR, vol. abs/1703.00420 (2017). http://arxiv.org/abs/1703.00420
11. Kahn, G., Villaflor, A., Ding, B., Abbeel, P., Levine, S.: Self-supervised deep reinforcement learning with generalized computation graphs for robot navigation. CoRR, vol. abs/1709.10489 (2017). http://arxiv.org/abs/1709.10489
12. Kruse, T., Pandey, A.K., Alami, R., Kirsch, A.: Human-aware robot navigation: a survey. Robot. Auton. Syst. **61**(12), 1726–1743 (2013)
13. van den Berg, J.P., Lin, M.C., Manocha, D.: Reciprocal velocity obstacles for real-time multi-agent navigation. In: 2008 IEEE International Conference on Robotics and Automation, pp. 1928–1935 (2008)
14. van den Berg, J., Guy, S.J., Lin, M., Manocha, D.: Reciprocal n-body collision avoidance. In: Pradalier, C., Siegwart, R., Hirzinger, G. (eds.) Robotics Research. STAR, vol. 70, pp. 3–19. Springer, Heidelberg (2011). https://doi.org/10.1007/978-3-642-19457-3_1
15. Phillips, M., Likhachev, M.: SIPP: safe interval path planning for dynamic environments, pp. 5628–5635, June 2011
16. Aoude, G.S., Luders, B.D., Joseph, J.M., Roy, N., How, J.P.: Probabilistically safe motion planning to avoid dynamic obstacles with uncertain motion patterns. Auton. Robots **35**(1), 51–76 (2013). https://doi.org/10.1007/s10514-013-9334-3

17. Kretzschmar, H., Spies, M., Sprunk, C., Burgard, W.: Socially compliant mobile robot navigation via inverse reinforcement learning. Int. J. Robot. Res. **35**(11), 1289–1307 (2016). https://doi.org/10.1177/0278364915619772
18. Everett, M., Chen, Y.F., How, J.P.: Motion planning among dynamic, decision-making agents with deep reinforcement learning. In: IEEE/RSJ International Conference on Intelligent Robots and Systems (IROS), Madrid, Spain, September 2018. https://arxiv.org/pdf/1805.01956.pdf
19. Chen, C., Liu, Y., Kreiss, S., Alahi, A.: Crowd-robot interaction: crowd-aware robot navigation with attention-based deep reinforcement learning (2018)
20. Kahn, G., Villaflor, A., Pong, V., Abbeel, P., Levine, S.: Uncertainty-aware reinforcement learning for collision avoidance. arXiv, vol. abs/1702.01182 (2017)
21. Ronneberger, O., Fischer, P., Brox, T.: U-net: convolutional networks for biomedical image segmentation. CoRR, vol. abs/1505.04597 (2015). http://arxiv.org/abs/1505.04597
22. Johnson, J., Alahi, A., Li, F.: Perceptual losses for real-time style transfer and super-resolution. CoRR, vol. abs/1603.08155 (2016). http://arxiv.org/abs/1603.08155
23. He, K., Zhang, X., Ren, S., Sun, J.: Deep residual learning for image recognition. CoRR, vol. abs/1512.03385 (2015). http://arxiv.org/abs/1512.03385
24. Zhu, J., Park, T., Isola, P., Efros, A.A.: Unpaired image-to-image translation using cycle-consistent adversarial networks. CoRR, vol. abs/1703.10593 (2017). http://arxiv.org/abs/1703.10593
25. Hornung, A., Wurm, K.M., Bennewitz, M., Stachniss, C., Burgard, W.: OctoMap: an efficient probabilistic 3D mapping framework based on octrees. Auton. Robots (2013). http://octomap.github.com
26. Min, P.: Binvox (2004–2017). http://www.patrickmin.com/binvox. Accessed 20 Feb 2017
27. Nooruddin, F.S., Turk, G.: Simplification and repair of polygonal models using volumetric techniques. IEEE Trans. Vis. Comput. Graph. **9**(2), 191–205 (2003)
28. Paszke, A., et al.: Automatic Differentiation in PyTorch (2017)
29. Rupprecht, C., Laina, I., Baust, M., Tombari, F., Hager, G.D., Navab, N.: Learning in an uncertain world: representing ambiguity through multiple hypotheses. CoRR, vol. abs/1612.00197 (2016). http://arxiv.org/abs/1612.00197
30. Hess, W., Kohler, D., Rapp, H., Andor, D.: Real-time loop closure in 2D LIDAR SLAM. In: IEEE International Conference on Robotics and Automation (ICRA) 2016, pp. 1271–1278 (2016)
31. Yamauchi, B.: A frontier-based approach for autonomous exploration. In: Proceedings 1997 IEEE International Symposium on Computational Intelligence in Robotics and Automation, CIRA 1997. 'Towards New Computational Principles for Robotics and Automation', pp. 146–151, July 1997
32. Bai, S., Wang, J., Chen, F., Englot, B.: Information-theoretic exploration with Bayesian optimization. In: 2016 IEEE/RSJ International Conference on Intelligent Robots and Systems (IROS), pp. 1816–1822. IEEE (2016)
33. Bai, S., Wang, J., Doherty, K., Englot, B.: Inference-enabled information-theoretic exploration of continuous action spaces. In: International Symposium of Robotics Research (2015)
34. Wirth, S., Pellenz, J.: Exploration transform: a stable exploring algorithm for robots in rescue environments. In: IEEE International Workshop on Safety, Security and Rescue Robotics: SSRR 2007, pp. 1–5. IEEE (2007)
35. Brockman, G., et al.: OpenAI Gym. CoRR, vol. abs/1606.01540 (2016). http://arxiv.org/abs/1606.01540

36. Chen, Y.F., Liu, M., Everett, M., How, J.: Decentralized non-communicating multiagent collision avoidance with deep reinforcement learning, pp. 285–292, May 2017

37. Fan, R.-E., Chang, K.-W., Hsieh, C.-J., Wang, X.-R., Lin, C.-J.: LIBLINEAR: a library for large linear classification. J. Mach. Learn. Res. **9**, 1871–1874 (2008). http://dl.acm.org/citation.cfm?id=1390681.1442794

38. Gupta, A., Johnson, J., Fei-Fei, L., Savarese, S., Alahi, A.: Social GAN: socially acceptable trajectories with generative adversarial networks. CoRR, vol. abs/1803.10892 (2018). http://arxiv.org/abs/1803.10892

39. Efron, B.: The Jackknife, The Bootstrap and Other Resampling Plans. ser. CBMS-NSF Regional Conference Series in Applied Mathematics. SIAM, Philadelphia (1982). Lectures Given at Bowling Green State Univ., June 1980. https://cds.cern.ch/record/98913

40. Gal, Y., Ghahramani, Z.: Dropout as a Bayesian approximation: representing model uncertainty in deep learning. In: Balcan, M.F., Weinberger, K.Q. (eds.) Proceedings of the 33rd International Conference on Machine Learning, ser. Proceedings of Machine Learning Research, PMLR, New York, NY, USA, 20–22 June 2016, vol. 48, pp. 1050–1059 (2016). http://proceedings.mlr.press/v48/gal16.html

41. Srivastava, N., Hinton, G., Krizhevsky, A., Sutskever, I., Salakhutdinov, R.: Dropout: a simple way to prevent neural networks from overfitting. J. Mach. Learn. Res. **15**(1), 1929–1958 (2014). http://dl.acm.org/citation.cfm?id=2627435.2670313

A Heterogeneous Ensemble Learning-Based Acoustic Fall Detection Method for Elderly People in Indoor Environment

XiaoLing Li$^{(\boxtimes)}$, JiaWei Li, JiaRui Lai, ZiMing Zheng, WeiWei Jia, and Bin Liu

School of Mechanical Engineering, Xi'an Jiaotong University,
Xi'an 710049, China
xjtulxl@mail.xjtu.edu.cn

Abstract. Falling is a severe hazard among elderly people, which always follows unpredictable consequences such as a permanent disability or even death especially for the people living alone. Accurate and reliable automatic fall detection based on sound in an indoor environment enables elderly people to receive instant treatment and can alleviate the severe consequences of falls. Aim to achieve this purpose, we propose a novel heterogeneous ensemble learning (HEL) method for indoor acoustic fall detection. Firstly, we pre-process the indoor fall acoustic in the dataset and extract the fall-like sound signals by short-time energy. Then, the MFCC and spectrogram is obtained as features. Finally, we adopt the HEL method to classify the daily fall-like signals and the actual human fall, which use bagging ensemble selection method and stacking method to combine three independent base classifiers. This paper demonstrates the stacking-based HEL method can improve the accuracy from 87.83% to 94.17% compared to the single component base classifier and it can recognize falling sounds with better performance, which greatly avoids the safety hazards of the elderly due to falls in an indoor environment.

Keywords: Heterogeneous ensemble learning (HEL) · Acoustic · Fall detection · Indoor environment

1 Introduction

Falling is one of the main causes of serious injury or even death for the elderly. Especially for elderly people living alone, the fall of the elderly at home face more serious consequences. The United Nations predicts that the elderly population in 64 countries will increase more than 30% by 2050 [1]. The World Health Organization reported that about 28% of 65-year-olds fall and about 32% of 70-year-olds fall each year [2]. Elderly people who live alone cannot alert anyone for help if a fall occurs due to any serious injuries sustained or if they were unconscious. Therefore, it is crucial for the elderly living alone to detect falls in the family, it can not only provide necessary assistance in a timely manner, but also effectively avoid life-threatening or complications caused by delay in detection.

The advancements in technology, in recent years, resulted in an increase in the research on various fall detection systems. Fall detection systems can be grouped into the following categories: camera-based, wearable sensors-based and acoustic-based.

© Springer Nature Switzerland AG 2020
H. Degen and L. Reinerman-Jones (Eds.): HCII 2020, LNCS 12217, pp. 369–383, 2020.
https://doi.org/10.1007/978-3-030-50334-5_25

The following sections provide a brief description of the existing research work related to these systems and discuss their pros and cons.

Among these methods, the wearable method is the most popular one. With the growth of micro-electro-mechanical system (MEMS), wearable devices become miniaturized, more compact, and cheaper. They can be easily integrated to other available alarm systems in the vicinity or to the accessories that the person carrier e.g. smartphones or smart watches which can achieve a kind of non-intrusive and non-invasive diagnosis and monitoring [3, 4]. The wearable device analyzes the tendency of the human activities by using accelerometers, gyroscopes and some health sensor (like electromyogram (EMG) sensors) to obtain corresponding fall information data [5]. The most important feature of a wearable solution is that collecting activity data from wearable sensors is not restricted to laboratory environment, which allows collection of real-world activities wherever you are [6]. However, for the elderly, if they go outdoors, they tend to be in a place with more people, but most of the time they are at home and they are often left unattended. If they fall, they will always be discovered after a long time, which is dangerous for an older. The wearable devices often cause additional physical burden and inconvenience [7], although these detection devices may be very small. It usually is considered an undesirable placement of device, and older adults neglect or even not want to wear them for its inconvenience to the movement. Additionally, wearable sensors generate a lot of false alarms when performing daily activities, which can lead to frustration of users due to the lack of context understanding [8].

The advancement in computer vision and image processing techniques can also be applied in fall detection problems, where camera sensors are used to monitor user behavior and detect fall activities without disturbing user routines. The camera-based detection can be divided into shape change, inactivity, posture, and 3D head motion [9]. Camera sensors can record the user's position and shape by RGB cameras, depth cameras or wide-angle cameras. The advantage of the Camera-based approach is that there is no intrusion on the users since these sensors do not need to be worn or remembered to be worn. It can also be used to monitor one or more people simultaneously, as well as fall monitoring in public areas. Compared with other methods, its biggest advantage is that it can monitor falls more accurately and has better robustness [10]. The problem of camera-based systems includes occlusions, light conditions, coverage, privacy, cost, and high processing [11]. One of the important impacts is the ethical issue. The ethical issues that are associated with camera-based methods includes confidentiality and privacy of the monitored person, which makes it difficult to monitor a person especially in the house. Even though privacy techniques are applied, based on the perception of the camera system, people still have the feeling of being "surveilled" [12].

Of the various fall detection approaches, an acoustic analysis of environmental sounds provides an effective alternative to overcome the drawbacks of both wearable-based and camera-based solutions, especially at an indoor environment [13]. The basic idea of acoustic-based method is to make use of a microphone sensor to capture the movements' sound of the users where different acoustic features are extracted to detect falls [14, 15]. Li, Ho et al. proposed an acoustic analysis for fall detection using the Mel-frequency Cepstral Coefficients (MFCC) features and nearest neighbor (NN) classifier [16]. Principi et al. combined ed floor vibration waves and fall sounds for fall detection [17]. Khan, Yu et al. presented a fall detection system using acoustic signals collected from sounds of footsteps [18]. Er, Poi Voon et al. classified fall detection by combining accelerometer with sound sensor using a fuzzy logic method [19].

As we can see, all of these methods commonly use supervised algorithms include naïve Bayes (NB), k-nearest neighbors (k-NN), support vector machines (SVM). Deep learning networks have also been attracting attention of researchers. Besides, another trend in machine learning is to increase the classification performance by using an ensemble of classifiers. In an ensemble system, a group of base classifiers is employed. If different types of classifiers are used as base learners, then such a system is called heterogeneous ensemble [20], otherwise homogenous ensemble. The former can significantly improve the text classification performance [6, 21].

We propose a heterogeneous ensemble method for acoustic fall detection that predicts an elderly person accident fall occurrence by classifying the fall sound from the fall-like sound. The functionality of this solution is monitoring a senior citizen's home for accidental fall activity, and to automatically request for assistance when a valid fall is detected.

2   HEL Method

2.1   The Base Learners

The frequency of environmental sounds similar to falls in life varies widely, which is a typical imbalanced classification problem. So to overcome the impact of data imbalance, the ensemble methods can be used for classification of sound signals. Compared to single classifier systems, combination-based methods generally have better performance because they weigh the predictions of a single sub-classifier before making a final decision, and they also have a tendency to recovery if the classifier fails to perform well. In order to set up an ensemble learning method, we need to select the base models to be aggregated. Most of the time a same single base learning algorithm is used so that lots of homogeneous weak learners are trained in different ways. The ensemble model obtained is then called "homogeneous". However, ensembles tend to yield better results when there is a significant diversity among the models. In this way, there also exist some methods that use different type of base learning algorithms: some heterogeneous weak learners are then combined into a "heterogeneous ensembles model". All the three heterogeneous base learners are combined into a "heterogeneous ensembles model", namely, the k-Nearest Neighbors (KNN), the Support Vector Machine (SVM) and the Convolutional neural network (CNN).

The KNN is a simple algorithm that stores all available cases and classifies new cases based on a similarity measure (e.g., distance functions). A case is classified by a majority vote of its neighbors, with the case being assigned to the class most common amongst its K nearest neighbors measured by a distance function. For the KNN algorithm, the selection of the k value is one of the most important ones. The appropriate k value is selected according to the effect of comparing the accuracy of different k values with the data. For the fall detection, the KNN algorithm has low time complexity, can guarantee fast operation speed, and is suitable for non-linear classification.

The SVM is binary classifier that divides an n-dimensional space with n features into two regions related with two classes [22]. The n-dimensional hyperplane separates two regions in a way that the hyperplane has the largest distance from training vectors of two classes called support vectors. The SVM can also be used for non-linear classification using a method called the kernel trick that implicitly maps input instances into a high-dimensional feature space that can be linearly separated. In SVM, different sets of kernel functions can be used to build a different set of classifiers with different decision boundaries. The model uses the following formula.

$$\min \frac{1}{2}\|\omega\|$$
$$s.t. y_i(\omega^T x_i + b) \geq 1, i = 1, 2, \ldots, m \tag{1}$$

Then, the RBF kernel is defined as follows:

$$\kappa(x_i, x_j) = \exp(-\frac{\|x_i - x_j\|^2}{2\sigma^2}) \tag{2}$$

SVM is widely used in traditional classification. The few support vectors of SVM determine the final result, which can not only help us to capture key samples and "remove" a large number of redundant samples, but also destined that the method is not only simple in algorithm but also more robust.

The CNN are made up of neurons that have learnable weights and biases. which architectures make the explicit assumption that the inputs are images, and allows us to encode certain properties into the architecture [23]. Furthermore, these make the forward function more efficient to implement and vastly reduce the number of parameters in the network. The CNN is a feedforward network with an input and output layer and hidden layers. Its architectures consist of a series of convolutional layers interleaved with pooling layers, followed by a number of fully connected layers. Convolutional layer applies a convolution filter to input data to produce a feature map to combine information with data on the filter. After convolution, a pooling layer reduces the number of samples in each feature map and retains the most important information. In this paper, the CNN uses the sound spectrum as the input layer of the network. In the training process, the classical optimization algorithm batch gradient descent method can update the parameters. For one class of environmental sound, feature spectrums of acoustic events are much more transformative than human speech, CNN can learn long contextual information [24].

2.2   HEL Strategies

The common ensemble learning methods include boosting, bagging and stacking. For the Boosting method, it is a serial computing relationship. On the one hand, it is not suitable for applications with high time delay requirements such as fall detection. On the other hand, it is based on the training of the previous model to generate a new model, and there is a risk of overfitting. To combine decisions of individual base leaners the KNN, SVM and CNN, bagging and stacking methods can be used in this study. In majority voting method, an unlabeled instance is classified according to the class that obtains the highest number of votes from collection of base classifiers.

In bagging method, results of these multiple models are also combined using average or majority voting, but each model is exposed to a different subset of data and ultimately use its collective output at the end. In stacking method, also called stacked generalization, a metalevel classifier is used to combine the decision of base-level classifiers [25]. The HEL can be applied to a parallel model where there is no strong dependency between the individual learners and can be generated simultaneously.

Table 1. The bagging method

Bagging algorithm.
Input:
1. Basic classifier: C,
2. The iteration of training: t. The total iteration T is 5,
3. Training set: S.
Output:
Ensemble of classifiers: C_t
1: t = 1
2: while t < T
3: S_t -- the subset of training set generated through bootstrap sampling
4: Using S_t to creat basic classifier C_t
5: t++
6: return C (Ensemble of classifiers C_t by simple voting measure)

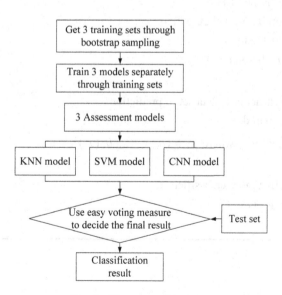

Fig. 1. Flowchart of bagging

We use the bagging and stacking method respectively. Bagging is an ensemble method that samples the training set with replacement multiple times and comes up with multiple training sets of size equal to that of the original training set. The bagging method effectively avoids overfitting and reduces variance compared to simple ensemble methods. Table 1 shows the complete bagging algorithm. The algorithm for building a bagging model is shown in Fig. 1.

The stacking method consists of two steps. In the first step, a set of base-level classifiers $C_1, C_2, \ldots, C_n$ is generated from a sample training set S that consists of feature examples $s_i = (x_i, y_i)$ where x_i is feature vector and y_i is prediction (class label). A meta-dataset is constructed from the decisions of base-level classifiers. The meta-dataset contains an instance for predictions of classifiers in the original training dataset. The meta-dataset is in the form of $m_i = (d_i, y_i)$ where d_i is the prediction of individual n base classifiers. The meta-dataset can also include both original training examples and decisions of base-level classifiers in the form of $m_i = (x_i, d_i, y_i)$ to improve performance. After the generation of meta-dataset, a metalevel classifier is trained with meta-dataset and used to make predictions. Table 2 shows the complete stacking algorithm. The algorithm for building a stacking model is shown in Fig. 2.

Table 2. The stacking method

Stacking algorithm.
Input:
Training data $D = \{x_i, y_i\}_{i=1}^m$
Output:
Ensemble classifier H
Step1: learn base-level classifiers
For t = 1 to T do
Learn h_t based on D
End for
Step2: construct new data set of predictions
For i = 1 to m do
$D_h = \{x_i', y_i\}$, where $x_i' = \{h_1(x_i), \ldots, h_T(x_i)\}$
End for
Step3: learn a meta-calassifier
Learn H based on D_h
Return H

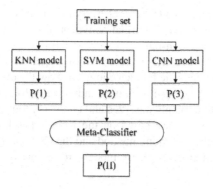

Fig. 2. Flowchart of stacking

3 Experiment

3.1 Data Acquisition

The proposed methodology for fall detection and recognition combines the conventional sound signal processing approach with ensemble learning to detect human fall indoor. The main contribution of the proposed method is to employ an acoustic sensor which is more sensible to fall events indoor by a novel heterogeneous ensemble learning algorithm. The method firstly collects the sounds of various events in the family through microphone, including the fall and some fall-like activities of daily life as the main identifiable signal. Secondly, the collected sound is preprocessed and feature extracted, and features such as MFCC in denoising and extracting sound are used for classification of subsequent sound events.

To evaluate the proposed algorithm, the environmental sounds indoor are recorded through a microphone ADMP401 at 44.1 kHz (Fig. 3). The sound data are grouped into 6 different sound classes. For fall detection experiments, different fall sounds through human subjects with associated events were recorded i.e. scream, and object falling e.g. door clapping etc. In order to reduce external sound interference, we specially record sounds at night time.

Fig. 3. Data acquisition equipment

For fall detection experiments, several everyday sounds similar to the sound of people falling indoors and several normal activities of daily living (ADL) are set as control group, calling these non-falling sounds as fall-like events, like door clapping, scream, chair, dishes, glass breaking. To our knowledge, no such ensemble methods have been used so far for acoustic fall detection. To show the effectiveness of ensemble methods, base classifiers have also been used individually for sound classification as a control group. This section mainly analyzes and compares four different algorithms for sound fall recognition, which are based on the KNN's baseline recognition system, SVM-based general machine learning method and the CNN-based deep neural network method. The implementation of these models relies heavily on the MATLAB's machine learning toolkit.

3.2 Signal Processing

The sound information contains a very rich amount of information, and the preprocessing and feature extraction based on sound information have a greater influence in the next steps. Most of the literature uses a more conventional method to classify signals directly, but after comparing the signals in the home, we find that unlike conventional sound event recognition, the indoor fall sound signal is relative to other admitted families. Activity is a kind of abrupt signal, so all the fall signals in the home environment can be obtained by extracting the abrupt signal of the environmental sound by energy entropy [26] (Fig. 4).

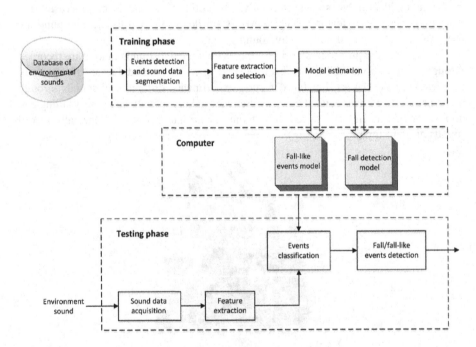

Fig. 4. Flow chart of fall detection

Then, the feature signals of the extracted fall-like events with different mutation properties are characterized and classified, which can simplify the data processing flow and sound feature parameters. Furthermore, two main features are used for classification. One is for the KNN and SVM algorithms, mainly through MFCC as the main feature vector of classification. For the CNN, the spectrogram is used as its input layer.

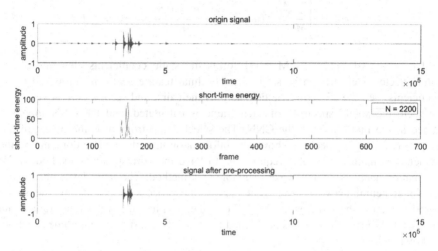

Fig. 5. Comparison between pre- and post-processing signal

Firstly, the signal is windowed and framed, and the signal is divided into frames with a frame length of 20 ms and a frame shift of 10 ms by a Hamming window function. The short-time energy of each frame is then calculated. Through the analysis of the energy entropy, the sound signal of the fall-like type is found (Fig. 5).

Despite the MFCCs are originally developed for speech and speaker recognition tasks, they have been successfully applied also for acoustic event classification and fall detection. The first processing step is the pre-emphasis of the input signal, which consists of applying a filter whose transfer function is

$$H(z) = 1 - \alpha z^{-1} \tag{3}$$

Usually $0.9 < \alpha \leq 1.0$ and here it can be set to 0.97. The purpose of pre-emphasis is to remove the DC component and improve the high-frequency portion of the spectrum. The signal is then split into 20 ms long frames that overlap by 10 ms and are multiplied by the Hamming window. For each frame, a discrete Fourier transform (DFT) is calculated and filtered using a filter bank consisting of 29 triangular filters evenly spaced on the mel scale.. Denoting with S(i) the DFT of a frame and i the frequency bin, the output of the "Mel Filter bank & Frequency Integration" block is

$$S(m) = \ln(\sum_{k=0}^{N-1} E(k)H_m(k)) \tag{4}$$

where $E(k)$ is the energy of the kth sub band, $H_m(k)$ is the frequency response of the kth filter, and m is the number of filters in the bank, which in this case is 29. The terms mel(k) are often named "mel coefficients". The final steps for the calculation of the jth MFCC c(j) is the logarithm and the Discrete Cosine Transform (DCT):

$$c(m) = \sqrt{\frac{2}{M} \sum_{n=1}^{M} S(m) \cos(\frac{\pi m(n-0.5)}{M})}, \ 1 \le m \le L \qquad (5)$$

The set $\{c(0), c(1),\ldots, c(M-1)\}$ forms the static coefficients elements of the feature vector. Here M can be set to 12. The final feature vector is composed of 36 coefficients, i.e., the 12 static coefficients plus their first and second derivatives.

Then, the sound spectrum of each frame is calculated, and the CNN model is trained as the input layer of the CNN. The selected spectrogram is the object of our analysis because the spectrum shows the information in both the time domain and the frequency domain, but it also requires us to have the corresponding method of 3D information analysis, which is very suitable as a method. The input layer of the convolutional neural network. The front part of the process of calculating the sound spectrum map is the same as the MFCC calculation. First, the window is framed and the discrete Fourier transform is performed to obtain the short-term amplitude spectrum as shown below.

$$X(n, w) = \sum_{m} x_n(m) \times e^{\frac{-2m\pi j\omega}{N}} \qquad (6)$$

Where, it is assumed that $x(n)$ is the original timing signal, $x_n(m)$ is the framed windowed signal, n represents a frame indication signal, m represents the time indication signal in the corresponding frame, $X(n, w)$ is a short-term amplitude spectrum estimation. The spectral energy density function at point m is $p(n, w)$.

$$p(n, w) = |X(n, w)|^2 = (X(n, w)) \times (conj(X(n, w))) \qquad (7)$$

A spectrogram is obtained by expressing the value of $p(n, w)$ as a two-dimensional image composed of a plurality of gray levels. Although the spectrogram is a two-dimensional image, it represents three-dimensional information. The shade of the color above the image indicates the amount of energy corresponding to the time and frequency, as shown in Fig. 6.

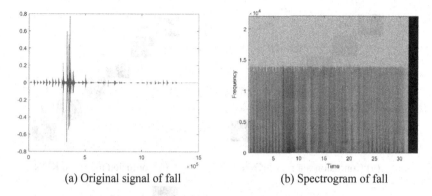

(a) Original signal of fall   (b) Spectrogram of fall

Fig. 6. The original time-frequency domain signal

3.3 Experiment and Volunteers

In the model establishment and verification stage, the experiments are set up. In order to distinguish the fall event from other fall-like events, dividing the sound data into six groups, five of which contained different fall-like sounds, respectively, door clapping, scream, chair, dishes, glass breaking. The five fall-like events easily generate impact sound signals like human fall. As it is harmful and unsafe for the elderly to simulate falls, all of the subjects are healthy young volunteers. Six volunteers of various genders (3 males and 3 females), heights (from 160 cm to 178 cm) and weight (from 46 kg to 68 kg) perform falls in experiment.

4   Experimental Results and Analysis

4.1   Data Analysis

In this work, cross-validation is employed for the analysis of the sound data, with using repeated holdout method in our experiments. We randomly divide a dataset into two halves where 80% of data is used for training and 20% for testing. To get a reliable estimation, we repeat the holdout process 10 times and an overall accuracy is computed by taking averages of each iteration. The confusion matrix is used to represent the results of the inheritance learning and the results of the base learners individually trained.

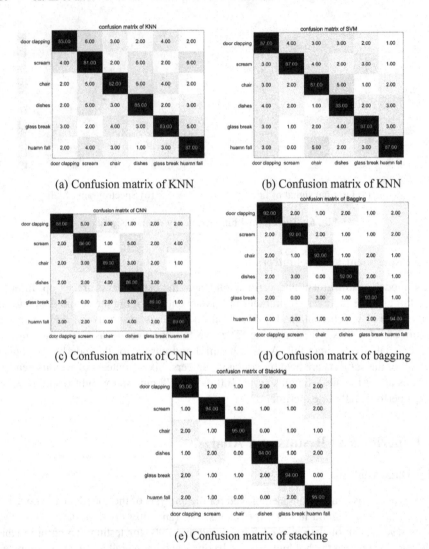

(a) Confusion matrix of KNN

(b) Confusion matrix of KNN

(c) Confusion matrix of CNN

(d) Confusion matrix of bagging

(e) Confusion matrix of stacking

Fig. 7. Confusion matrixes obtained for falling recognition using KNN, SVM, CNN, the bagging and stacking ensemble method

Figure 7 provides the confusion matrices for falling activity recognition when recognized using the KNN, SVM, CNN and HEL method by different ensemble strategies bagging and stacking while using both sensors data. It shows that stacking method delivered excellent results in recognizing the falling activities as compared to the KNN, SVM and CNN classifier and bagging method.

4.2 Result Assessment

To evaluate the fall detection performance, different quantitative performance metrics including precision, recall, F-1 score, accuracy and error rates are used. These measures are computed using the true positive (TP), true negative (TN), false positive (FP), false negative (FN) rates. The mathematical expressions are listed in Table 3.

Table 3. Performance metrics for evaluating classifier

Parameter	Description	Mathematical Expression
Sensitivity (SE)	True positive Rate	$\frac{TP}{TP + FN} \times 100\%$
Specificity (SP)	True Negative Rate	$\frac{TN}{TN + FP} \times 100\%$
Accuracy	A measure of true decisions in overall samples	$\frac{TP + TN}{TP + FN + TN + FP} \times 100\%$
Precision	Ratio of true positive to all positive results	$\frac{TP}{TP + FP} \times 100\%$
F1-score	A measure of test accuracy	$\frac{2 \times \mathrm{Precision} \times Sensitivity}{\mathrm{Precison} + Sensitivity}$

TP is defined as the success of the system to detect a fall or ADL when this one did happen. TN is defined as the success of the system to detect the absence of a fall or ADL when this one did not happen. FP is the failure of the system detecting a fall or ADL when this one, in reality, did not happen. And FN is the failure of the system in detecting a fall or ADL when this one did happen.

The performance of the different algorithms is reported in Table 4, the HEL (Stacking) algorithm can give high sensitivity and specificity which is important in fall detection. High specificity means low false positive rate of fall detection in daily living activities.

Table 4. Acoustic fall detection results obtained using different classifiers

Classifier	SE	SP	Accuracy	Precision	F1-score
KNN	50.29	96.96	83.50	87.00	63.74
SVM	57.62	97.10	87.17	87.00	69.33
CNN	58.94	97.55	87.83	89.00	70.92
HEL (Bagging)	71.71	98.72	92.67	94.00	81.36
HEL (Stacking)	76.00	98.95	94.17	95.00	84.44

We compared the HEL algorithm with the three base classify methods. The performance of the five algorithms is shown in Table 4. From the results, it is obviously that the stacking method outperforms the other algorithms both on sensitivity and specificity. Especially on F1-score, the HEL methods outperform significantly.

The values of this table are the average values obtained by applying different algorithms to the classification results of people falling and detecting similar falling sounds. In Table 4, the accuracy of the proposed algorithm is 94.17%, which is about 7% higher than the traditional single machine learning algorithms. On the one hand, for elderly people who easily fall in the family environment, the accuracy of classification is very important to reduce false positives. In our system, the false positive rate is only 5.83%. On the other hand, a higher F1 score also shows that the system can effectively distinguish between falls and fall-like sounds, and only in a few cases the fall-like sound will be regarded as falls, which reflects the system is capable of avoiding the trigger of the false alarm messages as much as possible.

5 Conclusion

we present a novel framework for fall detection indoor for elderly people by analyzing the sounds based on a HEL method. The proposed algorithm gives better performance than most of the acoustic fall detection methods. Compared to a single classification method, this HEL-based acoustic fall detection algorithm performs better in both accuracy and F1 scores. It shows that the kind of heterogeneous integrated learning based on stacking has better efficiency. In the future, this sound-based fall detection approach can be combined with wearable devices or video-based approaches to enhance the performance of fall recognition in different scenarios. It can also be used in some human activities' recognition at home.

Acknowledgment. This work is supported by the Key R&D project of Shaanxi Province in China under Grant No. 2018GY-142.

References

1. de la Concepción, M.Á.Á., et al.: Mobile activity recognition and fall detection system for elderly people using Ameva algorithm. Pervasive Mob. Comput. **34**, 3–13 (2017)
2. Vallabh, P., Malekian, R.: Fall detection monitoring systems: a comprehensive review. J. Ambient Intell. Hum. Comput. **9**(6), 1809–1833 (2018)
3. Chen, L., et al.: Intelligent fall detection method based on accelerometer data from a wrist-worn smart watch. Measurement **140**, 215–226 (2019)
4. Lee, J.S., Tseng, H.H.: Development of an enhanced threshold-based fall detection system using smartphones with built-in accelerometers. IEEE Sensors J. **19**(18), 8293–8302 (2019)
5. Hussain, F., et al.: Activity-aware fall detection and recognition based on wearable sensors. IEEE Sensors J. **19**(12), 4528–4536 (2019)
6. Yacchirema, D., et al.: Fall detection system for elderly people using IoT and ensemble machine learning algorithm. Pers. Ubiquit. Comput. **23**, 1–17 (2019). https://doi.org/10.1007/s00779-018-01196-8
7. Boutellaa, E., Kerdjidj, O., Ghanem, K.: Covariance matrix based fall detection from multiple wearable sensors. J. Biomed. Inform. **94**, 103189 (2019)
8. Wu, T., et al.: A Mobile Cloud Collaboration Fall Detection System Based on Ensemble Learning. arXiv preprint arXiv:1907.04788 (2019)

9. Fan, K., Wang, P., Zhuang, S.: Human fall detection using slow feature analysis. Multimed. Tools Appl. **78**(7), 9101–9128 (2019)
10. Gunale, K., Mukherji, P.: Indoor human fall detection system based on automatic vision using computer vision and machine learning algorithms. J. Eng. Sci. Technol. **13**(8), 2587–2605 (2018)
11. Min, W., et al.: Detection of human falls on furniture using scene analysis based on deep learning and activity characteristics. IEEE Access **6**, 9324–9335 (2018)
12. Hakim, A., et al.: Smartphone based data mining for fall detection: Analysis and design. Proc. Comput. Sci. **105**, 46–51 (2017)
13. Droghini, D., et al.: Few-shot siamese neural networks employing audio features for human-fall detection. In: Proceedings of the International Conference on Pattern Recognition and Artificial Intelligence ACM (2018)
14. Geertsema, E.E., et al.: Automated remote fall detection using impact features from video and audio. J. Biomech. **88**, 25–32 (2019)
15. Adnan, S.M., et al.: Fall detection through acoustic local ternary patterns. Appl. Acoust. **140**, 296–300 (2018)
16. Li, Y., Ho, K.C., Popescu, M.: A microphone array system for automatic fall detection. IEEE Trans. Biomed. Eng. **59**(5), 1291–1301 (2012)
17. Principi, E., et al.: Acoustic cues from the floor: a new approach for fall classification. Exp. Syst. Appl. **60**, 51–61 (2016)
18. Khan, M.S., et al.: An unsupervised acoustic fall detection system using source separation for sound interference suppression. Signal Process. **110**, 199–210 (2015)
19. Er, P.V., Tan, K.K.: Non-intrusive fall detection monitoring for the elderly based on fuzzy logic. Measurement **124**, 91–102 (2018)
20. Reid, S.: A Review of Heterogeneous Ensemble Methods. Department of Computer Science, University of Colorado at Boulder (2007)
21. Kilimci, Z.H., Selim A.: Deep learning-and word embedding-based heterogeneous classifier ensembles for text classification. Complexity **2018** (2018). https://doi.org/10.1155/2018/7130146
22. Burges, C.J.C.: A tutorial on support vector machines for pattern recognition. Data Mining Knowl. Disc. **2**(2), 121–167 (1998). https://doi.org/10.1023/A:1009715923555
23. Schmidhuber, J.: Deep learning in neural networks: an overview. Neural Netw. **61**, 85–117 (2015)
24. Zhang, X., Zou, Y., Shi, W.: Dilated convolution neural network with LeakyReLU for environmental sound classification. In: 2017 22nd International Conference on Digital Signal Processing (DSP). IEEE (2017)
25. Ren, Y., Zhang, L., Suganthan, P.N.: Ensemble classification and regression-recent developments, applications and future directions. IEEE Comput. Intell. Mag. **11**(1), 41–53 (2016)
26. Li, X., et al.: A novel signal separation and de-noising technique for Doppler radar vital signal detection. Sensors **19**(21), 4751 (2019)

Multi-view Visual Question Answering Dataset for Real Environment Applications

Yue Qiu[1,2(✉)], Yutaka Satoh[1,2], Ryota Suzuki[1], and Kenji Iwata[1]

[1] National Institute of Advanced Industrial Science and Technology (AIST),
Tokyo, Japan
`s1830151@s.tsukuba.ac.jp`
[2] University of Tsukuba, Tsukuba, Japan

Abstract. In this paper, we propose a novel large scale Visual Question Answering (VQA) dataset, which aims at real environment applications. Existing VQA datasets either require high constructing labor costs or have only limited power for evaluating complicated scene understanding ability involving in VQA tasks. Moreover, most VQA datasets do not tackle scenes containing object occlusion, which could be crucial for real-world applications. In this work, we propose a synthetic multi-view VQA dataset along with a dataset generation process. We build our dataset from three real object model datasets. Each scene is observed from multiple virtual cameras, which often requires a multi-view scene understanding. Our dataset requires relatively low labor cost and in the meantime, have highly complicated visual information. In addition, our dataset can be further adapted to users' requirements by extending the dataset setup. We evaluated two previous multi-view VQA methods on our datasets. The results show that both 3D understanding and appearance understanding is crucial to achieving high performance in our dataset, and there is still room for future methods to improve. Our dataset provides a possible way for bridging the VQA methods aiming at CG dataset with real-world applications, such as robot picking tasks.

Keywords: AI · Visual question answering · 3D vision · Deep learning

1 Introduction

The ability to interact with human operators through natural language plays an essential role in real environment Human-Robot Interaction (HRI) applications. Such as for domestic robot applications, the ability makes it possible to manipulate robots through natural language demands. For video surveillance systems, the ability to express changes occurred in the videos through natural language can help decrease the labor cost significantly.

The visual question answering task is one of the critical vision and language tasks, which is defined as an answer prediction process given an image along

© Springer Nature Switzerland AG 2020
H. Degen and L. Reinerman-Jones (Eds.): HCII 2020, LNCS 12217, pp. 384–395, 2020.
https://doi.org/10.1007/978-3-030-50334-5_26

with a question querying information about the image. The VQA task allows the machine to observe surroundings and offer the required information to human operators.

Existing VQA datasets either build from crowd-sourced real photos [1–3] or CG generated images [4]. Real image VQA datasets are relatively suitable for testing image understanding ability of VQA methods. However, constructing those datasets requires high labor costs, and those datasets often suffer from human reporting biases. In addition, those datasets have limited ability to precisely diagnose various VQA abilities. On the contrary, CG VQA datasets require less labor cost but often only consist of simple geometric objects; thus, they are unsuitable for evaluating image content understanding ability. Additionally, it is unclear how to adapt such CG VQA datasets to real-world applications. Moreover, most existing VQA datasets do not discuss the scene containing object occlusion. Those above issues make it difficult to adapt existing VQA datasets to real application situations.

To solve the above problems, we propose a multi-view VQA dataset consisting of real daily supply objects in occluded scene-setting. Our dataset is practical for training and evaluating the VQA abilities for real environment applications, such as robot picking. Inspired by the dataset generation process introduced in [4], we propose a four steps dataset generation process. We first obtained real daily supply object models from several reported object model datasets. Next, we annotated objects with their attributes and labels. Following that, we created scenes by randomly placing object models in simulated scenes and photographing scenes from multiple virtual cameras. Finally, we generated question-answer pairs for each scene based on pre-defined question templates along with the recorded scene information. Our dataset is useful for evaluating a range of critical VQA abilities, such as multi-view scene understanding, hierarchical object recognition, attribute recognition, and counting. In addition, the automatic dataset generation process allows users to adapt our dataset to a new environment with additional objects and question types.

We evaluated two previously proposed multi-view VQA methods on our dataset. Comparing to previous synthetic VQA dataset [4], the experiment results show that our dataset is challenging for various question types, especially for spatial-related questions that require an understanding of object spatial relationships. The experiment results also indicate that both 3D and appearance understanding could be critical for obtaining high performance on the dataset; thus, our dataset provides a useful testbed for the future VQA researching. Our dataset is suitable for training and evaluating various VQA skills aiming for real-world applications. The expandable automatic dataset generation process makes it possible to bridge the VQA methods aiming at CG dataset with various real-world applications.

2   Related Works

2.1   VQA Dataset

Real Image VQA Datasets. VQA_v2 and GQA dataset are two representative popular real images VQA datasets. VQA_v2 dataset consists of crowd-sourced images and question-answer pairs. VQA_v2 contains images ranging from indoor scenes to outdoor scenes, often containing massive visual information. VQA_v2 can be used for evaluating various VQA skills and also acts as an evaluation dataset for VQA challenges [5]. However, its human-made property makes it containing human-reported biases [4]. Similar to VQA_v2, the GQA dataset also is built from a crowd-sourced image dataset. The GQA dataset used Visual Genome dataset [6] as its dataset source. The detailed image information is recorded in scene graphs. The GQA dataset generates question-answer pairs based on recorded scene graphs and pre-defined grammar; thus, it is relatively less biased. However, both the two datasets require high labor costs and cannot avoid latent human-centered biases.

CG Image VQA Datasets. CLEVR is one of the representative CG VQA datasets. CLEVR defines an automatic scene generation engine that generates scenes with randomly placed geometric objects. CLEVR also proposes a question generation program that generates question-answer pairs based on recorded scene information. CLEVR strictly controls the dataset bias and provides detailed diagnose for various VQA abilities. However, the use of pure geometric objects makes it difficult for evaluating complicated image understanding. Moreover, it cannot be directly adapted to real-world applications with complicated visual information.

Most existing VQA datasets do not tackle the scenes with object occlusion, which is common in real-world applications. Based on the above, we propose a novel synthetic multi-view VQA dataset with more realistic and complicated objects comparing to CLEVR, and lesser labor costly comparing to conventional real image VQA datasets. The multiple virtual camera setting makes our dataset suitable for training and evaluating VQA methods for real applications use.

2.2   Object Models Dataset

The YCB [7], Bigbird [8], and NEDO item database [9] are well-known as scanned real object datasets. YCB is created for robot manipulation. It consists of daily supply objects (e.g., hammer, tennis ball, bowl) with different shapes, sizes, and textures. The authors created YCB object models through a high-resolution RGB-D scanner. Bigbird has similar object classes and dataset construction process with YCB. The Bigbird contains more packaged food and bottle-shaped object models (e.g., shampoo, detergent). The NEDO item database consists of daily supply object models with content shapes. Considering object classes, NEDO contains more food classes and office supplies. We adapted the above three datasets into our dataset generation process. We accomplished this by re-annotating object class labels and placing objects in CG scenes. It is noteworthy that our dataset can be further extended by adding more object models.

2.3   Multi-view VQA

Conventional VQA methods [10–12] predict answers from single-view images and questions. However, single-view images are inadequate for answering questions on various occasions, such as object occlusion, severe lighting conditions. Qiu et al. [13] proposed a multi-view VQA framework that predicts answers under a multi-view image scene-setting. The authors divided the multi-view VQA process into two separate components: multi-view image representation; question answering. In our work, we used Qiu et al. methods to benchmark the performance on our dataset.

3   Real Object Multi-view CLEVR Dataset

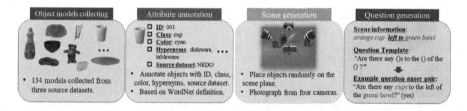

Fig. 1. Dataset generation process of the proposed dataset. This process allows us to extend the dataset by adding object models and question types.

3.1   Dataset Generation Process

Inspired by the dataset generation process introduced in [4], we propose a four steps dataset generation process. We show an overview of those four steps in Fig. 1. Each sample of our dataset consists of a CG scene observed from a multiple virtual camera setup, and a question-answer pair about scene contents. We started our dataset generation process by collecting 3D real daily supply objects models from three previously reported object model datasets. After the collecting process, we labeled object models based on the WordNet [14] hierarchical definition and annotated attributes for objects. Following that, we created CG scenes based on an automatic generation engine with those annotated objects. Finally, we generated question-answer pairs based on a series of pre-defined templates and recorded scene information. In the following sections, we dictate these steps in detail.

3.2   Object Models Collecting

In order to obtain realistic object models, we selected three open-sourced datasets: YCB, Bigbird, and NEDO item database introduced in Sect. 2.2 as our object model source datasets. Both of the three datasets consist of daily supply object models, ranging from food, playing things, washing materials, kitchenware to sports equipment. The YCB and Bigbird datasets are collected by an RGB-D scanner. This collecting process makes part of their models tending to be incomplete in shape, which is unsuitable for recognition related tasks. On the contrary, models in the NEDO item dataset are relatively complete in shapes. However, there is a considerable part of models are packed in boxed-packages, which makes it difficult to recognize those objects from the models' appearance. Considering the above problems, we removed models with incomplete shapes along with unrecognizable models packed in the packages. After the above step, we obtained a clean version of the object model set with 134 object models in total.

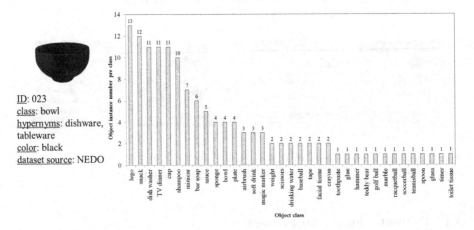

Fig. 2. Object annotation example (left) and object instances (model) number per object class (right).

3.3   Object Models Annotation

In order to generate meaningful question-answer pairs, we labeled the 134 object models with class labels and attribute. We followed the hierarchical object class definition defined in WordNet to label objects. In detail, for each object model, we observed its appearance to apply a leaf class label to it according to the WordNet hierarchical class structure. In addition, we added zero to three levels of inherited hypernyms in depth to further enabling referring objects through their hypernyms. Such as, for the question "Are there any foods visible?", if there is an apple, the answer for that question will be "yes" as "apple" is one of the hyponyms of "food." We also labeled each object with its dominant color.

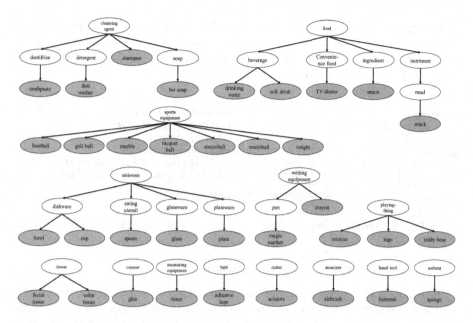

Fig. 3. Hierarchical object class definition of ROM_CLEVR_v1.0 dataset. Object classes are shown in gray ovals; hypernyms are shown in white ovals.

After this step, we constructed a hierarchical class definition with a total of 62 classes, which contains 35 leaf classes and 27 hypernym classes. We show one object annotation example in Fig. 2 left. Additionally, we show the object instance distribution in Fig. 2 right. All object classes, hypernyms, and their hierarchical relationships are shown in Fig. 3.

3.4 Scene Generation

Our scene generation process is based on the CLEVR scene generation engine. In detail, we created a base scene containing a ground plane along with ambient and spotlight lighting. Various scenes can be generated automatically by placing objects on the ground plane.

While creating a single scene, we placed objects with random numbers ranging from three to ten in the ground plane and arranged them randomly without object intersections. Unlike the original CLEVR setting, we adopted the multi-view CLEVR setup proposed in [4] and placed four virtual cameras above the ground plane. Those cameras take photos from evenly space viewpoints around the center of each scene. Moreover, in order to create scenes with high occlusion, we set a threshold of minimum pixel numbers to force each scene to have objects under the threshold pixel numbers from two camera viewpoints in minimum. This setup makes our dataset difficult to be resolved from single-view information.

Through the above processes, we obtained four images of each scene observed from four viewpoints along with a scene graph that records the scene information containing object positions; object attributes to enable the following question-answer pair generation process.

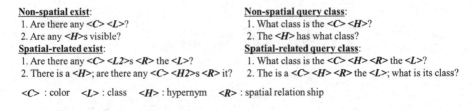

Non-spatial exist:
1. Are there any *<C>* *<L>*?
2. Are any *<H>*s visible?
Spatial-related exist:
1. Are there any *<C>* *<L2>*s *<R>* the *<L>*?
2. There is a *<H>*; are there any *<C>* *<H2>*s *<R>* it?

Non-spatial query class:
1. What class is the *<C>* *<H>*?
2. The *<H>* has what class?
Spatial-related query class:
1. What class is the *<C>* *<H>* *<R>* the *<L>*?
2. The is a *<C>* *<H>* *<R>* the *<L>*; what is its class?

<C> : color   *<L>* : class   *<H>* : hypernym   *<R>* : spatial relation ship

Fig. 4. Question templates examples of exist and query class question.

3.5 Question-Answer Pairs Generation

We introduced four question types, including exist questions (querying object existence in a scene), query color, query class, and counting questions. In addition, based on the existence of spatial relationship words (e.g., "left," "right," "front," "behind"), the questions can be further divided into spatial-related and non-spatial questions. In order to create questions, we first designed a series of question templates (78 in total) that provide the basic structure and question type of questions. We show eight templates in Fig. 4. Questions are instantiated by randomly choose words for the "colored" part (e.g., <C>, <H>). Next, we computed the answer for each question based on the pre-defined function program proposed in [4] and recorded scene information. Though the above process, we created 20 question-answer pairs for each scene. Then, we adjusted the overall dataset to keep the answer forming a uniform distribution. This adjustment makes our dataset hard to be answered without the image information understanding.

Table 1. Dataset statistics: Object (Obj).

Dataset	Scenes	Obj classes	Obj instances	Obj per scene	QA pairs
ROM_CLEVR_v0.5	53,000	8	16	2–8	527,906
ROM_CLEVR_v1.0	60,000	35	134	3–10	712,328

3.6 Dataset Statistics

We build ROM_CLEVR_v1 upon the above setup. Moreover, we also created a ROM_CLEVR_v0.5 with a smaller scale. We show the detailed statistics of these two versions in Table 1. We also show several examples of ROM_CLEVR_v1 in Fig. 5. Our dataset provides a way to train and evaluate VQA methods for real-world applications, such as robot picking. Moreover, the dataset can be adapted

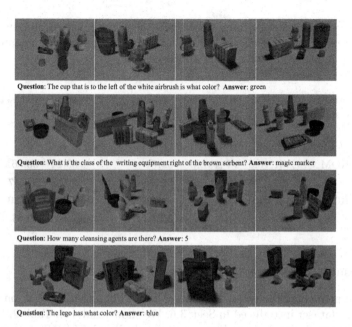

Question: The cup that is to the left of the white airbrush is what color? **Answer**: green

Question: What is the class of the writing equipment right of the brown sorbent? **Answer**: magic marker

Question: How many cleansing agents are there? **Answer**: 5

Question: The lego has what color? **Answer**: blue

Fig. 5. Four examples of ROM_CLEVR_v1.0 dataset: observed from default view, 90°, 180°, and 270° (left to right).

to user requirements by modifying the object models and question setting. It also has the ability to act as a pre-train dataset for real-world vision and language AI applications.

4 Experiments

4.1 Experimental Setup

In this section, we benchmark the two multi-view VQA methods proposed in [13] on our dataset. We also discuss the possible approach to improve the accuracy.

Implementation Details. There are two sub-tasks to answer questions in our dataset. First, multi-view image recognition is necessary. We implemented this by two approaches: view pooling operation (VP) [15], which combines multi-view image features (CNN features) via max or average pooling; scene representation network (SRN) [16], a conditional variational autoencoder-based method which embeds multi-view image information into a continuous scene representation. Second, we used FiLM [12] to predict answers from questions and integrated multi-view image information. In all experiments, we pre-trained SRN network for 200 epochs with batch size 36 and a starting learning rate of 0.0005. We trained FiLM network for 30 epochs with batch size 64 and a starting learning rate of 0.0005.

In the following subsections, we discuss the experiment results on datasets with different scales, the effect of different input image resolutions, and multi-view image information integrating approaches.

Table 2. Accuracy on ROM_CLEVR_v0.5 and ROM_CLEVR_v1.0 dataset: Spatial related question accuracy (S); Non-spatial question accuracy (NS).

Dataset	Method	Overall accuracy	S	NS
ROM_CLEVR_v0.5	VP_FiLM	89.74	89.24	90.36
	SRN_FiLM	**95.18**	**95.02**	**95.37**
ROM_CLEVR_v1.0	VP_FiLM	86.72	72.46	**95.36**
	SRN_FiLM	**87.61**	**79.48**	92.54

4.2   Results on Dataset with Different Scales

We first implemented the two approaches, VP_FiLM and SRN_FiLM, on v0.5 and v1.0 of our dataset introduced in Sect. 3.6. We show results on Table 2. Both two approaches obtained relatively lower accuracy on ROM_CLEVR_v1.0, especially for spatial-related questions. This result indicates that the previous approaches may have limited abilities for large scale scenes with more complicated visual information and object arrangements. This result also shows that it might be necessary to use more powerful models for more realistic dataset setups.

4.3   Results on Different Input Image Sizes

We conducted experiments with different input image resolutions and multi-view fusion approaches on ROM_CLEVR_v1.0. The experiment results are shown in Table 3. In this section, we first analyze the effect of input image resolution.

For the input image resolution of 64*64, both two approaches obtained the lowest accuracy comparing to the results under other resolutions. This trend is especially true for spatial-related questions. This result indicates that for the proposed dataset, input image resolution 64*64 might result in information deficiency.

In contrast, there were no apparent performance gaps for both approaches among resolution of 128*128 and 256*256. This result indicates that while the minimum resolution is satisfied, the performance boost cannot always be obtained by simply increasing the input image resolution. One possible reason is that the hyperparameter tuning for higher resolution input tends to be more difficult.

Table 3. Overall and per-question-type accuracy on ROM_CLEVR_v1.0 dataset: Resolution (Reso); Spatial related question accuracy (S); Non-spatial question accuracy (NS).

Methods	Reso.	Overall	Exist		Query color		Query class		Counting	
			S	NS	S	NS	S	NS	S	NS
VP_FiLM	64	73.81	56.83	86.92	91.61	86.71	93.30	90.64	35.29	58.01
VP_FiLM	128	86.72	72.57	97.72	94.86	98.25	96.53	98.63	51.59	81.03
VP_FiLM	256	85.25	58.98	**99.50**	96.59	**99.75**	98.29	**99.86**	47.40	**92.68**
SRN_FiLM	64	78.57	71.10	88.66	91.05	88.79	93.19	92.52	40.28	58.01
SRN_FiLM	128	86.06	**86.16**	92.35	95.58	90.49	97.13	94.24	**56.55**	69.41
SRN_FiLM	256	**87.61**	82.23	95.06	**97.31**	96.58	97.26	97.35	54.77	73.42

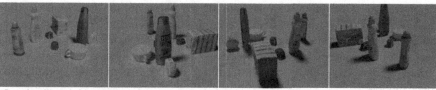

Question (1): Are there any cleansing agents in front of the food? **Answer:** yes
VP_FiLM: yes
SRN_FiLM: yes
Question (2): What color is the dishware? **Answer:** white
VP_FiLM: white
SRN_FiLM: white

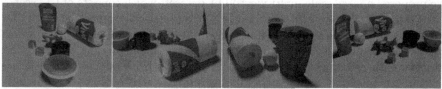

Question (3): What is the class of the cleansing agent? **Answer:** shampoo
VP_FiLM: shampoo
SRN_FiLM: shampoo
Question (4): There is a sports equipment; how many playingthings are on the left side of it? **Answer:** 3
VP_FiLM: 2
SRN_FiLM: 2

Fig. 6. Results examples on ROM_CLEVR_v1.0 dataset. The error answer predictions are shown in red. (color figure online)

4.4   Results on Different Input Image Features

In this subsection, we discuss the performance of two multi-view image integrating approaches. The SRN_FiLM outperforms VP_FiLM by a large margin for input image resolution of 64*64. The performance is significant, especially for spatial-related questions. Both two approaches achieved similar performance for input image resolution 128*128 and 256*256. These results might come from that the SRN network is relatively difficult to be directly applied to high image resolutions, such as 128*128.

For non-spatial questions, VP_FiLM performs slightly better than SRN_FiLM, while for spatial-related questions, SRN_FiLM performs far better. This result comes from that the SRN network has the ability to explore latent 3D information from multi-view images, which is challenging for view pooling structure. Integrating these two approaches might help improve performance. Both two approaches perform poorly for counting questions, which indicates that there is still room for the future method to improve.

4.5   Qualitative Results

We show several result examples in Fig. 6. For query and exist question types (eg., Question (1), (2), (3)), both two methods give a correct answer. Query and exist questions tend to be less challenging for these approaches. One possible reason is that these questions require a minimum dominant color or texture features, which are relatively easy to obtain through CNN structures. For counting questions, both methods performs relatively worse (e.g., Question (4)). It brings a challenge to improve the counting ability in scenes containing complicated object models.

5   Conclusion

We proposed a large scale multi-view VQA dataset, which consists of CG scenes with realistic daily supply object models and automatically generated questions. Existing CG VQA datasets are often built from simple geometric objects, which makes it difficult to evaluate complicated scenes understanding ability. VQA datasets with crowd-sourced images tend to suffer from human-centric biases and often require high labor costs for generating related questions. Comparing to the above datasets, our dataset consists of various realistic object models and also can be generated automatically with low labor costs. The hierarchical class definition of our dataset enables hierarchical object recognition, which is important in the real-world environment. The occlusion setting also makes our model more suitable for real-world environment applications, which always require multi-view understanding. We evaluate two previous multi-view VQA approaches on our dataset. The experiment results show that our dataset is still challenging for spatial-related questions and counting questions. We also found that ensembling scene representation approaches with traditional image feature extractors (e.g., CNNs) might provide a possible solution for achieving more leading performance.

References

1. Antol, S., et al.: VQA: Visual question answering. In: Proceedings of the IEEE International Conference on Computer Vision, pp. 2425–2433 (2016)

2. Goyal, Y., Khot, T., Summers-Stay, D., Batra, D., Parikh, D.: Making the V in VQA matter: elevating the role of image understanding in Visual Question Answering. In: Proceedings of the IEEE Conference on Computer Vision and Pattern Recognition, pp. 6904–6913 (2017)
3. Hudson, D.A., Manning, C.D.: GQA: a new dataset for real-world visual reasoning and compositional question answering. In: Proceedings of the IEEE Conference on Computer Vision and Pattern Recognition, pp. 6700–6709 (2019)
4. Johnson, J., Hariharan, B., van der Maaten, L., Fei-Fei, L., Lawrence Zitnick, C., Girshick, R.: CLEVR: a diagnostic dataset for compositional language and elementary visual reasoning. In: Proceedings of the IEEE Conference on Computer Vision and Pattern Recognition, pp. 2901–2910 (2017)
5. VQA Challenge Homepage. https://visualqa.org/challenge.html. Accessed 31 Jan 2020
6. Krishna, R., et al.: Visual genome: connecting language and vision using crowd-sourced dense image annotations. Int. J. Comput. Vis. 123(1), 32–73 (2017). https://doi.org/10.1007/s11263-016-0981-7
7. Calli, B., Singh, A., Walsman, A., Srinivasa, S., Abbeel, P., Dollar, A.M.: The YCB object and model set: towards common benchmarks for manipulation research. In: 2015 International Conference on Advanced Robotics (ICAR), pp. 510–517. IEEE (2015)
8. Singh, A., Sha, J., Narayan, K.S., Achim, T., Abbeel, P.: BigBIRD: a large-scale 3D database of object instances. In: 2014 IEEE International Conference on Robotics and Automation (ICRA), pp. 509–516. IEEE (2014)
9. Araki, R., Yamashita, T., Fujiyoshi, H.: ARC 2017 RGB-D dataset for object detection and segmentation. In: Late Breaking Results Poster on International Conference on Robotics and Automation (2018)
10. Fukui, A., Park, D.H., Yang, D., Rohrbach, A., Darrell, T., Rohrbach, M.: Multimodal compact bilinear pooling for visual question answering and visual grounding. arXiv preprint arXiv:1606.01847 (2016)
11. Anderson, P., et al.: Bottom-up and top-down attention for image captioning and visual question answering. In: Proceedings of the IEEE Conference on Computer Vision and Pattern Recognition, pp. 6077–6086 (2018)
12. Perez, E., Strub, F., De Vries, H., Dumoulin, V., Courville, A.: Film: visual reasoning with a general conditioning layer. In: Thirty-Second AAAI Conference on Artificial Intelligence (2018)
13. Qiu, Y., Satoh, Y., Suzuki, R., Kataoka, H.: Incorporating 3D information into visual question answering. In: 2019 International Conference on 3D Vision (3DV), Québec City, QC, Canada, pp. 756–765 (2019)
14. Miller, G.A.: WordNet: a lexical database for English. Commun. ACM 38(11), 39–41 (1995)
15. Su, H., Maji, S., Kalogerakis, E., Learned-Miller, E.: Multi-view convolutional neural networks for 3D shape recognition. In: Proceedings of the IEEE International Conference on Computer Vision, pp. 945–953 (2015)
16. Eslami, S.A., et al.: Neural scene representation and rendering. Science 360(6394), 1204–1210 (2018)

Social Dynamics in Human-Robot Groups – Possible Consequences of Unequal Adaptation to Group Members Through Machine Learning in Human-Robot Groups

Astrid Rosenthal-von der Pütten[(⊠)][iD] and Anna M. H. Abrams

RWTH Aachen University, 52078 Aachen, Germany
{arvdp,anna.abrams}@humtec.rwth-aachen.de
https://www.itec.rwth-aachen.de

Abstract. Social robots designed to live and work with humans will have to recognize, learn from, and adapt to multiple users, since humans live and organize themselves in groups. Social robots must consider the social dynamics that arise when humans interact in groups as well as the social consequences of their own behaviour in these groups. When trying to automatically adapt to its users, a robot might unintentionally favour one human group member. For instance, when in a work setting, a robot's implemented goal is to maximize team performance, it might decide to distribute more resources to those team members who are identified as high performers in the task, thereby discriminating low performers. Algorithm-based learning and decision-making can result in unequal treatment, intergroup bias and social exclusion of team members with severe negative outcomes for the emotional state of the individual and the social dynamics in the group. In this paper, we advocate for systematically investigating ingroup identification and intergroup bias in human-robot group interactions and their possible negative effects for individuals such as feelings of rejection, social exclusion, and ostracism. We review theories from social psychology on groups and outline future research lines to investigate social dynamics in human-robot mixed teams from the perspectives of psychology and computer science.

Keywords: Social dynamics · Human-robot mixed teams · Social exclusion · Intergroup bias

1 Motivation and Problem Statement

Robots are on the move into our everyday lives. Besides traditional application fields like industrial or search and rescue, a huge future market will be social robots. By 'social', we refer to the abilities of an autonomous robot to interact and communicate with humans by exhibiting social behaviours as well as being

© Springer Nature Switzerland AG 2020
H. Degen and L. Reinerman-Jones (Eds.): HCII 2020, LNCS 12217, pp. 396–411, 2020.
https://doi.org/10.1007/978-3-030-50334-5_27

able to interpret human social behaviours. Social robots are envisioned to provide assistance or service, to work together with humans in mixed teams in different working environments or to offer some form of companionship.

As a matter of fact, social robots will have to deal with more than one human in complex social environments. In utter contrast to this envisioned future scenario, research in human-robot interaction (HRI) has primarily focused on laboratory experiments, examining the interaction between a single human and a single robot, while research in HRI groups has only recently begun. As Jung and Hinds [22] pointed out this dyad-based research of HRI in laboratory settings "has helped establish a fundamental understanding about people as they interact with robots", but "our theories reflect an oversimplified view of HRI" (p. 1). The limited research on HRI groups so far neglected how social dynamics in HRI groups can have negative consequences on humans (cf. Fig. 1).

Fig. 1. Lee is excluded from group interaction

We claim that social robots must not only take into account the social dynamics that arise when humans interact in groups, but also the social consequences of their own behaviour in these groups. If a robot does not possess these abilities, we foresee unfairness in HRI:

1. When trying to automatically adapt to its users, a robot might unintentionally favour one human group member over another.
2. Algorithm-based learning and decision-making can result in intergroup bias and social exclusion of team members with severe negative outcomes for the emotional state of the individual and the social dynamics of the group.

Let us consider a working environment, in which the robot's implemented goal is to maximize team performance. The robot will monitor the performance of every single team member and their contribution to team performance. Based on the maximization goal, the robot might decide to distribute more resources to those team members who are high performers in the task, thereby discriminating low performers. Very likely, low performers will experience negative emotions, feel threatened in their self-esteem and their need to belong to the group, and will try to regain social inclusion.

A similar situation can arise in a family scenario. The user who spends more time at home potentially provides the largest training data base for the robot, is best known to the system, and their preferences can be easily determined and executed, while a user who spends less time at home might receive less often recommendations matching their preferences.

In both scenarios, algorithm-based learning and decision-making might result in intergroup bias and social exclusion of group or team members with severe negative outcomes for the emotional state of the individual and the social dynamics in the group. In this paper we advocate for systematically investigating ingroup identification and intergroup bias in human-robot group interactions and their possible negative effects for individuals such as feelings of rejection, social exclusion, and ostracism.

In the following we will briefly review the state of the art of research on human-robot groups (cf. Sect. 2), provide an argument for how and why unequal treatment of users is likely to occur in HRI groups (cf. Sect. 3) and outline the possible social consequences (cf. Sect. 3.2). We will present the I-C-E framework for researching group dynamics in human-robot mixed groups (cf. Sect. 4) and sketch research lines on HRI groups that will address the identified gaps (cf. Sect. 5).

2 Current Human-Robot Groups Research

HRI scholars have begun to tackle the research gap in human-robot groups from different perspectives. Most research has addressed technical challenges to enable robots to identify, keep track of and attend to multiple humans in interactions. Online studies and interaction studies addressed how humans perceive and evaluate robot groups and whether humans tend to prefer robots that were marked as ingroup members. In laboratory settings and observational studies in the field, researchers explored how interaction in dyads deviate from interaction in groups involving robots and humans with the goal to derive relevant concepts that need further investigation such as emotional climate, social signal modelling, and group norms. Further, robots have been used to positively shape interactions between humans.

2.1 Technical Solutions for Robots to Deal with Human Groups

New fields of research in HRI and other disciplines such as computer vision emerged in the last decade trying to find technical solutions to perception of and behaviour in multi-agent interactions. For instance, regarding computer vision, a robot has to identify multiple objects/people of interest [16], e.g., potential interaction partners, decide upon relevant objects/people [29], and keep track of these relevant objects/people [42]. Social signal processing comes into play when a robot takes on the challenge to recognize and interpret social behaviours exhibited by the identified interaction partners. After years of research on communication management (e.g., turn-taking, back-channeling) in HRI in dyads, research groups now have shifted to work on realising attention management, turn-taking gaze behaviour and other social gaze behaviour for robots in multi-party interactions (e.g. [5,21,31,45]). Motion in human groups has to be interpreted in real time to anticipate future actions of human group members and to synthesize the robots' own motion accordingly [19].

2.2 Humans' Perception of Robot Groups

Other research groups concentrate on humans' perception of entitativity of robot groups or social effects in minimal group paradigms. In online studies featuring pictures or videos of single and groups of robots, Wullenkord and Eyssel (manuscript in preparation) and Fraune and colleagues [15] examined aspects that contribute to a quantity of robots being perceived as a group. They found that number, type, similar colour, and synchronized behaviour lead to higher "groupness" (entitativity) perceptions of the observed robots. Synchronicity in movement and similarity in appearance within a group of robots was found to be perceived more negatively, i.e. threatening [13]. Eyssel and colleagues further investigated the impact of social categorization of social robots on its perception in an online study and found that German participants show an ingroup bias evaluating a robot that was developed in Germany more favourably than a robot from Turkey [12]. Tajfels' minimal group paradigm [39] also shows effect in HRI in dyad-based research [24]. Similarly, intergroup bias can significantly affect how close humans are approaching an ingroup robot and how much they trust the robot's recommendations regarding the task at hand [9]. However, previous research on perception of robot groups (online studies) and minimal group paradigms (one robot grouped with one human) has not been conducted in group settings that go beyond the dyad, yet.

2.3 Group Dynamics in Human-Robot Groups

Very few studies have begun to examine group dynamics in interactions between humans and robots. The research predominantly investigates how group interactions differ from dyadic interactions. For instance, engagement with or disengagement from the interaction is expressed differently according to the type of interaction, and it changes across the group size in HRI [25]. Hence, robots "should have different prediction models and, depending on the number of people around it, use the most appropriate" (p. 104). Alves-Oliveira and colleagues developed a framework to distinguish individual-level and group-level emotional expressions for interactions in HRI and introduced the concept of emotional climate to HRI [4]. Observational research of robots interacting with human individuals and groups in the wild show ample indicators of how the constellation of different groups encountered by a robot shapes interactions - often with the result that the robot is insufficiently equipped to handle the situation efficiently and socially adequately [14]. Moreover, in interaction studies researchers investigated the influence of the size of a robot group, for instance, with regard to how well participants can detect those robots that indicate attention toward the human by gaze behaviour [3]. Jung and colleagues investigated ways a robot could positively intervene during interactions between two or more humans with the aim to moderate working team conflicts [28], during conflicts between children [35] or for shaping conversational dynamics for equal consideration of all group members' contributions during a discussion [40].

3   Unfair HRI? - How Social Dynamics in HRI Groups Can Play Out Negatively for Humans

A new topic that has been recently identified [18] are potential negative consequences arising in HRI by robots that show unintended biases in favour of certain group members and thereby discriminating others. Recent research demonstrated in many application fields (e.g, financial credit, job application management) that algorithms often discriminate certain groups of people, for instance, based on gender or skin tone and thereby exhibit unintended and unexpected biases. Under the term Fair AI, researchers call out the computer science community to "identify sources of bias, de-bias training data and develop artificial-intelligence algorithms that are robust to skews in the data" [46]. Since computer vision and machine-learning are core technologies for robotic systems, it has been proposed that a similar threat is posed to HRI [32]. Interestingly, concerns about the negative effects of biased robotics systems are often seen from a more global societal perspective. For instance, autonomous cars could put people of colour to a greater risk due to biased person recognition and medical or service robots might reinforce certain discriminatory practices due to biased algorithmic decision-making [18]. I want to shift the viewpoint of unfair AI/HRI from a societal level to a small group and individual level.

3.1   Sources of Biases and Unfairness in HRI

Besides the issues already identified, new forms of biases are likely to emerge when the *training data base for machine learning are interactions with multiple humans over a longer time.* Let us explain: Robots are expected to learn from and adapt to their users, ideally while in operation during run-time. Hence, robots learning from humans means that robots learn from interactions and the more interactions the better the learning outcome. But humans might have more or less time or might be more or less motivated to provide these interactions that are needed for learning. Thus, training data sets differ in quantity and quality which has consequences for the learning outcome (e.g., knowing the user's preferences) and the robot's quality to adapt to different users. In a family scenario, the user who spends more time at home potentially provides the largest training data base for the robot, is best known to the system, and his/her preferences can be easily determined and served. A user who spends less time at home might receive less often recommendations and interactions matching his/her preferences. Consider the working team scenario described above, where the robot's implemented goal is to maximize team performance. The robot will monitor the performance of every single team member and their contribution to team performance and might decide to distribute more resources to those team members who are high performers in the task, thereby discriminating low performers.

These scenarios demonstrate that algorithm-based learning and decision-making can result in, for instance, perceived intergroup bias, i.e. the "systematic tendency to evaluate one's own membership group (the ingroup) or its members more favourably than a nonmembership group (the outgroup) or its members" [17], social exclusion or ostracism (the act of completely ignoring an individual) of individuals with severe negative outcomes for the emotional state of the individual and the social dynamics of the group.

In the following chapter, we will provide a brief overview over the social psychological processes that are involved in the above sketched scenarios.

3.2 Social Exclusion

According to Williams' Temporal-Need-Threat-Model [43] (Williams 2009, cf. Fig. 2), social exclusion and more extremely ostracism causes a reflexive pain response accompanied with negative affect (e.g., sadness, anger) and triggers threats to four fundamental needs: belonging, self-esteem, control over one's social environment, and meaningful existence. In a reflective stage, individuals' attention is directed to the ostracism episode and they reflect on its meaning and relevance. This may lead to coping responses such as compliance and conformity (to regain belongingness/self-esteem) or attracting attention, provoking, and attempts of controlling others (control/recognition) to fortify the threatened needs. Persistent exposure to ostracism over time consumes the resources necessary to motivate the individual to fortify threatened needs. Eventually, this leads to resignation, alienation, helplessness, and depression.

Humans tend to over-detect ostracism. Empirical studies have shown that rational or logical characteristics of the ostracism episode do not appear to moderate the detection of it. For instance, people felt ostracised when the source of ostracism were algorithms [44]. This hypersensitivity to ostracism has a reason, because the cost of perceiving ostracism when it is not actually occurring (false alarm) is lower than the cost of a miss (not detecting that exclusion is happening).

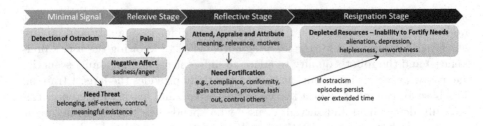

Fig. 2. Temporal-need-threat model by Williams 2009

Thus, it is extremely likely that humans detect ostracism in the above-mentioned AI scenarios where a robot favors one human over another and experience and engage in the described reflexive and reflective processes. However, research on human-human groups suggests that a prerequisite for this effect to happen is that humans identify (at least on a very shallow level) with human-robot mixed groups. Indeed, as we have learned above, humans show intergroup bias when rating a robot belonging to their ingroup more favorably than an outgroup robot. However, when working with another human and another robot in one team, can the robot be a source of social exclusion? Or is only the other human relevant for the "socialness" of the situation?

In the following, we review and transfer concepts from social psychology research on groups to the realm of HRI and discuss parallels and deviations in the applicability of these concepts for human-robot mixed groups.

4   I-C-E Framework for Researching Group Dynamics in Human-Robot Interaction

A group is commonly described as an assembly of two or more individuals, where two individuals are referred to as a dyad and three as a triad. Larger groups, namely mobs, crowds and other collectives classify as groups as well [36]. Dyads will be discarded here because they can be very intimate and unique groups, thus belonging to their own research category [26]. For this paper, we shift the attention to triadic and more interactions. Consequently, groups are defined as an assembly of three or more agents, while agents can be human or robotic. *Entitativity*, *cohesion*, and *ingroup identification* are amongst the most important underlying concepts that describe the characteristics of different groups and their members [1]. While these concepts were clearly distinct in the 1950s and 1960s, they later became vague and sometimes were circularly defined. Often, entitativity and cohesion were used interchangeably, while cohesion is used to define entitativity. For instance, [10] use the words "cohesive" and "unified entity" to give a definition for "entitativity", whereas [14] Fraune and colleagues (2019) state "entitativity is defined as cohesiveness [...]".

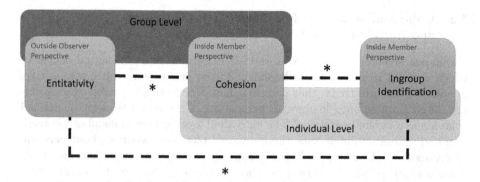

Fig. 3. I-C-E Framework for researching group dynamics in human-robot interaction

We proposed a clarification and integration of these core concepts to the HRI research community by introducing the I-C-E Framework for Researching Group Dynamics in Human-Robot Interaction (cf. Fig. 3; [1]). Within this framework, we differentiate between a group level, where the group is considered as a whole (e.g., how much a group appears to be a group), and an individual level (e.g., how much I identify with a specific group). We further differentiate an outside observer perspective and an inside member perspective when reflecting about a group. Importantly, these central concepts are correlated (see dotted lines in Fig. 3). If I strongly identify myself with a certain group (e.g., my family), cohesion of this group is likely to be high and outside observers will presumably evaluate the groupness (entitativity) of this group to be high. Nevertheless, they are separate concepts with distinct approaches to measure these concepts.

4.1 Entitativity: A Factor Localized on the Group-Level

Entitativity, defined as the perception of social groups in the I-C-E framework, is seen as a fundamental antecedent of many phenomena studied in social psychology [34]. Entitativity is the degree of having the nature of an entity. Groups are perceived differently concerning their entitativity or "groupness" [27]. Variables such as perceived interaction, common goals, common outcomes, similarity of group members, and importance of the group are strongly correlated with entitativity [27]. Moreover, size, duration and permeability are correlated to a weaker extent with perceived entitativity (ibid.). Rutchick et al. [34] postulated that a group can be perceived as entitative resulting from two distinct ways depending upon the observer's information: Perceived similarity of group members and perceived interaction. Furthermore, as an external observer only perceives the group as a whole, the description of groupness is based on the group level, rather than on an individual level.

4.2 Cohesion: A Factor Localized on both Group- and Individual-Level

Group cohesiveness is described in the I-C-E framework as the actual degree to which a group is unified and coherent [27] from an inside member perspective, in contrast to entitativity, that describes how a collective is perceived as a unified entity from an outside observer perspective. Carron and Brawley [7] defined cohesion as a twofold construct: The individual level involves a member's perception and evaluation, in specific the individual member's feelings about personal involvement in the group task, the group's goals and objectives, and his or her feelings about personal involvement and acceptance in the group's social activities. The group level includes the individual group member's perceptions about the group's similarity, closeness and bonding concerning its status as a social unit as well as his or her perception about similarity and closeness with regard to the group task at hand.

4.3 Ingroup Identification: A Factor Located on the Individual-Level

The concept of ingroup identification has been described as a form of social categorization of the self. Social identity theory (SIT, [38]) defines "that part of an individual's self-concept which derives from his knowledge of his membership of a social group (or groups) together with the emotional significance attached to that membership" (p. 69). Very little manipulation is needed for people to feel part of an ingroup which was shown by Tajfel's minimal group studies. Simply assigning participants to one group or the other is sufficient to make people think "we" instead of "I" and show intergroup bias, i.e. behave differently towards the own group and the other [11]. The question of why people tend to categorize themselves on a group-level rather than on an individual-level was answered by Abrams and Hogg [2] with the self-categorization theory (SCT). As an individual's self-esteem is dependent upon group membership, strategies to protect the group and differentiate it from other groups are important for the individual. SCT distinguishes between different levels of categorization (e.g., German, woman, psychologist; [11]). In the I-C-E framework, we conceptualize ingroup identification as an individual-level factor since it describes how strongly an individual identifies with the so far unknown situation of human-robot mixed groups [1].

5 Research Lines for the Future

When developing the future research lines that we regard important for research on HRI groups, we build upon the theoretical background of the I-C-E Framework for Researching Group Dynamics in Human-Robot Interaction [1] and the Temporal-Need-Threat-Model [43] to support our argument that human team members will very likely experience unequal treatment with potentially negative emotional outcomes. Hence, we propose the following:

Research Line 1 & 2: Systematically investigate *ingroup identification* and *intergroup bias* in HRI groups and their possible negative effects for individuals such as feelings of social exclusion (cf. Sect. 4) and examine strategies used by individuals in order to try regaining control and social inclusion.

Research Line 3: Identify different algorithm-based biases in robotic social behaviour and decision-making by observing those human behaviours that are used to regain social inclusion and develop and implement regulatory mechanisms in machine learning to promote "Fair HRI".

6 Research Line 1: Ingroup Identification

With robots entering the field as possible co-workers, servants and companions, new dynamics will emerge [23]. "Robots, as a new group of social agents, and human-robot groups, as unknown conglomerates, will not trigger defined mental representations" (p. 8) [1]. Variables on the group level (e.g., a group's societal status; its "coolness"; its relevance) are unlikely to cause a feeling of identification with robot groups and human-robot groups because these types of groups are unknown to the individual. There is no established information about the groups societal status or its relevance. Hence, this type of information is unlikely to influence an individual's decision to join the group [41]. It is more likely that initial identification processes rely on internal, personal representations of the group and the evaluation of the own individual fit. When a group's identity is unclear and undefined, the individual decides, consciously or subconsciously, to identify with one specific group because of an internal belief that group membership will be a good fit [1]. Future research should explore whether humans are capable of identifying with robot groups and human-robot groups. Do humans show ingroup identification with a robotic team member? In order to do so, the research community has to develop experimental settings that allow us to examine when and why ingroup identification takes place, explore the factors that might weaken or strengthen ingroup identification in human-robot mixed groups, and develop measures to capture these phenomena.

7 Research Line 2: Intergroup Bias and Social Exclusion

Intergroup bias refers to the systematic evaluation of groups consisting of two dimensions: ingroup bias and outgroup bias [17]. Favoring the own group and its members (ingroup favoritism) is typical for the phenomenon of ingroup bias. Discriminating or derogating the outgroup (outgroup discrimination) is commonly seen when the outgroup bias applies. These biases do not only encompass cognitive judgment (cognitive component) but cause a systematic tendency to treat groups and their members differently (behavioral component). Lastly, biases provoke different affect towards ingroup and outgroup (affective component; [17]).

An important factor that has been identified to play a role in intergroup bias is threat [6]. Threat can either result from intergroup competition over scarce resources or it can result from more symbolic factors, such as endangered ingroup values or differentiation from the outgroup [17]. When a relevant outgroup is perceived as similar to the ingroup, a threat to the ingroup's identity is conceived and differentiation attempts are the result [20]. When individuals' groups are threatened and their self-esteem is at stake, they engage in defense behaviour: ingroup favouritism and outgroup derogation (intergroup bias [2]. Intergroup bias is thus the consequence and result of threatened groups (e.g., when groups are ambiguous or undefined, when groups are under attack, when a group's worth is questioned) but also provokes threat towards an individual's self-esteem through a constant need to protect the group [2].

Fig. 4. Lee shows ingroup favouritism for Pepper 1

In HRI, ingroup favouritism was only studied in dyads with robots as the target of evaluation (the robot was either ingroup or outgroup; [9,12,24]. It has not been studied in small groups in which a human (e.g., Lee, cf. Fig. 4) would have both, a robot and a human, as interaction partner (e.g., Maria and the two pepper robots). Hence, we do not know whether ingroup favouritism shown in human-robot minimal group paradigm studies (i.e., groups established by arbitrary minimal characteristics, e.g., being assigned to the "blue" or "green" group, [39]) lead to favouring a robot over another human if that human is not a member of the minimal group (e.g., Pepper 1 and not Maria is in "my green group"; cf. [1]). We know that humans cooperate with robots and show empathy [30,33,37]. But does a human (Lee) extend trust, positive regard, cooperation and empathy *more to a robotic ingroup member* (Pepper 1) *than to a human outgroup member* (Maria) or does being in the group "human" override the experimentally established minimal "green" group? And if so, does Lee's ingroup favouritism for Pepper 1 lead to feelings of social exclusion in that human outgroup member (Maria)? Moreover, we do not know whether a robot's ingroup favouritism towards its human ingroup member (e.g., Pepper 1 favours Lee) really leads to feelings of social exclusion in other human outgroup members (Maria).

In case Maria experiences social exclusion, she will probably try to regain social inclusion. In the course of examining intergroup biases, it will be possible to examine strategies used by individuals in order to try regaining control and social inclusion (cf. Sect. 3.2). By detecting this coping behaviour, a robot might be able to identify episodes of social exclusion and regulate its behaviour to end its biased behaviour and thereby social exclusion.

7.1   Research Line 3: Identify Bias and Promote Fair HRI

A robot could use different information resources in order to detect potential biases. For instance, a robot system will have to know what kind of data sets already exist (which are used for machine learning), whether these data sets are prone to entail bias and more specifically which type of bias. Moreover, when a robot builds up a data set based on interactions with its user, it will need to identify whether the process of building this data set and the content that is stored therein might entail biases. A very simplified example would be that data sets of two users differ in the amount of data provided through interaction, for instance, because one user has limited time or access to engage in interactions. Learning on these data sets, the robot is probably better in predicting the behaviour, intentions or preferences of the user with the larger data set. This information can be used to inform the robot that it might exhibit a bias in favour for one user.

Sometimes we are not able to anticipate biases or identify biases as described above. Some unknown, unexpected bias might emerge over the course of a robot's interaction with multiple humans. The robot could use the human's behaviour as a source to estimate the likelihood that an undetected bias affected an individual or a group of users. Given that unequal treatment of one individual often leads to feelings of social exclusion within that individual with reflexive social pain responses and following coping behaviour that shall fortify threatened needs. A system that can detect coping behaviour will be able to use regulatory mechanisms to minimize bias.

Effects of these biased robot behaviours are unexplored in HRI. To our knowledge, only two recent studies have investigated this and found negative effects: 1) In a collaborative tower construction task, a robot distributed building blocks unequally between two participants which led to lower satisfaction of the human team members with the team relationship [22]; 2) In a collaborative Tetris Game, fair distribution (in contrast to unfair distribution) of resources led participants to trust the system more and resulted in higher overall team performance [8]. However, emotional responses and consequences for the self-perception and self-esteem of the neglected participant were not assessed. Nevertheless, these examples show how simple rules (e.g., defining a minimum percentage of building block or Tetris block distribution to each play) can already yield positive effects. Moreover, a robot could exhibit social strategies in order to mitigate social exclusion effects such as pointing out that the excluded individual is only excluded in this specific task on the basis of performance, but that this individual has other competencies or that this individual is a high performer in a different task.

8 Conclusion

Although a few researchers investigated robots interacting with humans in groups, the phenomena described above have not been theorized or studied in HRI, yet. In fact, although the need for a paradigm shift from studying dyadic interactions in laboratory settings to studying group interactions in complex environments has been identified and advocated for [22], research in human-robot mixed groups is still scarce. At the core of this paper are social psychological phenomena such as social exclusion and ostracism as negative consequences of a robot's unequal adaptation to group members through machine learning, thus representing a completely new perspective in research on HRI groups. This opens a new research line to the empirical investigation of human-robot groups and the influence of biased algorithms on individuals and social dynamics in the group. This future research line will elucidate currently unknown psychological processes in HRI group interactions.

While we focus on negative consequences for group dynamics in human-robot mixed groups induced by biased algorithm-based behaviour and decision-making on the side of the robot, the general notion of unfair or fair AI has been discussed intensively in recent years. In our modern, digitized world, we engage more and more in interactions with algorithms and artificially intelligent systems that learn and adapt based on these interactions. Our visits, views, clicks, and buying decisions provide training data for recommender systems on shopping websites (e.g., Amazon) or video streaming applications (e.g., Netflix). Recently, voice agents have entered our homes providing us with helpful information, services, and assistance while using these interactions as training data to learn and adapt to us. However, they also generalize this knowledge to predict preferences and intentions of groups of users. Especially in the latter area of voice agents, similar biases may emerge when algorithms try to categorize users into groups and provide these groups with personalized interactions. While the lack of diversity in the training data set used in machine learning originates from several different sources, it unequivocally causes a bias towards certain types of users at the cost of other users. On the other side, trying to de-bias algorithms might also raise ethical concerns of inequality. For instance, if a system detects that training data sets generated by interactions with two users differ in quantity and quality, it might try to de-bias by giving the low-quality data set a higher preference in the learning process. However, the user with the high-quality data set has spent considerably more time with the system in order to train the system to his or her needs. Is it fair, to diminish this personal individual effort by outweighing the data set during learning? This example shows that we need multidisciplinary approaches to tackle this problem.

References

1. Abrams, A.M.H., Rosenthal-von der Pütten, A.: I–C–E Framework: Concepts for Group Dynamics Research in Human-robot Interaction (2019). https://doi.org/10.31234/osf.io/jyue6
2. Abrams, D., Hogg, M.A.: Comments on the motivational status of self-esteem in social identity and intergroup discrimination. Eur. J. Soc. Psychol. **18**(4), 317–334 (1988). https://doi.org/10.1002/ejsp.2420180403
3. Admoni, H., Hayes, B., Feil-Seifer, D., Ullman, D., Scassellati, B.: Are you looking at me? Perception of robot attention is mediated by gaze type and group size. In: Staff, I. (ed.) 2013 8th ACM/IEEE International Conference on Human-Robot Interaction, pp. 389–395. IEEE, [Place of publication not identified] (2013). https://doi.org/10.1109/HRI.2013.6483614
4. Alves-Oliveira, P., et al.: It's amazing, we are all feeling it! Emotional climate as a group-level emotional expression in HRI. In: 2015 AAAI Fall Symposium Series (2015)
5. Bennewitz, M., Faber, F., Joho, D., Schreiber, M., Behnke, S.: Towards a humanoid museum guide robot that interacts with multiple persons. In: 2005 5th IEEE-RAS International Conference on Humanoid Robots, pp. 418–423. IEEE Operations Center, Piscataway (2005). https://doi.org/10.1109/ICHR.2005.1573603
6. Brewer, M.B.: Ingroup identification and intergroup conflict: when does ingroup love become outgroup hate? In: Ashmore, R.D., Jussim, L., Wilder, D. (eds.) Social Identity, Intergroup Conflict, and Conflict Reduction. Rutgers Series on Self and Social Identity, vol. 3, pp. 17–41. Oxford University Press (2001)
7. Carron, A.V., Brawley, L.R.: Cohesion. Small Group Res. **31**(1), 89–106 (2000). https://doi.org/10.1177/104649640003100105
8. Claure, H., Chen, Y., Modi, J., Jung, M., Nikolaidis, S.: Reinforcement learning with fairness constraints for resource distribution in human-robot teams. http://arxiv.org/pdf/1907.00313v2
9. Deligianis, C., Stanton, C.J., McGarty, C., Stevens, C.J.: The impact of intergroup bias on trust and approach behaviour towards a humanoid robot. J. Hum.-Robot Interact. **6**(3), 4 (2017). https://doi.org/10.5898/JHRI.6.3.Deligianis
10. Effron, D.A., Kakkar, H., Knowles, E.D.: Group cohesion benefits individuals who express prejudice, but harms their group. J. Exp. Soc. Psychol. **79**, 239–251 (2018). https://doi.org/10.1016/j.jesp.2018.08.002
11. Ellemers, N., Haslam, S.A.: Social identity theory. In: van Lange, P., Kruglanski, A., Higgins, E. (eds.) Handbook of Theories of Social Psychology, pp. 379–398. SAGE Publications Ltd., London (2012). https://doi.org/10.4135/9781446249222.n45
12. Eyssel, F., Kuchenbrandt, D.: Social categorization of social robots: anthropomorphism as a function of robot group membership. Br. J. Soc. Psychol. **51**(4), 724–731 (2012). https://doi.org/10.1111/j.2044-8309.2011.02082.x
13. Fraune, M.R., Nishiwaki, Y., Sabanović, S., Smith, E.R., Okada, M.: Threatening flocks and mindful snowflakes. In: HRI. HRI 2017, pp. 205–213. IEEE, Piscataway (2017). https://doi.org/10.1145/2909824.3020248
14. Fraune, M.R., Šabanović, S., Kanda, T.: Human group presence, group characteristics, and group norms affect human-robot interaction in naturalistic settings. Front. Robot. AI **6**, 3 (2019). https://doi.org/10.3389/frobt.2019.00048
15. Fraune, M.R., Sherrin, S., Sabanović, S., Smith, E.R.: Rabble of robots effects. In: Adams, J.A., Smart, W., Mutlu, B., Takayama, L. (eds.) HRI 2015, pp. 109–116. ACM, New York (2015). https://doi.org/10.1145/2696454.2696483

16. He, K., Gkioxari, G., Dollar, P., Girshick, R.: Mask R-CNN. In: Ikeuchi, K. (ed.) IEEE International Conference on Computer Vision, pp. 2980–2988. IEEE, Piscataway (2017). https://doi.org/10.1109/ICCV.2017.322

17. Hewstone, M., Rubin, M., Willis, H.: Intergroup bias. Annu. Rev. Psychol. **53**, 575–604 (2002). https://doi.org/10.1146/annurev.psych.53.100901.135109

18. Howard, A., Borenstein, J.: The ugly truth about ourselves and our robot creations: the problem of bias and social inequity. Sci. Eng. Ethics **24**(5), 1521–1536 (2017). https://doi.org/10.1007/s11948-017-9975-2

19. Iqbal, T., Rack, S., Riek, L.D.: Movement coordination in human-robot teams: a dynamical systems approach. IEEE Trans. Rob. **32**(4), 909–919 (2016). https://doi.org/10.1109/TRO.2016.2570240

20. Jetten, J., Spears, R., Manstead, A.S.R.: Intergroup norms and intergroup discrimination: distinctive self-categorization and social identity effects. J. Pers. Soc. Psychol. **71**(6), 1222–1233 (1996). https://doi.org/10.1037/0022-3514.71.6.1222

21. Johansson, M., Skantze, G., Gustafson, J.: Comparison of human-human and human-robot turn-taking behaviour in multiparty situated interaction. In: Al Moubayed, S., et al. (eds.) UM3I 2014, pp. 21–26. ACM (2014). https://doi.org/10.1145/2666242.2666249

22. Jung, M., Hinds, P.: Robots in the wild. ACM Trans. Hum.-Robot Interact. **7**(1), 1–5 (2018). https://doi.org/10.1145/3208975

23. Jung, M.F., Šabanović, S., Eyssel, F., Fraune, M.: Robots in groups and teams. In: Lee, C.P. (ed.) Companion of the 2017 ACM Conference on Computer Supported Cooperative Work and Social Computing, pp. 401–407. ACM, New York (2017). https://doi.org/10.1145/3022198.3022659

24. Kuchenbrandt, D., Eyssel, F., Bobinger, S., Neufeld, M.: Minimal group - maximal effect? Evaluation and anthropomorphization of the humanoid robot NAO. In: Mutlu, B., Bartneck, C., Ham, J., Evers, V., Kanda, T. (eds.) ICSR 2011. LNCS (LNAI), vol. 7072, pp. 104–113. Springer, Heidelberg (2011). https://doi.org/10.1007/978-3-642-25504-5_11

25. Leite, I., McCoy, M., Ullman, D., Salomons, N., Scassellati, B.: Comparing models of disengagement in individual and group interactions. In: Adams, J.A., Smart, W., Mutlu, B., Takayama, L. (eds.) HRI 2015, pp. 99–105. ACM, New York (2015). https://doi.org/10.1145/2696454.2696466

26. Levine, J.M., Moreland, R.L.: A history of small group research. Kruglanski, A.W., Stroebe, W. (eds.) Handbook of the History of Social Psychology 2012, pp. 383–405 (2012)

27. Lickel, B., Hamilton, D.L., Wieczorkowska, G., Lewis, A., Sherman, S.J., Uhles, A.N.: Varieties of groups and the perception of group entitativity. J. Pers. Soc. Psychol. **78**(2), 223–246 (2000)

28. Martelaro, N., Jung, M., Hinds, P.: Using robots to moderate team conflict. In: Adams, J.A. (ed.) Proceedings of the Tenth Annual ACMIEEE International Conference on Human-Robot Interaction Extended Abstracts, p. 271. ACM, New York (2015). https://doi.org/10.1145/2701973.2702094

29. Osep, A., Mehner, W., Voigtlaender, P., Leibe, B.: Track, then decide: category-agnostic vision-based multi-object tracking. In: Lynch, K., Automation, I.I.C.o.R.a. (eds.) 2018 IEEE International Conference on Robotics and Automation (ICRA), pp. 3494–3501. IEEE, Piscataway (2018). https://doi.org/10.1109/ICRA.2018.8460975

30. Reeves, B., Nass, C.: The Media Equation: How People Treat Computers, Television, and New Media Like Real People and Places. Cambridge University Press, Cambridge (1996)

31. Richter, V., et al.: Are you talking to me? In: Yau, W.Y., Omori, T., Metta, G., Osawa, H., Zhao, S. (eds.) HAI 2016, pp. 43–50. The Association for Computing Machinery, New York (2016). https://doi.org/10.1145/2974804.2974823
32. Righetti, L., Madhavan, R., Chatila, R.: Unintended consequences of biased robotic and artificial intelligence systems [Ethical, Legal, and Societal Issues]. IEEE Robot. Autom. Mag. **26**(3), 11–13 (2019). https://doi.org/10.1109/MRA.2019.2926996
33. Rosenthal-von der Pütten, A.M., Krämer, N.C., Hoffmann, L., Sobieraj, S., Eimler, S.C.: An experimental study on emotional reactions towards a robot. Int. J. Soc. Robot. **5**(1), 17–34 (2013). https://doi.org/10.1007/s12369-012-0173-8
34. Rutchick, A.M., Hamilton, D.L., Sack, J.D.: Antecedents of entitativity in categorically and dynamically construed groups. Eur. J. Soci. Psychol. **38**(6), 905–921 (2008). https://doi.org/10.1002/ejsp.555
35. Shen, S., Slovak, P., Jung, M.F.: Stop. I see a conflict happening. In: Kanda, T., Sabanović, S., Hoffman, G., Tapus, A. (eds.) HRI 2018, pp. 69–77. Association for Computing Machinery, New York (2018). https://doi.org/10.1145/3171221.3171248
36. Simmel, G.: The number of members as determining the sociological form of the group. II. Am. J. Sociol. **8**(2), 158–196 (1902)
37. Straßmann, C., von der Pütten, A.R., Yaghoubzadeh, R., Kaminski, R., Krämer, N.: The effect of an intelligent virtual agent's nonverbal behavior with regard to dominance and cooperativity. In: Traum, D., Swartout, W., Khooshabeh, P., Kopp, S., Scherer, S., Leuski, A. (eds.) IVA 2016. LNCS (LNAI), vol. 10011, pp. 15–28. Springer, Cham (2016). https://doi.org/10.1007/978-3-319-47665-0_2
38. Tajfel, H.: Social identity and intergroup behaviour. Inf. (Int. Soc. Sci. Counc. **13**(2), 65–93 (1974)
39. Tajfel, H., Billig, M.G., Bundy, R.P., Flament, C.: Social categorization and intergroup behaviour. Eur. J. Soc. Psychol. **1**(2), 149–178 (1971). https://doi.org/10.1002/ejsp.2420010202
40. Tennent, H., Shen, S., Jung, M.: Micbot: a peripheral robotic object to shape conversational dynamics and team performance. In: 2019 14th ACM/IEEE International Conference on Human-Robot Interaction (HRI), 11–14 March 2019, pp. 133–142. IEEE (2019). https://doi.org/10.1109/HRI.2019.8673013
41. van Veelen, R., Otten, S., Hansen, N.: A personal touch to diversity: self-anchoring increases minority members' identification in a diverse group. Group Process. Intergroup Relat. **16**(6), 671–683 (2013). https://doi.org/10.1177/1368430212473167
42. Wang, Q., Zhang, L., Bertinetto, L., Hu, W., Torr, P.H.: Fast online object tracking and segmentation: a unifying approach, pp. 1328–1338 (2019). https://arxiv.org/abs/1812.05050
43. Williams, K.D.: Ostracism: a temporal need-threat model. In: Zanna, M.P. (ed.) Advances in Experimental Social Psychology, vol. 41, pp. 275–314. Academic Press, London (2009). https://doi.org/10.1016/S0065-2601(08)00406-1
44. Zadro, L., Williams, K.D., Richardson, R.: How low can you go? Ostracism by a computer is sufficient to lower self-reported levels of belonging, control, self-esteem, and meaningful existence. J. Exp. Soc. Psychol. **40**(4), 560–567 (2004). https://doi.org/10.1016/j.jesp.2003.11.006
45. Zaraki, A., Mazzei, D., Giuliani, M., de Rossi, D.: Designing and evaluating a social gaze-control system for a humanoid robot. IEEE Trans. Hum.-Mach. Syst. **44**(2), 157–168 (2014). https://doi.org/10.1109/THMS.2014.2303083
46. Zou, J., Schiebinger, L.: AI can be sexist and racist - it's time to make it fair. Nature **559**(7714), 324–326 (2018). https://doi.org/10.1038/d41586-018-05707-8

What Emotions Make One or Five Stars? Understanding Ratings of Online Product Reviews by Sentiment Analysis and XAI

Chaehan So(✉)

Information and Interaction Design, Humanities, Arts and Social Sciences
Division, Yonsei University, Seoul 03722 South Korea
cso@yonsei.ac.kr

Abstract. When people buy products online, they primarily base their decisions on the recommendations of others given in online reviews. The current work analyzed these online reviews by sentiment analysis and used the extracted sentiments as features to predict the product ratings by several machine learning algorithms. These predictions were disentangled by various methods of *explainable AI (XAI)* to understand whether the model showed any bias during prediction.

Study 1 benchmarked these algorithms *(knn, support vector machines, random forests, gradient boosting machines, XGBoost)* and identified random forests and XGBoost as best algorithms for predicting the product ratings. In Study 2, the analysis of global feature importance identified the sentiment *joy* and the emotional valence *negative* as most predictive features. Two XAI visualization methods, *local feature attributions* and *partial dependency plots*, revealed several incorrect prediction mechanisms on the instance-level. Performing the benchmarking as classification, Study 3 identified a high *no-information rate* of 64.4% that indicated high *class imbalance* as underlying reason for the identified problems.

In conclusion, good performance by machine learning algorithms must be taken with caution because the dataset, as encountered in this work, could be biased towards certain predictions. This work demonstrates how XAI methods reveal such prediction bias.

Keywords: Explainable AI · Interpretable AI · Bias detection · Product reviews · Sentiment analysis

1 Introduction

Machine learning methods are known to be unrevealing of their learned knowledge due to their backbox nature. As they are frequently used to predict people's preferences to feed recommendation engines, it may be fruitful to scrutinize how they learned this prediction knowledge. To this aim, a new trend in artificial intelligence research caters to the emerging need for *interpretable or explainable AI (XAI)* [1, 2]. The present work applies such XAI methods to find out whether and how potential bias in models trained by machine learning algorithms can be detected and analyzed.

© Springer Nature Switzerland AG 2020
H. Degen and L. Reinerman-Jones (Eds.): HCII 2020, LNCS 12217, pp. 412–421, 2020.
https://doi.org/10.1007/978-3-030-50334-5_28

When people buy products online, they primarily base their decisions on the recommendations of others given in online reviews. To assess the usefulness of such user reviews, people rely on various factors such as the customer-rated helpfulness information [3]. To use the information contained in the review text for machine learning prediction, methods of *natural language processing (NLP)* have been applied. One popular NLP method, *sentiment analysis*, retrieves the emotional content in textual data. It has been applied to semantics like topics [4], aspects [5] or opinions [6], and domains including hotel reviews [7], movie reviews [8], or restaurant reviews [8].

The models of sentiment analysis differ in the sentiment categories. The most common category is *basic emotions*, a set of emotions from a theory by Ekman [9] believed to be universal in the sense of cross-cultural prevalence and inherited by all humans. The six basic emotions initially suggested by Ekman, namely happiness, surprise, fear, sadness, anger, disgust, were validated by neuroimaging research [10, 11]. Another sentiment category is *emotional valence*, i.e. the binary categorization of emotion as positive or negative [12], also validated by neurocognitive research on event-related potentials (ERPs) [13] and fMRI [14].

Taken together, the preceding considerations lead to a research question that can be formulated as follows:

How can XAI methods reveal potential bias in trained machine learning models for the prediction of product ratings?

To answer this research question, the current work analyzed Amazon online reviews by sentiment analysis and used the extracted sentiments as features to predict the product ratings by regression. These predictions, in turn, were disentangled by various XAI methods to understand whether the model showed any bias during prediction.

2 Method

The analysis was performed on a dataset on 28.332 consumer reviews on electronic products gathered by the data company Datafiniti on Amazon.com between February and April 2019. This dataset covered the complete range of electronic products branded by Amazon itself including the products Kindle, FireStick, and Echo.

2.1 Data Preprocessing

The data preprocessing encompassed the steps:

a) removing technical information (id, dateAdded, dateUpdated, name, asins, imageURLs, keys, reviews.date, reviews.dateSeen, reviews.id, reviews.sourceURLs, reviews.username, sourceURLs)

b) removing data with nearly 100% missing values (e.g. reviews.didPurchase)

c) cleaning the levels of categorical variables from special characters (e.g. "&") and delimiting characters (e.g. ".", ","), and replacing spaces by underscores

These three steps resulted in a final sample size of n = 20238.

2.2 Descriptive Statistics

The variable *brand* showed 43.04% *AmazonBasics* and 56.96% *Amazon* occurrences.

In *primaryCategories*, 49.40% observations were in *Electronics*, whereas only 0.65% in *Electronics, Media* and 0.01% in *Electronics, Furniture* (the latter two categories were later merged with the former category), 42.60% in *Health & Beauty*, 5.92% in *Toys & Games, Electronics*, 1.36% in *Office Supplies, Electronics*, 0.03% in *Office Supplies*, 0.02% in *Animals & Pet Supplies*, and 0.01% in *Home & Garden*.

The variables for "recommend this product", *reviews.doRecommend*, number of helpful reviews, and *reviews.numHelpful* were present for only 12.200 of 28.332 observations in the dataset (56.8%). This prevalence did not allow for the imputation of their missing values. The variable *reviews.doRecommend* was later removed after the pre-screening as will be explained in the corresponding section. To allow the inclusion of the variable *reviews.numHelpful*, the missing values were set to 0.

After analyzing the content of all categorical variables, the following three variables had to be removed for subsequent analyses:

The variable *manufacturer* was removed because it contained essentially the same information as brand.

The variable *categories* was removed because it had very lengthy category levels that very difficult to grasp in meaning (e.g. the two most frequent category levels of 259 and 268 characters referred to primary category *Health & Beauty*). Furthermore, the information was majorly overlapping with the variables *primaryCategories* and *asins*.

The variable *manufacturerNumber* had to be removed because it contained more than 53 class levels (65) which was incompatible with the machine learning library used in the benchmarking.

2.3 Design

The dataset was analyzed in three subsequent studies. Before these studies, a pre-screening of the features was performed.

- Study 1 conducted model training as regression on the reviews-rating variable
- Study 2 applied methods of explainable AI (XAI) to analyze the best model on a global and local level
- Study 3 reframed the prediction as a classification task and converted the target variable into five class levels.

2.4 Benchmarking Method

The present work compared the R implementations of the machine learning algorithms *knn* for k-nearest neighbors [15], *svmRadial* (method ksvm from library kernlab with radial kernel) [16] for support vector machines, *rpart* for CART decision trees [17], *rf* (library randomForest) [18] for Random Forests, *gbm* [19] for Gradient Boosting Machines and *xgbTree* [20] for XGBoost on decision trees.

2.5   Explainable AI (XAI)

Interpretability, in the machine learning context, is defined as the "ability to explain or to present in understandable terms to a human" [21].

The emerging need for interpretability of machine learning algorithms has led to the new branches of *interpretable AI* which has recently been referred to as *explainable AI (XAI)*. This trend can be witnessed at the most esteemed machine learning conferences in recent years. In 2017, Been Kim and Finale Doshi-VelezI published a paper [21] and offered a tutorial on *interpretable machine learning* at ICML, while Neurips had a same-named tutorial in the same year. In 2018, both conferences offered workshops that contained the term *explainability* in the titles.

Along with the explosive growth of explainable AI research, a multitude of programming libraries has become available. For Python, the popular python distribution platform *pip* has offered the libraries *xai. yellowbrick, ELI5, lime, MLextend,* and *SHAP*. For the R programming language, R package distribution platform *CRAN* has offered the libraries *breakdown, DALEX, lime, modelDown, pdp,* and *shapper,* among others. Although this list is not extensive, it shows already the interest of the machine learning community to develop programming tools to support explainable AI analysis.

The XAI methods applied in the present work shall be defined in the following.

Feature Importance

The variable or feature importance is a numeric value of a feature' prediction impact, i.e. its global relevance for generating the prediction in the trained model. This relevance is model-dependent, i.e. for tree-based models like gradient boosting machines or random forests, it corresponds to its role in splitting the trees, whereas for linear models, it corresponds to the normalized regression coefficient.

Local Attributions

The prediction of a trained model can be visualized to show each feature's local attributions to the averaged prediction of a few unseen observations. Such visualization can serve to uncover the local, i.e. instance-level, role of a feature that typically differs a lot between observations. In other words, a feature's variance, which is hidden by the analysis of global feature importance, can be understood by this feature's local attributions' visualization.

Partial Dependency Plot

The partial dependency plot (pdp) displays the marginal effect of several features on the target variable of a trained machine learning model [22]. The partial dependency is the degree to which the target variable partially depends on each feature individually, i.e. partially, and over its whole range.

All of the above three XAI methods may serve not only to understand the functioning of a trained model, but importantly, may also serve to make important decisions for model improvement. Features may e.g. be discarded due to low feature importance, overly high variance in local attributions, or wrong or weak relationships uncovered in partial dependency plots.

3   Results

3.1   Prescreening

Before the main studies, the current work performed a pre-screening of the prepro-cessed dataset's features on approximately half the dataset.

The prescreening encompassed the analysis of feature importance that showed by far the highest importance for the variable *reviews.doRecommend*. It is created when users (who have written their online review on Amazon.com) answer *Yes* or *No* to the statement *I recommend this product*. This variable had to be removed for two reasons:

First, it was only present in 56.8% of the dataset. Therefore, on the one hand, its missing values could not be imputed, and on the other hand, its inclusion as a feature would have dramatically reduced the training set by almost half its size.

Second, this variable is too obviously related with the target variable, the product rating. Answering *Yes* to a product recommendation is semantically a strong endorsement equivalent with a product rating of five stars. This strong relationship was further evidenced by transforming it into a numeric variable which revealed a very high correlation (r = .648) with the target variable. Since the focus of the current work was on the predictive power of NLP, the variable *reviews.doRecommend* had to be removed to enable the comparison of feature importance between sentiments.

3.2   Study 1

The benchmarking results for the regression task are displayed in Fig. 1. Random forests yield the best prediction (lowest RMSE), whereas support vector machines with linear kernel yield the worst prediction.

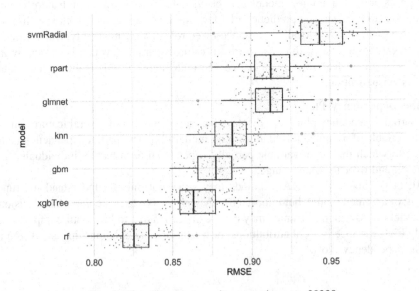

Fig. 1. Benchmarking results regression, n = 20238

The benchmarking results do not yield any explanatory value other than the algorithms' ranking. This black box characteristic was an expected result, and demonstrates the need for new methods to explain how the predictions were generated by the trained model. Such methods are provided by XAI methodology and shall be applied in the subsequent studies.

3.3 Study 2

The goal of Study 2 was to explain by XAI methods how the trained model of the best algorithm from Study 1's benchmarking, random forests, calculated its prediction. The explanation is performed both on the global and on the local level.

On the global level, the variable or *feature importance* can be retrieved from the trained model. As can be seen in Fig. 2, the visualization of feature importance reveals that the basic emotions *joy, trust, fear* and *anticipation,* as well as *negative* emotional valence yield the highest predictive value for random forests. In contrast, the *positive* emotional valence scores among the lowest, and the categorial variable *primaryCategories* shows the lowest feature importance.

Even though these feature importance scores reflect the overall importance of each feature, it should not disguise the fact that their prediction influence varies across all observations. This variance also means that an individual feature's impact on the target variable may reflect very differently in one observation from another.

Nevertheless, in the presence of many features, the feature importance scores can be utilized to shrink the feature set reasonably. In most cases, it would be pragmatic to discard features with feature importance scores lower than 10. This would concern features that have lower prediction impact than 10% of the most relevant feature.

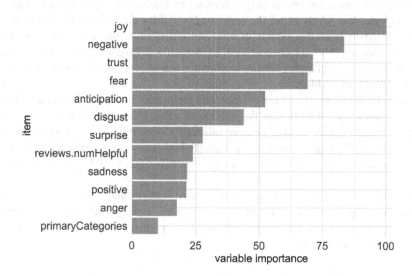

Fig. 2. Global feature importance, random forests, n = 20238

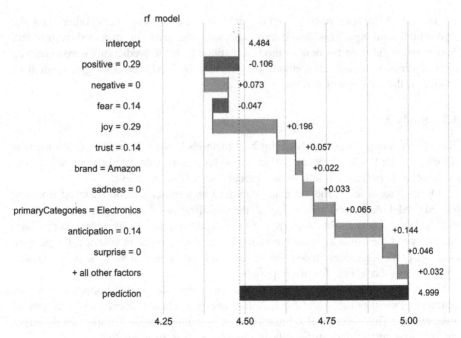

Fig. 3. Local attributions of features, random forests, n = 6

On the local level, the prediction of the trained random forests model was computed over six unseen observations.

The local attributions diagram in Fig. 3 shows that the prediction of 4.999 for the reviews-rating was mainly negatively influenced by low values of *positive* and *fear*. On the other side, low levels of all the remaining variables contributed positively to the prediction. Apart from that, although *trust* and *anticipation* had the same score from sentiment analysis (both 0.14), their local attribution was inverse to their global feature importance – *trust* with higher feature importance had a lower local attribution (+0.057) than *anticipation* (+0.144).

Generally speaking, it was not evident why the overall low emotional scores should lead to a prediction (4.999) near the maximum value (5.0). Furthermore, it was not plausible why a positive level of *positive* valence (0.29) should have a negative impact. Other mentionable aspects were the extremely high intercept (4.484) as well as the relative irrelevance of all other factors (with a contribution of +0.032 to the prediction of 4.999).

Taken together, it was not plausible why some features that should have a positive contribution had a negative one (positive valence), and features that had stronger feature importance had a lower local attribution. This puzzle required a more detailed analysis on the instance level.

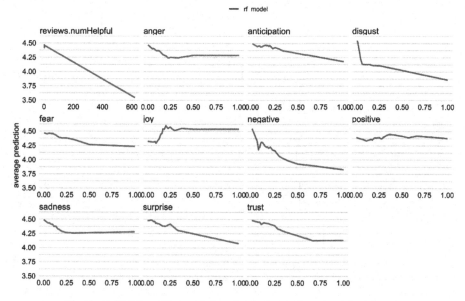

Fig. 4. Partial dependency plot on local observations – random forests

Apart from the local attribution analysis, another useful instance-level method is the analysis of *partial dependency*. This method can reveal the contribution to the prediction across the range of each feature.

The partial dependency plots (Fig. 4) detected systematic weaknesses, i.e. the algorithm did not correctly identify the relationships between several variables – e.g. *anticipation* and *trust* were incorrectly identified to have a negative relationship, Furthermore, although *anger, fear*, and *sadness* were correctly identified as negatively related to the target variable, the relationship was very weak and should be stronger. Besides, the variable *positive* (emotional valence) should have a strong relationship with the target but was identified to be not related at all (zero slope).

3.4 Study 3

To further understand the algorithm's functioning, the prediction task was reformulated as a classification task. This reformulation was permissible because the target variable, the reviews-rating, contained only integer values that were directly convertible into five classes with each of the five stars' rating as class level.

The benchmarking, visualized in Fig. 5, shows a similar result as Study 1. Again, random forests yield the best prediction, indicated by the highest accuracy on the holdout set of 72.9%. Nevertheless, the *no-information rate* showed a high value of 64.4%. This reveals a severe class imbalance in the dataset that explains the partially wrong relationships identified in the previous studies.

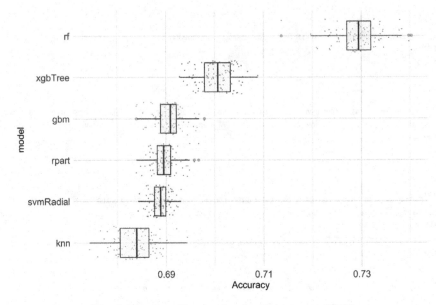

Fig. 5. Benchmarking results classification, n = 20238

4 Discussion

Online companies often use machine learning to make predictions on customer behavior and provide recommendations to users. The present work showed that such predictions can be severely biased, and that a global analysis of feature importance is insufficient to detect such bias. Only the analysis of local feature attributions and partial dependency plots could reveal that the predictions were severely biased towards positive ratings.

Acknowledgment. This research was supported by the Yonsei University Faculty Research Fund of 2019-22-0199.

References

1. Carvalho, D.V., Pereira, E.M., Cardoso, J.S.: Machine learning interpretability: a survey on methods and metrics. Electronics **8**, 1–34 (2019). https://doi.org/10.3390/electronics8080 832
2. Rudin, C.: Stop explaining black box machine learning models for high stakes decisions and use interpretable models instead. Nat. Mach. Intell. **1**, 206–215 (2019). https://doi.org/10. 1038/s42256-019-0048-x
3. Mudambi, S.M., Schuff, D.: What makes a helpful online review? A study of customer reviews on amazon.com. MIS Q. Manag. Inf. Syst. **34**, 185–200 (2010). https://doi.org/10. 2307/20721420

4. Bansal, B., Srivastava, S.: On predicting elections with hybrid topic based sentiment analysis of tweets. Procedia Comput. Sci. **135**, 346–353 (2018). https://doi.org/10.1016/j.procs.2018.08.183

5. Akhtar, N., Zubair, N., Kumar, A., Ahmad, T.: Aspect based sentiment oriented summarization of hotel reviews. Procedia Comput. Sci. **115**, 563–571 (2017). https://doi.org/10.1016/j.procs.2017.09.115

6. Hasan, A., Moin, S., Karim, A., Shamshirband, S.: Machine learning-based sentiment analysis for twitter accounts. Math. Comput. Appl. **23**, 11 (2018). https://doi.org/10.3390/mca23010011

7. Yu, Y.: Aspect-based Sentiment Analysis on Hotel Reviews. Arxiv Preprint 10 (2016)

8. de Kok, S., Punt, L., van den Puttelaar, R., Ranta, K., Schouten, K., Frasincar, F.: Review-level aspect-based sentiment analysis using an ontology. In: Proceedings of the ACM Symposium on Applied Computing, pp. 315–322 (2018). https://doi.org/10.1145/3167132.3167163

9. Ekman, P.: Are there basic emotions? Psychol. Rev. **99**, 550–553 (1992). https://doi.org/10.4081/jear.2011.169

10. Vytal, K., Hamann, S.: Neuroimaging support for discrete neural correlates of basic emotions: a voxel-based meta-analysis. J. Cogn. Neurosci. **22**, 2864–2885 (2010). https://doi.org/10.1162/jocn.2009.21366

11. Saarimäki, H., et al.: Discrete Neural Signatures of Basic Emotions. Cereb. Cortex **26**, 2563–2573 (2016). https://doi.org/10.1093/cercor/bhv086

12. Rucker, D.D., Petty, R.E.: Emotion specificity and consumer behavior: anger, sadness, and preference for activity. Motiv. Emot. **28**, 3–21 (2004). https://doi.org/10.1023/B:MOEM.0000027275.95071.82

13. Delplanque, S., Lavoie, M.E., Hot, P., Silvert, L., Sequeira, H.: Modulation of cognitive processing by emotional valence studied through event-related potentials in humans. Neurosci. Lett. **356**, 1–4 (2004). https://doi.org/10.1016/j.neulet.2003.10.014

14. Bohrn, I.C., Altmann, U., Lubrich, O., Menninghaus, W., Jacobs, A.M.: When we like what we know - a parametric fMRI analysis of beauty and familiarity. Brain Lang. **124**, 1–8 (2013). https://doi.org/10.1016/j.bandl.2012.10.003

15. Kuhn, M.: Caret: classification and regression training (2018)

16. Karatzoglou, A., Smola, A., Hornik, K., Zeileis, A.: kernlab – an S4 package for kernel methods in R. J. Stat. Softw. **11**, 1–20 (2004)

17. Therneau, T., Atkinson, B.: rpart: recursive partitioning and regression trees (2019)

18. Liaw, A., Wiener, M.: Classification and regression by randomForest. R News **2**, 18–22 (2002)

19. Greenwell, B., Boehmke, B., Cunningham, J., Developers, G.B.M.: gbm: Generalized Boosted Regression Models (2019)

20. Chen, T., Guestrin, C.: XGBoost: A Scalable Tree Boosting System. Arxiv (2016)

21. Doshi-Velez, F., Kim, B.: Towards a rigorous science of interpretable machine learning. 1–13 (2017)

22. Friedman, J.H.: Greedy function approximation: a gradient boosting machine. Ann. Stat. **29** (5), 1189–1232 (2001). https://doi.org/10.2307/2699986

Joking AI via Visual Cues

Ryota Suzuki[1]([⊠]), Kota Yoshida[2], Munetaka Minoguchi[2], Kazuki Tsubura[2], Takumu Ikeya[2], Akio Nakamura[2], and Hirokatsu Kataoka[1]

[1] National Institute of Advanced Industrial Science and Technology,
1-1-1 Umezono, Tsukuba, Ibakaraki, Japan
{ryota.suzuki,hirokatsu.kataoka}@aist.go.jp
[2] Tokyo Denki University, 5 Asahi-cho, Adachi City, Tokyo, Japan
{yoshida.k,minoguchi.m,tsubura.k,ikeya.t}@is.fr.dendai.ac.jp,
nkmr-a@cck.dendai.ac.jp

Abstract. We propose Artificial Intelligence (AI) based joking framework via visual cues. AI generates or retrieves funny captions relative to images which are shared by AI and humans for facilitating high level interaction between them. We also evaluate how funny the AI created funny captions using a social networking site (SNS).

Keywords: Artificial Intelligence · Sentimental sentence generation · Image captioning

1 Introduction

The recent development of AI technologies enables AI to perform high level cognition and expression. For example, a deep learning based AI [6] outperformed human [14] on image recognition. AI also has been advancing on generating sentences, which is even high quality and practically used such as Google Translation [19]. It will be expected for AI to understand social communication among humans for realizing high level communication between AI and humans.

As people practically use jokes [16], a joking function will facilitate smooth communication between AI and human beings. Whereas most of recent studies using AI aims to generate funny sentences from corpus (e.g. [21]), employing visual cues which are shared by AIs and users in real world will activate cooperative works between them.

We propose Artificial Intelligence (AI) joking framework via visual cues. AI recognizes and extracts features of the images and outputs funny captions of them.

At first, we construct a large scale dataset of pairs of images, funny captions and their funniness score (i.e. the FunnyJokeDB). We use Bokete [1], the Japanese SNS of submitting and evaluating funny captions for images submitted by users. We collected 27K images and 5.1M captions with their scores.

Supported by cvpaper.challenge.

H. Degen and L. Reinerman-Jones (Eds.): HCII 2020, LNCS 12217, pp. 422–436, 2020.
https://doi.org/10.1007/978-3-030-50334-5_29

Then we implemented two methods; Visual Funny Caption Generation (VFC-Gen) and Visual Funny Caption Retrieval (VFCRet). VFCGen generates a funny caption from an input image using deep learning. VFCRet retrieves a funny caption made by a human using relationship between image feature of an input image and image features among the database. The two methods have different characteristics. VFCGen can generate a funny caption based on an effectively extracted image feature, but it may not become fluent as well as human beings tell jokes. By contrast, VFCRet can retrieve a hand-made fluent funny caption, but it may not be consistent with an input image. We analyze characteristics the two methods how they induce feelings of humorous or funniness through evaluation by the Bokete users, who are the proficient on competing funny captions of images.

Here are the contributions of our work:

- Proposing a new viewpoint that generates funny captions from images.
- Constructing a large scale database of images and funny captions.
- Comparing two basic methods for discussing the effectiveness of inducing funniness through evaluation by the proficient SNS users.

2   Related Work

Our proposal is related to image captioning and human-like humor generation. Therefore, in this section, we review closely related work.

2.1   Image Caption

Recently, the cross-domain fields of image recognition and natural language processing have focused on both topics. Especially in computer vision, the most active technology is image captioning, which explains the contents of an image. Along this line, Vinyals et al. proposed a typical sentence generator with an encoder and decoder [18]. By using a sequence-to-sequence model [15], their architecture effectively optimized a large space between images and sentences with the Microsoft COCO dataset [11] (MS COCO). Generally, the encoder–decoder comprises concatenated convolutional neural networks (CNNs) and the Long Short-Term Memory (LSTM) architecture [8]. The following researches (e.g. [4,9,20]) have improved the performance rates on MS COCO and Flickr30k [13]. More important is to evaluate a generated caption. The existing methods, such as BLEU [12] and METEOR [2], seem to work well. However, vision and language researchers are struggling to evaluate their generated captions. According to Eqs. 1 and 2, existing evaluation methods, such as BLEU and METEOR, focus on the degree of matching of words with correct answer captions. However, since the correctness of image captions (and, of course, the funniness of jokes) is seldom objective, we think that the degree of matching of words with correct caption cannot be treated as an adequate evaluation. Methods for image captioning continue to improve, but here we focus on funny joke generation. Especially, laughter is a special and higher-order function that only humans possess; therefore, we should study the kind of image captioning technology that will evoke laughter from a human being. The task for computational humor, along with its evaluation, will be a next frontier.

2.2 Computational Humor

Recently, in the vision and language field, humor has been studied as computational humor. We here discuss humor in terms of both language and vision.

Language-Based Computational Humor. He *et al.* built a language-only database that contains a vocabulary of 137,773 words with 258,443 words total in 7,699 jokes written by American comedian Conan O'Brien [7]. Additionally, news articles were combined to generate jokes containing shifts of schema. As a result of questionnaire-based evaluation, their joke generation scored higher than a baseline model but lower than jokes written by humans. Zhiwei *et al.* trained a model to generate puns without any pun data [22]. The language model consists of two separate models, namely a joint model and highlight model.

Vision-Based Computational Humor. Chandrasekaran *et al.* [3] enhanced the humor of an image by constructing an analyzer to quantify "visual humor" in the image input. They also constructed datasets, including interesting (3,200) and non-interesting (3,200) human-labeled images, to evaluate visual humor. They used five stages to train the model to discern "funniness". However, their approach was limited to partial image modification, not image captioning. The study most similar to our proposal is Abel *et al.* [17], which generated a meme from an image input. Their system, however, only output memes, and assessment remained qualitative.

3 Funny Joke Database (FunnyJokeDB)

To achieve the concept of joke generation from an image input, we have collected pairs of image and joke as large as possible. We created the Funny Joke Database (FunnyJokeDB) by executing web scraping from the joking website Bokete. First we describe the joking website Bokete, and then we provide database details.

3.1 What About Bokete as a Joking Website

Bokete is a huge SNS-like website for posting and competing jokes in Japanese. As of October 2018, 66 million jokes and 3.8 million images have been posted on Bokete. Users can submit an image as a subject, and other users (or the posters themselves) can post a funny joke for the subjective image. Moreover, users can evaluate the posted funny jokes by giving a score from 1 to 3. Users compete for higher scores. Remarkably, Bokete has the system of picking up hot jokes, which attracts Bokete users and so increases the number of stars for "hot" jokes.

Table 1. Statistics of FunnyJokeDB.

Element	Frequency
# Funny joke	5,138,172
# Image	274,395
# Vocabulary	49,058,346
# Vocabulary per sentence	9.48
Average score	8.17
Minimum score	0
Maximum score	107,858

We believe that there are a lot of well-trained enthusiastic (proficient) Bokete users who daily submit subjective images and jokes. They do not award stars for less funny jokes. This produces results different from the tendency of evaluation by expected responses to questionnaires in any structured experiments, most of whom do not daily engage in Bokete.

The database is consists of sets of an image, jokes and scores. In the subsection, we explain web scraping, construction, and statistics.

Web Scraping. We developed a scraping tool for the Bokete website for automatically constructing FunnyJokeDB. First, we analyzed the structure of Bokete webpages in HTML, which consists of a subjective image, joke captions submitted by Bokete users, and cumulative scores (stars) given by other Bokete users (a sample page is depicted in Fig. 4). The Bokete website also has a catalogue of pages of jokes. The tool first retrieves all the pages of jokes from the catalogue and then extracts the contents of each page automatically. Moreover, it is also necessary to separate words in Japanese captions, because they do not include spaces as separators between words. Therefore, we employ the Japanese text morphology analysis tool MeCab [10] to automatically generate tokenized captions.

Database Structure. Pair of images and funny jokes were posted in temporal order on Bokete. We have collected a large number of images and funny jokes to make corresponding image and joke pairs. Thus, we obtained a database for generating funny jokes like an image caption one. Here are four main types of images: "photograph", "illustration", "comic", and "sentence". The image file name, text, and number of stars are managed by a JSON file. Each image and joke has a corresponding ID on Bokete.

Database Statistics. We show the statistics of FunnyJokeDB in Table 1. FunnyJokeDB contains 274,395 images, 5,138,172 jokes, and 49,058,346 unique words. The maximum star count is 107,858. Average score is 8.17. The standard deviation of stars is 230.5. Other properties are shown in Table 1.

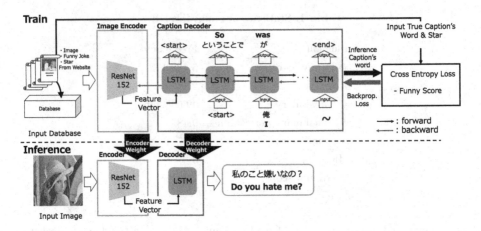

Fig. 1. Visual Funny Caption Generation.

4   Method

In this study, we implemented two methods, Visual Funny Caption Generation (VFCGen) and Visual Funny Caption Retrieval (VFCRet). The aim of implementing two methods is to investigate how differences between two methods affect the induction framework of feeling of humorous or funniness. Here we explain the two methods.

Visual Funny Caption Generation (VFCGen). VFCGen generates a funny caption from an input image based on a deep learning framework. We adopt a simple CNN+LSTM model [18]. It is a basic deep neural network model that realizes a function of image-to-sentence translation by learning relationship between images and sentences based on a large scale database. The Convolutional Neural Network (CNN) is a basic architecture for image processing, that is known to be a powerful module as an image feature extractor. The Long Short-Term Memory (LSTM) is also a basic architecture for natural language processing that realizes a sequence-to-sequence translation. The CNN+LSTM model combines them to extract an image feature and generate a sentence based on the image feature. We made two minor modifications to the model as follows: (i) To make the image representation as accurate as possible, under difficult situations, we employed ImageNet-pretrained ResNet-152 [5] as the CNN module. It is known to be more powerful for extracting image features. (ii) To easily optimize into the image-joke pattern space, we decreased the vocabulary scale (e.g., from 5 million to 1 million) by random sampling. We also alter the loss function to incorporate Funny Score, which let AI selectively learn funnier captions. Figure 1 shows an overview of the VFCGen.

Visual Funny Caption Retrieval (VFCRet). VFCRet retrieves the closest caption from the FunnyJokeDB using a query image. It retrieves a similar image to an

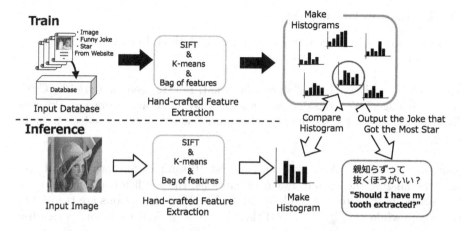

Fig. 2. Visual Funny Caption Retrieval.

Table 2. Result of quantitative evaluation using Bokete.

Method	Total stars	Average stars	Max stars	Winners against the other
VFCGen	1,734	1.74	19	168
VFCRet	1,797	1.80	12	191

input image via image features, and outputs the corresponding funniest caption. We use histogram matching for retrieving the closest funny caption. The equation shows the histogram similarity,

$$d(H_1, H_2) = \sum_I \min(H_1(I), H_2(I)) \tag{1}$$

whereas H_1, H_2 are the compared histogram that their size are the same, and I is an index of the bin of the histograms. The most similar image is searched on FunnyJokeDB with the extracted features. In this paper, we adopt human-crafted features (SIFT + Bag of Features) as an image feature descriptor. Figure 2 shows an overview of the VFCRet.

5   Evaluation

We conducted two experiments. We posted randomly selected jokes to Bokete for asking evaluation by Bokete users, who are enthusiasms to daily compete their jokes. We also made a structured questionary to analyze characteristics of the two methods on the viewpoints of consistency and fluency.

5.1   Evaluation Using Bokete

We posted randomly selected 997 jokes for each method. In this section, we show the results.

Quantitative Analysis. Table 2 shows the result. Bokete users preferred VFCRet on the average. We consider the reason that caption generation through CNN+LSTM degrades its fluency. However, fluency does not affect to max scores.

Qualitative Analysis. We picked up the best 10 samples for each method and show the images, the output Japanese captions, the English captions, and the stars scored by Bokete (see Table 3 and 4). The English captions are translated by authors while managing to hold their nuances. In VFCGen, some cases use personal pronouns frequently and it degrades fluency. But interestingly it got higher stars. VFCGen seems to extract image features at context levels. For example, VFCGen seems to have a manner to use the word "hate" and personal pronouns.

5.2   Structured Questionary

We conducted the other experiment that investigating how the characteristics of the methods affects to funniness. In the section, we explain experimental settings and and the result.

Experimental Setting. We asked 22 subjects to watch and evaluate jokes by the structured questionary. The subjects are male Japanese university students. We constructed the questionary using Google Forms, and we asked the subjects to answer it by their own comfortable terminals.

Content of Questionary. We picked up the evaluated jokes mentioned in the previous section. We select the jokes in the rules as:

1. Finding jokes of which images are used in evaluation of both VFCGen and VFCRet.
2. Selecting jokes of which stars are even as well as possible. In detail:
   (a) Calculating sum of stars of VFCGen and VFCRet for each images.
   (b) Randomly selecting 5 numbers from the above list of sum of stars.
   (c) Randomly selecting a image for each selected numbers.
   (d) For the purpose of grounding, we randomly selected a joke created by Bokete users for each selected images.

By the process, we constructed a list of comparable jokes of VFCGen, VFCRet and Human for the images. It consisted of 15 images and 3 corresponding jokes created by VFCGen, VFCRet and Human for each images. Finally, the max stars is 9 and the min stars is 0 among the selected jokes.

Table 3. Results of the top 10 funniest captions generated by the VFCGen method.

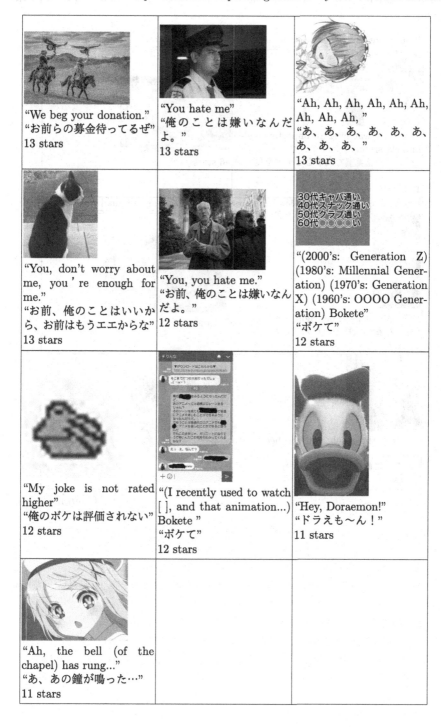

Table 4. Comparison between input image and retrieved original image on the VFCRet method.

Input image, retrieved caption and stars	Original image and original stars
"Girls are watching an important video in a classroom." "女子は視聴覚室で大事なビデオを見ています" 12 stars	46 stars
Input image, retrieved caption and stars	Original image and original stars
"The target is on my right, isn't it?" "右の写真の人物でいいんだな？" 11 stars	7 stars
"This is the result you are beastly to royal we." "わらわに歯向かうからそうなるのじゃ" 10 stars	3 stars

(*continued*)

Table 4. (*continued*)

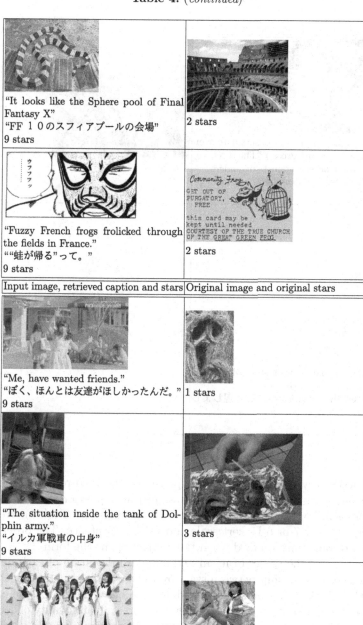

Input image, retrieved caption and stars	Original image and original stars
"It looks like the Sphere pool of Final Fantasy X" "FF１０のスフィアプールの会場" 9 stars	2 stars
"Fuzzy French frogs frolicked through the fields in France." ""蛙が帰る"って。" 9 stars	2 stars
"Me, have wanted friends." "ぼく、ほんとは友達がほしかったんだ。" 9 stars	1 stars
"The situation inside the tank of Dolphin army." "イルカ軍戦車の中身" 9 stars	3 stars
"You're just interested in our panty, right?" "あなた達、パンティ以外興味は無いの?" 9 stars	9 stars

(*continued*)

Table 4. (*continued*)

Input image, retrieved caption and stars	Original image and original stars
"(The app of [ ] that let users date even who are poor and gross.) "The three, relentless attackers against surrenders." "相手は降伏してるが容赦ない３人" 9 stars	4 stars
"A figure that shows history of songs of a certain woman singer." "八代亜紀代表曲をグラフに再現しました" 9 stars	4 stars

In a questionary, we show 15 funny captions and their corresponding images. The three types of the jokes are evenly assigned in a questionary, so they have 5 jokes for each. For each jokes, we asked four questions (see Table 5). We asked to answer Q1–3 by 7 or 6 Lickert scale and Q4 in a sentence. The order of the questions are randomly shuffled when the subject opens the form.

Figure 3 shows the values of mean and standard deviation of each question. We cannot see relationship between stars by Bokete and evaluation by the subjects. Although there are no significant difference between mean score of questions along the methods and humans, they seem to evaluate quality of sentences more seriously rather than consistency between images and jokes.

Figure 4 shows the mean values of each question and two methods. We also cannot observe relationship between stars and values of the answers. When we make attention on difference of the values,

Figure 5 shows subtraction score of Q1 minus Q2. Higher score shows that the mean score of Q1 is higher than the mean score of Q2. We can observe

Table 5. Questions and answering scale.

Q1	Consistency of the joke against the image	7. very consistent
		6. consistent
		5. more consistent
		4. not sure
		3. less consistent
		2. inconsistent
		1. very inconsistent
Q2	Quality of the sentence as a joke itself	7. very high
		6. high
		5. higher
		4. not sure
		3. lower
		2. low
		1. very low
Q3	Funniness of the caption against the image	6. very funny
		5. funny
		4. funnier
		3. cheesier
		2. cheesy
		1. very cheesy
Q4	Reason of your answer	

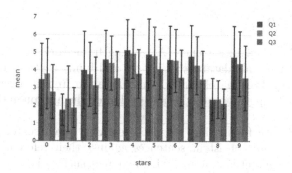

Fig. 3. Mean values of each question. Error bars are standard deviations ($\pm\sigma$).

which element of consistency and fluency is more important for VFCGen and VFCRet from it. Sum of the difference of VFCGen and VFCRet are 2.93 and -2.91, respectively. It shows that output jokes of VFCGen is higher-context than VFCRet, and by contrast VFCRet outputs more fluent and human-like sentences than VFCGen.

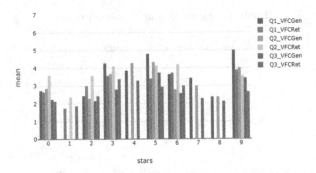

Fig. 4. Mean values of each question and method.

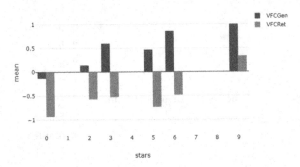

Fig. 5. Difference of questionary result between VFCGen and VFCRet. Higher value shows that score of Q1 is higher than score of Q2.

6   Conclusion

We proposed Artificial Intelligence (AI) joking framework via visual cues. We constructed a large scale database of images and funny captions using a joking SNS for successful learning of funny joke generation from a image. We implemented the two competitive methods and evaluated them through the two experiments.

In our study, we found that the deep learning based sentence generation method can generate consistent sentences against their referential cues, even while the target content is practically high-context such as joking. On the other hand, it was also found that the deep learning based method is still difficult to generate fluent and human-like sentence perfectly when it aims high-context sentence generation while high-level fluency is required for people. On the point of producing highly fluent joke, we proposed alternative method based on sentence retrieval tactics and we confirmed its effectiveness.

References

1. Bokete website (Japanese). https://bokete.jp/
2. Banerjee, S., Lavie, A.: METEOR: an automatic metric for MT evaluation with improved correlation with human judgments. In: Annual Meeting of the Association for Computational Linguistics (ACL) (2005)
3. Chandrasekaran, A., et al.: We are humor beings: understanding and predicting visual humor. In: IEEE Conference on Computer Vision and Pattern Recognition (CVPR) (2016)
4. Fortunato, M., Blundell, C., Vinyals, O.: Bayesian recurrent neural networks. abs/1704.02798. CoRR (2018)
5. He, K., Zhang, X., Ren, S., Sun, J.: Deep residual learning for image recognition. In: IEEE Conference on Computer Vision and Pattern Recognition (CVPR) (2016)
6. He, K., Zhang, X., Ren, S., Sun, J.: Delving deep into rectifiers: surpassing human-level performance on imagenet classification. In: Proceedings of the IEEE international conference on computer vision, pp. 1026–1034 (2015)
7. He, R., Quan, S.: Neural joke generation (2017)
8. Hochreiter, S., Schmidhuber, A.: Long short-term memory. Neural Comput. **9**(8), 1735–1780 (1997)
9. Karpathy, A., Fei-Fei, L.: Deep visual-semantic alignments for generating image descriptions. In: IEEE International Conference on Computer Vision and Pattern Recognition (CVPR) (2015)
10. Kudo, T., Yamamoto, K., Matsumoto, Y.: Applying conditional random fields to Japanese morphological analysis. In: Proceedings of the 2004 Conference on Empirical Methods in Natural Language Processing (EMNLP-2004) (2017)
11. Lin, T.-Y., et al.: Microsoft COCO: common objects in context. In: Fleet, D., Pajdla, T., Schiele, B., Tuytelaars, T. (eds.) ECCV 2014. LNCS, vol. 8693, pp. 740–755. Springer, Cham (2014). https://doi.org/10.1007/978-3-319-10602-1_48
12. Papineni, K., et al.: BLEU: a method for automatic evaluation of machine translation. In: Annual Meeting of the Association for Computational Linguistics (ACL) (2002)
13. Plummer, B.A., Wang, L., Cervantes, C.M., Caicedo, J.C., Hockenmaier, J., Lazebnik, S.: Flickr30k entities: collecting region-to-phrase correspondences for richer image-to-sentence models. Int. J. Comput. Vis. (IJCV) **123**(1) (2017)
14. Russakovsky, O., et al.: ImageNet large scale visual recognition challenge. Int. J. Comput. Vis. **115**(3), 211–252 (2015). https://doi.org/10.1007/s11263-015-0816-y
15. Sutskever, I., Vinyals, O., Le, Q.V.: Sequence to sequence learning with neural networks. In: NIPS (2014)
16. Tiberius, R.G., Billson, J.M.: The social context of teaching and learning. New Dir. Teach. Learn. **1991**(45), 67–86 (1991). https://doi.org/10.1002/tl.37219914509. https://onlinelibrary.wiley.com/doi/abs/10.1002/tl.37219914509
17. Peirson, V., Abel, L., Tolunay, E.M.: Dank learning: generating memes using deep neural networks. CoRR abs/1806.04510 (2018)
18. Vinyals, O., Toshev, A., Bengio, S., Erhan, D.: Show and tell: a neural image caption generator. IEEE International Conference on Computer Vision and Pattern Recognition (CVPR) (2015)
19. Wu, Y., et al.: Google's neural machine translation system: Bridging the gap between human and machine translation. arXiv preprint arXiv:1609.08144 (2016)
20. Xu, K., et al.: Show, attend and tell: neural image caption generation with visual attention. In: Proceedings of Machine Learning Research, pp. 2048–2057 (2018)

21. Yu, Z., Tan, J., Wan, X.: A neural approach to pun generation. In: Proceedings of the 56th Annual Meeting of the Association for Computational Linguistics (Volume 1: Long Papers), pp. 1650–1660. Association for Computational Linguistics, Melbourne, July 2018. https://doi.org/10.18653/v1/P18-1153, https://www.aclweb.org/anthology/P18-1153
22. Zhiwei, Y., Jiwei, T., Xiaojun, W.: A neural approach to pun generation. In: Annual Meeting of the Association for Computational Linguistics (ACL) (2018)

Interactive Method to Elicit Local Causal Knowledge for Creating a Huge Causal Network

Genki Yamashita$^{(\boxtimes)}$, Taro Kanno⑩, and Kazuo Furuta

The University of Tokyo, Tokyo, Japan
gyamashita@cse.t.u-tokyo.ac.jp

Abstract. Effective disaster drills and exercises require appropriate scenarios reflecting concrete disaster situations. It is however not easy to manually create such a scenario with enough details and validity, because it is fundamental difficult to comprehensively predict and assume disaster situations that may occur in various phases through a chain of causality from the primary damage. In order to make a scenario creation easier and more efficient, some support tools are necessary, in particular for predicting what kind of situations will happen through a causal chain from a base disaster assumption. In this paper, we proposed a simple and practical causal model consisting of three elements: cause, precondition, and effect, which can capture indirect causal relationships between two events by introducing the concept of preconditions. We also developed an interactive method with a GUI to elicit causal knowledge about disaster situations based on the model. Users can enter possible events that can occur in a disaster as well as countermeasures against those events by answering the questions presented on the GUI. Then the entered sentences are processed to identify causal elements automatically by a newly developed NLP techniques, and finally those elements are integrated into the database. The proposed method still has a room for improvement, however its performance is satisfying and can be expected to be utilized as a technical base for the creation of effective disaster scenarios.

Keywords: Causal model · Knowledge elicitation · Scenario creation

1 Introduction

In recent years, the concept of resilience has attracted attention in the field of disaster prevention. Bruneau et al. defined resilience as a generic term for ability to reduce failure probabilities, ability to reduce consequences from failures, and ability to reduce time to recovery [1]. In order for that, it is necessary for organizations to quickly establish an initial response system in a disaster and make appropriate and prompt decisions based on uncertain information. For developing this capacity to respond to disasters, it is not enough to simply read and understand a disaster response manual, but disaster drills and exercises are necessary. Effective drills and exercises require appropriate disaster scenarios that prescribe concrete disaster situations including

© Springer Nature Switzerland AG 2020
H. Degen and L. Reinerman-Jones (Eds.): HCII 2020, LNCS 12217, pp. 437–446, 2020.
https://doi.org/10.1007/978-3-030-50334-5_30

background situations of the organization, damage assumptions, the constraints caused by the damage, and so on.

It is however not easy to manually create such a disaster scenario with enough details and validity, in particular for people without special knowledge and experience. This is not only due to insufficient time or lack of knowledge on disasters, but also due to the fundamental difficulty for individuals to comprehensively predict and assume the extent of damage effects that may occur in various phases through a chain of causality. In disasters, different damages and events occur in a chain reaction from a certain damage and event, resulting in a chain failure caused by the dependency of the social systems and infrastructure, and unexpected events such as a chain reaction of events within a limited spatial scope.

Limousin et al. developed a support tool to create disaster scenarios using databases and matrices [2]. In this tool, cross impact analysis methodology is used to determine how relationships between events may impact resulting events. Since it is difficult for non-experts to use cross impact methodology, it is not easy to create scenarios considering the extent of damage effects that may occur in various phases through a chain of causality by using this tool. Judek et al. improved a crisis simulation approach called iCrisis and enabled the preparation of disaster scenarios considering cascading effects [3]. Using this tool, scenarios considering causal relationships can be created. However, this tool consists only of checklists and guidance, making it is still not easy for non-experts to create appropriate disaster scenarios.

To predict and describe a chain of causality is one of the biggest obstacles for non-experts in creating effective disaster scenarios. Therefore, it is necessary to support this by for example eliciting and reusing the knowledge obtained from many people.

There are two basic approaches for eliciting knowledge. One approach is automatic knowledge elicitation using AI techniques with natural language processing (NLP). There are many researches on knowledge elicitation from Web by text mining. This approach however has several problems. One is that current natural language processing techniques does not have enough accuracy. Another problem is that the information on the Web is more general and less specific to individual organizations although local and specific knowledge is required for individual organizations. Another approach is using manual methods such as interview, questionnaire, and model-based analysis. However, these methods require much time and effort, in particular in analyzing data and converting the knowledge into a reusable form. In addition, there are no good theoretical model for describing causal knowledge. For example, a simple cause and effect model is too simple to describe causal relationships behind an event. On the other hand, if we try to describe causal relationships in more detail, such as FRAM, a functional resonance analysis method, the model becomes complicated and difficult for non-expert to understand and use.

From this background, in this paper we propose a causal model consisting of three elements, cause, condition and effect, which is simple and practical to describe causal relationships. To solve the problems of the current manual and automatic knowledge elicitation method, we propose and develop an interactive method to elicit causal knowledge.

2   Causal Model

We propose a new causal model consisting of cause, preconditions, and effects.

FRAM describes six aspects of causal relationships, which makes the method difficult for non-experts to understand and use it. On the other hand, there are many phenomena that cannot be explained and understood by a simple cause and effect model. One of the example of such phenomena that cannot be explained by a simple model is that a medical equipment cannot be used due to blackout in a building with inadequate emergency power supply. "Blackout" is a direct factor that makes an effect (in this case, "medical equipment cannot be used"), but "inadequate emergency power supply" is not a direct factor for the effect. However, when "blackout" occurs, and if there is "inadequate emergency power supply", the effect occurs. But if there is not "inadequate emergency power supply", the effect does not occur. In this study, a direct causal factor is defined as "cause", while an event that is not a direct factor but is necessary for an effect to occur is defined as "precondition". In the above example, the cause is "blackout" and the precondition is "inadequate emergency power supply".

In our model, a precondition can cover four of the six aspects of function of FRAM (Time, Control, Precondition, and Resource). The remaining two aspects (Input and Output) correspond to a cause and an effect. This causal model consisting of causes, conditions, and effects is a simpler and more practical than FRAM. At the same time, this model has more descriptive power than a simple causal model consisting only of causes and effects. It is still difficult to consider and pre-identify preconditions behind events occurred in a disaster, which is the target causal relationships in this study. Therefore, we focus on countermeasures instead of preconditions, because counter-measures can be relatively easily elicited as ideas for preventing potential harmful events from occurring when a disaster occurs. In other words, we can say that coun-termeasures are interpretations of preconditions from different viewpoints. In the above example, the precondition is "inadequate emergency power supply" and the counter-measure is "installing an adequate emergency power supply".

3   Method to Elicit Causal Knowledge

We are developing an interactive method to elicit causal knowledge which describe the causal relationships behind events under disaster situations and to utilize the knowledge for creating detailed disaster scenarios. The knowledge elicited by the method is converted and stored in a database based on the causal model described in the previous section. This interactive method provides a GUI to ask questions on disaster situations and enter the answers, which is designed and developed for Japanese language. This method is intended to be used in a workshop.

At the beginning of a workshop, participants are asked to discuss possible events as well as their effects that can occur in a disaster and input them using the GUI, which aims to elicit causal knowledge. In order to enhance the usability and to avoid nar-rowing the scope of thinking, the participants can input any possible events that can occur in a disaster in free formants. Causal chains are extracted from input sentences automatically by the following two methods. As shown in Fig. 1, several causal candidates estimated by NLP are displayed on the GUI. First participants are asked to select whether input sentence has a causal relationship or not, then they are asked to select the appropriate cause and effect. If there is no appropriate candidate presented on the GUI, then participants are asked to enter an appropriate causal relationship manually. These procedures should be repeated until every conceivable event in a disaster is entered. The GUI then displays the previously entered pairs of causes and effects one by one Participants are also asked to enter as many countermeasures as possible to address these causes and effects. As described above, knowledge on countermeasures is elicited instead of preconditions in out method. This is not only because it is easier to come up with countermeasures than preconditions, but also because considering countermeasures becomes a good opportunity for learning about disaster response.

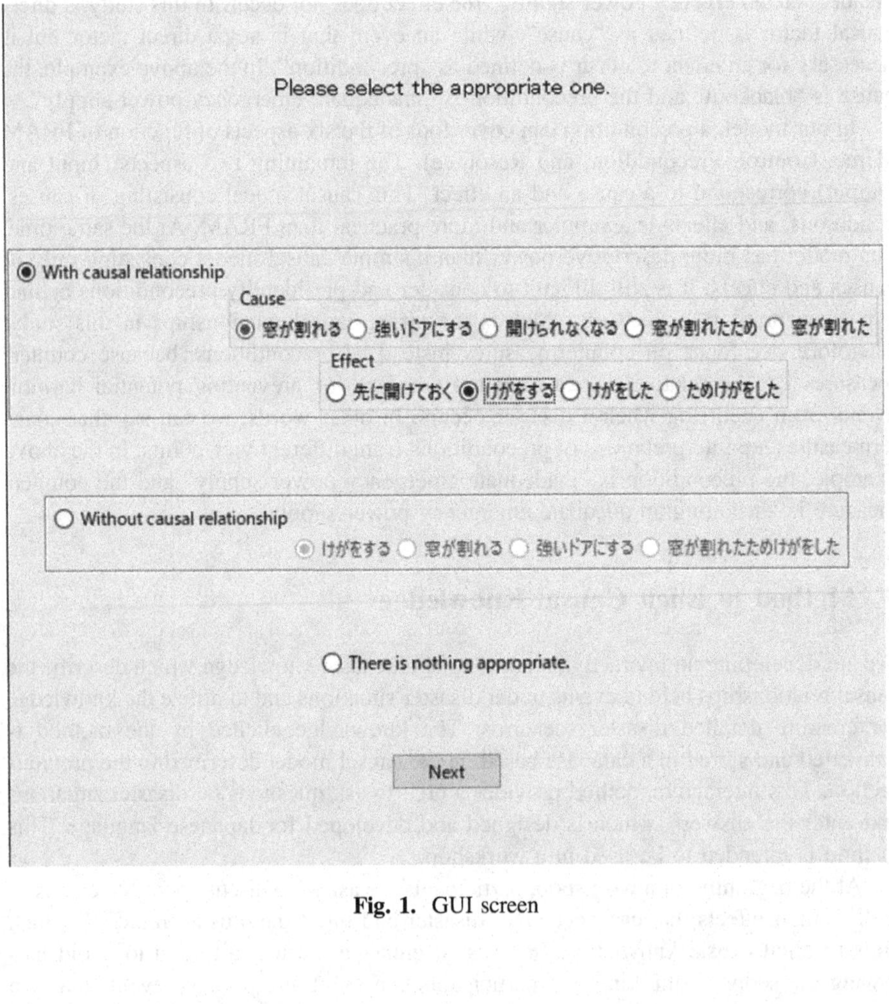

Fig. 1. GUI screen

3.1   Method to Extract Causal Relationship

This section describes the algorithms used in the method, especially for natural language processing. We incorporated a method developed by Sakaji et al. (hereinafter referred to as Method A) [5, 6] with a newly developed method (hereinafter referred to as Method B) to enhance the ability for knowledge elicitation. The purpose of Method A is to extract only certain causal relationship in the text, so it is not possible to comprehensively extract possible causalities. This is because causal relationship is often expressed in Japanese without using causal words such as conjunction. Therefore, Method B is developed to extract causal relationship that cannot be extracted by Method A.

Method A uses the sentence structure and clue expressions to determine and extract causal relationship. A clue expression, such as "No-de" in Japanese or "as" in English, is an expression that is an important clue to extract the cause and effect. Method A first looks for a clue expression in a target sentence. When a clue expression is found in the sentence, then a dependency analysis is conducted to determine the sentence structure. Dependency analysis is a type of syntax analysis that divides a sentence into morphemes and analyzes the modification relationships between morphemes. In this study, CaboCha [7] was used for dependency analysis. The sentence is categorized into five patterns based on the sentence structure. These five patterns are shown in Fig. 2. Based on them, the causal relationship is identified and extracted.

In Method B, a causal relationship is estimated and extracted by dividing an input sentence into several simple sentences. Although the original definition of a simple sentence means a sentence with only one set of a subject and a predicate, a sentence with a noun clause such as "I hear the news that an earthquake has occurred" is also treated as a simple sentence in Method B. In Japanese, noun clauses often play an auxiliary role in sentences rather than representing a single event, so Method B treats noun clauses as single nouns. In many Japanese sentences that express causal relationship without using clue expressions, the event described earlier tends to be a "cause" and the event described later tend to be an "effect". Therefore, in Method B, a preceding simple sentence in an input sentence is identified as a "cause" and the following simple sentence as an "effect". If an input sentence is divided into three sentences, it is assumed that the first sentence is a cause of the middle sentence and the middle sentence is a cause of the last sentence. It is the same even when it is divided into four or more simple sentences. The details of the algorithm is shown in Fig. 3. First, dependency analysis is performed using CaboCha. Next, a predicate is searched, and a modifier of the predicate is confirmed. If the modifier is not a noun, that is, it is not a noun clause, the input sentence is divided. If it is a noun, the input sentence is not divided. This procedure is done for all predicates, and causal relationship is extracted from an input sentence. While Method B can extract more causalities than Method A, it is more likely to extract wrong causalities that do not actually contain causal relationship. Therefore, in this study, as described above, causal candidates extracted by Method A and Method B are presented to participants, and they select the correct causal relationship in order to solve this problem.

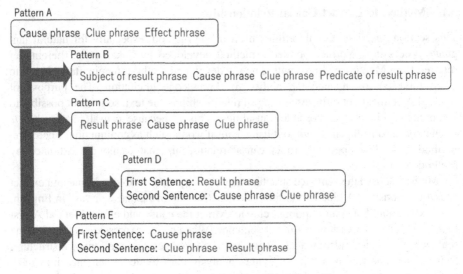

Fig. 2. An association chart of patterns [5]

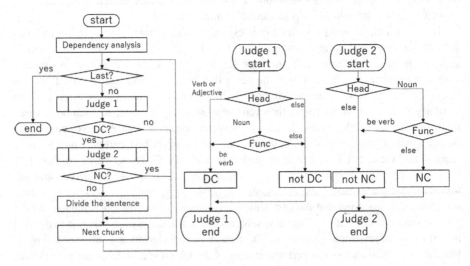

Fig. 3. Flowchart of NLP

3.2 Prevention of Duplication

Different people use different expressions for the same phenomenon. Some people describe "blackout" as "blackout occurs" and others describe "electricity stops". It is inconvenient if events with different representations are stored as different data in the database. In this study, therefore it is judged whether they are same event or not by evaluating the similarity of sentence vectors obtained by Word2Vec which is a model for converting words into discrete vectors. Since verb, adjective, and noun play main role in the meaning of a sentence in Japanese language, only vectors of verb, adjective, and noun are used to calculate sentence vectors. If distance between the two sentence vectors is closer than a fixed value, the sentence is determined to have the same meaning. The detailed procedure is as follows.

1. The target sentence (s) is morphemically analyzed.
2. Using a learned model, the vectors of morphemes are calculated.
3. A weighted average of these vectors is calculated to be the vector of s.
4. A vector data set (Dv) is created by repeating step 1 to 3 for a sentence group (D) collected in the past.
5. Steps 1 to 3 are performed on the new sentence (S), and a vector (V) is calculated.
6. Distance between V and the vectors in Dv is calculated, and sentences whose distance is less than a certain value is selected and displayed on the GUI.
7. Participants of the workshop select appropriate one. If there is no appropriate one, S is added to D.

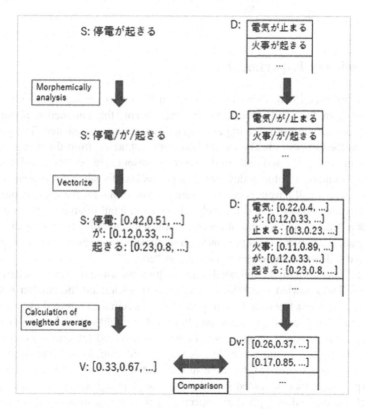

Fig. 4. Flow of similarity evaluation (Color figure online)

3.3   Verification

An experiment was conducted to verify the proposed method. "Kyoto University Web Documentation Lead Corpus" [8] was used as the test data. This corpus is a text corpus in which various language information, such as semantic relations, is added manually to the lead three sentences of various Web documents. In the verification, 100 sentences randomly selected from 628 sentences which contain causal relationships. Method A and Method B were applied to the selected sentences, and the correctness was judged manually.

Table 1 shows results of the experiment. Method A identified correct causal relationships in 46 sentences, while Method B did 63 sentences. Both methods failed to identify correct causal relationships in the same 14 sentences.

Table 1. Results of the verification experiment

Method A	Method B	Combining Method A and B
46	63	87

4   Preliminary Experiment

A preliminary experiment using the propose method was carried out to elicit causal knowledge from two participants. In the experiment, the knowledge about events which can occur in a room in a big earthquake was tried to be elicited. The procedure was as described in Sect. 3. The causal knowledge obtained from the two participants are shown in Fig. 4. The red node in the center represents the occurrence of disaster, in this time an earthquake, blue nodes represent events and damages that can be caused by the disaster, and small purple nodes represent preconditions for the event connected by an edge. An edge represents a causal relationship, and a tail of an edge between events represents a "cause" and a head of an edge represents an "effect". Where an event or disaster leads to an event via a precondition, an upstream event or disaster represent a "cause" and a downstream event represents an "effect".

Twenty events and 15 preconditions (countermeasures) were elicited in the experiment. The knowledge obtained from the first participant (hereinafter referred to as person A) and that from the second participant (hereinafter referred to as person B) were integrated and stored in a database. Person A thought that the earthquake would cause a fire, but person B thought that the gas stove would fall and the carpet would catch fire, then a fire would occur. In this way, by eliciting knowledge from multiple people, one person's knowledge can be supplemented by another person's knowledge. In this experiment, local knowledge of the room, such as a gas stove near a carpet, was elicited. If this method is applied to a specific facility or organization, it is expected to elicit local causal knowledge around that facility or organization (Fig. 5).

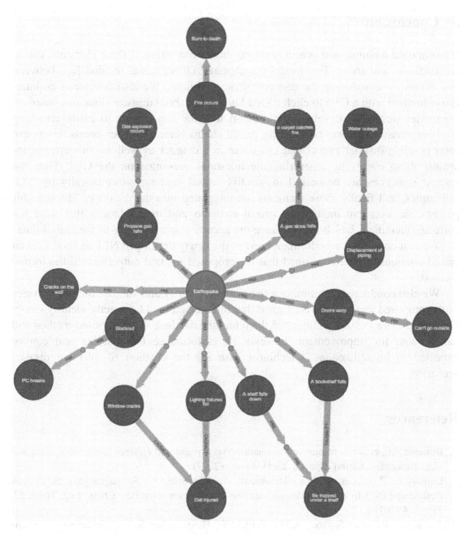

Fig. 5. Visualization of the causal knowledge

On the other hand, this method still has some limitations. One limitation is that the method does not have a function to help users to expand the imagination of events that can occur in a chain via three or more events ahead triggered by some other events. For example, person A thought that water outage would occur due to the displacement of piping, but neither A nor B thought about possible events that would occur due to water outage. In order to elicit further or deeper causal knowledge, the method need to provide some support, for example presenting a causal network to the users while they are working in a workshop. By presenting the causal network and let the users focus on the node where a water outage occurs, they are expected to be evoked to start thinking about what will happen when a water outage occurs.

5 Conclusion

We proposed a simple and practical causal model consisting of three elements: cause, precondition, and effect. This model can capture indirect causal relationships between two events by introducing the concept of preconditions. We also developed an inter-active method with a GUI to elicit causal knowledge about disaster situations based on the model, aiming at developing a support tool for non-experts to easily create an effective disaster scenario considering causal chains behind disaster events. Users can enter possible disaster events that can occur in a disaster as well as countermeasures against those events by answering the questions presented on the GUI. Then the entered sentences are processed to identify causal elements automatically by NLP techniques, and finally those elements are integrated into the database. Through this process, the user can modify the causal elements and their relations that were not correctly identified, which can enhance the accuracy and integrity of the causal data.

We first conducted a performance test of the newly developed NLP method to elicit causal relationship and confirmed that the proposed method outperformed the former method.

We also conducted a preliminary experiment to verify and validate the performance of the proposed method and confirmed that the method could correctly identify causal elements and successfully integrated them into the database. The proposed method still has a room for improvement, however its performance is satisfying and can be expected to be utilized as a technical base for the creation of effective disaster scenarios.

References

1. Bruneau, M., et al.: A framework to quantitatively assess and enhance the seismic resilience of communities. Earthq. Spectra **23**(1), 41–62 (2007)
2. Limousion, P., Tixier, J., Bony-Dandrieux, A., Chapurlat, V., Sauvagnargues, S.: A new method and tools to scenarios design for crisis management exercises. Chem. Eng. Trans. **53**, 319–324 (2016)
3. Judek, C., Edjossan-Sossou, A.M., Verdel, T., Heuserswyn, K.V., Verhaegen, F.: Crisis simulation scenario building methodology that considers cascading effects. J. Integr. Disaster Risk Manag. **8**(2), 24–43 (2018)
4. Hollnagel, E.: FRAM: the Functional Resonance Analysis Method. Ashgate Publishing Limited, England (2012)
5. Sakaji, H., Sakai, H., Masuyama, S.: Extracting causal expressions from PDF files of summary of financial statements. IEICE Trans. Inf. Syst. **98**(5), 811–822 (2015)
6. Sakaji, H., Takeuchi, K., Sekine, S., Masuyama, S.: Extraction of causal knowledge by using syntactic patterns. In: 14th Association for Natural Language Processing, pp. 1144–1147 (2008)
7. Kudo, T., Matsumoto, Y.: Japanese dependency analysis using cascaded chunking. Inf. Process. Soc. Jpn. **43**(6), 1834–1842 (2002)
8. Hangyo, M., Kawahara, D., Kurohashi, S.: Building and analyzing a diverse document leads corpus annotated with semantic relations. J. Nat. Lang. Process. **21**(2), 213–248 (2014)

Author Index

Printed in the United States
By Bookmasters